D1563694

Bureaucracy
and
the Public

BUREAUCRACY AND THE PUBLIC

A READER IN
Official-Client Relations

EDITED BY
Elihu Katz & Brenda Danet

Basic Books, Inc., Publishers

NEW YORK

© 1973 by Basic Books, Inc.
Library of Congress Catalog Card Number: 72–89283
SBN 465–00773–2
Manufactured in the United States of America
DESIGNED BY VINCENT TORRE

73 74 75 76 77 10 9 8 7 6 5 4 3 2 1

FOR

Peter M. Blau

The Authors

Gabriel Almond
Jean Bandler
Rivka Bar-Yosef
Bernard B. Berk
Peter M. Blau
David J. Bordua
Richard A. Brymer
Antoinette Catrice-Lorey
Felicia Clark
Brenda Danet
Milton S. Davis
S. N. Eisenstadt
Buford Farris
Robert Fellmeth
Florence Galkin
Walter Gellhorn
Erving Goffman
Kent Greenwalt
Lawrence Grossman
James M. Henslin

Lenore Jacobson
Alfred J. Kahn
Elihu Katz
Melvin L. Kohn
Arthur R. Matthews, Jr.
Stanley Milgram
Daniel R. Miller
Leonard I. Pearlin
Robert V. Presthus
Albert J. Reiss, Jr.
Morris Rosenberg
Robert Rosenthal
E. O. Schild
Philip G. Schrag
Gideon Sjoberg
Guy E. Swanson
James D. Thompson
Sidney Verba
Jonathan A. Weiss
William Foote Whyte

Preface

Most of the prefatory remarks that need saying are included in the Introduction and in our introductions to each of the parts. This preface is reserved, therefore, for saying thanks.

Primarily we are grateful to the authors who agreed to the reprinting of their work. While it turns out to be more difficult than we thought to edit a book of readings in an uncharted field, it is an inescapable truth that the editors are not the authors, and that the authors deserve the credit.

Then, we are grateful to those of our colleagues who participated in the formative stages of our thinking on the subject of bureaucracy and the public, particularly Peter M. Blau, S. N. Eisenstadt, Louis Guttman, and Everett C. Hughes. Joint seminars in Jerusalem and Chicago were the context for these exchanges. Indeed, so little account has been taken of the public in sociological writings on bureaucracy, that we decided to dedicate this volume to Peter Blau, whose pioneering work has always taken systematic note of the fact that bureaucracies deal with publics and that official-client interaction is a problem worthy of both scientific and social concern.

We thank the National Science Foundation whose grants (Nos. GS–1241 and GS–1385) supported our empirical research in this area. The focus of the early work was on the development of a generic scheme for the study of persuasive appeals directed by clients to officials. Later work focused on this and other aspects of official-client interaction, and something of all of these efforts is reported at various points in this volume. Michael Gurevitch and Tsiyona Peled were our partners in these studies.

William Gum of Basic Books encouraged us to include the very best material we could find, and then he encouraged us to take out most of it because the volume was too long. He, not we, owes apologies to a number of authors who are unrepresented, some of whom are our best friends. We are also grateful to him for his cheery and very nonbureaucratic letters, which are one of the fringe benefits of writing for Basic Books.

In organizing this book and planning its contents, we found aid and comfort in Ralph Kramer, who was visiting at the School of Social Work in Jerusalem, and in Harriet Hartman and Rafii Rosenstein. Brenda Danet's cleaning woman is responsible for our meeting deadlines, since she repeatedly threatened to quit unless we removed the papers and books which cluttered the living room.

1973   E. K. and B. D.

ix

Contents

PART I
Environmental Factors:
Culture and Community

PART II
The Influence of the Organization:
Goals, Roles, and Structures

PART III
Situational Influences:
The Physical and Social Setting

PART IV
Making Organizations Work for People: Strategies for Innovation and Change

Bureaucracy
and
the Public

Introduction

BUREAUCRACY AS A PROBLEM
FOR SOCIOLOGY AND SOCIETY

The word "bureaucracy" means different things to different people. In every-day conversation, to call something "bureaucratic" is to damn it. Bureaucracy implies red-tape, long lines, elaborate forms, unpleasant officials, and the cold sweat that comes with the feeling that you are not being understood. The popular image, in short, sees bureaucracy as inefficient, inhuman, and in-accessible. A more radical view holds that bureaucracy is dangerous—to the individual and to society.

For most social scientists, bureaucracy is neither efficient nor inefficient. It is, rather, a particular way in which people organize themselves and their resources to achieve some agreed-upon goal—like collecting income tax, or producing rockets, or healing the sick. Discovering how people go about this—and how efficiently—is a problem which has occupied social scientists.

These different usages reflect the fact that bureaucracy as the subject of social criticism and bureaucracy as a problem for empirical social science went off in different directions years ago, and have nearly lost sight of each other.[1] While social scientists have been observing what goes on *inside* bureaucracies, the social criticism of bureaucracy has been calling attention to what goes on *between* bureaucracy and the rest of society.

It is curious that social research should so largely have ignored the relationship between bureaucracy and the public. We all have read Kafka and Orwell. We all are clients of a large number of organizations. Indeed, one can hardly buy a loaf of bread these days, or see a doctor, or borrow a book without confronting a bureaucracy. Yet, the fact remains that among the very large number of studies of organizational structures and their functioning, there are only a very few which analyze the interaction between bureaucratic officials and their clients.[2]

Unfortunately, we do not have reliable information on the amount of time individuals in modern society spend as clients in organizational dealings. This must be considerable, however. Think, for example, of public utilities such as transportation, electricity, telephone; public and private service organizations such as medical clinics, libraries, welfare offices, schools, employment bureaus; commonweal organizations such as the police, income tax bureaus, driver's license bureaus; business organizations such as department stores, supermarkets, and banks.

These organizations, and their clients, are the subject of this book. Its aim is to combine the two approaches to bureaucracy outlined above—the approach of the social critic and the approach of the social scientist.

Bureaucracy As a Problem for Social Science

Bureaucracies, for the sociologist, are goal-oriented organizations based on a clearly defined division of labor whereby each job in the organizational chart is spelled out in detail. The chain of command is carefully specified, and people are assigned jobs on the basis of their objective qualifications to fulfill them. Individuals are expected to feel loyalty to the organization and to be motivated to advance through the ranks. Even the top managers of a bureaucracy are appointed rather than elected. But, usually, above the managers sits a cabinet minister or a board of trustees who are there, in a sense, to "represent" the interested public—that is, to remind officials that the organization has certain goals and to find out, now and then, what is being done to achieve them.

It is these aspects of bureaucracy which have attracted the attention of empirically minded social scientists. While political scientists have mainly been interested in *government* bureaucracy, sociologists have focused on the variety of formal organizations having these characteristics, whether a state employment agency or a private mental hospital. Many studies have analyzed the variety of organizational structures and their functioning. Research has dealt with such subjects as the effect on productivity of the centralization and decentralization of authority; the processes whereby informally defined work arrangements arise alongside those which are formally defined; the relationship between organizational structure and efficiency; the conditions under which lower-echelon officials communicate to their superiors; and so on.

These problems are fascinating indeed, but they are not the whole of what is interesting or what is problematic about bureaucracy. Implicit in the structure of bureaucratic organizations is a set of norms which are supposed to govern interpersonal relationships within the organization and between the organization and its clientele. These, too, are part of the definition of bureaucracy. They are usually summed up in the shorthand that puts off some people, by means of the labels "specificity," "universalism," and "affective neutrality."

Specificity means that person-to-person communications within formal organizations are supposed to be strictly limited to those things which are officially defined as relevant to the matter at hand. Thus, the authority of a supervisor over a worker in his department should not extend beyond office hours; a collector of income tax is not supposed to become interested in whether his client really believes in the principles of the church to which he makes tax-exempt donations; and a university, many people believe, has no right to give information about a student's grades to his draft board. It is perfectly relevant, however, for a mental clinic to pry into your love life, or for a policeman to find out whether you have committed a previous offense. The opposite of specificity is diffuseness, which is the kind of intimate, reveal-your-whole-self relationship characteristic of families and friends who communicate with each other over a wide range of mutual interests.

Universalism means that those people with similar attributes or qualifications—among those attributes defined as relevant to the organization—will be treated equally, on a first-come first-served basis. This means that all persons with a given amount and kind of income and with an equal number of dependents will pay the same income tax. It means that people with long or short hair will receive equal treatment in obtaining welfare benefits or service in a department store. The same criteria which apply to service apply to employment: relevant qualifications alone are supposed to be taken into consideration by the Civil Service Commission regardless of race, creed, or length of hair. Of course, the bureaucracy of a church or a political party may limit employment or service to persons of its own creed. So may private organizations—even bureaucratic ones—but then they will be denied contracts by the United States government.

Affective neutrality means that bureaucratic communications make room for calm and reason, but not the expression of passions. Thus, a salesgirl is not supposed to let herself be exasperated by a customer—or to show it if she is. Nor may she let the customer know how little she thinks of her taste in clothes. Decisions are supposed to be taken rationally, on the merits of the case.

It should be clear that these interpersonal orientations—universalism, specificity, and affective neutrality—are equally applicable to the study of relationships between officials and clients as they are to the relationships among officials. Although they have received far less attention than other attributes of formal organization, those social scientists who have shown particular interest in official–client interaction have found them useful.

There *are* sociologists interested in official–client interaction; obviously, this book could not have been compiled without them. One of them is Peter Blau. A leading student of formal organization, Blau has consistently taken account of interaction with clients in his studies of employment offices, tax bureaus, social work agencies, and other organizations which have regular dealings with the public (e.g., 1964, 1960). Students of occupations, such as Hughes (1958), Goffman (1961), Lombard (1955), and others, have provided perceptive insights into the relationships among service occupations —professional and business—and their client/customers. Indeed, orientations to clients have been most explicitly studied within the context of service or-

ganizations staffed by professionals. The recent volume of essays edited by
Rosengren and Lefton on the "sociology of service" (1970) is a prominent,
and perhaps the best, example. One of its major emphases is on the conditions
under which organizations relate to their clients segmentally or as "whole
persons." Interestingly, their concern is with the narrowness (the low degree
of "laterality," in their terminology) with which organizations deal with their
clients. In their view, human beings are treated too compartmentally. When
this concern is juxtaposed with the concern which decries the way in which
formal organizations trespass the boundaries of specificity in asking "too
much" of their clients, an important dilemma emerges.

There are other senses in which sociologists may also be said to be interested in bureaucracy–public relations. Litwak and Meyer's (1966) study of
the interdependence of bureaucracy and community is one example. Another
is expressed in studies of the impact of bureaucracy on the personalities of
its members (Merton, 1952; Kohn, 1971). Each of these problems will become clearer as we review the themes most frequently heard from the social
critics of bureaucracy.

Bureaucracy As a Social Problem

While most social scientists are interested primarily in what goes on *within*
bureaucracies, almost everybody else is concerned with what goes on between
bureaucratic organizations and the public. "Everybody else" includes kitchen-
table conversations, newspaper editorials, radical and not-so-radical critics of
mass society, and even off-duty social scientists.

Different kinds of people voice different kinds of criticism about bureaucracy, but if one listens closely, it is not difficult to hear that they are talking
about the ways in which formal organizations deal with their clients, or
beyond that, the ways in which formal organizations affect the environments
in which they exist, including the lives and personalities of their workers.
The most common complaints voiced against bureaucracies are that they
are inefficient, impersonal or inhuman, and inaccessible when really needed.

Unlike the social scientists who see in formal organizations the potential
for the rational and efficient pursuit of goals, everyday talk about bureaucracy
has to do with filling out forms, coping with red tape, punching time cards,
confronting yes-men, and being made to feel powerless. It may well be that
some of this kind of criticism has declined in recent years, at least among the
middle classes. One wonders whether this is because the bureaucracies of
government and big business have indeed become more efficient and service
oriented or whether it isn't because more and more of us have learned to
live with bureaucracies. Today, well over four-fifths of the population of

the United States, for example, consists of salaried employees, and the proportion of persons who work in bureaucratic organizations is constantly rising.

Hofstadter (1964) believes that there has been some decline in criticism and that it is because we have become accustomed to living with, and in, bureaucracies.

> It is this acceptance of the bureaucratic career that, more than anything else, tells us why there is no longer an antitrust movement. It is far more revealing than the law cases or the books on control of monopoly. And it is also a perfect illustration of how the problems of yesteryear are not solved but outgrown. Only a few people today are concerned about how to make the large corporation more competitive, but millions are concerned about how they are going to live inside the corporation framework. The existence and the workings of the large corporations are largely accepted, and in the main are assumed to be fundamentally benign. What is questioned, when anything is questioned, are matters of personal style: what can be salvaged, in the way of individualism or individuality, in an age in which the big corporation has become a way of life? [p. 52]

But if claims that bureaucracy is inefficient, unfair, or inaccessible have indeed declined in the middle classes and in the editorials, this criticism can still be heard very clearly among the more deprived groups—those who depend on the mechanics of the welfare state, whether it be for economic opportunity or for health. These concerns also preoccupy new nations which are struggling with the problem of how to superimpose a modern administrative apparatus on the patterns of social relations in their traditional cultures. One can hear the echo of these same concerns from the clients of bureaucracies in totalitarian regimes.

The debate over the impersonality of bureaucracy has, however, by no means subsided. The familiar outcry against the segmentation of human beings by bureaucratic categorizations has become a rallying cry of radical youth, among others, who object to the distance between person and person in modern society, and who see formal organizations as the major source of this evil. For them, bureaucracies can only make war, not love.

Ironically, some of the very same people are equally outraged over the invasion of privacy for which bureaucracies, it is said, are also to blame. While calling for more human relations and less segmentation in bureaucratic dealings with their clients, these critics fear the power which is concentrated in formal organizations and their imperialistic potential for taking over areas of society other than those officially assigned to them. (In totalitarian regimes, bureaucracy *is* society, or more exactly, all of life is dominated by an interlocking set of bureaucracies.) In a word, these critics fear that the norm of specificity is hardly enough protection, and that we are likely to wake up one morning to find ourselves powerless prisoners of organizations which know everything about us. Perhaps even more frightening is the thought of being happy with such a situation, as was the hero at the end of Orwell's *1984*.

Some Converging Themes

Having reviewed some of the ways in which social scientists and social critics look at bureaucracy, it is time to reunite these sets of concerns. For the purpose at hand, three sets of interrelated problems seem particularly salient. Each can be derived from the concerns of science and of society. The first of these is the dilemma of orientation towards clients: How much of the whole person should be taken into account?

The second problem flows from the first: How can bureaucracy be controlled? Can democracy control bureaucracy? Can bureaucracies be prevented from running off and setting their own goals or from forgetting about the goals set for them by society while continuing the comfortable routine of filling out forms and punching time clocks? How can the privacy of the individual be maintained in modern society when so many organizations are collecting and collating information about him?

The third problem is whether individual personalities can retain their independence in an organizational society. Can the personalities of individuals be protected from the constraints of working for bureaucratic organizations or being served by them? Or, is it possible that organizations are not as threatening as they seem? Each of the three problems is considered below.

SPECIFICITY VERSUS THE WHOLE PERSON

This is a genuine dilemma. The norms of bureaucracy call for a specific and affectively neutral relationship between official and client, or indeed, between professional practitioner and client. The job of the customs official, or of the salesgirl, or of the dentist is to focus on a very narrow segment of the client's personality. Yet, it is very clear that this is an emotionally unsatisfying relationship (as it was "meant" to be), and that people are less willing to tolerate it. They want to be treated as whole persons. Moreover, it becomes increasingly clear that it "pays" to treat people that way. That the ethnicity of clients may be a relevant factor for effective medical practice (Zola, 1966) may not be so surprising, but that their personalities are relevant for banking is rather more striking. A current advertisement for personalized checks in New York City reads:

> Show the world there's more to you than
> 911–0–456789.

Yet, as professional and commercial services move in the direction of personalization and human relations, the remaining vestiges of privacy move with them. One has revealed too much about oneself! The bank will tell the

Bureau of Internal Revenue, as indeed it will. The Bureau of Internal Revenue will tell the interagency computer—as it may or may not. And so on.

Just as an increase in "human relations" affects privacy and individuality, so does it affect universalism. Taking race, religion, or ethnicity into account—as we shall show in Part II—opens the door to the practice of "inequality," as the word is commonly understood.

So there is the dilemma. The more the whole person is taken into account, the less latitude is left for privacy and equality (specificity and universalism). The more segmented one's relationship with others, the more one wants to be treated as whole.

Some persons have tried to resolve the dilemma by "dropping out." They want both diffuseness and privacy—and the organization cannot give it to them. They opt for anarchy, or communes, or social movements—but not for the formal organization of social services. Others prefer the classical resolution: Organizations should stay as specific as they are; the whole person should piece himself together at home. Still others are willing to pay a price for human relations in organization: the risk of reduced privacy and increased inequality.

More optimistic, perhaps, is the possibility that certain kinds of services will become increasingly specific and segmented, anonymous and automated —like selling stamps or sandwiches by machine—while others will become increasingly personalized and lateral without too much threat to the self. We will return to this possibility—but it is by no means an easy one.

THE PROBLEM OF CONTROL

Granting, at least for the moment, that formal organization—with its specialized division of labor, hierarchial control, rules, and regulations, and peculiar forms of social relations—is the most rational way to achieve many societal goals, what kinds of checks exist to make certain that these goals are indeed the ones being pursued by the organization, that the organization is pursuing them effectively, and that the unanticipated consequences of this activity—pollution, for example, or the accumulation of power for its own sake —are kept at a minimum? In democratic theory, at least, goal setting is a matter of political decision while goal attainment is the job of formal organization. But policing the separation of these functions and supervising the workings of bureaucracy have become increasingly tenuous as organizations grow larger and managers play an increasingly large share in goal setting, not only in private corporations but in publicly owned organizations as well. Indeed, it is not at all unusual to find technocrats running the government itself.

The question is not limited to organizations which exist to serve the public, though this aspect is the one which will be given the most emphasis in this text. Responsiveness of organizations to their clients is a problematic matter as the organization grows, and as the distance between clients and managers or owners consequently grows (Etzioni, 1958). The problem is even more acute in monopolistic organizations, public or private, but especially so in public bureaucracies whose success is not measurable in terms of profit and loss.

A number of new ways of confronting this problem have been suggested in recent years, ranging from the decentralization of decision making in the public-serving bureaucracies (such as health, education, and welfare)—to allow for greater local, even neighborhood, control—to the introduction of an ombudsman to oversee the manner in which bureaucratic services are provided (Gellhorn, 1966; Rowat, 1965).

Connected to the problem of public control of bureaucracy is the current concern over the invasion of privacy implicit in the increasing bureaucratization of society (Westin, 1967; Rosenberg, 1969; Miller, 1971). Computers are the servants of bureaucratic organization, and as more and more information about individuals is accumulated and easily retrieved, the idea of the specificity of bureaucratic contacts and the privacy of the individual are increasingly threatened. Access to centralized information about an individual will be an easy matter, technologically speaking, with the establishment of data banks to facilitate the business of government, the administrative temptation of exchanging information, and the tendency toward a functional consolidation of the departments of government.

It has long been possible, of course, to obtain credit ratings on business firms, and the credit card, in effect, now makes it possible to obtain similar information on individuals. Life insurance companies, to take another example, virtually compel their would-be clients to give them unlimited access to private information, and so on.

Filling out forms is not the whole problem, of course. Security and loyalty programs have been continually refining the variety of electronic devices by which information can be obtained "unobtrusively," in addition to making full use of the more traditional means of investigation. The United States government, for instance, employs over 20,000 professional investigators (Westin, 1967:119). One-fifth of all job-holders in the United States is affected by some sort of loyalty program, including teachers in some states (Packard, 1964). Although these checks may be of a purely routine character, causing minimal inconvenience, they create an aura of surveillance, and by assigning identification cards and numbers, contribute to the general feeling that one is constantly being watched and that one's identity is becoming increasingly depersonalized.

In the company town of yesteryear (there are still some around), the employer or his representative was also one's banker, grocer, real-estate agent, preacher, and so on. Nowadays, people live at some distance from their places of work, but the long arm of the corporation is keeping pace. William H. Whyte's *Organization Man* (1956) describes the ways in which organizations invade the private lives of their employees, subtly directing them to certain kinds of social activities and certain kinds of neighborhoods, and even exerting influence on the choice of a spouse.

BUREAUCRACY AND PERSONALITY

A third major problem which confronts the society in which bureaucratic organization predominates is that of maintaining a balance between the kind of person who fits into the organizational life—but who also fits "out" of it. This is putting the problem at its simplest, implying as we are, that there is conflict between the two kinds of personalities. The organizational personality —so this argument goes—is one which knows its place, responding cheerfully and respectfully to the authority of superiors and exercising authority firmly and fairly over subordinates. This kind of personality accepts the rules as legitimate, and does not challenge or question why things are the way they are. Teamwork is another attribute of this kind of personality. The ability to establish and maintain distance—to keep personal relations from interfering —is considered desirable. Striving for success is admirable, too, but within the career line defined by the organization. Miller and Swanson (1958) have tried to show that parents who work in bureaucracies are preparing their children for organizational life by adopting more permissive and more gratifying child-rearing methods which presumably promote a more accommodative and adjustive personality. They compare these practices with the self-denying, ambitious, independent tasks demanded of the children of entrepreneurial parents.

If organizations "require" the kind of personality that analysis of the bureaucratic role implies, one wonders how desirable this same personality is as a citizen or a friend or a father. Although many writers agree that there is developing a modern personality that makes its way more easily among the tables of organization, some theorists fear this development. One source of concern is that the "fit" is an unnatural one. They believe that there persists a contradiction between individual needs and organizational needs. Whereas the individual requires opportunities for self-actualization, autonomy, creativity, and initiative, the organization requires commitment, conformity, and deference (Argyris, 1964; Presthus, 1965). Just as Freud postulated an irreconcilable conflict between the requirements of society generally—what he called "civilization"—and the striving of the id for libidinal freedom, so these theorists think that there is a basic contradiction, which might be paraphrased as "organization and its discontents" (Bennis, 1966).

Other theorists worry even more. They fear that personality can be adapted to the requirements of organization *too* successfully. Indeed, Weber himself, in a little-known statement (in Mayer, 1943), takes a very strong stand concerning the deleterious effects of bureaucracy on personality. In a speech delivered at the convention of the *Verein für Sozialpolitik,* an association devoted to research and action on social and political problems, Weber says,

Introduction

Imagine the consequences of that comprehensive bureaucratization and rationalization which already today we see approaching. Already now, throughout private enterprise in wholesale manufacture, as well as in all other economic enterprises run on modern lines, *Rechthaftigkeit,* rational calculation, is manifest at every stage. By it, the performance of each individual worker is mathematically measured, each man becomes a little cog in the machine and, aware of this, his one preoccupation is whether he can become bigger. . . . It is . . . horrible to think that the world could one day be filled with nothing but those little cogs, little men clinging to little jobs and striving toward bigger ones—a state of affairs which is to be seen once more, as in the Egyptian records, playing an ever-increasing part in the spirit of our present administrative system, and specially of its offspring, the students. This passion for bureaucracy, as we have heard it expressed here, is enough to drive one to despair. It is as if in politics the spectre of timidity—which has in any case always been a good standby for the German—were to stand alone at the helm; as if we were deliberately to become men who need "order" and nothing but order, who become nervous and cowardly if for one moment this order wavers, and helpless if they are torn away from their total incorporation in it. That the world should know no men but these: it is in such an evolution that we are already caught up, and the great question is therefore not how we can promote and hasten it, but what can we oppose to this machinery in order to keep a portion of mankind free from this parcelling-out of the soul, from this supreme mastery of the bureaucratic way of life. [pp. 96-97]

A related kind of argument—Merton's (1952) is still the best example of this position—holds that the individuals who ostensibly fit the organization best are the ones who may be the most likely to subvert the organization's own goals. Overspecialization, routinization of procedure, and rigid following of regulations cause the bureaucratic official to narrow his focus and thus to lose sight of the overall goals of the organization. The result is that procedures and means become ends in themselves.

The ultimate expression of this kind of personality is the "escape from freedom," the blind acceptance of the dictates of authority. Milgram's (1963)* well-known experiment on the limits of obedience to legitimate authority is a vivid exposition of the dilemma. In the experiment, a subject is asked by a person of seemingly legitimate authority to perform an act which would, under other circumstances, presumably outrage his conscience.

Opposing these gloomy theories of bureaucracy and personality is the surprisingly optimistic position of Kohn (1971)* who argues that individuals in bureaucratic organization, even in its present state, have a *better* chance for the expression of independence, creativity, intellectual striving, and openness to change than have individuals of comparable education working in non-bureaucratic contexts. One of the main troubles with this deviant argument is that it is supported by better empirical evidence than the positions it criticizes. If Kohn is correct, perhaps there is no problem. But if he is wrong—and it is difficult to give up the feeling that he is—the problem is obvious.

Our concern here is very largely with organizations which are supposed to serve clients. We want the client to be served well—by just regulations,

---

* Asterisks throughout the book indicate that the selection is included in this volume.

by humane treatment, by reasonable procedure. In short, instead of assuming that bureaucratic organizations are innately efficient or uniformly inefficient—indeed, instead of assuming that organizations are all alike—we want to know which kinds serve the client better than others. Why not assume that organizations serving the public might like to know the answers to these questions, too?

In short, we are posing a set of problems which require simultaneous solutions so that the advantages of optimizing one element are not cancelled out by the failure of the others. At one and the same time, that is, we want an organizational framework which can deal effectively and fairly with the problems with which it is asked to deal by individuals and society; to make certain that individuals and groups in society have the necessary countervailing power to constrain the organization from trespassing in areas of individual privacy or onto other public areas for which other kinds of organizations are more appropriate; to be certain that the kind of personality which grows up under the influence of formal organizations does not contribute to the downfall of the political and cultural values of democratic society—and, indeed, does not undermine the organization's ability to achieve its own goals.

Factors Affecting the Interaction of Official and Client

The object of this book of readings is to examine the variety of factors which influence the relationship between bureaucratic organizations and their publics. We propose to focus, as specifically as possible, on the interaction between officials and clients in a variety of organizational settings. In doing so, we shall go beyond the narrow definition of "officials" and include practitioners and professionals of all kinds who deal with clients within the context of formal organizations. The bus driver, the nurse, the army chaplain, the social worker are all salaried employees serving the clients of their organizations, along with the bank teller, the customs inspector, and the policeman. Our continual concern will be to identify, insofar as possible, the organizational and extra-organizational factors which influence the interaction and its outcome. Admittedly, we shall be taking the client's point of view rather more than that of the official, although we realize that officials sometimes have trouble with problematic clients, too.

Consider an extreme case. In the standard textbooks of introductory sociology, the relationship between bus driver and passenger is often used to illustrate the kind of relationship which is presumably characteristic of bureaucratic organizations. The bus driver and the passenger are supposed to be interested in each other only insofar as each does his own job. Their relationship is highly "specific," in other words. The driver does not really care whether passenger A or passenger B enters his bus, so long as one, or the other, or both, enters the bus in an orderly queue, has the proper fare ready, signals when he wants to alight, etc. The same thing holds true for the passenger: he has no interest whatever in whether today's driver is A or B, so long as the driver supplies the correct change, departs on time, drives safely, and so on.

Here, then, we have examples of specificity in interpersonal relations, universalism (the queue—first-come, first-served—is the epitome of universalism), and emotional neutrality (their interdependence is of a wholly rational and instrumental sort). There is a mutual awareness of the rules: that there is an established price and established route; that the money collected by the driver is handed over to the company and that he receives a salary; that there is a hierarchy of authority, in several echelons, supervising the driver; that agencies beyond the bus company itself—the police, the municipality which gave the franchise—have some interest in what goes on inside and outside the bus.

In the late 1950s, a group of sociologists at the Hebrew University became interested in the confrontation between new immigrants to Israel and the various bureaucracies with which they came into contact, including bus companies. In the early 1950s, large groups of immigrants had come to Israel from traditional societies, innocent of the norms and structures which apply to the peculiar kinds of relationships characterizing formal organizations. And, indeed, in those days it was not at all unusual to observe a new immigrant from, say, Yemen, bargaining with the bus driver over the fare, or asking to be let off in front of his home rather than at the bus stop. The outbreak of arguments, or worse, in queues was a common sight. Bus drivers, when interviewed, expressed concern over the problems of decorum inside the bus, and some suggested—not at all in keeping with the ideas of specificity—that they felt much more comfortable when they drove at fixed times so that they could establish personal relationships with their passengers than when they were simply anonymous bus drivers doing their jobs. Because they had large groups to control, the drivers often established personalized joking relationships with passengers, to keep their audiences amused. Supervisors took some account of this when assigning shifts.

And so, as the paper by Katz and Eisenstadt (1960)* points out, the drivers became socializing agents—teachers for a time—not out of any particular motive of patriotism or altruism, but in order to keep the buses running. They taught the ideas of a queue, fixed fares, and so on. It wasn't very long before traveling on a bus became boring again. In the process, though, some things had to be unlearned, probably at some expense. Elders and teachers who were used to deference found that they had to be satisfied with universalism, that may well have been interpreted as disrespect. People realized that they had less "power" than they were used to—that bargaining was to no avail, that persuasive talk did not help. Indeed, they discovered that even the driver himself had little or nothing to say—that power was beyond him, too—and thus that the individual was quite remote from the locus and the language of this new kind of authority. However, many people seem to have developed the feeling that the mysterious power in ultimate command is also benevolent, and that one can, and should, depend on it uncritically. In a sense, the learning of the passenger role—the role of client —was almost too one-sided.

Here, then, are some clues, from an admittedly piquant situation, to some of the factors affecting interaction among officials and clients. First, there are cultural factors that enter into the relationship: the expectations of each group were affected by their backgrounds. Secondly, there are some relevant organizational factors which made a difference: the structure of work within this organization was based on a rotation of drivers, but the structure was also flexible enough, apparently, to allow drivers and supervisors to take account of the unusual demands of the situation. Finally, in this case, the official must confront and control a large group of clients, more or less on his own. The driver does not have the protection of an office-full of colleagues.

Unusual as this case may be, it permits us to outline the three sets of factors which we feel are essential to an understanding of official–client interaction, and ultimately of the relationships of organizations with their publics: (1) environmental factors, such as cultural and subcultural influences bearing on the organization and on clients, the community context in which the official-client relationship takes place, whether the clients are organized or not; (2) organizational factors, such as the nature of formal control over the organization and its workings, the criteria by which performance is measured and supervision carried out, the goals of the organization (whether it is healing sick people or collecting income tax); and (3) situational factors, such as the affinities shared (or unshared) by a particular client and a particular official, whether the encounter takes place in relative isolation from other clients or officials, and so on.

Let us elaborate on each of these sets of factors, since they constitute the three main sections in which the readings in this book are organized. The fourth, and last, section is given over to reflections and suggestions—from the point of view of both social scientists and social reformers—of how to deal with the problems raised in the first three sections.

ENVIRONMENTAL INFLUENCES: CULTURE AND COMMUNITY

Different societies have different systems of values, and some, obviously, are more compatible with bureaucracy than others. As societies become more modern, they begin to introduce formal organizations, but like other innovations borrowed from abroad, the idea of organization is somewhat transformed during the process, and bears the imprint not only of the donor culture but of the culture of the borrower as well. We shall see that the official–client relationship is influenced by differences in cultural values.

A good illustration of the set of factors discussed here can be seen in the problems encountered, not so long ago, in the New York City school system. With the rise of militant black organizations, there came a demand for at least proportional representation of blacks on the teaching staff. That the low number of black teachers was heretofore highly disproportional was a fact, but the reason for this fact, it was argued, was universalism: that is, there were simply fewer blacks qualified to teach according to the city's standards for obtaining a license. Some blacks explicitly rejected this argument, claiming that particularism was an equally applicable criterion—black children *ought* to be taught by teachers of their own race. Others said that the supposedly universalistic standards were culture bound. Reflecting on this situation, Nathan Glazer (1964) points out that the stake which some groups have in the norm of universalism is much greater than that of others. Glazer says:

the liberal principles—the earlier ones arguing the democracy of money, the new ones arguing the democracy of merit—that have been so congenial to Jews and so much in their interest are being increasingly accepted by everyone else nowadays under the pressures of a technological world. We are moving into a diploma society where individual merit rather than family and connections and group must be the basis of advancement, recognition and achievement. The reasons have nothing to do directly with the Jews, but no matter—the Jews certainly gain from such a grand historical shift. . . . It is clear that one cannot say the same about the Negro interests. And so the Negroes have come to be opposed to these approaches. But when Negroes challenge—as they do in New York—the system of testing by which school principals and higher officials in the educational bureaucracy are selected and promoted, they are also challenging the very system under which the Jews have done so well. And when they challenge the use of grades as the sole criterion for entry into special high schools and free colleges, they challenge the system which has enabled the Jews to dominate these institutions for decades. . . . The Negro anger is based on the fact that the system of formal equality produces so little for them. The demand for economic equality is now not the demand for equality of opportunities for the equally qualified: it is the demand for equality of results—and it therefore raises such questions as why some businesses succeed and others fail, and how people are selected for advancement in large organizations. When we move into areas like that, we are not asking for abstract tolerance, or a simple desisting from discrimination. . . . Or consider the demand for equality in education, which has also become a demand for equality of results, of outcomes. Suppose one's capacity to gain from education depends on going to school with less than a majority of one's own group? Or suppose that it depends on one's home background? Then how do we achieve equality of results? The answers to this question and many similar ones suggest that the deprived group must be inserted into the community of the advantaged. For otherwise there is no equality of outcome.

Whether or not one agrees with Glazer that the trend in modern society is toward an ever-increasing implementation of the norms of universalism and achievement, it is plain that those interested in the survival of these values had better ensure the ability of bureaucratic organizations to respond sensitively to the problem he poses.

Just as some cultures are more hospitable to values implicit in bureaucratic organization—universalism, specificity, affective neutrality, centralized authority, and the like—so certain subgroups are better prepared than others to cope with bureaucracy. Even within modern, bureaucratically organized societies, some groups are more knowledgeable than others about the workings of bureaucracy, and some clients are better equipped than others, psychologically speaking, to encounter officials. Officials have personalities, of course, just as they have subgroup affiliations, and, naturally, these affect both the nature of the organization and the interaction between officials and clients.

As far as we know, the influence of culture, personality, and organizational structure are interdependent. If cultures and personalities affect organizational functioning, so organizational structures affect personality. And such effects, in turn, are transmitted by the parents who work and live in a given social structure to their children. Thus, in an indirect way, even the child-rearing methods which predominate in a given society or subgroup will be of relevance to the relationship between officials and clients.

Beyond culture and personality as elements of the environment in which bureaucracy functions, there is a societal context. Organizations function in communities: these may be small communities where everybody knows one another, or large ones. They may be stratified or highly egalitarian. They may depend on the organization—as in a company town—for access to resources, or they may have alternate channels of access. Whether clients are organized in any way is another important consideration. All these will affect the relationships between officials and clients.

ORGANIZATIONAL FACTORS: GOALS AND ROLES

The second set of factors which bear on the relationship between bureaucracies and their publics are the elements of the organizational structure itself. To begin with, one must consider the goals of the organization: does the organization exist to serve clients—as does a hospital, for example—or does it exist to serve society as a whole—as does the Bureau of Internal Revenue, for example? Obviously, the client has different rights vis-à-vis the one kind of organization than the other.

Again, one must ask whether the organization exists to provide resources which clients voluntarily apply for—as in a department store—or whether the interaction of the client with the organization is mandatory. Even in organizations as mandatory as prisons, it has been shown that custodial versus therapeutic orientations make an important difference. Following Thompson (1962)*, we shall also ask whether diagnosis of the client's problem can be done as a matter of routine, according to the letter of some law or a set of regulations (as in a customs inspection, for instance) or whether the right to diagnose and decide is more freely given to the official (as in a social welfare case, for example). These considerations have bearing not only on the nature of the interaction between officials and clients, but also on the question of who will come into contact with the public: Will it be a high-

ranking official or a low-ranking one? Will the job require professional training—as in the case of a hospital—or not?

Apart from the service rendered by the organization to the client or to
society at large, the nature of supervision within the organization will affect
official–client relations. Whether supervision is predicted on quantitative
criteria—how many job placements are made each day by an official in the
employment bureau—or whether it is predicated on specific criteria, such as
the "goodness of fit" between the job sought and the job offered, will obviously
make for different kinds of official–client relations. So will the nature of the
informal relationships among the officials themselves: If officials are integrated
in their peer groups, they are more secure vis-à-vis clients, and several
studies suggest that if group norms are service oriented, members are better
able to serve them and to empathize with their needs than are others less
accepted by their peers (Blau, 1964; Lombard, 1955).

Size of the organization appears to affect official–client relations, as does
the extent to which the organization is segmented and specific or total, as in
the case of prisons, hospitals, ships, etc., where clients, and often officials,
spend the full round of their lives within the context of organization. Goffman's (1961) famous essay on this subject analyzes how organizations behave when their clients eat, sleep, play, and make friends and enemies
inside the organization.

SITUATIONAL FACTORS

The third set of relevant factors which will be examined for their bearing
on official–client relations derives from the situation of interaction itself. A
key question here has to do with the extent of consensus in the expectations of
the official and the client of each other. Obviously, if each comes from different backgrounds, or, for whatever reason, with different expectations of the
other, communication between the two takes on an added difficulty.

Another kind of problem stems from what Gouldner (1957–1958) calls
"latent social identity," or what Katz and Eisenstadt (1960)* call "role
impingement." To what extent do roles which are officially irrelevant to the
interaction in question come into play? What happens when the client is of
a higher status than the official? Under what circumstances are official, or
client, or both, influenced in their behavior by common affiliation—kinship,
religion, political allegiance?

Clients sometimes try to influence the outcome of an interaction by making
these latent identities manifest, or they may employ "props"—to use
Goffman's (1959)* term—to make a more effective impression. The official,
too, may bolster his status with a set of symbols of office. Other types of
strategies may also be invoked by either side, for the sake of active persuasion
or of "self-defense."

Apart from expectations, latent identities, and strategies, however, there
are some situational influences on interaction which are far beyond the control

of either official or client. Consider, for example, the problems of interaction between a taxicab driver and his passenger compared, say, with those of a bus driver and his passengers. Unlike the passengers in a bus, the isolated dyad in a taxicab often experiences the pressure to converse. Perhaps this is to dispel the suspiciousness or anxiety that each holds about the other; perhaps it is to overcome the uncomfortable feeling of maintaining total impersonality in this kind of situation. In many societies, there is also concern on both sides about tipping, as Fred Davis (1959) suggests. Perhaps the ecology of this situation explains the loquacious cab driver. In more general terms, the absence of others—or the absence of supervision—makes for greater mutual dependence and, generally, for greater intimacy among the people involved. Altogether, spatial aspects of official–client interaction may be quite important in affecting the dynamics of the relationship and the mutual satisfaction with its outcome, and there is obviously much more room here for collaboration among architects, social scientists, administrators, and interested members of the public (Sommer, 1969).

Another situational variable is the channel or medium of contact—is it face-to-face or indirect, that is, through the mail or by telephone? The different channels provide different kinds of opportunities for mutual persuasion, for going "on the record," for saving time, and the like.

Interaction and Outcome

What we are suggesting, to this point, is that environmental factors, such as divergent or convergent expectations or seating arrangements, affect the dynamics of official–client interaction, and broadly speaking, the outcome of the encounter. But we haven't really given adequate definition of either interaction or outcome.

By *interaction,* we mean three things: (1) First, it is the *manner* in which officials and clients deal with each other. Do they greet each other? How much do they talk? Politeness and civility are decidedly included in this category. (2) Second, we are concerned with the *procedures* involved—number of forms filled out, number of different officials contacted, length of time invested by the client, and the like. (3) Finally, we are interested in the *resources* exchanged. Did the client get his license? Was he let off at his bus stop? How much did he have to pay—in money, in time, perhaps in self-respect? Did the official benefit in any way—in gratitude, in bribes? And so on.[3]

The evaluation of each of these elements of interaction will be called *outcome.* Each of the participants, or any observer (supervisor, spouse, social scientist) can ask, from the point of view of the client: Was he considerately treated? Was he efficiently treated? And was he treated fairly? (Almond and

Introduction

Verba, 1965).* In other words, the client can ask himself (or we can ask on his behalf): Was he treated in a civil, respectful *manner?* Were the *procedures* efficient? Were the *resources* allocated fairly? Obviously, one of these may be deemed satisfactory—by either or both criteria—and another less so. The procedure may be judged efficient but the manner impolite. Or, the manner may be perfectly polite but the procedure or the resources undesirable.

And what if the official is pushed to act favorably or unfavorably towards the client? The official may comply, he may spitefully do the opposite of what has been asked of him, or he may ignore the pressure altogether. And this applies, of course, with respect to each of the three dimensions of outcome. From the client's point of view, it is surely more important to receive a desired resource than to be treated considerately.

These three dimensions of interaction appear to be related to the three orientations which are supposed, ideally, to characterize interpersonal relations within organizations and between organizations and their clients: universalism, specificity, affective neutrality. Table 1 illustrates the connections.

TABLE 1

Three Aspects of Official-Client Interaction and Their Relation to the Norms of Universality, Specificity, and Affective Neutrality

	MANNER	PRO-CEDURE	RESOURCE
Universalism	X	X	X
Specificity	X	X	
Affectivity	X		

Universalism applies to all three dimensions of interaction, but especially, perhaps, to resources. That is to say, the interaction of officials and clients can be evaluated in terms of the degree of equality (or discrimination) shown by an official to a client in matters of civility, in the diagnostic and bureaucratic procedure, and in the allocation of the organization's resources. The notion of universalism seems especially important in connection with the last, since the allocation of resources—as we have already noted—is probably the ultimate concern of the individual and society. But unfair procedures—letting some go to the head of the line—is also a matter of obvious concern, as are the civilities and good manners with which human beings deserve to be treated.[4]

The notion of specificity cannot really be applied to resources, but it can be applied to both manner and procedure, especially the latter. If the form a client is asked to fill out requires him to submit personal information which goes beyond the organization's need for such information in the pursuit of its goals, such treatment may be said to deviate from the norm of specificity.

Specificity of treatment differs from specificity in manners in that the latter refers primarily to the style of interaction. An example might be a clerk at the post office who recognizes in his client a fellow countryman and addresses him in his native tongue, thus taking account not only of his client role but also of his ethnicity. Theoretically, at least, this need not be accompanied by any deviation from the norm of affective neutrality. He may simply go about the regular business of the organization without betraying either more or less emotion than is appropriate.

Affective neutrality, then, pertains almost exclusively to manner. It is a question of how a client and an official relate to one another emotionally. When the psychiatrist falls in love with his patient, it is a departure from affective neutrality.

Of course, the judgments of the outcome made by the client himself, by the client's wife, by the official's supervisor, or by the objective observer may be quite different. The client may feel that he has been discriminated against —in manners, in procedure, or in resources. Recalling Glazer's remarks about the black challenge to the New York City school system, it may be that an outcome will be considered fair by the client in the sense that it is admittedly equal, but nevertheless unsatisfactory. Or, as Glazer puts it, the client may demand not equality of opportunity, but equality of outcome—whether or not he qualifies for the outcome obtained by another.

Now let us try to organize the various things we have been talking about. We can conceptualize the structure of any given official–client encounter as a social system represented by the wedge in Figure 1. The first three parts of the wedge, from left to right, are the environment, the organization, and the situation. This graphic presentation makes it clear that the organization is a subsystem within the larger social system, and, in turn, the situation of the encounter is a subsystem of the organization. These three sets of variables constitute the input of the encounter. The interaction itself consists of the three elements we have discussed above: manner, procedure, and resources, all of which constitute aspects of the processing of the input. The outcome of this particular interaction is the evaluation of it in terms of these three elements, both by the official (and the organization) and by the client. We should also add that the environment can influence the encounter, independent of the organization, as when the client brings his general values into interaction.

Fragments of wedges at the left and right of center indicate that there is sequence and feedback: previous encounters influence the present one, and the outcome of the present one may influence any or all aspects of the next encounter, from the viewpoint of the client, or the organization, or both. This may entail a different strategy on the part of the client next time, a major change in the organizational structure, such as decentralization, or a situational change, like increasing the number of hours the office is open or having the matter taken care of by mail instead of in person. Although this model is designed mainly to describe face-to-face encounters, it seems quite applicable to telephoned or written ones as well.

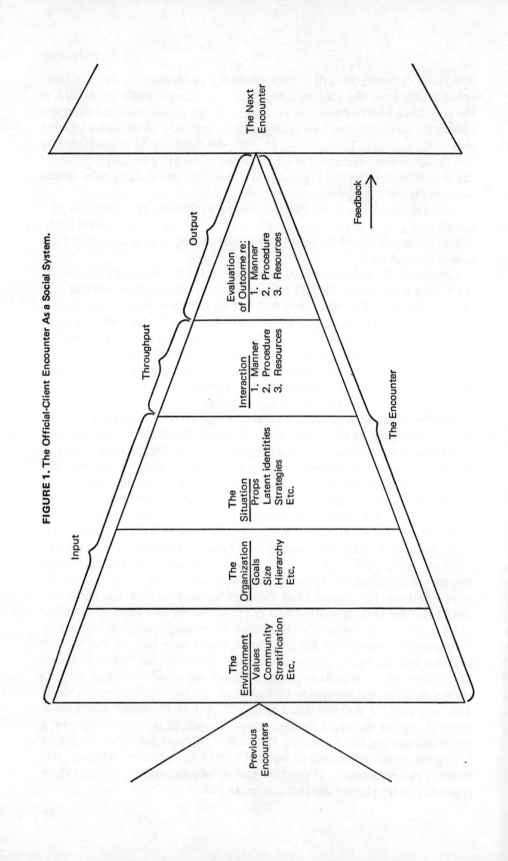

FIGURE 1. The Official-Client Encounter As a Social System.

What Can Be Done?

Each of the readings that follow points to a different kind of problem in the relationship between officials and clients, organization and publics, bureaucracies and democratic society. The final section of the book addresses itself to the sorts of things that might be done, that can be done, that are being done, to alleviate these problems.

Of course, what should be done depends very much on one's diagnosis of what, if anything, is wrong. Some people feel that most of the things that are wrong with bureaucracy can best be cured by more, and better, bureaucracy. Most of the problems, in this view, stem from the fact that many organizations deviate too far from the "ideal type" of bureaucracy. This may be because there is inadequate focusing on goals—in which case the board of directors and the supervisory process ought to be shaken up. Or, if the problem is that clients go away feeling that they have been badly dealt with, it may be because the system of categorization of people is too unrefined, and a more precise system of categorization with more subdivisions ought to be instituted.

Better socialization to bureaucratic rights and obligations is another sort of solution—not just for clients, but for officials as well. Thus, those who are most alienated from bureaucracy tend to be individuals who do not know their rights, do not know how to act in a bureaucratic situation, are not aware of proper bureaucratic channels of appeal—or even of the existence of such channels. They feel a general powerlessness in making bureaucratic organizations work in their interest. Several of the readings in the first section of the book deal with the determinants and consequences of bureaucratic socialization. The remedial aspects, such as the Citizens' Advice Bureaus in England, are presented in the last section (Kahn, *et al.*, 1966).*

An even stronger argument can be made for the resocialization of officials. Training in perceiving the needs of clients accurately and influencing the manner in which civil servants receive the public are a matter of continuing concern to the civil service commissions in different countries.

But it is unlikely that attitude and value change alone will make enough difference. More radical reformers want to see changes in the structures of bureaucratic organizations themselves, and a strengthening of organized control from without over the behavior of bureaucracies.

Those who feel that less bureaucracy is the remedy argue that decentralization will restore autonomy and initiative in the instrumental aspects of bureaucratic activity (procedures and resources) and add a human touch to the expressive aspect (manner). One leading advocate of this school of thought is Paul Goodman (1968). Another implication of the call for decentralization is a call for building formal organizations on the model of bureaucracies staffed by professionals where the official who deals with the public is a person who has high status and considerable discretionary power, unlike the low-level official who deals with the public in other kinds of organizations. This argument also stresses the need for developing feedback mechanisms within the organization, with respect both to the employee's own well-being and his views of the work situation. Such feedback would enable the organization to adapt more easily to changing circumstances and individual clients by staying in closer touch with the officials on the line who know the public best. A side effect, of course, is to give officials more sense of involvement and power within the organization, thus reducing the tendency to take it out on the client, and altogether having a desired effect on the official's personality. The hope, of course, is that such changes will make bureaucracies more responsive to their publics.

Still more radical organizational reform is proposed by some. Bennis (in Bennis and Slater, 1968) believes that bureaucracy will wither away due to its inability to cope with the rate of technological innovations and the growing awareness of its harmful effects. Cloward and Piven (1966) propose the nonviolent overthrow of the mammoth welfare bureaucracies by simply mobilizing all eligible persons to apply for the benefits legally due them. When the weight of these demands crushes the bureaucracy appointed to serve them, a system of guaranteed annual wage will be established, these authors believe, thus eliminating one of the more irksome types of bureaucratic contact. In a certain sense, of course, this proposal is as much for "better" bureaucracy as for "less."

More moderate proposals for the restructuring of bureaucratic organizations points to the success of organization-initiated efforts to facilitate the client's contact with the organization. Providing income tax information by telephone is an example. Patroling the queues to make sure that people are standing in the correct line is another. Enabling clients to telephone directly to organizational representatives on a radio program is still another. Listeners can learn from the answers given to these questions.

An alternative to organizational reform is counterorganization. This, of course, is the *raison d'être* of trade unions, consumer associations, and other types of "users" organizations. Members who belong and participate in such organizations feel far less powerless with respect to modern society and its bureaucracies.

The intensive efforts to create neighborhood organization within the ill-starred poverty program in the United States is another example of counterorganization, though the idea of spurring neighborhood organization and control is a long-standing one (Alinsky, 1946). It is not easy to arouse a community to action, and it is even more difficult to sustain such action for any length of time. There is no guarantee, of course, that successful community action—even when initiated by government in behalf of the people—will not turn against government itself. The vigilante groups organized for neighborhood protection, for example, are by no means always on the side of the police. Nor is the mobilization of this kind of community power limited to locally based bureaucracies; this countervailing power may extend far beyond the local community.

Still another kind of solution is that of regulating agencies and go-betweens. Rather than rely on socialization of either clients or officials, or reorganization of the bureaucracy or of its clients, a number of proposals are based on the idea of investing power in third parties. The best known of these reforms are associated with the idea of the ombudsman—which will be treated at length in Part IV—but other mediating mechanisms, some new and some well established, deserve examination as well. Where there is a cultural gap between officials of the bureaucracy and its clients, various intermediaries have proven successful on the community level: "detached workers" who mediate between neighborhood youth groups and the official world; the variety of health workers who intervene between traditionally oriented clients and Western medical practitioners (Simmons, 1955; Rosenblatt and Suchman, in Shostak and Gomberg, 1964); and ghetto lawyers (Matthews and Weiss, 1967).* Each is effective in its own way, and even the slightest of these efforts deserves respect.

To conclude: We are not proposing the abolition of formal organizations. We are pointing, rather, to the dilemmas which society must face as it assigns tasks and allocates resources to an organization, on the one hand, and tries to parry the undesirable consequences of their functioning, on the other. In other words, we are not "against" bureaucracy. We are against the kind of bureaucracy that is unresponsive to its clients, that usurps the goal-setting functions, that undermines autonomous and creative personalities, that invades domains which belong to the individuals or to other kinds of organizations. We are, in short, advocating continued attention to the harnessing of bureaucracy, but we are by no means advocating the retreat from the organizational society to the utopian socialism of the organized commune, and certainly not the anarchy of the disorganized commune.

NOTES

1. For a detailed discussion of the many meanings of "bureaucracy," see Albrow (1970).

2. The fact that "clients" is not an entry in the index to March's monumental *Handbook of Organizations* (1965) is evidence of this neglect.

3. Of course, the exchange model is in principle inapplicable to official–client relations; by "resource" we mean primarily the service or benefit the client comes to receive. The notion of resource is somewhat more difficult to apply in cases where the client comes to give something, as when he comes to pay a bill.

4. In certain kinds of interaction resources are indistinguishable from procedure, e.g., when the doctor in a health clinic spends more time examining one patient than another, even though both have exactly the same problem.

REFERENCES

Albrow, Martin. *Bureaucracy*. London: Pall Mall Press, 1970.

Alinsky, Saul. *Reveille for Radicals*. Chicago: University of Chicago Press, 1946.

Almond, Gabriel and Sidney Verba. *The Civic Culture*. Boston: Little, Brown, 1965.

Argyris, Chris. *Integrating the Individual and the Organization*. New York: Wiley, 1964.

Bennis, Warren G. *Changing Organizations: Essays on the Development and Evolution of Human Organization*. New York: McGraw-Hill, 1966.

Bennis, Warren G., and Philip E. Slater. *The Temporary Society*. New York: Harper Colophon Books, 1968.

Blau, Peter M. *The Dynamics of Bureaucracy*. Chicago: University of Chicago Press, 1964.

———. "Orientations toward Clients in a Public Welfare Agency." *Administrative Science Quarterly* 5 (1960): 341–361.

Cloward, Richard A. and Frances Fox Piven. "A Strategy to End Poverty." *The Nation* 202 (May 2, 1966): 510–517.

Davis, Fred. "The Cabdriver and His Fare: Facets of a Fleeting Relationship." *American Journal of Sociology* 65 (1959): 158–165.

Etzioni, Amitai. "Administration and the Consumer." *Administrative Science Quarterly* 3, no. 2 (1958): 251–264.

Gellhorn, Walter. *Ombudsmen and Others*. Cambridge: Harvard University Press, 1966.

Glazer, Nathan. "Negroes and Jews: The New Challenge to Pluralism." *Commentary* 38, no. 6 (1964): 29–34.

Goffman, Erving. *Asylums*. Garden City: Doubleday Anchor, 1961.

———. *The Presentation of Self in Everyday Life*. Garden City: Doubleday Anchor, 1959.

Goodman, Paul. *People or Personnel*. New York: Vintage, 1968.

Gouldner, Alvin. "Cosmopolitans and Locals: Toward an Analysis of Latent Social Roles." *Administrative Science Quarterly* 2 (1957–1958): 281–306; 444–480.

Hofstadter, Richard. "Antitrust in America." *Commentary* 38, no. 2 (1964): 47–53.

Hughes, Everett H. *Men and Their Work*. Glencoe: Free Press, 1958.

Kahn, Alfred J., Lawrence Grossman, Jean Bandler, Felicia Clark, Florence Galkin, and Kent Greenwalt. *Neighborhood Information Centers: A Study and Some Proposals*. New York: Columbia University School of Social Work, 1966.

Katz, Elihu, and S. N. Eisenstadt. "Some Sociological Observations on the Response of Israeli Organizations to New Immigrants." *Administrative Science Quarterly* 5 (1960): 113–133.

Kohn, Melvin L. "Bureaucratic Man: A Portrait and an Interpretation." *American Sociological Review* 36 (1971): 461–474.

Litwak, Eugene, and Henry J. Meyer. "A Balance Theory of Coordination between Bureaucratic Organizations and Community Primary Groups." *Administrative Science Quarterly* 11, no. 1 (June 1966): 31–58.

Lombard, George F. *Behavior in a Selling Group*. Cambridge: Graduate School of Business Administration, Harvard University Press, 1955.

March, James G., ed. *Handbook of Organizations*. Chicago: Rand McNally, 1965.

Matthews, Arthur R., and Jonathan A. Weiss. "What Can Be Done: A Neighborhood Lawyer's Credo." *Boston University Law Review* 67, no. 2 (1967): 231–243.

Merton, Robert K. "Bureaucratic Structure and Personality." In *Reader in Bureaucracy*, edited by Robert K. Merton et al., pp. 361–371. Glencoe: Free Press, 1952.

Milgram, Stanley. "Behavioral Study of Obedience." *Journal of Abnormal and Social Psychology* 67 (1963): 371–378.

Miller, Arthur. *The Assault on Privacy.* Ann Arbor: University of Michigan Press, 1971.

Miller, Daniel R., and Guy E. Swanson. *The Changing American Parent.* New York: Wiley, 1958.

Presthus, Robert V. *The Organizational Society.* New York: Vintage, 1965.

Rosenberg, Jerry M. *The Death of Privacy.* New York: Random House, 1969.

Rosenblatt, Daniel, and Edward A. Suchman. "The Underutilization of Medical-Care Services by Blue Collarites." In *Blue-Collar World,* edited by A. B. Shostak and W. Gomberg, pp. 341–349. Englewood Cliffs: Prentice-Hall, 1964.

Rosengren, William R., and Mark Lefton, eds. *Organizations and Clients: Essays in the Sociology of Service.* Columbus: Merrill, 1970.

Rowat, Donald C., ed. *The Ombudsman: Citizen and Defender.* London: Allen and Unwin, 1965.

Simmons, Ozzie. "The Clinical Team in a Chilean Health Center." In *Health, Culture and Community,* edited by Benjamin D. Paul, pp. 325–348. New York: Russell Sage Foundation, 1955.

Sommer, Robert. *Personal Space: The Behavioral Basis of Design.* Englewood Cliffs: Prentice-Hall, 1969.

Thompson, James D. "Organizations and Output Transactions." *American Journal of Sociology* 68 (1962): 309–324.

Weber, Max. "Bureaucratization." In *Max Weber and German Politics,* edited by J. P. Mayer, Appendix I, pp. 96–99. London: Faber and Faber, 1943.

Westin, Alan F. *Privacy and Freedom.* New York: Atheneum, 1967.

Whyte, William F., Jr. *Organization Man.* New York: Simon and Schuster, 1956.

Zola, Irving Kenneth. "Culture and Symptoms: An Analysis of Patients' Presenting Complaints." *American Sociological Review* 31, no. 6 (October 1966): 615–630.

PART I

Environmental Factors:
Culture and Community

THERE is a reciprocal influence between organizations and their environments. The environment in which organizations exist affects their character, but the organizations, in turn, also influence—and sometimes transform—their environment. This is obviously true of the natural resources of the environment, such as air or water, but it is equally true of social resources. The location of a factory, for example, may be influenced by the availability of waterpower, but pollution of the water may be a possible result. By the same token, a factory must draw upon the local community for its supply of manpower, and its success will be much influenced by the values and attitudes, and of course the skills, of those who come to work in it. In turn, the rhythms and rules of factory work may affect the personalities of its workers, as well as the families and communities from which they come. Indeed, some observers believe that, wittingly or not, bureaucratic organizations "pollute" their members' and their clients' personalities.

The readings collected in this chapter treat the mutual influence of bureaucratic organizations and social aspects of their environments. Three basic elements of the social environment are examined in turn: culture, community, and personality. We look first at bureaucratic organizations in different cultures to see how the organization—and particularly the relationship between official and client—is affected by the culture in which it resides. In a second section, we consider the effect of certain aspects of community organization on bureaucratic functioning. Then, we look more closely at individual personalities, the carriers of cultural values, how individuals are socialized by the societies to fit the requirements of bureaucratic organizations, and we debate the effect of bureaucratic socialization on the individual himself, on his culture and community, and on the organization in which he works.

The Influence of Culture and Social Structure

As far as culture is concerned, the problem is a classic one. The values appropriate to the functioning of bureaucratic organizations are not equally available in all cultures. The appropriate norms are those usually associated with modernity. Thus, institutional differentiation is a first requirement, meaning that kinship obligations or political affiliations are confined to the home

31

and community, respectively, and are not brought along to the office or the marketplace. Riggs' (1967) model of bureaucracy in developing societies makes use of the word "sala," which means both living room and office. In the office, universalism, specificity, and affective neutrality—terms which were explained in the Introduction—are supposed to govern interpersonal relations. As Weber pointed out (in Gerth and Mills, 1958:197), the maintenance of separate financial accounts for home and work fosters these interpersonal orientations in the office. The ideas of achievement and advancement based on merit are also prerequisite values, as is acceptance of the principle of hierarchical authority.

THE COMPATIBILITY OF BUREAUCRACY AND CULTURE

Some ancient societies possessed some of these values, but apparently, never all of them in combination. Ancient China, for example, had the idea of appointing people to office on the basis of achievement in a competitive examination. But they were tested not on technical knowledge needed by public officials, but on their general knowledge of Chinese culture (Weber, in Gerth and Mills, 1958: 416–444). McClelland (1961), too, provides many examples from other times and places of the presence of the "need for achievement," which undoubtedly creates a climate congenial to the establishment of bureaucracies.

In an analysis of the problems associated with the institutionalization of bureaucracy in the Middle East, Presthus (1959)* has elaborated on the theme of the compatibility of bureaucratic values with those of the wider culture. Where a person has little feeling of control over his destiny—where Allah's will is the ultimate determinant of human action and its consequences —then bureaucracy has trouble taking root. Similarly, bureaucracy flourishes where cultural values stress getting things done rather than simply savouring the pleasures of the moment or developing one's inner potentialities. And where individuals' loyalty extends only to kin and little more, the bureaucratic *esprit* cannot hope to thrive. Berger (1957) makes much the same point about the underdifferentiation of private and public spheres in modern Egypt and the resulting strain on officials, because they are not yet accustomed to looking upon others impersonally.

Marriott's (1955) analysis of the resistance to the introduction of Western medicine in Indian villages follows the same line of argument, except with a rather different emphasis. The traditional Indian healer has a very strong orientation to service; indeed, he is a saintly ascetic who does not often accept money from his patients—certainly not until after they have been cured. Mere technical competence does not qualify a man as a healer, and even makes him suspect if he does not possess the necessary spiritual qualities which are belied, in the case of the Western doctor, by the payment he demands, the impersonal (rather than custom-made) drugs he dispenses, his misplaced attention to the patient rather than to the family unit of which the patient is a part, and so on. It appears that the service orientation is deeply rooted in India; it is the rational part of the bureaucratic ethos that is missing.

Some cultures incorporate and modify the bureaucratic ideal more successfully. Abegglen's (1958) analysis of the paternalistic structure of a large number of Japanese factories is a well-known example in which wages and promotions are as much a function of family status and personal loyalty as of proven performance, and where the manager attends to education of the worker's children, the way in which he spends his money, and the like. Admittedly, there is less efficiency here—as there well may be in a family business in the West—but the successful adaptation of bureaucratic form to traditional values is the case in point. The same thing holds true for Caudill's (1961) study of the special nurse who attaches herself to mental patients in Japan, the *tsukisoi*. Of interest are the self-denying aspects of the *tsukisoi's* role, the intimacy and emotional expressivity which her relationship with the patient permits, as well as the buffer it provides for the patient from the impersonality and remoteness of professional, not to speak of bureaucratic, authority.

In the case of southern Italy, loyalty to family has proved hostile to bureaucratic values. According to Banfield (1958), traditional Italian familism explains much of the suspiciousness and resistance to all forms of regional or state officialdom, or, indeed, even to local attempts to organize individuals from different families for the purpose of economic development. Barzini (1965) claims that the Italian *is* heroic, altruistic, honest, etc., but does not grasp the idea of heroism in war, for example, or of patriotism.

Survey data on attitudes toward government bureaucracy reflect the varying institutionalization of bureaucratic values in different countries. Almond and Verba (1965)* compare attitudes of the public in five countries and conclude that Americans and British expect equal treatment from government officials and the police far more than Germans, Italians, and Mexicans, in that order. Mexicans expect neither equality of treatment nor considerateness from the police; Italians expect slightly more equality but low consideration. Although both the Americans and British expect equal treatment, the British are more likely also to expect considerate treatment. The Germans stand in the middle on both measures. Would the results be different for the United States today? It is difficult to say.

Two studies comparing Britain and the United States document the existence of variation in bureaucratic expectations and behavior within these two modernized societies. In a study of the police, Banton (1964) finds Americans less respectful of the law than the British, and, correlatively, finds American policemen exercising control much more informally. The American policeman tries to break down social distance by taking off his hat when entering a home; the British policeman does not do this. Richardson's (1956) cross-cultural study of merchant seamen found Britain's sailors more respectful of authority than Americans. The Americans did a good deal of regulating of their own behavior, and channeled their loyalties as well as their grievances through the unions, while the Englishmen left more of the deciding to their

33

superior officers. The American seamen tended to minimize the differences between themselves and the petty officers while the British were more at ease, apparently, with greater social distance.

Obviously, if official and client are of two different cultures, there may be problems of communication, whether in modern or traditional societies. Hall (1966) analyzes what he calls the "silent language" of overseas business and other cross-cultural contacts, referring primarily to implicit cultural differences in orientations to time and space, the definition of friendship, and how one conducts a business deal. He tells the story of an American businessman who went to Argentina to conclude a deal with a local executive. While the Argentinian could do business only with a man he could consider a friend and hence expected a series of purely social preliminaries, the American couldn't wait to get down to business, finding lengthy dinners and visits to night clubs a waste of time. End result: no sale.

CLASS AND SUBCULTURAL DIFFERENCES

The problem of subcultural differences within the same society is particularly characteristic of three types of situations: modernizing societies where there is a persistent gap between the elites and the more traditional masses; societies with an influx of new immigrants, especially of persons without prior socialization to bureaucratic ways; and modern societies with persistently different subcultures and classes.

The first type of society may be illustrated by the case of India, where low-status and rural persons have little contact with government services and have a low level of knowledge about these services, many of which exist to benefit them (Eldersveld, *et al.,* 1968). An example of the second situation is described by Katz and Eisenstadt (1960).* They analyze the process of cultural contact between Israeli officials and new immigrants recently arrived from Middle Eastern countries—as unsocialized to the ways of bureaucracy as Presthus (1959)* describes. During the period of mass immigration, the officials themselves had to take a hand in the bureaucratic socialization of their clients—such as teaching them the idea of a queue, or the expected behavior on a bus. The immigrants learned the role of client on the job, so to speak, but the result, at least temporarily, was *debureaucratization* of the official–client relationship.

Sjoberg and his colleagues (1966)* address themselves to problems raised by the third type of situation where subcultural differences lead to difficulties in official–client relations. Their main theme is that bureaucracy is a means by which the middle class has maintained its advantaged position vis-à-vis the lower class. Whether intentionally or not, middle-class organizations have often slanted their service to the detriment of the lower-class clients. For example, the least-qualified teachers tend to teach lower-class students, and the helping professions tend to encourage clients who best fit their middle-class values to use their services.

Even if one disagrees with the contention that middle-class organizations exploit or discriminate against their neediest clients, there is little doubt today that lower-class persons feel uncomfortable in impersonal, universalistic situations and have difficulties coping with the complexities of bureaucratic dealings. Sjoberg, *et al.,* point out the double disadvantage of these groups: neither do they know the rules of the game, nor do they have access to "pull" when necessary. Lower-status groups *know* less about their rights to services available to them, and are typically not reached by information campaigns through mass media. Their underutilization of these services is well documented (e.g., Rosenblatt and Suchman, 1964; Miller, *et al.,* 1970). There is a competing image of the lower class as disruptive and violent in bureaucratic encounters—strategies which often work. This is not so paradoxical as it sounds; however, when usually passive and apathetic individuals are provoked, they may well react explosively and outside the rules, shouting, making a scene, bringing the whole family, refusing to leave the office till their request is granted, and so on.

Ability to cope with bureaucracy is correlated with education and social status in other countries, too (Eldersveld, *et al.,* 1968; Almond and Verba, 1965*). Our own survey of attitudes toward government and public bureaucracy in Israel showed that better-educated, higher-status respondents, those of Western origin, men, and old-timers in the country all felt more capable of dealing with bureaucracy than did their counterparts (Danet and Hartman, 1972).

Ethnic or subcultural differences within modern society also may make a difference for official–client communication. Along the very lines described by Banfield (1958) and Barzini (1964), Zola (1966) finds that Italian patients in a Boston hospital experience more pain and complain about more symptoms than equally ill Irish patients (that is, even when the groups are matched on diagnosis). Thus, the definition of what constitutes illness and the response to that illness vary among ethnic groups, and affect the relationship between doctor and patient. And, as Zola points out, doctors who are unaware of such subcultural differences may fail to probe sufficiently in eliciting information about symptoms or respond inappropriately to the patient's "real" condition.

INFLUENCES OF THE COMMUNITY CONTEXT

While cultural values and structural characteristics of societies both influence official–client relations, the local community context also has implications of its own. For one thing, the size of the community has a bearing on the quality of interpersonal relations in its organizations. Officials in smaller organizations are usually more aware of their clients' needs and are more likely to know them personally. Size of community affects size of organization, which in turn affects relations with clients, which makes it difficult to sort out the effects of community size per se, as Thomas' (1959) study of role conceptions among social workers show.

Quite a different set of influences on official–client relationships stems from the social ecology of an organization's environment. Stinchcombe (in March, 1965) illustrates this by reference to the behavior of the police in places defined as "public" and "private." The latter still means no entry without a warrant, and the police therefore must obtain information from within to gain the right of entry. The former are directly accessible to the police so that when a public place is problematic, the police use their own sources in obtaining information and their own initiative in making decisions. Many of the crimes committed in public places would not be noticed if they had taken place in private. Rural areas have very few, if any, public places; large cities specialize in them.

The case of the police also serves as a good example of how organizations constitute environments for each other, or in other words, how the relationships among organizations affect official–client interaction. Both Banton (1964) and Reiss and Bordua* (in Bordua, 1967) point out that the courts in the United States frequently refuse to stand behind the police, and policemen are often made to feel that they are almost as much on trial as the person they have arrested. Consequently, the police learn that there is little reason to arrest someone who will not be convicted, and sometimes, as a result, they mete out on-the-spot punishment of their own. This is a good example of the countervailing power implicit in interorganizational checks and balances, but it also shows how difficult it is for bureaucracies and bureaucratic officials to work under such conditions of surveillance.

Informal relationships among clients—the network of friends, neighbors, and family which binds them to the community—often intervene between them and the services available to them. Freidson (1960) has described how the "lay referral system," in which individuals informally help one another to locate and evaluate available medical services, determines, among other things, how soon they come to the doctor. This informal referral system gives a doctor's patients more control over him than is sometimes realized.

When clients get together and form block clubs or consumers' unions, they gain bargaining power vis-à-vis the organizations of a community. Community organization has become a specialty, in fact, whose best-known proponent is probably Saul Alinsky (see, for example, Silberman, 1964). The Washington establishment of Kennedy and Johnson, together with assorted sociologists, political scientists, and social welfare people, urged communities to mobilize themselves as pressure groups to make their needs felt, and that users of different kinds of services get together to confront the bureaucracies as organized groups. Although the advocates of community organization did not propose the violent overthrow of bureaucratic organizations, they certainly proposed citizen participation in their administration, and, at least in one case (Cloward and Piven, 1966), they advocated the amassing of such a volume of legitimate demand as to cause the immobilization and ultimate collapse of one part of the welfare bureaucracy.

Bureaucracy and Personality

BUREAUCRATIC SOCIALIZATION IN CHILDHOOD

According to socialization theory, child-rearing techniques affect personality. In a pioneering study, fraught with methodological difficulties, Miller and Swanson (1958)* attempted to prove that the child-rearing methods of families in which the father is employed as a bureaucrat are affected, consciously or unconsciously, by the value orientations which are appropriate to the well-adjusted official or executive. Thus, parents who work in bureaucracies are found to be less strict than enterpreneurial parents about such things as feeding on schedule, or toilet training, or sexual self-indulgence. They are rather more likely to punish the child immediately and physically than to withdraw love and ask the child to think it over. Presumably, the more immediate gratifications of bureaucratic children, the greater permissiveness, less symbolic punishment, and lesser independence all work to produce a personality type which is more other-oriented, more easy-going, and sociable; has a weaker super-ego; is more trusting of the world, less ambitious, and more hedonistic than the model personality of the entrepreneurial child.

There are several more assumptions, here, of course, each of which can be turned into a hypothesis. They are (1) adults in a given occupational role will be constrained to adopt certain values and orientations, in short, their personalities will be affected; (2) having responded to these constraints, they will orient their children similarly by adopting appropriate child-rearing methods; (3) child-rearing methods of different kinds produce different kinds of personalities; (4) different kinds of personalities are differentially suited to occupational roles. In other words, the child-rearing methods used by bureaucratic parents will mold personalities which will both desire to work in such organizations and be suited to them.

Miller and Swanson's ideas have been influenced by Erikson's (1950) stage theory of socialization, which argues, for example, that at the conclusion of the oral phase the child will develop a basic trust or mistrust of his environment, depending on how he was cared for, while the anal phase will be resolved in terms of autonomy versus shame (again depending on how the child was managed), with correlative attitudes toward accumulation, orderliness, and the like. Eisenstadt (1956) suggests that the availability of the group appropriate to a given type of socialization will vary as a function of the need of the society for that kind of personality orientation. Thus, adolescent peer groups are not a universal phenomenon, he finds. Their presence is a sign that universalism is valued by the society. The family cannot socialize the child to this value, Eisenstadt argues, because the family is based on the principles of particularism and diffuseness. The function of the peer group in such societies is to give the child his earliest experience of independence of familial authority and to establish an egalitarian climate in which competition for achievement can take place. In societies where the peer group is absent, Eisenstadt concludes, an adult requires only the family-type orientations. We might add that Wilcox (1968) has shown that middle-class American children as young as the age of nine understand how organizational hierarchy works, who gives orders to whom, who has the most authority, and so on. Of course, it is possible that even children of the lower class or in less-bureaucratized countries might also understand hierarchy. Also, Wilcox did not check whether children younger than nine might grasp the principle.

EFFECTS OF BUREAUCRACY ON ADULT PERSONALITY

It is evident from the above description of Miller and Swanson's theory of child-rearing practices of bureaucratic parents that they believe that bureaucracy makes for happier, more relaxed, more well-adjusted people. This position is one which few writers have taken. On the contrary, some of the most eloquent writing about bureaucracy and bureaucratization has been a condemnation of the forces of bureaucratization as destructive of Western man's most precious values.

It is often thought that in formulating his "ideal model" of bureaucracy, Weber believed that bureaucracy was altogether good. On the contrary, as we saw in the Introduction, he was extremely worried about the fate of humanistic values in a world undergoing increasing rationalization and bureaucratization, and expressed profound fears that we would all become standardized cogs in the bureaucratic machine.

While Weber was worried about the effect that the production of bureaucratic personalities would have on the other institutions and values of society, Merton is concerned both with the subverting effect of bureaucratic structure on the personality of its workers and with the consequences of these personality changes for the organization itself. In his classic essay (1952) Merton has attempted to explain why the characteristics of bureaucratic organizations lead to overconformity, ritualism, arbitrariness, and concern with petty detail. In turn, this kind of behavior on the part of employees leads to *displacement of goals,* such that means become ends in themselves, resulting in a subversion of the original goals of the organization and conflicts with clients.

An elaborated and much more dramatic version of the Merton theory is found in the pessimistic analysis by Bensman and Rosenberg (1960) on the "meaning of work in bureaucratic society." They go beyond Merton by trying to develop a typology of responses to the constraints of work in a bureaucratic setting. More clearly than either Weber or Merton, we find an express concern with the effects of bureaucratic work on the individual, beginning with the assumption that there is a permanent conflict between organizational needs as expressed in bureaucratic role requirements, and the personality needs of individuals. The responses they observe are compulsive sociability; presentation of the self as a marketable product; the "happy" conformist; the search for identification with others in informal groups; alternately, *disidentification* with the organization or *overidentification* with it; feelings of powerlessness; authoritarianism. Whyte's *Organization Man* (1956) also pointed out some of these phenomena in the lives of corporation executives.

In a controversial series of experiments, Milgram (1963)* focused on the extent to which we are prepared to follow the dictates, however immoral, of a seemingly legitimate authority. His study questions the critical faculties of modern man both inside the organization and without. Indeed, Milgram's study has become known as the "Eichmann" experiment, and many people believe that he has called attention in a unique way to the ultimate moral problem of the "organization man." Is it beyond the capability of the organization man to experience the dilemma of obedience versus individual responsibility?

At the beginning of Orwell's *1984,* Smith, the leading character, harbors secret thoughts of rebellion against Big Brother. But these thoughts are purged out of him in a process of drastic resocialization, and Smith ends by loving Big Brother. This is reminiscent of Bettelheim's (1943) analysis of the concentration camp prisoners who identified with their Gestapo guards to the extent that they adopted their values and imitated their behavior.

To return to a less polemical level of discussion, the human relations school of industrial social psychology has been working for years on the problem of organizational needs versus individual needs, with varying degrees of optimism about the conflicts involved. In the last ten years, there has been a good deal of talk about the effectiveness of laboratory training, commonly known as "T-groups," in counteracting some of the negative aspects of organizational work (e.g., Schein and Bennis, 1965). In a sense, Bennis (in Bennis and Slater, 1968) takes the most optimistic position possible. He believes that bureaucracy is becoming obsolete and will actually disappear because it is unsuited to deal with rapid social change, and because it is hostile to the human needs of self-actualization, autonomy, and creativity in a democratic atmosphere.

The writers we have been talking about till now have depended mostly on their critical and observational powers to develop their theses. Kohn (1971)* is an exception. His is surely the most ambitious *empirical* study of the relationship between bureaucratic roles and personality so far. The results are a shock: instead of empirical confirmation of the negative stereotype of the conforming, rigid individual, Kohn finds that people who work in bureaucracies—defined as organizations with three or more levels of supervision—value self-direction *more* than nonbureaucrats; are *more* tolerant of nonconformity; *more* receptive to change; and *more* intellectually flexible. It is true, admits Kohn, that the higher educational level of workers in bureaucracy explains a large proportion of the differences he observed—but not all. Even after education is held constant, differences remain. Kohn feels that the best explanation for his findings lies in the relative complexity of the tasks with which bureaucrats deal, on the one hand, combined with the security of their tenure, on the other.

What are we to make of Kohn's results? It is premature to claim that the negative stereotype has been disproved. Further research is needed to check such things as the position of the individual in the organizational hierarchy and the kind of work he does. Thus, we need to know whether a doctor in a bureaucratic setting is more or less of a comformist outside the office than one having a private practice. And people doing other kinds of, perhaps less intrinsically satisfying work, should also be compared for the effects of working in bureaucracy. Another fact worth remembering is that bureaucracy is more than just hierarchy, which is the single organizational characteristic which Kohn studied. At any rate, we can conclude that Kohn himself is no conformist.

An Introduction to the Readings in This Part

The first pair of articles deals with the "goodness of fit" between bureaucratic organizations and different societies, and the ways in which bureaucratic organizations are shaped by their cultural contexts. Almond and Verba asked clients in five countries—the United States, England, Germany, Italy, and Mexico—to evaluate their contacts with officialdom according to the criteria of "considerateness" and "equality." Presthus tries to explain why bureaucracy is having a difficult time in the countries of the Middle East, while Katz and Eisenstadt report on the contacts of Jewish immigrants from these countries with the more Western-style Israeli bureaucracies.

The papers by Katz and Eisenstadt and by Sjoberg, *et al.,* are about sub-cultural differences within the same society. Whereas the former deals with migration, the latter analyzes the difficulties experienced by the resident poor in their bureaucratic contacts. Sjoberg argues that bureaucracies help keep the poor poor.

The influence of social and community contexts is represented in the paper by Reiss and Bordua. They discuss the concepts of public and private, and civil and criminal law, insofar as they affect the work of the police. They suggest that even in criminal cases, just as in civil ones, the police often wait for the initiative of the complainant before taking action, and try to settle some of their cases out of court. When the police find themselves being critically examined by the judge, rather than supported by him, they feel ambivalent about doing their jobs. This raises a dilemma for all agencies whose job it is to monitor the behavior of bureaucracies vis-à-vis their clients.

Then, we turn to the socialization of personality. Miller and Swanson attempt to prove that parents who work in bureaucracies raise their children to work in bureaucracies, and by virtue of their choice of child-rearing methods, the children will be better suited temperamentally than their parents are. Milgram's paper was chosen to represent the opposite threat: that over-adjustment to some of the interpersonal rules of bureaucratic behavior may have dangerous consequences. Kohn supports Miller and Swanson's implicit affirmation of the bureaucratic personality. He argues that people who work in hierarchical organizations are less conformist, more open to change, and more intellectually flexible than people who don't.

REFERENCES

Abegglen, James. *The Japanese Factory*. Glencoe: Free Press, 1958.

Almond, Gabriel, and Sidney Verba. *The Civic Culture*. Boston: Little, Brown, 1965.

Banfield, Edward C. *The Moral Basis of a Backward Society*. Glencoe: Free Press, 1958.

Banton, Michael. *The Policeman in the Community*. London: Tavistock, 1964.

Barzini, Luigi. *The Italians*. New York: Bantam, 1965.

Bennis, Warren, and Philip E. Slater. *The Temporary Society*. New York: Harper Colophon Books, 1968.

Bensman, Joseph, and Bernard Rosenberg. "The Meaning of Work in Bureaucratic Society." In *Identity and Anxiety: Survival of the Person in Mass Society*, edited by Maurice Stein, Arthur J. Vidich, and David Manning White, pp. 181–197. Glencoe: Free Press, 1960.

Berger, Morroe. *Bureaucracy and Society in Modern Egypt*. Princeton: Princeton University Press, 1957.

Bettelheim, Bruno. "Individual and Mass Behavior in Extreme Situations." *Journal of Abnormal and Social Psychology* 38 (1943): 417–452.

Caudill, William. "Around-the-Clock Patient Care in Japanese Psychiatric Hospitals— The Role of the Tsukisoi." *American Sociological Review* 26 (1961): 643–655.

Cloward, Richard A., and Frances Fox Piven. "A Strategy to End Poverty." *The Nation* 202 (May 2, 1966): 510–517.

Danet, Brenda, and Harriet Hartman. "Coping with Bureaucracy: The Israeli Case." *Social Forces* 50 (September 1972).

Eisenstadt, S. N. *From Generation to Generation*. Glencoe: Free Press, 1956.

Eldersveld, S. J., U. Jagannadham, and A. P. Barnabas. *The Administrator and the Citizen in a Developing Democracy*. Glenview: Scott, Foresman, 1968.

Erikson, Erik H. *Childhood and Society*. New York: Norton, 1950.

Freidson, Eliot. "Client Control and Medical Practice." *American Journal of Sociology* 65 (1960): 374–382.

Hall, Edward T. *The Silent Language*. New York: Fawcett Premier, 1966.

Katz, Elihu, and S. N. Eisenstadt. "Some Sociological Observations on the Response of Israeli Organizations to New Immigrants." *Administrative Science Quarterly* 5 (1960): 113–133.

Kohn, Melvin L. "Bureaucratic Man: A Portrait and an Interpretation." *American Sociological Review* 36 (1971): 461–474.

Marriott, McKim. "Western Medicine in a Village of Northern India." In *Health, Culture and Community*, edited by Benjamin D. Paul, pp. 239–268. New York: Russell Sage Foundation, 1955.

McClelland, David. *The Achieving Society*. New York: Van Nostrand, 1961.

Merton, Robert K. "Bureaucratic Structure and Personality." In *Reader in Bureaucracy*, edited by Robert K. Merton, *et al.*, pp. 361–371. Glencoe: Free Press, 1952.

Part I

Milgram, Stanley. "Behavioral Study of Obedience." *Journal of Abnormal and Social Psychology* 67 (1963): 371–378.

Miller, Daniel R., and Guy E. Swanson. *The Changing American Parent.* New York: Wiley, 1958.

Miller, S. M., Pamela Roby, and Alwin A. de Vos van Steenwijk. "Creaming the Poor." *Trans-Action* 7, no. 8 (June 1970): 39–45.

Presthus, Robert V. "The Social Bases of Bureaucratic Organization." *Social Forces* 38 (1959) 103–109.

Reiss, Albert J., Jr., and David J. Bordua. "Environment and Organization: A Perspective on the Police." In *The Police: Six Sociological Essays,* edited by David J. Bordua, pp. 28–55. London: Wiley, 1967.

Richardson, S. A. "Organizational Contrasts on British and American Ships." *Administrative Science Quarterly* 1 (1956): 189–207.

Riggs, Fred W. "The 'Sala' Model: An Ecological Approach to the Study of Comparative Administration." In *Readings in Comparative Public Administration,* edited by Nimrod Raphaeli, pp. 412–432. Boston: Allyn & Bacon, 1967.

Rosenblatt, Daniel, and Edward A. Suchman. "The Underutilization of Medical-Care Services by Blue-Collarites." In *Blue-Collar World,* edited by A. B. Shostak and W. Gomberg, pp. 341–349. Englewood Cliffs: Prentice-Hall, 1964.

Schein, Edgar H., and Warren G. Bennis, eds. *Personal and Organizational Change Through Group Methods.* New York: Wiley, 1965.

Sears, R. R., Eleanor E. Maccoby, and H. Levin. *Patterns of Child-Rearing.* Evanston: Row Peterson, 1957.

Silberman, Charles E. "Up from Apathy—The Woodlawn Experiment." *Commentary* 37, no. 5 (May 1964): 51–58.

Sjoberg, Gideon, Richard A. Brymer, and Buford Farris. "Bureaucracy and the Lower Class." *Sociology and Social Research* 50, no. 3 (April 1966): 325–377.

Stinchcombe, Arthur. "Social Structure and Organization." In *Handbook of Organizations,* edited by James G. March, pp. 142–193. Chicago: Rand McNally, 1965.

Thomas, Edwin J. "Role Conceptions, Organizational Size, and Community Context." *American Sociological Review* 24 (1959): 30–37.

Weber, Max. "Bureaucracy." In *From Max Weber,* edited by H. H. Gerth and C. Wright Mills, pp. 196–244. New York: Galaxy, 1958.

Whiting, J. W., and I. L. Child. *Child Training and Personality.* New Haven: Yale University Press, 1953.

Whyte, William F., Jr. *Organization Man.* New York: Simon and Schuster, 1956.

Wilcox, Herbert C. "The Culture Trait of Hierarchy in Middle Class Children." *Public Administration Review* 28 (May–June 1968): 222–235.

Zola, Irving Kenneth. "Culture and Symptoms: An Analysis of Patients' Presenting Complaints." *American Sociological Review* 31, no. 6 (October 1966): 615–630.

1

Gabriel Almond and Sidney Verba

EXPECTATIONS OF TREATMENT BY GOVERNMENT AND THE POLICE

The feelings that people have toward governmental authorities may be inferred from their expectations of how they will be treated by them. In constructing our interview we assumed that most people preferred to be treated fairly and considerately when in contact with officials. If they expected fair and considerate treatment, we could safely assume that at least in these respects they were favorably disposed toward governmental authority. And in the opposite case, we could assume that they were unfavorably disposed. Thus our questions were intended to discover what qualities our respondents imputed to the executive side of government.

We confronted our respondents with two hypothetical situations. In the first they were asked to imagine themselves in a government office with a problem that called for official action. How did they think they would be treated? Would they be treated equally, like everyone else? We then asked them to imagine that they were explaining their point of view to the official or officials. Did they expect that they would be listened to attentively and considerately? In the second situation they were asked to imagine themselves as having some minor trouble with the police. Did they expect to be treated equally and considerately by the police? The results of the questions on equality of treatment are summarized in Table 1-1.

The pattern that emerges is of great interest. The Americans and the British, who in large majorities perceived the significance of national and local government for their daily lives, who said they followed politics and political campaigns, and who most often spontaneously expressed pride in their political

Gabriel Almond and Sidney Verba, "Expectations of Treatment by Government and the Police," in *The Civic Culture* (Boston: Little, Brown, 1965), pp. 68–78. Tables and passages from Gabriel A. Almond and Sidney Verba. *The Civic Culture: Political Attitudes and Democracy in Five Nations.* Copyright © 1963 by Princeton University Press: Tables 2, 3, 4, and 5—pp. 108, 109, 110, and 112; text from pp. 106, 107, 110, 111, 112, 113, 114, 115, and 116. Reprinted by permission of Princeton University Press.

Expectations of Treatment by Government and the Police

TABLE 1-1

Expectation of Treatment by Governmental Bureaucracy and Police; by Nation*

PERCENT-AGE WHO SAY	U.S. BU-REAUC-RACY	U.S. PO-LICE	U.K. BU-REAUC-RACY	U.K. PO-LICE	GERMANY BU-REAUC-RACY	GERMANY PO-LICE	ITALY BU-REAUC-RACY	ITALY PO-LICE	MEXICO BU-REAUC-RACY	MEXICO PO-LICE
They expect equal treat-ment	83	85	83	89	65	72	53	56	42	32
They don't expect equal treat-ment	9	8	7	6	9	5	13	10	50	57
Depends	4	5	6	4	19	15	17	15	5	5
Other	—	—	—	—	—	—	6	6	—	—
Don't know	4	2	2	0	7	8	11	13	3	5
Total per-centage	100	100	98	99	100	100	100	100	100	99
Total number	970	970	963	963	955	955	995	995	1,007	1,007

*Actual texts of the questions: "Suppose there were some question that you had to take to a government office — for example, a tax question or housing regulation. Do you think you would be given equal treatment — I mean, would you be treated as well as anyone else?" "If you had some trouble with the police — a traffic violation maybe, or were accused of a minor offense — do you think you would be given equal treatment? That is, would you be treated as well as anyone else?"

systems, also in large majorities expect equality of treatment at the hands of government. In theoretical terms we can say that the British and Americans are high in output and input cognition, high in system affect, and high in output affect. The Germans again conform to the British and American pattern, although the proportions expecting equal treatment are somewhat lower. Though they are low in system affect, they are high in output affect, just as they were high in output and input cognition.

The responses in Italy and Mexico confirm the high incidence of output alienation in these countries. These people are alienated in their expectations of treatment at the hands of governmental authority and police. Again, on the output side, the Mexicans show more frequent alienation than the Italians—a repetition of the pattern in the dimension of output cognition.

Table 1-2 reports the frequency of expectations of considerate treatment at the hands of governmental officials and the police. Here we were concerned with whether or not our respondents imputed responsiveness to government officials, whether they felt they would be treated with dignity, on a "give and take" basis. Although there are structural differences in the bureaucratic and police organizations among our five countries, our questions were directed at those bureaucratic and police authorities with whom the respondents might come in contact in the hypothetical situations set up by the questions. (A more discriminating series of questions, which would get at differences in expectations of treatment by different levels of bureaucratic authority and

TABLE 1-2

Amount of Consideration Expected for Point of View from Bureaucracy and Police; by Nation *

PERCENT-AGE WHO EXPECT	U.S.		U.K.		GERMANY		ITALY		MEXICO	
	BU-REAUC-RACY	PO-LICE	BU-REAUC-RACY	PO-LICE	BU-REAUC-RACY	PO-LICE	BU-REAUC-RACY	PO-LICE	BU-REAUC-RACY	PO-LICE
Serious con-sideration for point of view	48	56	59	74	53	59	35	35	14	12
A little attention	31	22	22	13	18	11	15	13	48	46
To be ignored	6	11	5	5	5	4	11	12	27	29
Depends	11	9	10	6	15	13	21	20	6	7
Other	0	–	–	–	1	2	6	6	–	1
Don't know	4	2	2	1	8	11	12	14	3	4
Total per-centage	100	100	98	99	100	100	100	100	98	99
Total number	970	970	963	963	955	955	995	995	1,007	1,007

*Actual texts of the questions: "If you explained your point of view to the officials, what effect do you think it would have? Would they give your point of view serious consideration, would they pay only a little attention, or would they ignore what you had to say?" "If you explained your point of view to the police, what effect do you think it would have? Would they . . . [same choices as before]?"

different types of bureaucratic or police agencies, would no doubt have produced a more complex pattern and more reliable body of information.) Given the problem of interview length, we sought to attain comparability by specifying the type of problem (e.g., taxation, housing) or the type of offense (traffic violation, misdemeanor) that occasioned the bureaucratic or police encounter.

In all of our countries, with the exception of Mexico, the police were often viewed with as much favor as—if not more favor than—the general governmental authority. Mexican cynicism is particularly marked vis-à-vis the police, while in Britain the reported general confidence in the considerateness and responsiveness of the police is strikingly documented. It is of great interest that the Germans come out somewhat better than the Americans on expectations of considerate treatment at the hands of government and the police. Why Americans should, on the one hand, expect equality of treatment in such overwhelming proportions and then drop to only around 50 percent for expectations of considerate treatment is an intriguing question. We would like to suggest, though it will be treated in detail below, that Americans have not as fully assimilated the role of subject in relation to administrative authorities as have the Germans and the British. Certainly these data seem to support popular impressions of the American as uneasy in bureaucratic situations, fuming over inefficiency and red tape.

The distinction between the United States, Britain, and Germany, on the one hand, and Italy and Mexico, on the other, still holds. Only 35 percent of the Italians and 12 to 14 percent of the Mexicans expect serious consideration from governmental and police authority, should they try to explain their point of view, in contrast with 48 percent or more for the respondents in the other three countries.

Expectation of treatment by government and police also varies among educational levels. Table 1–3 shows these differences for the United States,

TABLE 1-3

Expectation of Treatment by Governmental Authorities and Police; by Education in the United States, United Kingdom, and Germany

PERCENT-AGE WHO EXPECT	U.S.			U.K.			GERMANY		
	PRIMARY OR LESS	SOME SECONDARY	SOME UNIVERSITY	PRIMARY OR LESS	SOME SECONDARY	SOME UNIVERSITY	PRIMARY OR LESS	SOME SECONDARY	SOME UNIVERSITY
Equal treatment in government office	80	84	88	81	87	88	64	73	77
Equal treatment by police	81	87	89	88	90	96	70	81	88
Consideration in government office	44	46	58	60	58	75	51	62	81
Consideration by police	50	59	60	75	72	71	58	65	81
Total number	338	443	188	593	321	24	788	123	26

Britain, and Germany. In the United States the proportion of university-educated respondents expecting equal and considerate treatment by the government and police ranges from 8 to 12 percentage points higher than for those respondents having primary school education or less. In England the difference is similarly small, and in the case of expectations of considerateness by the police the poorly educated come out better than the well educated. This suggests that in these two countries, not only is there a general widespread expectation of equal and considerate treatment, but the less educated have these expectations almost as frequently as the more educated. Table 1–3 also shows that Germany, which was high on the overall national percentage for expectations of treatment, has a sharper difference in expectation among educational levels. Furthermore, the difference is more marked in the dimension of considerate treatment than in equality of treatment. Though there is a difference of 13 to 18 percentage points in expectations of equality of treatment between Germans with primary school and those with university education, still around two-thirds of the less well-educated Germans expect to be treated equally by the government and the police. But only 51 percent of the less well-educated Germans expect to be considerately treated by governmental authorities, as compared with 81 percent of the university educated. The difference between these two groups with respect to considerate treatment by the police is also large—23 percent. The British figures present a striking contrast. Though almost three-fourths of all the British respondents expect to be considerately treated by the police, it would appear that this expectation is somewhat more widely distributed among poorly educated Britons than among the university educated.

These findings show that in the United States and Britain both the educated and the less well educated, in large and approximately equal proportions, tend to expect "good" treatment from government. In Germany the less well educated expect to be treated equally by governmental authorities, but the expectation of considerate treatment is more frequently concentrated among the educated elements of the population.

As Table 1-4 indicates, in Italy and Mexico the overall percentage of

TABLE 1-4

Expectation of Treatment by Governmental Authorities and Police; by Education in Italy and Mexico

PERCENTAGE WHO EXPECT	ITALY				MEXICO			
	NONE	SOME PRI- MARY	SOME SECON- DARY	SOME UNIVER- SITY	NONE	SOME PRI- MARY	SOME SECON- DARY	SOME UNIVER- SITY
Equal treatment in government office	30	51	65	59	19	45	58	68
Equal treatment by police	27	53	68	74	14	33	54	51
Consideration in government office	20	34	38	44	5	16	18	22
Consideration by police	17	34	43	48	8	13	17	22
Total number	88	604	245	54	221	656	103	24

those expecting fair and considerate treatment is low, but the differences between the advantaged and disadvantaged groups is relatively large. Thus in Italy 30 percent of those with no formal education expect to be treated equally by the police, as compared with 74 percent for those with some university education—a difference of 44 percentage points. In Mexico only 19 percent of those with no education expect equal treatment by government, as compared with 68 percent for the university educated—a percentage spread of 49 points. The difference among educational groups in expectations of equal treatment by the police is similarly high in both countries. Even on the upper levels of education, the expectations of considerate treatment are low

47

in both countries, but particularly in Mexico, where only 20 percent of the university educated expect considerate treatment at the hands of the government and the police.

From our analysis thus far we see that the American and British respondents tend, on the whole, to have relatively favorable expectations of government; and educational differences have a relatively small effect on such expectations. In Germany overall expectations proved to be relatively high, but class differences in expectations of considerateness of treatment are also relatively large. In Mexico and Italy, and particularly in the former, overall expectations of favorable treatment are relatively low, and educational differences in expectations tend to be relatively extreme.

In our life-history interviews we pursued a similar line of questioning, but in these cases we asked our respondents whether they had ever had any direct contact with government officials. We then pressed them to describe their experiences and indicate whether they were satisfied with the treatment they received. The life-history material, consequently, can provide us with reports of personal experience at the hands of governmental authority.

The pattern in Britain is illustrated in the experience of a British house painter who approached an official of the Inland Revenue. He asked him ". . . about starting our business. He was very fair. I asked him about scales for house purchase and rates of loan." When asked whether he was satisfied or felt fairly treated, he replied, "Very satisfied. It seemed too good to be true, this about housing loans." A garage mechanic referred to an experience with the police involving a "no parking" violation. When asked whether he was satisfied with his treatment, he replied, "Well, honestly, satisfied. I didn't like it at the time." When asked if he had been treated efficiently, he replied, "Yes, too much so." There were cases of dissatisfaction among the British respondents. Perhaps the strongest case of dissatisfaction was that of a small businessman. He referred to a contact with income tax officials: "The only way was to browbeat them. Politeness didn't work at all. In the long run, I was quite satisfied, but only through my own endeavors. I find the more minor the official you deal with, the less satisfaction you get." When asked whether he had been fairly treated, he replied, "Yes, I don't think there's any distinction made between various people. Only in the case of personal friendships, which is not only done in government offices."

The American respondents similarly reported favorable contacts on the whole, but with qualifications. Thus a salesman referring to his experiences with traffic tickets said his experiences had varied. "In some ways it was ideal, in others it was disgraceful the way I was treated. One guy was looking to give a ticket and he gave it. But the police force is adequate as could be expected. Some can be very arrogant." A manufacturer's representative referred to contacts with both an alderman and the sewer department. He reported: "The alderman fixed me up fine. As to the other—yes and no. Yes, insofar as the explanation I got. No, in that I was told the City Hall had to take care of the problem—this entailed much traveling." Pressed to state whether he was fairly treated, he replied, "Yes. That's the way everyone's treated." Southern Negroes' experiences of governmental treatment are illustrated in the case of a Negro woman who reported her effort to register as a voter. "The men were so harsh and gruff, I don't know. I mean, they used that tone of voice to me I guess trying to frighten me, but I just smiled to myself and acted like I did not notice it." When asked whether she was satisfied, she replied, "No, they could have been more pleasant."

The Italian and Mexican cases bring out a general pattern of experience with corruption, discrimination, and unresponsiveness:

AN ITALIAN HOUSEWIFE: I have spoken very often to governmental officials, but they take no interest in this town. My husband tried to get a pension for his father, but spent so much money that he had to stop. They don't take us into consideration. Here we advance only by recommendation.

AN ITALIAN TREE SURGEON: . . . my wife was sent back from the tax office. In the employment office things are not done right. . . . It is a month that I am without work, and am not on the employment list, as there is favoritism. The friends of the officials will be signed up first, and they will get the first jobs available. We are put on the list with a month and one-half delay.

AN ITALIAN GYMNASTIC INSTRUCTOR (COMMUNIST): For Heaven's sake! The last time I was at a government office there was a poor man with a paper to fill out. He was asking the official how to fill it out. The official wouldn't pay attention but told him, "Fill this paper out and that paper out and come back tomorrow." The poor man did not know what to do. So I told the official he was there because I was paying him; everyone was paying him to be there and give explanations. He didn't open his mouth, and filled out the paper for the man.

The themes are similar among the Mexicans.

A MEXICAN SMALL BUSINESSMAN: Normally the officials are not very competent. One doesn't see individuals with much education in the municipality. They are not very efficient in the way they do business. But in the local government they will do their duty for money. . . .

A MEXICAN BLACKSMITH: . . . the people that work in those places are not attentive. They don't do it willingly. They are despots and get angry.

A MEXICAN SCHOOLTEACHER: . . . the judges operate through money. As far as the state employees are concerned, they are generally just, although they take into account your personal appearance.

A Mexican housewife said she would go to the government authorities only if a member of her family was arrested. ". . . I would go to a judge or to a lawyer. If he [member of family] was guilty, they would let him free if I paid a big sum. If he was innocent, they would help me.". . .

2

Robert V. Presthus

THE SOCIAL BASES OF
BUREAUCRATIC ORGANIZATION

This chapter is broadly concerned with the problem of introducing Western bureaucratic organization into nonwestern cultures. It rests upon the assumption that economic change in such cultures is a function of their ability to superimpose upon a traditional social context new patterns of behavior that are more amenable to technical change and rational organization. While in a sense such cultures are already highly bureaucratized, existing values are often inapposite to the kind of social and economic development that under-developed countries have set for themselves. Social change is required to provide the basis for objective and rational patterns of organization. We shall try to show how such organizational changes rest upon deeper cultural change. The following analysis attempts to set existing social values in two Middle East states against the requirements of the Western bureaucratic model, which has become the common instrument for administering large-scale social and economic enterprise.

Such an analysis seems to require the broadest type of inquiry into traditional social values and their implications for bureaucratic structure and process in a given culture. It is not enough to investigate Middle Eastern organizations per se, since these are only the surface manifestations of deep-seated cultural values. Instead, one must begin at the culture-wide level since this illuminates the interrelationships between the bench-mark values of a society and its institutions. This kind of "pattern analysis" focuses upon the interplay among three critical variables: the whole culture of a society, a given organizational situation, and the modal personality type of the society. These critical variables are interdependent and changing, resulting in a very complicated analytical situation. Such a multidimensional context is hard to

Robert V. Presthus, "Social Bases of Bureaucratic Organization," *Social Forces* 38 (1959): 103–109. Reprinted by permission.

manage but it probably gives a truer image of organizational behavior than microscopic analyses that achieve rigor by exclusion.

Such an analysis might rest in part upon the formulations of so-called developmental psychology, which recognizes the biological underpinning of personality but regards personality as mainly the consequence of successive accommodations to authoritative interpersonal relations, shaped in turn by the peculiar values of a given society.[1] Such values include attitudes toward authority, family structure and child-raising methods, modal personality types, religious forms and values, class and status values, socioeconomic character of the society, concepts of time and the universe: i.e., are these regarded as changing and changeable by human effort or, alternatively, as static and timeless, and so on. While such a multifaceted approach demands big investments in skill and time, it seems the only way to avoid the disparate, fractured analyses that often characterize the research of any single discipline.

Experience suggests, too, that studies of particular organizations *in vacuo* leave unanswered the question of *why* such organizations have their own patterns of objectives, recruitment, rewards, and so on. It would seem that generalizations about organizational behavior in any given social context require the kind of broad cultural analysis suggested here. Otherwise, organizational objectives, values and procedures will often seem odd and even irrational, yet one soon learns that they have rational and functional bases in the traditions of the society. The problem is that such objectives, values, and behaviors are often inimical to the economic development that such societies have set for themselves, and it is in this nonnormative context that they are analyzed here.

It seems clear enough that until such critical variables are isolated and their relevance for organizational behavior assayed, the analysis of "foreign" organizations and values can only be random and particularistic, unguided by any selective theory that might give more meaning and direction to further research. While microscopic analyses of internal organization, small group behavior, status and authority patterns, recruitment, and so on, are obviously required, at the present stage in comparative research we must also work "downward" as the functional linkages between the culture, the given situation, and the individual point the way to more intensive and rigorous analyses.

The problem of economic development in poor countries provides a most useful framework for analyzing the social requirements of bureaucratic structure. This framework emphasizes the ecological context of organization and enables us to define organizations as social microcosms, as instruments for sharpening and validating the main values of the larger society. For example, interpersonal relations in any given organization provide insights into the structure of authority in the larger society. One of the manifest failures of technical assistance programs is the attempt to short-circuit the complicated social aspects of organization. Simply because organizations are regarded as independent systems, the discontinuities between bureaucratic values in Western and nonwestern cultures are overlooked or wished away.

My main proposition here can be stated operationally as follows: the West is attempting to introduce into exotic cultures such values as objectivity in personnel selection; greater rationality in linking means to ends; contract over against status as the main index of role, authority, and rights; and technical skill as the critical value in organizational relationships. In this context the question for both research and policy is the *adaptability* of existing nonwestern values to western bureaucratic organization. What are the major social values that affect organizational behavior, very broadly defined? Are such values consistent with the social and economic development that exotic societies have set for themselves?

The relationships between such values and the routine, operating attitudes and procedures of given organizations must be carefully traced. The dominant values of the society as these affect, or seem to affect, organizational behavior must be identified. At the outset some working definition of such values must be achieved before the critical task of determining their impact upon organizational forms and practices can be attempted. It is surprisingly difficult to find such agreement, not only about the bench-mark values of a society, but equally about the way they impinge upon organization. One of the reasons for this lack of consensus seems to be the varying time dimensions that observers use in gauging social change or "progress" in nonwestern areas. The rate of change for example looms quite differently if one uses fifty- or one hundred-year increments of time as opposed, say, to the technical assistance period since World War II, or similar relatively short-range indexes. Another related factor is whether exotic countries are measured in terms of their own standards or potential, or whether, as is often the case, they are measured in terms of some absolute criterion. While most of us would agree that the former standard is the more rational, the difficulties of abstracting oneself from his own historical context make the latter standard extremely common among Western observers.

The following analysis consists of some preliminary observations about values that seem to affect organizational behavior in the Middle East. While many of the assumed values may be seen in varying degree in Western society, it is precisely the differences in degree that account for different practices and results in the two cultures. Since many of the values are inconsistent with bureaucratic demands of rationality and technical supremacy, the following analysis tends to have a pessimistic bias. However, this need not impair its usefulness in suggesting a framework for comparative administration research and outlining the kinds of problems that Western technical assistance programs face.

While the following prescriptions are well known, it may be useful to begin with a resume of the ideal-typical bureaucratic model, against which related values of Turkey and Egypt may be set.[2]

1. Bureaucratic officials are personally free and subject to authority only with respect to their impersonal official obligations.

2. Each office has a clearly defined sphere of competence in the legal sense.

3. Officials are selected on the basis of technical qualifications, usually tested by examination or guaranteed by diplomas certifying technical training. In sociological terms, the bases of recruitment are "universalistic," i.e., recruitment is broadly based throughout the society and cuts across class, ethnic, and religious lines, since it is determined largely on objective bases of training and competence. Recruitment on subjective, class-oriented bases is called "particularistic."

4. The official is subject to strict and systematic discipline and control in the conduct of his office.

5. His office constitutes a career; only under defined circumstances can the employing authority terminate his employment.

6. Bureaucracies may be either "charismatic" or "legal-rational," but the former is merely a transitional stage in an inevitable movement toward the latter.[3]

7. Bureaucratic structure is legally and rationally based, and is thus merely an instrument controlled by some authority outside itself.

In a general and exploratory way, and without attempting to show specific connections in every case, we can now turn to several major values that appear relevant to the evolution of a rational bureaucratic model in the Middle East.

Since *objectivity,* defined for the moment as the capacity to identify and evaluate rationally the factors that impinge upon a decision, is a fundamental bureaucratic ideal, some observations on the state of this requirement in Middle Eastern culture provide a good starting point. There the foreign observer is struck by the extent to which personal and "political" factors influence behavior. Interpersonal relations are highly subjective as suggested by emotional forms of greeting, including embraces, etc. Family, school, race, religion, status, age, and other formal certifications tend to define decision-making situations. To win support for an idea, one often appeals directly to such prescriptions rather than to objective evidence. Personal status competes strongly with evidence or technical experience in deciding what is to be done. In an organizational context, respect for age results in formal interpersonal relations in which seniority dominates and communications are hampered by the variety of subtle forms used to mediate status. In part this may reflect a patriarchal family structure that prepares the individual for a submissive role in which his superiors may appear as a succession of "fathers."

Prestige and security seem to be bound up with the network of influence relations that characterize a culture in which kinship and family structure are just beginning to be shaken up by urbanization and industrialization. Probably because of the limited number of universities, as well as the strength of family ties, most members of the elite seem to know each other. As a result, civil service recruitment is influenced by interpersonal negotiations among a restricted group. In Egypt, as Berger shows, almost 40 percent of higher civil servants are the sons of civil servants[4]. In Turkey, similarly, Matthews found that just over 30 percent of civil servants had fathers in the government service.[5] In most organizations, including the public corporations that direct the major elements in the economy, the introduction of objective standards of recruitment through competitive examinations and specific requirements of training and experience, runs against such time-honored patterns of behavior.

Middle Eastern subjectivity is seen again in the pervasive role of religion, which influences social and economic development everywhere. As Tawney has shown, in the West the protestant ethnic gave capitalism a boost by enthroning values of thrift, industry, and personal responsibility. At the same time, religion was kept in its place: the differences between the ideal and the real were nicely rationalized. While this elasticity enabled the West to render unto Caesar what was Caesar's, in the Middle East for centuries religion and politics were inseparable. Moreover, in Turkey the Empire flourished under this theocratic system, which may in part explain the present tendency to revive traditional religious practices. In the long run, however, the attendant rigidity limited the ability of Turkey and its neighbors to adapt to the changing demands of history. Unlike Western Europe, there was no reformation which fostered the rise of skepticism and science.

In sum, while Christianity was somehow able to accommodate science, in the Middle East the impact of religion was sharply different. Islam became a *total* way of life, shaping thought and defining social relations in every context. This emphasis is suggested by the tendency of Muslims to catalogue all foreigners as infidels, that is, foreigners are *defined* in essentially religious terms. Islamic law sets up a distinction between those who believe and those who do not. And this distinction still provides a basis for defining situations. How one acts, how he evaluates the achievements and personal qualities of others, his attitudes toward social change—all are influenced by traditional religious values.

Most important of these values, perhaps, is the concept of fatalism. "Inshalla," the belief that God's will determines the course of human events, fosters a somewhat negative view toward self-aid and innovation. In the villages, when a new-born infant dies, primitive medical technology is not always held responsible, but often it is "God taking back his little angel."[6] The image of social possibilities is pessimistic, reinforced by a conviction that the real rewards are not of this world. There exists a deep-seated belief that men cannot really do much, and this view is held, I think, although less strongly, by intellectuals as well as by the mass.[7] While the opposing Western view, which regards all change as progress, is often naive, it provides nevertheless a firmer basis for personal effort. In both cultures, of course, such conclusions have been shaped by a reality which, on the one hand, encouraged faith in technical progress by generous material rewards and, on the other, encouraged resignation by denying them. But the theory was also important in posing the question whether individual effort was really worth while. In the Middle East it was easy to conclude that it was not.

This conflict between religious values and technical change is dramatized by religious holidays such as the month-long Ramazan. Many intellectuals and government officials honor this sacred period, which requires meditation and fasting from sunrise to sunset. Moreover, in Turkey, despite Ataturk's vigorous efforts to stamp them out, the ruling Democratic party is encouraging a revival of traditional religious practices among the peasants. Along with its support of agriculture, whose profits are tax free, this accounts in part for the party's impressive majorities in rural areas. By increasing the influence of the local *imams* at the expense of the teachers sent out by the central government, and thus placing roadblocks in the way of mass education, such a policy impedes change. The resulting ambivalence between traditional religious values and westernization is patent in Matthew's finding that over 75 percent of potential and junior administrators (average age 22 and 32 respectively) answered "Yes" to the question, "Is Islam adequate for modern life?"[8]

The impact of "Inshalla" is reinforced by skepticism insofar as technical change is concerned. The age of Turkish civilization and its historical perspective encourage a conservative posture that often rejects change or is, at best, ambivalent toward it. Throughout the Middle East there is a singular attitude toward time in which there is little differentiation between the past, the present, and the future. The world is viewed as essentially changeless, and this conception encourages resignation and an essentially pessimistic view of life. Certainly, when "tomorrow" may mean a month; western "crash" programs based on a five- or ten-year schedule are just not understood. The audacity of attempting to reshape historic patterns of culture in the short run may be regarded as a monument to the West's capacity to think positively, but in Muslim eyes it also reveals a relative insensibility to the impact of history.

Muslim ways of thinking also include an inclination to honor nonmaterialistic things. This view, which is apparent mainly among the educated elite, would not necessarily be inimical, but it often includes the *non sequitor* that industrialization necessarily means ethical and artistic poverty. This attitude may also reflect a reluctant acceptance of industrialization as a means to greater national power and income, but a fear of its egalitarian by-products which threaten the power monopoly Eastern elites have long enjoyed. Emerging peasant demands for medical care, education, and land reform assume a redistribution of wealth, requiring in turn a new ethic to replace the classical view that poverty and virtue go hand in hand.

That technical aid is also sometimes regarded as a form of political and cultural imperialism—as a way of getting the Western camel's nose under the tent—is not surprising. Here again, Turkish experience is illustrative. Since the revolution of 1922, Turkey has thrived on a diet of nationalism, nourished by the proud self-reliance and isolationism of Ataturk. This legacy helps explain Turkey's determination that her hard-won independence shall not be lost by a cultural invasion. Yet, the organizing and technical skill of the West clearly provide the ingredients of national strength and security. The resulting oscillation between Western and Eastern values has characterized

Turkish history throughout, and, even though Turkey has tended to lean toward the West in recent times, the religious and geographic factors that lie behind this ambivalence remain. As a result the technical aid issue tends to be posed as a choice between economic progress and honored cultural values.

We can now turn to educational values, another major instrument of social change and bureaucratic development. Here again we find an approach that leans in one direction as far as our own furiously practical system leans in the other. In the Middle East, university training is legal and historical, sprinkled with a generous dash of philosophy. Relying almost entirely on the lecture method, the system reinforces the submissive tendencies inculcated by the patriarchal family. The professor is looked upon as the source of most wisdom. Memorization is stressed rather than the questioning attitude that nourishes change. As a result, young university men are not always distinguished by self-reliance, nor are they likely to become acquainted with the operating conditions of government and commerce. When field research is done, it tends to be concerned with law and structure rather than with process. The Western idea of higher learning as a *preparation* for a career tends to be pushed aside by viewing the degree as conclusive evidence that one has arrived.

Equally significant is the antivocational bias of university graduates.[9] In part, such attitudes reflect the fact that many Turks have been trained in the classical tradition of Germany and France. Yet it is also a domestic product, nourished by class barriers and highly visible indexes of dress and ownership that will in time be minimized by mass production. It is not surprising, then, that technical knowledge is limited and that lawyers, philosophers, and historians sharply outnumber engineers, geologists, accountants, and chemists. In Turkey, moreover, socially devalued business and the trades have long been the preserve of Jewish, Greek, and Armenian minorities, while educated Turks served in government, higher education, and the military. Historically the Turkish military has always enjoyed great esteem. Not only is Islam a warrior-oriented faith, but, in an agricultural country with limited commerce and industry, the army and the bureaucracy were naturally among the few viable career avenues. Beyond this, during the Turkish struggle for survival during the late nineteenth and twentieth centuries, the Greeks and Armenians who had been entrusted with administrative posts had not always proved trustworthy. Thus the Turks felt obliged to replace them with Muslim Turks, even though the latter did not have comparable technical skill. As often happens during revolutionary times, bureaucratic demands for objective competence had to be sacrificed for political loyalty.

Throughout the Middle East these social and occupational values result in a scarcity of trained managers and scientists and only recently has there appeared any widespread desire among students to prepare for these occupations. While all governments are now encouraging the education of engineers and technicians, the absence of staff and facilities means that such training must be gotten abroad, under conditions that are often unlike those at home. For example, engineers trained in German and United States coal mines, where geologic conditions are relatively favorable and mechanization is highly advanced, find much of their experience irrelevant to difficult Turkish mining conditions.

In sum, the dominant educational philosophy tends to devalue practical training and this constitutes a barrier to bureaucratic evolution. Middle East youth prefer to become white-collar rather than blue-collar workers. This inapposite value has an immediate impact on technical and economic development, since it becomes difficult to build up the required force of skilled technicians. In the universities, subjects like statistics and research methods are resisted since they, too, tend to undercut the existing theoretical and subjective conception of learning. Such beliefs deny the demands of modern bureaucratic organization for precision, specialization, and scientific method.

Perhaps the most significant reason for the difficulty of change is the great gap in education and understanding between the tradition-oriented peasant and the urban intellectual. By sharpening the contrast between old and new ways of life and dramatizing the barriers to change, technical assistance, in the short run, may actually aggravate this gap. Here again, the link between bureaucratic patterns of behavior and deeper social values may be seen. It is often noted, for example, that the citizen in the Middle East views government negatively as an instrument of exploitation rather than as a positive aid to security and opportunity. The privatization of public office is regarded as natural. This lack of a "public interest" basis for official loyalty and identification reflects in part the strength of kinship and family ties in the Middle East. When the community is defined in kinship terms, interpersonal relations are likely to reflect particularistic claims, and loyalty to abstractions such as impartiality and community interest is likely to be tenuous.

Along with the evidence of the bureaucrat's preoccupation with self-interest,[10] this tendency toward bureaucratic "self-government" suggests that Middle Eastern systems fail to meet Weber's image of the true bureaucracy as an *instrument* subject to control by an articulate public whose interests are often mediated by an official "public interest" rationale. Insofar as the former type of bureaucracy is still in an evolutionary stage, we may say that it is charismatic, moving toward but not yet arrived at the legal-rational stage that defines the ideal typical bureaucracy.

Among intellectuals, a widespread personal insecurity tends to discourage the rise of a community spirit and to encourage subservience. This pervasive insecurity, the product of centuries of harsh social conditions, of limited career opportunity, of difficulty in dealing with large minorities whose values and loyalties were suspect although their competence was vitally necessary to prevent administrative breakdown, has a direct impact on economic development. In Egypt, for example, where the highest positions were held first by Turks and next by British conquerors, and where limited alternatives made bureaucratic posts a treasured possession, subservience became a functional behavior for the Egyptians.[11] Ottoman rule at home, with the possible exception of the sixteenth century when appointment by merit was practiced, was similarly calculated to encourage fear and subservience.[12] We may assume that this historical experience is reflected in contemporary patterns of official behavior among which anxiety and an upward-looking posture are noteworthy.[13]

Not only does this deep-seated anxiety increase resistance to changes that necessarily disrupt accepted ways of life and threaten high sunk costs in training and interpersonal alignments, but the general climate of insecurity leads to the concealment of private wealth needed for investment. Here again, the past is at work. In the words of a Turkish economic committee, "the reasons for this tendency should be sought . . . in the history of the Ottoman Empire during which confiscation formed one of the characteristics of the country's social and economic life." Personal insecurity, the lack of a community spirit, and a scarcity of private investment capital are thus built-in parts of Middle Eastern culture.

Summary and Conclusion

In setting these several Middle Eastern social values against the requirements of the typical Western bureaucratic model, one must conclude that contemporary exotic bureaucratic systems are at what Max Weber called the *charismatic* stage, in which subjective considerations remain prominent. A dependence upon personal rule rather than upon objective, technical imperatives is characteristic of this stage. From this stage, Weber assumed a logical evolution to a legal-rational type of organization, possessing most of the qualities outlined at the beginning of this chapter.

Perhaps the divergence of contemporary Middle Eastern bureaucracy from the ideal model is most clearly apparent in the precarious position of civil servants. In Turkey, for example, since 1956 civil servants have been subject to arbitrary dismissal.[14] For our purposes the vital point here is that subjective, political values outweigh objective, bureaucratic demands of skill and experience. The resulting insecurity will not only reinforce subjective behavior within the service, such as survival by conformity, but will tend to discourage the recruitment of superior young people into a bureaucracy which can ill afford to lose them.

Insofar as recruitment and the locus of bureaucratic loyalties are concerned, it is well known in Middle Eastern countries that subjective "particularistic" considerations compete strongly with objective standards in appointment and in policy determination. This is because Western "universalistic" concepts of impersonality, technical supremacy, and loyalty to some abstraction such as the "public interest" remain alien in societies in which primary loyalties are directed to members of one's family and personal friends. As a recent observer of the Egyptian civil service concludes, "in the Near

East, people are not yet accustomed to looking upon others impersonally in any situation. Their tendency to look upon others as individuals, with families, friends and communities behind them, is carried over into realms where recent changes have established different formal requirements."[15] The tendency to view bureaucratic employment in terms of self-interest is again apparent in replies to the question: "Do you think civil servants should have their own professional society such as doctors, lawyers, and engineers have?" Of 82 percent of higher civil servants answering "Yes," over 90 percent believed that such associations should be established to protect their economic interests rather than as an expression of professional position.[16]

Such evidences of the absence of ideal-typical bureaucratic loyalties and values are not unexpected, given the historical context of Middle Eastern bureaucracy. Their significance lies in their implications for the ability of states such as Egypt and Turkey to achieve the social and economic goals which they have set for themselves. Here, we assume that such goals can only be achieved by large-scale organizations operating mainly in terms of objective recruitment, technical skill, and rational decision making. For comparative research, Middle East bureaucratic orientations make clear the need to consider the relation between basic social values and the character of given organizations in a given society.[17] At both the levels of basic research and so-called action research, a "pattern analysis" approach such as that proposed here can help to show the functional relationships between such values and organizational behavior. Insofar as technical assistance programs are concerned, such a framework can help us isolate and possibly counteract the values that hinder the development of a more rational bureaucratic model.

NOTES

1. Perhaps the most comprehensive statement of developmental psychology is found in H. S. Sullivan, *The Interpersonal Theory of Psychiatry* (New York 1953); for an attempt to apply Sullivan's formulations to behavior in complex organizations, see Robert V. Presthus, "Toward a Theory of Organizational Behavior," *Administrative Science Quarterly,* 3 (June 1958), pp. 48–72.

2. Max Weber, *The Theory of Social and Economic Organization* (New York: Oxford University Press, 1947), pp. 328–334.

3. For an analysis of Weber's view of bureaucracy as being either "charismatic" or "legal-rational," see Helen Constas, "Max Weber's Two Conceptions of Bureaucracy," *American Journal of Sociology* (January 1958), pp. 400–409.

4. M. Berger, *Bureaucracy and Society in Modern Egypt* (Princeton, New Jersey: Princeton University Press, 1957), p. 45.

5. A. T. J. Matthews, *Emergent Turkish Administrators* (Ankara, Turkey: 1954), p. 14.

6. For a current statement of such resignation, see the *New York Times* account of a measles epidemic in Turkey, November 23, 1958, p. 11.

7. For example, in a recent study of young Turkish administrators (university graduates), it was found that 43 percent believed that "most of the important things that happen to people" are beyond human control. Among Cornell University students, on the other hand, only 17 percent expressed this attitude (Matthews, *op. cit.,* p. 65).

8. *Ibid.,* p. 57.

9. For example, 71 percent of junior administrators in Matthews' study believed the principal goal of schools and universities was "general education;" only 16 percent believed that training for a vocation should be paramount (Matthews, *op. cit.,* p. 52). While many of us would share the majority view expressed here, in the context of Middle Eastern aspirations for economic development it seems inapposite.

10. Berger, for example, found "self-protection" the biggest problem of the Egyptian higher civil service, *op. cit.,* p. 148.

11. For an authoritative account of Arab-Islamic, Ottoman, and British political and administrative domination of Egypt beginning as early as the seventh century, see H.A.R. Gibb and H. Bowen, *Islamic Society and the West* (London: Oxford University Press, 1950), Vol. I.

12. A. Milner, *England in Egypt* (London: 1893).

13. During the past five years the arbitrary dismissal of civil servants and university professors, and the fining and imprisonment of journalists for criticism of government policies have encouraged this climate of anxiety. See the *New York Times* for representative examples, March 13, 1957, p. 8; April 26, 1957, p. 5; November 27, 1957, p. 7; January 22, 1958, p. 7; March 5, 1958, p. 8; May 1, 1958, p. 5; October 21, 1958, p. 32; November 4, 1958, p. 4; January 13, 1959, p. 4; March 13, 1959, p. 1; April 9, 1959, p. 20; June 13, 1959, p. 4; July 17, 1959, p. 6. Despite such evidence, some American observers continue to define Turkey as a "stable," constitutional democracy with a viable party system.

14. For an analysis of the civil servant's position today, see Robert V. Presthus with Sevda Erem, *Statistical Analysis in Comparative Administration: The Turkish Conseil d'Etat* (Ithaca, New York: Cornell University Press, 1958), pp. 19–25.

15. Berger, *op. cit.,* p. 118.

16. *Ibid.,* pp. 127–128.

17. Robert V. Presthus, "Behavior and Bureaucracy in Many Cultures," *Public Administration Review,* 19 (Winter 1959), pp. 25–35.

3

Gideon Sjoberg, Richard A. Brymer, and Buford Farris

BUREAUCRACY AND THE
LOWER CLASS

Bureaucratic structures, so our argument runs, not only encounter major difficulties in coping with the problems of the lower class but also serve to maintain and reinforce patterns that are associated with the "culture of poverty."
Here we shall focus upon the relationships between client-centered bureaucracies[1] and the lower class in American society.

Sociologists have devoted little attention, on either the community or national level, to the impact of bureaucracy upon the stratification system. Yet
our experience, based on research among lower-class Mexican-Americans in
San Antonio,[2] points to the critical role of bureaucratic organizations in sustaining social stratification. Sociologists frequently compare lower- and middle-
class culture patterns, but they fail to recognize that bureaucratic systems are
the key medium through which the middle class maintains its advantaged
position vis-à-vis the lower class.

Our analysis of the effect of the client-centered bureaucracy upon the lower
class is cast in rather theoretical terms. However, illustrative materials from
our research project and the writings of other scholars indicate the kinds of
data that support our generalizations. After delineating the main elements of
the bureaucratic model, we discuss the lower class from the perspective of the
bureaucratic system and then bureaucracy from the viewpoint of the lower
class. These materials set the stage for a consideration of various emergent
organizational and political patterns in American society.

Gideon Sjoberg, Richard A. Brymer, and Buford Farris, "Bureaucracy and the Lower
Class," *Sociology and Social Research* 50 (1966): 325–337. Reprinted by permission.

The Nature of Bureaucracy

In the post-World War II era various sociologists[3] have questioned the utility of Weber's analysis of bureaucracy. Nevertheless, sociologists continue to assume that bureaucracy (as conceived by Weber) is positively associated with the continued development of an advanced industrial-urban order and that this bureaucracy is more or less inevitable.

Modern bureaucracies lay heavy stress upon rationality and efficiency. In order to attain these ends, men are called upon to work within a hierarchical system, with well-defined lines of authority, and within a differentiated social setting, with an elaborate division of labor that stresses the specialization of function. This hierarchy and division of labor are, in turn, sustained through a complex set of formalized rules which are to be administered in a highly impersonal and standardized manner. There is considerable centralization of authority, and as one moves from top to bottom there is greater specialization of function and adherence to the rules.

What is not as clearly recognized is that efficiency and rationality are predicated upon an explicit statement of the organization's goals. Only when an end is clearly stated can one determine the most efficient means for its attainment. Thus, because the corporate structure has had an explicit goal (i.e., profit), it has been quite successful in measuring the efficiency of its programs (i.e., means).

The corporate system has been the model that other bureaucracies have emulated. As a result, there has been considerable concern with efficiency within, say, the Federal Government. McNamara's reorganization of the U.S. Defense Department in the 1960's is a case in point. It is significant that McNamara has drawn heavily upon the work of Hitch and McKean[4] in developing his program, for Hitch and McKean argue that organizational goals must be spelled out in rather concrete terms in order to measure the effectiveness of various programs. An understanding of the interrelationships among measurement, objectification of goals, and efficiency and rationality is essential if we are to assess the impact of bureaucratic structures upon the lower class.

Orientations of Bureaucracies towards the Lower Class

Bureaucratic organizations frequently reinforce the class structure of the community and the nation through their staffing procedures. When a bureaucracy serves both upper- and lower-class groups, as does the school, the poorly qualified teachers tend to drift into lower-class neighborhoods, or, as frequently occurs, beginning teachers are placed in "hardship" districts, and then the most capable move up and out into upper-status school districts where higher salaries and superior working conditions usually prevail. Thus, the advancement of lower-class children is impeded not only because of their cultural background but because of the poor quality of their teachers.

In welfare bureaucracies, social workers have struggled to escape from their traditional identification with the poor, either by redefining their functions in order to serve middle-class clients or by moving away from clients into administrative posts. Once again, evidence suggests that the lower class comes to be served by the least qualified personnel.

In addition to staffing arrangements, the bureaucracy's method of selecting clients reinforces the class system. At this point we must remember that bureaucracies are under constant pressure to define their goals so that the efficiency of their programs can be measured. But unlike corporate systems, client-centered bureaucracies experience grave difficulties in specifying their goals and evaluating their efficiency. The client-centered bureaucracies meet the demands placed upon them through the use of simplified operational definitions. Universities, for instance, do not judge their effectiveness in terms of producing "educated men" but according to the ratings of their students on national tests, the number of students who gain special awards, etc. These operational criteria reflect the orientation or view of persons in positions of authority within the bureaucracy and the broader society. In turn, these criteria become the basis for the selection of clients. Through this procedure, a bureaucratic organization can ensure its success, and it can more readily demonstrate to the power structure that the community or society is "getting something for its money." The bureaucracy's success is likely to lead to an increase in funds and expanded activities. It follows that client-centered bureaucracies often find it advantageous to avoid lower-class clients who are likely to handicap the organization in the attainment of its goals.[5]

Several illustrations should clarify our argument. The Federal Job Corps program has been viewed as one means for alleviating the unemployment problem among youth, especially those in the lower class. This program has sought to train disadvantaged youths in various occupational skills. The success of the Job Corps is apparently to be evaluated according to the number of trainees who enter the industrial labor force. Consequently, the organization has sought to select those youths who have internalized some of the middle-class norms of upward mobility and who are likely to succeed in the occupational system. The Job Corps by-passes many persons who in theory stand in greatest need of assistance; for example, potential "troublemakers"— young men with criminal records—are not accepted as trainees. Because of this selection process the Job Corps leadership will likely be able to claim success and to convince Congressmen that the program should be continued and perhaps broadened.

A more subtle form of client selection can be found in child guidance clinics. Here clients are often accepted in terms of their "receptivity" to therapy.[6] However, this criterion favors those persons who have been socialized into the middle-class value orientation held by, for example, the clinic staff and the social groups who pay the bill. The poor, especially the families from ethnic groups within the lower class, who according to the ideal norms of these agencies should receive the greatest amount of attention, are quietly shunted aside. Moreover, one study has indicated a positive association between the social status of the client and the social status of the professional worker handling the case in the agency.[7]

The procedures by which school systems cope with their clients are perhaps central to understanding the community and national class system, for the educational variable is becoming increasingly significant in sustaining or advancing one's status. At this point we are concerned with the differential treatment of clients by the organization once they have been accepted.

School systems frequently employ IQ tests and similar instruments in their evaluation of pupils. These tests, however, have been constructed in such a manner that they articulate the values, beliefs, and knowledge of the middle class and the demands of the power elements of the society. That these tests are used to make early judgments on the ability of pupils serves to support the existing class system. Lower-class pupils often come to be defined as "dull," and, through a kind of self-fulfilling prophecy, this definition of the situation structures the students' future career. In fact, school counselors frequently interpret test scores according to their middle-class expectations; they, therefore, tend to discourage lower-class pupils from attending college even when their scores are relatively high.[8]

It is significant that the New York City school system has been forced to abandon the use of IQ tests.[9] It appears that the traditionally disadvantaged groups such as Negroes and Puerto Ricans have attained sufficient political power to challenge those methods that the school bureaucracy has used for determining success, methods that have been oriented to middle-class rather than lower-class norms.

Bureaucratized school systems place the lower-class clients at a disadvantage in still other ways. Various types of standardization or categorization, which are a product of middle-class expectations and which are viewed as essential for maintaining efficiency, limit the school's ability to adjust to the "needs" of lower-class pupils. We know of a special class, for example, that was established for the purpose of teaching lower-class and problem children, but in which the rules demanded that the teacher follow the same teaching plan employed in other classes in the school.

Actually, bureaucratic structures socialize the incumbents of roles in such a manner that they are frequently incapable of understanding the world-view of the lower-class client. Discussions of the bureaucratic personality, such as those by Merton and Presthus,[10] have given but scant attention to the difficulty of the bureaucrat's taking the role of the lower-class other. For as a result of his role commitment, the bureaucrat tends to impose his own expectations and interpretations of reality upon the client. He often comes to view the norms of the system as invariant. And bureaucrats in the lower echelons, those who have the greatest amount of contact with lower-class clients, are also the most bound by the rules. Faced with recalcitrant clients or clients having divergent value orientations, the typical office holder will say in effect, "If only clients would act properly, everything would be all right, and we could get on with our work."

The bureaucrat, oriented as he is to the middle- or upper-class life styles, usually lacks knowledge about the lower-class client's subculture. Moreover, he finds it difficult to step outside his formalized role. If he seeks to take the role of the client—in the sense of understanding the latter's belief and value system—he will ultimately have to challenge or at least question some of the rules that govern the operation of the system of which he is a part. For if he understands why clients act the way they do, he is likely to recognize that they have valid reasons for objecting to his conception of reality or, more specifically, to some of the bureaucratic regulations. Consequently, bureaucratic organizations tend to penalize those of their members who "overidentify" with clients.

Social workers who overidentify with their clients or teachers who overidentify with their students are considered to be indulging in nonprofessional action. Such action, so the reasoning runs, makes it impossible for the professional to adhere to the ideal norms of universalism and objectivity and thus to assist his clients effectively. Professional norms such as these reinforce those bureaucratic norms that impose barriers upon the lower-class person's advancement in the social order.

The controls exerted by the bureaucrats over members of the lower class are intensified because the office holders are constantly called upon to normalize and stabilize the system with an eye to maintaining the proper public image. One means of stabilizing and rationalizing the system's performance is to work within the context of established rules or categories. But to cope really effectively with such deviants as juvenile delinquents, the schools would have to alter radically their time-honored categories. Our experience suggests, however, that school systems stifle the grievances of deviant or lower-class groups, for these grievances, at least implicitly, challenge the bureaucratic norms that are supported by the groups that determine public policy.

The general insensitivity of bureaucracies to lower-class persons and their problems is highlighted in the "custodial function" adopted by many mental hospitals and even slum schools.[11] Because the bureaucracy's normative system runs counter to (or at best ignores) the norms and values of the lower class, a minimum of attention is given to socializing clients into the bureaucratic—or broader societal—norms. Bureaucratic systems adjust to this situation through the caretaker function.

Orientations of the Lower Class
towards Bureaucracies

Just as significant as the bureaucracy's orientation towards the lower class is the latter's orientation towards the bureaucracy. Our investigations, particularly depth interviews of Mexican-American families in San Antonio, support the conclusion of other social scientists—that members of the lower class encounter serious difficulties when they attempt to understand or to cope with the normative order of bureaucratic systems.

First and foremost, the lower-class person simply lacks knowledge of the rules of the game. Middle-class persons generally learn how to manipulate bureaucratic rules to their advantage and even to acquire special "favors" by working through the "private" or "backstage" (as opposed to the "public") sector of the bureaucratic organization. Middle-class parents teach by example as they intervene with various officials—e.g., the police or school teachers—to protect the family's social position in the community. In contrast, the lower-class person stands in awe of bureaucratic regulations and frequently is unaware that he has a legal and moral claim to certain rights and privileges. More often, however, it is the lack of knowledge of the system's technicalities and backstage regions that is responsible for the lower-class person's inability to manipulate a bureaucratic system to his advantage.

We mentioned earlier that in its lower echelons the bureaucracy is highly specialized and governed by numerous regulations. Therefore, the lower-class person, whose knowledge of the system is least adequate, must interact with the very officials who are most constrained by the formal rules. This situation is complicated by the fact that the problems the lower-class person faces are difficult to treat in isolation. The lack of steady employment, of education, and of medical care, for example, interlock in complex ways. Yet, the lower-class client encounters officials who examine only one facet of his difficulties and who, in the ideal, treat all cases in a similar fashion. After one agency (or official) has dealt with the special problem assigned it, the client is then referred to another agency which will consider another facet of the situation. It follows that no official is able to view the lower-class client as a whole person, and thus he is unable to point up to the client how he might use his strengths to overcome his weaknesses.

Middle-class persons, on the other hand, are in a position to deal with higher-status office holders, who are less encumbered by the rules and thus can examine their clients' problems in holistic terms. Delinquents from middle-class homes, for instance, are more apt than those from lower-class surroundings to be judged by officials according to their overall performance—both past and present.

The cleavage between modern bureaucracies and the lower class is intensified by various cultural differences. Gans,[12] for example, has found that lower-class persons typically relate to one another in a personal manner. Middle-class persons are better able to relate to others within an impersonal context. Thus, members of the lower class face a greater gulf when they attempt to communicate with middle-class bureaucrats who ideally must administer rules according to impersonal, universalistic norms.

This divergence between the lower class and bureaucratic officialdom in patterns of social interaction simply makes it more difficult for a lower-class person to acquire knowledge of how the system operates. It is not surprising that under these circumstances members of the lower class often experience a sense of powerlessness or alienation. This alienation in turn reinforces and is reinforced by the sense of fatalism that is an integral part of "the culture of poverty."[13] That is, those who live in the world of the lower class account for events in the social sphere in terms of spiritual forces, chance, luck, and the like; they have little or no sense of control over their own destiny.

Because bureaucratic officials find it difficult to understand the perspective of lower-class clients and because lower-class persons must increasingly cope with highly specialized and technically oriented systems, the social distance between the bureaucratically skilled members of American society and some elements of the lower class may well be increasing rather than decreasing.[14] A kind of "circular causation," in Myrdal's terms,[15] is at work, as various social forces tend to exaggerate the schism between at least some sectors of the lower class and the upper socioeconomic groups who control the bureaucratic organizations.

Organizational Implications

The dilemmas of client-centered bureaucracies which deal with lower-class persons are reflected in a variety of programs designed to eliminate poverty, juvenile delinquency, and other social problems. By examining these programs we can clarify some of the relationships between bureaucracy and the lower class discussed above and can bring to light other issues as well.

There have been two broad strategies for resolving the problems faced by the lower class on the national, state, and local levels. The dominant strategy emphasizes increased bureaucratization. The second approach, of theoretical rather than practical import at the present time, calls for a fundamental re-structuring of client-centered bureaucracies.

1. The primary means of overcoming the problems that have been associated with the lower class has been more and more bureaucracy. This pattern has taken two forms.

a. The social problems of the lower class that have resisted solution (in terms of the values and beliefs of the dominant groups in society) are to be resolved through expansion of existing bureaucratic structures or the addition of new ones. This has been the main thrust of most legislation on both the national and the state levels since the 1930's. The programs initiated during the New Deal era have reached their fruition in President Johnson's "Great Society." In one sense the problems generated by bureaucracy are to be met by more bureaucracy.

The efforts to resolve social problems through bureaucratization have proliferated in the nongovernmental sector as well. For example, some programs— e.g., the Y.M.C.A. Detached Workers Program in Chicago[16]—seek to combat delinquency among lower-class groups by fitting youth into an organizational apparatus.

The sociologist Glazer[17] views this organizational revolution as the basis of the new utopia. It is the model towards which men should strive. He, like many other sociologists, considers an industrial-urban order to be equivalent with a bureaucratic social order.

b. A small group of persons believe that the problems of the lower class require a counter-organizational solution. The Mobilization for Youth program in New York—as it has been interpreted by some social workers—is an instructive case in point.[18] Here a number of social workers, perhaps as a reaction to their traditional overidentification with middle-class norms, have been attempting to organize the poor in order to counter the problems generated by entrenched bureaucracies. In theory the new bureaucratic systems should side with the poor against the established bureaucracies which are controlled by the upper socioeconomic groups.

2. Along with this trend towards bureaucratization, there have been increased efforts to remake bureaucratic structures or to create nonbureaucratic systems in order to attain certain ends.[19]

a. Although the therapeutic community in the mental health field has not been specifically designed for lower-class clients, this development has been spurred by the sociological descriptions of custodial hospitals that have cared for lower-class patients. These highly bureaucratized systems have fallen far short of their stated goals; indeed, they have done much to stifle communication between therapists and patients.[20] The therapeutic community, which in extreme form calls for a complete breakdown of status barriers between therapist and patient, has thus emerged as a new organizational form in order to further the treatment of patients.

Somewhat similar communities have emerged in other areas as well. The Provo Experiment[21] with juvenile delinquents has displayed some of the characteristics of the therapeutic community. In at least the early stages of their contacts with delinquents, the workers in this project have placed considerable reliance upon informal groups (in sharp contrast to, say, the bureaucratized reformatory) as a mechanism for revising the delinquent's orientation.

b. In a similar vein, there have been efforts to set up organizations along collegial lines. Some writers, like Litwak, seem to regard this type of system as a "professional bureaucracy."[22] But if we take the Weberian model as our starting point, the very notion of a professional bureaucracy is a contradiction of terms. The collegial organization and the bureaucratic system are built on divergent principles. The former stresses, for example, equality among office holders and the need for generalists rather than specialists. The generalist, unencumbered by highly formalized rules, can view clients in holistic terms and thus examine their weaknesses relative to their strengths. There emerges here a type of rationality that is not encompassed by Weber's notions of "formal rationality" (typical of bureaucratic systems) and "substantive rationality" (typical of traditional paternalistic systems).[23]

Some mental hospitals are apparently being built along collegial lines—as a compromise between a bureaucratic system and a therapeutic community.[24] Our experience in a neighborhood agency indicates that a collegial organization is necessary if social workers are to function as "mediators" between divergent class elements.[25] Workers within a bureaucratic welfare agency, as depicted by Wilensky and Lebeaux,[26] must take the class structure (as defined by the upper socioeconomic groups) as their frame of reference. Because bureaucratic functionaries find it difficult to understand the role orientations of lower-class others, they can not mediate effectively between elements of different social classes.

Overall, the trends in the development of nonbureaucratic organizations suggest a close association between the system's internal structure and its relationships with clients. These trends also support our contention that bureaucratic systems have not been successful in working with lower-class clients.

Political Implications

The tensions generated by the bureaucratic solution to current social problems are highlighted by the efforts to resolve the difficulties encountered by the Negro lower class. The debate generated by the "Moynihan Report" is of special theoretical interest.[27] (This report, issued by the U.S. Department of Labor, was written by Daniel P. Moynihan, although he is not formally listed as author.) Moynihan argues that the family structure of the lower-class Negro—which is mother-dominated and highly unstable by societal standards —must be revised if Negroes are to adapt to the industrial-urban order or the bureaucratic school systems, economic organizations, etc.

Elements of the Negro leadership have sharply attacked the Moynihan Report. They believe that instead of restructuring the lower-class Negro family we must remake modern bureaucratic systems so that these will be more responsive to the "needs" of the Negro lower class.

Moynihan's position is in keeping with that of many sociologists who accept present-day structural arrangements as more or less inevitable. Sociologists often argue that social problems arise because lower-class individuals or families are committed to sociocultural patterns that make it difficult for them to accommodate to the demands of industrial-urban organizations. Although some scholars have analyzed the dysfunctions of bureaucratic systems,[28] they rarely, if ever, assume that basic structural reorganization is necessary or possible. But the Weberian model may not be a rational or efficient organization for coping with many of the problems that have emerged (and will emerge) in an advanced industrial order where the problems of production have been resolved and the issues dealt with by client-centered organizations loom increasingly larger.

Sociologists must reexamine their basic premises if they are to grasp the nature of current social trends. For one thing, politics in a postwelfare, advanced industrial-urban order may become oriented around pro-bureaucratic and anti-bureaucratic ideologies. The rumblings of minorities (including some intellectuals in England, the United States, and Sweden) suggest that this type of political struggle may be in the offing. It is of interest, for example, that in the United States elements of the New Left—e.g., Students for a Democratic Society—share a common "devil"—the bureaucratic system—with elements of the right wing. We would hypothesize that some relationship exists between these ideological concerns and the problems of client-centered bureaucracies. Certainly, these developments are worthy of serious sociological investigation—and before, not after, the fact.

Conclusions

Evidence indicates that modern bureaucracies, especially client-centered ones, stand between lower-class and upper-status (particularly middle-class) persons. These groups do not encounter one another within a vacuum but rather within an organizational, bureaucratic context. Even when they meet in relatively informal situations, the bureaucratic orientation of the middle-class person structures his response to the lower-class individual. It is through their positions in the key bureaucracies that the higher-status groups maintain their social advantages and even at times foster bureaucratic procedures that impede the advancement of lower-class persons into positions of privilege. While our illustrative data are limited to the United States, many of our generalizations seem to hold for other industrial-urban orders as well.

The social and political implications of the dilemmas that face bureaucratic systems require far more attention than they have received. Weber's conception of bureaucracy may have deflected sociologists from some significant concerns. There are, after all, other intellectual traditions to draw upon. For example, Spencer's[29] analysis of how "military organizations" emphasize the contributions of individuals to the system and of how "industrial organizations" emphasize the contributions of the system to individuals is of considerable relevance for an understanding of the link between formal organizations and their clients and, ultimately, formal organizations and social stratification. But whatever one's source of inspiration, the study of the impact of different kinds of formal organizations upon social stratification is central to the sociologist's major concern—that of understanding the nature of order.

NOTES

1. The term "client-centered bureaucracy" is derived from the classification scheme of Peter Blau and W. Richard Scott, *Formal Organizations* (San Francisco: Chandler

Gideon Sjoberg, Richard A. Brymer, and Buford Farris

Publishing Co., 1962). They employ the term "service organizations" for this type of structure.

2. Our main project, which focuses upon the evaluation of an action program for the prevention of juvenile delinquency, is supported by the National Institute of Mental Health: Grant No. R11-MH-1075-02 and 02SI. This project has, as a result of a grant from the Hogg Foundation, University of Texas, been broadened to include a study in depth of lower-class Mexican-American families.

3. Peter Blau, *The Dynamics of Bureaucracy* (rev. ed. Chicago: University of Chicago Press, 1963), and Alvin Gouldner, *Patterns of Industrial Bureaucracy* (New York: The Free Press, a Division of the Macmillan Co., 1965).

4. Charles J. Hitch and Roland N. McKean, *The Economics of Defense in the Nuclear Age* (Cambridge: Harvard University Press, 1960).

5. See e.g., Martin Rein, "The Strange Case of Public Dependency," *Trans-Action,* 2 (March-April, 1965), 16–23.

6. Based on the personal observations of Buford Farris who, as a social worker, has had extensive contact with these agencies.

7. Raymond G. Hunt, Orville Gurrslin, and Jack L. Roach, "Social Status and Psychiatric Service in a Child Guidance Clinic," *American Sociological Review,* 23 (February, 1958), 81–83.

8. Aaron Cicourel and John I. Kitsuse, *The Educational Decision-Makers* (Indianapolis: Bobbs-Merrill Co., 1963). For a general discussion of the bureaucratization of the school system see Dean Harper, "The Growth of Bureaucracy in School Systems," *American Journal of Economics and Sociology,* 23 (July, 1965), 261–71.

9. Fred M. Hechinger, "I.Q. Test Ban," *New York Times,* March 8, 1964, Section E, p. 7; Fred M. Hechinger, "Testing at Issue," *New York Times,* November 1, 1964, Section E, p. 9.

10. Robert K. Merton, *Social Theory and Social Structure* (rev. ed. New York: The Free Press, a Division of the Macmillan Co., 1957), 195–206 and Robert Presthus, *The Organizational Society* (New York: Vintage Books, 1965).

11. See, e.g., Ivan Belknap, *Human Problems of a State Mental Hospital* (New York: McGraw-Hill Book Co., 1956); Fred M. Hechinger, "Poor Marks for Slum Schools," *New York Times,* December 12, 1965, Section E, p. 9; Kenneth Clark, *Dark Ghetto* (New York: Harper and Row, 1965), chap. 6.

12. Herbert Gans, *The Urban Villagers* (New York: The Free Press, a Division of the Macmillan Co., 1965).

13. See, e.g., various essays in Frank Riessman, Jerome Cohen, and Arthur Pearl (eds.), *Mental Health of the Poor* (New York: The Free Press, a Division of the Macmillan Co., 1964).

14. U.S. Bureau of the Census, *Current Population Reprint Series P-60, No. 47, Income in 1964 of Families and Persons in the United States* (Washington, D.C.: U.S. Government Printing Office, 1965).

15. Gunnar Myrdal, *Economic Theory and Under-Developed Regions* (London: Gerald Duckworth and Co., 1957), 16–20.

16. Charles N. Cooper, "The Chicago YMCA Detached Workers: Current Status of an Action Program," Paper presented at a joint session of the annual meeting of the Society for the Study of Social Problems and American Sociological Association, Los Angeles, California, August, 1963.

17. Nathan Glazer, "The Good Society," *Commentary,* 36 (September, 1963), 226–34.

18. See, e.g., Charles F. Grosser, "Community Development Programs Serving the Urban Poor," *Social Work,* 10 (July, 1965), 15–21.

19. There has been considerable interest in reorganizing corporate bureaucracy in recent years, but this material does not bear directly upon the problems at hand.

71

20. See, e.g., Belknap, *op. cit.*

21. LaMar T. Empey and Jerome Rabow, "The Provo Experiment in Delinquency Prevention," *American Sociological Review,* 26 (October, 1961), 679–95.

22. Eugene Litwak, "Models of Bureaucracy Which Permit Conflict," *American Journal of Sociology,* 57 (September, 1961), 177–84.

23. *From Max Weber,* trans. and ed. by H. H. Gerth and C. Wright Mills (New York: Oxford University Press, 1946).

24. Research being carried out by James Otis Smith, J. Kenneth Benson, and Gideon Sjoberg as part of the Timberlawn Foundation Research Project, Dallas, Texas, will bear directly upon this issue.

25. Gideon Sjoberg, "The Rise of the 'Mediator Society'," Presidential address delivered at the annual meeting of the Southwestern Sociological Association, Dallas, Texas, March, 1964, examines the overall role of mediators in modern society.

26. Harold L. Wilensky and Charles N. Lebeaux, *Industrial Society and Social Welfare* (New York: The Free Press, a Division of the Macmillan Co., 1965), 238–40.

27. U.S. Department of Labor, *The Case for National Action* (Washington, D.C.: U.S. Government Printing Office, 1965). For reactions to this essay see: "The Negro Family: Visceral Reaction," *Newsweek,* 60 (December 6, 1965), 38–40 and John Herbers, "Moynihan Hopeful U.S. Will Adopt a Policy of Promoting Family Stability," *New York Times,* December 12, 1965, 74.

28. See, e.g., Harry Cohen, *The Demonics of Bureaucracy* (Ames, Iowa: Iowa State University Press, 1965).

29. Herbert Spencer, *The Principles of Sociology,* 3 vols. (New York: D. Appleton and Co., 1899).

4

Elihu Katz and S. N. Eisenstadt

SOME SOCIOLOGICAL OBSERVATIONS
ON THE RESPONSE OF ISRAELI
ORGANIZATIONS TO NEW IMMIGRANTS

This chapter has its origin in preliminary observations on the patterns of contact between Israeli organizations and recent immigrants from non-Western
countries. The pilot study resulting from these observations is concerned,
first with "the socialization of the client," that is, with the adaptation of newcomers from traditional familistic backgrounds to new role expectations such
as those implicit in becoming a factory worker, a hospital patient, a client of
a social welfare worker, or even a bus passenger. Secondly, the study is
equally concerned with the changes that occur in the organizations themselves
in response to the large influx of clients new to Western ways. It is to preliminary reflection on this second problem that the present chapter is devoted.

Rather than consider the organization as a whole, we are restricting our
focus to those officials having direct dealings with new immigrants. We are
concerned, in other words, with the official-client relationship where the of-

Elihu Katz and S. N. Eisenstadt, "Some Sociological Observations on the Response
of Israeli Organizations to New Immigrants, *Administrative Science Quarterly* 5 (1960):
113–133. Reprinted by permission.

NOTE: This chapter is a by-product of a collaborative effort to design research on the
developing bureaucratic framework of immigrant absorption in Israel. In 1957–1958
a research seminar on this topic was conducted by the authors at the Hebrew University
in Jerusalem. Participating in the seminar, and in the pilot study that emerged from it,
were the following faculty members and students: Rivka Bar-Yosef, Batsheva Bonné,
Esther Carmeli, Nina Toren, Arie Eliav, Uri Horowitz, Rivka Kaplansky, Yael Lissak,
Pnina Morag, Dorit Pedan, Ozer Schild, Dov Weintraub, and Rina Zabelevsky. Mr.
Schild and Mrs. Bar-Yosef are currently directing the pilot study, which is being supported, in part, by the Ford Foundation. We are indebted to Professors Peter M. Blau
and David Riesman for a critical reading of an earlier draft.

ficial is usually of European birth or parentage and where the client is a recent immigrant from a non-Western country.

According to sociological theory, there was good reason to expect that the rapid influx of large numbers of new immigrants would increase the bureaucratization of the organizations to which they came.[1] This meant that one could expect, first, an increasing impersonality of relations between bureaucrats and clients.[2] One could also expect an increase in the degrees of universalism—equality before the law—in the orientation of bureaucrat toward client. Similarly, the pressure of work resulting from the large influx ought to make the official more stringent in his enforcement of the rules. And, of course, one could expect official-client relations to become more businesslike and specific, becoming more narrowly limited to officially relevant concerns. Finally, one could expect the official to rely more heavily on the ascribed authority of his office and on the symbols and the power accompanying it to get his job done.[3]

These are some of the dimensions in which we expected to find changes in the official-client relationship as a result both of the large and rapid increase of clients and of the tensions arising from the radical cultural differences between officials and clients. We found such examples, of course, but we also found many examples of change in exactly the opposite direction. Rather than a marked increase in the degree of bureaucratization in official-client relations, we found evidence of debureaucratization. We often found officials relating to clients personally, taking sympathetic account of the status "new immigrant," and not confining themselves to their officially relevant roles. And frequently we found officials trying to get their job done, not so much by means of the power and symbols of office, but on the basis of exchange of services, or persuasion, or personal charisma.

In the pages that follow, we shall try to explain how such relationships appear to arise. But it is important to bear in mind that these are, so far, only impressionistic observations. The pilot study and, ultimately, the full-scale research, we hope, will be better founded.

Theory and Research on Bureaucratization

In the broadest sense, the theoretical problem here deals with the conditions affecting the degree of bureaucratization of an organization, specifically of the bureaucrat-client relationship. We are interested in the factors that make for varying degrees of bureaucratization as well as the factors (presumably the same ones) that influence the direction of organizational change. Indeed, in the writings of Max Weber and Robert Michels the problem of organizational change is essentially identical with the theme of bureaucratization.[4] If the classical sociological writings were concerned with bureaucratization, the later writings have devoted themselves to the problems of overbureaucratization. Thus, discussions of deviations from the ideal-type bureaucracy outlined by Weber focused on overbureaucratization as a threat to the attainment of the very goals for which the organizations were established. The leading character in these discussions, the official who converts means into ends, has been frequently described both in literary and scientific publications. The same is true for the accompanying manifestations of exaggerated hierarchy and red tape.[5]

Recently, however, with the beginning of empirical research on organizational behavior, these assumptions about the unidirectional evolution of organizations have been put into broader perspective. Thus, recent empirical research seems to suggest that (1) the trend toward total bureaucratization of organizations may sometimes be averted;[6] (2) actual bureaucracies are compounded of nonbureaucratic elements also;[7] (3) bureaucracies, once established, are by no means unchanging;[8] and (4) when changes do take place, they are not always in the direction of greater bureaucratization and formalism.[9]

FACTORS AFFECTING BUREAUCRATIZATION IN THE
OFFICIAL-CLIENT RELATIONSHIP

The literature provides a number of suggestions concerning the factors affecting bureaucratization in general. Weber's emphasis has already been noted.[10] Succession is another familiar example. When a new director takes over from a predecessor, he has little choice but to insist on relatively greater formal relations, to demand adherence to the appointed channels of communication, and the like.[11] Another factor is monopolization. When an organization has a monopoly on certain goods or services (as most public bureaucracies have, of course), there is little chance of effective protest on the part of the client and no possibility of recourse to a competitor; under such conditions, bureaucrats may permit themselves an attitude of detachment and ritualistic formalism vis-à-vis their clients.[12]

The reverse of each of these influences should be associated with a lesser degree of bureaucratization. Thus, a smaller organization or one which suffers a reduction in size ought to be less bureaucratic. So should an organization that is aware that its clients have a choice between it and a competitor.

Each of these factors, of course, has its impact on the official-client or the superior-subordinate relationships.[13] But there are other factors worth singling out for their specific impact on these relationships. It is well known, for example, that soldiers in combat relate to others and to their officers in a much less bureaucratic way than they do behind the front lines or in peacetime.[14] Closely related findings emerge from a study of the informal social organization that superseded the formal organization of a naval unit on a tiny, unpopulated Pacific island.[15] Similarly, workers on the night shift were treated differently by their supervisors than were day-shift employees,[16] just as, in Gouldner's study, workers in the mine successfully resisted greater bureaucratization while office workers in the same company did not.[17] The common elements in these situations would seem to be the relative danger or unusualness of the task, the relative isolation from social contacts outside the organization, and relative independence from the immediate presence of upper echelons in the hierarchy. One suspects that certain of these factors would also be appropriate to cases such as Diamond's study of the debureaucratization of a quasi-military group by early American settlers organized as the Virginia Company.[18]

As a final example of debureaucratization, Turner's study of the navy disbursing officer during wartime will serve particularly well.[19] Turner indicated several factors that influenced these officers to depart from the orientation prescribed by the rule book to establish more diffuse relations with some of their clients and to show favoritism. First, many clients of the disbursing officer were his superiors in rank and, consequently, his superiors in other role relationships. Secondly, he found it advantageous to help others who could reciprocate, such as the mess officer. This dependence, in part a function of his isolation from other social contacts, was embedded in a more general interdependence created by the war.[20] Finally, client and bureaucrat were dependent on each other because, especially during the war, the higher authorities who were to be consulted in case of doubt were both physically and psychologically distant.

This dependence of clients and officials on each other appears as a key factor in the other cases as well, and for much the same reasons.[21] The danger, the isolation, the aborted hierarchy of combat, the night shift, the mine, the Virginia Company, and the naval unit on the Pacific island made men dependent upon each other over and above the specific relations defined for them by their formal organizations. The attempt to enforce ordinary peacetime or daytime relations under such circumstances—that is, the attempt to behave in the accepted bureaucratic manner, or even more, to be overbureaucratic—is what apparently leads to desertion (where one is able to leave) or to mutiny (where one cannot).

ROLE IMPINGEMENT AS A CHARACTERIZATION OF
BUREAUCRATIZATION AND DEBUREAUCRATIZATION

The notion of dependence may be viewed sociologically as a special case of the impingement of other role relationships on a given bureaucratic relationship. In Turner's study, for example, the observed debureaucratization could be considered a product of the regularized contacts in other roles that existed between the disbursing officer and his clients. Moreover, if debureaucratization may be characterized in terms of the impingement of non-bureaucratic roles on bureaucratic ones, then overbureaucratization may be characterized as either the formalistic segregation of a bureaucratic relationship from all other role relations (even relevant ones) or, in its totalitarian form, as the imposition of the bureaucratic relationship on relations outside the scope of the bureaucracy. The bureaucratic ritualist would be an example of one who arbitrarily views all extrabureaucratic roles as irrelevant to the conduct of his office, while the totalitarian bureaucrat "takes his authority home," as, for example, the sergeant bullying his men off duty.

In effect, overbureaucratization and debureaucratization represent a disturbance in the relationship between an organization and its environment that is not envisioned by the classical model of bureaucracy. This model envisages the roles of both bureaucrat and client as segregated to some extent from their other roles; their roles are "specific" to the interaction setting and in this bureaucratic setting it is irrelevant, for example, that both bureaucrat and client belong to the same political club. However, even in the ideal-type bureaucracy a role is not completely independent of other roles; some outside roles clearly may be, or must be, considered. If an old man, obviously unable to wait his turn in a long queue, is given special attention by a clerk, this is not a case of an irrelevant role relationship being allowed incorrectly to impinge on the bureaucrat-client relationship. In general, the classic model of bureaucracy requires only that the bureaucratic organization not be directly dependent on external factors for its manpower, its resources, or its motivation for carrying out its organizational task. If an organization relies directly upon any one segment of the population for financing, or for political protection, these sources of support will clearly receive particularistic attention in the dispensation of the organization's services. It is such direct dependence that mechanisms such as boards of trustees, budget bureaus, and the like try to avert by insulating bureaucratic organizations from their sources of support. What is true for the organization as a whole is true for its members as well. If a bureaucrat receives direct rewards from outside the organization in addition to, or instead of, his rewards from within, obviously his independence of action as a bureaucrat is thereby reduced.[22]

Clearly, then, there is a very delicate balance—varying from organization to organization—between the specific roles defined as relevant to relations within the bureaucracy and those outside roles defined as irrelevant. Note the parallel to our notion of role impingement in Gouldner's concept of "latent identity."[23]

Israeli Officials and New Immigrants

Increasingly, in recent years, the contact between immigrants and the new societies to which they have come are mediated by professionals and bureaucrats. The customs agent, the social worker, the policeman, the public health nurse, the housing administrator, and the like, constitute the immigrants' main connections with the community to which they come, and it is these officials who provide aid and advice, which in earlier migrations were obtained more informally or not at all. This change is characteristic not only of the reception of immigrants in present-day Israel but also of the reception of Puerto Ricans and southern Negroes in New York and Chicago, and of other immigrant groups in the areas receiving them.[24] This change is in part a consequence of the greater bureaucratization of these areas in the last generation and in part a consequence of the theory and practice of the welfare state which, adapting itself to the immigrant, proffers many social services unknown to the immigrant of an earlier generation. In Israel, this change is also a consequence of the different pattern of motivation and different demographic composition of present-day immigrants compared with the "pioneer" immigrants of the turn of the century.[25]

The remainder of this chapter is devoted to a preliminary discussion of some of the problems arising out of the contact between immigrants to Israel and the officials with whom they deal, viewed against the theoretical considerations set forth in the first part of this chapter. The kind of immigrant with whom we are particularly concerned comes from non-Western countries (such as Yemen, Morocco, Iraq, and so on), where he is likely to have had little or no contact with formal organization.

The question to which we now turn is why so many of the official-client relations observed seemed to be moving in the direction of lesser bureaucratization. We do not mean to imply that Israeli organizations prior to the influx of the non-Western immigrants were close approximations of the Weberian ideal-type; for the small size of the country and the common struggle made for wide networks of interpersonal relations embracing officials and clients alike. The pioneering and egalitarian ideologies frowned on status differentiation, differential distribution of rewards, as well as on formalities of all sorts. Not least important, political parties exerted considerable influence on appointments to and conduct of the public bureaucracies.

As we have already said, the mere increase in organizational size and responsibility might have been expected to result in increased bureaucratization of relations between official and client, between supervisor and worker, and so forth. To this rapid increase in numbers add the divergence of cultural background between the majority of recent immigrants coming from non-Western countries and the European bureaucrats dealing with them, and one would certainly expect an increase in bureaucratic formalism.[26]

Yet our preliminary observations indicate that this is not the case. We have, of course, found some evidence of increasing bureaucratization as a response to the influx of new immigrants. Thus, in one co-operative organization, for example, the hierarchy became sharply elongated. Previously any member was able to reach the highest official of the organization rather directly and informally, nor was it particularly important whether he brought his problem to one or another of the top officials. Now, the same organization has developed a strict chain of command and a new immigrant with a problem must proceed strictly through the established channels and talk only to the relevant official. Yet, even in this organization, as far as the actual interaction between official and client is concerned, there is evidence of considerable debureaucratization.

Repeatedly, however, we have found in institutions as diverse as health clinics and bus companies, widespread evidence of debureaucratization in the relationship between officials and new immigrants. We have found cases where the official has assigned himself a greater number of tasks vis-à-vis his clients than those assigned him by his organization. We find considerable evidence of the growth of personal relationships between officials and new immigrants. We have even found cases where the official becomes the leader of a kind of "social movement" composed of new immigrants, thus completely reversing the expected trend which is supposed to lead from movements to bureaucracy. A major key to this unanticipated phenomenon is the notion of dependence we have developed, which takes quite a different form at this point. We shall try to describe what we think we have found and, in part, we shall do this in terms of case studies. In one case, officials assumed a teaching role vis-à-vis their clients. In another, officials departed from their prescribed role as agents of socialization in certain patterned ways. In the third case, officials became the leaders of an incipient social movement.

BUREAUCRATS AS TEACHERS: DEPENDENCE ON THE CLIENT'S PERFORMANCE OF HIS ROLE

The most characteristic form of debureaucratization in the relationship between bureaucrats and new immigrants in Israel is the assumption by the bureaucrat of the role of teacher along with (or at the expense of) his other functions. Consider, for example, the bus driver who gets out of the bus to teach the idea of a queue—"first come, first served"—an idea which is new to many of his new immigrant passengers. Similarly, the nurse at the well-baby clinic may be seen teaching women, informally, which of their needs are appropriate to the health services and which should be taken to other organizations. Or, the manager of the government-subsidized grocery in the new immigrant settlement may take the initiative and go into homes to teach housewives how to prepare certain foods with which they have had no previous experience.

In all these examples, the bureaucrat takes the time and effort to teach a client something about his (the bureaucrat's) expectations concerning how the client role is to be played. In other words, the bureaucrat teaches the client how to be a client so that he (the bureaucrat) can go on being a bureaucrat. This, it seems to us, is a form of dependence, but one which we have not considered so far; it is dependence on the client to act in a way which makes it possible for the bureaucrat to do his job.

In other words, it is expected by the bureaucrat and the bureaucracy that the client will bring with him to the bureaucratic context certain knowledge of expected roles from "outside," even though he may have had no previous contact with this particular bureaucracy. In Western society, for example, one is prepared for one's first encounter with a customs inspector by virtue of one's single-purpose relationships with other officials, tradesmen, and the like. When this preparation is lacking, the bureaucrat himself, in the examples cited, added a dimension—teaching—to his relationship with the client. And this change is an example of debureaucratization both because it adds another role to the specifically prescribed one and because the quality of interaction in the teacher-student relationship necessarily impinges on the more formal bureaucrat-client relationship. Yet these are the very elements which are officially alien to the ideal-type bureaucracy.[27] What is more, as we shall presently see, the teaching relationship may bring further debureaucratization, although conceivably it may simply permit the bureaucrat to perform his role as originally prescribed.

Consider the case of the bus driver. Introductory texts in sociology like to cite the driver-passenger relationship as an example of a purely instrumental, secondary relationship. Neither party matters to the other as an individual. One would not expect the bus driver to modify his behavior vis-à-vis new immigrants or anybody else, yet our preliminary observations seem to indicate that he does. Like other bureaucrats who come into contact with new immigrants, the bus driver tends to assume a teaching role, too. Besides trying to teach the idea of queuing, bus drivers were observed trying to persuade immigrant passengers that the cost of a ride on one bus was the same as the cost on the bus that had just gone by, or that the driver did not personally profit from each fare he collected, or that the decision for the bus to leave the terminal was not his. The consequences of the formal organization of a bus company that are understood by client and bureaucrat in modern society are simply not "obvious" to the non-Western immigrant.

Moreover, we have the impression—and the research now in progress will permit confirmation—that a kind of joking relationship grows up between drivers and new-immigrant passengers. This seems to be the case particularly where the passengers in the bus know one another—as in buses serving suburban settlements and city neighborhoods populated largely by new immigrants. Indeed, drivers on routes with concentrations of new immigrants have told us explicitly that they consider it desirable to get to know their passengers personally, because a new driver is likely to encounter "trouble" with non-Western immigrants, who may become unruly or begin to ask the usual questions anew: "How much is the fare?" "May I get off here?" and so on. In fact, we have had some indication that the bus companies recognize the desirability of less frequent changes of drivers on lines serving new immigrants. This "personalization" of the bureaucratic relationship represents a deviation from the impersonal, universalistic, specific relationship between driver and passenger which, in principle, ought to be unaffected by the substitution of one driver for another. It is an example of debureaucratization, which is the product of the dependence of the bureaucrat on the client's ability and motivation to perform his role as client.

It is important to note, however, that an official's dependence on the client to perform his role is probably of a different order from the kinds of dependence we discussed in the other examples reviewed in the first part of this chapter. In the earlier examples, the client actually had power over the bureaucrat—he could affect his well-being both as a member of the bureaucratic organization and as an individual. Thus, the clients of the disbursing officer were his superiors in other relationships, or the men in combat or in the mine could withdraw their reciprocal protection of their superior. In the present instance, however, the passenger has power over the driver in very much the same sense that a baby has power to disrupt the family schedule, and clearly this creates dependence of quite a different order.[28]

BUREAUCRATS AS SOCIALIZING AGENTS

The process of a bureaucrat stepping outside his role to teach a new immigrant how to act his role as client is highly reminiscent of the processes of socialization and social control as analyzed by Parsons.[29] In the socialization of the child, or in the process of psychotherapy, the socializing agent steps out of his place in the larger social system and assumes a role in the "deviant" subsystem. Thus, the mother is a member of the inclusive family system consisting of father, mother, and children. To bring a new child into this more inclusive system, she must use her role in the earlier mother-child subsystem and selectively reward the child for obedience and disobedience to the new expectations of the inclusive system while at the same time providing a basis of support for the child in his effort to learn the new role. At times, however, the mother may fail as a socializing agent, because she herself prefers to remain in the "deviant" subsystem and, ignoring the father and the rest of the family, acts to "keep the child for herself."

The parallel seems striking to us. The assumption of a teaching role by the bureaucrat and the "personalizing" of the bureaucrat-client relationship seems to function for the process of immigrant socialization as does the behavior of the socializing agent vis-à-vis the child. One of the objects of our empirical study will be to determine whether this kind of bureaucratic behavior (whatever its dysfunctions for the organizational routine) contributes more to the adaptation of the new immigrant than the unbending bureaucrat-client relationship.

Even more striking, perhaps, is the parallel to the kind of mother who "keeps the child for herself." Thus, a bureaucrat who has assumed a teaching role may fail to bring the new immigrant client to play the role expected of him by the bureaucracy and may, instead, remain a member of the "deviant" subsystem. This possibility is most conspicuous perhaps in the case of the village instructors who are assigned to each new settlement of immigrants. These instructors are part of a regional Settlement Authority which, in turn, is part of a nationwide Settlement Department. Sometimes, instead of mediating between the new immigrants and the authorities, the instructor becomes so much a part of his village community that his major effort is devoted to "representing" the interests of his clients vis-à-vis the authorities.

The village instructor typically lives among his clients and is potentially available all day long. His job, as compared with the bus driver's, is a highly diffuse one and includes teaching the settlers, who were semiskilled craftsmen or peddlers, to be farmers, co-operators (as this is understood in the *moshav*)[30] and Israelis. In this case debureaucratization is manifested not merely in the establishment of informal relations, but rather in the surrendering of part of the bureaucrat's commitment to his bureaucracy in favor of acceptance of a role in the system which he is expected to change.

Of course, this is only one of the ways that the instructor—given his highly diffuse and flexible role—can shape his relations with his clients. Some instructors, obviously, take quite the opposite position. Their control of the resources necessary for the very existence of their clients permits them to move in the direction of overbureaucratization. They may interfere in matters—religious observance, for example—which ought properly to be outside their (very broad) spheres of influence.

An even more complicating factor is that the instructor, apart from his bureaucratic role, is often eager to make his clients full-fledged members of the nationwide small-holders co-operative movement or even of his political party, and to have them identify with its ideology, participate in its activities, and so on. Among the instructors who play this double role—which is by no means always considered illegitimate by the upper echelon of the Settlement Authority—many tend to view the various aspects of their bureaucratic role of training immigrants in agriculture and administration as a means to the end of full citizenship. This goal, for the ideologically oriented Israeli, implies the assumption of political and ideological commitments. Such instructors aim at making their clients members of a solidary movement of which they themselves are a part. This subsidiary aim makes the instructor even more dependent on the settlers. They may easily threaten not to participate in the movement unless the instructor provides them with various benefits and allocations for which he is the intermediary, though these may not be their due. In response the instructor may either move in the direction of debureaucratization and succumb to these demands, or he may attempt to use his bureaucratic position to force the clients to assume the political and ideological roles he envisages for them.

BUREAUCRATS AS LEADERS

A bureaucrat serving as "representative" or as "organizer" of his clients is by no means the extreme example of the kind of debureaucratization which may result from the bureaucrat's assumption of the role of socializing agent. Sometimes bureaucrats become charismatic leaders of groups of their clients.

Consider, for example, the case of several nurses employed at a well-baby clinic in a relatively segregated immigrants' "transitional community" within one of the major cities. In this setting the nurse—like the village instructor —is expected to be a teacher and to establish the kind of relationship required for successful teaching. Thus, along with the curative and preventive medicine practiced in such clinics, she must teach the women how to care for themselves and for their children in the particular manner prescribed by the modern scientific and philosophical orientation of the well-baby clinic. The authority of the nurses observed, however, extended beyond these rather broadly defined functions. They became generalized counselors and the clinic soon took on the air of a kind of social center where women gathered to greet each other, to gossip, and to move within the orbit of the nurses.

Some of the nurses had become preoccupied with the position of women in non-Western families. Apparently, this particular problem had first attracted attention as a result of the frequently negative reactions of their clients' husbands to one or another of the practices recommended by the clinic. Having thus become sensitized to the subordinate role of their clients within their families, the nurses added the reconciliation of family conflict to their counseling efforts and, in fact, some of the nurses considered it part of their job to teach women their "rights" vis-à-vis their husbands. In several instances, we have even heard nurses recommending divorce to their clients! Step by step, then, these nurses seem to have moved out from their broad but relatively well-defined functions (which include teaching) to assume an even broader teaching and counseling role and, in some instances, to leadership of a kind of "suffragette" movement among their clients. In such cases, the leader does not appear adverse to illustrating her message with reference to her own private life or that of her friends. And to the extent that they follow, the clients look to their leaders for active support and guidance, and to sharing in the consequences of their behavior.

The leadership role, as played by the bureaucrat, represents a considerable degree of debureaucratization. It represents, in part, exchange of the authority vested in the bureaucratic office for the "voluntary" loyalty of clients; that is, such leadership exists not only by virtue of an "appointment" but by virtue of being "chosen" by followers as well. To that extent, the bureaucrat must submit himself to the authority, and to some of the norms, of his followers. Moreover, he has considerably extended the sphere of his influence from the specific tasks assigned to him to the wider, more diffuse, tasks inherent in the leadership role.

Direction of Future Research

The variety of official relations with new immigrants in Israel provides us with a unique opportunity to locate the conditions under which debureaucratization, overbureaucratization, or both these organizational changes take place. Thus, we would expect debureaucratization to occur more often in relatively isolated settlements of new immigrants than in immigrant communities within the larger cities. In the isolated settlement the bureaucrat is far more dependent on the voluntary cooperation of his clients, both for the performance of his task and for his social and emotional (i.e., non-bureaucratic) well-being. One would also expect a greater dilution of the bureaucratic role with the teaching role in situations where a community of immigrants is transplanted more or less at the same time, compared with situations where migration was stretched over a long period of time. Under the former conditions, the immigrant community will have had less opportunity to educate itself and to develop the leaders, intermediaries, and interpreters who permit the bureaucrat to play his role uninterruptedly. In both the isolated immigrant community and in the transplanted immigrant community, the "segregated" equilibrium between the organization and its environment is likely to be more upset, and hence more marked organizational change may be anticipated. In both these cases, one might argue that the direction of change might well be toward greater, rather than lesser, bureaucratization in the sense that the organization has a unique opportunity to impose itself on more aspects of its clients' lives than is usual. Our hypothesis holds otherwise, as we have tried to argue above, but the plausibility of the competing hypothesis illustrates how the two ostensibly opposite directions of organizational change stem from closely similar conditions.

Our study will enable us to make other comparisons, too. For example, we can compare bureaucrats who come into contact with clients of their own ethnic origin with bureaucrats whose clients are not of their own group. We can compare bureaucrats who are relatively isolated from contacts with their colleagues—instructors who live in the villages—with those who live among their colleagues in the newly built Rural Centers and commute daily to the nearby villages. In the same way, we can compare the pattern of official-client relations characteristic of the bus companies whose drivers have only sporadic and brief contact with their new immigrant clients to the behavior of bureaucrats in organizations which require more extended contacts.

Again, it is easier to choose the situations in which deviation from the ideal bureaucratic norm is more likely to occur than it is to predict the direction of the deviation. Thus, when the bureaucrat is confronted primarily by clients of his own group he is likely to move either in the direction of bureaucratic formalism, studiously seeking to demonstrate his rootedness in Israeli life and to resist the particularistic expectations of the relative newcomers to Israel, or he may move in the direction of debureaucratization in the sense of reaccepting portions of the pattern of traditional authority and behavior of which he was once a part. Compared to the bureaucrat dealing with members of his own ethnic group (who may, because of his better understanding of the group, be more successful in his task), the bureaucrat without an ethnic affiliation with his clients will display more affective neutrality, though this may still lead to overbureaucratization. Again, we expect to find that bureaucrats in close touch with their colleagues can maintain a more detached, objective, service-oriented attitude to their clients than bureaucrats dependent on their clients for social and emotional acceptance and interaction. And, for the same reason, we expect bureaucrats with more extended contacts with a given group of clients to depart from the norms of bureaucratic behavior to a greater extent than bureaucrats with relatively brief and less regular contact.

In this report of preliminary observations on the contact between Israeli organizations and the mass immigration from non-Western countries into Israel in recent years, we have tried to formulate an approach to the study of organizational change, particularly to change in the official-client relationship in response to this new kind of clientele.

Contrary to the expectations of classical sociological thinking, we have considerable impressionistic evidence pointing to a process of decreasing bureaucratization, at least in the relations between immigrant-clients and those parts of the bureaucracy which come into contact with them. We have tried to explain this finding by reference to the constraints operating on the bureaucrat who comes into contact with the public to train the immigrant client to perform the client role in order that he (the bureaucrat) may perform his own role adequately.

It seems to us that this process implies a certain kind of dependence on the client as far as the bureaucrat is concerned. Specifically, the bureaucrat is dependent on the client's proper performance of the client role, although in a different sense than the client is dependent on the bureaucrat's performance of his. Beyond this, the kinds of situations we are exploring include those where the bureaucrat may look to his client for sociability, or may recognize him as a member of the same ethnic group, or may seek to enlist his client in other organizations of which he is a member. All these exemplify situations of heightened dependence and, presumably, greater deviations from bureaucratic norms.

We have tried to suggest that the various forms of dependence which we found to be related to the process of debureaucratization may be subsumed under the more general heading of the articulation of role relations in modern society. The bureaucrat-client relationship is presumed to be segmented in certain ways from other kinds of social relations. Variations in the degree to which a given role relationship is insulated from other role relationships affects the degree of its bureaucratization. Thus, the process of debureaucratization may be characterized as an impinging of nonbureaucratic roles, or of other bureaucratic roles, on the specific bureaucratic role in question, while overbureaucratization may be expressed either in terms of the artificial insulation of the bureaucratic relationship from all other roles (however relevant) or, in its more totalitarian form, in the impinging of the bureaucratic relationship on relations not relevant to the bureaucratic role.

We have tried to set down some theoretical guidelines for a discussion of the problems of organizational change, with specific reference to the official-client relationship in a situation where there has been a rapid influx of immigrants having little previous contact with formal organization. We have tried to show that, in Israel, the process of decreasing bureaucratization is not an uncommon response in this situation, although we wish to emphasize that both increasing and decreasing bureaucratization may find simultaneous expression in different parts of the organization and, sometimes, in the very same relationship between official and client. It remains for the pilot study now in the field and the projected full-scale study to substantiate the general approach and the specific hypotheses we have proposed.

NOTES

1. An elaboration of the well-known Simmel hypothesis on the effects of the size of a group for the specific case of migration can be found in Frank E. Jones, "A Sociological Perspective on Immigrant Adjustment," *Social Forces*, 35 (1956), 39–47.

2. In general, our use of the terms official (or bureaucrat) and client is meant to refer also to superior-subordinate relationships within an organization.

3. Here and elsewhere we make use of Parsons' terminology. Although we make an effort to communicate the meaning of the several concepts we employ, for a full discussion see Talcott Parsons, *The Social System* (Glencoe, 1951), ch. ii.

4. Max Weber, "The Presuppositions and Causes of Bureaucracy," in Robert K. Merton, Ailsa P. Gray, Barbara Hockey, and Hanan Selvin, eds., *Reader in Bureaucracy* (Glencoe, 1952), 60–68. Of course, Weber was also concerned with the role of internal factors making for a greater degree of bureaucratization in the organization, a notable example being his discussion of "The Routinization of Charisma," which tends to develop when a group faces the problem of leadership succession, *ibid.*, pp. 92–100. This also gives a brief statement of Robert Michels' argument (pp. 88–92), as does his *Political Parties* (Glencoe, 1949).

5. The best known of these essays is probably Robert K. Merton, "Bureaucratic Structure and Personality," in Merton *et al.*, *op. cit.*, pp. 361–371.

6. Seymour M. Lipset, Martin T. Trow, and James S. Coleman, *Union Democracy* (Glencoe, 1956), try to specify the conditions that contribute, in at least one case, to the maintenance of trade-union democracy rather than oligarchic bureaucracy.

7. This, of course, refers to the dominant trend of present-day research, which has been concerned with the existence and the functions of informal social relations in the context of formal organization. But more important for our present purpose is the incipient concern for informal aspects of relationships between bureaucrats and the public. See, for example, Morris Janowitz, Deil Wright, and William Delany, *Public Administration and the Public* (Ann Arbor, 1958); Edwin J. Thomas, "Role Conceptions and Organizational Size," *American Sociological Review*, 24 (1959), 30–37; and George F. Lombard, *Behavior in a Selling Group* (Cambridge, Mass., 1955). For a recent critique of the assumption that the several elements of Weber's ideal-type bureaucracy are necessarily intercorrelated, see Stanley H. Udy, Jr., "'Bureaucracy' and 'Rationality' in Weber's Organization Theory," *American Sociological Review*, 24 (1959), 792–795.

8. See Peter M. Blau, *The Dynamics of Bureaucracy* (Chicago, 1955), esp. ch. iii.

9. See Ralph H. Turner, "The Navy Disbursing Officer as a Bureaucrat," in Merton *et al.*, *op. cit.*, pp. 372–379. Also compare Blau, *op. cit.*, for an example of the way in which variations in supervisory practice affected the extent to which employment agency officials used racial bias vis-à-vis their clients.

10. Max Weber, "The Presuppositions and Causes of Bureaucracy," in Merton *et al.*, *op. cit.*, pp. 60–68.

11. See Alvin W. Gouldner, *Patterns of Industrial Bureaucracy* (Glencoe, 1954), pp. 59–101.

12. See Merton, *op. cit.*, p. 369.

13. For a discussion on the effect of size, see Thomas, *op. cit.*

14. Samuel A. Stouffer, *et al. The American Soldier: Combat and Its Aftermath* (Princeton, 1949), p. 100.

15. Charles H. Page, "Bureaucracy's Other Face," *Social Forces*, 25 (1946), 89–91.

16. Lipset *et al., op. cit.*, p. 139.

17. Gouldner, *op. cit.*, pp. 105–154.

18. Sigmund Diamond, "From Organization to Society: Virginia in the 17th Century," *American Journal of Sociology*, 63 (1958), 588–594.

19. Turner, *op. cit.*

20. For example, Turner omits the interdependence based on the common danger.

21. Note again that we are using "bureaucrat-client" in a generic sense, implying superordinate-subordinate relations (such as in combat, the mine, the Virginia Company, etc.) as well.

22. To cite a familiar example, a civil servant looking to a political party for rewards for his performance in his role as civil servant may do so because he is a political appointee, because he is ideologically committed to his party, or for other reasons.

23. After developing this analysis of role impingement, we encountered Gouldner's concept and noted its close similarity. "It is necessary to distinguish," says Gouldner, "between those social identities of group members which are consensually regarded as relevant to them in a given setting and those which group members define as being irrelevant, inappropriate to consider, or illegitimate to take into account. The former can be called the manifest social identities, the latter, the latent social identities. . . . When group members orient themselves to the latent identities of others in their group, they are involved in a relationship with them which is not culturally prescribed by the group norms governing their manifest roles. . . . It would seem clear that latent identities and roles are important because they exert pressure upon the manifest roles, often impairing conformity with their requirements and endemically threatening the equilibrium of the manifest role system." Gouldner goes on to give an example concerning deference to elders in a universalistic setting which is very similar to the one we have presented. See Alvin W. Gouldner, Cosmopolitans and Locals: Toward an Analysis of Latent Social Roles, I and II, *Administrative Science Quarterly*, 2 (1957–1958), 281–306 and 444–480, esp. pp. 282–287. It should be noted also that the problem of role impingement or latent social identity differs from the problem of role conflict. Role impingement refers to the multiple role relations played by official and client vis-à-vis one another. Role conflict generally implies the multiple (and conflicting) roles of a given actor vis-à-vis several different others—e.g., the official's relationships to his wife and to his boss. Still a further distinction, recently introduced by Merton, is that of the role set, which has to do with the multiple role relations implicit in any given role—e.g., the official's relationship to his boss, his secretary, his colleagues, etc. Others who have employed analytic concepts similar to the concept of role impingement are Lloyd Fallers, *Bantu Bureaucracy* (Cambridge, Eng., 1957); Frank Jones, "The Infantry Recruit: A Sociological Analysis of Socialization in the Canadian Army" (unpublished doctoral dissertation, Harvard, 1956); and Thomas, *op. cit.*

24. A review, by Nathan Glazer, of several recent books treating Puerto Rican migration makes this point; see "New York's Puerto Ricans," *Commentary*, 26 (1958), 469–478.

25. See S. N. Eisenstadt, *The Absorption of Immigrants* (Glencoe, 1955), pp. 64–68, and 172 ff., "The Framework of Bureaucratic Absorption."

26. In 1948, at the time of the establishment of the state of Israel, persons born in Africa and Asia constituted 15 percent of the population; five years later, in 1953 they

constituted 38 percent of the population. See Moshe Sicron, *Immigration to Israel: 1948–1953* (Jerusalem, 1957), pp. 43–50.

27. This would be particularly true when a bureaucrat's aim is to bring his client to want the bureaucrat's services; thus, this might be more true of a storekeeper than a nurse, and more true of a nurse than a bus driver.

28. Replying to the query whether the "dependency" of the child does not sometimes confer power equal to or superior to that of the person on whom dependency exists, Parsons distinguishes between power defined as "relative importance in carrying out the functional performance of the system" and as the "ability to cause trouble by threatening to disrupt the system." In this latter sense, "the child, and other persons or groups in dependent positions have considerable 'power.'" See Talcott Parsons and Robert F. Bales, *Family, Socialization and Interaction Process* (Glencoe, 1955), p. 46, n. 18. It is this second type of power which concerns us at this point.

29. *Ibid.*, ch. ii.

30. See S. N. Eisenstadt, "Sociological Aspects of the Economic Adaptation of Oriental Immigrants in Israel: A Case Study of Modernization," *Economic Development and Cultural Change*, 4 (1958), 269–278; and Alex Weingrod, *From the Millah to the Moshav: Culture Contact and Change in a New-Immigrant Village in Israel* (unpublished doctoral dissertation, University of Chicago, 1959).

5

Albert J. Reiss, Jr., and David J. Bordua

ENVIRONMENT AND ORGANIZATION: A PERSPECTIVE ON THE POLICE

Introduction

This chapter presents a general perspective on the metropolitan police as an object of sociological research. The chapter is neither a detailed presentation of formal research hypotheses nor a presentation of research findings. An organizational perspective on the consequences of police relations to the environing system is presented as an orienting image within which more specific theoretical and empirical work can proceed.[1] Several topics are selected to illustrate the general application of the perspective. The facts are gleaned from general observation, research underway, and the literature on the police.

Police and the Environing System

The municipal police as an organizational system is especially adapted to an analysis that stresses its relations with the organized environment and its boundary transactions and moves from these to consideration of internal differentiation and problems of integration, coordination, and control. All organizations can be so studied, of course, but since Weber the broad fashion among sociologists has been to focus on the internal structure of organizations and on task differentiation as it is manifested within the organization. Unlike many organizations, however, the police have as their fundamental task the creation and maintenance of, and their participation in, external relationships.

Albert J. Reiss, Jr., and David J. Bordua, "Environment and Organization: A Perspective on the Police," in ed. David J. Bordua, *The Police: Six Sociological Essays* (New York: Wiley, 1967), pp. 28–48, 54–55 (abridged). Reprinted by permission.

Indeed, the central meaning of police authority itself is its significance as a mechanism for "managing" relationships.

Directing traffic, investigating complaints, interrogation, arresting suspects, controlling mobs and crowds, urging prosecutors to press or drop charges, testifying in court, participating with (or battling, as the case may be) probation officers in juvenile court, presenting budget requests to the city council, pressing a case with the civil service commission, negotiating with civil rights groups, defense attorneys, reporters, irate citizens, business groups, other city services, and other police systems—even such an incomplete list indicates the probable values of a perspective that emphasizes transactions and external relationships. The list also indicates something else of considerable significance. All of these transactions can be and often are antagonistic ones. Because of the complexity of organizational relationships with the environment, apparent even from a partial listing of police activities, we have chosen to concentrate our discussion of the external environment of the police and its internal consequences by selecting a few basic environmental features. These are the nature of the legal system, the nature of violative activity, and civic accountability. They are brought to bear upon a variety of organizational transactions and internal processes, especially on problems of production, strategy and tactics, and command and control.

The basic social mechanisms available to the police all flow from their role in the legal system. Yet, the legal system broadly considered is the source of some of the most severe problems of adaptation faced by the police. Because of this dual involvement with law, much of our early discussion of external relations deals with the police and the legal system. The legal system is not a seamless web of tightly articulated rules and roles, however, but a loose-jointed system held together at many points by microsystems of antagonistic cooperation and discretionary decisions.

Modern metropolitan police exist only in view of the fact that communities are legally organized.[2] The problem of the external parameters of police operation and organization, in its broadest sense, inheres both in the nature of the urban community and in the nature of the legal system. Indeed, the fundamental position of the police may be conceived as mediating between the two. On the one hand, the police are a fundamental representative of the legal system and a major source of raw material for it. On the other, the police adapt the universalistic demands of law to the structure of the locale by a wide variety of formal and informal devices.

Later we discuss several features of the modern urban community as they impinge on the social structure of law enforcement. In this section, we concentrate on some key aspects of the legal system and on the implications of the fact that the governance of communities is done by legal rather than other means. The broad designation "legal system" may be broken into the "legality" component, the "legal content" component, the "legal order" component and the "government" component.[3]

The value of these distinctions will perhaps be more apparent if we discuss first the one most familiar—the "legal content" component. By this we mean simply the actual content of laws. The importance for our purposes is that even modern societies differ considerably in the substance of the things they make illegal, and violations under them differ considerably in their impact on police strategy and tactics. A prime example is the well-known tendency of American society to make illegal many service crimes such as gambling.

By the "government" component we mean simply that the legal system is always organized politically into larger or smaller, more or less centralized, units. Even further, powers of government may be separated or combined in various patterns. Thus in the United States the police are organized to parallel the federal structure of local, state, and national government. Although the matter of levels of government has been widely discussed as a central "problem" in police administration, we are not particularly concerned with the matter here, since our focus is on the single community rather than inter-governmental aspects of the context of police operations.[4]

The third aspect of the legal system is the "legal order" component. By this we mean the complex apparatus involved in the administration of justice, especially those aspects with which the police are likely to come into contact routinely, such as the prosecutor and the courts. Because of the unique significance of this aspect of the legal system, we will devote considerable attention to it.

Finally, the "legality" component to which we now give special attention refers only to the procedural aspects of the exercise of legal power.

Legality, Police, and Community

In one sense, the police provide the primeval social service—protection of life and property. Unlike some other social services, however, the existence of a public agency largely precludes the performance of the service on a private basis. The very existence of the modern police signifies that in the broadest sense the exchange of property and the infliction of injury may take place only under definite rules. Moreover, disputes arising out of property exchange or personal altercation may be resolved only within definite limits. The body of legal rules that specify the acceptable modes of procedure in the resolution of disputes may collectively be deemed the canons of *legality*. The basic elements of legality—objective definitions of right, "due process," notice, citizen compliance, and official accountability—are primarily aspects of the ways citizens are treated rather than descriptions of specific statutes or judicial rulings. In the Anglo-Saxon tradition, the courts provide the primary definitions of legality in this sense with varying admixtures of legislative action and constitutional undergirding.

A society based upon such procedural and value premises, however, presents two closely intertwined problems. We can anchor the discussion of them by defining them very generally in terms of the subsystem relations involved. The first is the citizen-to-citizen relationship.

Within very broad limits, citizens must generally avail themselves of police services rather than resort to "self-help" in dealing with problems of person or property. The existence of police symbolizes not only that the citizen will be protected from the violator but that the violator will be protected from the citizen. One way the police serve the cause of legality, therefore, is to assure by their presence and performance that a set of rules prevails which make it *unnecessary* for the citizen to be continually prepared to defend himself or his property. We may, in fact, partly define the "maintenance of law and order"as the maintenance of a set of social conditions such that over the society as a whole, the expectation of attack on person or property has a probability below the level at which the citizenry resorts to "self-help." The maintenance of these conditions is always problematic, and in some localities of American society, "law and order" is sustained only with difficulty.

Comparison of the linkage among legality, police, and community in criminal law areas with the corresponding linkage in civil law is of sociological interest. The two great divisions of the law of civil wrongs—torts and contracts—involve much the same concern with the avoidance of "self-help" as a response to injury. Indeed, the traditional distinction in jurisprudence between civil remedies and criminal sanctions, with the former accruing to the injured party and the latter to the "state," obscures similarities between the two areas.

In the area of civil wrongs, especially tort law, the law is reactive rather than proactive, i.e., the legal system does not patrol or search out wrongs and take action but rather leaves to private initiative the invocation of the legal process. Closely related to the reactive stance of civil law is a very broad presumption favoring the private ordering of conduct and even of the resolution of disputes.[5] Thus legal ethics seem clear. The lawyer may not behave like a patrolman and search out tort victims or sufferers from breach of contract to encourage civil suits. Compare this doctrine of legal restraint with the doctrine of "aggressive patrol," which figures so prominently in modern police thinking.

On close examination many of the seemingly stark differences between the organization of civil remedies and the organization of criminal sanctions become less clear-cut. They perhaps can be seen most clearly if we look from the perspective of the private arrangement system itself. The determinants of the decision to call the police, for example, to deal with a neighborhood juvenile, are presumably complex but not totally unlike the decision to sue for damages.[6] A large part of police intervention is initiated by the victim. Moreover, the police have as one of their fundamental responsibilities the determination of when a "victim's" complaint in fact warrants formal action. No crime may have been committed, or if there is one, it may be so minor that department policy dictates only cursory attention. Like the civil lawyer, the policeman also becomes sensitive to subtleties of private vengeance masquerading as public duty.

Beyond these elements of "victims" initiating police activity, police "adjudication" policy, and their upholding of "disinterested" canons of legality, the operating procedures of police bear other similarities to civil procedure. Foremost among these is the tendency of police to let stand, or even to encourage, private settlement of disputes—even where violence may be present or likely. Among the "private arrangements" that the police may protect are their own relationships with categories of violators.

This aspect of policing is discussed in more detail later on, but at this point it is appropriate to indicate that the police in a sense are a service without clients. The police serve the public as a collectivity rather than distributively.[7] Enforcement must be initiated where there is no personal victim and/or complainant. Given the lack of guidelines either from the public as client or from a specific victim or complainant as client, the police can become in effect their own clients. We take this to be one of the fundamental features in the oft mentioned tendency of the police to develop a supermoralistic perspective and to see themselves as engaged in a "private" war on crime. Of basic significance here is that the courts and the police are in a relationship of "antagonistic cooperation" so that the legal order itself can be described only with difficulty as the "client" of the police.

Thus in many ways the respect for private ordering that is formal in civil law is informal in criminal law. Unlike the civil side, a large organized body of officials—the police—intervene between law and practice and may come to participate in such private arrangements themselves. From this perspective it is useful to see the police not as discretionless ministerial officers but as somewhat analogous to the practicing attorney, whose roles as advocate, counselor, and officer of the court are not totally dissimilar (though better legitimated) to the roles played by the policeman.[8]

Informal practice allows the police to vary their relationship to the many private dispute settling procedures available; hence, the degree to which formal legality is extended to (or imposed upon) different groups in the population varies considerably.[9] Among the private arrangements that the police may allow to stand is the use of violence among subordinate or peripheral groups in the society. The most outstanding instance until recently has been the willingness of the American police to respect intraracial violence among Negroes, thus implicitly defining the Negro population in a sense as a group "without the law." Correlatively, the police established private arrangements with the Negro violator that included their extrajudicial use of force as a substitute for "due process." Whether such private adjudication is less predictable, less merciful, and less just seems open to dispute, but such arrangements clearly imply that a segment of the population is operationally treated as outside the pale of legality.

The broader problem involved here is, of course, the central one of the conditions under which membership in the *state* supersedes membership in other collectivities as a determinant of both formal and operative rights. Historical developments for at least two centuries have tended to define state membership, that is, citizenship as prevailing over other statuses in determining individual rights. Nevertheless, here as elsewhere there have been many lags between formal declaration and informal practice.[10]

Up to this point we have tried to establish a general perspective that emphasizes the similarities between civil and criminal legal operations. The key points here are (1) that many features that are formal in the civil law are "informal" in the criminal law, (2) that the relations between private ordering and public determination are important in both areas, (3) that large areas of police operation are closer to the reactive model of civil adjudication than to the generally held proactive model of criminal process, (4) that the maintenance of legality as *between citizens* always involves some balance of police willingness either to "respect" or to override private arrangements, and (5) that the conditions under which citizens invoke the criminal process may determine the nature and boundaries of subsystem solidarity as well as of police behavior.

We purposely have emphasized the role of the police in securing as well as symbolizing legality as between citizens since this is a relatively neglected aspect of the larger problem. The other face of the legality problem is that of the relations between the citizenry and the police. Since this aspect of the problem has received much more attention, we will make only a few general remarks in the discussion of police in the legal order.

The Police in the Legal Order

Liberal democratic societies stemming from the English tradition formally organize enforcement of the law and the maintenance of order *within* the society in both the military and the police but principally in the police. The extension of the role of law in legality, due process, the exercise of discretion, and enacting justice when accusations or arrests are made is formally organized in the public prosecutor and the courts. This functional separation of powers in which ordinarily the police are expected to enforce the law and the judiciary to determine the outcome of events creates problems for both organizations and appears to account for some aspects of police organization and work.

Although the police are formally organized to enforce the law and maintain public order, it is apparent they are involved at the same time in enacting justice. It is important to note that all three key terms—order, legality and justice—are ambiguous terms in any social system. But what philosophers, social scientists, and lawyers have argued over for centuries, the police must do every day. The point requires little documentation. A policeman on duty, for example, when confronted with a situation of law enforcement or threat to public order must make decisions about the evidence and whether the act violates the law. Decisions to hold for investigation, to arrest or release, or to enforce order likewise require the extension of legality. His decision may, and often does, involve him at the same time in dispensing equity. Police, in short, make important decisions that affect outcome. They either do justice or limit the judicial function of courts, particularly by determining the nature of the evidence and who is to be held for adjudication.

Court decisions to dismiss charges are often viewed by the police as a rejection of their decisions. Such decisions may be particularly galling to the officer, since he regards his rules of knowing as more valid than the court's rules of evidence in making a decision. Furthermore, court decisions to dismiss offenders or to return offenders to the community often affect police work, as released offenders frequently create problems for continued law enforcement. The most obvious examples of this kind occur in police work with juveniles, vagrants, and habitual drunks. Police dissatisfaction with rehabilitation workers such as probation officers likewise stems in part from the fact that they have been unable to control disposition of the case; today's probationers are not infrequently tomorrow's work.

Police dissatisfaction with the administration of justice by the courts results in their doing justice, a tendency to settle things outside the courts to be sure that "justice is done." Nowhere is this more apparent than when police are expected to continue law enforcement involving violators that the court sends back to the community. The police then may take the law in their own hands and dispense justice, even if it means using violence. The continuing conflict between the police and the courts over admissibility of evidence, techniques of interrogation, the status of the confession, and the use of force, together with their separate definitions of justice, are likewise consequences of the separation of powers.

Transactions among police officers, public prosecutors, and the judiciary not infrequently have the effect of subverting the goals of law enforcement, since each is in a position to sanction the other's behavior. That individual or collective sanctions do not always achieve the intended goal is clear when the effect of sanctions of one part on another is examined. A single example may serve as an illustration.

Judges often negatively sanction police officers for failing to develop cases that meet court standards. It is not uncommon for a judge to criticize publicly from the bench an officer new to the service with a terse statement that fails to explain the grounds constituting an effective case. This judicial practice leaves the young officer in a quandary that often leads him to turn to the informal police system for advice about responses to judicial practice. Not infrequently this course of action leads to poor police technique and the development of cases where there is no intention to prosecute. Such responses lead to further judicial criticism that department administrators may ultimately perceive as an unwillingness by the court to convict. At this juncture, however, police practice may have deteriorated to the point where the court could not convict, if it would. Negative sanctions by the court and prosecutors thus lead to a deterioration of police practice which subverts judicial goals.

There is no necessary reason why these systems must be related in a cumulative set of negative sanctions. Police, prosecutors, and jurists sometimes take steps to cope with predicaments caused by negative sanctions, evolving practices that moderate these effects. They provide, for example, for prosecutors to advise officers prior to their appearance in court, though to be sure, prosecutors may use officers for their own intended sanctions of judicial behavior. The conflict between police practice and legality stems in part, however, from the fact that American courts traditionally resist giving advisory opinions and from the fact that jurists and prosecutors, as lawyers, do not perceive that they have an educational obligation toward the officers or their clients in the situation.

The legally defined end of a police department is to enforce the law. The measure of success of a police department is presumably some measure of the degree to which it has in fact enforced the law. There are two major ways that success gets defined for departments. The first kind is a measure of aggregate success, whether of a crime rate, arrests, crimes cleared by arrest, convictions, or value of stolen property recovered. The second is the success it has in meeting public demands to solve a particular crime problem as, for example, when a crime outrages the public conscience.

Police are relatively free to define their own criteria of success in crimes known to them, arrests made, and crimes cleared through arrest, despite national attempts to standardize the criteria. They can determine a successful arrest per se and satisfy themselves when a case has been cleared by arrest. They can recover stolen property incident to arrest and clearance, or independent of it, as is often the case for stolen autos. Their productivity record in these areas, however, can be compared with that of other cities through the uniform crime reporting system organized through the FBI. The media of communication hold the local police system accountable for its record in this system.

So far as the public is concerned police departments generally have a low success rate in the proportion of crimes cleared through arrest. Only about one in four offenses known to the police is generally cleared by arrest.[11] Clearance through arrest is greater for crimes against persons than crimes against property and for misdemeanors such as vagrancy, drunkenness, and disorderly conduct, though the latter bring few credits in the public ledger. The low success rate in crimes cleared by arrest creates a dilemma for the police administrators in their efforts to maintain a public image of themselves as productive in a market-oriented society. It is neither sufficient nor publicly acceptable for American police to justify themselves by their roles as simple representatives of moral or legal order.[12] They are under considerable pressure from local organizations such as the newspapers and crime commissions and from the FBI, who interpret the statistics in relation to their own goals, goals that not infrequently conflict with those of the police department.

The dilemma created by the necessity to maintain a public image of success in the face of aggregative measures of lack of success can readily lead to the manipulation of the statistics to create a favorable public image. Police departments, in fact, build up their *volume* of production largely out of misdemeanors rather than felonies, out of crimes against property rather than against persons, and in these days from juveniles and traffic. Tradition-oriented departments often artificially inflate their success rate by getting arrested persons to "cop out" to additional offenses or by charging offenses to an arrested person on the basis of a *modus operandi*.

The separation of enforcement from outcome creates additional dilemmas for the department in defining its success rate. Assuming legal police conduct, it is through convictions only that the penal sanctions presumed efficacious in reducing crimes can be forthcoming. And it is also through conviction only that the police's sense of justice can be vindicated. The conviction rate, however, is subject to police control only within narrow limits. Both prosecutors and courts intervene. The courts do so with the avowed purpose of scrutinizing police conduct, especially when legality as well as violation of the law is defined as an issue. While department arrest figures may define the policeman's success, acquittals in court may define his failures.

These dilemmas in defining success are partially resolved by the development of a complex bargaining process between police and prosecutors, the shifting of departmental resources in directions of maximum payoff from a conviction point of view, the development of a set of attitudes that define the police as alone in the "war on crime," and the elaboration of success measures that do not require validation by the courts.

All major metropolitan departments elaborate measures of success that they can manipulate independent of the prosecutor and the courts. Investigations of organized crime are publicized, though there is relatively little success in conviction in relation to the effort expended. Arrests under public pressure of well-known gangsters or crackdowns on prostitution, gambling, or narcotics peddling have their symbolic public relations value even if it is difficult to secure convictions, and they make undue claim on limited resources. Successful prosecution of the most serious or violent crimes against persons, such as homicide, forcible rape, and aggravated assault, likewise are used for their symbolic value, though they account for only a small volume of all crimes known to the police.[13]

Police concern for clearance of crimes through arrest is not infrequently a response to immediate public pressures that they maintain a safe community as well as to the more general and continuing one that they are an effective and efficient department. The police, for example, may come under fire when a neighborhood is plagued by a series of assaults or strong-arm robberies or when the "public" is offended by any specific crime. Police concern then shifts to clearing up these particular crimes so that they may reduce public pressure by an announcement that the perpetrators have been brought into custody.

Police administrators are confronted with a dilemma in their effort to manipulate the image of crime in the community. To justify increases in manpower and budget before municipal agencies, they are compelled to emphasize the high volume of crime in the community and the difficulties they face in meeting it with the resources available to them. At the same time, this emphasis can easily be interpreted as failure.

The individual policeman likewise is production oriented; his successes are arrests and acquittals are his failures. The successful policeman quickly learns what the police system defines as successes. These become his arrests. When he is not supported by the judicial system for what he regards as right action, he tends to take the law into his own hands, often by making a decision not to arrest or by making an arrest where there is no intention to prosecute.[14] In this way the police officer sanctions the judicial system for what he defines as its failure to make him a success.

Separation of enforcement from outcome also has an effect on police attitudes. The refusal of the courts to convict or of prosecutors to prosecute may rest on what seem to the police the most artificial of formalities. Police are aware as well that this lack of support attributes failure to them. Their sense of justice may be outraged. Collective subcultural modes of adjustment are a common protective response to such dilemmas and contradictions. For the police this adjustment consists in part in the development of a collective identity wherein the police are viewed as the true custodians of morality and justice. In the words of one police administrator:

Police get conditioned to the idea that we are the only people with our finger in the criminal dike in this country. They feel that everyone else "lets him go." Police differ from the D.A. The D.A. is satisfied with the conviction, finding him guilty. But police want him punished. They become outraged when the result of their work is ignored. "What if they let him off, I get him tomorrow: those bastards kiss him on the cheek and let 'em go," is their attitude of how the D.A. and the judge handle *their* cases.

Thus the police want an outcome that signifies for them that their effort has been appreciated and that morality has been upheld. This for them is what is meant by justice being done.

Many police see two broad classes of violators—those who deserve to be punished and those who do not. For the police, justice is done by *them* when they let a man go; he does not deserve to be punished. But justice must be done by *some other means* when they arrest. This they regard as the moral obligation of the prosecutor and the courts.

Mention has been made that the separation of enforcement from outcome forces the police into a bargaining situation that includes violators, prosecutors, defense attorneys, and courts. The public prosecutor is usually the central figure in this process. Bargaining relationships of the police are undoubtedly more complexly patterned and determined than current information allows us to assess. Three important points can be made here, however. The first is that the police are hedged in by officials whose formal discretion is greater than their own. The second is that although the prosecutor and the judge are the traditional figures, the system of justice has come to include others, such as probation officers and juvenile court officials, with whom the police must also enter into a bargaining relationship. Finally, all of these bargaining relationships are ones in which the role incumbents are potentially hostile to the police. As Stinchcombe has recently noted, adjunctive officials of the courts, particularly rehabilitation or welfare officials, are hired wholly or in part as a set of official opponents of the police.[15]

The formal linkage of the police to the prosecutor's office and the court has other implications for their adaptation. Interpersonal contact between police and court personnel involve both an inequality relationship and a reversal of roles. Normally, police are in a position of authority vis-à-vis the citizen; in a substantial number of situations, they are in a superior status position as well. When they are not, police use tactics to assert authority in the situation. Furthermore, police work generally places an officer in the role of interrogator, a role requiring that little information be given to suspects. Now in contacts with the courts, role situations are reversed. Police are generally below the status of officials they deal with in the courts, particularly with men of the bar and bench, and they are interrogated. Under certain circumstances, they are subject to cross-examination. This kind of contact brings with it all the suspicion and hostility generated between status unequals where roles are reversed and authority is displaced. The ambivalence of the police toward both the administration of justice and its role incumbents is further exacerbated under these conditions. This status reversal plus the generalized lower prestige of police when taken together with the institutionalized distrust of police built into the trial process creates a situation where the police not only feel themselves balked by the courts but perhaps, even more fundamentally, feel themselves dishonored.

The involvement of police in the legal order may also be looked at from the point of view of the legal remedies available in the event of illicit police conduct. For the citizen they are largely civil remedies as against the individual policeman. Usually, the citizen does not sue the police department for false arrest or battery; he sues the policeman. The officer's conduct, however, may have been well within the reasonable limits of departmental policy or regulation. The relatively unpredictable and *ex post facto* nature of judicial decision may exacerbate the problem for the policeman, even though the usually broad wording of applicable provisions of the law of arrest afford the officer much protection. This anomalous disjuncture between authority and liability is presumably one source of the oft-noticed solidarity of police systems. If effecting the department's mission lays the officer open to suit, clearly a norm of secrecy and mutual support is a highly likely result. The blue curtain descends between staff and line and the department and the outer world.

The balancing and correlative fact that police chiefs may be liable to sanctions by political and governmental officials even though immune from suit acts in much the same way. "Formal" informal mechanisms such as secret department trials, requests for resignation, and liability defense funds develop as ways of containing this dilemma.

Although the civil suit is in principle available to citizens, it is rarely used. There seem to be several reasons for this in addition to the fact that policemen are usually not able to pay large judgments. The segments of the population most likely to sue are (or were) least likely to be involved with the police. Those most involved with the police, the "depressed populations," are simultaneously unlikely to use the courts in general, because they are fearful of police reprisal and too impoverished to afford counsel.

The very structure of judicial control of the police means—as in recent U.S. Supreme Court decisions—that rulings about the illegality of police practices toward offenders must come in the form of upsetting the convictions of criminals.[16] Judicial rulings that announce new procedural limitations on the police are of necessity *ex post facto,* and therefore difficult to predict. Given this situation, it is no wonder that in the system for maintaining law and order other people have the law and the police get stuck with the order.

Recent decisions of the Court also highlight basic differences between the police and the courts regarding their organizational requirements for the legality and legal content components and set the stage for organizational conflict. The police organization generally requires high specificity of the legal content component in the decision to arrest but relative ambiguity of the legality component in enforcement and processing situations. The courts, in contrast, insist upon high specificity of the legality component in their position of judicial control of the police (or the protection of citizen rights) while tolerating relative ambiguity in the statement of legal content in the interest of case law.

Violative Activity and Organizational Strategy and Tactics

Police departments are organized primarily to carry out a reactive rather than a proactive strategy. This is in sharp contrast with some intelligence systems geared to a proactive strategy. A majority of the line in any major metropolitan police system is allocated to units that react to communications that the police are wanted at some time and place. The communications center is the heart of the modern operating system. Patrol is the single largest division. Geared essentially to react, patrol belies its name. To be sure, some units, such as tactical patrol, conduct both proactive and reactive operations, and others, such as vice control, are principally proactive, but on-balance patrol is organized to respond to commands that are reactions to requests originating outside the department. To understand how it happens that police departments operate primarily with a reactive strategy, we must turn to the organization of the environing system and the development of police transactions with individuals and organizations beyond its boundaries.

Before the evolution of modern police systems the citizen was paid for giving information on crimes and the whereabouts of criminals to proper authorities. But in Western societies there has been a gradual evolution from the citizen as paid informant and prosecutor to the citizen as a responsible complainant accompanied by a delegation of responsibility to the police for the enforcement of the law and to the prosecutor for pursuing formal charges. As a consequence of these changes the social sources of information on violations have changed. Police strategy and tactics become proactive, and special units—for example, vice and traffic control divisions—are developed to deal with violations where the individual citizen is not directly threatened and hence does not mobilize the police.[17] Information on crimes of this nature must generally originate, therefore, with police work, including the use of the undercover agent and the otherwise abandoned practice of paid informants. Correlatively, where police rely almost exclusively on the citizen complainant for origination of information on crimes against a person or his property, their strategy and tactics are generally reactive. Patrol is the initial unit assigned to respond, and the detective bureau follows.

Only in a superficial sense may police be said to solve crimes or to enforce the law. The organization of the society, the nature of violative activity, and the organization of a police department make it impossible to locate a population of subjects who have violated the law or to solve most crimes.

The social organization of behavior that violates the law and of how it is communicated to the police, when coupled with organizational problems in the allocation of limited resources to the solution of crimes, makes it impossible for the police to generate most of the inputs they process. These conditions also largely determine the internal differentiation of the police department and the strategy and tactics each unit adopts to process violations of the law. We shall turn first to examine ways in which communications about violations of the law create problems for the police in solving crimes and how the police organization adapts to these problems.

In a democratic society, the major volume of police work derives from an external source, the citizen complaint, rather than from an internal organizational source, police detection of crimes committed. The major element occasioning a complaint by an American citizen is that he sees himself as a "victim" experiencing a personal loss. Citizens are unlikely to mobilize the police or to report violations in which they are not actually a victim. In all other cases, the citizen tends to define enforcement of the law as a police responsibility. This means that many violations are known to citizens but not reported to the police because they lack direct personal involvement in the violative activity. Even when the person is a victim, he may not necessarily make his complaint known, since citizen complaint is responsive to public and police norms and expectations about communicating violations of the law.

Police definitions of the status of "victim" constitute one such set of expectations. Certain deviants—for example, homosexuals and prostitutes —do not usually report crimes against themselves, since they cannot afford to take the risk. In other cases, the citizen responds to collectively defined expectations of treatment by the police, as, for example, the Negro's response to expectations of "white man's" justice or police brutality. Indeed, much of the post Second World War reported increase in crime in American cities may be due to the changing relationship between the Negro public and the police rather than to an actual increase in violative behavior. Negroes now seem more willing to report crimes against themselves.

There are a number of norms that govern the role of citizen as complainant. Beyond the fact that enforcement of the law is defined primarily as a police and not a citizen responsibility, there are powerful norms governing the role of informants in our society. Norms about "squealing" and "minding one's own business" control the reporting of citizen information about violations. There are also norms about "not getting involved with the law" and general citizen distrust of involvement with interrogation by lawyers or policemen.

Indeed, the integrity of private systems and relations among them may require that citizens withhold complaint. Such matters as the protection of individual integrity, family honor, or the opportunity to continue in business have priority in the American normative system over the obligation to report violations or violators to the police. Finally, though we rely in our society on self-enforcement of conduct, the normative system works against reporting one's own violations. Though the police are charged with the detection of deviation, they are least likely to be sought out for confession of deviation. Deviation from the law may be acknowledged to the self, to the cleric, lawyer, friend, or therapist, but not to the police.

The nature of violative activity markedly affects the way police organization can cope with it. The popular image of how one effectively deals with crimes is through detective work. Yet, in a very important sense, police work does not rest on solving crimes through an inductive process of investigation beginning with evidence that leads ultimately to a violator. Rather, crimes are most often solved through a process of attaching persons known as violators to known violations.

Police work in response to citizen complaint usually begins and concludes solely as an intelligence operation; no arrest is made. The intelligence fed into the police system is on a crime that has been committed with, in many cases, little or no information on who may have committed it. The problem seemingly is one then, as the public says, of solving the crime. Though a majority of crimes must remain unsolved, for reasons under discussion here, even among those solved, only a minority can be said to be cleared through the inductive work of the detective division.

A majority of the cases that are cleared by arrest may be said to solve themselves in the sense that the violator is "known" to the complainant or to the police at the time the crime initially comes to the attention of the police. Whether the prosecutor and the courts will concur is another matter, but there is little doubt that the policeman operates in such situations by having a citizen sign a complaint or by making an arrest. Evidence technicians and detectives may work on such cases, but their task is one of linking the enforcement to the prosecution and adjudication systems by providing evidence, not one of solving crimes.

Though good data are lacking on the matter, there is good reason to claim that the second largest proportion of all crimes cleared by arrest is "solved" by arresting otherwise known violators. The arrest of a person for a crime often results in solving other crimes known to the police, since a major element of police practice is to utilize the arrested person and knowledge of his current offense as a means of clearing other crimes. Such well known police practices as interrogating the suspect to obtain confession to other crimes and presenting him for identification in a line-up are standard practices for clearing unsolved crimes as are well known ones such as charging the violator with unsolved crimes or simply assigning them to him in the department's records on the basis of a *modus operandi*. It is not uncommon to find that an arrest carries with it the solution to a half dozen other crimes, particularly for crimes of robbery and larceny.

One of the major problems for the modern metropolitan police force, as it centralizes command and control and draws its personnel away from operations that are based in local areas, is to maintain adequate intelligence on potential or known violators. There is good reason to conclude that the pattern of crimes solved by arrest changes with centralization of command and control, since it compels the department to place greater reliance on formal intelligence systems and means of crime solution.

The enforcement of the law is not simply a matter of maintaining an intelligence system on crimes and criminals and allocating organizational resources to deal with them in response to either citizen mobilization or police work. The organization of the larger society affects the organization of operating police units and their strategy and tactics in yet other ways.

Society is organized to make the detection of some violative behavior and the location of some violators more difficult than others. Consider just the matter of how a residential organization can affect the policing of the public. A public housing project with buildings twenty stories high, each containing several hundred families, poses somewhat different problems of crime detection and arrest than policing of the same area when it consisted of tenement houses.

Apart from considerations of the territorial and corporate organization of a population, the legal norms and order exercise an enormous impact on the exercise of coercive authority. A distinctive feature of modern liberal states is their use of the monopoly of violence to guarantee the boundaries of small, autonomous social systems like the private place and the citizen's right to privacy in public places. Police access to private places is guaranteed by the right of surveillance when there is reason to believe that a crime has been committed; and entry, search of the person and of places, and seizure of evidence are warranted under legally specified conditions. The right of the citizen to privacy and the right of state access to private matters forms one of the principal dialectical concerns in the organization of modern states and their police systems.

The laws defining police access to private places have consequences for the organization of staff and line units in police departments and in the strategy and tactics they adopt. Stinchcombe emphasizes that the differential distribution of crimes in public and private places when coupled with the greater legal accessibility police have to public as over and against private places, affects both the volume of police work and structural differentiation within the department.[18] He argues that police are organized through patrol in public places and therefore act much more on their own initiative in them; entry into private places is generally only on complaint or warrant.[19] It is true, of course, that police are in a better position to make an "on-view" arrest in a public rather than in a private place because of norms governing their access to private places. But it is also true that police are more likely to respond to complaints in both public and private places than they are to make an on-view arrest. This fact stems primarily from two conditions: the nature of occurrence of crime, and the allocation of limited organizational resources.

Whenever the nature of the crimes is such that the police cannot readily forecast a high probability of occurrence in a particular public or private location at a particular time, they must be organized primarily as a reactive organization. Many crimes in public as well as private places are of this form. These crimes are most likely to involve coercion in private life and disorders and nuisances in public places. Whether they are homicides, assaults, robberies, burglary, larceny, drunkenness, disorderly conduct, collective disturbances, or traffic accidents, police must in the nature of the case be organized to react to the occurrence of the crime when they are *not* present, for there is usually low predictability of occurrence of these types of crime, given the resources in manpower available.

A major problem police face in norms governing access to private places is the limitation it places on proactive strategies and tactics. Vice provides an excellent example. It operates "in the open" if a police department does not adopt a proactive strategy, since citizens who participate in such activities are unlikely to sign complaints that constitute a legal case. When a department "puts the heat on," however, vice can retreat into private places. This then necessitates an alteration in police tactics for dealing with vice. Progressively, as the legally acceptable means for access to these places become operationally difficult, the police resort to undercover roles or to use tactics designed to control public aspects of vice, for example, harassment.

Police organization and work, moreover, is substantially affected by the ways in which the violation is socially organized. To oversimplify, we might say that the more organized the violative activity, the less effective police are in dealing with the violation. Modern metropolitan police departments are perhaps least effective in dealing with organized crime. The literature on police work and the public press emphasizes that this is largely a consequence of the territorial limitations on operations of a metropolitan police force. By simple deduction, it is assumed that a police force coextensive with the organized activity would "solve" the problem of organized crime. Stinchcombe argues that it is difficult to deal with illegitimate businesses and dangerous organizations because of the barriers of privacy.[20]. . .

Conclusion

We have attempted to present a perspective on the metropolitan police that emphasizes the consequences of the external environment on police organization and operations. Such sociological study of the police may be of strategic value both for the sociology of law and of formal organizations. The police provide an unusual opportunity to develop and apply a transaction view of organizations, since, on the one hand, police departments have clearly defined boundaries, and yet, on the other, they must continually engage in the management of highly contingent relationships that arise outside them. At the same time, an organizational perspective that views the legal system in terms of transactions among organized subsystems that include the police rather than in terms of more formal imposition may make for a more viable sociology of law.

Our presentation concentrates on a few broad environmental features and traces their significance for police operations. Inevitably important areas have been scanted. Among those on which we would hope to concentrate more fully are those environmental features that affect the social sources and orientations of police personnel, the changing technologies of communication and intelligence, the increasing development and application of rational planning, and, indeed, the potential impact of sociology itself on police organization and behavior. The rationalization of police systems together with an increased emphasis on professional competence provides many opportunities for research on social organization and social order.

NOTES

1. We attempt to make explicit what is often left implicit in research programs—the generalized "image" out of which more specific work flows. See, for example, Daniel Glaser, "Criminality Theories and Behavioral Images," *American Journal of Sociology*, Vol. 61 (March 1951), pp. 433–44.

2. Something like police can occur in societies that would ordinarily not be termed legally organized. See Richard D. Schwartz and James C. Miller, "Legal Evolution and Societal Complexity," *American Journal of Sociology*, Vol. LXX (September 1965), pp. 159–69.

3. Except for the government component, the division follows closely that proposed by Roscoe Pound, who also discusses the confusions centering around the various uses of the terms "law" and "legal." Roscoe Pound, "The Sociology of Law," *Twentieth Century Sociology*, Georges Gurwitch and Wilbert E. Moore, eds., (New York, The Philosophical Library, 1945).

4. See the somewhat outraged treatment of Donald E. J. MacNamara, "American Police Administration at Mid-Century," *Public Administration Review*, Vol. X (Summer 1950), pp. 181–9.

5. For a jurisprudential discussion of the significance of private ordering with a sociological cast, see Henry M. Hart, Jr., and Albert M. Sacks, *The Legal Process: Basic Problems in the Making and Application of Law* (Cambridge, Mass., tentative edition, mimeo, 1958) Chap. 1.

6. Or, indeed, the decision to be sticky about formal contractual provisions in business dealings. Stewart Macaulay, "Non-contractual Relations in Business: A Preliminary Study," *American Sociological Review*, (February 1963), pp. 55–69.

7. See the discussion of commonweal organizations in Peter M. Blau and W. Richard Scott, *Formal Organizations* (San Francisco, Chandler Publishing Co., 1962), p. 54.

8. There is considerable law review literature on police discretion and what we have termed private arrangements involving the police. Most useful for the sociologist is the work of LaFave. Wayne R. LaFave, *Arrest: The Decision to Take a Suspect into Custody* (Boston, Little, Brown and Co. 1965). Also, Wayne R. LaFave, "The Police and Nonenforcement of the Law—Part I," *Wisconsin Law Review*, Vol. 1962, No. 1 (January), pp. 104–37 and "The Police and Nonenforcement of the Law—Part II," *Wisconsin Law Review*, Vol. 1962, No. 2 (March), pp. 179–239. See also Joseph Goldstein, "Police Discretion Not to Invoke the Criminal Process: Low-Visibility Decisions in the Administration of Justice," *The Yale Law Journal*, Vol. 69, No. 543 (1960), pp. 543–94, and Edward L. Barrett, Jr., "Police Practices and the Law—From Arrest to Release or Charge," *California Law Review*, Vol. 50, No. 1 (March 1962), pp. 11–55.

9. Informal practice in the police area may often be highly formalized. Indeed, it may even be written down. Formal, written department policy and procedure may be considered informal with respect to the law. Operating norms at all levels in police organizations may differ from either the law or department written rules. One of the more puzzling aspects of the control of police by the courts is the fact that the courts rarely take judicial notice of written police department rules and decide cases as though the individual policeman were a free agent. See the comparison of court rulings and police manuals in Goldstein, *op. cit.*

10. T. H. Marshall proposes a historical scheme from which much of the above has been drawn. He argues that the lower classes were first the recipients of civil legal status and then later of welfare or social rights as adjuncts of citizenship. In the United

States, at least, one can argue that large segments of the population had access to unemployment and old age insurance *before* developing any meaningful access to civil legality. This is true even in the formal sense for Negroes in the South, for example. T. H. Marshall, *Citizenship and Social Class* (Cambridge, Cambridge University Press, 1950).

11. Federal Bureau of Investigation, U.S. Department of Justice, *Crime in the United States: Uniform Crime Reports—1965* (Washington, D.C., U.S. Government Printing Office, 1964), Table 8, pp. 97ff. A total clearance rate of 26.3% is reported for seven major crimes. Clearance rates varied from 90.5% for murder to 19.6% for larceny. *Ibid.*, p. 97.

12. Compare Banton's analysis of the degree to which the police in Scotland justify themselves by simply existing as symbols of order. Michael Banton, *The Policeman in the Community* (New York, Basic Books, 1965).

13. Federal Bureau of Investigation, *op. cit.*, p. 47. These three offenses accounted for 8.1% of the total number of index crimes reported for 1965. The index crimes are all major crimes. The annual report of any large city department will show that these "public outcry" offenses are *quantitatively* a much smaller proportion of all crimes known to the police.

14. See the sources cited in footnote 8, *supra*.

15. Arthur L. Stinchcombe, "The Control of Citizen Resentment in Police Work." Unpublished paper, no date.

16. Mapp v. Ohio, 367 U.S. 643 (1961); Ker v. California, 374 U.S. (1963); Escobedo v. Illinois, 84 U.S. 1785 (1964).

17. As Skolnick notes, there are those violative acts where the individual citizen is directly offended: there is a crime against him as a private individual or against his property; and there are those violative acts where the citizen is involved only in the collective sense; there is some threat to the social order as defined by the legal norms. See Jerome H. Skolnick and J. Richard Woodworth, "Police, Suspects and Prosecutors." Paper read at the annual meeting of the American Sociological Association, Los Angeles, Calfornia, September 2, 1963.

18. Arthur L. Stinchcombe, "Institutions of Privacy in the Determination of Police Administrative Practice," *American Journal of Sociology*, Vol. LXIX (September 1963), p. 158.

19. *Ibid.*, p. 152.

20. *Ibid.*, p. 155.

6

Daniel R. Miller and Guy E. Swanson

CHILD TRAINING
IN ENTREPRENEURIAL AND
BUREAUCRATIC FAMILIES

In this chapter we shall present evidence that the old and new middle-class families in the Detroit area differ in their methods of rearing children. We were not at all certain that they are conscious of their techniques or of the effects those techniques are likely to have on children's conduct. We had some confidence, however, that we could forecast at least a portion of the difference in child care to be found between entrepreneurial and bureaucratic parents—a portion of the influence of a family's integration setting on the methods by which it shapes its children's behavior.

When our interviewers knocked on the doors of a sample of mothers in the Detroit area, they carried a set of questions designed to obtain information that would test some predictions we had developed. We were forecasting the behaviors that entrepreneurial families, as contrasted with bureaucratic families of upper middle-class status, would encourage in their children.

We predicted that, among whites, entrepreneurial middle-class mothers would be more likely than those with a bureaucratic integration to emphasize the child's development of strong self-control. Several of our questions relate to that emphasis. We call them Internalization Indices.

Similarly, we predicted that entrepreneurial middle-class mothers would train their children to take a more active and independent approach to the world than would their bureaucratic counterparts. We said that bureaucratic middle-class mothers should encourage children to adopt a more accommodating and adjustive way of life. A number of our questions seem related to this theme. We call them Activity Indices. We discuss Internalization and Activity Indices in that order.

Daniel R. Miller and Guy E. Swanson, "Child Training in Entrepreneurial and Bureaucratic Families," from *The Changing American Parent* (New York: Wiley, 1958), pp. 92–106 (slightly edited). Reprinted by permission.

Internalization Indices

Here (in Table 6–1) are the questions that we felt would give us evidence of the extent to which mothers in our sample taught their children self-control.

TABLE 6-1

Internalization Indices

ITEM NUMBER	ITEM
3	Mothers have different ways of handling a crying child of five months. Suppose that you were busy preparing the family dinner and the baby was cranky and crying — if you thought nothing was wrong with him (her), and he (she) only wanted attention, what would you do?
5, 5a	We'd like to know (name's) age at different times when you made changes in feeding. When did he (she) stop breast feeding as the main way of feeding at meal time?
5c, 6b	When did he (she) give up using the bottle entirely?
5d	When did he (she) give up breast feeding entirely?
5e, 6c	Did you feed him (her) at special times when he (she) was a baby, or when he (she) seemed to want to eat?
14	How old (in months) was he (she) when you began bowel training?
17	How old was your child when you began to train him (her) not to wet himself (herself)?
19, 19a	Think about a time when (name) will be (was) ten years old. He (she) has just done something that you feel is very good, or he (she) has been particularly good. What would you do at those times? Can you give me an example?
20, 20a	Now, please think about that same time when (name) will be (was) ten years old. He (she) has just done something that you feel is very wrong, something that you have warned him (her) against ever doing. What would you do at such times? Can you give me an example?

The sense in which each of these questions might reveal that the mother did or did not emphasize the child's acquiring self-control can now be summarized. We chose some items because they would refer to demands that the child give up present bodily pleasures for the mother's love or for other rewards in the future. These demands teach the youngster to curb the immediate expression of his desires in the interest of satisfying his long-range needs. The questions that we felt might refer to such training are those asking for the ages of weaning and of bowel and bladder training, and those inquiring about the use of scheduled as against demand feeding in infancy.

Types of reward and punishment that would use and reinforce the internal controls the child has acquired would be in keeping with such training in self-control. Thus, we expected that entrepreneurial middle-class parents would be more likely than their bureaucratic counterparts to praise the child or to let his virtue be its own reward instead of giving him some directly rewarding experience such as a piece of candy, or some money, or permission to stay out later than usual. We shall speak of this distinction as being one between symbolic and direct rewards.

Similarly, we can point to symbolic and direct types of punishment. We thought entrepreneurial middles would more probably use the symbolic disciplines of blame, appeals to guilt, and restriction of movement (for example, sending the child to his room to "think it over") instead of more direct punishments such as spanking. Items 19, 19a, 20, and 20a, in Table 6–1 get at these matters.

In connection with Item 3, we judged that the mother who is successful in teaching the child to control his immediate desires must be somewhat less warm and empathic toward her child, other things being equal, than mothers using less stringent and persistent measures, or she would be unable to bring herself to carry through with the task. Perhaps what is necessary is that, though she is equally warm, the entrepreneurial mother must be able to control the immediate expression of her sympathy for the child in distress. In any case, she must not be too completely gratifying to the child. She must not do what he would like without a price, or he will not learn strict self-control. Consequently, we expected that entrepreneurial middles would be less likely than bureaucratic mothers to give immediate care to an infant who cried for attention.

We did not try to predict whether differences would exist between the older and newer middle classes with respect to the time at which they completed the bowel or urinary training of their children. Evidence from earlier studies[1] suggested that such differences were unlikely.

Up to this point, we have spoken as if we were confident that these methods of rearing children would produce self-control, and as if we were equally confident that each of them would lead to that end. Actually, that gives far too simple a picture of the state of our thinking. We had several kinds of qualms and uncertainties. At the same time, we had serious reasons for thinking that early weaning and bowel training and symbolic rewards and the rest might lead a child to control his own behavior. We must say something about these conflicting thoughts so that our interpretation of the findings we are about to present will be clear.

First, then, consider the reasons we felt to be important in connecting these methods of training children with the mother's task of encouraging youngsters to examine their desires and modify or inhibit some of them. An important source of those reasons is found in the psychoanalytic idea of internalized controls.

"Controls" are standards the individual learns—standards like eating three meals a day or keeping clean or being honest—and which, once acquired, make it difficult for him to behave in alternative ways. Internalized controls are not simply those that are well learned or that are learned without contradiction. They are learned in ways that give them the characteristics of what, following Freud, is often called the superego. Where ways of behaving are well learned, but not internalized, they change if new conditions make them inappropriate. The change may be slow. The individual may be very unhappy and uncomfortable, but he does not blame himself for changing. He does not feel a guilt he cannot shake.

Ways of behaving that are internalized may also change under such special conditions as those provided in therapy. But the change is made especially difficult because the individual feels great guilt: an anxiety about forces within himself that are about to punish him. It is not simply that the outside world is upsetting and, perhaps, frightening. Silent, faceless threats within him make him pause.

Present knowledge of personality development suggests that there is a connection between learning a socially required pattern of conduct at a very early age and the internalization of that pattern. This is believed to be a significant feature of early weaning and toilet training. The child learns to give up pleasures. He is too young to understand why the parents force this deprivation on him. He needs their love. Therefore he must obey. They insist and persist. Thus a foundation is laid for his postponing immediate gratifications for future gains. In short, to the extent that the child does not understand why the demands that are put upon him are made, and to the extent that he finds that refusal to conform to seemingly irrational requirements leads to severe and persistent deprivations, whereas conformity brings reward and peace, he does conform. Since he may find obedience distasteful, he may have to control rebellious thoughts by denying their existence, by convincing himself that he always wanted to do what his parents now require. In later years, he still conforms even when there is not the faintest threat for nonconformity from the real world outside, or even when that world no longer demands that he continue behaving as he has. And he feels compelled to teach his children to behave as he does and is shocked and irrationally alarmed if they do not. It is believed that the person with internalized behavior patterns acts this way because he has learned those patterns under conditions[2] that make it impossible for him to think about their rationality or irrationality or to expect anything but great deprivation from nonconformity. As a result, he cannot control and change his conduct when new external conditions make it appropriate. Thus if he has internalized the standard of washing his face in the morning, he feels very uneasy and uncomfortable, and, possibly, guilty and depressed, if something interferes with this habit, even if his face is quite clean.[3] Such reasoning supports our belief that these early body regimens train children in self-control.

In describing the coming of the bureaucratic order, we have stressed the greater stability of the community and its larger potential for supervising and controlling its members. Once again parents may rely with some assurance on the ability of the groups the child meets to provide adequate controls and checks on his behavior. As a consequence, the need for his internalizing as extensive a set of controls in order to grow into a responsible adult is not so great.

We found the psychoanalytic picture of the internalization of some controls —of a special kind of learning of self-control and self-denial—highly suggestive. We recognize, however, that future research may modify it in whole or in part. The evidence in its favor resides in very suggestive reports from clinical records of therapy with children and adults, but these do not provide anything like conclusive evidence. Further, our own study contains no findings about the actual effects of early weaning or bowel training or the rest of these methods on the behavior of children. How, then, shall we interpret any findings obtained from the use of our Internalization Indices?

Our essential assumption is that these indices can reflect differences in the extent to which mothers use controlled and rationalized behavior with their children and that evidence of more extensive self-control in behavior will be found among entrepreneurial middle-class mothers than among bureaucratic mothers of the same social status. Our data enable us to test the existence of this connection between social positions and methods of child care. The data do not provide any evidence of the extent to which children adopt a pattern of conduct like that of their elders. The findings certainly give no evidence on the subject of whether, if children do acquire differences in self-control from their parents, those differences are learned through internalization or in some other fashion.

It is our personal judgment that children do learn a relatively impersonal and self-controlled style of behavior if parents set such a model for them and reward them for adopting it. We shall feel free to speak of our indices as reflecting themes that are taught to children. Yet, in strictest logic, we must admit that this way of speaking will represent what we believe to be the case, but not something that our data can establish or disprove.

Now, however, we come to a different problem. Were we certain that each of our questions was an equally good sample of the extent to which mothers practiced or taught self-control?

We were not. We appreciated that mothers might use any one of these techniques for reasons quite unconnected with exhibiting self-control in their own conduct or with teaching it to the child. Some women may wean or toilet train a child at an early age because they are ill and must simplify their housework. Perhaps the mother has a large family or plans to return to a job outside the home and must socialize the baby as rapidly as possible. It may be that the family's income has to be a certain size before parents will be likely to use many direct rewards such as giving the children candy or toys when they behave well. And these reasons can be multiplied manifold times.

What we did conclude was that some of these reasons, like that of a possible relation between family income and the use of direct rewards, would be less important when we controlled social class while comparing families with entrepreneurial and bureaucratic integrations. Other reasons, such as ill health, did not seem likely to be more frequent for mothers in one integration than the other. Finally, we judged that though we might be in error about the extent to which any particular technique of training children would reflect the theme of self-control, it was less likely that we were wrong about all of them or a significant number of them. It was also less likely that mothers who used several of these techniques would fail to be entrepreneurial in integration than would those who happened to use only one or two of them.

FINDINGS

With the uncertainties just mentioned, but with several reasons for believing that our predictions about internalization practices had a solid foundation, we proceeded to test their accuracy. Table 6-2 summarizes the results of that test.

The findings in Table 6-2 confirm most of our expectations. We find that

TABLE 6-2

Significance and Direction of Findings through the Use of the Internalization Indices*

ITEM NUMBERS	PREDICTION: ENTREPRE-NEURIAL MOTHERS ARE MORE LIKELY THAN BUREAUCRATIC MOTHERS TO:	AMONG UPPER MIDDLES p	AMONG LOWER MIDDLES p	AMONG ALL MIDDLES p
3	Give delayed attention to crying baby or give no attention.	+ < .01	+ < .005	+ < .0005
5c, 5d, 6b	Wean the baby by the end of twelve months.	< .90	< .95	< .90
5e, 6c	Feed the baby on a schedule.	+ < .05	< .70	+ < .03
14	Begin bowel training before the baby is ten months old.	< .95	+ < .10	+ < .10
17	Begin urinary training before the baby is eleven months old.	< .70	+ < .03	+ < .03
19	Use symbolic rewards.	< .95	< .80	< .70
20	Use symbolic punishments.	< .80	+ < .03	+ < .03

*The notation in this table gives a symbol for the direction of the findings followed by the level of probability. The direction symbols are as follows: a plus (+) means the results show the direction predicted; the absence of a symbol indicates that the p value is greater than .50, making hazardous any statement about trends. All p values reaching the .20 level or beyond and having the predicted direction, are presented using one tail of the probability distribution. The degrees of freedom in each χ^2 computation are one.

entrepreneurial mothers among the middle classes are significantly more likely than bureaucratic mothers of similar social status to feed babies on a schedule, to begin urinary training before the baby is eleven months old, and to use symbolic rather than direct punishments. They also are more likely to give a baby who cries when "nothing is wrong with him" some attention only after he sobs for a while or, in some cases, to pay no attention to him at all. Although it is not quite large enough to meet our standard for signifi-

cance (a confidence level of .05 or beyond), we find that the difference between entrepreneurial and bureaucratic mothers with respect to the age at
which bowel training is begun is in the direction we expected. Entrepreneurial
mothers are more likely to begin such training with their youngsters before
the baby is ten months old.

We find, however, that there is no difference of note between entrepreneurial and bureaucratic mothers with respect to two of our seven indices of
training for self-control. These have to do with the age at which the baby is
weaned and the use of symbolic as against direct rewards. We can only guess
as to the reasons why significant differences do not appear for the answers
to these questions. It may be, for example, that mothers do not usually think
of praise or a pat on the head when trying to remember how they reward
children. Perhaps, although they give these rewards, they fail to report them,
thus confounding our prediction. It may be, however, that age of weaning
and type of reward do not reflect the theme of self-control to the same extent
as do the other five questions. They may be inappropriate for other reasons.
We cannot be certain.

What is of more immediate interest is whether, despite these two failures
of prediction, we have obtained enough evidence at a high enough level of
significance to conclude that our expectation of large differences between
entrepreneurial and bureaucratic mothers with respect to this set of seven
questions is fulfilled. There are many technical and statistical problems involved in making such a judgment. . . . We consider it correct and conservative
to conclude that our prediction is upheld. Entrepreneurial middle-class
mothers are more likely than those in a bureaucratic integration to use practices which emphasize self-control in training children.

Table 6–2 shows something else of interest. It shows that there are far
more significant differences in the expected direction on these Internalization
Indices between mothers of lower middle-class status than between upper
middle-class mothers in the two integration settings. The reason for this
trend is quite unexpected. Contrary to our earlier beliefs, we find that the
older and newer upper middles are rather like each other in being more strict
than lower middles in their training on these Internalization Indices.

We said earlier that upper middles, whether entrepreneurial or bureaucratic,
have considerable economic security. We observed that they occupy positions
in society that give upper middles some appreciation of the whole complex
organization of modern life and of their place in it. From these facts we
expected upper middles, generally, to strive and struggle less than lower
middles; to have fewer experiences of being lost and confused in an urban
society.

Now, however, we must revise our judgment. It may be that we have underestimated the extent to which American upper middles, whether of the older
or newer type, still have reason to stress self-control in training their children.
Perhaps the pressures of the kinds of work they do—work in which the
individual has considerable responsibility even in the framework of a large

enterprise—forces an emphasis on the control of impulses. Perhaps there are subtle but important pressures on upper middles as a consequence of their relatively superior social positions; that is, it may be that they feel called upon to behave as elites and with a corresponding gravity and self-restraint. Our present data do not allow us to decide among these and other possibilities.

Table 6–3 gives the answer to a different question. Is it true that mothers

TABLE 6-3

Significance of Entrepreneurial-Bureaucratic Comparisons in Cumulative Internalization Scores

SCHEDULE FORM	GROUPS COMPARED	χ^2	df	ONE-TAILED p
A	Upper middles	.33	1	< .35
A	Lower middles	3.76	1	< .05
A	All middles	6.17	1	< .01
B	Upper middles	.54	1	< .25
B	Lower middles	8.03	1	< .005
B	All middles	8.26	1	< .005

who answer several of the Internalization Indices in a way that we feel leads to training the child in self-control are more likely to be entrepreneurial than are other mothers? Table 6–3 supports an affirmative answer. To understand that answer, however, we must describe how it was obtained.

In order to increase the number of questions we could ask mothers in our sample, we asked some questions of only a random half of that sample and still other questions of the remaining mothers. Three groups of items from our Internalization Indices (Items 3, 5c and 5d and 6b, and 5e and 6c) were asked of the half of the sample who answered the questions on Schedule Form A. The remaining four groups of items (Items 14, 17, 19, and 20) were asked of the half of the respondents who were interviewed by means of Schedule Form B.

Our procedure for obtaining the results in Table 6–3 was quite simple. Let us take the case of mothers answering Schedule Form A. For each of the three groups of questions in that form that were included among our Internalization Indices, mothers' responses were categorized as likely or less likely to train a child in self-control or as "uncodable." For example, beginning to teach the child to urinate in the toilet before he was 11 months old was considered as likely to train him in self-control, while teaching him this skill at 11 months of age or later was considered less likely to train him in self-control. Mothers who said they could not remember when they began this training were classified as uncodable. Mothers responding to Schedule Form A could have answered as many as three questions in such a way as to suggest that they were interested in teaching the child to control himself. But they might have answered in that fashion with respect to two, one, or none of the three possible opportunities. When the same approach is applied to mothers answering the questions from Schedule Form B, we find that there were four questions in our Internalization Indices in that form. Hence, these mothers may have responded in ways we feel indicative of an interest in teaching self-control to their youngsters on four, three, two, one, or none of those questions. Our prediction is that the larger the number of questions to which a mother responds with an answer indicative of an effort to train the child to control himself, the more likely it is that mother is entrepreneurial.

Table 6-3 reports the findings from mothers responding to each of the schedule forms. The results support our prediction. They also show that our prediction holds more clearly for lower middle-class mothers than for upper middles.

Activity Indices

At the beginning of this chapter we predicted that the same pattern of socio-economic conditions that leads to an emphasis on self-control pushes the entrepreneurial middle classes toward activity instead of toward an accommodative style of behavior. As we see it, the individual in the older middle classes is taught to change himself if he must, but, when possible, to impose his will on the world rather than simply to adapt to his environment. This should be especially true for entrepreneurial males, since they are expected to be the risk takers and to lead in winning higher status for their families. There actually are pressures against a woman becoming as independent and manipulatory as her husband. Parsons has observed[4] that, when the economic system emphasizes extreme competition and involves comparisons of the relative success and superiority of the competitors, the stability of the marriage relation is enhanced if only the husband participates in the economy. In that circumstance, he does not compete with his wife, nor she with him. His is the active, aggressive, independent role. Hers is the more integrative, passive, accommodative one. Because these roles are complementary, they gain in stability.

That long-time Detroit resident and poet of America's entrepreneurial middles, Edgar A. Guest, once spoke of the need for active mastery of one's future in these terms:[5]

> So long as men shall be on earth
>   There will be tasks for them to do,
> Some for them to show their worth;
>   Each day shall bring its problems new.
> And men shall dream of mightier deeds
>   Than ever have done before:
> There always shall be human needs
>   For men to work and struggle for.

And the kind of man who can grasp opportunity:[6]

A man doesn't whine at his losses.
   A man doesn't whimper and fret,
Or rail at the weight of his crosses
   And ask life to rear him a pet.
A man doesn't grudgingly labor
   Or look upon toil as a blight;
A man doesn't sneer at his neighbor

   ·   ·   ·   ·   ·   ·

A man looks on woman as tender
   And gentle, and stands at her side
At all times to guard and defend her,
   And never to scorn or deride.
A man looks on life as a mission.
   To serve, just so far as he can;
A man holds his noblest ambition
   On earth is to live as a man.

As we have seen, the bureaucratic situation strips from the worker much of his potentiality for striving and achievement and for the active shaping of his own future through planning and risk taking. It becomes, then, increasingly possible for women to participate in the economy without as serious a threat to the marital relationship.[7] Together with the previously mentioned increase in the number of clerical jobs, the declining requirements for heavy muscular skills in industry, the freeing of women from many older household duties, and the decline of striving and competition lead to greater similarity of participation by men and women in the economy, and in the home.

We concluded that, relatively speaking, the entrepreneurial middle classes would show greater devotion to activity and independence and mastery than would bureaucrats of the same social classes, and that they would also prefer sharper differences between masculine and feminine roles. It is these differences in emphasis that the Activity Indices listed in Table 6–4 were grouped to expose.

Among these Activity Indices, Items 11 and 35 and their subparts are efforts to catch the sharpness of the distinction between the sex roles, with its implication for the greater mastery required of male behavior. Items 2 and 7 reflect the efforts of the parents to prevent a child from finding pleasures in a passive manipulation of his own body instead of in control of the world outside himself. It may be objected that the major reason parents try to prevent children's explorations of their genitals is their fear that the child will become too interested in sex as such. This objection seems doubtful, since we do find significant differences by social position in their answers to Item 7, but no differences by those positions in their responses to a question asking if they permit the child to follow the parent of opposite sex into the bathroom. It is improbable that the latter item has no connotations relating to a stimulation of the child's interest in sex.

It may be wondered why we did not include length of nursing as well as items on thumb-sucking and genital exploration among these questions assembled to reflect the parents' toleration of passivity in their children. We

TABLE 6-4

Activity Indices

ITEM NUMBER	ITEM
2	Did (child's name) ever suck his (her) thumb, or arm, or hand, or something like that?
2*a*	(If yes) Have you thought it necessary to do anything about it?
2*b*	(If yes) What was that?
7	Have you or your husband done anything at any time when (name) was five years old or younger and he (she) touched his (her) sex organs?
7*a*	(If no) Did he (she) ever do that?
9	Suppose a mother has a very good woman who will stay with her three-year-old boy two afternoons a week while she goes shopping and visiting. She decides not to do this because she feels three-year-olds are too young to be away from their mothers so often. How do you feel about this?
9*a*	Why would that be?
10	We hear a lot these days about different ways to bring up children. Some people think children should be on their own as early as possible to work out their own problems. Do you agree or disagree?
11	Here are some things that might be done by a boy or a girl. Suppose the person were about thirteen years old. As I read each of these to you, I would like you to tell me if it should be done as a regular task by a boy, by a girl, or by both.
11*a*	Shoveling walks.
11*b*	Washing the car.
11*c*	Dusting furniture.
11*d*	Fixing light cords.
11*e*	Making beds.
35	Here are some things that might be done by a husband or wife. As I read each of these to you, I would like you to tell me if, in your home, it is usually done by you, by your husband, or by both of you.
35*a*	Painting rooms in the house.
35*b*	Getting up at night to take care of the children if they cry.
35*c*	Deciding where to go for a holiday or celebration.
35*d*	Punishing the children, if necessary.
35*e*	Picking out more expensive things like furniture or a car.
35*f*	Washing dishes.

cannot exclude the possibility that some parents who wean their children late are more tolerant of passivity. However, we do find that there is not a significant relation between the age at which a child is weaned and his parents' answers to these questions on what they did if he touched his sex organs or sucked some part of his own body. It may also be useful to give our original reason for excluding age of weaning from the Activity Indices. We felt that most parents would consider nursing to be an activity the child carries on in relation to the environment. In this sense, as contrasted with thumb-sucking or genital exploration, nursing involves gaining satisfactions through manipulating the environment in the service of the infant's needs, not getting satisfactions without making efforts to control the outer world.

The reasons for including Item 10 seem clear without explanation. Item 9 was not added for the direct answers which respondents gave to the question it posed. On reading the interviews, we discovered that the vast majority of mothers added a comment to their answers. Almost all mothers told the interviewer *why* they agreed or disagreed with the hypothetical mother in the question. Of course, a mother might agree or disagree and we still would have no basis for predicting whether she would feel that her child should be active or accommodative. However, if she said that she disagreed because it would be good for the mother to get away from the child, we felt this was a plausible reflection that she felt somewhat detached from, and independent of, the child. We assumed that the child, in turn, would have to become independent of a mother with such an attitude; that he would not become overly attached to any single adult on whom he would then be dependent.

FINDINGS

Table 6–5 summarizes the findings we got from using the Activity Indices. Of the twelve Activity Indices, nine show trends in the direction predicted. Six of these trends are strong enough to make it improbable that they occurred merely by chance. These significant differences show that entrepreneurial middle-class mothers are more likely than bureaucratic mothers of the same social class to use harsh means to stop a child from sucking his body, to declare that their children did not touch their sex organs, and to say that they took measures to stop a child who touched his sex organs. Mothers in the older middle classes are also more likely to feel that it is desirable for his mother's sake that a child frequently be left at home with a competent woman while the mother shops, and to say that children should be put on their own as soon as possible to solve their own problems. Finally, the entrepreneurial mothers more often state that, among adolescents, only males should perform activities traditionally associated with their sex, like washing the family car and shoveling sidewalks.

Three trends occur as we expected except that they are not significantly large. Thus entrepreneurial mothers are less likely than those of bureaucratic integration to say that their children ever sucked any part of their bodies. Moreover, among entrepreneurial and bureaucratic respondents who report that their children were seen sucking their fingers or arms or feet, the mothers in the older middle classes frequently declare that they did something to stop the child's sucking. This older type of middle-class mother is also more likely to feel that, among adolescents, girls and only girls should perform activities traditionally associated with their sex—activities such as making beds and dusting furniture.

Whether as a result of widespread teaching, or because of a growing tolerance for sexual exploration, or for some other reason, we do not find differences of any note between mothers in the old and new middle classes with respect to the use of harsh means to stop the child who touches his sex

TABLE 6-5

*Significance and Direction of Findings Obtained through the Use of the Activity Indices**

ITEM NUMBERS	PREDICTION: ENTREPRE-NEURIAL MOTHERS ARE MORE LIKELY THAN BUREAUCRATIC MOTHERS TO:	AMONG UPPER MIDDLES	AMONG LOWER MIDDLES	AMONG ALL MIDDLES
2	Say the child never sucked parts of his body.	+ < .50	< .95	+ < .50
2a	Say the parents felt it necessary to do something about the child sucking his body if he did so.	†	1.00	+ < .50
2b	Use harsh means (mechanical and chemical) to stop the child who sucked his body.	†	+ < .05	+ < .05
7	Say the child did not touch his sex organs.	+ < .30	+ < .005	+ < .005
7a	Say the parents felt it necessary to do something when the child touched his sex organs.	†	+ < .05	+ < .03
7b	Use harsh means (spankings, threats) if they did something when the child touched his sex organs.	†	< .80	< .70
9a	Feel it is good to leave a child at home frequently with a competent woman while the mother shops or visits because the mother benefits.	+ < .005	< .90	+ < .05
10	Agree that a child should be on his own as soon as possible to solve his own problems.	< .70	+ < .03	+ < .005
11a, b, d	Feel that only males should perform activities traditionally associated with their sex among adolescents.	+ < .30	+ < .10	+ < .03
11c, e	Feel that only females should perform activities traditionally associated with their sex among adolescents.	< .95	< .80	+ < .50
35a	Feel that only males should perform activities traditionally associated with their sex among adults.	< .70	< .70	< .99
35b, f	Feel that only females should perform activities traditionally associated with their sex among adults.	+ < .03	< .80	< .70

*The notation in this table gives a symbol for the direction of the findings followed by the level of probability. The direction symbols are as follows: a plus (+) means the results show the direction predicted; the absence of a symbol indicates that the p value is greater than .50, making hazardous any statement about trends. All p values reaching the .20 level or beyond, and having the predicted direction, are presented using one tail of the probability distribution. The degrees of freedom in each χ^2 computation are one.

†The number of cases is too small to warrant computation.

organs. Almost no middle-class mother uses spanking or threats in such situations.

Another point at which a prediction failed deserves attention. It may well be that the absence of any important difference between the integration settings with regard to the degree to which adult sex roles are sharply separated is due to the way Item 35 is written. In retrospect, it seems like a question that is badly designed for the purpose to which it was put. Too many of the activities listed in its six subparts are performed jointly by husbands and wives. This is conspicuously true for such matters as deciding where to go on a holiday or choosing expensive purchases. As a result, these items may be insensitive to the definitiveness with which male and female behaviors are distinguished from each other. On the other hand, we cannot discount the possibility that Item 35 is valid and our prediction was incorrect. Deciding between these accounts will require further research.

NOTES

1. Allison Davis and Robert J. Havighurst, "Social Class and Color Differences in Child-Rearing," *American Sociological Review* 11 (December, 1946): 698–710.

2. There is some uncertainty whether these conditions should be stated as involving the child's lack of symbols with which to conceptualize his experiences or as involving his repression of feelings that he has conceptualized. Perhaps both situations are involved. Arguments for the former appear in such sources as: Alfred R. Lindesmith and Anselm L. Strauss, *Social Psychology* (New York: The Dryden Press, 1949); Ernest G. Schactel, "On Memory and Childhood Amnesia," *Psychiatry* 10 (February, 1947): 1–26; David C. McClelland, *Personality* (New York: William Sloane Associates, 1951), pp. 544–549. Some results of making demands on the child at a very early age are presented in Wesley Allinsmith, "The Learning of Moral Standards," unpublished doctoral dissertation, Department of Psychology, University of Michigan, 1954.

3. We recognize, of course, that people differ in their responses to experiences of guilt. Some of these differences are discussed in Daniel R. Miller and Guy E. Swanson, *Inner Conflict and Defense* (New York: Schocken Books, 1966).

4. Talcott Parsons, "An Analytical Approach to the Theory of Social Stratification," *The American Journal of Sociology* 45 (May, 1940): 852–853.

5. Edgar A. Guest, "Opportunity," in *Collected Verse of Edgar A. Guest* (Chicago: The Reilly and Lee Company, 1938), p. 23. Reprinted with permission.

6. "A Man," *ibid.*, p. 90. Reprinted with permission.

7. This may be one of the conditions that has resulted in unprecedented numbers of women entering and remaining in the labor force in prosperous times. Previously women came into the economy in large numbers only in time of war or depression and they left as soon as the emergency was over.

7

Stanley Milgram

BEHAVIORAL STUDY OF OBEDIENCE

Obedience is as basic an element in the structure of social life as one can point to. Some system of authority is a requirement of all communal living, and it is only the man dwelling in isolation who is not forced to respond, through defiance or submission, to the commands of others. Obedience, as a determinant of behavior, is of particular relevance to our time. It has been reliably established that from 1933–1945 millions of innocent persons were systematically slaughtered on command. Gas chambers were built, death camps were guarded, daily quotas of corpses were produced with the same efficiency as the manufacture of appliances. These inhumane policies may have originated in the mind of a single person, but they could only be carried out on a massive scale if a very large number of persons obeyed orders.

Obedience is the psychological mechanism that links individual action to political purpose. It is the dispositional cement that binds men to systems of authority. Facts of recent history and observation in daily life suggest that for many persons obedience may be a deeply ingrained behavior tendency, indeed, a prepotent impulse overriding training in ethics, sympathy, and moral conduct. C. P. Snow (1961) points to its importance when he writes:

When you think of the long and gloomy history of man, you will find more hideous crimes have been committed in the name of obedience than have ever been committed in the name of rebellion. If you doubt that, read William Shirer's "Rise and Fall of the Third Reich." The German Officer Corps were brought up in the most rigorous code of obedience . . . in the name of obedience they were party to, and assisted in, the most wicked large scale actions in the history of the world [p. 24].

Stanley Milgram, "Behavioral Study of Obedience," *Journal of Abnormal and Social Psychology* 67 (1963): 371–378. Copyright 1963 by the American Psychological Association, and reproduced by permission. Also used by permission of Stanley Milgram.

NOTE: This research was supported by a grant (NSF G–17916) from the National Science Foundation. Exploratory studies conducted in 1960 were supported by a grant from the Higgins Fund at Yale University. The research assistance of Alan C. Elms and Jon Wayland is gratefully acknowledged.

While the particular form of obedience dealt with in the present study has its antecedents in these episodes, it must not be thought all obedience entails acts of aggression against others. Obedience serves numerous productive functions. Indeed, the very life of society is predicated on its existence. Obedience may be ennobling and educative and refer to acts of charity and kindness, as well as to destruction.

GENERAL PROCEDURE

A procedure was devised which seems useful as a tool for studying obedience (Milgram, 1961). It consists of ordering a naive subject to administer electric shock to a victim. A simulated shock generator is used, with 30 clearly marked voltage levels that range from 15 to 450 volts. The instrument bears verbal designations that range from Slight Shock to Danger: Severe Shock. The responses of the victim, who is a trained confederate of the experimenter, are standardized. The orders to administer shocks are given to the naive subject in the context of a "learning experiment" ostensibly set up to study the effects of punishment on memory. As the experiment proceeds the naive subject is commanded to administer increasingly more intense shocks to the victim, even to the point of reaching the level marked Danger: Severe Shock. Internal resistances become stronger, and at a certain point the subject refuses to go on with the experiment. Behavior prior to this rupture is considered "obedience," in that the subject complies with the commands of the experimenter. The point of rupture is the act of disobedience. A quantitative value is assigned to the subject's performance based on the maximum intensity shock he is willing to administer before he refuses to participate further. Thus for any particular subject and for any particular experimental condition the degree of obedience may be specified with a numerical value. The crux of the study is to systematically vary the factors believed to alter the degree of obedience to the experimental commands.

The technique allows important variables to be manipulated at several points in the experiment. One may vary aspects of the source of command, content and form of command, instrumentalities for its execution, target object, general social setting, etc. The problem, therefore, is not one of designing increasingly more numerous experimental conditions, but of selecting those that best illuminate the *process* of obedience from the sociopsychological standpoint.

RELATED STUDIES

The inquiry bears an important relation to philosophic analyses of obedience and authority (Arendt, 1958; Friedrich, 1958; Weber, 1947), an early experimental study of obedience by Frank (1944), studies in "authoritarianism" (Adorno, Frenkel-Brunswik, Levinson, and Sanford, 1950; Rokeach, 1961), and a recent series of analytic and empirical studies in social power (Cartwright, 1959). It owes much to the long concern with *suggestion* in social psychology, both in its normal forms (e.g., Binet, 1900) and in its clinical manifestations (Charcot, 1881). But it derives, in the first instance, from direct observation of a social fact; the individual who is commanded by a legitimate authority ordinarily obeys. Obedience comes easily and often. It is a ubiquitous and indispensable feature of social life.

Method

SUBJECTS

The subjects were 40 males between the ages of 20 and 50, drawn from New Haven and the surrounding communities. Subjects were obtained by a newspaper advertisement and direct mail solicitation. Those who responded to the appeal believed they were to participate in a study of memory and learning at Yale University. A wide range of occupations is represented in the sample. Typical subjects were postal clerks, high school teachers, salesmen, engineers, and laborers. Subjects ranged in educational level from one who had not finished elementary school, to those who had doctorate and other professional degrees. They were paid $4.50 for their participation in the experiment. However, subjects were told that payment was simply for coming to the laboratory, and that the money was theirs no matter what happened after they arrived. Table 7-1 shows the proportion of age and occupational types assigned to the experimental condition.

TABLE 7-1

Distribution of Age and Occupational Types in the Experiment

OCCUPATIONS	20-29 YEARS n	30-39 YEARS n	40-50 YEARS n	PERCENTAGE OF TOTAL (OCCUPATIONS)
Workers, skilled and unskilled	4	5	6	37.5
Sales, business, and white collar	3	6	7	40.0
Professional	1	5	3	22.5
Percentage of total (age)	20	40	40	

Note: Total $N = 40$.

PERSONNEL AND LOCALE

The experiment was conducted on the grounds of Yale University in the elegant interaction laboratory. (This detail is relevant to the perceived legitimacy of the experiment. In further variations, the experiment was dissociated from the university, with consequences for performance.) The role of experimenter was played by a 31-year-old high school teacher of biology. His manner was impassive, and his appearance somewhat stern throughout the experiment. He was dressed in a gray technician's coat. The victim was played by a 47-year-old accountant, trained for the role; he was of Irish-American stock, whom most observers found mild-mannered and likable.

PROCEDURE

One naive subject and one victim (an accomplice) performed in each experiment. A pretext had to be devised that would justify the administration of electric shock by the naive subject. This was effectively accomplished by the cover story. After a general introduction on the presumed relation between punishment and learning, subjects were told:

But actually, we know *very little* about the effect of punishment on learning, because almost no truly scientific studies have been made of it in human beings.

For instance, we don't know how *much* punishment is best for learning—and we don't know how much difference it makes as to who is giving the punishment, whether an adult learns best from a younger or an older person than himself—or many things of that sort.

So in this study we are bringing together a number of adults of different occupations and ages. And we're asking some of them to be teachers and some of them to be learners.

We want to find out just what effect different people have on each other as teachers and learners, and also what effect *punishment* will have on learning in this situation.

Therefore, I'm going to ask one of you to be the teacher here tonight and the other one to be the learner.

Does either of you have a preference?

Subjects then drew slips of paper from a hat to determine who would be the teacher and who would be the learner in the experiment. The drawing was rigged so that the naive subject was always the teacher and the accomplice always the learner. (Both slips contained the word "Teacher.") Immediately after the drawing, the teacher and learner were taken to an adjacent room and the learner was strapped into an "electric chair" apparatus.

The experimenter explained that the straps were to prevent excessive movement while the learner was being shocked. The effect was to make it impossible for him to escape from the situation. An electrode was attached to the learner's wrist, and electrode paste was applied "to avoid blisters and burns." Subjects were told that the electrode was attached to the shock generator in the adjoining room.

In order to improve credibility the experimenter declared, in response to a question by the learner: "Although the shocks can be extremely painful, they cause no permanent tissue damage."

Learning task. The lesson administered by the subject was a paired-associate learning task. The subject read a series of word pairs to the learner, and then read the first word of the pair along with four terms. The learner was to indicate which of the four terms had originally been paired with the first word. He communicated his answer by pressing one of four switches in front of him, which in turn lit up one of four numbered quadrants in an answer-box located atop the shock generator.

Shock generator. The instrument panel consists of 30 lever switches set in a horizontal line. Each switch is clearly labeled with a voltage designation that ranges from 15 to 450 volts. There is a 15-volt increment from one switch to the next going from left to right. In addition, the following verbal designations are clearly indicated for groups of four switches going from left to right: Slight Shock, Moderate Shock, Strong Shock, Very Strong Shock, Intense Shock, Extreme Intensity Shock, Danger: Severe Shock. (Two switches after this last designation are simply marked XXX.)

Upon depressing a switch: a pilot light corresponding to each switch is illuminated in bright red; an electric buzzing is heard; an electric blue light, labeled "voltage energizer," flashes; the dial on the voltage meter swings to the right; various relay clicks are sounded.

The upper left-hand corner of the generator is labeled Shock Generator, Type ZLB, Dyson Instrument Company, Waltham, Mass. Output 15 Volts–450 Volts.

Details of the instrument were carefully handled to insure an appearance of authenticity. The panel was engraved by precision industrial engravers, and all components were of high quality. No subject in the experiment suspected that the instrument was merely a simulated shock generator.[1]

Sample shock. Each naive subject is given a sample shock on the shock generator, prior to beginning his run as teacher. This shock is always 45 volts, and is applied by pressing the third switch of the generator. The shock is applied to the wrist of the naive subject, and has its source in a 45-volt battery wired into the generator. This further convinces the subject of the authenticity of the generator.

Shock instructions. The subject is told to administer a shock to the learner each time he gives a wrong response. Moreover—and this is the key command —the subject is instructed to "move one level higher on the shock generator each time the learner flashes a wrong answer." He is also instructed to announce the voltage level before administering a shock. This serves to continually remind subjects of the increasing intensity of shocks administered to the learner.

Preliminary and regular run. Pretests revealed that the procedure of reading words and administering shocks requires some practice before it can be handled smoothly. Therefore, immediately preceding the regular run, the teacher is given a preliminary series of 10 words to read to the learner. There are 3 neutral words in the practice series (i.e., words that the learner answers correctly), so that shocks are administered for 7 of the words, with the maximum shock at 105 volts (moderate shock). Almost all subjects master the procedure by the time the preliminary run is over.

Subjects are then presented with a second list, and are told that the procedure is the same as for the first list; the experimenter adds, however, "When you get to the bottom of the list, repeat it over again, and continue giving shocks, until the learner has learned all the pairs correctly." The experimenter instructs the subject to "start from 15 volts and increase the shock level one step each time the learner gives a wrong answer."

Feedback from the victim. In all conditions the learner gives a pre-determined set of responses to the word pair test, based on a schedule of approximately three wrong answers to one correct answer. In the present experimental condition no vocal response or other sign of protest is heard from the learner until Shock Level 300 is reached. When the 300-volt shock is administered, the learner pounds on the wall of the room in which he is bound to the electric chair. The pounding can be heard by the subject. From this point on, the learner's answers no longer appear on the four-way panel.

At this juncture, subjects ordinarily turn to the experimenter for guidance. The experimenter instructs the subject to treat the absence of a response as a wrong answer, and to shock the subject according to the usual schedule. He advises the subjects to allow 5–10 seconds before considering no response as a wrong answer, and to increase the shock level one step each time the learner fails to respond correctly. The learner's pounding is repeated after the 315-volt shock is administered; afterwards he is not heard from, nor do his answers reappear on the four-way signal box.

Experimenter feedback. At various points in the experiment the subject may turn to the experimenter for advice on whether he should continue to administer shocks. Or he may indicate that he does not wish to go on. It was important to standardize the experimenter's responses to these inquiries and reactions.

If the subject indicated his unwillingness to go on, the experimenter responded with a sequence of "prods," using as many as necessary to bring the subject into line.

Prod 1: Please continue. *or* Please go on.
Prod 2: The experiment requires that you continue.
Prod 3: It is absolutely essential that you continue.
Prod 4: You have no other choice, you *must* go on.

The prods were always made in sequence: Only if Prod 1 had been unsuccessful, could Prod 2 be used. If the subject refused to obey the experimenter after Prod 4, the experiment was terminated. The experimenter's tone of voice was at all times firm, but not impolite. The sequence was begun anew on each occasion that the subject balked or showed reluctance to follow orders.

Special prods. If the subject asked if the learner was liable to suffer permanent physical injury, the experimenter said: "Although the shocks may be painful, there is no permanent tissue damage, so please go on." [Followed by Prods 2, 3, and 4 if necessary.]

If the subject said that the learner did not want to go on, the experimenter replied: "Whether the learner likes it or not, you must go on until he has learned all the word pairs correctly. So please go on." [Followed by Prods 2, 3, and 4 if necessary.]

DEPENDENT MEASURES

The primary dependent measure for any subject is the maximum shock he administers before he refuses to go any further. In principle this may vary from 0 (for a subject who refuses to administer even the first shock) to 30 (for a subject who administers the highest shock on the generator). A subject who breaks off the experiment at any point prior to administering the thirtieth shock level is termed a *defiant* subject. One who complies with experimental commands fully, and proceeds to administer all shock levels commanded, is termed an *obedient* subject.

Further records. With few exceptions, experimental sessions were recorded on magnetic tape. Occasional photographs were taken through one-way mirrors. Notes were kept on any unusual behavior occurring during the course of the experiments. On occasion, additional observers were directed to write objective descriptions of the subjects' behavior. The latency and duration of shocks were measured by accurate timing devices.

Interview and dehoax. Following the experiment, subjects were interviewed; open-ended questions, projective measures, and attitude scales were employed. After the interview, procedures were undertaken to assure that the subject would leave the laboratory in a state of well being. A friendly reconciliation was arranged between the subject and the victim, and an effort was made to reduce any tensions that arose as a result of the experiment.

Results

PRELIMINARY NOTIONS

Before giving an account of the experimental results, it is instructive to consider how persons predict others will perform when commanded to administer powerful shocks to another person. Fourteen Yale seniors, all psychology majors, were provided with a detailed description of the experimental situation. They were asked to reflect carefully on it, and to predict the behavior of 100 hypothetical subjects. More specifically, they were instructed to plot the distribution of obedience of "100 Americans of diverse occupations, and ranging in age from 20 to 50 years," who were placed in the experimental situation.

There was considerable agreement among the respondents on the expected behavior of hypothetical subjects. All respondents predicted that only an insignificant minority would go through to the end of the shock series. (The estimates ranged from 0 to 3%; i.e., the most "pessimistic" member of the class predicted that of 100 persons, 3 would continue through to the most potent shock available on the shock generator—450 volts.) The class mean was 1.2%. The question was also posed informally to colleagues of the author, and the most general feeling was that few if any subjects would go beyond the designation Very Strong Shock.

RESULT OF EXPERIMENT I

Subjects accept situation. With few exceptions subjects were convinced of the reality of the experimental situation, that they were administering shocks to another person, and the most potent shocks were extremely painful. In the postexperimental interview subjects were asked: "How painful to the learner were the last few shocks that you administered to him?" Subjects were instructed to indicate their answers on a printed 14-point scale ranging from "Not at all painful" to "Extremely painful." The modal response was 14 (Extremely painful) with the mean at 13.42.

Signs of extreme tension. Many subjects showed signs of nervousness in the experimental situation, and especially upon administering the more powerful shocks. In a large number of cases the degree of tension reached extremes that are rarely seen in sociopsychological laboratory studies. Subjects were observed to sweat, tremble, stutter, bite their lips, groan, and dig their fingernails into their flesh. These were characteristic rather than exceptional responses to the experiment.

One sign of tension was the regular occurrence of nervous laughing fits. Fourteen of the 40 subjects showed definite signs of nervous laughter and smiling. The laughter seemed entirely out of place, even bizarre. Full-blown, uncontrollable seizures were observed for 3 subjects. On one occasion we observed a seizure so violently convulsive that it was necessary to call a halt to the experiment. The subject, a 46-year-old encyclopedia salesman, was seriously embarrassed by his untoward and uncontrollable behavior. In the postexperimental interviews subjects took pains to point out that they were not sadistic types, and that the laughter did not mean they enjoyed shocking the victim.

Distribution of scores. It had been conjectured that persons would not, in general, agree to administer shocks beyond the level designated as Very Strong Shock. The distribution of maximum shocks for this experiment is shown in Table 7–2. The obtained distribution of scores deviates radically from the prediction.

Upon command of the experimenter, each of the 40 subjects went beyond the expected breakoff point. No subject stopped prior to administering Shock Level 20. (At this level—300 volts—the victim kicks on the wall and no longer provides answers to the teacher's multiple-choice questions.)

Of the 40 subjects, 5 refused to obey the experimental commands beyond the 300-volt level. Four more subjects administered one further shock, and then refused to go on. Two broke off at the 330-volt level, and 1 each at 345, 360, and 375 volts. Thus a total of 14 subjects defied the experimenter.

TABLE 7-2

Distribution of Breakoff Points

VERBAL DESIGNATION AND VOLTAGE INDICATION	NUMBER OF SUBJECTS FOR WHOM THIS WAS MAXIMUM SHOCK
Slight shock	
15	0
30	0
45	0
60	0
Moderate shock	
75	0
90	0
105	0
120	0
Strong shock	
135	0
150	0
165	0
180	0
Very strong shock	
195	0
210	0
225	0
240	0
Intense shock	
255	0
270	0
285	0
300	5
Extreme intensity shock	
315	4
330	2
345	1
360	1
Danger: severe shock	
375	1
390	0
405	0
420	0
XXX	
435	0
450	26

It is instructive to reprint their remarks at the point of defiance, as transcribed from the tape recordings:

[0124] I think he's trying to communicate, he's knocking. . . . Well it's not fair to shock the guy . . . these are terrific volts. I don't think this is very humane. . . . Oh, I can't go on with this; no, this isn't right. It's a hell of an experiment. The guy is suffering in there. No, I don't want to go on. This is crazy. [Subject refused to administer more shocks.]

[0123] He's banging in there. I'm gonna chicken out. I'd like to continue, but I can't do that to a man. . . . I'm sorry I can't do that to a man. I'll hurt his heart. You take your check. . . . No really, I couldn't do it.

These subjects were frequently in a highly agitated and even angered state. Sometimes, verbal protest was at a minimum, and the subject simply got up from his chair in front of the shock generator, and indicated that he wished to leave the laboratory.

Of the 40 subjects, 26 obeyed the orders of the experimenter to the end, proceeding to punish the victim until they reached the most potent shock available on the shock generator. At that point, the experimenter called a halt to the session. (The maximum shock is labeled 450 volts, and is two steps beyond the designation: Danger: Severe Shock.) Although obedient subjects continued to administer shocks, they often did so under extreme stress. Some expressed reluctance to administer shocks beyond the 300-volt level, and displayed fears similar to those who defied the experimenter; yet they obeyed.

After the maximum shocks had been delivered, and the experimenter called a halt to the proceedings, many obedient subjects heaved sighs of relief, mopped their brows, rubbed their fingers over their eyes, or nervously fumbled cigarettes. Some shook their heads, apparently in regret. Some subjects had remained calm throughout the experiment, and displayed only minimal signs of tension from beginning to end.

Discussion

The experiment yielded two findings that were surprising. The first finding concerns the sheer strength of obedient tendencies manifested in this situation. Subjects have learned from childhood that it is a fundamental breach of moral conduct to hurt another person against his will. Yet, 26 subjects abandon this tenet in following the instructions of an authority who has no special powers to enforce his commands. To disobey would bring no material loss to the subject; no punishment would ensue. It is clear from the remarks and outward behavior of many participants that in punishing the victim they are often acting against their own values. Subjects often expressed deep disapproval of shocking a man in the face of his objections, and others denounced it as stupid and senseless. Yet the majority complied with the experimental commands. This outcome was surprising from two perspectives: first, from the standpoint of predictions made in the questionnaire described earlier. (Here, however, it is possible that the remoteness of the respondents from the actual situation, and the difficulty of conveying to them the concrete details of the experiment, could account for the serious underestimation of obedience.)

But the results were also unexpected to persons who observed the experiment in progress, through one-way mirrors. Observers often uttered expressions of disbelief upon seeing a subject administer more powerful shocks to the victim. These persons had a full acquaintance with the details of the situation, and yet systematically underestimated the amount of obedience that subjects would display.

The second unanticipated effect was the extraordinary tension generated by the procedures. One might suppose that a subject would simply break off or continue as his conscience dictated. Yet, this is very far from what happened. There were striking reactions of tension and emotional strain. One observer related:

I observed a mature and initially poised businessman enter the laboratory smiling and confident. Within 20 minutes he was reduced to a twitching, stuttering wreck, who was rapidly approaching a point of nervous collapse. He constantly pulled on his earlobe, and twisted his hands. At one point he pushed his fist into his forehead and muttered: "Oh God, let's stop it." And yet he continued to respond to every word of the experimenter, and obeyed to the end.

Any understanding of the phenomenon of obedience must rest on an analysis of the particular conditions in which it occurs. The following features of the experiment go some distance in explaining the high amount of obedience observed in the situation.

1. The experiment is sponsored by and takes place on the grounds of an institution of unimpeachable reputation, Yale University. It may be reasonably presumed that the personnel are competent and reputable. The importance of this background authority is now being studied by conducting a series of experiments outside of New Haven, and without any visible ties to the university.

2. The experiment is, on the face of it, designed to attain a worthy purpose —advancement of knowledge about learning and memory. Obedience occurs not as an end in itself, but as an instrumental element in a situation that the subject construes as significant, and meaningful. He may not be able to see its full significance, but he may properly assume that the experimenter does.

3. The subject perceives that the victim has voluntarily submitted to the authority system of the experimenter. He is not (at first) an unwilling captive impressed for involuntary service. He has taken the trouble to come to the laboratory presumably to aid the experimental research. That he later becomes an involuntary subject does not alter the fact that, initially, he consented to participate without qualification. Thus he has in some degree incurred an obligation toward the experimenter.

4. The subject, too, has entered the experiment voluntarily, and perceives himself under obligation to aid the experimenter. He has made a commitment, and to disrupt the experiment is a repudiation of this initial promise of aid.

5. Certain features of the procedure strengthen the subject's sense of obligation to the experimenter. For one, he has been paid for coming to

the laboratory. In part this is canceled out by the experimenter's statement that:

Of course, as in all experiments, the money is yours simply for coming to the laboratory. From this point on, no matter what happens, the money is yours.[2]

6. From the subject's standpoint, the fact that he is the teacher and the other man the learner is purely a chance consequence (it is determined by drawing lots) and he, the subject, ran the same risk as the other man in being assigned the role of learner. Since the assignment of positions in the experiment was achieved by fair means, the learner is deprived of any basis of complaint on this count. (A similar situation obtains in Army units, in which—in the absence of volunteers—a particularly dangerous mission may be assigned by drawing lots, and the unlucky soldier is expected to bear his misfortune with sportsmanship.)

7. There is, at best, ambiguity with regard to the prerogatives of a psychologist and the corresponding rights of his subject. There is a vagueness of expectation concerning what a psychologist may require of his subject, and when he is overstepping acceptable limits. Moreover, the experiment occurs in a closed setting, and thus provides no opportunity for the subject to remove these ambiguities by discussion with others. There are few standards that seem directly applicable to the situation, which is a novel one for most subjects.

8. The subjects are assured that the shocks administered to the subject are "painful but not dangerous." Thus they assume that the discomfort caused the victim is momentary, while the scientific gains resulting from the experiment are enduring.

9. Through Shock Level 20 the victim continues to provide answers on the signal box. The subject may construe this as a sign that the victim is still willing to "play the game." It is only after Shock Level 20 that the victim repudiates the rules completely, refusing to answer further.

These features help to explain the high amount of obedience obtained in this experiment. Many of the arguments raised need not remain matters of speculation, but can be reduced to testable propositions to be confirmed or disproved by further experiments.[3]

The following features of the experiment concern the nature of the conflict which the subject faces.

10. The subject is placed in a position in which he must respond to the competing demands of two persons: the experimenter and the victim. The conflict must be resolved by meeting the demands of one or the other; satisfaction of the victim and the experimenter are mutually exclusive. Moreover, the resolution must take the form of a highly visible action, that of continuing to shock the victim or breaking off the experiment. Thus the subject is forced into a public conflict that does not permit any completely satisfactory solution.

11. While the demands of the experimenter carry the weight of scientific authority, the demands of the victim spring from his personal experience of

pain and suffering. The two claims need not be regarded as equally pressing and legitimate. The experimenter seeks an abstract scientific datum; the victim cries out for relief from physical suffering caused by the subject's actions.

12. The experiment gives the subject little time for reflection. The conflict comes on rapidly. It is only minutes after the subject has been seated before the shock generator that the victim begins his protests. Moreover, the subject perceives that he has gone through but two-thirds of the shock levels at the time the subject's first protests are heard. Thus he understands that the conflict will have a persistent aspect to it, and may well become more intense as increasingly more powerful shocks are required. The rapidity with which the conflict descends on the subject, and his realization that it is predictably recurrent may well be sources of tension to him.

13. At a more general level, the conflict stems from the opposition of two deeply ingrained behavior dispositions: first, the disposition not to harm other people, and second, the tendency to obey those whom we perceive to be legitimate authorities.

NOTES

1. A related technique, making use of a shock generator, was reported by Buss (1961) for the study of aggression in the laboratory. Despite the considerable similarity of technical detail in the experimental procedures, both investigators proceeded in ignorance of the other's work. Milgram provided plans and photographs of his shock generator, experimental procedure, and first results in a report to the National Science Foundation in January 1961. This report received only limited circulation. Buss reported his procedure 6 months later, but to a wider audience. Subsequently, technical information and reports were exchanged. The present article was first received in the Editor's office on December 27, 1961; it was resubmitted with deletions on July 27, 1962.

2. Forty-three subjects, undergraduates at Yale University, were run in the experiment. The results are very similar to those obtained with paid subjects.

3. A series of recently completed experiments employing the obedience paradigm is reported in Milgram (1964).

REFERENCES

Adorno, T., Frenkel-Brunswik, Else, Levinson, D. J., and Sanford, R. N. *The authoritarian personality*. New York: Harper, 1950.

Arendt, H. What was authority? In C. J. Friedrich (Ed.), *Authority*. Cambridge: Harvard University Press, 1958. Pp. 81–112.

Binet, A. *La suggestibilité*. Paris: Schleicher, 1900.

Buss, A. H. *The psychology of aggression.* New York: Wiley, 1961.

Cartwright, S. (Ed.) *Studies in social power.* Ann Arbor: University of Michigan Institute for Social Research, 1959.

Charcot, J. M. *Oeuvres complètes.* Paris: Bureaux du Progrès Médical, 1881.

Frank, J. D. Experimental studies of personal pressure and resistance. *J. gen. Psychol.,* 1944, 30, 23–64.

Friedrich, C. J. (Ed.) *Authority.* Cambridge: Harvard University Press, 1958.

Milgram, S. Dynamics of obedience. Washington: National Science Foundation, 25 January 1961. (Mimeo)

Milgram, S. Some conditions of obedience and disobedience to authority. *Hum. Relat.,* 1964.

Rokeach, M. Authority, authoritarianism, and conformity. In I. A. Berg and B. M. Bass (Eds.), *Conformity and deviation.* New York: Harper, 1961. Pp. 230–257.

Snow, C. P. Either-or. *Progressive,* 1961 (February), 24.

Weber, M. *The theory of social and economic organization.* Oxford: Oxford University Press, 1947.

8

Melvin L. Kohn

BUREAUCRATIC MAN: A PORTRAIT
AND AN INTERPRETATION

Bureaucratic Man: A Portrait and an Interpretation[1]

It is often asserted that bureaucracy makes for unthinking, literalistic conformism. So self-evidently correct does this view seem that Webster's Third New International Dictionary defines bureacracy as, among other things, "a system of administration marked by . . . lack of initiative and flexibility, by indifference to human needs or public opinion, and by a tendency to defer decisions to superiors or to impede action with red tape." Moreover, there is plausible theoretical reason why bureaucracy should have such effects. As Merton (1952) pointed out, the social psychological corollary of the efficiency, rationality, and predictability that Weber prized in bureaucratic organizational practice must be a certain "overconformity" in the behavior of bureaucrats.

But does working in a bureaucracy merely make automatons of men, or are there compensating features that encourage individualistic qualities? Surprisingly, there has been little empirical study of how bureaucracy affects those who spend their working hours in its employ.[2] One objective of this chapter is to ascertain whether "bureaucrats" really are conformist in their values and in their appraisal of social reality, resistant to innovation and change, literalistic in their moral judgments, and inflexible in their thinking.

A further and more important objective is to discover *how* bureaucratization exerts its social psychological impact, whatever that impact may be. The overall structure of the organization can matter for those who work there only through its impact on occupational conditions that bear directly on men's lives—"proximate" occupational conditions, such as closeness of

Melvin L. Kohn, "Bureaucratic Man: A Portrait and an Interpretation," *American Sociological Review* 36 (1971): 461–474. Reprinted by permission of the American Sociological Association and by the author, Melvin L. Kohn.

supervision, time pressure, and the substantive complexity of the work. Bureaucratization affects many of these conditions, but most discussions seem to have arbitrarily focused on only one. In this inquiry, we attempt a systematic examination of the many occupational concomitants of bureaucratization, to see which of them contribute to its impact.

We are not here concerned with the efficiency of bureaucratic organization for getting things done, with the effect of the system on outsiders who must deal with it, nor even with the adequacy of bureaucrats' performance in their occupational roles. We deliberately limit our attention to how (and why) the experience of working in a bureaucracy affects men's values, social orientation, and intellectual functioning.

Research Methods

The research is based on interviews with 3,101 men, representative of all men throughout the United States employed in civilian occupations. These interviews were conducted for us by the National Opinion Research Center in the spring and summer of 1964 (cf. Sudman and Feldman, 1965, for a general description of the sampling methods). About half the interview questions were directed to job, occupation, and career, the remainder to background information, values, and orientation.[3]

BUREAUCRACY: DEFINITION AND INDEX

Our conception of bureaucracy is derived from Weber's classic analysis (cf. Gerth and Mills, 1946: 196–244; Weber, 1947: 329–341). As summarized by Merton (1952: 362), the main characteristics of bureaucratic structure are that: "[B]ureaucracy involves a clear-cut division of integrated activities which are regarded as duties inherent in the office. A system of differentiated controls and sanctions is stated in the regulations. The assignment of roles occurs on the basis of technical qualifications which are ascertained through formalized, impersonal procedures (e.g., examinations). Within the structure of hierarchically arranged authority, the activities of 'trained and salaried experts' are governed by general, abstract, clearly defined rules which preclude the necessity for the issuance of specific instructions for each specific case."

In this study, we are able to index only one of these several dimensions of bureaucracy, the hierarchical organization of authority. This limitation is the price we pay for a sample sufficiently large and diverse to permit a systematic assessment of the occupational conditions attendant on bureaucratization. In studying a multitude of organizations, we cannot assess their structure at firsthand, but must rely on reports by the men who work there, some of whom know little about their employing organization except insofar as it directly impinges on them. The one facet of organizational structure that necessarily impinges on all men is authority.

How much is lost by our inability to index other dimensions is uncertain, because there is contradictory evidence as to whether or not bureaucracy's several dimensions are highly intercorrelated (cf. Hall, Hall and Tittle, 1966; Miller, 1970). But even the research that finds low intercorrelations concludes that the hierarchical organization of authority "may be the central dimension ... of the overall degree of bureaucratization" (Hall, 1963: 37). Moreover, hierarchy of authority is conceptually central: bureaucracies can operate with greater or lesser specialization, with more or less impersonality, with or without a multiplicity of codified rules and procedures, but it is basic to the very idea of bureaucracy that authority be hierarchically organized (cf. Gerth and Mills, 1946: 197; Rheinstein, 1954: 336–337; Blau, 1970: 203). Although our analysis will yield only a partial picture of bureaucratization, that part is fundamental.

We treat the hierarchical organization of authority as operationally equivalent to the number of formal levels of supervision. Although many men do not have a comprehensive view of the authority structure of the firm or organization in which they work, even the man at the bottom of the hierarchy knows whether his boss has a boss and whether that man is the ultimate boss. So we asked the respondents: "Is this [an organization] where everyone is supervised directly by the same man, where there is one level of supervision between the people at the bottom and the top, or where there are two or more levels of supervision between the people at the bottom and the top?"[4]

To distinguish further, we assume that when an organization reaches at least three levels of formal authority, greater differentiation of structure is roughly proportional to size, at least in organizations of about one hundred to one thousand employees—an assumption given some empirical support by Blau's (1970: 205) recent work. (We cannot make the same assumption about organizations of more than one thousand employees; nor would we even trust respondents' estimates of size when the number surpasses a thousand.) Thus, the index of bureaucratization is as follows:

1 One level of supervision.
2 Two levels of supervision.
3 Three or more levels of supervision, fewer than 100 employees.
4 Three or more levels of supervision, 100–999 employees.
5 Three or more levels of supervision, 1,000 or more employees.

This index makes explicit what is in any case implicit: that it is impossible to index hierarchical structure without also indexing size—their correlation (0.71) is too great. For now, we simply accept as empirical fact that bureaucratization implies large size; later we shall attempt to separate the consequences of bureaucratic structure, as such, from those of size.

INDICES OF VALUES, SOCIAL ORIENTATION,
AND INTELLECTUAL FUNCTIONING

Valuation of conformity. By values, we mean standards of desirability—criteria of preference (cf. Williams, 1960: 402–403). Specifically pertinent here, because of the assertion that bureaucracy breeds conformism, is men's relative valuation of self-direction or of conformity to external authority. The index is based on a factor analysis of the men's rankings of the relative desirability of a number of generally valued characteristics.[5] Self-direction, as thus indexed, means regarding as most desirable such characteristics as curiosity, good sense and sound judgment, and the ability to face facts squarely; valuing conformity means giving priority to respectability.

Social orientation. At issue here is whether bureaucratization is conducive to intolerance of nonconformity, literalism in moral positions, and resistance to innovation and change. We attempt to measure all three, by means of the following indices:[6]

1 "Authoritarian conservatism," that is, men's definition of what is socially acceptable—at one extreme, rigid conformance to the dictates of authority and intolerance of nonconformity; at the other extreme, open-mindedness. It is indexed by agreement or disagreement with such assertions as: The most important thing to teach children is absolute obedience to their parents. Young people should not be allowed to read books that are likely to confuse them. There are two kinds of people in the world: the weak and the strong. People who question the old and accepted ways of doing things usually just end up causing trouble.

2 "Criteria of morality," by which we mean a continuum of moral positions, from believing that morality consists of strict adherence to the letter of the law, to holding personally responsible moral standards. This dimension is indexed by answers to the question, Do you believe that it's all right to do whatever the law allows, or are there some things that are wrong even if they are legal? and by agreement or disagreement with such assertions as: It's all right to do anything you want as long as you stay out of trouble. If something works, it doesn't matter whether it's right or wrong. It's all right to get around the law as long as you don't actually break it.

3 "Stance toward change," that is, men's receptiveness or resistance to innovation and change. It is indexed by responses to the questions: Are you generally one of the first people to try out something new or do you wait until you see how it's worked out for other people? are you the sort of person who takes life as it comes or are you working toward some definite goal? and by agreement or disagreement with: It generally works out best to keep on doing things the way they have been done before.

Intellectual functioning. The most serious charge against bureaucracy is that it inhibits men's readiness to think for themselves. As one test of this assertion, we have measured men's intellectual flexibility, evidenced in several appraisals of actual performance deliberately built into the interview. These include cognitive problems that require weighing both sides of an economic or a social issue; a test involving the differentiation of figure from ground in complex color designs; and a test of men's ability to draw a recognizably human figure whose parts fit together in a meaningful whole.[7] We also asked the interviewers to evaluate each respondent's "intelligence"; and we did a simple count of the respondent's propensity to agree with agree-disagree questions. All these we take to reflect, in some substantial part, intellectual flexibility.

As a single index, we use scores based on a factor analysis of these diverse measures. We also extracted from these same data two rotated factors, which provide measures of two distinct aspects of intellectual functioning.[8] One is "perceptual," based primarily on inferences drawn from the figure-drawing and form-perception tests. The other is "ideational," manifested primarily in problem solving and in impressing the interviewer as being an intelligent person.

One final index examines the demands men put on their intellectual resources, no matter how great or limited those resources may be. This index, based on a factor analysis of questions about a wide range of leisure-time activities, focuses on how intellectually demanding are those activities. The relevant factor contrasts spending a large amount of one's leisure time watching TV and reading popular magazines, with engaging in such intellectually active pursuits as going to museums and plays, reading books, and working on hobbies.[9] Some of the latter activities are facilitated by education and income; that will be taken into account in our analyses.

The Social Psychological Concomitants of Bureaucratization

The most difficult problem in assessing the social psychological impact of bureaucratization is deciding who to compare with whom. Who are bureaucrats? The narrowest definition would be that they are the higher, nonelective officialdom of government. But there is reason and ample precedent to expand that definition to include all employees of all organizations that are bureaucratic in structure—blue-collar as well as white-collar workers, employees of profit-making firms and nonprofit organizations as well as government. To whom should bureaucrats be compared—entrepreneurs, employees of nonbureaucratic organizations, or both? Again, the answer is not self-evident.

Rather than make a priori decisions, we prefer to deal with these questions empirically. We begin at the simplest descriptive level, seeing what relationship there may be between bureaucratization, as we have indexed it, and those aspects of values, orientation, and intellectual functioning on which it has been thought to bear.[10] No man employed in a civilian occupation is excluded from this analysis, whether he be employee or entrepreneur, whether he work in a profit-making firm, a nonprofit organization, or a governmental agency.

The correlations[11] of bureaucratization with values, orientation, and intellectual functioning are small, ranging from only 0.05 to 0.17; they are nonetheless impressive, because they consistently contradict preconception (Table 8-1). Men who work in bureaucratic firms or organizations tend to value, not conformity, but self-direction. They are more open-minded, have more personally responsible standards of morality, and are more receptive to change than are men who work in nonbureaucratic organizations. They show greater flexibility in dealing both with perceptual and with ideational problems. They spend their leisure time in more intellectually demanding activities. In short, the findings belie critics' assertions.

Now we can consider what difference it makes if the definitions of bureaucrat and nonbureaucrat be altered.

Ownership. Many discussions of bureaucracy assume or assert that the antithesis of the bureaucrat is the entrepreneur. We find, to the contrary, that entrepreneurs are remarkably similar to bureaucrats, particularly to bureaucrats of comparable occupational status. (The one notable difference is that bureaucrats are more intellectually flexible—another refutation of stereotype.) The real contrast is not between bureaucrats and entrepreneurs, but between both these groups and the employees of nonbureaucratic organizations.

To properly assess the effects of bureaucratization, we must limit the analysis to employees, comparing the employees of bureaucratized organizations to those of nonbureaucratic organizations. Thus limiting the analysis strengthens the contrast between bureaucrats and nonbureaucrats (Table 8-2). Most of the correlations are increased in magnitude, the overall (canonical)[12] correlation increasing by one-third. The picture of the bureaucrat as self-directed and intellectually flexible becomes a little more sharply etched.

Sector of the economy. Just as the entrepreneur has been thought to be the antithesis of the bureaucrat, the government official is usually thought to be its prototype. In fact, employees of government (and of nonprofit organizations) do exemplify the social psychological characteristics associated with bureaucratization: they are more tolerant of nonconformity, have more personally responsible moral standards, evidence greater flexibility in dealing with ideational problems, and make more intellectually demanding use of their leisure time than do employees of equally bureaucratized profit-making firms.

To examine the impact of bureaucratization separately from that stemming from employment in the public or the private sphere, we further limit the analysis to profit-making firms—the one sector of the economy where there is any substantial variation in conditions of bureaucratization. We find (Table 8-2) the correlations of bureaucracy with values, orientation, and intellectual functioning to be nearly the same for employees of profit-making firms as for all employees.[13] Thus, our earlier findings do not simply reflect the bureaucratization of the public sector of the economy, for bureaucracy's influence extends to the private sector as well.

Occupational position. Many discussions of bureaucracy have been addressed only to its salaried, its white-collar, or its professional staff. It is therefore necessary to see if bureaucratization bears the same relationship to values,

TABLE 8-1

Values, Social Orientation, and Intellectual Functioning by Bureaucracy—Total Sample

	MEAN SCORES FOR:									
	VALUES AND ORIENTATION				INTELLECTUAL FUNCTIONING					
	Valuation of self-direction/conformity (+ = conformist)	Authoritarian conservatism (+ = authoritarian)	Criteria of morality (+ = personally responsible)	Stance toward change (+ = receptive)	Perceptual component of intellectual flexibility (+ = flexible)	Ideational component of intellectual flexibility (+ = flexible)	Overall index of intellectual flexibility (+ = flexible)	Intellectual demandingness of leisure-time activities (+ = demanding)	Canonical correlation[a]	Number of cases[b]
Index of Bureaucracy:										
One level of supervision	1.01	0.91	−0.59	−0.57	−1.47	−0.74	−2.17	−0.49		(840)
Two levels	−0.12	0.16	−0.63	0.01	−0.69	−1.06	−2.34	−1.22		(121)
Three or more levels:										
< 100 employees	0.23	0.12	0.50	0.33	0.68	−0.03	0.15	−0.32		(307)
100-999 employees	−0.97	−0.36	0.08	0.13	0.26	1.07	0.54	−0.07		(456)
1,000 + employees	−0.61	−1.29	0.66	0.68	1.20	1.82	1.78	1.35		(1,023)
Degree of Association (Eta):										
Linear component of bureaucracy	.07**	.09**	.05**	.05*	.11**	.11**	.17**	.08**	.17**	
All components of bureaucracy	.08**	.09**	.06	.05	.11**	.12**	.17**	.09**	.17**	

[a] The canonical correlation excludes the overall index of intellectual flexibility, because it is a linear function of the two component indices.

[b] 354 respondents for whom data are incomplete are excluded from this and subsequent tables.

$* = p < 0.05.$

$** = p < 0.01.$

TABLE 8-2

*Correlations of Bureaucracy with Values, Social Orientation, and
Intellectual Functioning — for Specified Samples*

CORRELATIONS[a] OF BUREAUCRACY AND:	ALL MEN EMPLOYED IN CIVILIAN OCCUPA- TIONS (OWNERS AND EMPLOYEES)	EMPLOY- EES ONLY	EMPLOYEES OF PROFIT- MAKING FIRMS		
			ALL	WHITE- COLLAR	BLUE- COLLAR
Values and Orientation					
Valuation of self-direction/ conformity	.07**	.09**	.08**	.07*	.09**
Authoritarian conservatism	.09**	.09**	.07**	.08*	.00
Criteria of morality	.05**	.11**	.11**	.00	.15**
Stance toward change	.05*	.09**	.10**	.07*	.09**
Intellectual Functioning					
Perceptual component of intellectual flexibility	.11**	.09**	.08**	.08*	.06*
Ideational component	.11**	.17**	.18**	.14**	.14**
Overall index of intellectual flexibility	.17**	.19**	.19**	.17**	.13**
Intellectual demandingness of leisure-time activities	.08**	.15**	.15**	.07*	.13**
Canonical correlation[b]	.17**	.23**	.24**	.19**	.23**
Number of cases	(2,747)	(2,268)	(1,855)	(702)	(1,140)

[a]*Eta* or the canonical correlation for the linear component of bureaucracy.

[b]The canonical correlation excludes the overall index of intellectual flexibility (see note to Table 8-1).

* = $p < 0.05$

** = $p < 0.01$

Note: Mean scores are not presented in this table. The direction of all relationships is the same as indicated by the mean scores in Table 8-1.

orientation, and intellectual functioning for blue-collar as for white-collar employees. To do this, we examine the two groups separately, recognizing that in so doing we partially control variables correlated with occupational position, such as education, the substantive complexity of the work, and the job protections attendant on unionization. Even so (Table 8-2), bureaucracy's social psychological correlates are similar for blue-collar and for white-collar workers.[14] Moreover, the canonical correlation is as strong for blue-collar as for white-collar workers. Thus, any explanation of the social psychological impact of bureaucratization must apply to the entire work force, not just to the white-collar portion. It is true, of course, that the explanation need not be the same for both groups.

We conclude that bureaucratization bears essentially the same relationship to values, orientation, and intellectual functioning wherever and to whomever it occurs. Why? What is there about working in a bureaucratic organization that makes men more self-directed, open to change, and intellectually flexible?

We must also ask: why are the correlations so small? The comparable correlations for several other aspects of occupation are much stronger (cf. Kohn, 1969: 165–182). Does the small size of bureaucracy's correlations imply that we have used an inadequate index, or does bureaucratization have a weaker impact than had been supposed?

Explaining Bureaucracy's Impact

Bureaucrats and nonbureaucrats are drawn from rather different segments of the population. Bureaucrats necessarily live where large firms are located: disproportionately in big cities along the Great Lakes and in the Northeastern and Pacific states. Not only are they now urban, but they grew up in urban places. Their forebears are more likely to have come from northern or western Europe than from southern or eastern Europe. Few are black; few are Jews. They are disproportionately Catholic. Those who are Protestant are a little more likely to be members of large, established denominations than of smaller sects. Most notable of all, bureaucrats are more highly educated than are nonbureaucats.

Of all these differences in the composition of bureaucratic and nonbureaucratic work forces, only education seems to matter for explaining why bureaucrats differ from nonbureaucrats in values, orientation, and intellectual functioning (Table 8–3). That is, statistically controlling education markedly reduces bureaucracy's impact: the canonical correlation is reduced by nearly 30 percent and the correlations with authoritarian conservatism and the specifically perceptual component of intellectual flexibility are reduced to statistical nonsignificance. Additionally controlling any or all of the other measures of social background reduces the correlations little more than does controlling education alone. Thus, education is clearly implicated in explaining why bureaucrats differ from nonbureaucrats; but aside from bureaucracies' employing more educated men, the composition of the work force appears to have little explanatory relevance.

Important though education may be, it can provide only a partial explanation of the differences between bureaucrats and nonbureaucrats. That is, even with education statistically controlled, bureaucrats are found to value self-direction more highly than do nonbureaucrats, to have more personally demanding moral standards, to be more receptive to change, to be intellectually more flexible (especially in dealing with ideational problems), and to spend their leisure time in more intellectually demanding activities. The explanation of these differences must lie either in bureaucracies' somehow recruiting more self-directed, intellectually flexible people (a possibility to which we shall return), or in bureaucracies' subjecting their employees to occupational conditions that foster these social psychological attributes.

TABLE 8-3

*Effects on Bureaucracy Correlations of Controlling Education, Region,
Size of Community, Race, National Background, Religion, and Rurality of Childhood
(Limited to Employees of Profit-making Firms)*

	INITIAL CORRELA-TION WITH BUREAUC-RACY[a]	PARTIAL CORRELATION WITH BUREAUCRACY, CONTROLLING:	
		EDUCA-TION	EDUCATION + REGION, SIZE OF COMMUNITY, RACE, NATIONAL BACK-GROUND, RELIGION, AND RURALITY OF CHILDHOOD
Values and Orientation			
Valuation of self-direction/ conformity	.08**	.07**	.06*
Authoritarian conservatism	.07**	.00	.01
Criteria of morality	.11**	.09**	.07**
Stance toward change	.10**	.07**	.06*
Intellectual Functioning			
Perceptual component of intellectual flexibility	.08**	.05	.03
Ideational component	.18**	.11**	.10**
Overall index of intellectual flexibility	.19**	.11**	.09**
Intellectual demandingness of leisure-time activities	.15**	.08**	.09**
Canonical correlation[b]	.24**	.17**	.16**
Number of cases = 1,855 in columns 1 and 2 and 1,807 in column 3			

[a]*Eta*, or the canonical correlation, appropriately controlled, for the linear component of bureaucracy.

[b]The canonical correlation excludes the overall index of intellectual flexibility (see note to Table 8-1).

$* = p < 0.05$

$** = p < 0.01$

Note: Mean scores are not presented in this table. The direction of all relationships is the same as indicated by the mean scores in Table 8-1.

Bureaucratization does make for widespread and in some instances substantial differences in the conditions of occupational life, few of them attributable to educational disparities and most of them applicable (although not always in equal degree) to both the white-collar and blue-collar work forces (Table 8–4). These are, principally, that the employees of bureaucracies tend to work at substantively more complex jobs than do other men of comparable educational level,[15] but under conditions of somewhat closer supervision;[16] to work under an externally imposed pressure of time that results in their having to think faster; to work a shorter week; to work in company of, but not necessarily in harness with, co-workers; to face greater competition; to

145

TABLE 8-4

The Occupational Concomitants of Employment in Bureaucratic Organizations
(Limited to Employees of Profit-making Firms)

	CORRELA-TION[a] WITH BUREAUCRACY	PARTIAL CORRELA-TION, EDU-CATION CONTROLLED	WHITE-COLLAR EMPLOYEES ONLY	BLUE-COLLAR EMPLOYEES ONLY
1. Substantive Complexity	.40**	.31**	.37**	.33**
2. Supervision				
a. Closeness of supervision	.02	.05*	.04	.04
b. Positional disparity between man and his effective supervisor	.17**	.18**	.13**	.18**
3. Time Pressure				
a. Frequency of time pressure	.10**	.05	.10**	.06*
b. Determinants of time pressure: workflow, not own volition	.10**	.13**	.12*	.19**
c. Consequences of time pressure: think faster, not make faster movements or work longer hours	.19**	.14**	.21**	.16**
4. Average Hours Worked per Week	−.28**	−.29**	−.20**	−.29**
5. Interpersonal Setting				
a. Time spent in the company of five or more co-workers	.22**	.24**	.11**	.27**
b. Time spent alone	−.12**	−.13**	−.03	−.15**
c. Participation in coordinated workteam	.02	.04	.01	.04
6. Amount of Competition	.17**	.13**	.19**	.11**
7. Job Protection				
a. Tenure, or seniority guaranteed by union contract	.37**	.42**	.16**	.56**
b. Formal grievance procedures	.39**	.45**	.20**	.57**
c. Sick pay	.33**	.30**	.25**	.34**
d. Job protection: overall index	.50**	.52**	.30**	.60**
8. Income and Income Fluctuations				
a. Job income	.27**	.21**	.19**	.31**
b. Fluctuations in income	−.04*	−.02	−.07*	.02
9. Routinization of Work	.08**	.09**	−.18**	.15**

[a]*Eta*, or (in the case of 1, 3b, 3c, 7d, and 9) the canonical correlation, for the linear component of bureaucracy. In column 2, a partial correlation, controlled on education, is reported. Columns 3 and 4 report total correlations, computed for the appropriate subgroups. In lieu of presenting a multitude of mean scores, we have arbitrarily used signs to indicate the direction of relationships.

  * = $p < 0.05$
  ** = $p < 0.01$

Note: N's vary from 1,826 to 2,059 for the sample of all employees of profit-making firms, from 646 to 749 for the white-collar subsample, and from 1,169 to 1,289 for the blue-collar subsample.

enjoy much greater job protections;[17] and to earn more than other men of similar educational background (even when in jobs of comparable occupational status).

In assessing the possible explanatory relevance of these occupational conditions, we statistically control education throughout[18] and limit the analysis to those social psychological correlates of bureaucracy that remain significant even with education controlled. From one point of view, this procedure gives undue weight to education, which may matter primarily because it is a precondition for certain types of jobs—substantively complex jobs, for example. But since most men come to their jobs only after completing their educations, it is incumbent on us to show that occupational conditions matter above and beyond any effect that might be attributed to education.

Three of the occupational concomitants of bureaucracy—job protections, income, and substantive complexity—prove to have substantial pertinence (Table 8–5). The combined effect of controlling all three is to reduce the canonical correlation of bureaucracy with values, orientation, and intellectual functioning by two-thirds and to render this and all the individual correlations statistically nonsignificant.

Further analysis, using multiple regression techniques,[19] shows that all three occupational conditions contribute independently to bureaucracy's social psychological impact (Table 8–6). Job protections contribute notably to bureaucracy's relationships with social orientation, but also to its relationship with the overall measure of intellectual flexibility. It thus appears that men who are protected from some of the dangers that change might bring are less fearful of the new and the different, are better able to accept personal responsibility for their acts, and are even able to make fuller use of their intellectual talents. Substantive complexity is more specifically pertinent for explaining bureaucrats' flexibility in dealing with *ideational* problems and their making intellectually demanding use of leisure time. The experience of working at substantively complex jobs thus appears to have direct carryover to the use of one's intellectual resources in nonoccupational endeavors. And job income is most pertinent for explaining bureaucrats' high valuation of self-direction; the higher income enjoyed by employees of bureaucracies appears to facilitate their feeling sufficiently in control of their lives to think self-direction an attainable goal.

We conclude, then, that job protections, substantive complexity, and income all contribute to, and together may largely explain, the social psychological impact of bureaucratization. Separate analyses of the white-collar and blue-collar work forces do indicate, though, that job protections contribute more to bureaucracy's impact on blue-collar workers, substantive complexity to its impact on white-collar workers. It would seem that the job protections afforded by bureaucracy matter most for men in occupations that do not already enjoy a substantial measure of security. Substantive complexity comes to the fore only when some degree of security has been attained.

TABLE 8-5

Effects of Controlling the Principal Occupational Concomitants of Bureaucracy
(Limited to Employees of Profit-making Firms)

VALUES, ORIENTATION, AND INTELLECTUAL FUNCTIONING	Partial correlation with bureaucracy, education controlled[a]	PERCENTAGE REDUCTION IN THIS PARTIAL CORRELATION WHEN CONTROLLING:								
		Job protections	Job income	Substantive complexity	Amount of competition	Time pressure	Hours of work	Interpersonal setting	Closeness of supervision and positional disparity	Job protections, income, and substantive complexity
Valuation of self-direction/conformity	.07**	17	20	14	−06	08	20	−03	06	44
Criteria of morality	.09**	50	24	25	−02	05	12	00	−08	85
Stance toward change	.07**	39	19	08	21	10	−19	10	12	80
Ideational component of intellectual flexibility	.11**	24	21	29	05	03	01	−06	−03	64
Overall index of intellectual flexibility	.11**	32	12	16	05	−05	−07	−01	−05	66
Intellectual demandingness of leisure-time activities	.08**	11	35	33	00	05	01	−01	05	71
Canonical correlation	.17**	29	21	18	03	02	00	00	−01	66
Number of cases	(1,855)	(1,774)	(1,662)	(1,823)	(1,829)	(1,846)	(1,762)	(1,761)	(1,804)	(1,569)

[a]From Table 8-3. In the computations that follow, these partial correlations (*etas*) have in each instance been recomputed for all respondents for whom the relevant occupational data are known.

* = $p < 0.05$

** = $p < 0.01$

TABLE 8-6

Summary of Multiple Regression Analyses of the Independent Effects of Controlling Occupational Conditions

VALUES, ORIENTATION, AND INTELLECTUAL FUNCTIONING	STANDARDIZED BETA-COEFFICIENT[a] FOR BUREAUCRACY			INDEPENDENT CONTRIBUTION OF EACH OCCUPATIONAL CONDITION TO REDUCING BETA-COEFFICIENT FOR BUREAUCRACY[b]							
	Uncontrolled	Controlled on education	Controlled on education and all relevant occupational variables[c]	Job protections	Job income	Substantive complexity	Amount of competition	Time pressure	Hours of work	Interpersonal setting	Closeness of supervision
Valuation of self-direction/											
conformity	.074	.051	.027	.004	.011	.001	-.008	.000	.012	-.005	-.004
Criteria of morality	.109	.083	.010	.021	.005	.008	-.005	.000	.003	-.006	-.012
Stance toward change	.099	.063	.003	.030	.000	.016	.009	-.001	-.004	.004	-.006
Ideational component of intellectual flexibility	.181	.085	.041	.012	.004	.022	.002	.000	.004	-.008	-.005
Overall index of intellectual flexibility	.185	.091	.056	.018	.002	.012	.003	-.001	.000	-.007	-.002
Intellectual demandingness of leisure-time activities	.138	.059	.009	.007	.011	.024	-.003	-.001	.005	-.002	.000

[a]Signs omitted.

[b]The amount by which the standardized beta-coefficient for bureaucracy would be raised (or lowered) if the given occupational variable were not included in the equation.

[c]That is, controlled on all occupational variables whose inclusion in the equation reduces the beta-coefficient for bureaucracy.

Discussion

Observers of bureaucracy, impressed by its need to coordinate many people's activities, have assumed that a primary effect of bureaucratization must be to suppress employees' individuality. We have found, to the contrary, that bureaucratization is consistently, albeit not strongly, associated with greater intellectual flexibility, higher valuation of self-direction, greater openness to new experience, and more personally responsible moral standards. In part, this seems to result from bureaucracies' drawing on a more educated work force. In larger part, it seems to be a consequence of the occupational conditions attendant on bureaucratization—far greater job protections, somewhat higher levels of income, and substantively more complex work. Job protections matter particularly for bureaucracy's impact on blue-collar workers; substantive complexity, for its impact on white-collar workers.

There are four issues that our data do not fully resolve. The first is whether the effects we have attributed to the experience of working in a bureaucratic organization might really be an artifact of what types of people bureaucracies recruit. We have found that the educational disparities between bureaucratic and nonbureautic work forces cannot provide a sufficient explanation, and that other disparities in the social and demographic compositions of the work forces have little relevance. But there remains the possibility that bureaucracies may hold a special attraction for self-directed, intellectually flexible men who are receptive to innovation and change. Perhaps, for example, intellectually active people seek jobs in bureaucratic organizations because that is where challenging work is to be found.

We cannot test this interpretation, because we have no information about the men's values, orientation, and intellectual functioning prior to their employment in bureaucratic (or nonbureaucratic) organizations.[20] There are, however, two reasons to doubt that "self-selection" can explain our findings. The interpretation assumes that men have more complete and accurate knowledge of working conditions in bureaucratic organizations, before starting to work there, than is usually the case—especially in light of widely held stereotypes about bureaucracy. The interpretation also assumes that men have a fuller range of choice in deciding on jobs than is usually the case—particularly when one remembers that our findings apply to men of all educational and skill levels and that many types of jobs can be found only in bureaucratic or only in nonbureaucratic settings. It would be more consonant both with our broader knowledge of occupational realities and with the specific data of this study to conclude that bureaucrats differ from nonbureaucrats primarily because they have experienced different conditions of occupational life.

The second issue is why the correlations are so small. We may have underestimated their size by limiting this investigation to one dimension of bureaucracy or by employing an inadequate index of that dimension. Our data, however, suggest an alternative explanation: that bureaucracy really does have a smaller social psychological impact than had been assumed. The psychologically most potent occupational conditions are those that maximize men's opportunities for self-direction in their work: freedom from close supervision, substantively complex work, and a varied array of activities (cf. Kohn, 1969: 139–167). Bureaucracies do provide substantively complex work. They conspicuously fail to provide freedom from close supervision. And although they provide a wide variety of complexly interrelated jobs to their white-collar workers, they tend to entrap their blue-collar workers in a routinized flow of simply organized tasks. It is ironic and probably self-defeating that bureaucracies hire educated men, give them complex jobs to perform, and then fail to give them as much opportunity for occupational self-direction as their educational attainments and the needs of the work allow. To this important extent, they are surely wasteful of human talent.

The third issue is whether our findings reflect bureaucratization or only size. Two of the three occupational conditions that have come to the fore in our analyses—income and substantive complexity—may be only ancillary features of bureaucracy. It is not intrinsic to bureaucratic organization that it pay its employees more or that its work be substantively more complex. These are, instead, products of the very conditions that give rise to bureaucracy itself —large size, technology, the need for highly skilled employees, and the problems of coordination, planning, and record keeping that result from size and technology. Job protections, though, are an essential feature of bureaucracy. As Weber long ago recognized (cf. Gerth and Mills, 1946:202–203), it is necessary to bureaucratic organization that its authority be circumscribed. The principal findings of this research—that job protections are central to the impact of bureaucratization on its employees—cannot be attributed to size alone; they necessarily reflect the structural essentials of bureaucracy.[21] (It is perhaps ironic that these structural essentials may be more important for the blue-collar work force, whom theories of bureaucracy have largely ignored, than for the white-collar work force.)

Last, and most important, is the issue of whether our focus on one dimension of bureaucratic structure—the hierarchical organization of authority— produces so partial a picture as to be misleading. Had we also studied such facets of bureaucracy as impersonality of procedures or specificity of rules, proximate occupational conditions other than (or in addition to) job protections, income, and substantive complexity might have come to the fore. The picture we have presented may be seriously incomplete.

Even if this is true, our findings are so at variance with common presuppositions as to require a rethinking of how bureaucracy impinges on its employees. Many writings about bureaucracy assert that a system based on the hierarchical organization of authority necessarily imposes tight discipline, leaving little leeway for initiative. Our data do indicate a tendency in this direction—employees of bureaucratic firms are supervised a little more closely than are other men of their educational levels, and close supervision does have the constricting effects ascribed to it. But the propensity of bureaucracies to supervise employees too closely is more than offset by the protections it affords from the arbitrary actions of superordinates.

Bureaucracies must ensure that superordinate officials are limited in what facets of their subordinates' behavior they are allowed to control and how they may exercise that control: superordinates cannot dismiss subordinates at will, and questionable actions can be appealed to adjudicatory agencies. The power of nonbureaucratic organizations over their employees is more complete and may be more capricious. Thus, the alternative to bureaucracy's circumscribed authority is likely to be, not less authority, but personal, potentially arbitrary authority. What is notable about bureaucratic practice is not how closely authority is exercised, but how effectively it is circumscribed.

NOTES

1. I am indebted for critical advice and essential help to my associates, Carmi Schooler, Lindsley Williams, Elizabeth Howell, Margaret Renfors, Carrie Schoenbach, and John Westine; and, for carrying out the survey on which the research is based, to Paul Sheatsley, Eve Weinberg, and the staff of the National Opinion Research Center.

2. The few relevant studies give apparently contradictory results. Whyte (1956) argued that large corporations co-opt junior executives, to the detriment of their individuality; and Miller and Swanson (1958) found that bureaucratization leads parents to deemphasize self-reliance in favor of accommodation as values for children; but Blau (1955: 183–200) found that the job securities provided to the employees of a government bureaucracy generate favorable attitudes toward change; and Bonjean and Grimes (1970) failed to find any consistent evidence to support the hypothesized relationship between bureaucracy and alienation.

3. For the full interview schedule, and further information on sample and research design, cf. Kohn, 1969: 235–264.

4. Men who told us that they work in a firm or organization employing fewer than ten people were not asked about supervisory structure, because pretest interviews had shown these men to take it so completely for granted that there can be only one boss that they find such questions baffling. We simply assume that such firms have only one level of supervision. Correspondingly, we assume that firms or organizations employing as many as 500 people must have at least three levels of formal authority.

5. For the derivation of this index, cf. Kohn, 1969: 73–75 or Kohn and Schooler, 1969: 664–666. This and subsequent factor analyses are orthogonal principal component factor analyses, rotated to simple structure through the varimax procedure, based on the computer program developed by Clyde, *et al.* (1966: 15–16). The procedure used for calculating factor scores (cf. Ryder, 1965) preserves the orthogonality of the factors.

6. The indices that follow are based on a factor analysis of a set of fifty-seven questions, mainly of the "agree-disagree" and "how often?" types. For the derivation of these indices, cf. Kohn, 1969: 265–269 or Kohn and Schooler, 1969: 666–669.

7. Specifically, we asked: "Suppose you wanted to open a hamburger stand and there were two locations available. What questions would you consider, in deciding

which of the two locations offers a better business opportunity?" and "What are all the arguments you can think of for and against allowing cigarette commercials on TV? First, can you think of arguments *for* allowing cigarette commercials on TV? And can you think of arguments *against* allowing cigarette commercials on TV?" The perceptual test consists of a portion of Witkin's (1962) Embedded Figures Test, selected by Witkin. The Figure-drawing Test (cf. Witkin, 1962: 117–129) consists simply of asking the respondent to draw a figure of a man on a standard-size card with a standard pencil. Respondents are reassured that artistic ability is not required. The meaningful coherence of the figure is what we appraise.

8. The factor loadings for the single index are: hamburger-stand problem, 0.37; cigarette-commercials problem, 0.41; Embedded Figures Test, 0.67; Draw-A-Man Test: summary score, 0.75; Goodenough estimate of intelligence, based on the Draw-A-Man Test (cf. Witkin, 1962: 127–129), 0.78; interviewer's rating of respondent's intelligence, 0.60; "agree" score, .52. In the two-factor solution, the first factor is based primarily on the Draw-A-Man Test (summary score, −0.91; Goodenough estimate of intelligence, −0.91) and the Embedded Figures Test (−0.43). The second factor is based on the interviewer's appraisal of the respondent's intelligence (0.69), the cigarette-commercials problem (0.61), the respondent's "agree" score (−0.56), the hamburger-stand problem (0.54), and the Embedded Figures Test (0.52).

9. The factor loadings are: frequency of visits to plays, concerts, and museums (−0.60); number of books read in the past six months (−0.54); time spent working on hobbies (−0.35); amount of magazine reading (−0.61); and time spent watching television (0.35).

10. This and subsequent analyses of variance are based on the computer program initially developed by Dean J. Clyde, Elliot M. Cramer, and Richard J. Sherin (1966: 20–28) and further developed by Cramer. The test of statistical significance is the F-ratio. We are treating all dependent variables in these analyses as interval scales (for justification, cf. Blalock, 1964; Cohen, 1965; Labovitz, 1967).

For more general discussions of the logical bases of the statistical procedures we have used, cf. Blalock, 1960, Chapters 15–21; Blalock, 1964; Cohen, 1968.

11. The measure of association that we use is *eta,* the square root of the ratio of the "between groups" sum of squares to the total sum of squares, as calculated in an analysis of variance. When one deals with the linear component of the independent variable, *eta* is identical to the product-moment correlation coefficient, except that its sign is always positive—the direction of relationships can be determined only by an examination of the means. (Cf. Blalock, 1960: 266–269; Cohen, 1965; Peters and Van Voorhis, 1940: 312–324 and 353–357.)

It is apparent in Table 8–1 (and has been confirmed in more detailed analyses) that the *etas* for the linear component of bureaucratization, in its relationships with the several aspects of values, orientation, and intellectual functioning that we have investigated, are nearly as large as those for all components. It is therefore appropriate to treat our index of bureaucratization as an essentially linear variable.

12. The canonical correlation is a multiple correlation of one or a set of independent variables with a set of dependent variables. More precisely, it is the maximum correlation between linear functions of the two sets of variables (cf. Cooley and Lohnes, 1962: 35).

13. It could hardly be otherwise, since employees of profit-making firms constitute two-thirds of the total sample. For the same reason, all conclusions drawn from analyses of this subsample apply as well to the sample as a whole. We focus on employees of profit-making firms, not to secure different empirical findings, but for conceptual clarity. There is no advantage in further focusing the analysis on particular types of industries, for bureaucracy has essentially the same social psychological correlates in

all types of industry. Moreover, excluding nonurban occupations from the analysis has no noticeable effect.

14. The index of occupational position is taken from Hollingshead and Redlich, 1958: 387–397. For validation of the index, cf. Kohn, 1969: 13–15.

It should also be noted that the social psychological correlates of bureaucracy are essentially the same regardless of men's own positions in the supervisory hierarchy (as measured by the number of subordinates they have).

15. The index of substantive complexity is a linear combination of seven constituent indices, which measure the complexity of the man's work with data, with things, and with people, the overall complexity of his job, and the amount of time he spends working with data, with things, and with people. The first three of these indices are based on those of the third edition of the *Dictionary of Occupational Titles* (U.S. Department of Labor, 1965). For a discussion of the concept and index of substantive complexity, cf. Kohn, 1969: 139–140, 153–155, 271–276.

16. Closeness of supervision is indexed by a Guttman Scale based on five questions about how much latitude men's supervisors allow and how supervisory control is exercised (cf. Kohn, 1969: 153). Note, too, that many employees of bureaucracies are effectively supervised by men who are one or two steps removed from them in formal position.

17. In particular, bureaucrats are more likely to enjoy the basic job protections given by tenure or by contractual guarantees based on seniority; by the existence of formal grievance procedures; and by sick pay. These correlations are more pronounced for blue-collar than for white-collar workers, and are linked to the greater unionization of the blue-collar work force. Even for nonunion and for white-collar workers, though, job protections are decidedly greater in bureaucratic firms. (And they prove to be as important for younger as for older men.)

It is noteworthy that the critical difference bureaucratization makes is not in the *risks* to which men are subject but in the *protections* that their jobs afford. Bureaucrats are no less exposed to occupational risk than are nonbureaucrats, but they are better protected, should those eventualities occur.

18. Since bureaucrats are more educated than are nonbureaucrats, they are necessarily higher in social class position, too. But we regard education, not class, as the appropriate variable to control in these analyses, because education is what men bring to the job. Other components of class, notably occupational position, are conferred by the job. (In fact, if education is controlled, occupational position has little importance.)

19. The multiple regression program employed here is that by Norman H. Nie, Dale H. Bent, and C. Hadlai Hull (1968: Chap. 15). To do this analysis, we constructed a single index of job protections by adding the dichotomized scores for job security, grievance procedures, and sick pay, giving each equal weight. For a single index of substantive complexity, we used scores based on a factor analysis of the seven constituent elements. The results shown in Table 8–6 are based on the standardized beta-coefficients for bureaucracy; analyses using the unstandardized beta-coefficients yield essentially the same results.

20. We do find, though, that the correlations of bureaucracy with values, orientation, and intellectual functioning gradually increase in size, as men have worked for their present employer for greater and greater lengths of time (at least until approximately six years, when the correlations begin to decline). The picture is the same whether or not age and education are controlled. But this evidence is hardly definitive, for most of the men have had previous jobs, and we do not know whether these jobs were in bureaucratic or nonbureaucratic organizations.

21. It is hardly crucial to the argument (but nonetheless reassuring) that the correlations of bureaucracy with all our principal indices of values, orientation, and intel-

lectual functioning remain statistically significant not only when we employ a truncated version of the bureaucracy index that makes no use of information about the size of the organization, but even when we impose the extreme restriction of statistically controlling size of organization.

REFERENCES

Bialock, Hubert M., Jr. 1960. *Social Statistics.* New York: McGraw-Hill.
———— 1964. *Causal Inferences in Nonexperimental Research.* Chapel Hill: University of North Carolina Press.
Blau, Peter M. 1955. *The Dynamics of Bureaucracy: A Study of Interpersonal Relations in Two Government Agencies.* Chicago: University of Chicago Press.
———— 1970. "A Formal Theory of Differentiation in Organizations." *American Sociological Review* 35 (April): 201–218.
Bonjean, Charles M., and Michael D. Grimes. 1970. "Bureaucracy and Alienation: A Dimensional Approach." *Social Forces* 48 (March): 365–373.
Clyde, Dean J., Elliot M. Cramer, and Richard J. Sherin. 1966. *Multivariate Statistical Programs.* Coral Gables, Fla.: Biometry Laboratory of the University of Miami.
Cohen, Jacob. 1965. "Some Statistical Issues in Psychological Research." Pp. 95–121 in Benjamin B. Wolman (ed.), *Handbook of Clinical Psychology.* New York: McGraw-Hill.
———— 1968. "Multiple Regression As a General Data-Analytic System." *Psychological Bulletin* 70 (December): 426–443.
Cooley, William W., and Paul R. Lohnes. 1962. *Multivariate Procedures for the Behavioral Sciences.* New York: John Wiley.
Gerth, H. H., and C. Wright Mills (eds.). 1946. *From Max Weber: Essays in Sociology.* New York: Oxford University Press.
Hall, Richard H. 1963. "The Concept of Bureaucracy: An Empirical Assessment." *American Journal of Sociology* 69 (July): 32–40.
Hall, Richard H., and Charles R. Tittle. 1966. "A Note on Bureaucracy and Its 'Correlates' ". *American Journal of Sociology* 72 (November): 267–272.
Hollingshead, August B., and Frederick C. Redlich. 1958. *Social Class and Mental Illness: A Community Study.* New York: John Wiley.
Kohn, Melvin L. 1969. *Class and Conformity: A Study in Values.* Homewood, Ill.: The Dorsey Press.
Kohn, Melvin L., and Carmi Schooler. 1969. "Class, Occupation, and Orientation." *American Sociological Review* 34 (October): 659–678.
Labovitz, Sanford. 1967. "Some Observations on Measurement and Statistics." *Social Forces* 46 (December): 151–160.
Merton, Robert K. 1952. "Bureaucratic Structure and Personality." Pp. 361–371 in Robert K. Merton, *et al.* (eds.), *Reader in Bureaucracy.* Glencoe, Ill.: The Free Press.
Miller, Daniel R., and Guy E. Swanson. 1958. *The Changing American Parent: A Study in the Detroit Area.* New York: John Wiley.
Miller, Jon P. 1970. "Social-psychological Implications of Weber's Model of Bureaucracy: Relations among Expertise, Control, Authority, and Legitimacy." *Social Forces* 49 (September): 91–102.
Nie, Norman H., Dale H. Bent, and C. Hadlai Hull. 1968. *Statistical Package for the*

Social Sciences: Provisional Users Manual. Chicago: National Opinion Research Center (mimeo).

Peters, Charles C., and Walter R. Van Voorhis. 1940. *Statistical Procedures and Their Mathematical Bases.* New York: McGraw-Hill.

Rheinstein, Max (ed.). 1954. *Max Weber on Law in Economy and Society.* Cambridge, Mass.: Harvard University Press.

Ryder, Robert G. 1965. "Scoring Orthogonally Rotated Factors." *Psychological Reports* 16 (June): 701–74.

Sudman, Seymour, and Jacob J. Feldman. 1965. "Sample Design and Field Procedures." Pp. 482–485 of Appendix 1 in John W. C. Johnstone and Ramon J. Rivera (eds.), *Volunteers for Learning: A Study of the Educational Pursuits of American Adults.* Chicago: Aldine.

U.S. Department of Labor. 1965. *Dictionary of Occupational Titles.* Washington, D.C.: U.S. Government Printing Office. Third edition.

Weber, Max. 1947. *The Theory of Social and Economic Organization.* New York: Oxford University Press.

Whyte, William H. 1956. *The Organization Man.* New York: Simon and Schuster.

Williams, Robin M., Jr. 1960. *American Society: A Sociological Interpretation.* New York: Knopf. Second edition.

Witkin, H. A., R. B. Dyk, H. F. Faterson, D. R. Goodenough, and S. A. Karp. 1962. *Psychological Differentiation: Studies of Development.* New York: John Wiley.

PART II

The Influence of the
Organization: Goals,
Roles, and Structures

T HIS SECTION, like the previous one, is divided into normative influences and social-structural influences bearing on the official–client relationship. But, this time, we are looking at the problem closer up, from within the organization itself. The normative aspect is implicit in the influence of the goals of an organization on its dealings with the public, and the social-structural aspect has to do with the effects on the interaction of officials and clients resulting from the variety of ways in which bureaucracies are organized and internally controlled.

Organizational Goals and Their Influence

A number of attempts have been made to classify formal organizations in terms which have direct bearing on the official–client relationship. One of the most useful, we find, is Blau and Scott's (1962) *cui bono?*—who benefits?—criterion. Four types of organizations are suggested, based on prime beneficiaries. Thus, there are organizations whose prime beneficiary is the *client,* in the sense that their reason for being is to provide services to the individuals with whom they have contact. Hospitals and welfare organizations are examples. A second type of organization exists to serve its *owners,* and includes all the profit-making organizations such as department stores, banks, and the like. The prime beneficiary may also be *members* of the organization, as in trade unions or churches. Or, the organization may exist primarily to serve *society at large,* rather than its immediate clients. Such commonweal organizations as the customs or the police have a right to be suspicious of the individuals with whom they deal directly because their client—that is, the prime beneficiary—is the public as a whole.

Blau and Scott hasten to point out that organizations all have secondary beneficiaries—the department store may have to show a profit first of all, but obviously, the customer-client is next on line. It is ironic, these authors suggest, that the motto, "the customer is always right" originated in those organizations which may legitimately consider its owners and managers as prime beneficiaries, whereas the service organizations—whose prime beneficiary is the client in contact—do not, in general, allow their "customer" either to diagnose or to prescribe. These service organizations, typically, are manned

159

by professionals who are presumed to know the client's true needs better than he.

Thompson (1962)* classifies organizations according to the extent to which their dealings with the client are "programmed" or "heuristic"—that is, the extent of ambiguity present in the client's situation, and the discretionary power required of the official in dealing with it—and according to whether the client's contact with the organization is voluntary (he wants a hunting license) or mandatory (he is required to file an income tax report). Cross-tabulation of these elements generates a four-fold typology. The heuristic-voluntary type, obviously, resembles Blau and Scott's client-oriented service organizations, while the programmed-mandatory type are the bureaus of income tax or the customs, which serve society as a whole. This type clearly resembles Weber's "ideal type."

Other authors have looked at the range of goals which may be adopted by the *same* kind of organization. Students of "total institutions" such as prisons or mental hospitals have taken the lead in showing that a "custodial" orientation to inmates is quite different from a "therapeutic" orientation, or, in other words, that a particular prison may take the client-in-contact, rather than society at large, as its prime beneficiary. The ideological basis for such a commitment, of course, is that society will benefit no less, and perhaps even more, as secondary beneficiary.

The value of these classificatory schemes from our point of view is in their implications for understanding interaction and outcome in official–client encounters. Thompson's (1962)* paper is very explicit on this point, speculating, as it does, on the kinds of interaction that are most likely in each type of organization, the paths that lead to different sorts of outcomes, and the strategies of persuasion available to clients. For the heuristic-mandatory situation, for example, Thompson cites Joseph Eaton's perceptive suggestions that the client may influence the outcome by "presenting a challenge" to the professional or semiprofessional worker, saying, in effect, "I am no ordinary case, and you should find me quite interesting." Or, the client may offer the worker the promise of compliance (and thus the promise that the worker's therapeutic effort will be scored as successful).

A similar kind of derivation has been made from Blau and Scott's typology. While Blau and Scott do not spell out their expectations concerning inter-action process in each *cui bono?* type, we have tried to do so (Katz and Danet, 1966),* and then to study whether people actually behave that way. We ask, in effect, whether clients dealing with an organization whose avowed goal is to serve the client are aware that they have more power than when confronted by the official of an organization whose prime beneficiary is the society as a whole.

The ways in which organizations of different kinds control their clients (or inmates, or lower-level members) is the basis for Etzioni's (in March 1965) typology of identitive power (universities), utilitarian power (business concerns), and coercive power (prisons). But, again, there are those who prefer to look more closely at variation within a single institution and consider, as does Berk (1966),* the implications for interaction in prisons of variations in staff orientations. Berk's findings show, for example, that the custodial orientation of staff gives rise to strong counter-organization among inmates, and as a result, the need to bargain and make concessions to inmate leaders in order to maintain effective formal control. In the therapeutically oriented prison, the norms of the informal grouping of inmates were congruent with the formal ones.

Along the same line are several studies which compare the differing orientations of parallel departments within the same organization. Coser (in Freidson, 1963), for example, compares the orientations of nurses toward patients in two wards of a regular hospital, one for chronic diseases, the other for nonchronic diseases. Nurses in the chronic ward were more alienated from their work, and interacted less with their patients. In the chronic ward, "good" patients were those who were physically neat and made no trouble; in the other, "good" patients were the more active ones. Blau's (1964) comparison of the orientations of two departments of a state employment agency is another good example. One department was oriented to quantitative achievement, that is, to placing as many people in jobs as quickly as possible. The other was oriented more qualitatively, seeking to "fit" applicants and jobs in an optimal way. One of the ironic consequences of the more qualitative orientation was that although there was less conflict with clients, there was apparently more, rather than less, actual discrimination on a racial basis. Thus, the "human relations" approach to bureaucracy has its dangers: the more one tries to take account of the whole person the more likely one is to see him as an Italian or a Negro or a hippie. The qualitative orientation in the employment office which led clerks to ask whether an applicant would "fit" well in a given job, also allowed them to take account of the color of his skin.

MIXED GOALS

It would be incorrect to leave the impression that most organizations have a single clear-cut goal. Not only do many organizations have mixed goals, as was mentioned above, but some of these goals conflict with each other. For example, conflict between service to the individual and responsibility to the public-at-large is illustrated by Blau's (1960)* study of a public welfare agency. Here the conflict was between providing needy persons with aid and checking their eligibility to receive it. The police are another example. Ostensibly, they serve the general public with prime emphasis on their function of social control but the public is often unaware of the helping or service function of the police. Banton (1964) has made explicit this dilemma of the built-in tension between the helping and control functions; a citizen may be reluctant to ask a policeman for help, for example, for fear that the policeman will find his behavior suspect in some way. Yet, in another study of the police,

Cumming, Cumming, and Edell (1965) conclude that the public is almost totally unaware that the greater part of the policeman's duties consists in "social work" in which he gives advice or support in personal problems.

Mixed goals in organizations can give rise to role conflicts in officials, not the kind where your boss wants you to work late and your wife wants you to come home, but the kind where the conflict resides in one and the same role and in one and the same social setting. Little's (1956) study of the role of the medical ward officer in the army is a case in point: as a physician, his first responsibility is to the health of his patient; yet as an army officer, his obligation is to suspect malingering and, insofar as possible, to keep the man on active duty. An analogous kind of problem is posed by Burchard (1954) in his study of the conflicting goals in the role of the military chaplain.

Even a family physician in private practice has certain responsibilities to the larger society (reporting a communicable disease, for example, or being parsimonious about giving patients medical certificates to explain their absence at work), just as a priest has obligations to the larger society while listening to the confessions of his parishioners. Pressure to take explicit account of society's benefit is much greater on physicians in the Soviet Union (Field, 1953). The balance of primary and secondary beneficiaries is different still in the case of the doctor employed by an insurance company to check on an applicant's insurability, and it is hopelessly inverted in the case of the concentration camp physician.

Organizational Structure and Its Influence

Ostensibly, the goals of an organization and its structure ought to be inextricably related; yet, there is some reason to suspect that bureaucratic organization does not vary as much as it might, or should, to achieve different kinds of goals. It is certainly a legitimate question to ask whether it makes sense to organize a television station like a bureau of internal revenue when the goal of one is creativity and the other tax collection, or like a department store, even if both the store and the TV station share the goals of serving stockholders and serving the client-in-contact. But a bureaucracy is a bureaucracy, it seems, and the strain is toward similar kinds of organization regardless of goal.

HIERARCHICAL VERSUS COLLEGIAL STRUCTURES

Nevertheless, there are important structural variations in the organization of bureaucracy, and we propose to examine some of their effects. Where variations can be seen to be most closely related to goals, perhaps, is in the structural difference between service organizations whose prime beneficiary is the client-in-contact and commonweal organizations whose prime beneficiary is society-at-large. The key to the difference, as has already been implied, is in the tendency to staff the service organization with professionals. Hospitals, social work agencies, schools, and the like, therefore, are bureaucracies where the "official" who deals with the public is of relatively high status within the organization. This is also one of the important differences between therapeutic and custodial institutions, in that the former is more likely to have professionals on its staff.

Professionals differ from other kinds of officials in that they are not usually supervised directly by a superior officer, but are subject only more generally to the professional ethic which they have presumably internalized and to the informal scrutiny of their colleagues. They are oriented to serve clients by virtue of their professional commitment, and are trained—more than other kinds of officials—to cope with the individual aspects of each case. They are supposed to know how to listen, and to understand a problem from the client's point of view, though they may differ with the client over what they think is good for him.

The introduction of professionals into a bureaucracy brings with it a continuing struggle between two competing principles of organization: the decentralized service orientation of the professional and the hierarchical procedure-oriented principle of the official. The client may experience this tension in the professional's occasional helplessness when the organization denies him access to a resource he feels appropriate to a given case, as when a socialized health scheme decides centrally on what pharmaceuticals it will stock, or—to use Ben David's (1958) example—when the doctor is forced to refer certain kinds of cases to specialists even if he would prefer to treat them himself. There is a tendency, in such organizations, for the professional to think of the bureaucrat as having no sense of the organization's mission, and for the official to think of the professional as unable or unwilling to face up to, or cope with, the realities of budgets and politics.

It may be argued that the tension between service-oriented professionals and procedure-oriented officials is a healthy one, as Litwak's (1961) label, "organizations which permit conflict," suggests. In other words, the checks and balances which are implicit in this kind of organizational conflict serve the twin goals of efficiency and service, and moreover, may keep the professionals' spirit alive. However, one may argue—with equal cogency—that the organization would be even healthier and more useful if the administrative personnel could also be induced to share the service-oriented goals to which the organization is dedicated.

But whichever side one takes in this argument, and in the absence of studies which can help us decide, there nevertheless remains a gnawing concern that organizational life may dampen the professional spirit, after all. The independent professional—the doctor, the lawyer—is fast disappearing in our society as more and more professionals set up practice within an organization, or are affected by the constraints of such organizations as health insurance schemes and the like. Ben David's (1958) and Shuval's (1962) analyses of the frustrated and bureaucratized physician in the medical scheme to which most Israelis belong are good examples. Becoming a *salaried* employee rather than receiving a fee-for-service also makes a difference for professional–client relations, as Roemer's (1962) article on methods of payment to doctors shows. While some professions hardly exist at all outside an organizational framework—the social worker, the priest, and the teacher—it is still relevant to be concerned over what bureaucratization does to them. Independence and creativity are not the only victims of the bureaucratization of the professions. Something as sacrosanct as the "professional secret"—which sealed the lips of the professional in private practice—has almost no chance of survival in a bureaucracy where a host of subprofessionals and officials have legitimate access to records.

Rosengren (1970) has expressed a particularly pessimistic view of the chances for survival of a humane, *gemeinschaft* orientation toward clients in bureaucratized service professions. Even if there is an explicit ideological commitment to cultivate and preserve such an orientation, he argues, the dynamics of organizational change and interorganizational relationships lead service organizations to become increasingly specific in orientation over time.

What is of concern here is not limited to professionals alone; the concern is no less applicable to untrained officials who deal with clients, and particularly to those in situations which require considerateness, discretion, diagnosis, and prescription. Indeed, we might suggest that more and more of the truly "programmed" contacts with clients should be given over to machines —selling postage stamps, for example—while the more "heuristic" contacts (including appeals from negative decisions, and the breakdown of the machines) should be placed in the hands of increasingly well-trained semi-professionals within supportive organizational frameworks. Catrice-Lorey's (1966)* report on the problems of official–client relations in the French social security offices provides an example. It was widely expected that these contacts would be highly satisfactory to the public: the organization was new and idealistic; it was decentralized and owned by its members; it provided for member participation; it dealt with clients-in-contact. But the facts went otherwise. The clients were less happy with their own social security scheme than with the workings of the post office or the bank. Among other possible causes, the author speculates that the trouble may be related to the intimacies which clients are required to reveal to officials in the social security office. These require a much more understanding ear, and a much more trust-inspiring atmosphere, than are necessary at the post office, or even at the bank. Yet, as if in fear of the tensions implicit in the demands of the situation and the growing dissatisfaction of their clients, the officials asked that counters be installed to separate them from their clients.

Admittedly, some writers are more optimistic. Professionals in organizations can do their job better; they have greater access to colleagues, to needed equipment, and the like. Indeed, in some ways they seem more innovative than others: for example, it has been shown that physicians who shared offices with others, practiced in group clinics, or who were on appointment at the local hospital together with physicians who were simply popular among their peers, were earlier to adopt a new antibiotic than those practicing alone (Coleman, Katz and Menzel, 1966); but this did not hold true, one should add, with respect to the adoption of a less conventional innovation—psychosomatic theories of patient management (Menzel, 1960). As has already been noted, Kohn (1971)* is equally optimistic about bureaucratic officials, in general. To the surprise of all, his study finds officials more receptive to change, more flexible, more tolerant of nonconformity, and the like. While this comparison of individuals working in frameworks with varying degrees of bureaucratization (defined by number of levels of supervision) is far less compelling after education is taken into account (bureaucrats are better educated), enough remains of the original differences to require serious consideration.

Though professional and bureaucratic orientation differ in many ways, they have in common the tendency toward specialization, or a complex division of labor. In both cases specialization is supposed to make the work more efficient, and indeed it does in many ways. But both kinds of specialization can also be dysfunctional. Merton's (1952) analysis of the constraints of bureaucratic structure on personalities includes a discussion of what happens when the division of labor in carrying out the organization's goals is so complex that each individual loses sight of the total picture. This narrowing of focus is one of the factors which leads to an overconcern with procedures and an excessive rigidity and conformity with the rules, often to the detriment or chagrin of clients. While professional specialization is supposed to provide the client with expert service, Simon (1959) has documented at least one case where it had an effect quite opposite to the one usually expected. Chronically ill patients being treated in a number of different clinics for different ailments improved when they were transferred to a comprehensive clinic which treated the whole person.

Even when organizations are staffed with large numbers of professionals, bureaucratic hierarchy still exercises certain constraints. Thus, Seeman and Evans have demonstrated that the stratification system of a hospital makes a difference for medical care. For instance, where status differences were less stressed, interns told of communicating more with patients, spending more time explaining their problems and the nature of the treatment they were receiving, and giving psychological support (Seeman and Evans, 1961a). De-emphasis of status differences was also associated with greater consultation with members of other departments (Seeman and Evans, 1961b). Rosenberg and Pearlin (1962)* report that lowest-status attendants were more likely than higher status workers to invoke their organizational authority in trying to persuade patients to do their bidding. The latter—highest-status nurses and supervisors—were more likely to prefer what the authors call "benevolent manipulation" to pulling rank. Several studies have shown that hierarchical status affects one's view of organizational goals. In mental hospitals, for example, it was found that the attendants had a more custodial orientation than nurses, who in turn, were more custodial than doctors (Levinson and Gallagher, 1964; Stein and Oetting, 1964). If Janowitz and Delaney (1957) are correct in supposing that the higher the status of official, the less information he has about clients, the anomaly of certain organizational situations becomes clear: the most service-oriented officials in a bureaucratic structure have least knowledge of clients' problems.

Typically, the chain of command in a hierarchy transmits orders from the top down. In restaurants, things are different. Orders are initiated from the bottom up—from client to waitress to counterman to chef. This reversal is a source of repeated conflict between the higher-status male kitchen staff and the waitresses. Whyte's (1946*; 1948) analysis of the problem led him to propose an organizational innovation: that direct interaction between waitress and chef be minimized by substituting written orders for verbal ones and placing them on a spindle which the counterman or chef could deal with as he saw fit. This case raises the question, once more, of whether the structure of professional organizations, which gives high status to the worker who deals with clients, might not be extended to other service-oriented bureaucracies as well.

In any event, conflicts among the staff often have negative consequences for the client. Both Caudill (1958) and Stanton and Schwartz (1954) have studied the effect of staff disagreements on mental patients. Caudill reports that when there was conflict among the staff, all role groups restricted their participation and withdrew from each other; relations among patients broke down and the result was collective disturbance. Stanton and Schwartz found that patients who were the subject of secret staff disagreement became pathologically excited, and when the disagreement was resolved, their excitement subsided.

STYLES OF SUPERVISION AND OTHER METHODS OF CONTROL

One of the manifest functions of hierarchical authority in bureaucracy is to maintain control, or, in other words, to ensure that each higher level in the organization supervises the activity of the level below. What's more, the higher levels are ultimately responsible for what happens at lower levels, and they are also expected to evaluate workers' performance and to propose appropriate sanctions, positive and negative.

Still, there are supervisors and supervisors. Variations in the style of supervision may depend on the structure of the organization as a whole—for example, how much discretionary authority is vested formally in the lower echelons?—in the behavior and attitudes of the supervisors' supervisors, and in the supervisors' own personalities. Although studies of the relationship between supervisory styles and worker productivity tend to show a positive relationship between "democratic"-style supervision and productivity, these results are of lesser interest here. We are after the relationship between supervisory style and officials' behavior toward clients. Scott (1961), for example, found that social welfare workers under authoritarian supervisors were procedure oriented, while those working under nonauthoritarian supervision showed a desire for greater individual responsibility.

In Blau's (1964) study of the employment agency, the effect of supervisory style is clearly reflected in the work of the two departments. One department, it will be recalled, had a supervisor who relied heavily on statistical records of performance for evaluation of his subordinates. The other department was supervised by an individual who paid rather more attention to the whole person—both worker and client—and was more interested, therefore, in the quality of performance. While the workers in the latter group had many fewer conflicts with uncooperative clients, and were less punitive towards them, it is also true—as has previously been noted—that the human relations approach allowed a certain amount of apparently unwitting discrimination to creep into the job-placement procedure. Where the supervisor enforced productivity most completely by basing his evaluation on statistical records of performance, the competitive race overshadowed any discriminatory tendencies that might have existed, just as Weber implies in his ideal model. The statistically oriented supervisor, incidentally, was better liked, probably because the unpleasant task of evaluating associates was shifted to the statistical record.

Blau makes a point of distinguishing between prejudiced attitudes and discriminatory behavior, implying that it is quite possible to be prejudiced and still not discriminate when the situation makes discrimination difficult. Shuval's (1962) study of doctors in Israel's bureaucratized health system helps make this point clearer. Comparing doctors with light and heavy case loads, Shuval finds that doctors with the lighter loads (fewer than 100 patients per week) were far less likely to concur that members of a recently arrived ethnic group possessed the undesirable characteristics (uncleanliness, irresponsibility towards children, etc.) often attributed to them. Acceptance of the negative stereotype was most likely among doctors with heavy case loads which included a large proportion of patients from that particular group. The interpretation proposed is that the heavy case load heightens the effect of bureaucratization of medical service creating pressure to spend less time with each patient and increasing the paperwork, and so the acceptance of negative stereotypes is an inevitable result. The interpretation is strengthened by the discovery of a strong relationship between these prejudiced attitudes and doctors' perceptions of the extent to which working in a bureaucracy interferes with their medical practice.

Taking the Blau and Shuval studies together suggests that bureaucratization may, at one and the same time, increase prejudice but reduce discrimination. In other words, the pressure to keep the line moving may lead to equitable results, but less personalized ones, while stereotyped images of the clientele are breeding in the minds of the officials in charge. If it were enough to dismiss

167

each patient with an aspirin or to give routine references to job applicants, the solution would be easy. It is where universalism, or equality, requires personalized treatment that the dilemma arises.

PEER GROUP INTEGRATION

One of the most interesting things about peer group relations among workers is the extent to which they encourage or discourage a service orientation toward clients. Blau (1960)* tried to specify the conditions under which officials in client-serving roles developed such "professionalized" orientations. In his study of untrained workers in a public service agency, he demonstrates that workers who were more integrated in groups of their peers were more likely to take the initiative in offering their clients casework service rather than limiting their contacts to procedure-oriented checking on eligibility. Experience on the job also led to this kind of orientation—up to the point where "too much" experience apparently induced apathy and even overcame the influence of peer group integration. Although they dealt with clients with appropriate professional detachment, the integrated workers were also more likely than their unintegrated colleagues to take their work home with them —to worry about, or mull over, problems of clients even while they were off the job.

Perhaps it is no accident that solidarity with peers encourages a service orientation. For, as we have noted, one of the defining characteristics of professional work is the dominance of *collegial* rather than hierarchical authority. In the case of full professionals, informal peer group ties *overlap* with formal collegial ones; in less professionalized organizations informal peer group relations stand in contrast to the formal hierarchical structure.

Acceptance into a group of peers has other consequences as well. It gives the worker a feeling of security, for one thing. Several studies have shown that this feeling is associated, in turn, with more professional behavior toward clients. Lombard (1955), for example, reports that saleswomen in a department store are better able to empathize with their clients' needs—rather than impose their own prejudgments of what they think the client should need—the more they feel acceptance in the group. Similarly, it has been noted that integration with colleagues leads to an attitude of proper detachment in dealing with clients, one which is neither too domineering (Blau, 1964), nor too dependent. Again, in a comprehensive analysis of police–community relations both in the United States and Great Britain, Banton (1964) has shown that particularly because of the genuine danger of some police work, staff solidarity is crucial for job satisfaction and for acquiring the confidence and skill necessary to deal with the public.

Two things may work *against* the development of a service orientation among integrated members of peer groups. One is the development, for whatever reason, of negative norms toward clients. In such cases, the integrated member of a work group which is hostile toward its clients will be loyal to the group in this respect as well. Another source of negative influence is simply the creation of a self-satisfied professional community which loses sight of its clients. Thus, Croog, *et al.* (in Freeman, *et al.,* 1963) found that the total amount of interaction between patients and nurses increases when more nurses are added to hospital wards. But when more than five nurses are placed together, interaction among themselves increases at the expense of interaction with patients.

ORGANIZATIONAL SIZE

The huge size of many modern organizations is often considered to be one of the major sources of their dysfunctional consequences, yet we actually know very little about the effects of size per se, particularly as it affects relationships with clients. The Thomas (1959) study which we have already discussed reports that the larger a social welfare agency, the lower the extent of agreement among staff and supervisors about how things should be done, and the less personal the orientation toward clients. Thomas suggests that the real factor behind the results may be size of community. Unlike the smaller communities where the rate of worker turnover was low and the sense of belonging to the same community or even actual personal acquaintance were prevalent, the setting of the larger agency in the larger community made it more subject to the impersonality of big-city life. In such cases, only the reinforcement of professional commitments, manageable caseloads, and a supportive bureaucracy can overcome the pressures toward a formalistic procedure orientation.

This would seem to be the point of Shuval's (1962) aforementioned study of doctors in bureaucratized medical clinics. Where heavy caseloads increased the strains of bureaucratization by minimizing time spent with patients and multiplying the paperwork, doctors' views of their patients became more and more stereotyped. Indeed, where it is impossible to deal with individuals individually, stereotyping may function as a substitute for the more relevant categorizations required for professional diagnosis. We do not know whether the work of these physicians was actually impaired by negative stereotyping, but the danger is there.

PAYMENT IN SALARIES

Another of the defining characteristics of bureaucracy is that its officials receive a regular salary. As more and more practitioners move into bureaucratic settings, we can ask, what difference does it make for their relations with clients whether they receive a fee directly from the client, as in private practice, or they are guaranteed a regular monthly wage, independent of the particular clients they serve? Field (1953) and Roemer (1962) have both analyzed the consequences of payment arrangements for doctor–patient relations. The principal ways doctors are paid are fee-for-service, salary, or capitation (the number of persons for whose health the doctor is responsible during a certain period). Roemer uses five types of criteria to evaluate the pro's and con's of the three systems: the quantity of medical care provided, the quality of care, the costs, the administrative process, and the larger politics of the medical care field.

THE STRUCTURE OF TOTAL ORGANIZATIONS

Earlier in this chapter we made a distinction between *limited* and *total institutions*. The latter term, made famous by Erving Goffman (1961) refers to all those organizations in which a group of inmates lives together in an enforced, formally managed round of life. Inmates of these institutions do not go home at night, and home is often far away, whether the organization is a prison or a hospital, or whether it is a ship, boarding school, military camp, or monastery. Despite the obvious differences between total organizations where entrance is voluntary or mandatory, they have a number of interesting things in common. From the client's point of view there are the "degradation" ceremonies associated with entrance in which the new inmate checks his identity at the door and takes on the identity assigned to him by the institution. Then, the new member must begin to find his way through the formal and the informal status systems and learn its language. He must learn what degree of social distance from staff members is appropriate to certain times and certain places. For its part, the staff must wrestle with the dilemmas of maintaining distance and exercising authority and yet recognizing the humanity of their wards—or at least giving the impression that such recognition is being shown to those who look in occasionally from outside.

The total organization is a company town whose members are constantly under surveillance and whose loyalty and achievements are ever being measured. Work in the ordinary sense takes second place to the process of the transformation of identity. Indeed, some of these total institutions have succeeded so well that their inmates do not easily reassume identities which are familiar and acceptable to members of the outside world. It was in response to this problem that the therapeutic community (Jones, 1968) and the half-way houses were created to desocialize the desocialized, and to resocialize once more.

Introduction to the Readings in This Part

The first three chapters deal with the effect of organizational goals on official–client interaction. The paper by Katz and Danet asks whether the approach of clients to a service organization (a medical clinic, for example) is different from their approach to a commonweal organization (the police, for example) or to a profit-oriented organization like a bank or department store. Blau and Scott's *cui bono?* (who benefits?) typology implies that it should be, and this study asks whether it actually is.

Thompson's paper presents a different way of classifying organizations according to whether the services they offer are routine, such as selling postage stamps, or must be individually tailored to the client, such as social work, and spells out the implications of each for official–client relations. Berk, however, treats only one kind of organization—prisons—arguing that the same type of organization may have very different goals with very different consequences for clients.

Two factors—integration with peers and years of tenure—are found by Blau to be related to the development of a professionalized service orientation among social workers in a public welfare agency. Catrice-Lorey, concerned with the same problem, asks why workers in the French social security organizations are not more service oriented. The organizations are owned by their beneficiaries, we are told, and their goals are modern in conception—then why do their officials rate lower in the eyes of the public than officials in the post office and in the bank? One of the problems, Catrice-Lorey suggests, is the low social status of the officials who deal with clients. This disconcerts their clients, considering the kinds of intimate problems with which they must deal. The low status of another kind of worker—the waitress—is the subject of Whyte's paper. The problems of waitresses, Whyte suggests, result both from the structure of the restaurant and from their own personal backgrounds.

REFERENCES

Banton, Michael. *The Policeman in the Community*. London: Tavistock, 1964.

Ben David, Joseph. "The Professional Role of the Physician in Bureaucratized Medicine." *Human Relations* 11 (1958): 255–274.

Berk, Bernard. "Organizational Goals and Inmate Organization." *American Journal of Sociology* 71 (1966): 522–534.

Blau, Peter M. *The Dynamics of Bureaucracy*. Chicago: University of Chicago Press, 1964.

———. "Orientation toward Clients in a Public Welfare Agency." *Administrative Science Quarterly* 5 (1960): 341–361.

Blau, Peter M., and W. Richard Scott. *Formal Organizations: A Comparative Approach*. San Francisco: Chandler, 1962.

Burchard, Waldo W. "Role Conflicts of Military Chaplains." *American Sociological Review* 19 (1954): 528–535.

Catrice-Lorey, Antoinette. "Social Security and Its Relations with Beneficiaries: The Problem of Bureaucracy in Social Administration." *Bulletin of the International Social Security Association* 19 (1966): 286–297.

Caudill, William. *The Psychiatric Hospital as a Small Society*. Cambridge: Harvard University Press, 1958.

Part II

Coleman, James S., Elihu Katz, and Herbert Menzel. *Medical Innovation: A Diffusion Study*. Indianapolis: Bobbs-Merrill, 1966.
Coser, Rose L. "Alienation and the Social Structure: Case Analysis of a Hospital." In *The Hospital in Modern Society*, edited by Eliot Freidson, pp. 231–265. Glencoe: Free Press, 1963.
Croog, Sidney H. "Interpersonal Relations in Medical Settings." In *Handbook of Medical Sociology*, edited by Howard E. Freeman et al., pp. 241–271. Englewood Cliffs: Prentice-Hall, 1963.
Cumming, Elaine, Ian M. Cumming, and Laura Edell. "The Policeman as Philosopher, Guide and Friend." *Social Problems* 12, no. 3 (Winter 1965): 276–286.
Etzioni, Amitai. "Organizational Control Structure." In *Handbook of Organizations*, edited by James G. March, pp. 650–677. Chicago: Rand McNally, 1965.
Field, Mark G. "Structured Strain in the Role of the Soviet Physician." *American Journal of Sociology* 58 (1953): 493–502.
Goffman, Erving. "On the Characteristics of Total Institutions." In *Asylums*, edited by Erving Goffman, pp. 1–124. Garden City: Doubleday Anchor, 1961.
Janowitz, Morris, and William Delaney. "The Bureaucrat and the Public: A Study of Informational Perspectives." *Administrative Science Quarterly* 2 (1957): 141–162.
Jones, Maxwell et al. *The Therapeutic Community*. New York: Basic Books, 1968.
Katz, Elihu, and Brenda Danet. "Petitions and Persuasive Appeals: A Study of Official-Client Relations." *American Sociological Review* 31 (December 1966): 811–822.
Kohn, Melvin L. "Bureaucratic Man: A Portrait and an Interpretation." *American Sociological Review* 36 (1971): 461–474.
Levinson, Daniel, and Eugene B. Gallagher. *Patienthood in the Mental Hospital*. Boston: Houghton-Mifflin, 1964.
Little, Roger W. "The 'Sick' Soldier and the Medical Ward Officer." *Human Organization* 15 (1956): 22–24.
Litwak, Eugene. "Models of Bureaucracy Which Permit Conflict." *American Journal of Sociology* 57 (September 1961): 177–184.
Lombard, George F. *Behavior in a Selling Group*. Cambridge: Graduate School of Business Administration, Harvard University, 1955.
Menzel, Herbert. "Innovation, Integration and Marginality." *American Sociological Review* 25 (1960): 704–713.
Merton, Robert K. "Bureaucratic Structure and Personality." In *Reader in Bureaucracy*, edited by Robert K. Merton et al., pp. 361–371. Glencoe: Free Press, 1952.
Roemer, Milton I. "On Paying the Doctor and the Implications of Different Methods." *Journal of Health and Human Behavior* 3 (1962): 4–14.
Rosenberg, Morris, and Leonard I. Pearlin. "Power Orientations in the Mental Hospital." *Human Relations* 15, no. 4 (November 1962): 335–350.
Rosengren, William R. "The Careers of Clients and Organizations." In *Organizations and Clients: Essays in the Sociology of Service*, edited by William R. Rosengren and Mark Lefton, pp. 117–135. Columbus: Merrill, 1970.
Scott, W. Richard. "A Case Study of Professional Workers in a Bureaucratic Setting." Ph.D. dissertation, Department of Sociology, University of Chicago, 1961.
Seeman, Melvin, and John W. Evans. "Stratification and Hospital Care: Part I. The Performance of the Medical Intern." *American Sociological Review* 26 (1961): 67–79.
———. "Stratification and Hospital Care: Part II. The Objective Criteria of Performance." *American Sociological Review* 26 (1961): 193–204.
Shuval, Judith T. "Ethnic Stereotyping in Israeli Medical Bureaucracies." *Sociology and Social Research* 46 (1962): 455–465.
Simon, Abraham J. "Social Structure of Clinics and Patient Improvement." *Administrative Science Quarterly* 4 (1959): 197–206.

Stanton, Alfred H., and Morris S. Schwartz. *The Mental Hospital.* New York: Basic Books, 1954.

Stein, William W., and E. R. Oetting. "Humanism and Custodialism in a Peruvian Mental Hospital." *Human Organization* 24 (1964): 278–282.

Thomas, Edwin J. "Role Conceptions, Organizational Size, and Community Context." *American Sociological Review* 24 (1959): 30–37.

Thompson, James D. "Organizations and Output Transactions." *American Journal of Sociology* 68, no. 3 (November 1962): 309–324.

Whyte, William F. "When Worker and Customer Meet." In *Industry and Society,* edited by William F. Whyte, pp. 123–147. New York: McGraw-Hill, 1946.

————. *Human Relations in the Restaurant Industry.* New York: McGraw-Hill, 1948.

9

Elihu Katz and Brenda Danet

PETITIONS AND PERSUASIVE
APPEALS: A STUDY OF
OFFICIAL-CLIENT RELATIONS

The burgeoning literature on formal organizations gives prominent attention to the interaction of officials within the organization but only scant attention to what goes on between the organization and its clients. Yet, in an increasingly bureaucratized society, the relationship between officials and clients is of obvious importance both as a social and as a theoretical problem. The exploratory study to be reported on in this paper is part of a larger set of studies being carried out in Israel on relations between bureaucracy and the public, with particular reference to problems associated with the socialization of new immigrants from traditional backgrounds to the unfamiliar role of "client." This study analyzes the strategies employed by clients to influence bureaucratic decisions in their favor. Specifically, the focus is on the kinds of reasons or persuasive appeals which clients offer to substantiate their requests.

Suppose, for example, that an individual approaches an official of the Customs and asks to be allowed to import an automobile free of duty. He

Elihu Katz and Brenda Danet, "Petitions and Persuasive Appeals: A Study of Official-Client Relations," *American Sociological Review* 31 (1966): 811–822. Reprinted by permission.

NOTE: Support for this research came from the National Science Foundation (Grant Number NSF-GS-41). The work was carried out during 1963–1964 at the Israel Institute of Applied Social Research. We wish to thank our colleagues on this project, Dr. Michael Gurevitch, Mrs. Tsiyona Peled, and Miss Ilana Hirsch, for their advice and assistance, and Professors Peter M. Blau and S. N. Eisenstadt for their comments. The data were gathered through the generosity of Dr. Jona Rosenfeld; he allowed us to append several questions to his study on the use of social services in Israel.

might then offer the official a bribe, or threaten him with bodily harm. He might seek to motivate the official by indicating how destitute he was, or by implying that God will reward the official for his favor, or, perhaps, that the petitioner will see to it that the official is rewarded by his boss. Alternatively, the request might be based on the individual's insistence on his legal "right" to the particular benefit, or, by the same token, on the official's "duty" to provide it. Something about the individual's perception of the organization and/or the official, as well as of his own role as a client, can be inferred by analyzing the reasons which he gives to support his requests for favors or services. An offer of reciprocity such as a bribe or a threat obviously implies a different conception than does an appeal to the official's altruism. Mention of the official's boss implies some sophistication about the hierarchical structure of the organization. Insistence on legal "rights" obviously reflects some socialization to bureaucratic norms and a belief in their efficacy—though it is widely thought in Israel that new immigrants from even the most traditional backgrounds learn very quickly to say "it's my right," whether it is or not.

Under what kinds of circumstances are persuasive appeals likely to appear in official-client interaction? First, there are situations in which it is *legitimate* and even *necessary* to present a "reason" designed to activate an organizational obligation. The client of a bank who requests a loan is asked to state why he needs the money, or the department store customer returning a purchased article claims, "It's the wrong size." Second, whenever the rules do not guarantee automatic transfer of resources and officials have *discretionary power,* we can expect appeals to appear. Third, clients are likely to attempt to influence officials' decisions after a *refusal* or when they know they have no legal right to what they want. If a request alone, or a request accompanied by an appropriate (normative) strategy, fails on the first try, clients are likely to increase their efforts to influence officials. In addition, a refusal is likely to encourage the switch to an inappropriate appeal like a bribe or a request for a favor.

There are at least two other conditions under which appeals are likely to occur. People who lack experience with formal organizations may offer reasons, even when these are unnecessary or inappropriate, simply because they are "ignorant" of the role and continue to behave as they would in informal interaction. Thus a new immigrant may plead, "Have pity on me. Life is hard and I am new in this country." In contrast, there are clients who *do* know better. They know which appeals are appropriate in a given situation, and whether appeals are appropriate at all, but they intentionally break the rules of the game in order to get what they want. The classic example here is "pulling strings," as in the case of the anxious father who pressures an old friend, the dean of a college, to see that his son is accepted. In more precise terms, "pulling strings" is the calculated manipulation of *role impingement*—the impingement of informal relationships, of officially irrelevant latent social identities and nonbureaucratic norms, on the official-client dyad.[1]

Design of the Study

Four hypothetical situations were designed, in each of which a client petitions an official for services or help. The basic idea is to examine (a) the types of appeals invoked by clients of varying background characteristics, and (b) the influence of type of organization on the choice of appeals. The organizations were chosen in accordance with the typology of formal organizations developed by Blau and Scott.[2] Since the typology is based on the criterion of *cui bono?* ("who benefits?") the identity of the prime beneficiary differs in each situation. The four situations are as follows:

Police. Let's say that you are a driver. A traffic policeman stops you and claims that you have broken a traffic law. He wants to give you a ticket. What would you do?

Factory Workers' Committee. Let's suppose that you are a worker in a factory and it seems to you that you deserve a raise. You go to the secretary of the workers' committee and explain your case. The secretary says that at the moment he does not see that it is possible to request this from the management. What would you do to get what you want?

Bank. Let's say that you go to a bank to request a loan. The manager of the bank listens to what you say and then refuses to grant the loan. What would you do to get what you want?

Sick Fund. Suppose you are sick and request emergency medical treatment in the Sick Fund clinic. It turns out that your membership card entitling you to service is not valid because you have forgotten to pay your monthly dues. The clerk refuses to let you see the doctor. What would you do in order to be treated by the doctor?[3]

The prime beneficiary of the police situation (and of most government bureaucracies) is the *public-at-large*. The beneficiary of the second situation is the *member* of a mutual-benefit organization, a union in this case. The bank belongs, of course, to the category of business concerns, or profit-oriented institutions, where the prime beneficiary is the *owner*. Finally, the Sick Fund represents service institutions, whose prime beneficiaries are their *clients-in-contact*.

These four situations were presented to a group of 116 male Army reservists, aged 25 to 30, who had been called up for one day's service. Respondents were asked how they would behave in order to persuade the official in each case to act in their favor. If they did not suggest a *verbal* appeal to him, interviewers were instructed to ask a second question to elicit a specific response of this type. They asked, "What would you say to the policeman (secretary, manager, clerk) to convince him to grant your request?" Respondents were from a wide variety of socioeconomic backgrounds. Information was collected with regard to their country of origin, education, occupation, and length of time in Israel. Answers as to whether respondents had ever been in situations resembling the hypothetical ones serve as a fifth independent variable, crudely called "experience."

The coding scheme. The persuasive appeals addressed to the various officials were coded according to the seven categories which are illustrated in Table 9–1. These seven categories may be collapsed into three types. First,

TABLE 9-1

Illustrations of the Various Types of Appeals

CATEGORY	EXAMPLE
1. Promise to organization	"I won't do it again."
2. Request for special consideration, favor	"Please forgive me this time."
3. Plea of personal need	"I'm sick—it's an emergency."
4. Diffuse claim of rights	"I deserve a raise."
5. Activation of norm of reciprocity	"I have had an account in your bank for the last ten years."
6. Activation of specific organizational commitment	"Giving loans is part of the service a bank is supposed to provide."
7. Threats	"If you don't let me see the doctor, I'll knock you down."

there are the appeals to *self-interest,* which take both a positive form (as in category 1) and a negative form (category 7). It is very important to note, however, that the appeals in category 1 are typically directed to the organization rather than the official. Second, there are appeals to the *altruism* of the official (or the organization) as expressed in categories 2 and 3, where one describes one's plight or throws oneself on the mercy of the official or the organization. Finally, there are appeals to *norms* as reflected in categories 4, 5, and 6. Note that these normative appeals are frequently based on the client's insistence that the organization owes him something not by virtue of his status as a client but by virtue of his having served the organization or contributed to it in some way in the past. For example, suppose the request for a loan is supported by the appeal, "I have had a savings account at this bank for the past ten years." Here the appeal is to a presumed obligation of the bank based not simply on a law or rule but stemming rather from the *norm of reciprocity.* In large measure, the difference between appeals based on reciprocity and appeals based on norms (since both are directed to the organization rather than the official) is the difference between "I *will* reward the organization," for example, with future cooperation, and "I *have* rewarded the organization." Despite this kinship between appeals to reciprocity and appeals to the norm of reciprocity, they have been kept separate, and appeals to the norm of reciprocity have been combined with other types of norms in this analysis.[4]

Rhetoric and motivation: analyzing the forms and content of appeals. There are two aspects to persuasive communications. One aspect deals with the motivational bases of appeals, that is, why they should convince the person addressed to comply with the speaker's wishes. The other aspect focuses on the rhetorical forms used by the speaker, the explicit phrasing of the appeal. The relevant literature to date has largely been oriented toward the first of these approaches. French and Raven, Thibaut and Kelley, Heider, Rosenberg, and Blau are among those who have attempted to analyze the bases of power and influence in social interaction.[5] In particular, one attempt which has influenced our own thinking is that of Talcott Parsons in his typology of "ways of getting results."[6]

Parsons distinguishes between "situational" and "intentional" influence-attempts, on the one hand, and between positive and negative on the other. In "situational" attempts, X seeks to induce Y to perform in a certain way by either offering (positive) or threatening (negative) to change his situation —to pay him, for example, or to block his promotion. In "intentional" attempts, X may influence Y by suggesting the ways in which Y will reward *himself* by complying (positive). Or, conversely, X may point out that if Y does *not* comply, he will punish himself in some sense by violating a commitment he has already made (negative). Parsons labels these four types: "inducements" (situational-positive), "deterrence" (situational-negative), "persuasion" (intentional-positive), and "activation of commitments" (intentional-negative). Our normative categories (4, 5, and 6) correspond to his "activation of commitments" and our reciprocity categories (1 and 7) correspond to his "inducements" and "deterrence."[7] Interestingly, the situations which we have studied do not evoke the strategy of "persuasion"; apparently, it does not occur to a client to try to motivate an official by pointing out that compliance with his (the client's) wishes would be rewarding to the official. This is probably because clients perceive their interests as clearly and legitimately different from those of officials and feel no need to mask them.

On the other hand, the present study gives prominence to the category of "altruism" which does not appear in the analysis of Parsons or the others. This is because the "motivating mechanism" implicit in appeals to alter's altruism is by no means clear, a point to which we shall return in a moment. But it serves to underline the fact that we are as interested in what people *say* as in what they *mean*. This orientation—which stresses, ultimately, the relation between form and content—thus moves toward some of the concerns of the areas of psycho- and socio-linguistics, though these specialties, to our knowledge, have hardly begun to consider linguistic aspects of the communication of intention.

The semantic problem in content analysis. While we are interested in the rhetoric of appeals, there is no escaping the fact that we are also ascribing meaning to what is being said. And, as in most content-analytic efforts, the problems of inferring meaning from manifest content are extremely difficult, and this study, perhaps, provides particularly good examples.

First of all, there is the problem of interpreting the motivational "theory" implicit in the several rhetorical forms. Appeals to the self-interest of the other pose almost no problem: a request followed by an inducement or a threat is clear evidence of the motivating mechanism of exchange or reciprocity. Appeals to norms are somewhat more difficult. If a request is supported by ego's argument that he has rewarded alter in the past without explicit reference to alter's obligation to reciprocate, it requires an inference to code such statements as appeals to the norm of reciprocity. But even more to the point is the controversy about whether norms—the appeal to obligation—are motivating mechanisms in their own right or whether they are "translated" by speaker and hearer alike into the more primitive calculus of self-interest, either in the sense that alter realizes that he must repay others if he wants them to repay him, or in the more general case of conformity to obligation, that he will be rewarded (by ego, by society, or by his own superego) for conformity to a norm.

The case of altruism is most difficult of all, because on a rhetorical level the appeal asks for alter to *sacrifice* his self-interest, or at very least, it implies that alter has nothing to lose in helping ego. Conceivably, one might want to postulate an altruistic motive. Alternatively, one might prefer to "translate" altruistic appeals either into the motive of self-interest ("If you grant my request, you will reward me and thereby reward yourself") or the motive of obligation ("If you grant my request, you will reward me and thereby fulfill the *norm of* altruism"). The first of these translations corresponds to Parsons' "persuasion," the second to Parsons' "activation of commitments." In order to decide when to stop translating, it is not enough for the observer to have his own theory of motivation; he must also know the appellant's theory.

But even if these semantic problems could be solved for a given situation, the problem of meaning would reemerge in comparing rhetorically identical appeals in different kinds of situations. Thus altruistic, normative, and reciprocal appeals may mean rather different things in an organizational setting than in informal interaction. We have already indicated, for example, that inducements and deterrents—the appeals to reciprocity or self-interest—are not generally addressed to the official at all, but rather to the organization. Their content does not so much reflect the client's command of desirable resources as it does his essential weakness: he has not much more to offer than the promise "to be good."

Moreover, the meaning of the different appeals may vary in the confrontation with different types of organizations. Thus, an altruistic appeal to an official of the Sick Fund, however, may simply be another way of saying, "Grant my request because the organization exists to serve sick people like me"—that is, it may be an appeal to the *norm* of altruism which is at the basis of the organization's legitimacy, rather than an appeal for special consideration by either the official or the organization. Thus, an altruistic appeal to the Sick Fund may not reflect the same kind of powerlessness vis-à-vis the organization as an altruistic appeal to the police.

Finally, a given appeal may have several levels of meaning, even in the same setting. An appeal to the altruism of a police officer—"Do me a favor this one time"—may also be perceived as flattering. In other words, the most altruistic of appeals—reflecting the powerlessness of the client—also has a component of reciprocity: status or subservience is being offered in return for the official's hoped-for compliance.[8]

Hypotheses

Two main sets of hypotheses guide this study. One set deals with the relationship between background characteristics of the respondents and variations in the appeals they address to officials. The other set considers the relationship between types of appeals on the one hand, and types of organizations on the other. We are also interested in the *variability* of appeals: Do some clients discriminate more than others in what they say to different organizations? Are certain organizations distinguishably similar or different, judging from the variability in the types of appeals addressed to them?

As far as the behavior of different types of respondents is concerned, our overall hypothesis is that those of more "modern" background (oldtimers in Israel, of Western origin, with at least some high school education, and in the higher occupations) will use more normative appeals.[9] Ranking appeals in terms of the degree of their presumed legitimacy in a bureaucratic setting, we consider the normative type most bureaucratic, and altruistic appeals least so.[10] Appeals to reciprocity are difficult to classify in this study since they are not, as we have already pointed out, appeals directed to the official as a profit-oriented individual, but, typically, promises to the organization to be a "better" client in the future—that is, promises of conformity. Those hypotheses have to be qualified, as we shall see below, by type of organization.

We expect the "traditionals" (newcomers from Middle Eastern and North African countries, those with only elementary education, and in the lower occupations) to be more passive—that is, to give fewer reasons altogether— than the "moderns." This is in line with Judith Shuval's finding that immigrants of Eastern origin, short stay in Israel, and low education are more likely to have passive orientations to their environments.[11]

In addition, we expect that the more "modern" groups will distinguish among the several organizations in their appeals—directing different kinds of appeals to each of the organizations—while the "traditional" groups will tend to address the different organizations more similarly.

Finally, contact with Israeli bureaucracy should teach clients without previous experience to refrain from using altruistic appeals and to invoke more appropriate norms instead. Over time, Westerners may not change much in their behavior and attitudes toward Israeli organizations, since their cultural background is not so different from that of Israel. Easterners, on the other hand, should learn to cite more norms and/or obligations as they acquire experience with Israeli officials. Consequently, Eastern newcomers should be the *least* bureaucratic, i.e., give most altruistic and least normative appeals.

The *cui bono?* criterion provides a key to hypothesizing about organizational differences. Inasmuch as it points to the basis of legitimacy on which the organization rests, it implicitly defines the extent of the client's power vis-à-vis each type of organization, and the rhetoric of appeals that might be more likely to work in each case. With regard to appeals to the different organizations, the client should be guided by the interest of the organization. In appealing to a bank, for example, it would be legitimate to use threats and inducements, since the organization is profit-oriented. Therefore, we might expect a high proportion of appeals to reciprocity in the bank situation, where a refusal on the part of the bank manager to grant a loan can be countered by the client's threat to take his business elsewhere. Where the prime beneficiary is someone other than the owner, norms become the proper language of bargaining. Thus, clients may be expected to appeal to the mutual-benefit organizations in terms of obligation to serve their members (in return for faithful membership). One can appeal to client-serving organizations such as the Sick Fund in terms of the obligation to serve their clients, and, theoretically, one should appeal to the traffic policeman in terms of the public interest.[12]

Our data, and the classificatory system which we have devised, are neither rich nor subtle enough to distinguish among the different types of normative appeals. What we can do, however, is to infer the extent to which the appeals to a given organization reflect the client's feeling of relative powerfulness or powerlessness. Employing appeals to the official's altruism as a measure of powerlessness, we would expect those organizations which serve the client to be low in appeal to altruism, while organizations which are "against" the client should be highest in altruism.[13] Ranking the organizations in these terms, we should find the police situation highest in altruism, and the Sick Fund and workers' committee situations lowest; the bank should fall in between because its *secondary* beneficiary, after the owner, is the client. If we separate the Sick Fund and the workers' committee on the basis that the former is a client-serving organization where one must deal with professional decision-makers and a set of imposed rules while the latter is a membership organization where the individual's power is presumably greater, we predict that the proportion of altruistic appeals will follow the order: police, bank, Sick Fund, workers' committee.

The *cui bono?* hypothesis is not the only one that speaks to the client's differential power vis-à-vis the several organizations. Consider, for example, the rank order of client's "bargaining power" resulting from the extent to which each of the four organizations holds a monopoly.[14] The client's bargaining power should be greatest in the bank and workers' committee situations since he presumably can take his business or his employment elsewhere. It should be less great in the Sick Fund, since it is more difficult (although not impossible) to change health plans, and it should be lowest vis-à-vis the police. In this case, the ranking of client's power would be as follows (from least to most appeals to altruism): police, Sick Fund, workers' committee, bank. The data will enable us to choose between the hypotheses of "normative power" and "bargaining power."[15]

Background Differences and Appeals

Beginning with the first set of hypotheses relating background variables to the content of persuasive appeals, Table 9-2 reports the relationship between

TABLE 9-2

*Types of Appeals by Ethnic Origin, Time in Israel, Education,
and Occupation, for All Situations Together*

	TYPE OF APPEAL			
PERSONAL ATTRIBUTE	ALTRUISM	NORMS	RECIPROCITY	TOTAL APPEALS* (= 100%)
Ethnic origin				
Westerners	31%	41%	27%	(164)
Easterners	39	33	28	(229)
Time in Israel				
Oldtimers	26	44	30	(116)
Newcomers	38	35	28	(257)
Education				
High school	26	42	32	(194)
Elementary	45	32	24	(188)
Occupation				
High	25	47	28	(75)
Medium, low	39	34	27	(277)

*Note that this and subsequent tables are based on total responses (appeals) rather than total respondents, since they sometimes offered more than one appeal.

ethnic origin, length of time in the country, education and occupation, and different types of appeals.

The comparison of groups reveals a consistent pattern: the more "modern" groups—those presumably more socialized to bureaucratic behavior—exceed the more "traditional" groups in the giving of normative reasons, while the latter tend to give more appeals to altruism. This is in line with our view that altruistic appeals are least appropriate to bureaucratic encounters, while normative appeals are most appropriate.

The joint effect of ethnic origin and length of residence on the use of normative appeals is presented in Table 9-3. A comparison of the four groups of respondents shows that the newcomers from Asia and Africa differ markedly from the other three groups—which do not differ very much among themselves. In trying to cope with three of the four hypothetical situations, this group is least likely to invoke a normative appeal, and most likely to invoke an appeal to the altruism of the official or organization.[16] (The one exception, the case of the bank, shows the Eastern newcomer group somewhat more likely to invoke normative appeals, suggesting—as we shall argue below—that the bank is a rather different kind of organization from what we originally anticipated.)

Table 9–3 also examines the "change over time" in the use of normative

TABLE 9-3

Joint Effect of Ethnic Origin and Time in Israel on the Use of Normative Appeals

SITUATION	WESTERN NEW- COMERS	WESTERN OLD- TIMERS	"CHANGE"*	EASTERN NEW- COMERS	EASTERN OLD- TIMERS	"CHANGE"*
Police	33% (12)	37% (24)	+4%	19% (48)	42% (12)	+23%
Workers' committee	68 (22)	81 (16)	+13	53 (43)	86 (7)	+33
Bank	26 (19)	22 (18)	−4	30 (37)	20 (10)	−10
Sick Fund	33 (27)	35 (26)	+2	27 (59)	31 (13)	+4

*See footnote 17 (page 190).

appeals for Westerners and Easterners, proceeding on the assumption that the newcomers will become more like the oldtimers as time goes by.[17] It is apparent from the table that the increase in normative appeals between oldtimers and newcomers is concentrated primarily in the Eastern groups, though only in their hypothetical dealings with the police and the workers' committee. There are similar differences between newcomers and oldtimers among the Western group, and they are in the same direction and in the same two situations. While the amount of "change" in the Sick Fund is negligible, the bank situation shows a small *negative* change in both groups: oldtimers are less likely than newcomers to plead that the bank "owes" them a loan because they have been "faithful members of the bank."

One further hypothesis which we tested was whether Westerners in general tend to discriminate in their appeals to the four organizations more than individuals with Middle Eastern or North African backgrounds. Our assumption, again, is that offering different appeals to various kinds of organizations represents more socialized behavior. The two matrices of rank order correlations in Table 9–4 suggest that the Eastern groups show greater similarity in their appeals than do the Western groups: in the three pairs of organizations in which the correlations for the two groups differ substantially (bank and police; bank and workers' committee; workers' committee and Sick Fund), it is the Western groups who discriminate more. We also subjected this hypothesis to the test of Kendall's W, which measures the overall concordance of the rankings for all four situations. Since this coefficient varies from 0 to 1,

TABLE 9-4

*Rank-Order Correlations of Appeals to All Pairs of
Institutions by Ethnic Origin* *

	POLICE	WORKERS' COM- MITTEE	BANK	SICK FUND
Westerners				
Police		− .36	− .14	+ .42
Workers'				
committee			− .50	− .15
Bank				+ .28
Easterners				
Police		− .50	+ .44	+ .38
Workers'				
committee			− .03	+ .06
Bank				+ .32

*Based on 7 ranks as in Table 9-1.

the higher the value, the higher the concordance in the ranks compared. For Westerners we found a value of $W = 0.20$; for Easterners it was $W = 0.29$. Although both of these values proved not significantly different from 0 (with an F test at the 0.05 level), the difference between the groups is at least in the right direction, i.e., it suggests greater similarity among the answers of the Easterners in the four situations.

We would have liked to infer from these data that there is an overall socializing effect operating on new immigrants such that newcomers are less bureaucratic in their behavior than oldtimers. *Some* kind of socializing effect is in evidence—in the "levelling" which seems to make the two groups more alike over time. (See Table 9-3.) The initial difference between Western and Eastern newcomers is considerably less for the two corresponding groups of oldtimers. The fact that the oldtimer-newcomer difference is especially apparent among the Eastern groups seems to validate our thesis of a greater initial cultural gap for Easterners. The trouble is, however, that when we compare those individuals within the two ethnic groups who report having had *actual experience* in the kinds of hypothetical situations we described, the oldtimer-newcomer difference is completely reversed.[18]

As Table 9-5 shows, those with experience in the police and in the workers' committee situations tend to give *fewer* normative responses (and correspondingly higher altruistic responses) while there is an *increase* in normative responses to the bank. Even more surprising is the finding that it is the respondents of Western origin who change most as a result of experience, rather than the Easterners.[19] It seems that the levelling among those with experience (see Table 9-5) is a product of the *debureaucratization* of the Western group rather than the socialization of the Easterners to bureaucratic ways. It is difficult to reconcile these two tables. One can only suggest that newcomers, particularly those from traditional backgrounds, do tend to learn that norms are the appropriate rhetoric of communication in organizations, but that actual

TABLE 9-5

*Joint Effects of Experience and Ethnic Origin on the Use of
Normative Appeals in the Police, Workers' Committee, and Bank Situation**

	WITHOUT EXPERIENCE	WITH EXPERIENCE	"CHANGE"
Westerners			
Police	45% (18)	31% (16)	−14%
Workers' committee	85 (21)	59 (17)	−26
Bank	13 (15)	32 (22)	+19
Easterners			
Police	24 (38)	23 (22)	−1
Workers' committee	60 (20)	55 (27)	−5
Bank	10 (20)	42 (26)	+32

*The Sick Fund is omitted since only three respondents reported experience.

experience at the same time creates an opposite constraint. Possibly new-comers simultaneously learn both the rules and how to get around them!

Organizational Differences and Appeals

From the data presented so far, it is evident that there are significant differences in the kinds of appeals addressed to the different organizations. Thus, it is evident from Tables 9–3 and 9–5 that bank officials are not often appealed to in normative terms, whereas the workers' committeemen in the factories are. Table 9–6 gives the overall distribution of appeals over the four organizations.

Looking first at the rank order of appeals to altruism, we find the organizations arrayed (from most to least altruism) as follows: police, bank, Sick

TABLE 9-6

Types of Appeals in the Four Situations

TYPE OF APPEAL	POLICE	WORKERS' COMMITTEE	BANK	SICK FUND
Altruism	52%	22%	44%	26%
Reciprocity	21	13	30	44
(Inducements)	(18)	(2)	(25)	(40)
(Deterrents)	(3)	(11)	(5)	(4)
Norms	28	66	26	30
Passivity*	26	6	12	13
Total appeals (= 100%)	(96)	(87)	(84)	(125)

* Percentage of the 116 respondents who gave passive responses such as "It's no use" or "There's nothing you can do."

Fund, and workers' committee. This fits the *cui bono?* prediction precisely. Where the client is weaker, he uses more appeals to altruism; as his position gains strength, he uses fewer such appeals, and, correspondingly, more normative appeals. Thus, the *cui bono?* hypothesis fits these data better than the hypothesized rank order based on the extent of each organization's monopolistic position vis-à-vis the client; the predicted rank order from the point of view of "bargaining power" (from most to least altruistic appeals) was: police, Sick Fund, workers' committee, bank. In other words, it appears that the client's strength vis-à-vis these organizations is based more on his "normative power" than on his "bargaining power"—more on his "rights" in the organization than on his ability to reward or deprive the organization.[20]

Although the *cui bono?* hypothesis seems to give a good fit, there is reason to exercise considerable caution in interpreting these data in a conclusive way. This cautionary note can be amplified by reference to our expectations with respect to each of the organizations and the actual patterns of appeals that emerge in Table 9-6.

The police situation is the one in which the client is objectively weakest. He has least power because the organization is "against" him and "for" the general public. However, his power is low for other reasons as well. First, the organization with which he is dealing is a monopoly. Second, the situation presented to the respondent implies that the client is in the wrong; the policeman stops the driver and alleges that he violated a traffic ordinance. All of these influences lessen the client's power, and it would certainly be incorrect to attribute the high rate of altruistic appeals directed to the police official to the *cui bono?* mechanism alone. Further evidence of the client's weakness in this situation can be seen in the extent of "passivity"—the percentage of respondents who indicated that they would not try any persuasive appeal at all (bottom line of Table 9-6).

The factory workers' committee has not only the fewest altruistic appeals, it also has the highest rate of normative appeals, providing support for the argument that clients have greatest "normative power" in mutual-benefit associations in which they hold membership. While the data give clear support for the *cui bono?* hypothesis, there is reason to be cautious in this situation too: at least some of our respondents—we do not know how many—perceived this situation incorrectly and thought they were being asked to address the foreman or the boss rather than the chairman of the workers' committee (shop steward). Had we predicted for the situation in which an employee appeals to his employer, we would have placed the factory alongside the bank. In other words, we would have predicted a higher rate of altruistic appeals according to the *cui bono?* hypothesis. The success of the hypothesis in this case, then, clearly depends on how the situation was actually perceived by respondents.

The high rate of reciprocity in appealing to the Sick Fund is a surprise. In line with the *cui bono?* criterion, the client should experience considerable power vis-à-vis the Sick Fund, since it is an organization designed to serve *him.* Hence, the low rate of appeals to altruism. We expected to find, however, that the client expressed his power through appeals to norms (including the norm of altruism, "it is your duty to help me"). Instead we find the client offering promises of future cooperation, promises to pay the dues that are in arrears, and so forth. It must be reiterated that appeals to reciprocity only serve to emphasize that the client does not really have much to offer a bureaucratic organization. Nevertheless, to our surprise, our respondents preferred appeals to reciprocity over appeals to norms in the Sick Fund situation.[21]

While we expected the bank to exceed the workers' committee and the Sick Fund in appeals to altruism—by virtue of the client's lesser "normative power" vis-à-vis the bank—we expected to find a very high rate of reciprocity, certainly higher than the Sick Fund. Instead, we find that the rate of altruistic appeals approaches that of the police, and the rate of reciprocity is short of that of the Sick Fund (although it is still rather high). Retrospectively, it seems likely that we have overrated the power of the client vis-à-vis the present-day Israeli bank. The reality of the Israeli situation is such that the client's power to bargain with the bank is probably quite limited. The existence of tight controls on credit makes it rather less likely than we originally thought for a client to threaten to take his business elsewhere. Indeed, it appears that clients perceive the bank as having a large amount of power and perceive themselves as relatively limited in their ability to bargain.[22]

Thus, altogether, the *cui bono?* hypothesis seems to work—although we are not altogether sure that it always works for the right reasons. Another test we can make is to examine the rank-order correlations of all pairs of situations to see whether the factory workers' committee and police are indeed most different, as the *cui bono?* hypothesis would predict, and whether the workers' committee and Sick Fund are most alike (since the prime beneficiary, in both cases, is the client). Table 9–7 shows that only the first half of the prediction

TABLE 9-7

*Rank-Order Correlations of All Pairs of Situations**

	POLICE	WORKERS' COMMITTEE	BANK	SICK FUND
Police		− .50	+ .07	+ .42
Workers' committee			− .14	− .15
Bank				+ .67

*Based on 7 ranks, as in Table 9-1.

is borne out; the correlation between police and workers' committee is −0.50; but, surprisingly, the Sick Fund and bank turn out to be most alike (+0.67). This, as we already have discovered, is because of the unexpectedly high proportion of appeals to reciprocity in the Sick Fund and the unexpectedly high proportion of altruistic appeals in the bank.

Conclusion

To summarize, we have presented evidence from this study that the type of organization influences the appeals of clients in trying to get what they want. The content of these appeals, it appears, is more influenced by the normative basis on which the organization rests—the prime beneficiary whom it is serving—than on the client's ability to offer his resources in exchange for the organization's.

We found that people presumed to have had greater contact with organizations, whether in Israel or in other Western countries, more often base their appeals on activation of normative commitments of the organization and less often on altruism than do their counterparts. But analyzed more closely, the evidence for the nature of the socializing effect which contact with Israeli organizations has on clients is not clear-cut, since part of the data support the idea that clients learn through experience that it pays to ask for a favor.

In discussing the limitations of this study, we have pointed out the small nonrepresentative sample, the content-analytic problems of inferring meaning from rhetorical statements, and some flaws in the design of the hypothetical situations. A more general limitation of these data is that they are based on what people *said* they would do in four *hypothetical* situations, not on actual behavior. This is not the case in a larger study which we are now carrying out, a content analysis of letters written by clients to the Israeli Customs and Income Tax Authorities.

NOTES

1. For a more complete discussion of role impingement, see Elihu Katz and S. N. Eisenstadt, "Some Sociological Observations on the Response of Israeli Organizations to New Immigrants," *Administrative Science Quarterly*, 5 (1960), pp. 113–133.

2. Peter M. Blau and W. Richard Scott, *Formal Organizations: A Comparative Approach*, London: Routledge & Kegan Paul, 1963.

3. Most of the Israeli population belongs to the Histadrut, or the General Federation of Labor, a very large union which provides virtually free medical service to its members.

4. Like other norms, the norm of reciprocity appeals to obligation. The difference is that it explicitly points to the origin of the obligation in direct exchange rather than ignoring origin altogether or locating origin in tradition, law, and so forth.

5. John R. P. French, Jr. and Bertram Raven, "The Bases of Social Power," in Dorwin Cartwright and Alvin Zander, eds., *Group Dynamics: Research and Theory*, Evanston, Ill.: Row, Peterson, 1960, pp. 607 ff.; John W. Thibaut and Harold H. Kelley, *The Social Psychology of Groups*, New York: Wiley, 1959, especially p. 119;

Fritz Heider, *The Psychology of Interpersonal Relations*, New York: Wiley, 1958, pp. 245 ff.; Morris Rosenberg, "Power and Desegregation," *Social Problems*, 3 (1955), pp. 215–223; Peter M. Blau, *Exchange and Power in Social Life*, New York: Wiley, 1964, especially pp. 118–125.

6. Talcott Parsons, "On the Concept of Influence," *Public Opinion Quarterly*, 27 (Spring 1963), pp. 37–62.

7. See Parsons, *ibid.*, pp. 42 ff. Rosenberg and Pearlin employ similar categories in their study of how nurses in mental hospitals motivate recalcitrant patients. They refer to "coercive power" based on actual sanctions or the threat of sanctions (corresponds to "deterrence"); "legitimate authority" ("activation of commitments"); "persuasion" (the same term in Parsons' typology); and "benevolent manipulation," which is not really relevant in the present context. See Morris Rosenberg and Leonard I. Pearlin, "Power Orientations in a Mental Hospital," *Human Relations*, 15 (November 1962), pp. 335–349. Schmitt has done an empirical study which focused only on what he called the "invocation of a moral obligation,"—again parallel to Parsons' "activation of commitments" and our "normative" appeals. His attempt to isolate the conditions under which this type of strategy is used, while not entirely successful, is suggestive of one direction which research on the differential use of various types of appeals may take. See David R. Schmitt, "The Invocation of Moral Obligation," *Sociometry*, 27 (September 1964), pp. 299–310.

8. In a personal communication to one of the authors, Blau has suggested that appeals to altruism, like inducements, acknowledge one's indebtedness to the other, thus offering him status or power.

9. Respondents were dichotomized on each of the four background variables. Roughly half were classified as "Western" in origin (respondents born in Europe, North and South America, and natives of Israel whose parents are from Europe, North and South America, or Israel) and the other half as "Eastern" (those born in Asia or Africa, and those born in Israel whose parents are from Asia or Africa). This classification, of course, is very gross, and entirely overlooks the important distinction between rural and urban residence in country of origin. Those with at least nine years of schooling (about half the respondents) were assigned to the "High School" category while the others were classified as "Elementary School." Subjects were divided into "High" versus "Medium and Low" occupations, with professionals, businessmen, clerical and sales workers constituting the "High" group, and skilled manual employees, semiskilled, and unskilled workers in the other group. Note that the young age of the respondents probably lowers their occupational level; furthermore, the heavy concentration in the skilled labor category (60 of 114) somewhat distorts the distinction between groups: there are only 29 "High," while 85 fall into the other occupational group. As for length of time in the country, respondents were again separated into two groups, oldtimers and newcomers, according to whether they had come to Israel before or after the establishment of the state in 1948.

10. As has been pointed out, some of the appeals to norms which appear in the data actually tend to activate the norm of reciprocity, rather than a strictly rational-legal norm.

11. Judith T. Shuval, "Values of Israeli Immigrants," *Sociometry*, 26 (June 1963), pp. 247–259.

12. For example, "Don't write the ticket, because I am a civil defense worker hurrying to my post."

13. The decision to use altruism as a basis for testing the *cui bono?* hypothesis follows upon the realization that we cannot easily distinguish among the several types of appeals to norms. The hypothesis, therefore, is partly *ex post facto*, and was not formulated prior to examination of the data.

14. It should be noted that this ranking might differ in other times and places where

medical practice, for example, might be more or less monopolistic, the labor market more open or more closed, and so forth. In fact, as we shall note below, we are probably wrong even for the present day Israeli situation in our placement of the bank.

15. Still another way to rank client's power in these four situations is according to the extent of institutionalization of mechanisms for appealing against the official's decision—high in the police situation, low in the bank.

16. Altruistic appeals increase as normative appeals decrease; appeals to reciprocity do not vary with these background variables (as was shown in Table 9-2).

17. This is a questionable assumption, of course, although it is often found in the empirical literature. Use of "difference" rather than "change" would be more accurate though somewhat less interesting.

18. Since only three respondents had actually experienced the situation in the Sick Fund, the analysis of the effects of experience is restricted to the three other situations.

19. There is some face validity in the measure of experience by virtue of the fact that one would expect Westerners—who have more cars—to have had greater contact with traffic policemen. Similarly, one would expect greater experience among Easterners with the workers' committee situation.

20. As was noted above in the presentation of hypotheses, we are using rate of appeals to altruism as a general measure of the client's strength. It is ironic that we cannot use the rate of appealing to norms as a measure of "normative power" and the rate of appealing to reciprocity as a measure of "monopolistic power" or "bargaining power." To do so, however, would raise more problems than would be solved.

21. With the wisdom of hindsight, we now realize that the client's "guilt" in this situation, and his alleged guilt in the case of the police situation, probably increase the number of promises "to be good."

22. We are aware that the study would have been strengthened by empirical validation of our view of the salient prime beneficiary in each organizational situation presented. That is, we might have asked respondents to indicate the identity of the prime beneficiary in each case. To our knowledge this type of validation of the *cui bono?* typology of Blau and Scott, *op. cit.*, has not been attempted.

10

James D. Thompson

ORGANIZATIONS AND OUTPUT

TRANSACTIONS

Complex purposive organizations receive inputs from, and discharge outputs to, environments, and virtually all such organizations develop specialized roles for these purposes. *Output roles,* designed to arrange for distribution of the organization's ultimate product, service, or impact to other agents of the society thus are *boundary-spanning* roles linking organization and environment through interaction between member and nonmember.

Organizational output roles are defined in part by reciprocal roles of non-members. Teacher, salesman, and caseworker roles can only be understood in relation to pupil, customer, and client roles. Both member and nonmember roles contain the expectation of closure or completion of interaction, leading either to the severance of interaction or bringing the relationship into a new phase.[1] Each output role, together with the reciprocating nonmember role, can be considered as built into a *transaction structure.*

Because output roles exist in structures that span the boundaries of the organization, they may be important sources of organization adaptation to environmental influences. Empirical studies reflect this fact more than do theories of organization.

Classic bureaucratic theory is preoccupied with behavioral relations ordered by a single, unified authority structure from which the client is excluded,[2] and only recently has an explicit correction for this one-sided approach been introduced by Eisenstadt's theory of debureaucratization.[3] Another strain of organization theory, following Chester Barnard, clouds the significance of input-

J. D. Thompson, "Organizations and Output Transactions," *American Journal of Sociology* 68 (1962): 309–324. Copyright 1962 by The University of Chicago Press. Reprinted by permission of The University of Chicago Press and J. D. Thompson.

NOTE: I am indebted to my colleagues—Robert Avery, Carl Beck, Richard Carlson, Joseph Eaton, Robert Hawkes, Axel Leijonhufvud, Morris Ogul, and C. Edward Weber —for helpful reactions to earlier versions of this chapter.

output problems by lumping investors, clients, suppliers, and customers as members of the "co-operative system."[4] The developing inducements-contributions theory of March and Simon has so far been directed primarily at the problem of recruiting and motivating members or employees.[5]

One purpose of this chapter will be to focus theoretical attention on boundary-spanning behavior by way of output roles. A second will be to indicate that there are several types of transaction structure, each having peculiar significance for the comparative analysis of organizations. A third aim will be to indicate that transaction processes can be studied profitably through sequential analysis. Finally, some larger consequences of output relationships will be suggested.

Consideration will be limited to those transaction structures that call for face-to-face interpersonal interaction between member and nonmember, thus ignoring the cigarette "salesman" who may periodically load a vending machine without seeing his customers or knowing who they are, and the soldier who may deliver destruction to an enemy he neither sees nor could identify. Consideration will also be limited to those cases in which the output role is occupied by an employed agent of the organization.

Characteristics of Transaction Structures

For any transaction structure there appear to be three possible transaction outcomes: (1) *completion* of a transaction as defined by organizational norms, (2) *abortion*, in which interaction is terminated without completion of the transaction, or (3) *side transaction*, in which member and nonmember complete an exchange not desired or approved by the organization.[6] Which of these three outcomes emerges will in part be determined by the desires, attitudes, and actions of the two parties involved. But the likely paths from initiation of interaction to termination, and the branching points which lead to one or another outcome, are largely defined by the type of transaction structure.

Elements of a Typology

The organization cannot predict in advance of any specific encounter just what desires, attitudes, or actions the nonmember will bring to the transaction structure, but the organization can estimate in advance with reasonable accuracy two things: (1) the extent to which it has armed its agents with routines, and

(2) the extent to which the nonmember is compelled to participate in the relationship.

The first dimension will be labeled one of *specificity of control over member.* Undoubtedly this forms a continuum, but it will be discussed here only in its extremes. At one extreme the member is equipped with a single, complete program—a standard procedure which supposedly does not vary, regardless of the behavior of the nonmember. At the other extreme, the member's behavior is expected to be guided primarily by the behavior of the nonmember, although always in relation to some organizational target or goal.[7] The supermarket check-out clerk approximates the *programmed* role, while the social caseworker illustrates the *heuristic* variety.

The second dimension, also a continuum but here dichotomized, will be labeled *degree of nonmember discretion.* At one extreme the nonmember finds interaction *mandatory,* at the other it is *optional.* It may be presumed that the prisoner, for example, finds interaction with the guard mandatory. To be sure the prisoner may evade interaction by escape or by behavior which results in transfer to another cell block or prison. But short of these extremes, the prisoner cannot choose whom he will interact with or whether to interact; the relationship is mandatory.

The optional state is exemplified by the salesman-customer relationship under conditions of "perfect competition," where the prospect has a wide choice of salesmen. Not only does the customer have discretion over whether to interact, but he also may terminate it at will, before completion of a transaction.

When these two dichotomized dimensions are combined, four types of output structures emerge:

DEGREE OF NONMEMBER DISCRETION	SPECIFICITY OF ORGANIZATIONAL CONTROL	
	MEMBER PROGRAMMED	MEMBER HEURISTIC
Interaction mandatory	I	III
Interation optional	II	IV

Temptation to label each cell is strong, since there are familiar categorizations readily available which appear to correspond to each. Cell I, for example, might be considered "clerical," Cell II "commercial," Cell III "semi-professional," and Cell IV "professional." The temptation has been resisted, however, because casual, traditional categorizations may in fact hide some of the distinctions which this typology attempts to bring out. Thus, transactions which might typically be lumped under the term "commercial" may, in fact, appear in any of the cells defined here.

Occurrence of Transaction Structures

Organizations which develop elaborate programs for those in output roles appear to be those that either (1) provide services for large numbers of persons and, therefore, face many nonmembers relative to each member at the output boundary, or (2) employ a mechanized production technology which places a premium on large runs of standardized products, attaches heavy costs to retooling, and, therefore, depend on a large volume of standardized transactions per member at the output boundary.[8] The first condition seems appropriate for clerical activities, such as the issuance of licenses or permits by a government bureau, and is especially likely when the organization holds a monopoly position, as a government often does. This seems to correspond to Cell I in the typology above, and to classic bureaucratic theory.

The second condition seems to describe commercial transactions of mass-produced products under competitive conditions and corresponds to Cell II in the typology. When competition is removed, as in the seller's market for automobiles after World War II, the role of salesman can be redefined into a clerical role, with the salesman merely writing orders and adding names to the waiting list—and perhaps adding a side transaction to give the customer a priority rank in exchange for private payment.[9] Under competitive conditions, however, the sales person expresses one or more organizational programs governing size, style, color, price, terms, delivery schedules, and so on, and the customer either takes it or leaves it to search among other organizations for a more suitable program.

Neither of these transaction structures is appropriate for the organization which must "tailor" its output, for here the exigencies make it impractical if not impossible to develop standard programs in advance. Instead the organization must rely on the judgment of the member at the output boundary. Such roles tend to be assigned to professionally trained or certified persons, for it is believed that the professional type of education qualifies individuals to make judgments or exercise discretion in situations appropriate to their specialization.

When nonmember participation is mandatory the transaction structure corresponds to Cell III in the typology above. Examples would include the therapy-oriented prison and the military hospital, the public school, and the *public* (as distinguished from "voluntary") welfare agency. In each case, the nonmember (prisoner, patient, pupil, or applicant) is obliged to participate in the structure, and in each case the member is expected to vary his behavior to suit the particular condition of the nonmember.

When interaction of the heuristic variety is optional for the nonmember, the transaction structure corresponds to Cell IV in the typology. This would encompass the "voluntary" (nongovernmental) welfare agency and the voluntary hospital. Many of the services which fit this category are dispensed by private entrepreneurial arrangements—by private practitioners—rather than in large-scale oganizational contexts. It appears that this reflects the relative complexity of the process in this kind of transaction structure, which makes it especially difficult when subjected to the additional constraints of an organizational context.

It is suggested that in the order listed above, and numbered in the typology, the four types of transaction structures are increasingly difficult to operate.

Transaction Processes

The same three types of outcomes—successful transaction, abortion, and side transaction—are available for all of the transaction structures, but significant contrasts appear in the possible courses of interaction. The final state, and the paths to it, *depend in each case on contingencies and on responses to contingencies.*

Our conceptual apparatus for analyzing contingent interaction is ill-developed, since interaction theory has been preoccupied with structure-maintaining behavior, that is, with behavior conforming to stable norms and with social control mechanisms to correct deviation. The contingencies and possible paths of interaction, therefore, will be shown in flow diagrams. These are offered as hypothetical, for literature search did not reveal sufficient data to "test" them, but illustrative citations will be made.

For illustration, the possibilities for Type I, where the member is programmed and the nonmember finds interaction mandatory, are shown in Figure 10–1. Once contact is made, the nonmember may respond in one of three ways, and each, in turn, presents several response possibilities to the member. *If,* following initial contact, the nonmember responds appropriately by offering necessary information, the member may routinely complete the transaction. Instead of responding appropriately, however, the nonmember may resist or offer a bribe. *If* the nonmember resists, the member applies punishments, and the nonmember may respond by increasing resistance, by cooperating, or by offering a bribe. The bribe attempt thus may be made immediately upon initial contact or following an exchange of activity. In either case, however, the member may elect one of three alternative responses to the bribe offer: accept it, apply additional punishments, or explore the pros and cons of the bribe possibility. And so on, as is indicated in Figure 10–1. In each flow diagram we have attempted to depict as the central pattern that course of interaction most desired by the organization. In each, however, there are several possibilities for the interaction to digress from the desired path, swinging either to the right or left. In the more complex transaction structures, the course of interaction may swing from one stream to the other several times before the final outcome

FIGURE 10-1.

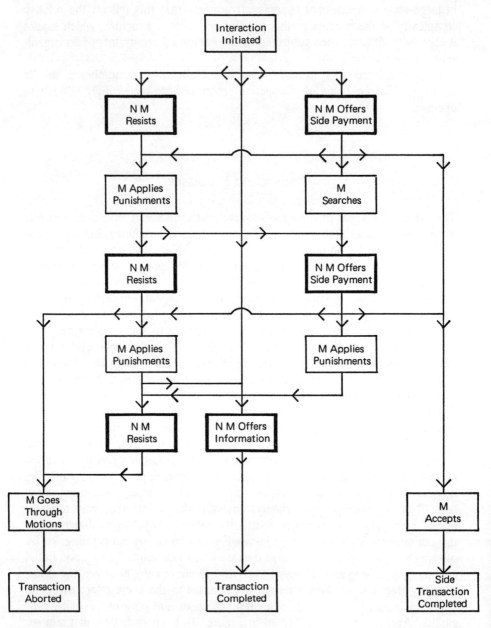

Key

Sequence flows from top to bottom — arrows indicate possible paths of interaction

M   Indicates activity of member

N M   Indicates activity of nonmember

is reached, and one of the major problems for the member is to counter each digression so that it returns to the central path and ultimately results in a successful transaction.

Why members and nonmembers elect one route rather than another at each switching point is a subject for microanalysis and is beyond the scope of this chapter.

The number of "ifs" or contingencies—even in this simplest type of transaction—is impressive when diagrammed, but too large to make verbal reproduction possible. The following discussion will focus, therefore, on certain implications of contingencies for behavior within each type of transaction structure.

Interaction in Type I Structures

Here the nonmember's participation is mandatory, the member is programmed, and the organization expects a large number of output transactions from the member (see Figure 10–1).

The course of interaction is simplest if the nonmember chooses to complete the transaction speedily, for he appears to the member to be cooperative. The member scores a completed transaction in a minimum of time, which contributes toward maximizing the number of transactions in serial and not only puts the member in line for organizational rewards but may provide the personal satisfaction of a "job well done." Blau, for example, noted that employment interviewers in a government agency avoided operations that took time without helping to improve their statistical records. Since the records served as the basis for evaluating performance, concentration on this goal made interviewers "unresponsive to requests from clients that would interfere with its attainment."[10]

If the nonmember chooses to seek concession from the member, he must offer personal satisfactions sufficient to induce the member to risk penalties that the organization can apply if deviation from programs is detected. Blau found that at times the social reward of the client's appreciation led governmental employment interviewers to offer extra help,[11] and students of prisons have reported favored treatment by guards of prisoners who could exercise (or withhold) informal control over other inmates.[12]

That the opposite result—penalties for seeking too much help—can occur is suggested by the analysis of another employment office. Francis and Stone note that the client's eligibility for unemployment compensation is in effect determined by the interviewer's report, and that this report reflects the interviewer's *judgment* as to whether the claimant has given an accurate or exaggerated account of his history and present circumstances.[13] Blau also reports the use of punitive measures to vent *antagonism against aggressive clients.*[14]

The bribe attempt involves risk for both member and nonmember. If the inducements offered by the nonmember are insufficient, the member may

197

regard him as uncooperative and therefore apply penalties. If, on the other hand, the nonmember's offer is sufficiently inducing, the member must somehow hide his deviation from the program, and runs the risk of being caught. The bribe attempt, therefore, often calls for a rather delicate "sounding out process."[15]

If neither party is able to marshal enough power to bring a transaction or a side transaction to a conclusion, this mandatory relationship is likely to settle into a going-through-the-motions, with each party seeking to maximize his rewards or minimize his costs.[16] From the standpoint of official organizational goals, then, the transaction is aborted. If interaction must be sustained, as in the prison, it is likely to become a struggle for control. That the struggle for control can be most subtle is brought out by Gresham Sykes' study of the corruption of authority in the maximum security prison.[17]

Interaction in Type II Structures

In this case the nonmember's participation is optional, the member is programmed, and the organization expects a large number of output transactions from the member (see Figure 10–2).

Since the relationship is not mandatory, the organization usually develops an *array* of programs, one to appeal to each class or category of potential customer. The nonmember, in interacting with this organization, is foregoing interaction with another, and hence seeks to determine rapidly whether a satisfactory program is available. The "gambit," or "opening move," is therefore a crucial issue in this interaction process. Lombard reports some of the difficulties salesgirls faced in "sizing up" prospective customers. In a children's clothing department, for example, "each customer presented . . . a different set of values that determined her taste in the clothes she bought for her children." Knowledge of style was not alone sufficient to make a sale, for the salesgirl could not express this in a way that criticized the customer's taste. With respect to price, the store suggested that "unless a customer made some other request, a salesgirl would do well to show her clothes in a middle price range."[18]

The simplest situation in this output transaction occurs when the gambit is successful, either because the nonmember offers enough accurate information or the member "sizes up" the nonmember correctly. On either basis the most suitable program is offered and the nonmember accepts or rejects. The transaction has been completed successfully in short order, or has been aborted clearly and speedily, permitting the member to devote attention to other prospects and the nonmember to seek a more satisfactory supplier.

A complication arises when the member selects from his repertoire of programs an unsuitable one because of inaccurate "size up," incorrect interpretation of the information given by the nonmember, or false or misleading

FIGURE 10-2.

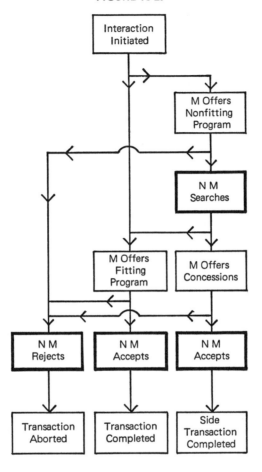

Key

Sequence flows from top to bottom — arrows indicate possible paths of interaction

[M] Indicates activity of member

[N M] Indicates activity of nonmember

information offered by the nonmember. The result may be (*a*) further exploration until a fitting program is identified, which is relatively costly to both parties, (*b*) withdrawal of the nonmember from the output structure, in which case a potential transaction is lost to a competitor, or (*c*) continued interaction on the basis of false optimism, with mounting frustration for one or both parties as they find the investment mounting and the possibility of satisfaction dwindling.[19] In the latter case, the eventual abortion of the transaction is likely to be unpleasant, reducing the possibility of future interaction between member and nonmember. It is in this frustrating situation that the member is most likely to deviate from approved programs, misrepresenting the product, offering inferior substitutes, or finding ways of offering arrangements not approved by the organization, such as special deliveries or price reductions by shaving commissions. Another possible outcome of this situation is for the nonmember to reduce his standards—accepting another color, style, or settling for a different size, delivery date, and so on. When this occurs, the transaction is completed, although perhaps at the expense of future transactions.

Because prolonged search behavior is "costly," requiring investment of time and energy where the outcome is problematic, ability to "close the deal" as early as possible becomes almost as crucial as the gambit.

Interaction in Type III Structures

Here the nonmember's participation is mandatory, the member must tailor his service to the particular needs of the nonmember, and the organization must therefore judge the member's performance in terms of results rather than in terms of conformity to prescribed procedures (see Figure 10–3).

The straight-forward and relatively easy case occurs when the nonmember elects to complete the transaction with least effort and responds appropriately. The ability of the nonmember to take *active* part in the heuristic process seems frequently to be important, and especially so in comparison with the Type I output structure. Nurses were found to prefer an active patient who could make his needs and wants known, if for no other reason than to help his own treatment. In contrast, ward aides, whose duties defined the patient as "something like a necessary evil, preferred the passive patient above all others."[20]

When the nonmember's responses are appropriate, both parties achieve a satisfactory outcome at minimum cost, and the member has the additional reward of evidence that his skills were instrumental—that he did a job well. But what happens when the response of the nonmember is inappropriate?[21] The inappropriate response might come either from a nonmember with a sincere desire to cooperate or from a nonmember who is resisting. Cooperation by the nonmember does not guarantee his appropriate response, for he may be incapable of articulating appropriate information, may not understand which responses are desired by the member, or may zealously offer a flood of irrelevant information. Extreme status differences between member and nonmember, often found in the "helping professions," can lead to this situation. Fanshel concludes that casework help is tailored more for the verbal, communicative group than it is for "the significantly large group of clients who find difficulty in expressing their feelings and their basic ideas about the problems that bring them to the agency."[22]

When an inadequate or inappropriate response is made, therefore, the member must form a judgment (or leap to a conclusion) about the reason. If he defines the nonmember as uncooperative he may apply punishments, while if he defines the nonmember as sincere but inept, he may search for

FIGURE 10-3.

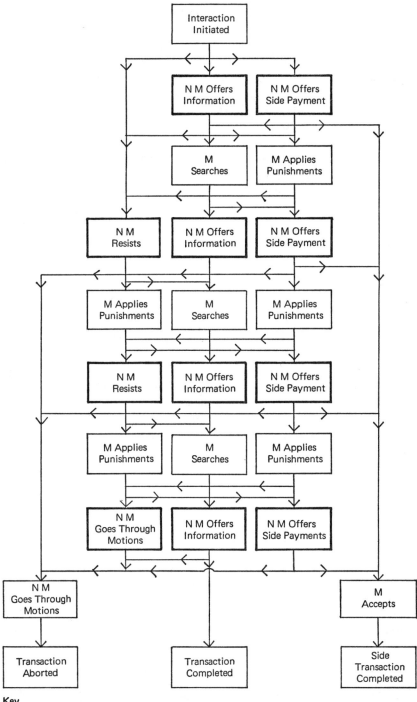

Key

    Sequence flows from top to bottom — arrows indicate possible paths of interaction

        M   Indicates activity of member

        N M Indicates activity of nonmember

relevant information by seeking to educate the nonmember to the appropriate role. This educational activity under such circumstances is clearly brought out by Israeli responses to large numbers of immigrants who had yet to learn client roles,[23] but there is no reason to believe that it does not occur in more "normal" or less striking situations.

Whether the member will search for information or, rather, punish the nonmember for inappropriate responses, will depend largely on the member's conclusions regarding the reasons for inappropriate responses. If the nonmember's search for the proper role is unsuccessful, or if he responds to punishment by resisting (or increasing resistance), the interaction process in this output structure is likely to degenerate into a struggle for control. This would appear, perhaps, in the relationship between high-school students and teachers, in the therapy-oriented prison, and in the therapy-oriented mental hospital.[24] Often the nonmember will resist "help" but will "go through the motions," appearing to cooperate to escape punishments. Eaton has suggested that for the social caseworker the client may effectively control the relationship by "presenting a challenge," by "showing appreciation," or by promising to change his behavior at some future time—provided that the caseworker keep trying.[25]

The abortive struggle for control can also occur when the nonmember offers inadequate bribes for a side transaction. A bribe offer that is rejected, however, gives the member added leverage in avoiding the stand-off and, instead, completing a transaction successfully. Blau reports that being offered a bribe constituted a special tactical advantage for the field agent of a law enforcement agency. A nonmember who had violated one law was caught in the act of compounding his guilt by violating another one. He could no longer claim ignorance or inadvertence as an excuse for his violations, and agents exploited this situation to strengthen their position in negotiations.[26]

Interaction in Type IV Structures

Now the interaction is heuristic, the relationship is optional for the nonmember, and the member must attract clients and maintain interaction before he can complete a transaction (see Figure 10–4).

Whether interaction is initiated by the member or by the nonmember, making the initial contact is likely to be a difficult experience. Lack of knowledge of appropriate role behavior may indeed lead many individuals who need "professional help" to avoid interaction with appropriate professionals. In a sample survey seeking to determine "normal" American attitudes toward mental health, "lack of knowledge about means" of seeking professional help was a major reason given by those who felt they could have used help but did not seek it.[27] A study of "well-trained" life insurance underwriters con-

FIGURE 10-4.

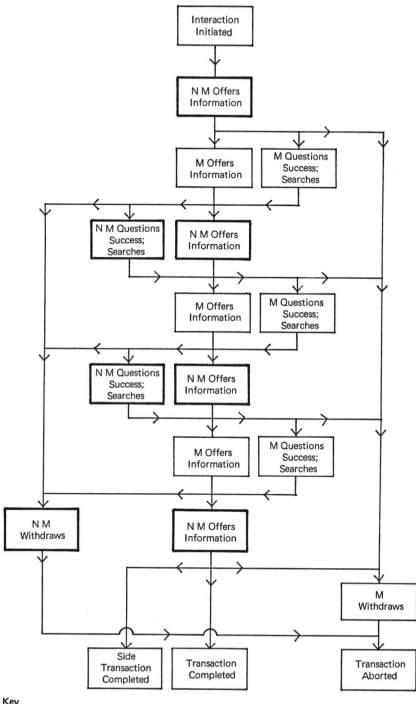

Key

Sequence flows from top to bottom — arrows indicate possible paths of interaction

M Indicates activity of member

N M Indicates activity of nonmember

cluded that "anxiety over intrusion on prospect privacy," was a major deterrent to making contacts,[28] and it has been reported that "a salesman of accident and health insurance is expected to make at least 36 prospect contacts by cold canvass each week. If he can sell four of these, he is regarded as performing very well. Thus he must steel himself to an average of 32 rejections 50 weeks in the year."[29]

Initial contact, at best, simply sets the stage for further exploration. Freidson concludes that the first visit by urban patients to a medical practitioner is often tentative, a tryout. Whether the physician's prescription will be followed, and whether the patient will come back, seem to rest at least partly on his retrospective assessment of the professional consultation.[30] Kadushin reports a considerable amount of shopping around by individuals undertaking psychotherapy.[31] The organizational counterpart of shopping around is exercised, for example, by the intake committee of the psychiatric clinic that, on the basis of initial exploration, may select those most likely to succeed as patients.[32]

Nevertheless, both parties enter this transaction structure with a measure of uncertainty, because the behavior of each must be keyed to information possessed by the other. The potential client seeks a personalized transaction for which there may be no standard pattern, and hence, no readily available schedule of costs or of probabilities of satisfactory outcome. The member's diagnosis and prognosis depend on the unfolding of information during the interaction process; hence the member cannot at the outset guarantee success, nor can he predict the complete costs to the nonmember. The member must hold out enough hope of results to maintain interaction in the face of uncertainty—but he also needs "escape clauses." The client likewise must disclose enough information and motivation to enable the member to make estimates—but without irrevocable commitment to the transaction.

If the nonmember becomes fully committed to the transaction he can make few choices and exercises little control. Freidson notes that when the patient penetrates into "organizational practice" such as found in hospitals, he is well into the professional referral system, which involves maximal restriction on client choice of services, and his efforts at control are most likely to take the form of evasion.[33] In other words, when the client becomes fully committed to the transaction structure, the transaction structure is converted into a Type III structure.

Short of this conversion, however, there is a fully developed sounding-out process. In the early stages of interaction, a large proportion of behavior of both parties is oriented toward establishment of *rapport* and a small proportion to the substance of the transaction relationship. As the interaction process nears successful achievement the proportions are reversed, but en route the joint search may yield information that changes the prognosis of one or both parties, either making costs appear higher than anticipated or making success appear less likely. When the unfolding of the relationship in this way changes the conditions for the client, the transaction may be aborted. Each successive time the relationship is thus challenged by the unfolding of information which bears on costs and rewards, *rapport* must be reestablished. Eaton notes that an evaluation of the actual results of treatment is often impossible until a good deal of time has elapsed. "Along the way, during this protracted search for happiness, both practitioner and client want to know if there is evidence of progress, and often a judgment is made with an implied presumption that the *quality of the therapeutic relationship* is predictive of its outcome."[34]

Each successive time that the relationship is questioned, additional investment has been made and thus the magnitude of the dilemma is greater. This may be true for the member as well as for the nonmember, for crisis over rapport is likely to be personally dissatisfying to the practitioner as well as threatening to his organizational rewards; thus, he may be reluctant to alter early diagnosis and prognosis (in a direction more costly to the client) so long as there appears to be a possibility of success on the original terms. This would operate, then, to diminish the heuristics of the interaction process; the early prognosis becomes a program not easily disrupted.

The possibility of a side transaction occurs when the member has exclusive access to something desired by the nonmember, such as drugs that only a licensed physician can prescribe, or when the nonmember seeks some form of attention rather than technical treatment. In medicine, under these circumstances, the placebo may satisfy the patient's need for attention and maintain the physician-patient relationship. Freidson notes that whether their motive be to heal the patient or to survive professionally, physicians dependent on the lay referral system will feel pressure to accept or manipulate lay expectations by administering harmless placebos or by giving up unpopular drugs.[35]

Because of the uncertainties of the heuristic transaction process and the difficulties of establishing and maintaining rapport, it would appear that the distinction between a process leading toward side transaction often is difficult to distinguish from one leading toward transaction. For this reason, Figure 10–4 does not distinguish a separate flow for transactions and side transactions.

The theme of the Type IV transaction structure thus appears to be rapport, and members must not only be able to establish and maintain rapport but, it would seem, to "cool out" the nonmember if rapport cannot be reestablished at one of the crisis points;[36] that is, when the transaction is aborted, the member needs some means of convincing the disappointed nonmember that the attempt was a reasonable one.

Dynamics of Output Relations

Because disposition of its products is imperative for any complex, purposive organization, the transaction structure is crucial. It may dictate or place significant constraints on (*a*) the acquisition of necessary inputs by the organization, (*b*) the internal arrangements for allocation and coordination of resources and activities, and (c) the political or "institutional" requirements of the organization. The pivotal nature of the output relationship thus claims the attention not only of those in output roles but also of those at the several administrative levels.

Significance of Supervision

At the technical level of the organization is found not only the output role but, inevitably, a supervisory role—charged with direct responsibility for evaluating, facilitating, or modifying the behavior of those in output roles vis-à-vis nonmembers. The foregoing analysis has suggested differences in the role of the supervisor for each type of transaction structure. For the Type I structure, supervisory responsibility revolves around enforcement of conformity to program and detection of deviation. The supervisory focus on the Type II structure is on subordinates' skills in gambits and in closing transactions. For the Type III structure, the supervisory problem centers on the maintenance of heuristics—and preventing the development of *ad hoc* programs. For the supervisor of a Type IV relationship, the concern is with balancing rapport and treatment.

Though the content of the supervisory role differs from one type of structure to another, its significance is common to all; the supervisory role reinforces the organizational dimension in the definition of the output role. Since the nonmember also is important in defining the role of member, the stage is set for a three-person game, with the supervisor having to make sure that the coalition always is between himself and the member in the output role, and not between member and nonmember, that is, a side transaction.

Even when the coalition includes the supervisor, however, satisfactory disposal of output is not assured, for perfomance at the output boundary always is subject to the constraints of the transaction structure. If the structure departs from one of the "pure types" discussed above, members at the technical level can only adapt to those impurities, but administrators at other levels of the organization may have the resources necessary to reinforce or "purify" the structures. If it is to the organization's advantage to convert from one type of structure to another, that too must result from administrative decision and action. Finally, if the organization faces a changing environment for which existing transaction structures are inadequate, the necessary adaptation can come only from administrative action.

Mixed Structures and Managerial Action

Poetic license was exercised earlier to deal only with the polar extremes of two variables that in reality are continuous. The four pure types yielded by this maneuver may indeed describe the "ideal models" toward which organizations strive—but often only approximate. Impurities may stem from the situation of the nonmember or of the member.

Nonmembers may be *more or less* under compulsion to interact with members, rather than at the mandatory or optional poles. Even where the government has a monopoly on licensing certain activities, the potential nonmember may choose to risk illegal activity rather than to negotiate for a license. The member in the output role and his supervisor are powerless to combat this. If the transaction structure is to be reinforced in this case, it requires managerial policies and commitment of resources to find and punish evaders. Prisoners may be unable to effect escape, but the fact that they are *batched*[37] makes rioting possible, and the fact that they and their guards engage in a prolonged series of transactions gives prisoners a certain subtle bargaining power that can place limits on the complete arbitrariness of the prison.[38] If the transaction structure is to be reinforced in this case, it requires managerial policies and commitment of resources to provide for segmentation of prisoners or rotation of guards.

Potential customers may, of course, "do without" or find alternative sources of supply, but there are inconveniences of time and place involved in both alternatives. Potential clients may have a choice of suffering without professional help or seeking out other professionals, which often is difficult for the layman, and there are costs attached to these alternatives also. If the transaction structure is to be purified in these cases where the nonmember's discretion is limited, policies stressing service or professional norms must be adopted and emphasized by managers.

Impurities can be introduced into the transaction structure from the organization's side also. The programmed member can be furnished with such a large number of programs that he must, in fact, behave heuristically. If this situation is to be purified, it must be through managerial action to reduce the number of programs or, more likely, to departmentalize, with nonmembers initially screened and routed to the appropriate department. Scarcity of prospects, in the Type II structure, also leads to impurities, for this structure operates on a statistical rather than an absolute basis, that is, a percentage of interactions are expected to abort. When prospects are scarce, members in the output role may be reluctant to permit an abortion, seeking instead to complete a side transaction. If this situation is to be purified, it is likely to be through managerial action to increase the flow of prospects. Advertising, extension of credit, or emphasis on convenience are among the tactics employed.

An overload on the member in the structure calling for heuristics also introduces impurities by limiting the time available to engage in heuristics and encouraging the use of *ad hoc* programs. Here again, if impurities are to be removed, managerial action is required. In the Type IV structure managerial policies can turn away prospective clients, but in the Type III structure the most likely course is to increase the size of the output staff.

Management of Organizational Posture

Managerial or administrative influence over transaction structures rests less on authority to dictate standards or procedures than on ability to negotiate changes in *organizational posture,* that is, a relationship between the organization and its relevant environment resulting from the joint action of both.[39]

Hawkes has shown, for the psychiatric hospital case, how the contractual negotiations of the administrator can significantly influence transactions at the boundaries. Both patient input and patient output are affected by the administrator's activities outside the hospital.[40] Levine and White have indicated that administrative negotiations can affect the *domain* of a welfare agency within the larger welfare system, and hence affect what are here termed transaction structures.[41] Economic evidence clearly indicates that administrative negotiation can arrange for monopoly or cartel systems, which in turn have important implications for output relationships.

While most of the illustrations given above were of actions that rectify some imbalance caused either by (*a*) a positive advantage held by the prospective nonmember or (*b*) a disadvantage imposed on the member, administrative maneuvers can sometimes result in a posture more favorable to the organization than to the nonmember. It can be hypothesized that organizations faced with Types II or IV transaction structures will attempt to reduce the freedom of prospective nonmembers, thus converting the structures into Types I or III. Achievement of a monopoly, of course, accomplishes this immediately.

While monopoly is illegal for certain types of American organizations, many others are not subject to such constraints. Governments usually operate monopolistic agencies, and public school systems are monopolistic or quasi-monopolistic. Hospitals, clinics, and voluntary social welfare organizations are monopolistic in many nonmetropolitan settings. In larger cities they may achieve monopoly or near-monopoly by actions of the referral system, if referring agencies recognize the organization's claim to exclusive domain or jurisdiction for certain types of cases.

Even in the commercial sphere where legal codes prohibit economic monopoly, social-psychological monopoly can be achieved or approached through brandname advertising, or by the achievement of *extrinsic prestige* by the organization.[42]

Conclusion

It is hoped that this chapter has called attention to the need for further consideration by organization theorists of the output relationship, by showing that it occurs in transaction structures built in part of elements not within the organization and hence that it cannot be authoritatively dictated.

Finally, it is hoped that a case has been made for the necessity of developing or adapting analytic tools—such as flowcharts—for the investigation of contingent interaction in social roles.

NOTES

1. Role theory has devoted much more attention to structure-maintaining behavior than to transaction behavior, in spite of the variety and quantity of transaction in modern societies. See, however, William J. Goode, "A Theory of Role Strain," *American Sociological Review*, XXV (August 1960), 483–96; George C. Homans, *Social Behavior: Its Elementary Forms* (New York: Harcourt, Brace & Co., 1961), and John W. Thibaut and Harold H. Kelley, *The Social Psychology of Groups* (New York: John Wiley & Sons, 1959).

2. Max Weber, *The Theory of Economic and Social Organization* (Glencoe: Free Press, 1957), and Robert K. Merton, *Social Theory and Social Structure* (rev. ed.; Glencoe: Free Press, 1957), chap. vi.

3. S. N. Eisenstadt, "Bureaucracy, Bureaucratization, and Debureaucratization," *Administrative Science Quarterly*, IV (1959), 302–20.

4. Chester Barnard, *The Functions of the Executive* (Cambridge, Mass.: Harvard University Press, 1938).

5. James G. March and Herbert A. Simon, *Organizations* (New York: John Wiley & Sons, 1958).

6. This concept was suggested by that of "side payment" as developed by R. M. Cyert and J. G. March, "A Behavioral Theory of Organizational Objectives," in Mason Haire (ed.), *Modern Organization Theory* (New York: John Wiley & Sons, 1959).

7. March and Simon make a similar distinction by referring to programs specifying activities (means) and programs specifying product or outcome (ends). They observe that the latter allow discretion to the individual (*op. cit.*, p. 147).

8. I am indebted to Axel Leijonhufvud for contributing this insight from economic theory.

9. When competition returned to this field, dealers complained frequently that their "salesmen" had forgotten how to "sell."

10. Peter M. Blau, *The Dynamics of Bureaucracy* (Chicago: University of Chicago Press, 1955), pp. 43, 70.

11. *Ibid.*, p. 70.

12. See summary in Lloyd E. Ohlin, *Sociology and the Field of Corrections* (New York: Russell Sage Foundation, 1956), pp. 20–21.

13. Roy G. Francis and Robert C. Stone, *Service and Procedure in a Bureaucracy* (Minneapolis: University of Minnesota Press, 1956), pp. 83–84.

14. *Op. cit.*, pp. 24, 87.

15. For analysis in another context of the "sounding out process" see James D. Thompson and William J. McEwen, "Organizational Goals and Environment," *American Sociological Review*, XXIII (February 1958), 23–30.

16. Thomas C. Schelling, *The Strategy of Conflict* (Cambridge, Mass.: Harvard University Press, 1960), reports an unusual case. This involved a club for motorists, and the membership card identified the holder as a person who would keep quiet if his bribe offer was accepted by a policeman. Schelling also reports, however, that if the police could identify card-carrying motorists by sight, they could concentrate arrests on card-carrying drivers, threatening a ticket unless payment were received! (See pp. 140–41.)

17. "The Corruption of Authority and Rehabilitation," in Amitai Etzioni (ed.), *Complex Organizations* (New York: Holt, Rinehart & Winston, 1960), pp. 191–97.

18. George F. Lombard, *Behavior in a Selling Group* (Boston: Harvard Business School, 1955), pp. 176–80.

19. *Ibid.*, p. 177. When "merchandise which a customer liked was not available in the desired color or size, the situation could quickly become most difficult for both salesgirl and customer."

20. Reported in Leonard Reissman and John H. Rohrer (eds.), *Change and Dilemma in the Nursing Profession* (New York: G. P. Putnam's Sons, 1957), p. 143.

21. This dilemma frequently arises in treatment-oriented organizations which also have a custodial responsibility. Oscar Gursky notes that if an inmate in a traditional prison system violates the rules, the guard simply writes up a "ticket" and the inmate is punished by a central disciplinary court or a disciplinary officer; the transaction fits our Type I. However, if the same violation occurs in a treatment-oriented prison, it complicates the guard's response and creates conflict, for he must decide whether he ought to write up a ticket or whether, for treatment reasons, he ought to let the inmate "express his emotions" [see "Role Conflict in Organization," *Administrative Science Quarterly, Vol. III* (March 1959)].

22. David Fanshel, "A Study of Caseworkers' Perceptions of Their Clients," *Social Casework, XXXIX* (December 1958), 543–51.

23. Elihu Katz and S. N. Eisenstadt, "Some Sociological Observations on the Response of Israeli Organizations to New Immigrants," *Administrative Science Quarterly*, Vol. V (June 1960).

24. Morris S. Schwartz and Gwen Tudor Will describe "mutual withdrawal" in a mental hospital ward, with the withdrawal of the nurse perpetuating the withdrawal of the patient and the withdrawal of the patient reinforcing the nurse's withdrawal. Withdrawal in this case was described as affective, communicative, and physical [see "Low Morale and Mutual Withdrawal on a Mental Hospital Ward," *Psychiatry*, XVI (November 1953), 337–53].

25. Joseph W. Eaton, private conversation.

26. Blau, *op. cit.*, p. 151.

27. Gerald Gurin, Joseph Veroff, and Sheila Feld, *Americans View Their Mental Health* (New York: Basic Books, 1960), chap. xi.

28. Herbert E. Krugman, "Salesman in Conflict," *Journal of Marketing*, XXIII (July 1958), 59–61.

29. Robert N. McMurry, "The Mystique of Super-Salesmanship," *Harvard Business Review*, XXXIX (March-April 1961), 113–22.

30. Eliot Freidson, "Client Control and Medical Practice," *American Journal of Sociology*, LXV (January 1960), 374–82.

31. Charles Kadushin, "Individual Decisions to Undertake Psychotherapy," *Administrative Science Quarterly*, III (December 1958), 379–411 (see also his "Social Distance

between Client and Professional," *American Journal of Sociology,* LXVII (March 1962), 517–31.

32. Kadushin, "Individual Decisions to Undertake Psychotherapy," *op. cit.*

33. *Op. cit.,* p. 381.

34. Joseph W. Eaton, "The Client-Practitioner Relationship As a Variable in the Evaluation of Treatment Outcome," *Psychiatry,* XXII (May 1959), 189.

35. *Op. cit.,* p. 378.

36. The "cooling out" concept appears to have been first introduced into sociological literature by Erving Goffman in his analysis of confidence games, in "On Cooling the Mark Out: Some Aspects of Adaptations to Failure," *Psychiatry,* XV (November 1952), 451–63. The concept appears to be relevant to other types of activities where, acting in good faith, the practitioner must disappoint the client and faces the need to "let him down gently." For the application of the cooling-out concept in the junior college see Burton R. Clark, "The 'Cooling-Out' Function in Higher Education," *American Journal of Sociology,* LXV (May 1960), 569–76.

37. See Goffman, "On the Characteristics of Total Institutions," *Proceedings of the Symposium on Preventive and Social Psychiatry* (Washington: Walter Reed Army Institute of Research, 1957).

38. For a discussion of the substitution of functional diffuseness and particularism for functional specificity and universalism under similar conditions, see Peter B. Hammond, "The Functions of Indirection in Communication," in James D. Thompson *et al.* (eds.), *Comparative Studies in Administration* (Pittsburgh: University of Pittsburgh Press, 1959), pp. 183–94.

39. For a discussion of the concept of organizational postures see James D. Thompson, "Organizational Management of Conflict," *Administrative Science Quarterly,* V, No. 4, (March 1960), 389–409.

40. Robert W. Hawkes, "The Role of the Psychiatric Administrator," *Administrative Science Quarterly,* VI (June 1961), 89–106.

41. See Sol Levine and Paul E. White, "Exchange As a Conceptual Framework for the Study of Interorganizational Relationships," *Administrative Science Quarterly,* V (March 1961), 583–601.

42. For the concept of extrinsic prestige and its implications for output relationships see Charles Perrow, "Organizational Prestige: Some Functions and Dysfunctions," *American Journal of Sociology,* LXVI (January 1961), 335–41.

11

Bernard B. Berk

ORGANIZATIONAL GOALS AND

INMATE ORGANIZATION

While sociological interest in informal organization dates back to the time of Cooley, there has been little exploration of the relationships between formal and informal organization. Earlier research efforts have been more concerned with documenting the existence of informal organization and demonstrating that it had an impact upon organizational functioning than in trying to establish relationships between it and the organizational context. Different conclusions have been reached in regard to its contribution to the formal organization's ability to achieve its goals, with Roethlisberger and Dickson highlighting its subversive aspect in limiting productivity in economic organi-

Bernard B. Berk, "Organizational Goals and Inmate Organization," *American Journal of Sociology* 71 (1966): 522–534. Copyright 1966 by The University of Chicago Press. Reprinted by permission.

NOTE: The author would like to acknowledge indebtedness and gratitude to: Dr. Oscar Grusky of the University of California at Los Angeles both for his earlier work which stimulated this research and for his comments and aid in clarifying this chapter; also my intellectual indebtedness to Professor Morris Janowitz of the Center for Social Organizational Studies and the University of Chicago and to Professor Guy E. Swanson of the University of Michigan. Naturally, I am to be held solely accountable for any errors or defects in this chapter. I would also like to thank the National Institute of Mental Health which supported this research (Grant MF-8943) along with the Michigan State Department of Corrections, the camp staff, and inmates for their kind cooperation. This research was based upon "Informal Social Organization among Inmates in Treatment and Custodial Prison Camps: A Comparative Study" (unpublished Ph.D. dissertation, University of Michigan, 1961), which formed part of a research program under the direction of Professors Robert Vinter and Morris Janowitz dealing with the treatment potentials of correctional institutions [Vinter and Janowitz, "Effective Institutions for Juvenile Delinquents: A Research Statement," *Social Service Review*, XXXIII (June 1959), 118–130]. Comments by Allan Silver, Halowell Pope, and Harwin Voss of an earlier draft are gratefully acknowledged.

zations, while Shils and Janowitz suggest it can facilitate the goals of military organizations by developing social cohesion.[1] Reconciling these findings rests upon the notion that organizations with different goals, structures, and contexts should produce different patterns of informal organization, and informal organization would also have different effects upon the functioning of such diverse types of organizations. What is needed is specification of relationships between the parameters of formal and informal organization and identification of those aspects of organizations which generate oppositional informal organization. By limiting this investigation to one particular type of organization and by examining variation in one of its parameters—its goals—it is hoped some clarification of the problems may emerge.

Specifically, this chapter examines relationships between organizational goals and informal organization in a variety of correctional institutional settings. The study had two major objectives. First, we sought to replicate Grusky's study of the consequences of treatment goals for the informal organization of prison inmates.[2] Second, we were concerned with extending existing formulations concerning the relationship between the formal and informal structure of total institutions and, in particular, the conditions which generate informal organizations that are fundamentally opposed to the existing administration.

Description of Research Sites

The three institutions selected for study were minimum-security prisons which differed in their emphasis of treatment goals. The criteria used to determine the extent to which treatment goals were dominant were: (1) the presence of a full-time counselor or of treatment personnel; (2) the existence of a rehabilitative program; and (3) the active implementation of educational, vocational, or other auxiliary-type programs. The three prisons (to be called Benign, Partial, and Lock) were ranked on a continuum ranging from a strong treatment orientation to a strong custodial orientation.[3]

Camp Benign ranked as the most treatment-oriented institution, as all three criteria were present. In addition, it was the smallest, containing only ninety-seven inmates. This prison was characterized by considerable staff-inmate interaction, maximal opportunities for counseling and guidance,[4] and a sincere effort directed at changing the inmate. Camp Partial was slightly larger (127 inmates) and had both a full-time counselor and a limited educational program. However, it did not have an official treatment program. Treatment techniques employed in this institution tended to be subverted to custodial ends, such as securing inmate conformity. Camp Lock, which had 157 inmates, was the most custodially oriented institution, the sole rehabilitative program being an Alcoholics Anonymous group. Its primary goal was containment, and there was little official pretense or concern about treatment or rehabilitation. The officials sought to run an institution which attracted as little attention as possible from the community.

The Findings

INMATE ATTITUDES

The first area investigated was the differences in attitudes of inmates of the treatment and custodial prisons. Numerous observers have asserted that the relationship between guards and inmates in custodial institutions is characterized by hostility, mistrust, suspicion, and fear, promulgated by both the official dictates of the prison and the informal norms among the inmates.[5] Grusky, Vinter and Janowitz, and others have argued that a positive and cooperative type of staff-inmate relationship is a prerequisite for and a consequence of treatment goals. This is due primarily to accepting attitudes on the part of the staff, the overall replacement of formal controls by more informal ones, and the general reduction of inmate deprivations.

Grusky found support for the hypothesis that more positive attitudes among inmates are found in treatment, rather than in custodial institutions. By comparing attitudinal responses of inmates in three institutions, each situated in a different position along the treatment-custodial continuum, we were able to test this same hypothesis more carefully than could be done in the original case study.

As in the original study, inmate attitudes in three areas were examined: attitudes toward the prison, staff, and treatment program. Table 11–1 demon-

TABLE 11-1

Inmate Attitudes toward the Prison, Staff, and Program

	BENIGN (PERCENT)	PARTIAL (PERCENT)	LOCK (PERCENT)
Attitudes toward the prison:[a] favorable (scale types I-II)	63.1	48.2	39.1
Attitudes toward the staff:[b] favorable (scale types I-II)	44.3	29.2	23.4
Attitudes toward the program:[c] favorable (item response "yes")	88.8	81.9	74.8
N =	(95)	(124)	(138)

[a]For a description of scale see O. Grusky, "Treatment Goals and Organizational Behavior" (unpublished Ph.D. dissertation [University of Michigan, 1958]), p. 141. The coefficients of reproducibility for this scale were Benign .91, Partial .90, and Lock .93. The coefficients of scalability were .54, .77, and .81, respectively. A difference of over 12.5 percent between the camps is significant at the .05 level by a difference-of-proportions test.

[b]The coefficients of reproducibility for this scale were Benign .88, Partial .91, and Lock .92; for scalability, they were .53, .75, and .77, respectively.

[c]Only a single item, "Do you feel (the program) has helped you in any way?" was available. No answer: Benign 2, Partial 3, Lock 19.

strates a positive relationship between favorable inmate response toward the prison and the degree of development of its treatment goals. Where about six out of ten of Benign's inmates were positively oriented toward the prison (63 percent), not quite five of ten of Partial's inmates (48 percent) and less than four of ten of the inmates at Lock (39 percent), the most custodially oriented prison of the three, had positive feelings toward their institutions. A similar pattern is revealed concerning attitudes toward the staff. At Benign, 44 percent of the men had favorable attitudes toward the staff, whereas only 29 percent at Partial and 23 percent at Lock were as positively oriented toward the staff. The third area of inmate attitudes investigated were those toward existing programs. These attitudes were also found, as expected, to be related to the goals of the prison. At Benign, 89 percent of the men felt that the program had helped them, as compared with 82 percent of the men at Partial, and 75 percent of the men at Lock who expressed similar views. Attitudes toward the programs were the most positive and reflected, in part, the salience of the program which, in turn, was due to the official support for treatment goals. In short, Grusky's original hypothesis was strongly confirmed.[6] Significant differences were found between the prison which was most custodially oriented and the one most treatment-oriented.

THE EFFECTS OF SOCIALIZATION

In order to give a sharper test to the proposition, the length of residence in the institution was held constant. In this manner, the consequences of official socialization could be examined. It would be expected that the longer the inmate was exposed to the values and programs of the prison, the more likely he would be influenced by them; that is, inmates who have spent a long time in the prison should most clearly reflect the impact of the prison on their attitudes, and those who have been there only a short time should be least affected.

The data presented in Figure 11-1 show a strong relationship between attitude toward the staff and length of time spent in the prison. Inmates who had spent longer time in the custodially oriented prison were more likely to hold negative attitudes than those who had only been there a few months, whereas the reverse was true at the treatment-oriented prison where inmates who had spent a long time in the prison were more likely to hold positive attitudes than negative ones.[7] When those inmates at Benign who had spent fewer than three months in the prison were compared with those who had spent more than eight months there, we found that only about one of three (35 percent) of the former, as contrasted with about half (56 percent) of the latter, fell into the most favorable scale type. At Camp Lock the reverse was found true. The proportion of positive responses dropped sharply from 27 percent of the inmates who had been there less than three months to less than 9 percent of those who had been there eight or more months. Camp Partial exhibited a mild positive influence, reflecting its intermediate position.[8]

In Figure 11-2, the same general relationship is revealed with respect to

FIGURE 11-1. Relationship of Attitudes toward Staff to Length of Time Spent in Prison. The *N*'s from Which Percentages Were Based for the 0-3 Month Period Were: Benign 26, Partial 33, and Lock 55. For the 4-7 Month Period, They Were 36, 35, and 44, Respectively. And for the 8⁺ Month Period, They Were 30, 59, and 35.

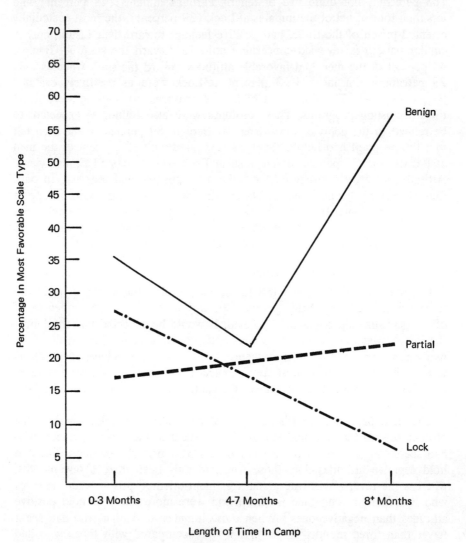

Length of Time In Camp

attitudes toward the prison, but not quite as clearly. The proportion of inmates at Lock who were favorably oriented decreased slightly from 36 percent of those whose stay was short-term to 31 percent of those having a longer-term stay in the prison. In contrast, the percentage of favorable responses increased at Benign from 50 percent of those having less than three months' experience to 64 percent of those who had eight or more months in prison. However,

FIGURE 11-2. Relationship of Attitudes toward Prison and Length of Time Spent in Prison. The *N*'s from Which Percentages Were Based Are the Same As for Figure 11-1.

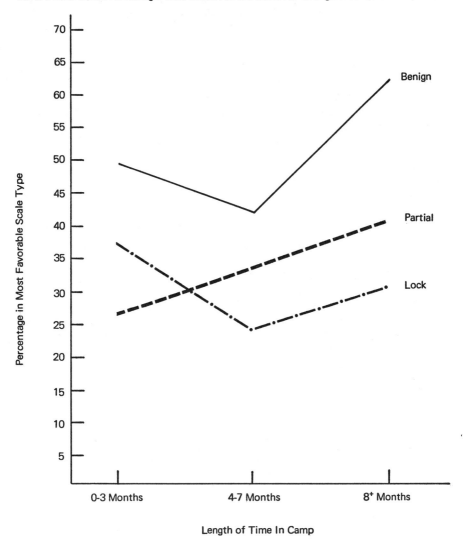

Length of Time In Camp

in both prisons, inmates with four–seven months' experience were most negative.[9]

INFLUENCE OF OTHER VARIABLES

Before any conclusions could be drawn from these findings, it was necessary to control for other relevant variables, since an important obstacle to studies of this nature is that inmates are not usually randomly assigned to treatment institutions. This was true of this study as well, in that inmates at Benign were younger and likely to have been less serious offenders. However, this type of selectivity does not appear to have accounted for the results obtained in this study. *Age:* Initially, it might have been argued that the older age of the inmates at Lock and Partial would be sufficient to account for the more negative attitudes found there. Our findings, on the contrary, show age to be inversely related to negative attitude at both Lock and Benign, with the younger inmates in both camps more likely to hold negative attitudes. No difference was found at Partial. Furthermore, young inmates were more positive at Benign than their counterparts at Lock. The same was true for older inmates. This would suggest that selectivity in regard to age would operate against the hypothesis. *Type of offender:* It similarly could have been argued that inmates at Partial and Lock were more experienced and hardened criminals, well indoctrinated in the ways of crime and would, therefore, exhibit more negative attitudes. We may ask, first, whether this is true and, second, if so, is this factor large enough to account for the differences obtained between the prisons? Again, the findings show, in contradiction to what is commonly believed, that the more serious offenders, by a variety of measures, did not have more negative attitudes. On the contrary, these two variables were generally unrelated. In the few cases where differences were found, they were small and variable. Furthermore, the direction of this relationship was reversed in the treatment institution, where the more serious offenders were more likely to hold more positive attitudes than the less serious offenders. And, finally, when comparable groups of types of offenders were compared in the various camps, they were more positive in their attitudes at Benign than at Lock.[10]

It would appear (see Table 11-2) that the selectivity in regard to age and

TABLE 11-2

Inmate Attitudes toward the Prison by Age and Type of Offender
(Percent in Most Favorable Scale Type)

	BENIGN (PERCENT)	N	PARTIAL (PERCENT)	N	LOCK (PERCENT)	N
Age:						
25 years and under	47.6	(86)	36.3	(11)	11.1	(18)
26+	77.7	(9)	35.4	(111)	35.9	(114)
Number of prison sentences:						
1	48.6	(70)	37.1	(62)	34.2	(76)
2 or more	56.0	(25)	35.1	(61)	29.3	(58)
Number of charged crimes:						
1-3	45.9	(61)	31.9	(47)	35.5	(45)
4+	65.3	(26)	39.6	(63)	33.3	(70)
Seriousness of crimes[a]						
Less serious crimes	50.0	(18)	47.5	(59)	30.8	(39)
More serious crimes	50.0	(74)	34.7	(59)	31.6	(76)

[a]When more than one crime was charged, the most serious was coded. Serious crimes were regarded as murder, rape, and assault. The less serious crimes consisted in robbery, burglary, larceny, etc.

type of offender would not be sufficient to account for the differences obtained in this study, and certainly could not account for the differences between Partial and Lock, since there was little difference in the types of inmates sent to those two camps. It should be pointed out, however, that inmates at Benign were more positive during the early period than inmates at the other camps, which may have been partly due to a selectivity, or may have resulted from the camp having had an initial positive impact on inmate attitudes. In any case, whatever differences existed in the nature of the inmates in the organization initially as a result of differential recruitment procedures, inmates became more positive over time in the treatment institution and more negative in the custodial one, reflecting the differential impact of the organization upon its members.

By these tests, then, it appears that, regardless of any selectivity in input, the differences between prisons were responsible for attitudinal differences.

INFORMAL ORGANIZATION

These attitudinal differences between prisons reflected major differences in the nature of the informal organization among prison inmates.

Support for this assertion is reflected in the finding that attitudes of inmates were related to the degree of their involvement in the inmate subculture. Attitudes appeared to be acquired as a result of informal socialization and participation in prison subculture, and reflected those informal standards held by its members.

Involvement and participation in the subculture was measured by the number of friendship choices the inmate received from other inmates. Three types of inmates were distinguished: the uninvolved or isolate who received no choices, the moderately involved who received from one to three choices, and the highly involved who received four or more friendship choices. Table 11-3 shows that at Benign isolates were the most negative and the highly involved inmates the most positive in their attitudes toward the prison. At Lock, the reverse was true with the highly involved inmates the most negative and the uninvolved inmates the most positive in their attitudes. At Partial, negative attitudes were related to both high and low involvement in the subculture. It is not immediately clear why moderately involved inmates at Partial were more positive than isolates. In all three prisons, however, favorableness of attitude was related to degree of involvement with the informal organization.[11]

INFORMAL LEADERSHIP

Further evidence of the impact of custodial and treatment goals on informal organization among prison inmates was found in the kinds of attitudes held by informal leaders in the various prisons.

Both Schrag's[12] and Grusky's studies dealt with the relationship between leaders and organizational goals. Schrag asserted that leaders were uniformly

TABLE 11-3

Degree of Involvement in Informal System and Attitudes toward the Prison[a]
(Percent in Most Favorable Scale Type)

	BENIGN (PERCENT)	N	PARTIAL (PERCENT)	N	LOCK (PERCENT)	N
Isolates (received no choices)	33.3	(15)	32.4	(37)	33.3	(75)
Moderately involved (received 1-3 choices)	50.6	(63)	38.5	(78)	30.2	(59)
Highly involved (received 4+ choices)	64.6	(17)	25.0	(12)	20.0	(5)

[a]Involvement measured by the number of friendship choices received by the inmate.

selected from among the most negative inmates. In contrast, Grusky hypothesized that orientation of the leader would vary with the type of total institution; specifically, informal leaders in treatment institutions were seen as more likely to be cooperative than their counterparts in custodially oriented prisons.

Consistent with Grusky's hypothesis, leaders at Benign were more positive in their attitudes than were leaders at Partial who, in turn, were more positive than those at Lock.[13] However, this might have been true for any sample of inmates, because inmates were, as a whole, more positive at Benign than at Lock. By comparing the leaders with the nonleaders within each prison, a more precise test of this relationship was obtained. Tables 11–4 and 11–5 show leaders were more positive than the nonleaders at Benign, while the reverse was true at Lock where the leaders were more negative than the nonleaders. This relationship was found to hold both for attitudes toward the prison and the institution's programs.

TABLE 11-4

Leadership and Attitudes toward Prison
(Percent in Most Favorable Scale Type)

	BENIGN (PERCENT)	N	PARTIAL (PERCENT)	N	LOCK (PERCENT)	N
Leaders	61.3	(31)	47.5	(50)	23.3	(37)
Nonleaders	45.3	(66)	35.5	(77)	34.3	(97)

TABLE 11-5

Leadership and Attitudes toward Program[a]
(Percent Favorable)

	BENIGN (PERCENT)	N	PARTIAL (PERCENT)	N	LOCK (PERCENT)	N
Leaders	74.2	(31)	47.6	(50)	39.3	(37)
Nonleaders	62.5	(66)	48.0	(77)	63.5	(97)

[a]The particular item asked if they thought the programs in the camp were a good idea.

Bernard B. Berk

Observations about Informal Organization

THE FUNCTION OF INFORMAL ORGANIZATION
IN TOTAL INSTITUTIONS

Having replicated Grusky's study and substantiated the hypothesis, we sought to develop a fuller explanation of the findings. Inmate attitudes reflect the nature of inmate subculture and informal organization which, in turn, is conditioned by formal organizational characteristics, such as the formal structure and the official objectives.

Informal organization develops in prison because: (1) inmates are isolated from society; (2) institutionalization generates common problems of adjustment[14] which require cooperation for their solution while simultaneously providing a situation with opportunity for effective interaction with others similarly situated;[15] and (3) inmates are members of a formal organization which, by its very nature as a system of action, can never fully anticipate or coordinate all behavior through the formal system alone; hence, informal organization serves to close the gaps of the formal organization.

Two kinds of informal organization have been identified in the prisons studied—one supportive of the official structure and the other in opposition to it. We submit that the goal of treatment encourages the development of the former, and the goal of custody the latter.

Inmate subcultures develop as solutions to the problems and deprivations experienced by inmates in the prison situation. They would, therefore, differ in their form and content as the nature of the problems experienced by inmates, patricularly those created by the institutional experience itself, differ. The two different types of informal organization developed because the inmate subsystem performed contrasting functions in the treatment and custodial institutions.

Two reasons may be suggested to explain the character of the inmate subculture in the custodial institution; first, the problems faced by inmates tend to be more severe there; in addition, inmates perceive the custodial institution itself to be responsible for their problems. As a result, they band together in opposition to the prison and its administration, which they see as the source of their frustrations.[16] Consequently, inmate subcultures tend to become more and more dominated by the values of professional criminals which already emphasize a strict demarcation between the guards and inmates, since these groups are seen as fundamentally in opposition to one another.

The emergence of this subculture compounds an already difficult problem— a central concern, in fact, of the custodial institution—that of maintaining social control within the prison. Since techniques for insuring conformity are inadequate, guards resort to various methods of accommodation and bargain for conformity with the means available to them.[17] One method, as Sykes points out, is to "buy compliance at the cost of tolerating deviance." In return for the guards overlooking selected infractions of the rules, inmates are expected to comply with the rest. In this fashion, inmates begin to regulate their own behavior and, in so doing, begin to fulfill, in part, the formal organization's task of maintaining internal order. The more effectively they are able to exert control over their behavior, the more advantageous is their bargaining position vis-à-vis the guards—a process which itself has a further consolidating effect upon inmate subculture. In this manner, inmates are able to gain some degree of freedom from the demands and pressures of the formal organization, thereby increasing the relative amount of control they can exercise over the conditions of their existence.[18] This newly gained mastery over their environmental conditions is, however, illusory. It would appear that they have merely traded their previous situation and its attendant deprivations for subjugation to an even more despotic ruling group—other inmates who have less compunctions and fewer limitations about the use of force and violence to gain compliance with their ends. Thus, in reality, freedom is usually only temporary, as inmate leaders quickly replace the official demands for conformity with new demands for conformity to new rules which sustain their dominance.

In contrast to this picture of informal organization in custodial institutions, we can view the development of informal organization in treatment institutions. While inmate organization can also be found in treatment institutions, it does not generally take on an oppositional character. It does not simply because many of the psychological deprivations of imprisonment have been reduced, and a shift in patterns of control has occurred. Inmates are treated with more respect by the organization and, as a result, the institution is not perceived by inmates to be totally against them or antithetical to their interests. In addition, the treatment institution is more flexible in regard to its rules, and treatment needs of inmates are considered in its demands for conformity. Furthermore, in its attempt to regulate behavior, formal methods of controls are replaced by more informal ones, thus reducing resentment and hostility. This leads to a greater tolerance in the range of inmate conformity and, concomitantly, "control" becomes less important in the hierarchy of organization objectives. Accordingly, there is little payoff from the administration for inmates' regulation of their own behavior.

Selected aspects of the formal organization's structure also have an impact on informal organization. Particularly in total institutions, the formal authority structure serves as a model for the informal. The custodially oriented prison, which is usually highly centralized, tends to produce a similar type of informal inmate leadership; for such an adaptation serves, on the one hand, to strengthen official control and administration of the prison and, on the other, to stabilize inmate relations by focusing attention on the deprivations inflicted by the authorities. Because inmate subculture there is dominated by criminal values emphasizing a strict demarcation between guards and inmates, informal

leadership must thereby justify itself by securing special concessions from
the oppressors, the "screws," in return for which the leaders prevent their
men from stepping too far out of line. The typical inmate in such a situation
is confronted with few alternatives and usually accepts the values and the
leadership as it is presented to him, thereby perpetuating the subculture.

The inmate subsystems are seen as performing different functions within
their respective institutions which, as we have seen, are directly linked to the
goals of the prison. In the custodial prison, even though oppositional and
subversive to the organization, it also functioned to assist it in the maintenance of internal order by regulating inmate behavior, though this is usually
at the cost of the "corruption of the formal authority system." In contrast,
control of inmate behavior was not a primary function of informal organization in the treatment institution. Informal organization there was more compatible with the formal organization and was more oriented toward meeting
the particular needs of inmates and integrating and coordinating their behavior.

The functioning of informal leaders was, in turn, directly linked to the
functions performed by the inmate subsystem, and, as a consequence, the
informal leaders' main task in the custodial prison was one of exercising control over the behavior of other inmates. In order to effectively implement
this end, the informal leadership employed the same techniques as the formal
organization and developed a highly consolidated and centralized power
structure. And, like the formal organization, it also relied upon coercion and
force, rather than on consensus or cooperation, to insure conformity.

In contrast, the informal leaders in the treatment institution, because the
treatment goal allowed for a broader range of inmate adaptation, performed
a variety of functions depending on the particular needs of the inmates, and
functioned more as coordinators and integrators of behavior rather than as
controllers, as they did in the custodial prison. Not only did the informal
leaders play very different roles in the two types of prisons, but techniques
of leadership differed as well, since the inmate subsystem in the treatment
institution tended to be based more upon consensus and cooperation than
was true of the custodial prison.

These speculations led to a new hypothesis about the structure and functioning of informal leadership in the different types of prisons. As we have
pointed out, one of the techniques for maintaining order in the custodial
prison was the *centralization of control* by informal leadership. Because this
function was less important for the inmate subsystem in the treatment institution, it was hypothesized that the more treatment-oriented the prison, the less
centralized the informal leadership structure would be and the proportionately
greater number of inmates who would emerge as top leaders.

The data supported this hypothesis. At Benign, 9.3 percent of the inmates
were chosen as top leaders (that is, received nine or more choices), while at
Partial 6.3 percent were chosen, compared with only 1.3 percent of the inmates at Lock. When inmates were asked: "Who were leaders?" similar
results were obtained. Forty-three percent of the inmates at Benign were

named, compared with 38 percent at Partial and 23 percent at Lock.[19] Both measures indicated greater concentration of power and centralization of control in the custodial prison.

A second technique, adopted by inmate leaders in the custodial prison to control inmate behavior, was the use of coercion to secure conformity and to maintain power. This led to a hypothesis dealing with types of persons likely to rise to positions of leadership or influence in the two types of prisons. Because *control* was an important function of the inmate leaders in the custodial prison, individuals disposed toward such behavior would be more likely to rise to positions of leadership there than would be true of treatment prisons where a more charismatic, socioemotional, or consensus-oriented type of leader would be expected to develop. Therefore, it was hypothesized that leaders in the custodial institution would be more authoritarian, reflecting their "tough-minded" orientation toward the use of power, and would be "less well liked," due to their reliance upon coercion and emphasis upon control than leaders in treatment institutions. Support for this hypothesis comes from the finding that leaders were selected from the most authoritarian inmates at Lock, whereas the reverse was true at Benign, where leaders were selected from the least authoritarian inmates.[20] Not only was the leadership structure more decentralized at Benign, but the leadership positions were occupied there, as well, by less authoritarian persons. Furthermore, leaders at Benign were less authoritarian than those at Partial who, in turn, were less authoritarian than the leaders found at Lock. No difference in authoritarianism was found between the general population of inmates at the three prisons. In addition to their being less authoritarian, the leaders at Benign were liked better, friendlier, and more approachable by other inmates than was true of the leaders at Lock.[21] This style of leadership is reflected in the findings that leaders at Benign were more likely to be chosen by other inmates as "well liked," a "best buddy," and as someone with whom they could discuss their personal problems, than was true of the leaders at Camp Lock. Camp Partial once again was found to exhibit an intermediate position with regard to its leaders.

Summary and Conclusions

The purpose of this study was twofold: (1) to replicate a study conducted by Grusky; and (2) to examine the consequences of treatment and custodial goals upon the inmate subsystem within correctional institutions, with particular emphasis on the conditions generating oppositional informal organization. Three areas of concern were inmate attitudes, the effect of socialization, and the development of informal leadership:

1. The findings on the whole supported Grusky's major hypothesis: Inmates were more positive in their attitudes toward the institution, staff, and programs in the treatment institution than those in the custodial one. Furthermore, they became more positive or negative with the length of time they spent in the prison, depending upon the type of organizational goal, thereby suggesting that it was the prison experience which was primarily responsible for the development of negative attitudes.

2. Differences between prisons were found to be related to differences in inmate organization. Two facts suggested this: First, attitudes were found to be related to degree of involvement with inmate organization, and second, leaders' attitudes were found to vary systematically with the prison's goals, being more positive in the treatment institution and more negative in the custodial one.

3. The informal leadership structure was also found to be more centralized in the custodial institution in an attempt to maintain more effective control over inmate behavior. The informal leaders among the inmates played different roles, depending upon organizational goals and contexts; and these roles were directly linked to the function of the inmate sub-culture within the prison. Leaders in the custodial prison were also found to be more authoritarian and less well liked than leaders in the treatment prison, reflecting the differences in their roles.

The goal of "custody," with its concomitant centralized- and formal-authority structure and increased deprivations for inmates, contributed significantly to the development of the hostile informal organization in the custodial prison. The disenfranchisement of inmates from possible rewards of the institution encouraged the development of negative attitudes and a hostile informal leadership.

NOTES

1. F. J. Roethlisberger and W. J. Dickson, *Management and the Worker* (Cambridge, Mass.: Harvard University Press, 1939); Edward A. Shils and Morris Janowitz, "Cohesion and Disintegration of the Wehrmacht in World War II," *Public Opinion Quarterly*, XII (1948), 280–315. Informal organization has also been found to contribute positively to economic organizations by reducing absenteeism, and negatively to military ones by generating norms which foster "goldbricking." Lewin's study contrasting the consequences of different patterns of control upon informal relations specifies in more detail relationships between organizational parameters and informal relations [K. Lewin, R. Lippitt, and R. K. White, "An Experimental Study of Leadership and Group Life," in G. E. Swanson, T. M. Newcomb, and E. L. Hartley (eds.), *Readings in Social Psychology* (rev. ed.; New York: Holt, Rinehart & Winston, 1952)]. For an excellent study dealing with similar concerns in juvenile institutions which was published too late for comment in this chapter, see David Street, "Inmates in Custodial and Treatment Settings," *American Sociological Review*, XXX (February 1965), 40–56.

2. The replicated study was: Oscar Grusky, "Organizational Goals and the Behavior of Informal Leaders," *American Journal of Sociology*, LXV, No. 1 (July 1959), 59–67. Sociology is characterized by a lack of replication studies, particularly in the area of social organization. In his analysis of replication studies, Hanson noted fewer than twenty-five such studies in the field of sociology, with fully one-third of these

Organizational Goals and Inmate Organization

refuting the original hypothesis. This would appear to leave sociology in the position of having relatively few sets of propositions which have been independently tested in different research sites. This condition neither contributes to the development of a cumulative fund of reliable knowledge, nor does it permit of the development of a set of standardized instruments which can be used to compare different types of organizations. See Robert Hanson, "Evidence and Procedure Characteristics of 'Reliable' Propositions in Social Science," *American Journal of Sociology*, LXIII (January 1958), 357–71. This replication was enhanced by the use of the same instruments in two new prison camps in addition to a repeat investigation of the prison originally studied by Grusky. Moreover, we utilized Grusky's questionnaire items and Guttman scales.

3. It is important to keep in mind that all three prison camps would be located on the treatment end of the continuum if compared with maximum-security institutions.

4. One cannot overlook the possible importance of the size of the prisons, which could provide an additional explanation to the one offered in this paper. However, the fact that Benign almost doubled in size between the original study and the replication, while inmate attitudes remained relatively unchanged, casts some doubts on its usefulness in accounting for our findings. Also, similar data collected on three other juvenile institutions did not show attitudes to be related to size as such; rather, it confirmed the importance of organizational goals. This is not to discard the importance of size, since it may have important ramifications for organizational structure which, in turn, influences informal organization. There was also a selectivity in the inmates sent to Benign, which was dealt with in this chapter.

5. Donald Clemmer, *The Prison Community* (New York: Holt, Rinehart & Winston, 1958), chap. ii; Donald Clemmer, "Observations on Imprisonment As a Source of Criminality," *Journal of Criminal Law and Criminology*, XLI (September–October 1950), 311–19; R. J. Corsini, "A Study of Certain Attitudes of Prison Inmates," *Journal of Criminal Law and Criminology*, XXXVII (July–August 1946,), 132–42; Donald Cressey (ed.), *The Prison: Studies in Institutional Organization and Change* (New York: Holt, Rinehart & Winston, 1961); Lloyd W. McCorkle and Richard Korn, "Resocialization within the Walls," *Annals*, CCXCIII (May 1954), 88–98; Hans Reimer, "Socialization within the Prison Community," *Proceedings of the American Prison Association* (1937), pp. 151–55; Gresham M. Sykes, *The Society of Captives* (Princeton, N.J.: Princeton University Press, 1958); Gresham Sykes, and Sheldon L. Messinger, "The Inmate Social System" in *Theoretical Studies in Social Organization of the Prison* [Social Science Research Council Pamphlet No. 15 (March 1960)], pp. 5–19; Robert Vinter and Morris Janowitz, *op. cit.*

6. In comparing Grusky's results with our own there was remarkable agreement in the percentages of positive responses.

7. In an excellent study of socialization within the prison, Wheeler demonstrates similar findings in regard to "prisonization," a phenomenon related to both attitudes toward society and the prison. His findings show that the longer the time the inmate spent in the prison, the less conforming his attitudes were with those of the staff, reflecting his internalization of the prison culture. See Stanton Wheeler, "Socialization in Correctional Communities," *American Sociological Review*, XXVI (October 1961), 697–712.

8. It should be pointed out that a smaller proportion of fairly recent (0–3 months) inmates of Partial than those from the more custodial Lock demonstrated favorable attitudes toward the staff. However, the percentage of favorable responses increased steadily with experience in the former institution, and decreased steadily in the latter. A greater proportion of favorable responses was evidenced at all time periods among inmates of the highly treatment-oriented Benign than among those of both the other prisons. We inferred that inmates of Benign were apparently more receptive to the staff initially, their receptivity then declined, but ultimately were most favorable among

those inmates with eight or more months of experience. Of course, the sample survey design which we used has the weakness of providing data only for a particular slice of time. Resurveys or panel studies are required to assess clearly the effect of prison experience on attitudes.

9. Wheeler, *op. cit.*, found a similar U-shaped pattern in regard to conforming attitudes held by inmates and attributed this to the stage of the inmate's institutional career. Inmates in the last phase of their institutionalization were believed to shed prison culture as they anticipate leaving the prison and returning to society.

10. The total time spent by the inmate in confinement in any institution was also found to be related to negative attitudes; the longer the time spent in custodial institutions, the more negative the attitude. This, of course, supports the argument that it is the prison experience as such which is largely responsible for the development of negative attitudes. Selectivity did exist, however, in that all inmates sent to prison camps to begin with were not believed to be security risks by the prison officials. It should be pointed out in this connection that inmates in all camps were, as a whole, positively oriented toward their institutions, staff, and programs. Whether this finding can be attributed to an initial selectivity in inmates sent to camps, or whether this is a reflection of the differences between maximum- and minimum-security prisons, generally, cannot be settled by this research design. The amount of variance accounted for by characteristics of members in an organization has not been clearly established by research findings.

11. Wheeler's study, *op. cit.*, also demonstrated a relationship between the speed and degree of "prisonization" and involvement in informal inmate organization.

12. Clarence Schrag, "Leadership among Prison Inmates," *American Sociological Review*, XIX (February 1954), 37–42.

13. Leaders were designated in accordance with Grusky's and Schrag's studies, *op. cit.*

14. In the typical custodial prison, social rejection; pervasive and rigid social control; and loss of liberty, autonomy, respect, affection, heterosexual relationships, security, and self-esteem have been identified as problems which inmates experience. Because these problems often require the cooperation of others for their solution, strong pressures for a collective response are built up. As cohesion develops among the inmates, a reduction of deprivations is experienced; and, conversely, as it decreases, an increase in the irritants of prison life is experienced. In this manner systematic pressures for a collective solution are created (cf. Sykes and Messinger, *op. cit.*).

15. Cf. Albert K. Cohen, *Delinquent Boys* (Glencoe, Ill.: Free Press, 1956), chap. iii, for a penetrating analysis of the formation of subcultures.

16. McCorkle, for example, has argued that the major problem the inmate social system attempts to cope with is social rejection and that inmates defend threats to their self-esteem by "rejecting the rejectors," a process which allows inmates to maintain favorable self-images in a situation where the formal organization imposes self-definitions which are unacceptable or threatening. This is accomplished by devaluing either the importance or legitimacy of persons imposing such definitions. L. S. McCorkle and R. Korn, *op. cit.*, pp. 86–95.

17. Gresham Sykes, *op. cit.*; Richard Cloward, "Social Control in the Prison," in *Theoretical Studies in Social Organization of the Prison, op. cit.*, and others have pointed out problems endemic to the custodial institution in maintaining social control, the most important of these being the lack of an internalized sense of duty on the part of inmates, the limitations upon the use of force, the difficulties involved in segregating rule violators, the lack of effective inducements, and the strains inherent in the role of the guard.

18. See Richard McCleery, "Communication Patterns As Bases of Systems of Authority and Power," in *Theoretical Studies in Social Organization of the Prison, op. cit.*, for a discussion of relations between formal and informal power structures.

19. In part, some of the differences between camps in the proportions of top leaders

were a function of the numbers of nominations made by respondents in the different camps. Whether the number of nominations reflects the number of actual leaders is directly linked to the difficult problem of validity in the use of sociometric techniques which cannot be dealt with here.

20. Leaders were more authoritarian than nonleaders at Lock and less authoritarian than nonleaders at Benign. At Lock, 48.3 percent of the leaders as compared with 39 percent of the nonleaders gave authoritarian responses to a question asking if they would harshly discipline an angry employee while, at Benign, only 33.3 percent of the leaders as compared with 47.6 percent of the nonleaders responded in such an authoritarian fashion. At Partial, 40.5 percent of the leaders and 52.0 percent of the nonleaders responded in an authoritarian fashion.

21. Leaders were also less well liked and more socially distant from nonleaders in the custodial institution. At Benign, 77.4 percent of the leaders were also chosen as a "best buddy" by other inmates as compared with 66 percent of the leaders at Partial and 40.6 percent of those at Lock. The same pattern was found in regard to being chosen as "best liked" by other inmates, where 77.8 percent of the leaders at Benign, 52 percent of the leaders at Partial, and only 48 percent of the leaders at Lock were so chosen. These relationships were also found to hold in regard to a qustion asking who they would discuss personal problems with in the prison, where inmates at Lock were much less likely to discuss personal problems with their leaders than were inmates at Benign.

12

Peter M. Blau

ORIENTATION TOWARD CLIENTS IN
A PUBLIC WELFARE AGENCY

Public assistance differs in important respects from other branches of social work. Since furnishing financial aid to those in need is legally recognized as a public responsibility, such assistance is administered by public welfare agencies, whereas case work and group work are generally carried out by private agencies. The welfare agencies in metropolitan communities are larger and more complex than private social work agencies, often having one thousand employees or more and consisting of numerous divisions, which provide many services besides financial assistance. Another distinctive characteristic of public welfare is that most of the "case workers" who administer assistance are not professionally trained social workers but have only a college degree and possibly a few courses in social work. Welfare agencies have not been successful in attracting professionally trained personnel not only because of their low pay but also because the ideology of professional social workers depreciates work in public assistance.

This chapter is concerned with the orientation of case workers toward clients in a public welfare agency in a large American city, and particularly with the ways in which the organizational and social context of the agency influenced their orientation.[1] Merton's concept of role set calls attention to the "complement of role relationships which persons have by virtue of occupying a particular social status."[2] Thus the status of case workers in the welfare agency involves individuals in role relationships with superiors in the organization, with clients, and with co-workers, and each of these relationships has some bearing upon the way they perform their role as case worker.

The first question to be raised is that of bureaucratic constraints. The administrative procedures that have necessarily become established in such a complex organization impose limits upon role relationships and operations.

Peter M. Blau, "Orientation toward Clients in a Public Welfare Agency," *Administrative Science Quarterly* 5 (1960): 341–361. Reprinted by permission.

Training, supervision, and accumulated experience help the case worker to adapt his role to the bureaucratic requirements. What are the consequences of these bureaucratic conditions for orientation toward recipients of public assistance? A second problem is posed by the role relationship between case worker and clients. How does the experience of meeting recipients and encountering difficulties in dealing with them affect the worker's approach? His relationships with peers and integration in his work group constitute a third important source of influence upon the case worker's orientation toward recipients. Finally, the significance of the absence of a role relationship should be noted. Since they are not professionally trained, case workers are not actual members of a professional group of colleagues (although professional social work is a meaningful reference group for some of them).

The data for the study were collected in 1957 in a large public welfare agency.[3] The agency was responsible for administering general public assistance, but it also provided medical and legal aid, help with employment, industrial training, child placement, and several other services. The main duty of the case worker was to determine whether new applicants were eligible for public assistance and to continue to check whether recipients remained eligible. He was also expected to furnish sufficient case-work service to encourage clients to become self-supporting again and to see that they obtained the services from other departments as needed. These tasks required familiarity with agency procedures and involved a considerable amount of paper work in the office as well as visiting clients in their homes. Case workers spent about one-third of their time in the field. Large case loads and high turnover of personnel created special difficulties for discharging these responsibilities. More than one-half of the case workers were men, and one-third were Negroes.

The research concentrated on twelve work groups, each consisting of five or six case workers under a supervisor. After a three-month period of observation devoted to collecting some systematic data as well as general impressions, pertinent information was abstracted from agency records, and the members of the twelve work groups were interviewed. A central focus of the interview, which lasted from one to two hours, was the respondent's orientation toward clients. Only those items which analysis revealed to be salient as well as reliable are used in this chapter. Although such interview responses cannot hope to capture all subtle aspects of the case worker's approach to clients, they do indicate some basic differences in approach.

Bureaucratic Constraints

Case workers often complained about the bureaucratic restraints under which they had to operate. Many of them felt that the agency's emphasis on following procedures, and particularly the requirement to investigate closely each recipient's eligibility, made it impossible for them to provide the kind of case-work service which would benefit clients most:

They always talk about social work, but actually you can't do anything of the kind here. For instance, I had one case which I wanted to send to . . . [another agency], but my supervisor said, "You can't. You would have to make a case plan first, and we can't do that."

These were the words of a worker who had been with the agency only a few months. Newcomers not only voiced such complaints most often (although they were by no means alone in doing so), but they also frequently criticized old-timers for having grown callous and inflexible in the course of having become adapted to the bureaucratic organization.

Implicit in the opinions of case workers were two contradictory explanations of compliance with official procedures. On the one hand, compliance was ascribed to externally imposed restraints that prevented workers from following their own inclinations and furnishing good case-work service. On the other, the old-timers' conformity to procedures was attributed to their rigidity resulting from their overadaptation to the bureaucratic organization. As a matter of fact, neither of these explanations is entirely accurate. Bureaucratic constraints actually became internalized, but adaptation to them did not increase rigidity.

The impact of the bureaucratic organization on service to clients cannot be directly determined without comparing different agencies that are more or less bureaucratized. While this is not possible in a study confined to case workers in one organization, an indirect estimate of this impact can be made. Since bureaucratic pressures are, in large part, transmitted to workers through their supervisors, their influence can be inferred from a comparison of the orientations of workers under supervisors who stress strict adherence to official procedures and under supervisors who interpret procedures more liberally. On the basis of their description of a day in the field, workers were classified as being primarily oriented either toward checking eligibility in accordance with procedures or toward providing some case-work service. Only 7 of the 29 workers under supervisors who emphasized procedures were oriented toward case-work service, in contrast to 19 of the 31 under less procedure-oriented supervisors.[4]

Some case workers were subject to less bureaucratic pressure than others, and this was reflected in their work, but few if any escaped the penetrating impact of bureaucratization. The summer camp program illustrates this. A number of free placements in children's camps were made available to the agency each year. Case workers who often deplored the lack of funds that made it impossible to help clients beyond supplying them with the bare necessities of life, and who sympathized particularly with the plight of children, would be expected eagerly to take advantage of this opportunity to provide special services and to compete for the few placements available. Actually, most workers were not at all interested in making camp referrals, looking upon it as an extra burden rather than an opportunity, although the actual amount of work involved was quite small. Moreover, service-oriented workers were no more likely to make referrals to summer camps than others.

This general apathy toward the camp program indicates that, although many case workers complained about being restricted in their endeavors to serve clients by bureaucratic restraints *externally* imposed upon them, they had actually internalized bureaucratic constraints to a considerable degree. To be sure, some workers defined their responsibilities less narrowly than others, partly in response to differences in their superiors' interpretations of agency policies. But even a broader definition of the case worker's bureaucratic responsibilities limited their scope to certain recurrent services, and referring children to camps was an extraordinary service, not part of the regular routine.

The very complexity of official procedures in this large organization served to promote adaptation to bureaucratic practice. In order to help his clients, a case worker had to know agency procedures and to work within their bounds. But it was impossible in a few days or weeks to learn to understand, let alone to administer, the many rules and regulations that governed operations. New employees were overwhelmed by the complexity of their administrative duties and had to devote several months, often much of their first year, to becoming familiar with agency procedures. Newcomers who were unable or unwilling to master the pertinent regulations and perform their duties in accordance with them either found their job so unsatisfactory that they soon left or, more rarely, performed their tasks so poorly that they did not survive the probation period. Most of the case workers who remained with the agency for any length of time had come to accept the limitations of official procedures and, indeed, to incorporate them into their own thinking, because doing so was a prerequisite for deriving satisfaction from the job and performing it adequately.

Internalized bureaucratic constraints tended to govern the decisions and actions of case workers, their protestations against bureaucracy notwithstanding. But as an examination of the data reveals, this does not mean that adaptation to the organization and its requirements increased rigid adherence to procedures at the expense of case-work service. Case workers who had been with the agency for a long time could be assumed to be better adapted to it than newcomers, for reasons already noted. (The fact that less than one-half of the workers with more than one year of employment, compared to three-quarters of the newcomers, mentioned bureaucratic conditions as one of the things they liked least about the job supports this assumption.) Old-timers, however, were less likely than newcomers to confine their work to checking eligibility. Twelve of the 21 newcomers, 10 of the 21 workers with one to three years of service, and only one-third of the 18 workers with over three years of service were primarily oriented toward eligibility procedures. Another finding indicates a similar decrease in rigid compliance with official procedures with increasing experience. Agency rules required workers to be on time, and repeated tardiness was penalized. The time sheets showed that none of the newcomers were late for work more than once every other month, whereas nearly half (19 of 39) of the workers with more than one year seniority were.

Apparently, adjustment to the organization did not lead to greater bureaucratic rigidity; on the contrary, it was the insecurity of the newcomer, not thoroughly familiar with procedures and not yet adapted to the bureaucratic organization, that produced rigid adherence to official procedures. The more experienced worker's greater understanding of procedures and better adaptation to them made him less confined by them,[5] with the result that he was more likely than a newcomer to go beyond checking eligibility in his contacts with clients and provide some case-work service.

Reality Shock

There are two things you learn on this job, particularly if it is your first job. First, you become less idealistic. You realize that people are not always honest—that you cannot always accept what they say. Then, you learn to work within a framework of rules. You realize that every job has rules and that you have to work within that framework.

This statement of a perceptive case worker who had been with the agency for not quite one year indicates the two major problems that confront the newcomer. Often fresh out of college, not only is he faced by a complicated set of procedures, but he also encounters clients who are very different from what he had expected and with whom he must establish a working relationship.

Most persons who took a job in the welfare agency were partly motivated by an interest in working with and helping poor people. They tended to look forward to establishing a warm, although not intimate, relationship with deserving and grateful clients, and considered the case worker as the agent of society who extended a helping and trusting hand to its unfortunate members. Newcomers generally deplored the "means test" and cared little about protecting public funds by investigating whether clients meet eligibility requirements, feeling that a trusting attitude should accompany financial aid in the best interest of rehabilitation. While a few case workers were motivated to seek their job by very different considerations, such as a desire to dominate people, they were the exception, and the attitudes of most new case workers toward clients were strongly positive, if somewhat sentimental and idealistic. Contacts with clients put these views to a severe test, which often resulted in disillusion.

Recipients of public assistance constitute the most deprived segment of the population, especially in a period of relative prosperity. In this northern metropolis, disproportionate numbers of them were Negroes, in-migrants from the South, unmarried mothers, alcoholics, and generally people with severe handicaps in the labor market. The mores and folkways of most of these people were quite different from those prevailing in the American middle or working class. Strong moral condemnation of desertion, illegitimacy, or physical violence, for example, was not part of the values of their subculture. Such differences in values and customs made it difficult for middle-class workers to maintain their positive feelings for clients, but another factor was even more important in changing their orientation. Clients were in dire need, since the assistance allowance, originally set low, never caught up with the inflationary trend. They were, therefore, under strong pressure to conceal what slim resources they might have had and try to get a little more money from the agency, even if this required false statements. People under such deprived conditions tend to look upon government organizations as alien forces that must be tricked into yielding enough money for survival, and consequently some clients, although by no means all, tried to cheat. In fact, the situation in which recipients found themselves made honesty a luxury.

The new case worker was typically full of sympathy for clients' problems. But as he encountered clients who blamed him personally for not helping them enough, even though agency procedure limited him, and clients met his trusting attitude by cheating and lying, the newcomer tended to experience a "reality shock,"[6] just as new teachers do whose first assignment is an overcrowded class in a slum.[7] This disillusioning experience might make a worker bitter and callous, or induce him to leave the job, and even those who did not have either of these extreme reactions tended to change their orientation to clients.

Finding out that people one has trusted have lied is a threatening experience. It implies that one has been made a fool of and that others are laughing behind his back at his naïveté. To protect his ego against these threats, a case worker is under pressure to change his orientation toward clients. If he anticipates deception by distrusting the statements of recipients, their lies no longer pose a threat to his ego. And if he loses his personal interest in them, their attitudes cease to be significant for his self-conception, making his ego still more immune against possible deception and other conflicts. In short, the *situational context* of public assistance, by producing a reality shock, tends to create a distrustful and uninterested orientation toward recipients.

The conception of reality shock implies that case workers lose some of their interest in clients and concern with their welfare during their first year in the agency. The empirical data confirm this hypothesis. Of the newcomers, 57 percent reported that they worried sometimes or often about their cases after working hours; of the workers with more than one year of service, only one-third did (this proportion was the same for those with one to three years and those with more than three years seniority). Personal involvement with clients, that is, the proportion of workers who considered it important to be liked by clients, decreased similarly after one year of service.

A less simple pattern, however, was revealed by the relationship between seniority and deriving satisfaction from clients, as Table 12–1 shows. Contacts with clients were a major source of work satisfaction for three-quarters of the newcomers; this proportion decreases, as expected, to considerably less than one-half for workers with one to three year seniority; but it increases again to more than three-quarters for old-timers with more than three years of employment. The proportion of workers who in particular enjoyed helping clients manifests the same pattern—a drop after one year and a rise after three years. Again, workers with one to three years of seniority were somewhat more likely to think that clients often cheat than either newcomers or old-timers. These findings suggest that the reality shock has some effects that are temporary as well as some permanent ones.

TABLE 12-1

Seniority and Source of Work Satisfaction

MAJOR SOURCE OF WORK SATISFACTION	NEWCOMER	1-3 YEARS	OLD-TIMER
	%	%	%
Client contacts	76	43	83
Other sources	24	57	17
Number of cases	21	21	18

Having come to the agency with idealistic views about poor people, newcomers tended to be much concerned with helping recipients. Contacts with clients constituted the most gratifying aspect of their work, not only because of their positive feelings toward clients, but also because they had few alternative sources of satisfaction on the job. Still unsure about procedures and not yet having become friendly with many colleagues, newcomers were not likely to find much gratification in their work at the office, where the necessity to make decisions and submit them to the supervisor aroused their anxieties, and where the friendly interaction among other case workers underlined their own relative isolation. The disillusioning experience of the reality shock often alienated the case worker from clients. After he had been with the agency for about a year, therefore, he tended to lose much of his concern with helping clients and to derive less satisfaction from working with them. But as the worker learned to adapt to the reality shock by becoming less involved with clients, contacts with them ceased to be a threatening and unpleasant experience. Moreover, as he became increasingly conversant with agency procedures and acquired skills in applying them less rigidly, the worker could furnish more effective case-work service, and this made contacts with clients once more a source of work satisfaction for him. The continuing lack of involvement of the old-timer may be considered a residue of the reality shock. After 3 years of experience the old-timer was again at least as apt as the newcomer to find satisfaction in his work with clients. But whereas the gratification of the newcomer was rooted in his interest in recipients and their welfare, that of the old-timer, who generally lacked such a personal interest in clients, stemmed from his superior skill in providing effective service. The workers who did not find the exercise of this skill an interesting challenge probably left the agency in disproportionate numbers, and this selective process may well partly account for the finding that those who had remained with the organization for more than three years obtained more satisfaction from contacts with clients than those with one to three years seniority.

Peer Group Support

The finding that newcomers, despite their positive feelings, were less likely than other workers to go beyond checking eligibility and to offer case-work services to clients has been interpreted by suggesting that lack of experience and familiarity with procedures engendered insecurities and anxieties, and that these anxieties led to rigid adherence to procedures. If this interpretation is correct, then conditions other than experience that lessen feelings of insecurity should also promote case-work service.

Friendly relations with colleagues are a source of social support which helps reduce the anxieties and insecurities that arise in the work situation. Individuals who were somewhat isolated from colleagues, therefore, were expected to be less oriented toward case-work service than those with extensive informal relations with peers. Indeed, this seemed to be the case. Two measures of social support from peers were the case-worker's popularity in the organization (how often others named him as a colleague with whom they were friendly) and his integration in his work group (whether he was called by his first name by other members of his own work group). Whichever index was used, over one-half of the workers with social support from peers were service oriented, in comparison with not quite one-third of those without such social support.

Apparently, friendly relations with peers decreased the tendency of workers to confine themselves rigidly to checking eligibility,[8] just as accumulated experience did. The influence of both social integration in the peer group and experience (seniority) on the service orientation of workers[9] is presented in Table 12-2. The data in adjacent pairs of columns show that social support from integrative relations with co-workers encouraged case-work service only among workers with less than three years of experience, but not among old-timers. If the two categories of case workers who had been with the agency less than three years are combined, 22 percent of the unintegrated, in contrast to 54 percent of the integrated, were service oriented. But after three years, whether workers were integrated among peers or not, the proportion of service-oriented ones was 50 percent. This suggests that social support from colleagues is significant for service to clients only as long as lack of experience

TABLE 12-2

Seniority, Integration, and Orientation

ORIENTATION TOWARD CLIENTS	NEWCOMER INTEGRATION		1-3 YEARS INTEGRATION		OLD-TIMER INTEGRATION	
	LOW	HIGH	LOW	HIGH	LOW	HIGH
	%	%	%	%	%	%
Eligibility procedure	67	50	67	33	13	50
Intermediate	11	8	11	0	38	0
Case-work service	22	42	22	67	50	50
Number of cases	9	12	9	12	8	10

engenders anxieties that impede service. Since the worker who has become fully adapted to the organization and its procedures in several years of employment experiences little anxiety in his work, the anxiety-reducing function of friendly relations with peers has no bearing upon his performance.

Experience decreased rigid concern with procedures considerably among unintegrated case workers but had much less impact on the orientation of integrated workers, as a comparison of alternate columns in Table 12–2 shows. Among the integrated, the proportion of procedure-oriented workers declined somewhat after the first year only to increase again after the third. Among the unintegrated, in contrast, two-thirds of the workers were procedure oriented for the first three years, but this proportion dropped sharply to one out of eight after three years of experience. This finding probably indicates that experience frees the worker from being rigidly restricted by procedures, and thus fosters case-work service, not simply because it increases a worker's technical competence but specifically because his increased competence lessens his feelings of insecurity and anxiety. The unintegrated worker, whose anxieties are not already relieved by social support from peers, is therefore the one most apt to become less rigid with increasing experience.

Social support from colleagues and accumulated experience can be considered functional substitutes for each other with respect to service to clients. Both seemed to reduce anxieties and rigidities, and thus to foster case-work service, but their effects were not cumulative. If workers were experienced, integration did not increase their tendency to be service oriented, and if they were integrated, experience hardly increased service. As a matter of fact, there is some indication that the combined influence of much experience and social support from peers was the very reverse of that of either condition alone. After three years of employment, integrated workers were somewhat *more* likely to be procedure oriented than unintegrated ones. This could be interpreted as showing that a certain amount of anxiety serves as an incentive to go beyond merely checking eligibility. Workers who were too secure had no incentive to do more than that, and those who felt too insecure were too rigid to do more. The integrated workers without several years of experience and the highly experienced but unintegrated ones, on the other hand, whose anxieties presumably had been mitigated without having been entirely eliminated, were most apt to go beyond checking eligibility and provide some case-work service.[10]

While the implication of social integration among peers for case-work service was largely similar to that of years of experience, the significance of integration for the concern workers expressed about helping clients was opposite of that of experience. Fully 28 of the 34 integrated workers were sufficiently concerned to worry, at least occasionally, about their cases after working hours, in contrast to only 12 of the 26 unintegrated workers. Integration in the work group was, then, directly related to this manifestation of interest in the welfare of clients, but experience, as previously noted, was inversely related to it, and this remains true if the associations of both factors with worrying are examined simultaneously, as Table 12–3 shows. Case workers who were integrated among peers were more apt to be greatly concerned about their cases than unintegrated workers, whatever their seniority (compare adjacent pairs of columns). Experience, on the other hand, reduced the tendency to worry much about recipients, both among integrated workers (from 67 percent for newcomers to 40 percent for old-timers) and among unintegrated ones (from 44 to 25 percent).

These findings suggest that peer group support served to absorb some of the impact of the reality shock. The unintegrated worker, without such social support, experienced the full force of the reality shock, which constrained him to shield his ego by developing a hardened attitude toward clients. Ego support from integrative relations with peers made a worker less vulnerable, enabling him to cope with disagreeable experiences with recipients without feeling threatened and thus reducing his need for protecting his ego by becoming indifferent toward clients. Among unintegrated workers, therefore, the proportion who never worried increased from 11 percent during the first year of employment to 75 percent after three years, but there was no corresponding increase among integrated workers (compare alternate columns in the third row of Table 12–3). Social support from colleagues helped integrated workers withstand the reality shock and thus permitted them to maintain a greater concern for clients and their fate. Moreover, workers whose interest in helping clients led to worrying and made them vulnerable had particularly strong

TABLE 12-3

Seniority, Integration, and Concern

CONCERN: WORRY ABOUT CASES	NEWCOMER INTEGRATION		1-3 YEARS INTEGRATION		OLD-TIMER INTEGRATION	
	LOW	HIGH	LOW	HIGH	LOW	HIGH
	%	%	%	%	%	%
Often or sometimes	44	67	22	42	25	40
Rarely	44	25	22	25	0	50
Never	11	8	56	33	75	10
Number of cases	9	12	9	12	8	10

incentives to seek social support by fostering integrative relations with colleagues. The data do not enable us to tell whether integration increased concern or concern enhanced the chances of integration, or whether both influences occurred. In any case, however, they point to the conclusion that integration in the work group served to lessen the impact of the reality shock.[11]

Does this finding imply that the colleague groups discouraged a detached approach toward clients? It does not, because professional detachment is quite distinct from lack of concern with helping clients. As a matter of fact, the question about worrying was originally intended as a measure of detachment, but further reflection as well as examination of the answers revealed that it is not a valid indication of an impersonal professional approach. Professional detachment involves lack of personal identification and emotional involvement with clients, but not lack of concern with their welfare or lack of interest in helping them. How much a worker worried about his cases appeared to be not so much indicative of his emotional involvement as of his concern with providing effective service to clients, as the example given by respondents of what they worry about showed.[12] The social contacts of 20 case workers with an average of four clients each were observed, and an index of detachment was derived from these observations. To be sure, there was a direct relationship between detachment and lack of concern. However, integrated case workers were more apt than unintegrated workers to remain detached in their interviews with clients,[13] whereas they were also less apt than unintegrated ones to be unconcerned with clients by not worrying about their work after office hours, as we have seen. Although the number of workers directly observed is small, the finding suggests that worrying expresses an aspect of the orientation to recipients that is distinct from, although not unrelated to, lack of professional detachment.

The way the colleague group promoted adjustment to the reality shock was apparently by encouraging its members to displace aggression against clients in conversations among themselves. Case workers often expressed very callous attitudes toward recipients in joking and talking with one another. For instance, when a worker went to interview a neurotic client, a colleague bid farewell to her with the words, "Don't push him over the brink," to which she responded, "Anything to get your case load down." Or, a worker proudly displayed his strictness by telling another about having discontinued assistance for a recipient when finding a Christmas tree and presents at his home, and ended by saying, "A dirty thing to do, right at Christmas." Workers often seemed to be actually bragging to colleagues about how unsympathetic they felt toward clients and how harshly they treated them. Indeed, even those workers who had impressed the observer with their sympathetic and understanding attitude toward recipients joined in this aggressive banter. To be sure, these workers might have deceived the observer by simulating a positive orientation in their statements to him and their behavior with clients when under observation by him; a systematic check, however, confirmed the initial impression. In five of the twelve work groups, a quantitative record was kept of all anticlient statements made during section meetings and conferences with the supervisor. A worker's tendency to make anticlient statements in these interactions with colleagues was not at all related to his attitude to clients, as indicated in the interview.

Aggressive jokes or remarks about clients were typically made at these meetings and conferences after some disagreement or conflict, and the common laughter or indignation helped to reunite the conflicting parties. In other words, anticlient statements were a mechanism for reaffirming social solidarity among colleagues. Since they readily served this function, case workers had incentives to make aggressive statements against recipients, regardless of their attitudes toward them, as a means for healing breaches in interpersonal relations that might otherwise fester and become disruptive conflicts. Moreover, since older workers, who had generally less considerate attitudes toward clients than newcomers, tended to occupy dominant positions in the work groups, newcomers were under pressure to prove that by joining in the anticlient raillery they were "regular fellows" and disprove the suspicion that they were naïve and sentimental about clients.

Displacing aggressive feelings aroused by conflicts with clients in the fairly harmless form of ridiculing them and displaying a hardened attitude toward them in discussions with colleagues may have helped to prevent such aggressive reactions from crystallizing into an antagonistic attitude to clients; but a case worker's opportunity for doing so depended on the extent of his informal relations. The unintegrated worker's inability readily to relieve the tensions produced by conflicts with recipients in this fashion may be one reason why he was more prone than the integrated worker to develop a callous, unconcerned attitude toward clients as a means of avoiding such tensions. Processes of selection, however, may also have contributed to the observed differences in worrying about the welfare of clients. Perhaps workers who worried left the agency in disproportionate numbers, and unintegrated worriers were even more apt to do so than integrated ones, whose friendly relations with peers made the job relatively more attractive. This pattern of turnover could also account for the findings presented in Table 12-3.

Discussion and Conclusion

Two important components of a professional orientation, in social work as well as in other occupations, are an interest in serving clients and the ability to furnish professional services. These are, of course, not the only elements in professionalism, but they are of special interest in the study of public assistance, because they become particularly problematical in the context of the administration of public welfare. The necessity to adapt to the bureaucratic procedures of complex welfare organizations creates obstacles for service, partly by diverting energies to learning the official regulations and administering them, partly by engendering anxieties and rigidities, and partly by the limitations imposed by internalized bureaucratic constraints. Furthermore, conflicts with clients, resulting primarily from the requirement to check their eligibility for assistance, jeopardize the interest in extending services to them. Finally, since the large majority of the personnel of public assistance agencies are not professionally trained, it is especially pertinent to ask what substitutes for such training, if any, promote a concern with the welfare of clients and an ability to serve them.

To be sure, untrained workers cannot be expected to have the skills to provide intensive case work, and there is no measure of such professional competence available in any case. We are concerned here merely with the worker's ability to cope with official procedures without restricting himself simply to checking eligibility—his ability to maintain an orientation to case-work service. Although newcomers were most vociferous in their criticism of agency procedures, their approach to clients tended to be most limited by them. Experience, including the training that workers received from their supervisors as well as from training officials, was a functional substitute for professional training, which enabled workers to render more extensive services to clients. It apparently reduced the case worker's anxieties about his work and thus freed him from being rigidly confined by procedures. Social support from integrative relations with peers also lessened anxieties and inflexibilities and, consequently, encouraged service to recipients.

Concern with the welfare of clients, too, was reinforced by integrative relations with colleagues, probably because peer group relations mitigated the impact of the reality shock that workers experienced in their early contacts and conflicts with clients, which obviated the need to adapt to such conflicts by developing a callous attitude toward clients. Experience, however, did not contribute to an interest in the welfare of clients; on the contrary, it reduced concern with their welfare.

In sum, experience increased the case worker's ability to serve recipients but decreased his interest in doing so. Peer group support on the other hand, promoted the worker's concern with helping clients as well as his ability to help them. Friendly relations with peers, moreover, constituted a source of work satisfaction which may well have reduced turnover.[14] This possibility raises the question of how differences in the tendency to leave the agency affected the findings.

The relationships between seniority and the orientations of case workers to recipients were in all likelihood not entirely due to the influence of experience but partly to processes of selection. Since friendly relations with colleagues make the job more attractive, integrated workers have more reason to remain than unintegrated workers. Hence, factors that make the job unsatisfactory would be expected to increase the quitting rate of unintegrated workers, whose interpersonal relations do not hold them back, more than that of integrated workers.[15] One such dissatisfaction might be a worker's inability to extend the scope of his activities beyond the fairly routine and uninteresting task of checking eligibility; another one might be the anxiety caused by contact with severely deprived recipients. If workers who feel restricted by procedures leave the agency in disproportionate numbers, there will be fewer procedure-oriented workers among those with several years seniority than among those with little seniority. And if the restrictions of procedures increase the quitting rate of unintegrated workers more than that of integrated ones, the differences in procedure orientation between old-timers and newcomers will be pronounced among unintegrated but not among integrated workers. This is precisely what Table 12–2 shows. Similarly, if worry about clients encourages quitting, and if worry exerts a stronger influence on the turnover of unintegrated than that of integrated workers, it follows that there are fewer worries left after several years, and that the difference in worrying associated with length of service is greater among unintegrated than among integrated workers. This is precisely what Table 12–3 shows. In short, the pattern of findings may be due either to these processes of selection or to the influence of experience discussed earlier. The most plausible assumption is that both factors contributed to the observed differences.[16]

Professional training in social work not only imparts knowledge and skills but also has an important socializing function; namely, to inculcate an orientation toward clients that combines impersonal detachment with serious concern for their welfare. The untrained workers in the agency studied probably suffered even more from not having undergone this process of socialization than from lack of professional knowledge and skills. To be sure, beginners were typically much concerned with helping clients, but they were not prepared for the shock of actually meeting recipients and, particularly, for coping with their own reactions to either the sympathy-evoking plight or the threatening aggression of recipients. The worker's untutored response to the tensions produced by these experiences was to become emotionally involved, or to escape by leaving the agency, or, perhaps most often, to lose concern with the welfare of clients as a means of avoiding these tensions. Such ego-defensive reactions would probably have been much rarer if the initial concern of workers with the welfare of recipients had been fortified by a detached attitude which made them less dependent on clients, just as ego support from integrative relations with colleagues reduced the likelihood of such reactions. To produce a detached service approach—the peculiar combination of a strong interest in furthering the welfare of clients and a detached attitude toward them—is an important function of professional training in social work.

NOTES

1. For a study that deals extensively with the orientation to clients in a public employment agency, see Roy G. Francis and Robert C. Stone, *Service and Procedure in Bureaucracy* (Minneapolis, 1956). A study that deals with the influence of the community on the orientations to recipients in a public welfare agency is reported in Edwin J. Thomas, "Role Conceptions and Organizational Size," *American Sociological Review*, 24 (1959), 30–37.

2. Robert K. Merton, *Social Theory and Social Structure* (rev. ed.; Glencoe, 1957), p. 369.

3. I am indebted to Philip M. Marcus for assistance in the collection and analysis of the data, and to the Ford Foundation as well as to the Social Science Research Committee of the University of Chicago for financial support. I also want to acknowledge William Delaney's helpful suggestions for revising the chapter.

4. Supervisors were classified on the basis of descriptions by their subordinates. But regardless of how a given worker described his supervisor, the worker was less apt to be service-oriented if the other subordinates described the supervisor as emphasizing procedures than if they did not.

5. The same relationship between knowledge of procedures and lack of rigidity was observed in another bureaucracy; see Peter M. Blau, *The Dynamics of Bureaucracy* (Chicago, 1955), pp. 197–198.

6. This concept has been introduced by Everett C. Hughes in his studies of professional careers.

7. See Miriam Wagenschien, "Reality Shock" (unpublished Master's thesis, University of Chicago, 1950).

8. An alternative interpretation of the finding would be that service orientation made workers more popular among colleagues, but other data suggest that the interpretation presented is probably the valid one. Thus this interpretation implies a direct relationship between popularity and self-confidence, and also one between self-confidence and a service orientation, and the data confirm both of these inferences.

9. The pattern of findings is quite similar if the index of popularity rather than that of integration is used, and also if several other measures of orientation to clients are substituted for the one shown in the table. (Integration in the ingroup rather than popularity in the organization is the measure presented in the tables, because there are too few popular newcomers to make meaningful comparisons.)

10. Although it is hazardous to venture an explanation of a single reversal, this one deserves to be mentioned, because it calls attention to forces that are often neglected in sociological studies of administrative organizations, including my own. In our reaction against scientific management and purely rational models of administrative behavior, we have tended to overemphasize the significance of informal relationships and paid insufficient attention to the formal administrative structure, the significance of incentives, and related problems. See on this point Alvin W. Gouldner, "Organizational Analysis," in Robert K. Merton, *et al.*, eds., *Sociology Today* (New York, 1959), pp. 400–412.

11. The findings permit, however, still another interpretation from which this conclusion would not follow. Perhaps certain personality types, as for example dependent individuals, were more likely than others to worry about clients and also more likely to foster integrative relations with colleagues. The assumption made in the text is that the relationship between integration and worrying is not spurious, that is, not simply due to personality differences that affect both these factors.

12. Few examples revealed personal involvement with clients ("Somebody gets under your skin and bothers you. . . ."); the majority expressed a more impersonal concern with effective service ("Did I do everything so that they can get their checks?"); and some referred not to clients but only to the respondent's own work or performance ("Too much paper work; we are under great pressure; heavy load"). It is worth noting that newcomers did not differ from old-timers in the proportion of their examples that referred only to their own problems. This indicates that the observed difference between newcomers and old-timers in *extent* of worrying is not simply due to the fact that experienced workers had less reason to worry about their performance, as one might otherwise suspect.

13. See Blau, "Social Integration, Social Rank, and Processes of Interaction," *Human Organization,* 18 (1959–1960), 152–157. In this paper, which is primarily based on observational data, I mistakenly assumed, on the basis of an inconclusive analysis of some of the interview data, that amount of worry is an index of detachment. I want to correct, and apologize for, the erroneous statement reported there.

14. Over one-third of the integrated workers, but less than one-tenth of the uninte-grated ones, spontaneously mentioned friendly relations with colleagues as one of the things they liked best about the job.

15. Lack of integration in combination with another source of job dissatisfaction might have motivated workers to leave. By itself, lack of integration in the ingroup evidently did not have this effect, as shown by the findings that the proportion of unintegrated did not increase with seniority (see last row of Table 12–3). Lack of popularity in the organization, on the other hand, might have induced workers to leave; for the proportion of the unpopular did decrease with seniority (from four-fifths among newcomers to one-third among workers with more than one year of service).

16. There is still another factor that may have contributed to these differences, namely, promotions to supervisor. Perhaps the promotion chances of procedure-oriented workers were better than those of workers who showed little interest in official procedures; perhaps individuals who worried about their cases were more likely to be promoted to supervisor than those who expressed less concern with their work; and perhaps popularity among colleagues decreased a worker's interest in becoming a supervisor. These processes of selective advancement might have contributed some-what, though hardly very much, to the observed differences between newcomers and old-timers.

13

Antoinette Catrice-Lorey

SOCIAL SECURITY AND ITS
RELATIONS WITH BENEFICIARIES:
THE PROBLEM OF BUREAUCRACY
IN SOCIAL ADMINISTRATION

The problem of the relations of social security administrations with their beneficiaries cannot, unfortunately, in the present state of research into the microsociology of social security, be approached at the level of comparative sociology; the task is still at the stage of close analysis of the working of the different national systems. This study is therefore centered on the French system, but includes an attempt to present in more general terms the problems of public relations in social security administration.

The description which follows is based on a series of social security studies which have been undertaken at the Institute of Labor Social Sciences (*Institut des Sciences Sociales du Travail*). The research has progressed in three stages. The first was a public opinion poll among insured persons under the General Scheme, based on a national representative sample. At the second stage, research was conducted within the social security bodies; questions were put to all the Directors of Social Security Funds in France concerning their relations with the public. The third stage is now in progress, attempting to consider the problem at a deeper level; whereas the first two stages were essentially descriptive, an effort is now being made to find explanations. This stage of research is being conducted both among insured persons and within

Antoinette Catrice-Lorey, "Social Security and Its Relations with Beneficiaries: The Problem of Bureaucracy in Social Administration," *Bulletin of the International Social Security Association* 19 (1966): 286–297 (slightly abridged). Reprinted by permission.

NOTE: This chapter is based on a recording of the address delivered at the Round Table Meeting on "Cross-National Sociology."

the social security bodies by means of smaller samples, and the ideas which follow constitute the guiding thread of this third stage.

Relations between Social Security Administration and Insured Persons in France

The problem of relations between social security administration and insured persons involves the question of contact between an administrative body and those on whose behalf the administration is conducted. It may be thought that a social security body would meet with fewer difficulties of communication with the public than would be the case with another type of administration. Social security administration is young and of recent origin; it is social in nature and is rendering service to the public; the subjects of administration are in this case the beneficiaries. For both these reasons the problem of relations between the administration and insured persons might be expected to appear in a favorable light. But another consideration has to be taken into account, that of the unusual structure of the French social security system, whereby the users are invited to participate in the management of the funds. The social security bodies, which are private organizations responsible for a public service, are in effect managed by elected administrative councils on which the representatives of wage-earners are in the majority (the employers' representatives constitute only one-quarter of the members of the councils). In face of the autonomous position of the social security bodies, the state has indeed reserved to itself powers of guidance and control. In its original conception, these powers were intended to be loosely exercised and thus to respect the autonomous management of the funds. Since 1945, however, development has been accompanied by a constant and growing strengthening of state control and by increasing state intervention in the operations of the social security bodies. As will be seen below, the gap which now exists between present realities and the initial conception of social security as an institution constitutes a permanent source of difficulties which react on the public mind.

It is important to recall that the decision in 1945 in favor of participation by users in the management of social security bodies was not a new idea; it is rooted in French social history and is related to the prominence of the mutual benefit society, the organized solidarity of the workers which preceded the establishment, first of compulsory social insurance, and later of social security. Thus when social security was introduced, the association of insured persons in the management of the institutions set up for their protection was a heritage of the mutual funds, the continuation of a tradition founded on action by the workers themselves.

These particular characteristics of "Social Security" as an administration might seem to facilitate contacts with the public, but the question may be asked as to whether in fact normal relations have been established in a climate of confidence and participation. It cannot be said that this has been the case. In spite of the close attachment of insured persons to their institution, tense relations often develop between the administration and insured persons. It cannot be said that social security administration is considered as popular by public opinion. A gap has developed between the institution and its beneficiaries and the reasons for this state of affairs will now be investigated. The attitudes which have arisen will be described and analyzed and an effort will be made to explain them in view of the special needs of insured persons in relation to social security, needs which are more definite than under other forms of administration. In the light of these needs, a study will be made of possible defects, which may react on the public, in the working of social security. The concept of bureaucracy will then be used to determine the extent to which social security administration is tending to deviate from its original and basic purpose.

THE MENTALITY OF INSURED PERSONS IN FRANCE:
INVOLVEMENT WITHOUT PARTICIPATION

It would appear to be a characteristic of the mentality of insured persons in France that a gap exists between their ideological attachment to social security, because of the security which it represents, and their attitude as consumers, or users, of the services. Research already undertaken has given results which indicate clearly that for insured persons social security has become an accepted fact which now forms an integral part of the wage-earner's condition. Is this attachment to the institution accompanied by an interest on the part of insured persons in the functioning of social security or at least by a favorable attitude? It would seem that this is not the case. The attitude of insured persons towards the functioning of the institution is characterized by various forms of nonparticipation already noted, whether this arises from misunderstanding of the aims, from ignorance of the internal working, or from a propensity to constant criticism or even to aggressive attitudes.

Insured persons are usually well informed as to their rights and as to the procedure to be followed, but they are certainly not well-informed about the institution itself or its aims. Most of the directors who were interviewed complained that insured persons considered the social security administration simply as a payments organization for the reimbursement of benefits and not as a social institution engaged in constructive work in the field of health. This misconception of the purposes of the social security administration is accompanied by ignorance of its internal operational mechanism. A single example may be cited for its special significance, since it concerns the machinery which has been devised to ensure democratic functioning: the vote of users in social security elections. If insured persons are asked whether it is important to vote in these elections, 73 percent reply that it is important to vote. Other results, however, show that they do not know the meaning of the vote, its significance or its consequences. If the question is asked "Do you know the composition of the administrative council responsible for your fund?" 75 percent are unable to reply. They do not see any connection between the vote and the fact that the administrative council is composed of their representatives. What, then, is the sense of voting? Perhaps at least a wish to demonstrate their attachment to the institution and perhaps also, as will be explained below, a confused affirmation of a certain feeling of ownership.

The tendency to constant criticism has been mentioned as another indication of nonparticipation. Blame is easily cast by public opinion on the social security administration. Since 1945, however, the institution has had to face difficulties of all kinds connected with the introduction and simultaneous acceleration of the system, but opinion has not taken into account these extenuating circumstances. Subjects such as the social security deficit have become fixed ideas in public opinion and are associated with bad management and waste. Another illustration of the same tendency is that, in opinion polls on the comparative functioning of several public services, social security administration is always in the lowest place. After an inquiry by the French Institute of Public Opinion (on the administration of the Posts and Telegraph Department) certain questions were presented again for purposes of the present study to different sample groups, with similar results. For example, 5 percent only of the public considered that the administration of the Posts, Telegraph, and Telephones functioned badly or very badly, but 33 percent thought that the social security administration functioned badly or very badly. A final fact noted during the investigations seems evidence of a tendency to aggressiveness on the part of the public, with consequences for the reactions of the counter clerks in social security funds. The counter clerks have hitherto usually insisted, as regards the reception arrangements, that they should be separated by a partition from the clients with whom they are concerned; this gives the impression that they feel the need of some protection against possible aggressive reactions.

PARTICULAR REQUIREMENTS OF SOCIAL SECURITY ADMINISTRATIONS: THE
DEMAND FOR A PERSONAL APPROACH AND THE DEMAND FOR CONTROL

The tendencies referred to above in the mentality of insured persons may appear paradoxical. The explanation may possibly be that the public has particular expectations from the social security administration and is more exacting than towards other administrations. What is exacted may be summarized under two headings: the demand for a personal approach, and the demand for control. It may be objected, as regards the personal approach, that the public has bureaucratic contacts with other administrations about which there are fewer complaints. It should be pointed out, however, that at the Bank or at the Post Office people do not have to reveal their personal position, whereas at the Social Security Office it is a question of personal problems and thus insured persons feel a special need for an administration which is really social, human and accessible. The following question was recently put to insured persons: "In your opinion, should one feel more at home in a Social Security Fund than in another administration, or is there no reason for any difference?" Fifty-seven percent of the sample of insured persons replied in the affirmative, considering that "one should feel more at home at the Social Security Office."

As concerns the demand for control, this seems to arise partly from consciousness of payment of contributions. In France, social security is not financed by taxation but by bipartite contributions from employers and wage-earners; these latter seem to be well aware that they are personally contributing to the working of the services. The demand for control may also have originated in the history of social security administration and its antecedents. It is widely felt among workers that social security belongs to them, because it has been won by the workers; it is indeed true that social security owes much to long and patient working-class activity in trade unions and mutual funds. Thus for both these reasons—the past and the present contribution—insured persons may have a feeling of ownership in relation to social security; hence the demand for control.

In face of these demands, what is the position of the insured person and how is he treated by social security administration? As regards the personal approach, it seems that there has long been much to say as to the manner in which insured persons have been received in the offices of the funds. The bad state of the premises, the wait, sometimes long, at the counter, the inadequate information given to the public and the lack of a proper reception are matters which have been examined in detail in the works to which reference has been made. The situation was such that the ministry responsible recently launched an official "humanization" campaign. The terms of the minister's circular may be of interest: "I have been struck," he said, "by the fact that although the participation of elected representatives of insured persons in the management of the social security bodies had the express purpose of establishing a close link between these bodies and the users of a public service, the Social Security Administration has been generally regarded as more impersonal and lacking in human qualities than some of the traditional state departments. . . ." The insured person has thus, because of certain deficiences, felt himself neglected, disregarded, treated as a number.

Where, then, is the control which is supposed to exist? It seems that, far from being in a position to follow and understand what is happening in social security, the insured person has, on the contrary, a feeling that he is totally dependent on an anonymous authority and that he has no control over social security administration. He is the "insurable person," he is the subject of administration and not the beneficiary. It should be noted in this connection that the directors of the funds, in their replies, insisted strongly on the complexity of the rules applicable to insured persons. They considered that the administrative formalities to which insured persons are subject are both too numerous and too complicated. The users do not see the necessity or the sense of these formalities, which have come to be regarded as sheer vexation. To this must be added the fact that the regulations are often notified to insured persons in a language which they do not understand. For them, the authority is anonymous; the public does not know where, when or how decisions are made on its behalf. Decisions are usually imputed to the fund itself, but the fund merely transmits them and shelters behind the authority of the responsible administration.

Where, then, is the democratic participation in the institution? It seems that this has no effective reality for the insured person. As has already been seen, the insured person does not feel that he has representatives on the administrative councils. The elected representatives are far removed from the insured persons and there is no real contact between them; this problem will be further considered below.

THE GAP BETWEEN EXPECTATION AND REALITY

As concerns the problem of relations between the Social Security Administration and insured persons, the existence of a wide gap between expectation and reality is confirmed by the foregoing remarks. This gap may be responsible for the attitudes of withdrawal adopted by insured persons, who seem to have decided to remain strangers to the life of the institution. This may also explain the characteristic grasping mentality, the underlying idea in the user's mind that he must recover from social security the sums which he has been obliged to pay and use it to obtain the utmost advantages, in an effort to restore the balance between what he has given and what he receives. This grasping mentality regards social security, not from its true aspect of solidarity, but from the aspect of contributions paid and benefits received by the individual concerned.

Social Security and Bureaucracy

The second part of this chapter will consider to what extent the attitudes, already described, of insured persons in France may be a response to defective working of the institution. Instead of analyzing the attitudes of insured persons, the functioning of the institution will be examined.

BUREAUCRACY, PATHOLOGY OF ORGANIZATIONS,
REFLECTIONS ON THEIR PURPOSE

This study of the working of social security administration will make use of the concept "bureaucracy." In view, however, of the many senses of the term and in view of the development of the concept since Max Weber, it is important to define the sense in which the term will be understood. Differing from Max Weber, bureaucracy will not be considered as a type of organization, even an ideal type. It will be considered rather as a pathological type of functioning found in organizations. In this sense the expression "bureaucratization," or the process of "bureaucratization," rather than bureaucracy, will be used. Deriving inspiration from the ideas of Alain Touraine in his book "Sociology of Action," it will be suggested that an organization becomes bureaucratic when it deviates from its purposes and from its original objectives and is no longer adapted to the purposes for which it was conceived and which it should serve. An organization is effective, says Touraine, when it is adapted to its social ends, but when it becomes independent of its purposes, exists for itself alone and forgets the reason for its existence, then it becomes bureaucratic. There is a constant tendency in organizations to become bureaucratic, that is to say, to deviate from their original direction and in the course of their development to forget their essential aims. An attempt will be made to determine in which sense and by what means social security administration tends to become bureaucratic and how far it has departed from the fundamental reason for its existence. The study of the pathology of organizations therefore centers on their aims. The aims of social security will now be considered.

The first purpose of social security is basically, as its name suggests, to afford security, not only material security in actual sickness, but moral security in face of the possible materialization of the risk and therefore a feeling of security which certainly includes psychological security in dealings with the administrative bodies to which claims are made. The mission of the social security administration is to render service and this it effectively does, but what has been said above concerning its purpose involves the manner in which the service is rendered. It is a question of preoccupation with the improvement of the quality of the service, the concern to help insured persons rather than to treat them as subjects for administration.

It will be asked whether in the working of social security administration there are not factors which turn it from fundamental purpose, preoccupation with the insured person and with the quality of the service rendered to him. With this in view, an attempt will be made, by dismantling the mechanisms of the institution, to discover what "malfunctioning" at present exists in social security administration and at what levels. Malfunctioning in the structure of the institution will first be studied and then consideration will be given to malfunctioning which may arise from the individual attitudes of those responsible in the different grades.

STRUCTURAL MALFUNCTIONING IN SOCIAL SECURITY ADMINISTRATION

Structural malfunctioning arises from difficulties in relations between the central authority and the social security bodies. The central administration and the funds are too self-contained and lack intercommunication, each working in a closed circle adjacent to the other. The rules applicable to insured persons are formulated and imposed by the central administration, which tends to operate in its own closed universe; there is thus a temptation to consider the rules as an end in themselves, oblivious of the points of view both of those who have to apply the rules and of those who are subject to them. The central administration lacking any real contact with those in charge of the funds, is liable to become enclosed in a legalistic and abstract formalism. Again, still at the structural level, mention must be made of the permanent state of tension which exists between the decentralized institutions—the funds —the central authority. This arises from the increase of state control, until a supervisory authority has become almost a hierarchic power. Self-management in the funds is reduced to almost nothing and the administrative councils which should, in principle, exercise management functions, feel themselves more and more transformed into figureheads. The result is that the funds have a sense of frustration and work under tension; their initiative is slackened and neutralized by state shackles on their activity. It may be concluded that all this is evidence of maladjustments in the functioning of the bodies which compose the institution, tending to distract it from service to the public. The primary objective—service to the insured person—eventually becomes overridden by other preoccupations.

MALFUNCTIONING ARISING FROM THE ATTITUDES OF THOSE
RESPONSIBLE FOR THE WORKING OF THE FUNDS

The matter will now be considered at the level of the funds, bodies which are themselves in contact with the public. Although, as has already been noted in connection with the management of risks, the funds have little room for initiative in some respects, they have much wider margin of initiative as regards relations with insured persons. The style adopted for relations with the public may vary greatly from one fund to another. As regards the ways in which social security funds may become bureaucratic, it may be suggested that they become bureaucratic bodies when they are tempted to become self-centered and preoccupied with internal operational problems rather than with their beneficiaries, who thus receive scant attention. These bureaucratic tendencies in social security bodies arise from the individual attitudes of those responsible in the different grades for the operations, and from their conception of their role.

A review will now be made of the attitudes towards their functions of managers of funds, of trade union representatives on the administrative councils, and of employees in contact with the public. The managers, by which term is understood all management staff, will first be considered.

Managerial positions. In past and in current studies two types of attitudes have been noted in management: one may be described as the managerial attitude, the other as the public service attitude. A different mode of behavior is observed according to which attitude dominates the minds of those responsible. When the managerial attitude predominates, management staff are primarily concerned with the internal working problems of the fund, with the organization of the departments and with the realization of economies in management. In brief, they are much more concerned with the running of their concern and with its good management than with service to the public. Problems arising from satisfaction of the public are apt to be considered as disturbing factors, partly because innovations of this kind may upset the daily administrative work, partly because innovations always cause additional expenditure. On the other hand, managers are found who are fully convinced that they are at the head of a social organization and are devoted to the service of insured persons. These managers will always be preoccupied with improvements in the quality of service rendered to the public.

In the course of this research, an attempt has been made to find indications of the extent to which those responsible for the funds show consideration for the public, though only a brief outline can now be given. One indication is whether or not there exists a general policy for public relations in the funds; if no such policy exists problems are treated piecemeal in proportion to their urgency. A second indication is the scope of measures taken to improve relations and to make the administrative bodies more accessible to the public. A third indication concerns information and it is of interest to consider the attitude of the management of a fund which tends either systematically to underestimate the public, or which thinks that the public can be improved. The way in which information is expressed and distributed may also be noted. In this respect a distinction has been made between routine information, which could be described as bureaucratic, and information of a dynamic type with varying modes of expression both in basis and form.

Trade union representatives on the councils. The attitudes of the trade union representatives on the administrative councils will now be considered. These administrators, it will be recalled, have to play a double role of management on the one hand and mediation on the other. The management functions of the administrative councils and the limitations imposed on them by the state have already been referred to, but their role as mediators remains: the mission entrusted to them of maintaining contact between the users whom they represent and the social security administration. Their mediation has a two-way role; as social security administrators they must reflect within the administrative bodies the needs and reactions of insured persons, but they must also demonstrate externally to the beneficiaries the activities of the funds on their behalf. It does not seem, however, that this mediatory function is fully assumed. Brief reference will be made to several factors which play a part in deflecting the trade union representatives from the accomplishment of this mission.

Their role as spokesmen for insured persons within the administrative bodies may be said to be in some measure fulfilled, but there are some distracting factors which become major preoccupations for the administrators, to the detriment of an essential aspect of their function. Within the council, the administrators are trapped by trade union conflicts; working-class divisions arise in the councils because there is no trade union unity in France. To this must be added eventual tensions in the councils with the employers' representatives. It may also happen that, by a kind of professional reflex, the trade union representatives may be motivated by the claims of the social security personnel, employees of the fund, and this influence may counteract the improvement of the service for insured persons. A single example may be cited: the hours during which the offices of social security funds are open. It would seem that the hours of opening are arranged to suit the personnel rather than the users. In contrast to some public services, such as the post offices, which have made the effort to be open on Saturdays until four o'clock, the social security offices are usually closed all day on Saturdays, mornings and afternoons.

The education of insured persons, which should be an external task of the trade union representatives, so that a true picture of the institution may be presented to public opinion, is a particularly delicate problem. Reference has already been made to the distance which separates trade union leaders in the administrative councils from the general mass of people. This may be partly explained, no doubt, by the position of trade unions in France, their low numerical representation, their lack of material means, and so on. But it may also be true that the mission of educating the public to some extent in social security has not so far been given the place it deserves in trade union preoccupations.

Employees at the counters. The attitudes of social security employees may now be considered, especially as concerns those who work at the counters and are in direct daily contact with the public. The counter clerk is the hinge between the institution and the public. The manner in which he performs his task is therefore of great importance, for his attitude will to some extent indicate in the mind of the user the intentions of the social security administration in his case. The question of the attitudes of counter clerks amounts to this: is their interest centered solely on their work, their techniques and their department, or do they also consider the point of view of the user? In their daily relations with insured persons, do they seek to help them or to exercise power over them? In other words, study is needed of the comportment of the counter clerks in relation to the rules and the factors which lead them to adopt a more or less disciplinary tone in the application of the regulations. It is clear that the work of these officials requires on their part, if it is to be satisfactorily performed, a degree of psychological and moral involvement. The work is not of a kind that can be mechanically performed, as work studies actually in progress will fully demonstrate. Observation shows that this work should in some respects be considered as "social" and thus involves some participation and motivation on the part of the personnel. This factor, which has been brought to light by American studies among hospital personnel, leads to the question as to who are, in fact, the social security counter clerks? What motives have led them to work in social security administration? Why and how did they choose this occupation and what was their previous work? If they could begin again, what would their attitude be? These are the questions which are being presented to them. The funds complain of difficulties in recruitment and also of problems of absenteeism. It would seem that the qualifications of social security personnel as a whole are not high enough and may even be lower than in other administrations. The low starting salaries may explain this; absenteeism may be explained by the fact that three-quarters of the personnel are women. Other explanations must, however, be sought; for example, the job of social security employee does not seem to be held in esteem by public opinion. If the question is put to insured persons: "Which do you consider the best job for a young man or a young girl: to work in the post office, in a bank, or in the social security administration?" the social security office is by far the last choice.

Two essential problems result from the preceding study of the attitudes of social security employees and of their consequences. If it is desired to obtain a satisfactory functioning of the institution, it is important first to recruit personnel with a certain level of qualifications and general culture and with an aptitude for human relations, and then to give them a special training. This training should aim to create among social security officials an attitude of mind in harmony with the purposes of the organization, that is, to obtain their participation in the fundamental values which belong to the institution.

To recapitulate, this study of the institution of social security at its different levels has indicated instances when concern for the public has been lost sight of at each level. They show that social security administration is in danger of becoming bureaucratic when it departs from the fundamental reason for its existence, to give to insured persons the feeling of the greatest possible security. At present, the attitudes of withdrawal and estrangement adopted by insured persons are justifiable when those responsible for the organization tend to forget or at least to neglect the users. *In sum,* the attempt has been made in this study, after describing certain reactions which are characteristic of insured persons in France, to explain them in the light, on the one hand, of the heavy demands made by the public on social security administration and, on the other hand, of the defective functioning of the institution, a tendency in social security to become bureaucratic.

It is not intended, however, that this study should leave a final impression unfavorable to the French social security system nor that it should be interpreted as a facile criticism of its working. The attempt to define the bureaucratic tendencies in social security and to throw light on the deviations which are the cause of these tendencies, has been deliberately made from the standpoint of optimum or ideal functioning of the institution. It may be considered salutary for an organization to take stock of the distortions and deviations of which it should beware. It would in any case be salutary to verify from other examples the therapeutic advantages of such a study.

A movement towards "debureaucratization." In conclusion, suggestions may be made for the launching of a process of "debureaucratization" in French social security administration. The case may be quoted of the above-mentioned humanization campaign set in motion during the last two years by the responsible ministry and spontaneously adopted by the funds as a whole. This campaign has aroused consciousness of certain gaps in the services rendered to insured persons, and more especially in the manner in which they are received at the offices of the funds. It is clear that the campaign has already given quite spectacular results and has led to important practical improvements. It may be remarked in passing that it is sometimes called "Operation Hostesses and Green Plants." This should call attention to the deeper aspects of the problem of humanizing the institution. The humanization of social security by inner improvements will only be achieved by the effort to create, at all levels of responsibility, a state of mind centered on the rendering of service. It must also be realized that the humanization of social security requires, this time on the part of the central administration, difficult reforms of legislation and regulation so as to adapt them better to the needs of the public. It must be foreseen that the "debureaucratization" of social security administration will sooner or later necessitate structural reform. This point raises controversy; some may think that it would be desirable to rationalize the institution by making it a public state service. However, it may be wondered whether this would be the best solution or whether indeed it would solve the problem of bureaucracy in social security administration. At the present time, social security administration seems to be at the cross-roads. How can the system recover its coherence? Is the answer to be found in a return to the sources, that is, to the concept of 1945, or is it in radical change, such as some form of state administration? The suggestion in mind, in mentioning structural reform, is not state administration of social security but, on the contrary, a relaxing of state control and its replacement in large part by internal control. The pleasant surprise which would be produced by such a reform would certainly arouse a new dynamism in the funds, and would thus put them in a better position to accomplish the mission which was laid down for them in the legislation. Finally, does not the fact that social security in France is managed by private bodies, and the fact that medicine preserves its liberal character, bound to the state only by agreements, constitute a cultural reality which is not only characteristically French but also an imperative for the future?

14

William Foote Whyte

WHEN WORKERS AND
CUSTOMERS MEET

. . . When workers and customers meet, in the service industries, that relationship adds a new dimension to the pattern of human relations in industry.
When the customer takes an active part in business activity, the whole organization must be adjusted to his behavior.

While all service industries have the customer relationship in common,
there are nevertheless important structural differences among industries in
this group. For example, the restaurant industry differs from the others in
certain respects that make it particularly interesting for human relations
research.[1]

The restaurant is a combination production and service unit. In this it
differs from the factory, which is solely a production or processing unit, and
it also differs from the department store, which is solely a service unit.

The restaurant deals in a perishable commodity, which can be produced
only a little in advance of its consumption, and it must serve customers whose
numbers can never be exactly foreseen. If the food estimates prove to be
low, then the kitchen runs out of a number of popular items, and there are
delays in providing new orders or substitutions. This upsets the customers,
who in turn upset the waiters or waitresses, and so on until the pressure is
carried right into the kitchen. On the other hand, if the food estimates prove
to be too high, then food is wasted, costs go up, and the restaurant loses
money. Consequently the restaurant always faces a difficult problem of
coordination of production and service departments—a problem, which, so
far as I know, is to be found in no other industry.

The human relations problem faced by the worker is also quite unique.

When Workers and Customers Meet

Nearly every restaurant worker must adjust to people in at least two different relationships—in addition to getting along with fellow workers on his own job. For example, the cook responds to the directions of the kitchen supervisor and also must respond to requests for food from kitchen runners or supply men. Similarly, the pantry worker is under the pantry supervisor and responds to orders for food from waitresses. For the waitress, the problem is a good deal more complex. She must adjust herself to supervisor and to other waitresses and in addition she has to deal with between 50 and 100 customers a day, many of them complete strangers; and she has to adjust to service pantry workers or cooks to get the food out, and to bartenders to get her drinks, if the restaurant serves liquor. Clearly it requires a high degree of social adaptability to handle this assignment successfully.

As far as the workers are concerned, the factory is characterized by a predominantly straight line authority. The restaurant has that straight line but, in addition, it has what we might call a diagonal line of action extending from customer straight through to dishwasher (see Figure 14–1).

We might expect this situation to give rise to special problems of adjustment, and that is indeed what we have found. However, before we explore these problems, it should be pointed out that only a part of the behavior we

FIGURE 14-1. The Restaurant (Simplified Diagram).

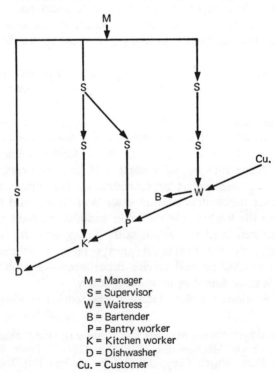

M = Manager
S = Supervisor
W = Waitress
B = Bartender
P = Pantry worker
K = Kitchen worker
D = Dishwasher
Cu. = Customer

observed in our restaurant study could be attributed to the distinctive structure of the restaurant itself. Our research was carried on during the war when restaurant people were working under the "abnormal" pressures of wartime. However, in some respects this is an advantage, for much of our knowledge of normal individuals is derived from the study of abnormal psychology. Similarly, we can expect to increase our understanding of human reactions to the ordinary tensions of everyday life through observing the breakdowns that occur under abnormal pressure.

Faced with acute food shortages, additional work to meet new government regulations, and with a labor force short in numbers and experience, restaurant organizations faced extraordinary difficulties in meeting their record volume of consumer demand. To one who has seen the industry from the inside, the remarkable thing is not that there were frictions and tensions but rather that restaurants managed to function so well under such severe handicaps. However, there were extra pressures, and there were some people who broke down under pressure. It is to these individuals and to the high-tension situations they faced that I will give my attention.

Since there is not space to consider the whole organization, let us look at the problem at the point of customer contact, where the waitress meets the customers. (To simplify the story, waiters will not be considered here, though their problems are quite similar.) That raises several questions. How do waitresses react to customers? How do customers react to them? How does the customer relationship affect the behavior of the waiter or waitress in contacts with supervisors or other workers? And finally, what role does the supervisor play in handling customer relations?

To answer these questions, I shall give special attention to the crying waitress. Of course, it should be understood that even under wartime pressure only a small minority of waitresses were subject to crying spells. However, crying is worth attention because it furnishes quite an objective manifestation of behavior. As we explore that, we can ask what situations give rise to crying and then ask further which waitresses cry and which do not. As we answer those questions, we shall be able to draw conclusions upon the nature of the human relations situation and also upon the relationship between the social background and social ties of the waitress and her behavior under pressure.

What nervous tension means to the waitress can hardly be explained in general terms. We must go to the girls themselves to get that story. Here is an example that brings out most of the elements common to the crying situation. The waitress in this case is a girl of about twenty-one, with a year of experience in a large and busy Loop restaurant. She put it this way:

You know, I was so mad! I finally broke down Tuesday and cried. That was really a terrible day. The guests were crabby, and I wasn't making any money, and we kept running out of food in the kitchen.

Once I went past one of my tables just when a new party was sitting down. One of the women picks up 50 cents and puts it in her pocket. She says, "Look, the people here must have forgot and left their money." I could have screamed, but what could I do?

Well the guests were yelling at me all day, trying to get my attention. Everybody had trouble. Sue cried too.

The waitress was asked if she could remember the particular incident that set the crying off.

Yes, it was like this. I was rushed, and I came in to the service pantry to get my hot plates. There were three hot plates standing up there on the counter, and, when I called my order in, the woman standing behind the counter just said, "Take them," so I put them on my tray and started out. I thought I was doing all right, but then Sue comes in. You see she had been stuck all day. She had orders for hot plates for her whole station all at once, and she couldn't carry it all out, so she left some of her hot plates at the counter and told the woman behind the counter to save them for her.

When she came back and saw the hot plates all gone with a long line of girls waiting to get them, she started to cry. Well, when I saw that the plates were really hers, I gave them right back to her, and a couple of other girls gave plates back to her, so she got her hot plates right back, and she didn't have to leave the floor.

But that upset me. You know, I was getting out of a hole with those hot plates, but then all of a sudden I had to give them up and get right at the end of a long line. I just started to bawl.

I had to go down to the rest room. Well, the way I am, I'm just getting over it when I think again what one of the guests said and the way they were acting, and then I get feeling sorry for myself some more, and I start to cry all over again. It took me an hour to get back on the floor Tuesday.

Here we see that there is no one cause for crying. Rather it is a combination of pressures. This was a bad day in the coordination of production and service. The food was not ready when the waitresses needed it, and, when it did come up, there was a failure of adjustment between waitresses and counter people. Related to this problem, a number of the girls were having trouble in getting along with their customers.

The waitress brought up one important aspect of the customer relations problem: the matter of tipping. Her experience with customers pocketing the tip left by their predecessors was unusual. Her comment that on this particular day she was not making any money was a remark that we heard all the time. Even in high-quality restaurants there are always a certain number of "stiffs"—customers who don't tip.

Since it is well known that the waitress's income depends upon tips more than wages, we might be tempted to put down the "stiff" as an economic problem. However, when we get the girls to talk about the situation, it is clear that this is not the case. We asked one girl to explain how she felt when she was "stiffed." She said,

You think of all the work you've done and how you've tried to please those people, and it hurts when they don't leave anything for you. You think, so that's what they really think of me. . . . It's like an insult.

260

A restaurant owner told me that in a place he operated where "stiffing" was quite rare, he would find one of his best waitresses in tears from time to time. She would always explain, "I failed, Mr. Blank, I failed today. After all I did for them, they didn't like me."

Waitresses, like other people, are conditioned by their experiences in growing up to expect recognition when they are of service to someone. The recognition need not necessarily be a material reward, but it is the custom, under the tipping system, to put it in that form. Consequently, the waitress can't help feeling a sense of personal failure and public censure when she is "stiffed." She may try to look at the situation rationally, saying that some people just never tip, or perhaps they just forgot it, or they may not have had the right change, and so on, but this does not alter the fact that her expectations were frustrated.

The relationship between expectations and events is clearly an important one. Factory studies have shown that the development of certain routines in handling the job and a certain pattern of adjustment to fellow workers and supervisors help to give the worker emotional stability and a sense of satisfaction. The restaurant job and its human relations can never be fitted into a pattern of routine. The experienced waitress develops certain skills in organizing her work so as to keep her various customers occupied and get the food out of the service pantry, but these skills must be continually put to the test in meeting changing conditions in the dining room and in the service pantry. There are always new problems to be solved. And—perhaps most unsettling of all—there are the solved problems that suddenly become unsolved, as in the case of this waitress who thought she was getting out of a hole, only to find herself more deeply involved than ever.

The waitress in this case says that she could have screamed. If she had screamed, probably she would not have had to cry. The relationship is well recognized by the waitresses themselves. As one of them said,

The trouble is, when the guests get nasty with you, you can't tell them off. You have to keep it all inside you. That's what makes it so nerve-racking. It would be much easier for us if we could talk back.

It is clear that the pressures upon the waitress cannot simply be absorbed. In one way or another, they must come out, and crying is one outlet.

The waitress who told us this story was talking about "one of those days" when everything seems to go wrong. There are days when everything seems to run along fairly smoothly, and then there are days when something goes wrong at the start and everybody is under great pressure all day long. Tension and confusion, when once under way, tend to build up and reinforce each other. If the waitress once gets upset in her relations with her customers, she is likely to have trouble all day.

This was clearly shown in one restaurant we studied. There the difficult customers seemed to run in series. We often heard the girls comment, as they finished work, "What a night! Just one of them after another." We have no statistics on the percentage of unpleasant to total customers from one night to another, but the wide fluctuations in the waitress's feelings towards customers certainly do not refer just to the personalities of the customers. She is reacting to a relationship. Whenever a difficult incident arises to upset this relationship, the waitress is thrown off balance and is more likely to get into difficulties with her next customers, so that social equilibrium may readily be destroyed for the whole working period.

The background gives us an idea of the situation in which crying takes place, but it must be noted that waitresses react to these tensions in varying ways. Some cry fairly frequently, some seldom cry, and there are some who never cry. If we are to understand this behavior, such differences must be explained.

The broadest generalization we can make is that crying behavior is related to length of waitress work experience. There are a number of reasons why this should be so. In the first place, there is a selective process at work, with girls who break down under the strain tending to drop out of the industry. The more experienced girls have more skill in organizing their work and have had practice in coping with almost any problem that may arise. Furthermore, in some restaurants where stations are assigned on a seniority basis, the more experienced girls tend to work in the same general location, where they are able to help each other. Inexperienced girls may be concentrated together too, but they generally have their hands so full with their own work that they can't provide each other with the help over rough spots, which is so important when the pressure is on.

As a rule, the more experienced girls are much more aggressive toward service pantry workers and bartenders, so that they are able to get some of the pressure off in that direction.

There are also important differences in relations with customers and with supervisors. Most experienced waitresses build up a following of steady customers. Sometimes the relationship becomes a very cordial one, and the appearance of a steady customer may completely change the situation for a waitress who has been in difficulty with strangers. Even when the steady customer is an unpopular one, at least he is not an unknown quantity, and the waitress knows what to expect from him.

Experienced waitresses have generally made their adjustment to the standards of the restaurant and do not make many mistakes in their work. They are thus much less subject to criticism and enforcement of rules from supervisors. In fact, where we have observed it, the comparison is quite striking. The experienced waitresses proceed with little if any regulation of their behavior by supervisors, whereas inexperienced girls tend to be subjected to a good deal more attention from the supervision.

The matter of experience accounts for a great deal, but it does not tell the whole story. We find among inexperienced waitresses some who never cry and among experienced waitresses some who break down fairly frequently. If we look into these deviations from the expected behavior, and if we give close attention to several other cases where the factor of experience is held constant, then we should be able to come to grips with the dynamics of this crying behavior.

The first point that stands out is that the waitress who bears up under pressure does not simply respond to her customers. She acts with some skill to control their behavior. The first question to ask when we look at the customer relationship is, "Does the waitress get the jump on the customer, or does the customer get the jump on the waitress?" The skilled waitress realizes the crucial nature of this question. One of them gave these instructions to a new girl:

Get a clean cover on the table, give them their water, take the order, and then leave them if necessary. Once they have a feeling that you have taken charge, they will be all right.

The skilled waitress tackles the customers with confidence and without hesitation. For example, she may find that a new customer has seated himself before she could clear off the dirty dishes and change the cloth. He is now leaning on the table, studying the menu. She greets him, says, "May I change the cover, please?" and, without waiting for an answer, takes his menu away from him so that he moves back from the table, and she goes about her work. The relationship is handled politely but firmly, and there is never any question as to who is in charge. Most customers react favorably to this approach. While we have not interviewed them on the subject, it appears that it gives them a feeling of security when the waitress moves right in and shows that she knows how to handle her work.

Getting the jump on customers involves not only such concrete moves as changing the tablecloth. It also involves giving the proper emotional tone to the relationship. This is a difficult matter on which to present objective data, but skilled waitresses know what they are doing and explain it along these lines:

The trouble with a lot of girls is that they're afraid of the guests. They wouldn't admit it, but they really are. You know, if you're timid, the guests can sense that, and I guess it's just human nature that people like to pick on you when you're timid. That way you get off on the wrong foot from the beginning, and you never get things right all day. I know how it is because I used to be afraid of people when I first started and I cried a few times the first month or two. But I've got more confidence now. I know there isn't any situation I can't handle.

A lot depends upon the way you approach the guest. I can tell it myself. If you go up to them as though you are afraid of them or as though you don't want to wait on them at all, they can sense that, and it makes them nervous and fussy. So I always go up to a guest as if I was happy to wait on the person. I try to make them feel comfortable and at ease to start with, and then I don't have any trouble.

While we need not accept the waitress's observation upon human nature, we can observe the behavior she describes. Apparently it is up to the waitress to seize the initiative in customer relations—to set the pattern for the relationship. This she does by the things she does, the things she says, the way she uses her voice, and the expression on her face. If she fails to seize the initiative in this manner, the customer senses her uncertainty and seems to feel uneasy himself. This is likely to lead to trouble.

However, the generalization needs this qualification. We can observe three general types of waitress-customer relationships. In one, the waitress holds the initiative from beginning to end. In another, the customer holds the initiative throughout. In the third, it is uncertain who is taking the lead and the initiative passes back and forth or remains in dispute. From the standpoint of the emotional stability of the waitress, either of the first two relationships is feasible, provided that the customer who takes the initiative frames his demands in a manner that will not bring the waitress into conflict with other employees and supervisors. It is the third type of relationship that seems to be the troublesome one, and this, incidentally, is most often a problem of the woman customer. The customer does not know what she wants yet refuses to accept the waitress's suggestions. She is not ready to give her order when the waitress wants to take it, and she wants to give her order when the waitress is occupied with other duties. And then she changes her mind. She does not want coffee with her main course, but when that course arrives she wants coffee after all. She will have the broiled scrod, but when her friend's chicken salad arrives it looks so good that she will have that instead. Such a relationship leads to a good deal of fencing between waitress and customer, and forces the waitress to reorganize her plan of work with every move the customer makes. It also gets the girl in trouble in the service pantry, as the employees there do not like to change orders. Such a customer therefore gives rise to a number of particular problems, but beyond that the basic difficulty seems to be that the waitress does not know where she stands and does not know what to expect.

While the waitress may get along well with the customer who seizes and maintains the initiative, that alone will not solve her problems. She must be able to lead those who want to be led and to get the jump on the uncertain and recalcitrant customers. She will always have difficult customers to deal with, but, with this approach, she will find that there are not enough of them to upset her equilibrium.

This would lead us to expect that girls with some leadership experience —with some experience in taking the initiative in human relations—would make the best adjustment to waitress work. We found that this did prove to be an important factor.

In one of the restaurants studied, we were fortunate in finding two sets of twins. In both cases, one of the pair broke down on the job fairly often, while the other never or hardly ever cried. Being able to hold the age and experience factors constant, and taking the girls from the same general family and community environment, we should be able to explore individual differences in patterns of interaction.

The Swansons, Ruth and Sally, were identical twins, and both said that they had always been "very close," doing nearly everything together. While both girls were considered shy and quiet, we found in interviewing them that Sally was decidedly more articulate. We drew Sally out on their relationship, asking how they decided what they were going to do. "Well," she said, "sometimes we would have arguments about it, but we would always decide to do the same thing in the end." We asked who usually won out in the arguments. She smiled and said, "I guess I usually did." Ruth was the girl who cried. Sally never cried. We asked for an example of the sort of arguments they had. She said,

Well, lots of times it would be about clothes. Ruth would want to wear one dress, and I'd want to wear another dress. We'd argue it out, and she would finally wear the dress I wanted her to wear.

The Careys, Rita and Lucille, were not identical. Both were quite attractive, talkative, and popular with the other waitresses, but in the matter of social initiative, there were striking differences. This may best be illustrated with part of an interview we had with both of them together:

RITA: Ever since I was little I had to take care of my small cousins and other kids in the neighborhood. I used to like to take care of kids. It never bothered me when they cried or got into some kind of trouble. I used to do a lot of running errands to the store for my mother too, and I took care of a lot of things around the house. I always used to enjoy doing things like that.
INTERVIEWER: Did you both take care of your little cousins?
RITA: We both did, but I did it more than Lucille.
LUCILLE: They always liked Rita better than me. I don't know why it was, but it was always Rita first and then me. I guess Rita just had a way with kids. She always liked to take care of kids. Rita took care of me too. (*She laughed.*) She fought my battles for me.
INTERVIEWER: How was that?
LUCILLE: Well, just to give you an example, sometimes we'd be out swimming, and some kid would duck me for no good reason at all. Rita would come up and give them hell. She'd tell them they couldn't get away with something like that on her sister.
RITA: You see, I was always bigger than Lucille. I was a regular tomboy. It wasn't that I had to fight very often. Most times I would just tell people, and they'd lay off Lucille.
LUCILLE: Yes, that's the way it was.
RITA (*sternly, to Lucille*): Don't bite your nails!
LUCILLE (*removes them quickly*): Well, I'm so nervous I have to do something.

It is hardly necessary to comment that in this case Lucille was the one who couldn't take it. In fact, she found the job so upsetting that she quit shortly after this interview, whereas Rita appeared always cheerful and in control of her situation.

To explore further this matter of initiative, let's compare Sue Tracy and Estelle Wolinski. Sue had been a waitress in this particular restaurant for over three years, which made her one of the longer service employees. She was an intelligent and very attractive girl. She had an unusually large number of steady customers. And yet, with all this in her favor, she was easily upset and broke down fairly often. Estelle had worked for only several months, not long enough to build up any following, and she was not attractive enough to make a favorable impression on customers through her appearance. Nevertheless, she took everything in her stride and never cried.

If we explore the patterns of human relations to which the two girls had become accustomed, we can explain their differing reactions.

There are two children in the Tracy family, Sue being four years younger than her sister. When Sue was growing up, her family moved around a great deal, so, she says, she did not make any close friendships with children. Most of her time was spent with adults, with whom she got along very well. Her father was a commercial artist. On her relations with her parents, she had this to say:

Well, when I was growing up, I was sick a lot of the time, and my mother was always there taking care of me. I got a lot of attention. I wasn't spoiled—that is, I don't think I was spoiled—but my parents tried to give me everything. That is, everything except a bicycle I wanted. Mother said she wouldn't give me that because I wasn't safe on the streets. Even now it's terrible the way I cross streets. I'm a regular jaywalker. It's just luck that I haven't been run over. I was knocked down by a car once, but I only got a bump out of it. Mother always would say that I wasn't safe on streets, and that's why I didn't get the bicycle. You see, they always treated me like the baby of the family.

In growing up, then, Sue had no experience in initiating action for others, was kept under close parental control, and became very dependent upon adult approval of her behavior. When customers failed to give her that approval, she was unable to manage the situation.

Estelle's background was quite different. She comes from a large family of Polish extraction, the seventh of nine children. When she was growing up, she always went around with a large gang of boys and girls. When she was with her group of girls, she took the lead. As she explained it,

Well, just to give you an example, suppose one of the girls said, "Let's go to a show." I might say, "Let's go boat riding," and then I'd try to convince the girls. I'd tell them, "Look, we put in a dollar between us, and we can go and get sodas, but if we go to a show, it'll be 35 cents apiece, and that'll be all we can do." I'd work on one girl to convince her first and then the two of us would work on somebody else. That way we'd get all the girls convinced. Most of the time they took my suggestions.

When we say that a girl has been a follower all her life, we mean that other people have been making her social adjustments for her. When she is placed in a position where that support is withdrawn, she breaks down. When we say that a girl has had a good deal of leadership experience, we mean that she has had to adjust herself and adjust others to a variety of social situations. She learns then to manipulate the restaurant situation so as to take some of the pressure off herself.

However, there are other factors besides leadership involved in this situation. Take the cases of Mary and Frances, small-town Ohio girls who came to the city for restaurant work. Mary had always been a follower and was very much dependent upon Frances. She explained herself in this way.

I always just stayed in the background. I followed along and did what other people wanted to do. I was always very shy, but I've changed a lot since being with Frances.

I admire Frances. She has so much initiative. I don't know what would have become of me if it hadn't been for Frances. I would still be stuck in that small town. I never would have had the nerve to go to the city by myself.

From the time that they left the small town, Mary and Frances had always lived and worked together. In the restaurant where we met them, they had begun work in the same dining room. This way they were able to work closely together, and Mary had no serious trouble. But then they were transferred into separate dining rooms and Mary began having trouble. One busy noon time, she had to leave the floor to cry. In the rest room she had hysterics. It was four days before she felt able to return to work. After that she and Frances were again set to work in the same dining room, and Mary had no further serious trouble.

There seem to be two interrelated factors involved here. Frances helped Mary with her work, and that lightened her load. However, it seems unlikely that the specific acts of helping out were the significant matter, for in the dining room where Mary broke down, the waitresses all prided themselves on the way they pitched in to help each other. Of course, Mary and Frances knew each other so well that they were able to help each other more efficiently than any other person could, but it appears that a major part of this help was simply in the nature of social support—blowing off steam to a sympathetic audience, knowing that someone close to you understood your problems and was with you in spirit.

This suggests that social integration into the work group is of great importance in easing the nervous tensions of work. There is another sort of integration, the social adjustment outside the work situation, which is also important, as the case of Ann Lindstrom will indicate.

Ann was the leader of a large informal group of the younger waitresses, who always ate together in the afternoon and frequently got together outside of work. Growing up in Chicago in a Scandinavian neighborhood, she had been the leader of a group that had included only one other girl. She had never cried when with the gang. She could not have held her position if she had done so. Such a highly developed social initiative and such a strong conditioning against crying would seem to be a good guarantee against this sort of breakdown at work. Nevertheless, Ann did cry—and fairly often.

The problem in her case seemed to be two-sided involving downward social mobility and the disruption of her social ties outside the work situation. Her father had been a small businessman, ruined by the depression, who then became a factory worker. Ann had always been hostile to her mother, who tried to suppress the tomboy in her and make her a lady. In her late teens she married a young man who had been born in Europe, and this was thought to be a step down for her. Neighbors said to her mother, "Couldn't she do any better for herself than that?"

While Ann was very much on the defensive concerning her marriage, she nevertheless led a very active social life with her husband and his friends. Their home was the meeting place of the gang. However, after half a dozen years the marriage broke up. This cut her off not only from her husband but also from her gang.

Ann had been working in the credit department of a large firm, holding quite a responsible white-collar job. At about this time she had an accident that impaired her vision for close work, and she had to find a job that did not put such a strain on her eyes. It was that which led her into waitress work.

In the restaurant where we encountered her, she had become popular with a large group of employees, and yet she had not really accepted her new position. The first words she said to us were, "This is definitely not my type of work."

Finally, she suffered through a change in supervision. When she started work, she was close to her supervisor. She felt that the supervisor understood her, and the supervisor felt that she could count on Ann to help out whenever an extra bit of work needed to be done. Then there was a change, the new supervisor distrusted her, and thought that she was a bad influence for the other waitresses. Ann developed a great hostility toward the new supervisor, felt that she was under pressure from that source, and began to have more and more trouble in her work, until she told us, "It's getting to be just one crying jag after another." Shortly after this she quit.

The meaning of downward mobility to the waitress is again illustrated in the case of Alice Franklin. She was thirty-seven and unmarried, the fourth child in the family of a small-town schoolteacher. Her parents expected her to go to college, but at the time of her high-school graduation, they could not afford to send her away to the state university. Rather than start college in the local institution, she continued with a summer waitress job. In part, this was a rebellion against her parents, whom she considered puritanically strict.

Alice had been a waitress for 18 years. She had traveled all over the country, working in all types of restaurants. Since she had learned all the tricks of her trade, we might have expected her to handle her job without difficulty, and yet she was one of the few experienced girls who could not stand the strain without occasionally breaking down.

Alice had never been able to accept for herself the position of waitress. It seemed a serious comedown to one who had been brought up to think in terms of a professional career.

This had affected her social relations both on the job and outside of work. She had no intimate ties on the job. As she said,

I get along with them all right inside the restaurant, but I don't see many of them outside. You know, I don't believe in being too intimate with the people you work with. That leads to jealousy, and that leads to friction on the job. You begin going out with one particular girl, and then you have some kind of fight, and you take that right back to where you work. I think it's much better if you don't go around with the people you work with.

Even outside the work situation, she had few ties. She explained that the work tired her so much that when she was finished, she just wanted to rest. Thus, when she met the pressures of waitress work, she met them alone. Without any kind of social support, she could not stand up under the tension.

The importance of social mobility requires a further explanation. In a restaurant that prides itself on maintaining standards of refinement, the waitress learns the sort of behavior that is highly useful in moving up in the world. The restaurants where we gave particular attention to the crying waitress, recruit their girls largely from small towns, rural areas, and from the urban working class. To wait on tables properly, the girls must discard lower-class or rural behavior and attitudes toward food, service, and etiquette, and adapt themselves to middle-class standards. More important still, they must learn to adjust themselves to their social superiors. They must appear to subordinate themselves and at the same time learn to manipulate people and situations to their own advantage. Girls who can absorb this sort of social learning find that their new pattern of behavior brings its own reward. Many former waitresses in this particular restaurant have married business or professional men or white-collar workers and have consolidated their social positions in the lower or even in the upper middle class.

The girl of middle-class background clearly faces a different situation. She finds herself taking orders from people whom she feels to be her equals and, in some cases, her inferiors. Nor do they recognize her former status. She finds it exceedingly difficult to adjust to this unaccustomed type of sub-ordination.

This effort to explain the crying waitress has been long and involved—but necessarily so. We have long since ceased to look for *the cause* for any particular manifestation of human behavior. We always must deal with a number of interdependent variables, and we never see one of them operating quite isolated from the others. However, we have been able to discriminate three factors that seem of the greatest importance.

The waitress requires some leadership experience in order to take the play away from the customers and to fit them into the pattern of her work. She needs to be integrated into some group where she works and also in her life outside of work, so that she has some social support and some outlet for the tensions that arise in her job. (In some cases, the same group may serve to integrate her both at work and outside of it. We do not have enough data to know exactly what the social requirements are. We can only point to their importance.) And finally, the waitress needs security in her social position. If she is holding her own or moving up, she can adjust herself to the peculiar social pressures she faces much better than if she is downwardly mobile.

Of course, as we concentrate our attention upon the crying problem, we

must remember that that is only one of a number of possible waitress reactions. To work out her problems, the waitress may (1) talk back to the
customers, (2) yell at service pantry workers and bartenders, (3) break
down and cry, get "the shakes," or other nervous reactions, (4) take the
pressure off herself by controlling her customers, or (5) blow off steam to
the supervisors.

It is clear that these first three reactions do not constitute solutions to the
problem. We have, it is true, studied one lower-class restaurant where a
waitress informed us, "In this place the customer is always wrong, and he
knows it—God bless him." In this restaurant we found no crying waitresses,
but the middle-class restaurant cannot afford to allow its waitresses to tell
the customers off.

When the waitress yells at people in other departments, she simply transfers
the pressures to other people in the organization. When she cries, she has
to leave the floor, and other waitresses must take over her station.

We have seen that a skillful waitress can take a good deal of pressure off
herself through controlling her customers, but this in itself is not a solution
to the problem; for there are always customers who cannot be controlled,
and there are always waitresses who are not very successful in their attempts
at control.

That raises a practical question for management: What can be done to
improve the social skills of the waitress? Most managements have grappled
with his problem in one form or another. Many of them have tried to solve
it through inspirational talks on the psychology of salesmanship. There are
several men who have made a nationwide reputation as salesmanship lecturers
to employee groups, and many owners, managers, and supervisors have tried
to serve this function in a more casual and less professional manner.

There are several difficulties inherent in this approach. In the first place,
the principles of salesmanship are rather simple and generally familiar to
most people. Therefore, even if employees get an emotional lift from a good
talk on the subject, such talks become repetitious and boring if they are
repeated often. Our experience so far is that salesmanship talks get a mixed
response from employees. Some enjoy them. Others are unmoved. And
some resent them. At best these programs are simply a temporary "shot in
the arm."

The second difficulty is far more serious. We can illustrate it in this way.
The salesmanship lecturer tells the waitresses that they will get along better
with customers if they approach them with a pleasant smile. That is quite
true. However, the assumption seems to be that the smile can be put on
simply by an act of will. That is not true. A girl may be able to apply a smile
to her face just as she puts on her lipstick, but unless she feels it inside her
she won't be able to maintain it through the tensions of her work. Our research clearly shows that the girls who are successful with their smiles and
pleasant manner really enjoy their work. While they may face many disagreeable situations, fundamentally they get pleasure out of pleasing and

controlling customers. The other girls feel that customers are hostile and menacing forces, and an effective smile does not go with such a feeling.

The real problem then is: how can we help the girl to feel like smiling, to enjoy her work? A good deal of experimentation needs to be done in this area, but I think we can answer the question along general lines.

First it should be pointed out that this is not a problem peculiar to the restaurant industry. It crops up wherever the customer relationship is involved, and it is particularly important wherever the employee has the responsibility of making a sale, for in those cases management has a yardstick to measure the effectiveness of the salesman. When the records show that the salesman is not making his quota of sales, many managements take action in one of two ways. They may threaten the salesman with dire consequences if he does not improve. Or they may try to stimulate him through inspirational lectures.

Inspirational or not, a lecture is a lecture, and the salesman, who is falling down on the job because he is not adjusting well to customers or is preoccupied with some personal problem, will see in the lecture only just so much more pressure bearing down on him. Since he already feels worried and under pressure, more pushing from management only makes the situation worse.

This is not to argue that "pep talks" have no place in industry. The point is simply that pep talks don't solve human relations problems. When a man is under pressure, he cannot act with skill and confidence. Only when the pressure is relieved will he find inspiration in pep talks from management.

How then can management act to take the pressure off? That is a problem in supervision, and it has many aspects that we cannot take up here; but it should be emphasized that skillful supervision begins with giving employees an opportunity to talk their problems off their chests. If the worker cannot be allowed to express his emotions to the customer, then some other outlet must be provided, for bottled up emotions inevitably take their toll on the nervous system and reflect themselves in poor work performance.

The supervisor who looks upon nervous tensions as the inevitable products of human nature, as problems in the technical organization of work, or as problems in salesmanship will never be able to cope with the situation in a constructive manner. On the other hand, the supervisor who looks upon restaurant or factory as an organization of human relations, as a system of personal communications, will be able to make the necessary adjustments in order to minimize the frustrations and add to the satisfactions of work in industry.

NOTE

1. The National Restaurant Association sponsored the research on which this chapter is based. However, the views expressed are the sole responsibility of the author.

PART III

Situational Influences:
The Physical and
Social Setting

WE ARE now at the point where client and official are face to face, or talking over the telephone. We know that each brings with him a supply of expectations and rules of conduct concerning such encounters which were picked up all along the way. We know that the larger community in which the two are embedded has shaped each one's view of the other. We have also seen something of the ways in which organizational goals and structures bear upon their predispositions and affect their interaction.

We want to keep these factors in the background now, and focus on the constraints of the situation-of-contact itself. We will examine the ways in which certain elements of the situation—including the furniture—affect the expectation of official and client, their interaction, and its outcome. We will consider how these situational variables are "managed" by officials or clients or both. We will also analyze some *unwitting* effects of certain latent characteristics of the participants on the outcome of the encounter. Then we will look at the intersection of the expectations of official and client and at the extent of their congruence, and explore the consequences of these expectations for interaction and outcome.

Situational "Settings" and Their Management

This is Goffman territory. Goffman (1959) has made popular the dramaturgical approach to interaction which uses such words as "props," "settings," "backstage," and so on, to describe the "performance" of individuals in their social roles. Note that the word "role," itself, is a theatrical term borrowed by social science. Many roles are played in costume: physicians wear white coats, policemen wear blue ones. But even when there is no uniform that goes along with a role, people present to others, and look for in them, the external signs of who they are. It is the mundane things like clothing, accent, the newspaper one carries, which tell the story.

In addition to "personal fronts," many roles have more permanent props, including a frontstage and backstage. The front region, like the personal front, is designed to create an impression and also to mark off an area which is the backstage. The waiter is a different person in the dining room than he is in the kitchen, and customers, indeed, are not allowed into the kitchen at all. The doctor's waiting room is carefully stocked with certain kinds of magazines, its walls have certain kinds of pictures, and, farther inside, are the doctor's credentials, duly sealed and delivered.

All this has to do, wittingly or not, with what Goffman calls "impression management." It helps to establish authority and to press towards the outcome desired by the performer. Clearly, a person well-familiar with a stage will have the upper hand over another who is entering it for the first time. To return to clients and officials, the client is no less involved in "impression management" than is the official. Indeed, the client may dress for the occasion, or put on his best accent, carry a prestigious newspaper, or wear his American Legion button—if he thinks that that might make a favorable impression. He may, on the other hand, act purposely casual and superior. Or, if he is writing a letter, he may go out of his way to have it typed or use an especially florid phrase to achieve the same effect. Both client and official, we may assume, are trying to manipulate the situation to maximum advantage, making whatever use they can of available props. The experienced waitress, according to Whyte (1946),* will make it clear to a customer that she is in charge.

In brief, both officials and clients vary (1) in the extent to which they consciously attempt to manipulate what happens during the encounter, and (2) in their choice of what is to be manipulated—their own behavior, the social situation, or the physical situation. Thus, the helpless expression on a client's face may or may not be a calculated means to influence the social worker—but it may have such an influence. Similarly, the social worker's large desk may serve to keep clients at bay, but the social worker may not have planned it that way, or at least may not be admitting it to himself or herself. A person who brings his or her family along to the office is thereby changing the social situation, but again he or she may not necessarily be aware of that. In the discussion that follows we shall be talking about three kinds of strategies: actions consciously calculated to influence, actions which are unwittingly influential, and nonactions (aspects of one's identity) which have the effect of influencing the others. The last kind of strategy will be called *latent identity*. The two types of action, in turn, may relate to the individual's own behavior (a client's threat, for example) or to strategic manipulation of the physical or social setting.

Interaction Styles and Strategies

It is often difficult to judge intentions, and some intentions are subconscious anyway, so we shall not bother much with this distinction, even though it is an important one. Some authors, such as Berne in *Games People Play* (1964), give us their own analysis of other people's strategies; other authors tell us what people say about themselves. We shall have to rely on both types.

Rosenberg and Pearlin (1962),* for example, studied the persuasive strategies of nurses in a mental hospital. They asked about the strategies that might be used to influence a recalcitrant patient to comply with their wishes. What they found was that different types of appeals were related to the position of the nurse within the stratification system of the hospital. There was also a marked disparity between the strategies which the nurses said they would most like to use and those they thought most effective.

The study of officials' persuasive attempts is related to Bar-Yosef and Schild's (1966)* work on the strategies used by officials to "defend" themselves against demanding clients. They found three basic types of defense: the individualistic use of the official's personal ideology; the "joint" defense, in which the worker invokes the aid of his peers; and the "buffer" defense, in which one official in the organization specializes in the handling of problematic clients.

While officials seek to control clients in various ways, clients find ways to rebel against bureaucratic constraints, and to manage interaction to suit their own ends. This is the theme of Goffman's (1961)* essay on the underlife of total institutions. The secondary adjustments which inmates develop are subtle ways of keeping the self alive in organizations like prisons and mental hospitals. The implications of this essay, and of Goffman's other work, go far beyond the mere question of management of interaction in bureaucratic settings, suggesting that bureaucratization—whether in total institutions or in totalitarian societies—can never be complete. Goffman thus takes an optimistic stance, implying that an Orwellian world of complete control is, in fact, impossible.

Clients' strategies and styles of interaction in everyday bureaucratic encounters are the focus of our own studies of official–client communication in Israel. In our own paper (Katz and Danet, 1966)* we looked at the ways in which clients' sociocultural background and the type of organization both influenced the verbal strategies chosen to influence an official. In the more detailed study of Israeli Customs officials, variations in types of persuasive appeals (Danet, 1971) and in styles of presentation of self (Danet and Gurevitch, 1972) were examined. Generally, "moderns" (clients of Western origin and in high-status occupations) used a more bureaucratic approach to Customs officials—they appealed to the laws of the organization and presented themselves to officials in a highly specific capacity—talking about themselves as clients and not as Jews or fathers or VIP's—while "traditionals" (clients of Middle Eastern origin and in low-status occupations) appealed more often to the altruism of officials and revealed many officially irrelevant things about themselves.

The effects of situational constraints were also evidenced in the Customs study. Although all clients were constrained to appeal to the officials' altruism because the Customs is a commonweal organization, the push toward altruism derived in part from the fact that clients' requests had already been refused at a lower level in the organization. Second, moderns and traditionals responded differently to their situations: moderns appealed to altruism to the same extent regardless of how serious their legal predicament was, while traditionals increasingly appealed to altruism as the legal difficulties in their cases became worse (Danet, 1971).

Clients' interaction styles have consequences for their outcomes, even when these styles are not necessarily calculated or planned. Zola's (1966) paper on ethnic differences in patients' presentation of a "sick" self to doctors has implications here. If doctors are not aware of such ethnic differences, they may fail to diagnose and treat properly the illness of a person who makes little of what may be a serious condition. Miller and Schwartz (1966) found that in hearings whose purpose was to determine whether defendants should be declared insane and committed to an institution, the behavior of defendants during the hearing made a difference for the outcome. Those defendants who acted in a controlled and effective manner were less likely to be committed than those who either did not object openly or objected in violent or abusive ways.

Our study of Customs officials and their clients also analyzed whether what clients said and how they said it had any effect on the results. On the whole (these findings are not included in the selection in this part), form and content of letters per se had little effect, with the legal merits of the case mostly determining the outcome. But there were some interesting exceptions to this general picture. Clients having a legal difficulty actually did better when writing a longer letter. And a letter written in "nonbureaucratic style" paid off especially well for clients with a *serious* legal difficulty; in particular it paid to appeal to the altruism of Customs officials (for further details, see Danet, 1972).*

Still another way in which strategies of interaction can influence the outcome is illustrated by Davis's paper (1968).* He found that patients were less likely to conform to their doctors' orders when there were communication difficulties during the visit to the doctor. Patients who became increasingly active with repeated visits and vied with the doctor for control of the relationship tended not to comply with his orders. Another factor influencing patients' compliance was whether or not the doctor gave the patient feedback on the information elicited from him on symptoms and medical history.

Latent Identities

Symbols of identity may be influential, of course, even when they are not manipulated in a calculated way. This means nothing more than that an official may take notice of certain "irrelevant" characteristics of his client, even if the client did nothing to call his attention to them. If these characteristics affect the decision he makes or the service he renders, we say that he is taking account of his client's "latent social identity" (Gouldner, 1957–1958). Plainly, this is called "discrimination"—though the discrimination may not be conscious, it may not be negative, and it may have nothing to do with race or ethnicity. For example, an official may notice an old lady or a woman carrying a child waiting in the queue, and he may decide to take her out of turn or offer her a seat. Sometimes such deviations from bureaucratic etiquette seem so legitimate that they even become institutionalized, as when women with young children are allowed to board an airplane ahead of other passengers. No such legitimation is available for the case of a pretty girl, however, or for somebody one knows personally, or for somebody of one's own ethnic group or religious faith.

Several studies deal explicitly with the way in which bureaucratic systems take unwitting account of latent social identities. For example, Evans's (1963) study of insurance salesmen and their clients finds that a sale is more likely if both salesman and prospective customer are about the same height or of the same political persuasion. Haney *et al.* (1969) and Nagel (1966) both analyze the effect of latent identity in the courts. One of Nagel's findings is that blacks are less likely to be let out on bail. Second, they are more likely to be given a quick trial. But quick trials more often bring negative decisions. The courtroom scene depicted by Haney *et al.* is more complex, for it involves the identities of two persons—that of a person brought before the court for commitment to a mental institution and that of a relative petitioning for the commitment. For example, women petitioners were more likely to be successful when petitioning for the commitment of a woman than of a man. In other words, it is the *combination* of the two identities that seems to create the effect.

It is no surprise that face-to-face interaction makes room for the illegitimate intrusion of latent social identities, but it is only after somebody notices the repeated cases of bias that much can be done about it. Blau (1964) cautions that mere rhetoric—proclaiming that discrimination will not be tolerated—is often less effective than the creation of constraints which make discriminatory behavior unlikely. In his study of a state employment office (as we noted in the Introduction to Part II), he finds that the department in which statistical records were used was unwittingly less likely to discriminate against blacks than the department which was more concerned with finding the right person for the right job. Thus, statistical records constrained officials to be universalistic, regardless of their attitude toward black people.

The effect of latent social identities is visible even in written communications between clients and officials. In the Customs study, Danet (1972)* discovered a small but systematic tendency to be more lenient with *lower* status clients. Given two similar requests, Customs officials were somewhat more likely to say "yes" to the client of Middle Eastern origin, to a person of lower occupational status, to the unemployed, and to women, than to Europeans, professionals, the currently employed, or men. Danet calls this the "underdog effect"—or "giving the underdog a break"—and it is interesting that it operates via the mails—the medium which is ostensibly least likely to transmit bias.

The Physical Settings

Partitions exist in many bureaucratic settings to separate customers or clients from officials. Lombard (1955) points out that counters help saleswomen in a department store keep control of the situation; for the same reason the French social security workers studied by Catrice-Lorey (1966)* (see Part II) asked that counters be installed. A partition, now said to be bullet-proof, separates urban taxicab drivers from their passengers. And many a bureaucracy is still operated via the awkward window openings which force one to tiptoe and squirm and twist in the hope of aiming one's message into an official's ear and one's money and/or papers into his hand. If there is anything calculated to make a client feel disembodied, it is these windows which, while apparently disappearing from the United States, are still on view in bureaucracies throughout the world.

The physical setting not only sets the stage for the interaction between officials and clients; it also affects the course of interaction. The architecture of waiting rooms, parks, public transportation, or banks, to choose a few random examples, all have implications for the values of privacy, interaction, surveillance, and the like. Sometimes such arrangements are very close to the major goal of the organization itself. Sommer's (1969) analysis of the therapeutic implications of seating arrangements in a geriatric ward is an example.

Of course, such settings have their effect not only by virtue of the physical channelling of behavior, but also by virtue of the norms which are attached to them. Customers are not allowed to enter the restaurant's kitchen areas nor air passengers the plane's cockpit without permission. These are norms designed to reinforce the sanctity of the backstage regions to which clients are not given access.

More generally, norms exist to define the areas which are public and private. As Stinchcombe (1963) points out, the thinnest partition may mark the door to a man's house, but the norms honoring that partition make it the equivalent of a steel barricade. Stinchcombe demonstrates the relevance of the public–private distinction by analyzing the ways in which the police act with respect to the two kinds of situations. Police have direct access—information, surveillance, and entry—to public situations, while they must have search warrants or be asked inside before entering private property. The ratio of public to private space varies from culture to culture. Indeed, even the proper distance to be maintained between two interacting people is governed by social norms and varies in different societies (Hall, 1966).

The Social Setting

The social setting—the human ecology—is affected by the physical setting, as was just shown, but it is also affected directly by the organization's goals and structure. Thus, one of the first things of which clients and officials become aware is whether or not they are alone. They may be alone in a room, but aware that others are next door. Or they may be much more alone —in a taxicab, for example. If the client is surrounded by fellow-clients but the official is alone—as in the classroom or on a bus—it is one thing. Or if the client is alone and the official is surrounded by colleagues—as in the operating room of a hospital—there is still another kind of situation to reckon with. These examples hardly begin to exhaust the possibilities, but they give some idea of the range.

How is behavior affected in each kind of situation? The taxi, for example, is loaded with ambiguity. In the metropolis, there is an urgent need to first establish trust; both driver and passenger want to make certain that it is safe to be alone with each other (Henslin, 1968).* One of the functions of organization among cabdrivers is surely for the purpose of mutual protection. Another ambiguity during the taxi ride is whether or how much the passenger will tip the driver (Davis, 1959). Still another source of ambiguity was evident in Israel at the time of the mass immigration: neither driver nor passenger knew the exact definition of his role. Thus, some passengers expected drivers to help carry their suitcases to their doors while some drivers expected passengers to place their luggage, by themselves, in the trunk of the cab. These conflicting expectations arose from the fact that many of the drivers had entered the taxi business only after immigration, that drivers and passengers came from a large assortment of different cultures, and that it is difficult to learn proper norms in a two-person relationship.

The bus driver is in quite a different situation, of course. He is safer, in a sense, even though his back is turned to dozens of clients. But, like the school teacher, he may have serious problems of control—as was pointed out in the example cited in the Introduction. If he cannot manage, he has to have recourse to a policeman, although that is a lot more difficult than sending a child to the principal.

Another aspect of the social situation is not simply the presence or absence of others, or of kindred spirits, but the presence or absence of the hierarchy to which the official is responsible. In a variety of situations, the official finds himself without the benefit of hierarchy and must manage on his own. On the night shift, for example, when management is home in bed, foremen tend to establish more diffuse relations with their men and exercise control of more informal kinds. The same relaxation of formality holds true in situations of danger, such as work in a mine or police work. Renee Fox (1959) describes a situation in which patients, in effect, became collaborators and consultants to their doctors in the context of volunteering for medical experimentation on an incurable disease. When officials or professionals must act on their own, it is only natural that their dependence on the support of subordinates or clients increases.

Timing

There are several time-related variables which also play a part in shaping official–client encounters. One of these is the duration of the encounter. Of course, length of contact is in large part determined by the nature of the goal involved—whether receiving medical treatment, buying groceries, or having a tooth pulled. It is the extremes of the continuum that are particularly interesting, the very brief encounter and the extended contact over many hours, if not days or weeks. We noted earlier that the situation of contact between taxi drivers and their passengers is quite a special one because of the need to establish trust. Another factor which characterizes this relationship is its "fleetingness" (Davis, 1959) which, in combination with the mutual risk taking and physical and social isolation of the pair, introduces strains of its own. In an early study, Cressey (1932) showed similar tensions in the fragmentary contractual relationship between taxi dance hall girls and their customers. At the other end of the continuum, shipboard romances can blossom because the ship's officers and female passengers find themselves in a floating total institution.

Frequency of interaction also affects the quality of the official–client relationship. Again, the nature of the goal involved may determine how many times the client has to come back—the number of cavities the dentist has to fill, or the number of different books needed from the library. We all know that people who come together often get to know, and sometimes get to like, one another. Thus, personalization of the relationship is likely with frequent contacts. On a somewhat less common-sense level, Lennard and Bernstein (1960) showed that with repeated contact over time psychotherapists and their patients became increasingly more alike in verbal behavior.

Channels of Communication

We talk most of the time as if officials and clients always meet each other face to face, but obviously this is not true. In certain societies, the public makes a point of going in person to arrange matters which elsewhere are usually arranged by mail or by telephone. The mails are useful for people who need a written record. Entrusting one's case to the mails means that one has at least a minimum of faith that the postal bureaucracy will deliver the letter and that the addressee will answer it. Indeed, of all the media, the written word is probably the one most compatible with the norms of bureaucracy: it maximizes affective neutrality by avoiding the biases of face-to-face conflict, gives the organization a chance to deal with the case calmly and coolly, and fits nicely into the bureaucratic proclivity for record keeping.

In some ways, the telephone is a debureaucratizing device. For "moderns," at least, it requires the least expenditure of energy, reducing the proportion of one's lifetime spent standing in line or writing letters to organizations. Moreover, it masks or hides otherwise-evident latent characteristics of clients, thus fostering universalization. Use of the telephone, however, implies a large measure of trust that the person on the other end will really deal with one's problems. To think that one has no other record of having made an airplane reservation than the confirmation proffered by an anonymous clerk would make people in a more traditional society pale with shock. To shop by telephone would be equally upsetting to the more traditional *hausfrau* who enjoys haggling with the fruit seller in the outdoor market. But things seem to be changing now. With the projected linkages of telephone, television, cable, and computer, one can make a call and have both face-to-face contact and a written confirmation.

It would be interesting to compare different societies and different kinds of people with respect to their use of, and preference for, different media for contacting bureaucracies. At the same time, one would want to study the effect of using several media on client outcomes: Was the client treated considerately? Were the procedures efficient? Was satisfaction obtained? We noted above that discrimination can and does occur through the mails (Danet, 1972).* So Weber may be right that written communication fosters universalism, but it certainly doesn't guarantee it.

Mutual Expectations and Their Implications

So far, we have been discussing the elements of situational setting or structures, which have bearing on the expectations of clients and officials, their interaction and outcome. We have added landscaping, interior decoration, and human ecology to the environmental and organizational influences which bear upon the client–official interaction. In this section, we take still another step and look at the operation of expectations. More specifically, we want to examine how expectations arise, whether in the environment, in the organization, or in the situation itself. We want to look, too, at the effect of congruence of expectations—that is, the conditions under which official and client each expect of the other what the other expects of himself—and effect of such congruence.

A number of studies have analyzed the importance of congruence of expectations between various practitioners and their clients for successful interaction. Thus, Kutner (in Jaco, 1958) and Mechanic (1961) both argue for the need for compatible expectations between surgeon and patient, and between psychotherapist and patient. Kadushin (1962) comes to much the same conclusion about the clientele of ministers, physicians, and psychotherapists. In Wheeler's study (in Cressey, 1961) of role conflict between inmates and staff in a state reformatory, the *perceived* amount of conflict was greater than the actual amount. Note, however, that none of the studies examine the actual consequences of congruence or incongruence of expectations for interaction and its outcome, as do the various studies we review next. While the above studies merely *imply* that there must be consequences, the next group makes them explicit.

Lennard and Bernstein (1960) have demonstrated empirically that the more dissimilar the expectations of therapist and patient for therapy, the more socializing behavior the therapist introduces to teach the patient his role. This is reminiscent, in some ways, of Katz and Eisenstadt's (1960)* paper on bureaucratic officials in Israel functioning as teachers for new immigrants from Middle Eastern countries. We know also that one of the major reasons why lower-class patients often drop out of psychotherapy is that their expectations are not met by the middle-class therapist. While the patients typically want a medical, action-oriented approach, the middle-class therapist wants to talk—and lower-class people are generally less verbal (Overall and Aronson, in Reissman *et al.*, 1965).

One study on the effect of expectations on outcomes stands out from most others. It is Rosenthal and Jacobson's (1968)* *Pygmalion in the Classroom.* In an ingenious experiment, they planted in the minds of schoolteachers expectations concerning the future performance of certain of their students. The teachers thought the researchers' predictions were based on the intelligence test they had just administered, whereas in fact the assignment of students to the "will-blossom" category was entirely random. Although the process which determined the outcome is by no means clear, it *is* clear from this study and from several recent replications that the students who were expected to improve *did* improve, to a greater extent than those who were not expected to. There appears to be a kind of "altercasting" here, to use Weinstein and Deutschberger's (1963) term, whereby ego "assigns" a role to alter which alter successfully assumes. This is not essentially different from the process by which an experienced waitress constrains the customer to act the way she thinks he should.

A frequent situation in bureaucratic settings is for ego to think that alter should behave in a certain way, alter thinks otherwise, but ego thinks alter thinks as he does. This is the situation described by Foa (1955) as "projection." Contrary to this situation is the one labeled "empathy" in which ego thinks that alter should behave in a certain way, alter thinks otherwise, but ego knows that alter differs with him. Translating this abstract formulation onto the floor of a large department store, we find exactly the situation described by Lombard (1955). The saleswoman in the sports department thinks the customer should be submissive and take her sophisticated advice; the customer thinks she should be assertive; but the saleswoman is unaware that the customer is of a different mind. Lombard suggests that this kind of projection is a product of inexperience and insecurity. The older saleswomen in infants' wear who were more experienced and, as a group, more confident, were also more empathic. They understood their customers' needs even when they disagreed with them, and were better able to serve them therefore.

Introduction to the Readings in This Part

The chapters by Bar-Yosef and Schild and by Rosenberg and Pearlin are empirical studies of strategies used by officials when clients prove difficult. Bar-Yosef and Schild analyze types of defenses used by officials to resist the pressure from clients, while Rosenberg and Pearlin study the strategies of persuasion which the staff of a mental hospital uses in managing recalcitrant patients. The selection from Goffman's "The Underlife of a Public Institution" summarizes the strategies by which inmates of total institutions manage to keep the self alive.

The chapter by Danet deals with the theme of latent social identity and its consequences for interaction. Her analysis of the response of Customs officials to requests of a group of clients reveals a tendency to "give the underdog a break." Henslin's chapter focuses on a large number of situational variables, including clients' latent identities, which determine whether a taxi driver trusts his passenger or not. These variables are reflected in the verbal and nonverbal cues given and "given off" by the passenger.

Davis correlates behavioral strategies with *outcome*. He relates certain aspects of both the doctor's and the patient's behavior during the encounter to the patient's compliance with the regimens prescribed for him. For example, patients who vied with the doctor for control were less cooperative with his instructions. The influence of expectations for interaction on its outcome

Part III

is the subject of the selection by Rosenthal and Jacobson. They find that students can be made to improve if their teachers can be made to expect them to improve.

REFERENCES

Bar-Yosef, Rivka, and E. O. Schild. "Pressures and Defenses in Bureaucratic Roles." *American Journal of Sociology* 71, no. 6 (May 1966): 665–673.
Berne, Eric, M.D. *Games People Play: The Psychology of Human Relationships.* New York: Grove Press, 1964.
Blau, Peter M. *The Dynamics of Bureaucracy.* Chicago: University of Chicago Press, 1964.
Catrice-Lorey, Antoinette. "Social Security and Its Relations with Beneficiaries: The Problem of Bureaucracy in Social Administration." *Bulletin of the International Social Security Association* 19 (1966): 286–297.
Cressey, P. *Taxi Dance Hall.* Chicago: University of Chicago Press, 1932.
Danet, Brenda. " 'Giving the Underdog a Break:' Favoritism or Flexibility?" *Administrative Science Quarterly,* in press.
———. "The Language of Persuasion in Bureaucracy: 'Modern' and 'Traditional' Appeals to the Israel Customs Authorities." *American Sociological Review* 36 (October 1971): 847–859.
Danet, Brenda, and Michael Gurevitch. "Presentation of Self in Appeals to Bureaucracy: An Empirical Study of Role Specificity." *American Journal of Sociology* 77, no. 6 (May 1972): 1165–1190.
Davis, Fred. "The Cabdriver and His Fare: Facets of a Fleeting Relationship." *American Journal of Sociology* 65 (1959): 158–165.
Davis, Milton S. "Variations in Patients' Compliance with Doctors' Advice." *American Journal of Public Health* 58 (1968) 274–288.
Evans, F. B. "Selling as Dyadic Interaction." *American Behavioral Scientist* 7 (1963): 76–79.
Foa, Uriel. "The Foreman-Worker Interaction: A Research Design." *Sociometry* 18 (1955): 226–244.
Fox, Renee. *Experiment Perilous.* Glencoe: Free Press, 1959.
Goffman, Erving. *The Presentation of Self in Everyday Life.* Garden City: Doubleday Anchor, 1959.
———. "The Underlife of a Public Institution." In *Asylums,* edited by Erving Goffman, pp. 171–320. Garden City: Doubleday Anchor, 1961.
Gouldner, Alvin. "Cosmopolitans and Locals: Toward an Analysis of Latent Social Roles." *Administrative Science Quarterly* 2 (1957–1958): 281–306; 444–480.
Hall, Edward T. *The Hidden Dimension.* New York: Doubleday, 1966.
Haney, C. Allen, Kent S. Miller, and Robert Michielutte. "The Interaction of Petitioner and Deviant Social Characteristics in the Adjudication of Incompetency." *Sociometry* 32 (1969): 182–196.
Henslin, James M. "Trust and the Cabdriver." In *Sociology and Everyday Life,* edited by Marcello Truzzi, pp. 138–158. Englewood Cliffs: Prentice-Hall, 1968.
Kadushin, Charles. "Social Distance Between Client and Professional." *American Journal of Sociology* 67, no. 5 (March 1962): 517–531.
Katz, Elihu, and Brenda Danet. "Petitions and Persuasive Appeals: A Study of Official-Client Relations." *American Sociological Review* 31 (1966): 811–822.

Katz, Elihu, and S. N. Eisenstadt. "Some Sociological Observations on the Response of Israeli Organizations to New Imigrants." *Administrative Science Quarterly* 5 (1960): 113–133.

Kutner, Bernard. "Surgeons and Their Patients: A Study in Social Perceptions." In *Patients, Physicians, and Illness,* edited by E. Gartly Jaco, pp. 384–397. Glencoe: Free Press, 1958.

Lennard, Henry L., and Arnold Bernstein. "Expectations and Behavior in Therapy." In *Anatomy of Psychotherapy,* chap. 4. New York: Columbia University Press, 1960.

Lombard, George F. *Behavior in a Selling Group.* Cambridge: Graduate School of Business Administration, Harvard University Press, 1955.

Mechanic, David. "Role Expectations and Communication in the Therapist-Patient Relationship." *Journal of Health and Human Behavior* 2 (1961): 190–198.

Miller, Dorothy, and Michael Schwartz. "County Lunacy Commission Hearings: Some Observations of Commitments to a State Mental Hospital." *Social Problems* 14, no. 1 (1966): 26–35.

Nagel, Stuart S. "The Tipped Scales of American Justice." *Trans-Action* 31, no. 4 (1966): 3–9.

Overall, Betty, and H. Aronson. "Expectations of Psychotherapy in Patients of Lower Socio-economic Class." In *Mental Health of the Poor,* edited by Frank Riessman, Jerome Cohen, and Arthur Pearl, pp. 76–87. New York: Free Press, 1965.

Rosenberg, Morris, and Leonard I. Pearlin. "Power Orientations in the Mental Hospital." *Human Relations* 15, no. 4 (1962): 335–350.

Rosenthal, Robert, and Lenore Jacobson. *Pygmalion in the Classroom.* New York: Holt, Rinehart and Winston, 1968.

Sommer, Robert. *Personal Space: The Behavioral Basis of Design.* Englewood Cliffs: Prentice-Hall, 1969.

Stinchcombe, Arthur L. "Institutions of Privacy in the Determination of Police Administrative Practices." *American Journal of Sociology* 69, no. 2 (September 1963): 150–160.

Weber, Max. "Bureaucracy." In *From Max Weber,* edited by H. H. Gerth and C. Wright Mills, pp. 196–244. New York: Galaxy, 1958.

Weinstein, Eugene A., and Paul Deutschberger. "Some Dimensions of Altercasting." *Sociometry* 27 (1963): 454–466.

Wheeler, Stanton. "Role Conflicts in Correctional Communities." In *The Prison: Studies in Institutional Organization and Change,* edited by D. R. Cressey, pp. 229–259. New York: Holt, Rinehart and Winston, 1961.

Whyte, William F. "When Workers and Customers Meet." In *Industry and Society,* edited by William F. Whyte. New York: McGraw-Hill, 1946.

Zola, Irving Kenneth. "Culture and Symptoms: An Analysis of Patients' Presenting Complaints." *American Sociological Review* 31, no. 6 (October 1966): 615–630.

15

Rivka Bar-Yosef and E. O. Schild

PRESSURES AND DEFENSES IN
BUREAUCRATIC ROLES

Blau and Scott[1] have pointed out that officials (particularly in "service organizations") frequently face a dilemma between "adherence to and enforcement of procedures" and becoming "captives of their clientele." On the one hand, they are exposed to pressures from organizational superiors that impel them toward conformity with the policy and regulations of the organization. On the other hand, clients exert pressures and present demands which may deviate considerably from the bureaucratic norms.

This dilemma is alleviated to the extent that clients are well socialized in their role as clients of a bureaucracy.[2] A bureaucratic organization makes certain assumptions as to the behavior of its clients. The client is expected to accept the authority of the organization as legitimate, and to conform in his dealings with officials to certain norms of interaction. In particular, he is supposed to acknowledge that the line-bureaucrat is restricted by the organization in his freedom to concede requests and demands. If so, the pressures which the client will exert on the bureaucrat will be restrained. Schelling[3] has pointed out that if one of the parties in a bargaining situation is committed to his stand, and if this commitment is recognized by the second party, the second party will frequently forego threats or promises which he might otherwise have profitably employed. The bureaucratic regulations serve as such "commitment" for the line-bureaucrat.

But if the client does not, or only insufficiently does, recognize the existence of this commitment, the bureaucrat's position is only worsened. He is, in fact, committed to the organization—but at the same time he is exposed to pressures as if he were a free agent. Thus, when clients are imperfectly socialized—when they recognize neither the organization's criteria for al-

Rivka Bar-Yosef and E. O. Schild, "Pressures and Defenses in Bureaucratic Roles," *American Journal of Sociology* 75 (1966): 665–673. Copyright 1966 by The University of Chicago Press. Reprinted by permission.

locating services nor the rules of interaction—the client-bureaucrat encounter is likely to turn into a field of unrestrained pressures.

Katz and Eisenstadt[4] have, in this context, analyzed the interaction between officials of public institutions in Israel and new immigrants. The new immigrants, who have little previous experience with bureaucratic organizations, present demands which deviate considerably from the organizational norms; moreover, as (at least in the initial stages of absorption) they have not learned to accept the organization as a legitimate authority, they will exert strong pressures to make the bureaucrat accede to their demands.

Katz and Eisenstadt suggest that in this situation the bureaucrat has two choices: He may "overconform" to the organizational regulations, disregarding considerations of the interests of the clientele; or he may disregard organizational norms, and "debureaucratization" will be found.

However, whatever the choice of the bureaucrat, whether he elects to resist organizational pressures or to resist client pressures, he will always be in need of defense. Whyte[5] presents a case of the possible outcome when a member of an organization is caught in cross-pressures without appropriate defenses. Waitresses, subject to pressures from both customers and superiors, were likely—when pressures became very intense—to "break down" and cry. A different example of the need for defenses is presented by Blau,[6] who reports how workers in a public employment agency defend themselves against the impact of conflicts with clients by a mechanism of psychological tension release: complaining to colleagues and joking about the clients.

Defense can have either or both of two functions: (*a*) to reduce the pressures exerted (i.e., make threats and/or sanctions applied by client or organizational superior fewer or more lenient); (*b*) to lessen the impact of the pressures (e.g., the psychological tension release does not reduce pressures actually exerted by the clients, but makes them easier to bear). But whatever its functions, resistance to pressures presupposes the existence of appropriate mechanisms of defense.

What are the possible mechanisms of defense for the line-bureaucrat? Thompson[7] has pointed to the possibility of *ideology* as a defense (obviously fulfilling the second of the two functions mentioned above). And indeed, in regard to the Israeli case, Katz and Eisenstadt have suggested that a general societal ideology may serve as what is here termed "defense." Societal values held by the bureaucrat may legitimize his decisions—above and beyond, or in contradiction to, organizational (and/or professional) values.[8] The existence of such legitimation will reduce the impact of the pressures. Evidently, the fact that the line-bureaucrat holds a societal orientation as part of his role image does not in itself predict whether he will conform to the organizational requirements or accede to the clients' demands. The societal values may, depending upon their content, predispose to conformity to the organization or to resistance to the organization. The important point in the present context is that these values make it easier for the bureaucrat to resist pressures against a decision made in accordance with the values, and thus serve as a mechanism of defense.[9]

This mechanism of defense is an *individual* one; it is not dependent on the interaction of the bureaucrat with his peers (beyond, perhaps, social support for his societal values), nor is it linked to any structural change, even informal, within the organizational framework. But if it is true that defense against pressures fulfils a crucial function for the bureaucrats who are caught up in cross-pressures, then we might expect to find some structural adjustment, too. In other words, we may look for *structural* (formal or informal) mechanisms of defense.

It is well known that the peer group may support the bureaucrat in deviations from the organizational regulations. There seems, however, to be no reason why such informal peer organization should provide defense against superiors only. Bureaucrats who conform to the bureaucracy are in need of defense against client pressures; hence, we may inquire into the possibility that this kind of defense, too, may develop on the basis of the peer group.

In defense based on the peer group, all bureaucrats perform identical roles in the defense. But a defense mechanism can also be developed by appropriate division of labor; certain bureaucrats assume the informal role of "handling pressures" and thereby reduce the pressures exerted on the colleagues.[10]

In the present chapter we shall present findings which exemplify and elaborate on such mechanisms of defense. Whatever the mechanism, however, we must—as stressed above—expect a correlation between the existence of some kind of defense and the resistance to pressures. The two responses envisaged by Katz and Eisenstadt—(*a*) overconformity and (*b*) debureaucratization—seem linked, in the first case to defense against clients and lack of defense against superiors, and in the second case to defense against superiors and lack of defense against clients. But logically, at least, we may expect two further response types: (*c*) The bureaucrat may pursue an almost *independent* policy. He will decide, and legitimize his decisions, on the basis of criteria rooted in his own values or those of the unit to which he belongs (as opposed to the values of the organization as a whole or those of the clients). It would seem that such behavior on the part of the bureaucrat is contingent upon the existence of effective defenses against *both* clients and superiors. (*d*) If *no* effective defenses exist, either against clients or against superiors, we may expect the bureaucrat's behavior to be *erratic*. Whichever pressure is the strongest at any given moment will impel the bureaucrat to act in that direction. The existence of strong cross-pressures will then frequently lead to inconsistent behavior—sometimes conformity to organization, sometimes conformity to clients' demands. The "independent" bureaucrat, too, conforms to different sources of demands in different situations; his decision, however, is consistent in accordance with certain criteria—while the "erratic" bureaucrat "bows with the wind."[11]

The data to follow will offer some evidence on these two additional types of responses to the cross-pressures.

Data

The study was carried out in two development towns in Israel where the great majority of the residents are new immigrants. Town A had, at the time of study, a population of about 30,000; town B, a population of about 5,000. The location of the two towns—at some distance from the national centers of population and activity—made for a certain isolation from headquarters of the organizational units in the towns; thus organizational pressures were less in these units than in units located closer to big cities.

Table 15-1 shows the institutions in which the study was carried out. The respondents comprise practically all of the line-personnel in these institutions. Each line-bureaucrat was given a structured interview lasting about two hours, and replied to a brief questionnaire containing closed questions. All interviewing was carried out by the same two interviewers.

TABLE 15-1

Line-Bureaucrats Interviewed, by Town and Organization

ORGANIZATION	ROLE OF LINE-BUREAUCRATS	RESPONDENTS (N = 67) TOWN A	TOWN B
Social welfare office	Social welfare officers	12	4
Immigrant absorption department	Absorption officials	7	4
Health insurance clinic	Doctors and nurses	14	3
Labor exchange	Work-placement officers	8	3
Municipal department of taxes and water supply	Collectors	8	
A and B district public health office	Public health inspectors	A and B = 4	

Each interview was analyzed and rated by three coders: (*a*) the interviewer herself; (*b*) the second interviewer (who had had no personal contact with the respondent to be rated); and (*c*) a rater who had met none of the respondents.

Each respondent was classified in one category on each of the following two dimensions:

1. Conformity and resistance
    a) Consistent conformity to organization and resistance to clients
    b) Consistent conformity to clients and resistance to organization
    c) Independent policy—conformity sometimes to clients and sometimes to organization, in accordance with criteria extraneous to organizational regulations
    d) Erratic behavior—conformity sometimes to clients and sometimes to organization, *without* criteria beyond the strength of pressure exerted
2. Individual defense
    a) Individual defense primarily against clients' pressures
    b) Individual defense primarily against organizational pressures
    c) No individual defense

While this coding was done for each *respondent,* each of the *units* was also rated on the basis of all interviews with members of that unit. The categories were as follows:

3. Defense mechanism in units
    a) Defense by division of labor
    b) Defense by peer group without specialization
    c) No structural defense

The intercoder consensus was quite high—about 80 percent. Disagreements were resolved by the authors. Five cases could not be classified on the conformity-resistance dimension, and three cases could not be classified on the individual defense dimension.

The questionnaire included three items designed to tap the societal orientation of the respondents. These items were phrased in parallel for the different organizations, allowing for the modification of specific details in accordance with the functions of the organization. The items (each providing four response categories: very important, important, not important, and it should not be done at all) were as follows:

1. To what extent is it important that a ——— [the role of the respondent] should instruct clients in their rights and duties as citizens of Israel?
2. To what extent is it important that a ——— [the role of the respondent] should educate the clients to general societal values?
3. To what extent is it important that a ——— [the role of the respondent] should persuade the client to ——— [do something against his own wishes and not required by the organization in question, but desirable according to Israeli values]?

After dichotomization of the items, they scaled in a Guttman scale with reproducibility of .90. By foldover technique the zero point was found, and the respondents were classified as holding "high" or "low" societal orientation. Two respondents did not reply to all three items and are, therefore, excluded from the analyses referring to this scale.

Individual Defense

A respondent was classified as utilizing individual defense when he tended to legitimize his decisions by values extraneous to the bureaucratic organization. The following may serve as illustrations: "If I know that what I do is for the best in helping the immigrant to his *long-run* adjustment, then I don't care what he says." "Those people in Tel Aviv don't know what the situation is here. They have the best intentions, but their demands are not realistic. I have a clear conscience because what I do is the best possible under the given circumstances. In my way I encourage the people to stay here in town rather than moving north—and that's the important thing, isn't it?"[12]

It may be mentioned that the use of this defense is, by definition, a deviation from classical bureaucratic principles. The latter assume, in regard to any decision, first that it will be made in accordance with the organizational regulations and second that these regulations in themselves provide all legitimation needed. If the decision made was one of conformity to the regulations, it should by this very fact be legitimized, and the extra-bureaucratic considerations involved in "individual defense" have no place as independent legitimizing criteria. If the decision was in violation of the bureaucratic rules, it should not have been made in the first place; and if brought about by *force majeure,* it should certainly not be legitimized. Thus, if the bureaucrat sees his decisions as having a source of legitimization beyond the organizational framework, this is a deviation from classical bureaucratic attitudes.

Katz and Eisenstadt suggested that this deviation may be correlated with the general societal ideology of the bureaucrat. The role image of the bureaucrat may include role goals of a general societal character not identical with the specific functions of the organization. The inclusion of such goals may aid the bureaucratic legitimation (defense against clients) or support the bureaucrat in resisting the hierarchy (defense against organization). The hypothesis may then be phrased, that a bureaucrat with a general societal orientation is more likely to have individual defense than a bureaucrat without this orientation.

Tables 15–2 and 15–3 present the relevant data. In Table 15–2 respondents with individual defense against clients are compared to respondents with no individual defense (i.e., either against clients or against organization). It is seen that a respondent with high societal orientation is more likely to have individual defense against clients than is a respondent with low societal orientation.

Table 15–3 parallels 15–2, this time for respondents with individual defense against organization. It is seen that a respondent with high societal orientation is more likely to have individual defense against organization than is a respondent with low societal orientation.

Thus, societal orientation—as hypothesized—predisposes the bureaucrat to individual defense. However, as seen by comparing Tables 15–2 and 15–3,

TABLE 15-2

*Societal Orientation and Individual Defense Against Clients**

	NUMBER OF RESPONDENTS CLASSIFIED AS APPLYING		
	INDI-VIDUAL DEFENSE AGAINST CLIENTS	NO INDI-VIDUAL DEFENSE AT ALL	TOTAL
High societal orientation	14	15	29
Low societal orientation	6	18	24
Total	20	33	53

*$Q = .47$; $\chi^2 = 3.03$; p (one-tailed) $< .05$.

the societal orientation does not influence the *direction* of the defense. In general, respondents are more likely to use individual defense against clients (38 percent) than against organization (18 percent); but there is no difference in this respect between respondents with high and respondents with low societal orientation ($\chi^2 = .19$, $p > .60$).

We may thus conclude that to the extent that the bureaucrat's role image includes general societal goals, he is more likely to be able to apply individual defense, be it against clients or against organization.

TABLE 15-3

*Societal Orientation and Individual Defense Against Organization**

	NUMBER OF RESPONDENTS CLASSIFIED AS APPLYING		
	INDI-VIDUAL DEFENSE AGAINST ORGANIZA-TION	NO INDI-VIDUAL DEFENSE AT ALL	TOTAL
High societal orientation	7	15	22
Low societal orientation	2	18	20
Total	9	33	42

*$Q = .62$; $\chi^2 = 2.96$; p (one-tailed) $< .05$.

Structural Defense

The existence of individual defense is thus a question of the orientation of the individual and need not be correlated with the structure of the organization in which he serves. (Indeed, the occurrence of individual defense was found to be independent of the organizational unit.)

The story is a different one when we turn to structural defense. The respondents themselves, most of whom explicitly recognized the existence of strong pressures, suggested the initial idea in the analysis of structural defense. One respondent said: "Every Friday we have a meeting of the whole staff. Each of us presents cases, or the difficult ones he is presently working on, and we decide jointly what should be done. [Interviewer: How do you decide?] Well, usually, you see, the official who is dealing with the case knows it best, so we follow his recommendation. [Interviewer: So why couldn't he decide without a meeting?] Well, it's nicer to have a *staff* decision, and then you aren't tempted to back down later."

We see here the peer group actually formalized as a mechanism of defense. The "staff decision," or rather the stamp of approval by colleagues, makes it easier to bear pressures. Like individual defense, it provides support—this time social support—consonant with the decision. But this defense may in addition *actually reduce* the pressures exerted, and not just alleviate their impact.

First, the "collective" decision-making may assure consistency among the bureaucrats; otherwise a concession on the part of one bureaucrat may be used by clients as a precedent to extract the same concession from other bureaucrats. Second, the staff decision provides the bureaucrat with the *commitment* he previously lacked. While commitment to abstract regulations may make little impression upon the client, the fact that the bureaucrat is bound by a staff decision in the concrete case may more easily be recognized. The "bargaining position" of the bureaucrat is thereby improved, and the potential pressures may not be exerted in full.

This mechanism of defense—we may call it "joint defense"—may thus be more effective than individual defense. But the important difference is in the type of mechanism—that the "joint defense" involves the structure of interaction in the unit. Structurally, it may seem rather primitive; but the crucial step is taken from purely psychological-attitudinal defense to a mechanism based on restructuring of role relations.

Even in units with joint defense, however, no new roles are created, and no specialization is found. But some respondents could also tell of such phenomena. A respondent reported that when he was faced with strong pressures from a client, and in particular when the pressure was backed up by the leaders of the client's ethnic group (a not infrequent occurrence in immigrant towns), he "would send him [the client or ethnic leader] to X [a colleague of the respondent]." Other respondents from the same unit told the same story. It turned out that X had become a "pressure specialist," handling all cases in which his colleagues felt difficulty in resisting. Moreover, this informal role of X's was being recognized outside the unit. Representatives of clients would turn to X even if the case was being handled by another official. Organizational superiors, too, tended to use X as a channel for dealing with suspected or actual violations of the organizational norms.

Here then, and in the other units where a similar set-up was found, a new pattern of interaction has developed to handle pressures. One of the officials acts as a "buffer" between his colleagues and sources of major pressures (particularly organized pressures). He thereby evidently releases the colleagues from a major part of the pressures, thus effectively improving their position.

Moreover, the deflection of pressures into an institutionalized channel, with consequent postponement of the immediate clash, may in itself alleviate the conflict; in this respect the "buffer defense" shows similarity to grievance procedures in industry.[13] As far as the "buffer" himself is concerned, it may paradoxically be that the very concentration of demands and pressures upon him facilitates resistance to the demands. Schelling has pointed out that a person exposed to similar demands from many sources may be in a better bargaining position in respect to each source than a person exposed to the demand from one or a few sources only. The fact that each decision, by creating a precedent, has far-reaching implications—implies a kind of commitment.

It may thus be that "buffer defense" is the most effective of the three mechanisms discussed. Certainly it is structurally the most radical. It changes the division of labor in the unit and reshuffles role definitions.

We have thus found two types of structural defense. These mechanisms are established on the basis of the organizational unit; it is, therefore, of interest to inquire into the distribution of the units studied according to type of structural defense, if any. Table 15–4 presents this distribution. It is seen that

TABLE 15-4

Distribution of Organizational Units According to Types of Structural Defense

BUFFER DEFENSE	JOINT DEFENSE	NO STRUCTURAL DEFENSE
Social welfare, town A	Health clinic, town B	Absorption department, town B
Social welfare, town B	Absorption department, town A	Labor exchange, town A
Public health, A and B	Labor exchange, town B	Municipality, town A
Health clinic, town A		

structural defense in one or the other form is frequent indeed, being found in seven of the ten units studied.

Inspection of Table 15–4 indicates a relationship between the professional background of the personnel in the unit and the type of defense applied. All of the units with professional or semiprofessional personnel have structural defense—primarily buffer defense. No nonprofessional unit has buffer defense, and some have no structural defense at all. Table 15–5 summarizes this finding. Although due caution is needed because of the small number of units studied, the difference seems striking.

An interpretation may be suggested by recalling that specialization is the central characteristic of buffer defense. Professionals are, by their training, predisposed to specialization; and it may, therefore, be "natural" for them

TABLE 15-5

Type of Structural Defense According to Professional Background of Personnel*

	NUMBER OF UNITS		
	BUFFER DEFENSE	JOINT DEFENSE	NO STRUCTURAL DEFENSE
Professional and semiprofessional	4	1	0
Nonprofessional	0	2	3

*$\gamma = 1.00$.

to have recourse to specialization in dealing with pressures also. Moreover, structural defense in general is based on a notion of coordination and increased interdependence between officials—a notion certainly familiar to those performing professional roles.

Defense and Resistance

In the introduction it was suggested that there may be more types of response to cross-pressures than those of conformity to clients (and resistance to organization) and conformity to organization (and resistance to clients). Two additional types were suggested: "independent" and "erratic" behavior.

The coding of the interviews did indeed allow for classification of certain respondents as using the two latter types. Although the distinction between "independent" and "erratic" behavior was not always easy (but apparently successful, as indicated by the findings presented below), the distinction between these two types and the two originally suggested by Katz and Eisenstadt was rather clear-cut. Of a total of sixty-two classifiable respondents, thirteen were classified as "independent" and fifteen as "erratic."

The stress placed thus far on mechanisms of defense as a necessary adjunct to resistance to pressures leads naturally into the question of the relation between types of defenses and types of response to cross-pressures.

The existence of defense against either organization *or* clients should incline the bureaucrat to consistent conformity to that source of pressures against which he is not defended. Independent behavior is contingent upon *effective* defense against both organization *and* clients, while erratic behavior is the outcome of *weak* defense against *both* sources of pressures.

It was implied above that the mechanisms of defense might be ordered according to efficiency. Any kind of structural defense was seen as more effective than no structural defense, and buffer defense was seen as more effective than joint defense. This then leads to a hypothesis that *independent* behavior will be particularly frequent in units with *buffer defense,* while *erratic* behavior will be particularly frequent in units *without* structural defense.[14] The relevant data are presented in Table 15-6.

TABLE 15-6

*Response to Pressures According to Type of Defense: Percentage of
Bureaucrats in Units with Given Type of Defense Showing**

UNITS	INDE-PEN-DENT BEHAV-IOR	CON-FOR-MITY TO ORGANI-ZATION	CON-FOR-MITY TO CLIENTS	ERRATIC BEHAV-IOR	TOTAL (PER-CENT)	N
Buffer defense	36	24	21	18	99	33
Joint defense	9	55	18	18	100	11
Structural defense	0	39	22	39	100	18

*$\chi^2 (df = 6) = 13.04$; $p < .05$. Considering only independent versus erratic behavior: $\gamma = .88$ ($p < .05$).

It is seen that buffer defense is indeed the mechanism predisposing to independent behavior. Only one independent bureaucrat was found in units without buffer defense. On the other hand, the absence of structural defense predisposes to erratic behavior. Erratic bureaucrats were found in other units, too, but with relatively less frequency.

It should be mentioned that the frequency of independent behavior in units with buffer defense also allows of an alternative explanation. It was previously found that buffer defense was correlated with the professional background of the personnel. May it not be that this professional background, rather than the type of defense, is the factor predisposing to independent behavior? The data do not enable us to prove or disprove this alternative explanation. The only unit that could provide a test case is the Health clinic in Town B. It has no buffer (and hence, according to the approach of the present paper, independent behavior should be scarce); on the other hand, its personnel are professional (and should, according to the alternative explanation, tend toward independence). However, this unit has only three members. We may note that none of these three shows independent behavior —thus at least not contradicting our argument on the defense-response correlation; obviously, however, the number involved does not allow for any conclusion.

NOTE: We are greatly indebted to our two interviewers, Mrs. Rachel Seginer and Mrs. Rina Zamir, for their intelligent and stimulating cooperation throughout the study. We also want to thank Professors S. N. Eisenstadt and Elihu Katz, Dr. Y. Dror and Dr. D. Kahnemann for their valuable comments on a previous draft of this chapter.

NOTES

1. Peter M. Blau and W. Richard Scott, *Formal Organizations* (San Francisco: Chandler Publishing Co., 1962), p. 52.

2. In this case, the clients may indeed be considered as participants ("low participants") in the bureaucracy; see Amitai Etzioni, *A Comparative Analysis of Complex Organizations* (Glencoe, Ill.: Free Press), 1961.

3. T. C. Schelling, *The Strategy of Conflict* (Cambridge, Mass.: Harvard University Press), 1960.

4. Elihu Katz and S. N. Eisenstadt, "Some Sociological Observations on the Response of Israeli Organizations to New Immigrants," *Administrative Science Quarterly,* 5 (1960), 113–33.

5. William F. Whyte, *Human Relations in the Restaurant Industry* (New York: McGraw-Hill Book Co., 1948), pp. 64–81.

6. Peter M. Blau, *The Dynamics of Bureaucracy* (Chicago: University of Chicago Press, 1955), pp. 82–96.

7. Victor B. Thompson, *Modern Organization* (New York: Alfred A. Knopf, Inc., 1961), pp. 114–37.

8. In particular when the organization is a "commonweal" one (cf. Blau and Scott, *op. cit.,* p. 54).

9. In modern psychological language: the societal values add cognitive elements consonant with the decision and thus reduce dissonance.

10. The school principal has been described as performing such a role in respect to pressures exerted by parents on teachers. See Howard S. Becker, "Social Class Variations in the Teacher-Pupil Relationship," *Journal of Educational Sociology,* XXV (1952), 451–65.

11. The erratic bureaucrat may seem similar to the "expedient" type described in Neal Gross, Ward S. Mason, and Alexander W. McEachern, *Explorations in Role Analysis* (New York: John Wiley & Sons, 1958). In fact, however, our entire analysis refers to "expediency" in the sense of the control of role behavior by pressures. Only the "individual defense" by a societal ideology is relevant to "moral" behavior.

12. Much value is ascribed in Israel to the immigrants' remaining in development towns, rather than moving to the populated centers of the country.

13. See, for example, A. Kornhauser, R. Dubin, and A. M. Ross, *Industrial Conflict* (New York: McGraw-Hill Book Co., 1954), pp. 57 and 282–83.

14. It was found above that societal ideology also may function as defense. However, when controlling for structural defense, no significant relationship was found between the prevalence of societal ideology and independent versus erratic behavior.

16

Morris Rosenberg and Leonard I. Pearlin

POWER-ORIENTATIONS IN THE

MENTAL HOSPITAL

Among the various interpersonal processes in which sociologists have legitimate interest, power must stand among those in the front rank. Power has been defined, probably most appropriately, as the ability to influence the behavior of others in accord with one's intentions (Goldhamer & Shils, 1939, p. 171). The requirements of social function and social control in the mental hospital make it imperative that nurses direct the behavior of patients in certain ways, i.e., that they exercise power. This is unavoidable and indispensable. It is not a question of *whether* nursing personnel will exercise power, then, but what *means* they will employ.

In the present report we do not have information regarding actual power exercise, but we do have data dealing with the methods different nurses *say* that they actually would use in a particular situation. For this reason we shall not be concerned with actual power exercise, which connotes an act involving the behavioral compliance of one person with the intention of another, but with *power-orientations*.

Sample and Method

The subjects of the study are all members of the nursing service below the level of supervisor in a large public mental hospital in the Middle Atlantic region. There are approximately 7,500 inpatients on the hospital's rolls; approximately half are white and half are Negro. The questionnaires were self-administered and anonymous; of the 1,315 nursing personnel who received

Morris Rosenberg and Leonard I. Pearlin, "Power-Orientations in the Mental Hospital," *Human Relations* 15 (1962): 335–350. Reprinted by permission.

questionnaires, 1,138, or 86 percent, returned completed and usable questionnaires. In addition, selected questionnaire topics were examined by means of intensive interviews.

Three ranks are represented among the personnel included in the study, each differing in responsibilities, authority, and rewards. The lowest rank is called nursing assistants; next to them are charge attendants who have been given the charge of wards on the basis of experience and demonstrated ability. The third group, smallest in number, is composed of registered nurses. This group has authority over the preceding ranks and is usually responsible for running the wards. These three groups are collectively referred to as nursing personnel. Forty percent of them are males and 60 percent are females.

One of the topics covered in these questionnaires was the power-orientations of nursing personnel toward patients. The respondents were presented with a hypothetical situation and were asked to rank each of five power methods from the one they would be most likely to employ to that which they would be least likely to employ. The hypothetical situation was the following:

What would you do in this situation? Patient J. R. is a male schizophrenic, 25 years of age. He has been in the hospital seven months. Recently he has gotten into the habit of sleeping much of the day and is up during the night walking around and disturbing the other patients. You feel that the patient is not especially nervous or depressed and he can understand perfectly anything you tell him. However, in the past he has shown an unwillingness to go along with ward routine and you expect him to be stubborn about changing his sleeping habits. Nevertheless, you feel that the patient *should* change his sleeping habits—that it would be best for him and the other patients. Let's say that you could not ask for advice or help from the doctors or anyone else, but that you had to decide for yourself how you would get this stubborn patient to change his sleeping habits. Which of these things would you *actually* do?

The alternatives presented were:

1. "I would force him to go to bed when everybody else does." (This statement was intended to serve as an index of *coercive power*, i.e., power based on compulsion, sanctions, or the threat of sanctions.)
2. "Since a nurse or nursing assistant has the right to tell a patient what to do, I would simply tell him to change his sleeping habits." (This was the index of *legitimate authority*, i.e., the individual's right to control the behavior of another by virtue of his objectively defined status in a formal organization.)
3. "I would offer him certain privileges or grant him certain benefits if he changes his sleeping habits." (This was the index of *contractual power*, i.e., power based upon a system of reciprocal obligations.)
4. "I would try to explain to him the reasons for changing his sleeping habits and try to convince him that it is for his own good or the good of other patients." (This was the index of *persuasion*, i.e., power based upon the ability to convince another to behave in the desired way.)
5. "I would try to figure out some ways to keep him busy during the day so he would *want* to sleep at night." (This was the index of *manipulation*,[1] i.e., a method of getting someone to behave in the desired way without this person being aware that this is the power-wielder's intention.)

Power-Orientations in the Mental Hospital

Respondents were asked to indicate which of these methods they would actually use first in this situation, which they would actually use second, and so on up to the fifth method. Since various considerations or criteria inevitably enter into a power decision of this sort, they were also asked to rank these methods in terms of which method had the "best chances of working" (the criterion of *effectiveness*), which method involved the "most work and trouble" (the criterion of *effort*), and which method they personally "like best" (the criterion of *values*). (This differentiation among modes of power and criteria for power decisions is drawn from Rosenberg, 1956.)

It should be emphasized that we are dealing with a single hypothetical situation which, though quite realistic, cannot be taken to represent all possible situations requiring the exercise of power in the mental hospital. Our aim, then, is to learn something about how nursing personnel tend to *think* about power—what criteria are likely to be brought to bear or what factors taken into account when a power decision is required. While the responses are necessarily influenced by the nature of the situation presented, they may still serve the central purpose of this paper, *viz.* to illustrate and elaborate some of the mental operations used by nurses when confronted with situations requiring the exercise of power.

Preferences for Power Modes

Table 16–1 indicates the proportions selecting the various power modes as their first choices in terms of their predicted actual behavior and in terms of the criteria of effectiveness, effort, and values. Nursing personnel, we find, are most likely to say that they would actually use persuasion; the second

TABLE 16-1

Modes of Power Selected As "First Choice" in Terms of Predicted Behavior and According to Power Criteria

	METHOD WOULD ACTUALLY USE	METHOD CON-SIDERED MOST EFFECTIVE	METHOD CON-SIDERED MOST WORK AND TROUBLE	METHOD WOULD LIKE TO USE
Persuasion	54	37	13	54
Benevolent manipulation	38	47	27	32
Legitimate authority	5	4	3	12
Contractual power	1	7	3	1
Coercion	2	4	55	2
Total percent	100	100	100	100
Number	(1,033)	(1,037)	(1,035)	(1,040)

most frequently chosen alternative is manipulation. With regard to the criterion of effectiveness, manipulation is most often chosen, followed by persuasion. With regard to the method considered the most work and trouble, coercion is most frequently chosen; manipulation is next most likely to be selected. With regard to the method the respondents would most like to use, persuasion is most frequently chosen, followed by manipulation.

In general, then, nursing personnel are most likely to say that they would use persuasion; this method is most highly valued and is second most likely considered effective. Manipulation is the method second most likely to be used and second most likely to be valued; although manipulation is considered the most effective of all methods, it is, next to coercion, viewed as involving the most work and trouble. Few nurses say that they would actually use coercion, contractual power, or legitimate authority as their first choice; only about a sixth value any of these methods most highly and an equally small proportion consider them most effective. Authority and contractual power are rarely considered the most work and trouble, but coercion stands first in this regard.

The question we now wish to raise is: Why are some modes of power so frequently selected and, equally important, why are others so consistently avoided? In order to obtain a clearer understanding of the bases of these various selections and rejections, let us consider these various power modes in greater detail.

COERCION

One of the most striking findings in the study of power-orientations in the mental hospital is the general repugnance felt about the use of coercion. This is not to say, of course, that coercion is not used. In dealing with psychotics there is often no alternative. A patient in an uncontrollable destructive rage must often be constrained by sheer physical force. In addition, of course, sadistic nursing personnel who obtain pathological satisfaction from the use of coercion are not unknown. But it is impressive how strongly the hospital norms are opposed to the use of force. In our hypothetical example, fully 68 percent said they would use force only as a last resort. However much nursing personnel may actually employ force, they do not freely admit to its use; overwhelmingly, they express repugnance at the exercise of brute power.

One might be inclined to suspect that this apparent distaste for the use of coercion is less a reflection of the nurses' actual attitudes than of their belief that this is the "right" thing to say. We found, however, that our respondents very rarely rejected the use of coercion with pious proclamations of lofty and ethical motives. On the contrary, pragmatic and self-interested considerations assumed first priority. For example, we asked our respondents which of the five power modes they would consider the "most work and trouble." Far more than any other single method—indeed, *more than all four other methods combined*—the coercive solution is viewed as producing the maximum difficulty *for the nurse*.

One obvious reason for avoiding force is that it is likely to elicit physical resistance. In the ensuing struggle, both sides may often end up spent, exhausted, injured, and resentful. A male nursing assistant said:

Well, forcing the patient, in my opinion, I don't like to force nobody to do nothin'. Sometimes the situation arises, you have to force the patient to do certain things. ... But sometimes you start to force the patient, that's when the patient starts swinging on you. Then he may hurt you, or you get tangled up together, you may hurt him. ... One of these times you can be on the ward by yourself and ... he'll clobber the devil out of you. I always find it best to try to talk to him.

A second objection to coercion appears to lie in the *impermanence* of its consequences. In other words, while coercion many accomplish the nurse's immediate purposes, it is often viewed as having deleterious effects in the long run. A male head nurse said:

If a nursing assistant ordered him to go to bed, and he didn't, he tried to take him by the hand and lead him to bed and he didn't, he'd call for some help. If he called me, chances are I'd be back up four or five times during the night. And the next night. ... Some patients will get up just to be doing the opposite of what he told them to do.

A third consideration in the use of coercion is that it is believed to generate resentment, which, by reducing voluntary cooperation, compounds the difficulty it was designed to alleviate.

Yes, the problem, I think, once you force the patient, if you ever ask (him) to do something else, he'll say: "No, I'm not going to do it" or "I don't want to do it"—especially if they have the choice—because "You made me go to bed when I didn't want to go to bed." If he has the choice, he won't do it.

A fourth objection mentioned by the nursing staff is that coercion not only bears upon the resistant patient but may have consequences for the entire ward; these consequences, in turn, react back to plague and afflict the nursing staff.

When force was used to put the patient to bed, the patient became loud, combative, disturbing the other patients, and naturally the other patients got upset and, as a result, the whole ward was upset, causing the other patients to remain up all night.

Nursing personnel pointed out another consequence of the involuntary compliance which attends the use of coercion. The patient may indeed yield, but it is the nature of his compliance which is affected, *viz.* if the patient reluctantly yields to the threat, he may tend to sabotage or undermine its purpose. He may in fact do what is desired, but do it in such a half-hearted, inefficient, reluctant manner that the purpose of the coercion is often defeated. Thus, one male nurse reported that many patients were compelled to seek work outside the hospital. They immediately told their prospective employers, who were initially disposed to hire them, that they were mental patients; they were almost certain to be refused employment. They could then return to the hospital and report that they had been unable to obtain employment.

Finally, one broad, long-range consequence considered by the nursing staff is that the use of coercion may tend to poison the atmosphere on the ward. Although compliance might be achieved in the immediate situation, coercion may render the ward an unpleasant place *for the nurse* to work in. A female nurse said:

Certainly if you try to force him to do something without any explanation, you just generate extreme hostility and resentment, and this can lead to all sorts of repercussions. I certainly don't like to handle a ward that has discontented, sullen, irritable people. Your ward atmosphere is one thing that can be poisoned by a small group of malcontents.

Nursing personnel thus do not reject coercion with pious proclamations of horror; their emphasis rather is on the fact that it has definite *practical* disadvantages. There is, first of all, the danger of immediate resistance, with possible injury to the nurse or patient. Second, there is the generation of resentment, which may call forth future violent reprisal, lack of cooperation in situations in which the patient has an option, or half-hearted compliance. Third, although coercion may achieve its immediate purpose, it may be necessary to repeat it time after time, at great cost to the nursing staff. Fourth, the use of force may produce general confusion and consternation on the ward, thus expanding the nurse's problem from the resistant patient to the entire ward. Finally, coercion may generate a sullen resentment which makes work unpleasant for the nurse. Over the long haul, then, it is easier and more effective to get someone to *want* to do as you like, or to be willing to do as you like, than to force him to do as you like. It is no wonder that nurses are inclined to employ force only when all else fails, when no other recourse remains. In the mental hospital, coercion is not only impolite; it is downright dangerous and difficult.

CONTRACTUAL POWER

In advanced societies, one of the most common methods of affecting the behavior of others is by means of contractual power. Specifically, contractual power involves gaining compliance with one's will by providing rewards or advantages in return. In the present context, it was expressed in the phrase: "I would offer him certain privileges or grant him certain benefits if he changes his sleeping habits." Despite its general popularity, however, this mode of control is firmly opposed by the nursing personnel of the mental hospital. Only 5 percent said that they would actually use this method as one of their first two choices and only 10 percent said that this was either their first or second value preference.

Why, then, are nurses so reluctant to use this method? It is certainly not considered much work and trouble—indeed, it ranks with legitimate authority as the easiest method of all. The simplicity and parsimony of using contractual power are indicated by the male nurse who said:

I know a lot of nursing assistants do (use this method)....I do too. If I ask a patient would he mind helping me, he'll say no. Well, I'll just automatically say: "Well, I'll give you a cigarette if you do," and he'll help, because most of the people here will respond to tobacco.

Nothing could be simpler. Nor is contractual power considered particularly ineffective—indeed, more nurses feel that it works well than consider authority or coercion effective.

The main opposition to contractual power stems from a quality it possesses which is not characteristic of other power modes, *viz.* that each party influences the behavior of the other to some degree. If, in order to get someone to do what we want, we agree to do what he wants, then we are subject to his control and thereby sacrifice some of our own freedom. This is obviously a desirable form of power from the viewpoint of the power-subject, but not from the viewpoint of the power-wielder. One male nursing assistant stated:

Oh yeah, that works well. If you say, "I'll give you parole" or "You can have cigarettes" or whatever he wants—something like that, you know—it'll work, but you always got a kickback. When you don't have no cigarettes or some candy, the patient won't do what you ask him. So when you come to a problem like that, you're leaving yourself open for the kickback. If you don't start it, you won't have the problem to confront with.

With reference to this mode of power, an assistant said:

If you start a patient—go and give him cigarettes and candy or buy him a Coca-Cola—he start lookin' for that. And when you stop doin' that for him, he's going to be demandin' that he wants it. And it cause bad friendship between you and patients.

Another limitation to the use of contractual power stems from the requirement of objective treatment in a formal organization. If this form of power, so desirable from the viewpoint of the patient, is applied to one patient, then other patients, occupying the same status, may claim the same privilege for themselves. A male nursing assistant reported:

It has a tendency to change the whole morale on the ward, too. If one patient can get privilges and candy and stuff for doing something, the rest of them, they want the same thing. When they don't get it then they resent you too. So it pays—no favors....Once you start giving them candy, this one will get candy, that one will get candy, they going to tell you about it.

A third reason for the reluctance to employ contractual power in the mental hospital is that it is seen as an ethically dubious method. In this context it smacks of bribery, a method which to many nurses is morally repugnant.

The rejection of the use of contractual power is thus based upon both ethical and pragmatic grounds. To yield to the use of this method places the nurse under an obligation to the patient; a new set of expectations are established based on the fact that the nurse, in exercising power over the patient, at the same time places himself in the power of the patient. And since large organizations tend to develop impersonal and abstract rules, the advantages of contract to one patient are liable to be claimed by all. Contractual power, if it is to be exercised, must either be employed generally or not at all. Hence the nurse's resistance to the use of contract is based emphatically on his *self-interest* as well as on moral opposition to the method.

LEGITIMATE AUTHORITY

Legitimate authority refers to the *right* of an individual to direct the actions of another by virtue of his objective, impersonal position in a social system. The essential underpinning of most formal organizations is legitimate authority, usually supported by implicit coercion. We may say that most formal organizations tend in the direction of the increasing use of legitimate authority for both ethical and pragmatic reasons. In the present study, it was indexed by the statement: "Since a nurse or nursing assistant has the right to tell a patient what to do, I would simply tell him to change his sleeping habits."

It is thus interesting to note that only 13 percent of the respondents said that legitimate authority would be either the first or second means of power they would employ. Is this attributable to an ethical repugnance about the use of this method? The answer is no; for we find that twice as many respondents (28 percent) say they would *like* to use this method as their first or second choices as claim they would *actually* do so. Nor is it due to the difficulty of employing authority; authority shares almost equal rank with contractual power as the *easiest* method to apply. The main reason why so many people who would like to use legitimate authority do not do so is that they feel it *will not work.*

It should be pointed out that this relationship between values and effectiveness is not generally true of other methods of exercising power. We find, for example, that only 17 percent of those who valued authority most highly also thought it was most likely to work. This contrasts with 79 percent of those who most valued manipulation, 56 percent of those who most valued persuasion, and 53 percent of those who most valued coercion. The only comparable alternative is the contractual method, which was considered most effective by only 15 percent of those who valued it most highly.

Why is legitimate authority considered so ineffective by members of the nursing staff? One reason is that legitimate authority is always based upon a system of mutual expectations and the acceptance of rights. When nurses therefore say that they consider legitimate power relatively ineffective, they are essentially saying that patients do not accept the *right* of the nurse to tell them what to do. This is illustrated in the response of a male nurse:

I think that many of the patients feel that hospital employees are nothing but bosses and such, and that they don't want to be told what to do by hospital employees. I hear it once in a while: "Well, who does he think he is, just because he happens to be a hospital employee or an attendant or a nurse—tell me what to do." And it comes from the whole group, not just one type of patient. "You better not boss me around."

Not only are nurses inclined to doubt that patients will acknowledge their right to direct their actions, but there are many nurses who do not *claim* this right; they, too, deny that their position entitles them to use this mode of power.

Well, I'm not so sure that we really do have a right. Sometimes I don't sleep all night and I wouldn't want someone to force me to go to bed if I wanted to stay up. If someone gave me a logical reason for going to bed, then, if it was necessary for somone's convenience, that I could help them—then I would go. But if someone said: "All right, let's go to bed," then I (would start) swinging.

It should be recognized that the relatively small number saying that they would use legitimate power is probably more a function of the difficulty of the hypothetical situation posed than the actual frequency with which it is employed. In the routine day-to-day and moment-to-moment situations on the ward, legitimate authority is almost always the most common mode of power exercise, but this does not mean that it is most likely to be employed when a difficult situation arises. It is under these conditions—special, extraordinary, nonroutine situations—that nursing personnel are likely to doubt that their claims for legitimacy will be honored or should even appropriately be invoked.

Why, under such conditions, do nursing personnel so often expect legitimate authority to fail in its purpose? For one thing, most mental patients do not enter the hospital voluntarily and therefore do not accept its authority structure. They may yield to coercion or persuasion, but they may refuse to acknowledge rights. If a patient rejects the institution and his position in it, then the entire basis of legitimacy is undermined.

An additional factor is that the scope of one's life which comes under the authority system in a "total institution" (Goffman, 1957) tends to be vaguely defined. In a university, for example, a professor has the right to tell a student to read a certain book but he has no right to tell him to date a certain girl or to eat a certain food. In the mental hopital, on the other hand, the limits as to what a nurse can or cannot control are more vaguely defined. The nurse may feel he has certain rights of control which the patient denies are legitimate. In these circumstances quite different forms of power must be invoked.

BENEVOLENT MANIPULATION

The least overt form of power, the one least violating the individual's sense of freedom, is manipulation. The essence of the manipulative mode of power lies in the fact that A gets B to do what he wants without B being aware of the fact that this is A's intention; in this situation, B cannot feel that his freedom is abridged or violated. This mode of power exercise, we find, is one of the most frequently selected; it ranks second only to persuasion among the five power alternatives presented. Fully 38 percent of our sample said that this was the means they would be most likely to employ, and an additional 50 percent ranked it second. In other words, seven out of every eight respondents indicated that this was one of the two methods they would be most disposed to use.

The term "manipulation," of course, was not used in the questionnaire, since it tends to smack of trickery, indirection, and below-board maneuvers. In the situation under consideration, the alternative did involve manipulation, but it might more appropriately be called "benevolent manipulation." The distinctive characteristic of benevolent manipulation is that the power-wielder exercises power over the power-subject for the benefit of the subject or of the institution, not for his own benefit, and the manipulation does the power-subject no harm. It is this sort of manipulation which achieves such popularity in the mental hospital.

On what basis do we conclude that the manipulation under consideration actually has this benevolent property? (i) Next to coercion, manipulation was said to involve the *greatest* effort and difficulty. Twenty-seven percent considered it the *most* work and trouble and an additional 29 percent said it was the second most difficult. If the nurses were selfishly motivated in their selection of this means, they would hardly choose a method which they personally considered more time-consuming and energy-consuming than almost any other. (ii) Next to persuasion, manipulation is characterized as the most *desirable* form of power exercise. This mode of power is thus hailed by nurses as corresponding to their highest ideas. (iii) There is some indication that this mode of power is selected by those nurses who are most kindly disposed toward patients. Those who completely *denied* that "patients don't have the same feelings as others" ($p < .10$) and that "patients are on the lookout to get around the ward rules" ($p < .10$) were more likely to choose manipulation than those who agreed with these statements. It is further relevant to note that those who had high faith in people were more likely to select manipulation that those with low faith in people ($p < .01$). The manipulation suggested here, then, is not a self-interested manipulation based on contempt for, and hostility toward, patients; on the contrary, it is one motivated by kindness, respect, and a desire to help.

It is interesting to note that the method of benevolent manipulation is selected not because it is thought to be easy but in spite of the fact that it is considered difficult. A male nurse explains this fact in the following way:

Well, if you have 45 or 50 patients and are trying to figure out something for one patient when you're worried about the others and you have medicines ... you find that these people can (wander) off awfully easy and you're spending your time looking for them and finally find them in a corner somewhere sleeping. ...

Then, too, to keep them busy, actually busy, once you do find them is about as bad as getting them to go to bed—forcing them to go to bed.

The complexity of the problem is amplified by the fact that it is so often necessary to take account of the unique, idiosyncratic qualities of each patient.

Well, I wouldn't try to follow courses of action which are truly make-do methods —work for work's sake sort of thing. I think I would try to find courses of action which would concern his interest, his previous background which would include such things as his hobbies, and his work background, what sort of tasks were assigned to him. I certainly wouldn't expect a man who was interested in botany to be interested in cleaning out latrines. Nor would I expect a man only capable of cleaning out latrines to do statistical work.

Given the idiosyncrasies of each patient, the large number of patients requiring care, and the variety of institutional regulations limiting the range of solutions potentially available, benevolent manipulation is understandably difficult to use. What, therefore, may account for the popularity of benevolent manipulation as a mode of power in the mental hospital?

One factor is probably the general suspicion of power which tends to characterize a democratic society. Where power must be exercised, the value system prescribes that it be made as palatable and inoffensive as possible. When manipulative power is employed, the power-subject's sense of abridgement of freedom is at a minimum.

The second reason has to do with the image of the relationship of the nurse to the patient. In a sense, it is seen as similar to the relationship of the parent to the child or the doctor to the patient, i.e., power is exercised for the benefit of the power-subject rather than for that of the power-wielder. In order to avoid the less desirable techniques of force or bribery, and recognizing the ineffectiveness of rational persuasion, a mother may often resort to indirect means, such as distraction, to keep her child from harm or otherwise to advance his interests. The nurse may tend to see her relationship to the patient in a similar way. Benevolent manipulation achieves the desired end with no harm to the patient or anyone else and with the minimum of patient resistance and resentment. Despite the difficulty in its use, then, benevolent manipulation is considered a happy solution to the problem of power in the mental hospital, for it is the least overt, least conspicuous, least evident form of power.

PERSUASION

The most favored method of exercising power in the mental hospital is persuasion. Fifty-four percent of our respondents said this would be the first method they would actually employ and an additional 39 percent ranked it second. Persuasion appeals particularly to the *value* system of the nursing staff—54 percent saying it was the method they most like to use and 39 percent ranking it second. It is also deemed relatively effective; three-quarters of the respondents considered it one of the two surest ways of inducing the patient to comply with their wishes. Nor is it deemed unusually time- or energy-consuming; it is not thought to take as much work and trouble as coercion or manipulation, although it is seen as more work and trouble than contractual or authoritative power. Among the five modes of power, then, persuasion ranks first by the value criterion, second by the effectiveness criterion, and third by the effort criterion. We can thus see why nursing personnel are so likely to say that they will employ it.

The strong value emphasis placed upon persuasion reflects a system of ideals springing from manifold sources. First, the nursing ideology of "tender loving care" is sharply opposed to blatant or coercive modes of power exercise. Kindness and respect for the individual are watchwords of this creed. "Angels of mercy" are not expected to bludgeon, command, or bribe people to do their bidding; but they have their ways.

Second, the value of democracy, fundamentally resting on assumptions concerning the rationality and perfectibility of men, also favors persuasion. Democracy is founded on the assumption that men are and should be moved by reason, not by force or authority; hence, the negative valuation of coercion and the positive ideal of persuasion.

One surprising finding is the very widespread belief among nursing personnel that persuasion is effective with mental patients. This finding is especially impressive because it is precisely the irrationality of mental patients which has induced society to expel and segregate them. Despite this, nursing personnel tend to feel that patients are fundamentally rational. A male nursing assistant averred:

He (the mental patient) may be sick, but he's still got plenty sense. And he's still got feelings. . . . Many times the patient may be so sick, but you sit down and talk to him—he understand what you say.

A female nurse expressed it as follows:

Well, I think that you get much more cooperation from the patient. No matter how ill the patient is I do think that you get through to him. Not in total maybe, but at least in part.

Mental patients thus tend to be seen as amenable to persuasion, responsive to reason. Such persuasion, of course, is not always "rational" persuasion; patients do not yield only to the power of strict logic. On the contrary, as in all communications, a wide variety of "appeals" are utilized: (i) Appeals based upon positive feelings for the nurse; e.g., the patient should comply because this will help the nurse. (ii) Appeals emphasizing the benefits accruing to the patient himself, e.g., the argument that sleeping at night will make the patient feel better. (iii) Appeals emphasizing the consequences for other patients, e.g., the argument that it is not fair to other patients for the individual not to shower daily. (iv) Appeals referring to the necessity for compliance with institutional rules, e.g., that patients must dress, remain tidy, trim their beards, wear shoes, etc. In addition to such appeals, it was noted that simply talking to the patient could so modify the emotional state of the patient, calm him down, that he would then be willing to comply. Finally, the desirability of persuasion often appears to be based upon emphatic identification with the patient. The nurse states that if he were a patient, he would like to have the reasons for action explained to him; the same courtesy should be accorded the patient.

Why is persuasion considered to be relatively little work and trouble? It is, after all, easier to tell a patient what to do or give him something than to go into a long explanation. The advantage, it appears, lies in its *long-term* benefits. A male nurse expressed it as follows:

How much work is involved in each of these? Well, I think that in the final analysis, explaining things to them, although it may seem time-consuming initially, is not really time-consuming. Because working on the assumption that most patients are reasonable, once things are explained to them, I feel that the very next time the problem comes up I will spend far less time in securing his cooperation.

The Repercussions of Power Acts

In presenting our respondents with a specific hypothetical situation, the following point captured our attention: that nursing personnel do not tend to react to the situation solely as an immediate and specific problem to be dealt with entirely on its own terms—an event isolated from all others, with a specific end point—but rather are very alert to the possible repercussions of the act.

Thus, the *present* act was consistently interpreted in the light of *future* consequences. For example, one might coerce a patient now, but this might make the patient more hostile, violent, or uncooperative in the future; the simplicity of the immediate solution had to be weighed against the anticipated increased difficulty in time to come. Or one might offer a patient candy or certain privileges (contractual power) in order to gain immediate compliance, but the danger was foreseen that the patient would continue to demand these as a condition for compliance in the future. Conversely, persuasion might be more difficult in the immediate situation, but it was seen as producing increased cooperation in the future. In responding to the criteria of power, then, nursing personnel characteristically adopted the "long view"; it was recognized that a direct and simple solution might solve the current problem but compound the nurse's difficulties in the future.

A second consideration in the selection of criteria was the concern with the "spreading effect" of the act, i.e., its consequences for other patients. Thus, a nurse might be reluctant to use coercion because this would upset the other patients, thereby vastly multiplying the nurse's problems. Similarly, many nurses shied away from offering patients benefits as a price for compliance because they anticipated that all patients would then demand the same advantages.

We thus see that the power act is not based upon a decision divorced from time and society but is, on the countrary, consistently evaluated in terms of potential repercussions. While this is true of most situations involving interpersonal interaction, it is probably accentuated in the present situation because nurse-patient interaction on the mental hospital ward is of such extended duration. Just as G. H. Mead (1934) has shown that the later stages of a social act are implicit in, and influence, the earlier stages, so it would appear that future possible acts are given serious consideration, and influence the immediate power decision.

Hospital Status and Preference for Power Modes

Which people are disposed to use which power methods in the mental hospital? Registered nurses, it appears, are most likely to favor benevolent manipulation, whereas nursing assistants are least likely to do so (Table 16-2). On the other hand, legitimate authority, while not highly favored by

TABLE 16-2

Position in Hospital and Preference for Benevolent Manipulation

WOULD ACTUALLY USE BENEVOLENT MANIPULATION	POSITION		
	NURSING ASSISTANTS	CHARGE ATTENDANTS	HEAD NURSES
First choice	35	40	51
Second choice	50	53	47
Third, fourth, or fifth choice	15	7	3
Total percent	100	100	100
Number	(694)	(168)	(156)

$\chi^2 = 30.9; df = 4; p < .001$

any group, is more likely to be selected by nursing assistants than by any other group (Table 16-3).

The higher status nurses, we see, prefer to proceed by indirection, by applying their interpersonal skills, by foreseeing possible difficulties and evading them in advance. The lower status people, on the other hand, show a greater tendency to rely on formal roles in dealing with patients.

The use of legitimate authority is apparently also related to the amount of time one has worked in the mental hospital. Generally speaking, those who have worked longer in this environment (4 to 20 years) tend to show a greater preference for this effortless and impersonal mode of power than

TABLE 16-3

Position in Hospital and Preference for Legitimate Authority

WOULD ACTUALLY USE AUTHORITY	POSITION		
	NURSING ASSISTANTS	CHARGE ATTENDANTS	HEAD NURSES
First or second choice	16	9	3
Third choice	47	44	45
Fourth or fifth choice	37	47	52
Total percent	100	100	100
Number	(640)	(156)	(150)

$\chi^2 = 30.4; df = 4; p < .001$

those who are relative newcomers to the job (under 4 years). Among the small number who have worked in the hospitals for over 20 years, however, the number selecting this method again goes down (Table 16–4).

TABLE 16-4

Length of Service and Preference for Legitimate Authority

WOULD ACTUALLY USE LEGITIMATE AUTHORITY	LENGTH OF SERVICE		
	a 1-4 YEARS	b 4-20 YEARS	c OVER 20 YEARS
First or second choice	4	17	3
Third choice	53	44	43
Fourth or fifth choice	44	39	53
Total percent	100	100	100
Number	(262)	(615)	(58)

a vs. b: $\chi^2 = 27.8; df = 2; p < .001$

b vs. c: $\chi^2 = 8.6; df = 2; p < .02$

Those who have served in the mental hospital a shorter period of time, on the other hand, tend to show some preference for the method of benevolent manipulation. This is the "preferred," the "idealistic" approach, and it is not too surprising to find it embraced more by those who have not been jaded by experience (Table 16–5).

In the course of time, it would appear, the more imaginative and idealistic approach of benevolent manipulation appears to give way to the more bureaucratic and standardized approach of legitimate authority. The exception, once again, is among those who have worked in the hospital over 20 years.

The preference for a particular mode of power is, as one might anticipate, also related to a broader orientation toward one's work and what one hopes to get out of it. Those who are interested in the extrinsic rewards of their

TABLE 16-5

Length of Service and Preference for Benevolent Manipulation

WOULD ACTUALLY USE BENEVOLENT MANIPULATION	LENGTH OF SERVICE		
	a UP TO 4 YEARS	b 4-20 YEARS	c OVER 20 YEARS
First choice	45	36	41
Second choice	51	49	54
Third, fourth, or fifth choice	4	15	5
Total percent	100	100	100
Number	(271)	(672)	(63)

a vs. b: $\chi^2 = 25.0$; $df = 2$; $p < .001$

b vs. c: $\chi^2 = 5.3$; $df = 2$; $p < .10$

job—its economic or prestige aspects—are more likely to say they would employ the method of legitimate authority than those who are concerned with its service aspects. For example, we asked our respondents what they liked best about their jobs. Those who selected as their first choice the fact that it represented "clean, dignified work" or "steady, secure pay" were characterized as concerned with the "extrinsic rewards" of the job; those who said that it gave them a chance to "do something for others" or "help people in trouble" were considered to show special concern for "service." We find that those emphasizing the extrinsic rewards of work are significantly more likely than those concerned with service to say they would use legitimate authority ($p < ·02$).

Legitimate authority is an objective, impersonal method of influence, based on formal rank and position, and operating independently of those who occupy the position. We would thus expect that those people who do not wish to get close to patients, who do not wish to be intimate with them, to give of themselves in the relationship, would be relatively inclined to favor this power mode. Our data suggest that the less the nurse's feelings of intimacy for patients and the greater his status distance from them, the more likely is he to favor the use of authority ($p < ·10$). (See Pearlin and Rosenberg, 1962, for a more complete description of this "status distance" scale.)

Lower formal position in the hospital structure, greater length of experience (with the exception of the over 20 years group), concern with the extrinsic rewards of work, and attitudes of status distance toward patients are thus all associated with a tendency to favor the use of legitimate authority. Authority thus appears to appeal more to those who are themselves more powerless in the hospital, who are more alienated from its purposes, or, with some exceptions, who have more experience in learning to use this method effectively.

Conclusion

In the mental hospital, as in any area of life involving human interaction, power must be exercised. The question thus becomes: What *means* do people use to influence the behavior of others in accord with their intentions and what considerations or criteria enter into their selection of various means? The present study has been confined to the examination of *power attitudes*. In order to obtain a more complete understanding of power in the mental hospital, further studies based on observations of actual power exercise, joined with motivational investigations of nurses at the time of power exercise and with analyses of patient compliance, would be required.

NOTE

1. Though the term "manipulation" has, in common parlance, pejorative connotations, we indicate that this is actually a form of "benevolent manipulation."

REFERENCES

Goffman, E. (1957). On the characteristics of total institutions. *Symposium on preventive and social psychiatry.* Washington, D.C.: Walter Reed Army Medical Center.

Goldhamer, H., and Shils, E. A. (1939). Types of power and status. *Amer. J. Sociol., 45,* 171.

Mead, G. H. (1934). *Mind, self and society.* Chicago: University of Chicago Press.

Pearlin, L. I., and Rosenberg, M. (1962). Nurse-patient social distance and the structural context of a mental hospital. *Amer. Sociol. Rev., 27,* 56–65.

Rosenberg, M. (1956). Power and desegregation. *Soc. Prob., 3,* 215–23.

17

Erving Goffman

THE UNDERLIFE OF A
PUBLIC INSTITUTION

I

In every social establishment, there are official expectations as to what the participant owes the establishment. Even in cases where there is no specific task, as in some night-watchman jobs, the organization will require some presence of mind, some awareness of the current situation, and some readiness for unanticipated events; as long as an establishment demands that its participants not sleep on the job, it asks them to be awake to certain matters. And where sleeping is part of the expectation, as in a home or a hotel, then there will be limits on where and when the sleeping is to occur, with whom, and with what bed manners.[1] And behind these claims on the individual, be they great or small, the managers of every establishment will have a widely embracing implicit conception of what the individual's character must be for these claims on him to be appropriate.

Whenever we look at a social establishment, we find a counter to this first theme: we find that participants decline in some way to accept the official view of what they should be putting into and getting out of the organization and, behind this, of what sort of self and world they are to accept for themselves. Where enthusiasm is expected, there will be apathy; where loyalty, there will be disaffection; where attendance, absenteeism; where robustness, some kind of illness; where deeds are to be done, varieties of inactivity. We find a multitude of homely little histories, each in its way a movement of liberty. Whenever worlds are laid on, underlives develop.

II

The study of underlife in restrictive total institutions has some special interest. When existence is cut to the bone, we can learn what people do to flesh out their lives. Stashes, means of transportation, free places, territories, supplies for economic and social exchange—these apparently are some of the minimal requirements for building up a life. Ordinarily these arrangements are taken for granted as part of one's primary adjustment; seeing them twisted out of official existence through bargains, wit, force, and cunning, we can see their significance anew. The study of total institutions also suggests that formal organizations have standard places of vulnerability, such as supply rooms, sick bays, kitchens, or scenes of highly technical labor. These are the damp corners where secondary adjustments breed and start to infest the establishment.

The mental hospital represents a peculiar instance of those establishments in which underlife is likely to proliferate. Mental patients are persons who caused the kind of trouble on the outside that led someone physically, if not socially, close to them to take psychiatric action against them. Often this trouble was associated with the "prepatient" having indulged in situational improprieties of some kind, conduct out of place in the setting. It is just such misconduct that conveys a moral rejection of the communities, establishments, and relationships that have a claim to one's attachment.

Stigmatization as mentally ill and involuntary hospitalization are the means by which we answer these offenses against propriety. The individual's persistence in manifesting symptoms after entering the hospital, and his tendency to develop additional symptoms during his initial response to the hospital, can now no longer serve him well as expressions of disaffection. From the patient's point of view, to decline to exchange a word with the staff or with his fellow patients may be ample evidence of rejecting the institution's view of what and who he is; yet higher management may construe this alienative expression as just the sort of symptomatology the institution was established to deal with and as the best kind of evidence that the patient properly belongs where he now finds himself. In short, mental hospitalization outmaneuvers the patient, tending to rob him of the common expression through which people hold off the embrace of organizations—insolence, silence, *sotto voce* remarks, uncooperativeness, malicious destruction of interior decorations, and so forth; these signs of disaffiliation are now read as signs of their maker's proper affiliation. Under these conditions all adjustments are primary.

Furthermore, there is a vicious-circle process at work. Persons who are lodged on "bad" wards find that very little equipment of any kind is given them—clothes may be taken from them each night, recreational materials may be withheld, and only heavy wooden chairs and benches provided for furniture. Acts of hostility against the institution have to rely on limited, ill-designed devices, such as banging a chair against the floor or striking a sheet of newspaper sharply so as to make an annoying explosive sound. And the more inadequate this equipment is to convey rejection of the hospital, the more the act appears as a psychotic symptom, and the more likely it is that management feels justified in assigning the patient to a bad ward. When a patient finds himself in seclusion, naked and without visible means of expression, he may have to rely on tearing up his mattress, if he can, or writing with feces on the wall—actions management takes to be in keeping with the kind of person who warrants seclusion.

We can also see this circular process at work in the small, illicit, talisman-like possessions that inmates use as symbolic devices for separating themselves from the position they are supposed to be in. What I think is a typical example may be cited from prison literature:

Prison clothing is anonymous. One's possessions are limited to toothbrush, comb, upper or lower cot, half the space upon a narrow table, a razor. As in jail, the urge to collect possessions is carried to preposterous extents. Rocks, string, knives—anything made by man and forbidden in man's institution—anything—a red comb, a different kind of toothbrush, a belt—these things are assiduously gathered, jealously hidden or triumphantly displayed.[2]

But when a patient, whose clothes are taken from him each night, fills his pockets with bits of string and rolled up paper, and when he fights to keep these possessions in spite of the consequent inconvenience to those who must regularly go through his pockets, he is usually seen as engaging in symptomatic behavior befitting a very sick patient, not as someone who is attempting to stand apart from the place accorded him.

Official psychiatric doctrine tends to define alienative acts as psychotic ones—this view being reinforced by the circular processes that lead the patient to exhibit alienation in a more and more bizarre form—but the hospital cannot be run according to this doctrine. The hospital cannot decline to demand from its members exactly what other organizations must insist on; psychiatric doctrine is supple enough to do this, but institutions are not. Given the standards of the institution's environing society, there have to be at least the minimum routines connected with feeding, washing, dressing, bedding the patients, and protecting them from physical harm. Given these routines, there have to be inducements and exhortations to get patients to follow them. Demands must be made, and disappointment is shown when a patient does not live up to what is expected of him. Interest in seeing psychiatric "movement" or "improvement" after an initial stay on the wards leads the staff to encourage "proper" conduct and to express disappointment when a patient backslides into "psychosis." The patient is thus reestablished as someone whom others are depending on, someone who ought to know enough to act correctly. Some improprieties, especially ones like muteness and apathy that do not obstruct and even ease ward routines, may continue to be perceived naturalistically as symptoms, but on the whole the hospital operates semi-officially on the assumption that the patient ought to act in a manageable way and be respectful of psychiatry, and that he who does will be rewarded by improvement in life conditions and he who doesn't will be punished by a reduction of amenities. Within this semi-official reinstatement of ordinary organization practices, the patient finds that many of the traditional ways of taking leave of a place without moving from it have retained their validity; secondary adjustments are therefore possible.

III

Of the many different kinds of secondary adjustment, some are of particular interest because they bring into the clear the general theme of involvement and disaffection, characteristic of all these practices.

One of these special types of secondary adjustment is "removal activities" (or "kicks"), namely, undertakings that provide something for the individual to lose himself in, temporarily blotting out all sense of the environment which, and in which, he must abide. In total institutions a useful exemplary case is provided by Robert Stroud, the "Birdman" who, from watching birds out his cell window, through a spectacular career of finagling and make-do, fabricated a laboratory and became a leading ornithological contributor to medical literature, all from within prison.[3] Language courses in prisoner-of-war camps and art courses in prisons can provide the same release.

Central Hospital provided several of these escape worlds for inmates.[4] One, for example, was sports. Some of the baseball players and a few tennis players seemed to become so caught up in their sport, and in the daily record of their efforts in competition, that at least for the summer months this became their overriding interest. In the case of baseball this was further strengthened by the fact that, within the hospital, parole patients could follow national baseball as readily as could many persons on the outside. For some young patients, who never failed to go, when allowed, to a dance held in their service or in the recreation building, it was possible to live for the chance of meeting someone "interesting" or remeeting someone interesting who had already been met—in much the same way that college students are able to survive their studies by looking forward to the new "dates" that may be found in extracurricular activities. The "marriage moratorium" in Central Hospital, effectively freeing a patient from his marital obligations to a non-patient, enhanced this removal activity. For a handful of patients, the semiannual theatrical production was an extremely effective removal activity: tryouts, rehearsals, costuming, scenery making, staging, writing and rewriting, performing—all these seemed as successful as on the outside in building a world apart for the participants. Another kick, important to some patients—and a worrisome concern for the hospital chaplains—was the enthusiastic espousal of religion. Still another, for a few patients, was gambling.[5]

Portable ways of getting away were much favored in Central Hospital, paperback murder mysteries,[6] cards, and even jigsaw puzzles being carried around on one's person. Not only could the ward and grounds be taken leave of through these means, but if one had to wait for an hour or so upon an official, or the serving of a meal, or the opening of the recreation building, the self-implication of this subordination could be dealt with by immediately bringing forth one's own world-making equipment.

Individual means of creating a world were striking. One depressed, suicidal alcoholic, apparently a good bridge player, disdained bridge with almost all other patient players, carrying around his own pocket bridge player and writing away occasionally for a new set of competition hands. Given a supply of his favorite gumdrops and his pocket radio, he could pull himself out of the hospital world at will, surrounding all his senses with pleasantness.

In considering removal activities we can again raise the issue of over-commitment to an establishment. In the hospital laundry, for example, there was a patient worker who had been on the job for several years. He had been given the job of unofficial foreman, and, unlike almost all other patient workers, he threw himself into his work with a capacity, devotion, and seriousness that were evident to many. Of him, the laundry charge attendant said: "That one there is my special helper. He works harder than all the rest put together. I would be lost without him." In exchange for his effort, the attendant would bring from home something for this patient to eat almost every day. And yet there was something grotesque in his adjustment, for it was apparent that his deep voyage into the work world had a slightly make-believe character; after all, he was a patient, not a foreman, and he was clearly reminded of this off the job.

Obviously, as some of these illustrations imply, removal activities need not be in themselves illegitimate; it is the function that they come to serve for the inmate that leads us to consider them along with other secondary adjustments. An extreme here, perhaps, is individual psychotherapy in state mental hospitals; this privilege is so rare in these institutions,[7] and the re-sulting contact with a staff psychiatrist so unique in terms of hospital status structure, that an inmate can to some degree forget where he is as he pursues his psychotherapy. By actually receiving what the institution formally claims to offer, the patient can succeed in getting away from what the establishment actually provides. There is a general implication here. Perhaps every activity that an establishment obliges or permits its members to participate in is a potential threat to the organization, for it would seem that there is no activity in which the individual cannot become overengrossed.

Another property is clearly evident in some undercover practices and possibly a factor in all of them: I refer to what Freudians sometimes call "over-determination." Some illicit activities are pursued with a measure of spite, malice, glee, and triumph, and at a personal cost, that cannot be accounted for by the intrinsic pleasure of consuming the product. True, it is central to closed restrictive institutions that apparently minor satisfactions can come to be defined as great ones. But even correcting for this reevaluation, something remains to be explained.

One aspect of the overdetermination of some secondary adjustments is the sense one gets of a practice being employed *merely* because it is forbidden.[8] Inmates in Central Hospital who had succeeded in some elaborate evasion of the rules often seemed to seek out a fellow inmate, even one who could not be entirely trusted, to display before him evidence of the evasion. A patient back from an overlate foray into the local town's night life would be full of stories of his exploits the next day; another would call aside his friends and show them where he had stashed the empty liquor bottle whose contents he had consumed the night before, or display the condoms in his wallet. Nor was it surprising to see the limits of safe concealment tested. I knew an extremely resourceful alcoholic who would smuggle in a pint of vodka, put some in a paper drinking cup, and sit on the most exposed part of the lawn he could find, slowly getting drunk; at such times he took pleasure in offering hospitality to persons of semistaff status. Similarly, I knew an attendant who would park his car just outside the patient canteen—the social hub of the patient universe—and there he and a friendly patient would discuss the most intimate qualifications of the passing females while resting a paper cup full of bourbon on the differential covering, just below the sight line of the crowd, drinking a toast, as it were, to their distance from the scene around them.

Another aspect of the overdeterminism of some secondary adjustments is that the very pursuit of them seems to be a source of satisfaction. As previously suggested in regard to courtship contacts, the institution can become defined as one's opponent in a serious game, the object being to score against the hospital. Thus I have heard cliques of patients pleasurably discuss the possibility that evening of "scoring" for coffee,[9] accurately employing this larger term for a smaller activity.[10] The tendency of prison inmates to smuggle food and other comforts into the cell of someone suffering solitary confinement may be seen not only as an act of charity but also as a way of sharing by association the spirit of someone taking a stand against authority.[11] Similarly, the time-consuming elaborate escape planning that patients, prisoners, and POW internees engage in can be seen not merely as a way of getting out but also as a way of giving meaning to being in.

I am suggesting that secondary adjustments are overdetermined, some of them especially so. These practices serve the practitioner in ways other than the most evident ones: whatever else they accomplish these practices seem to demonstrate—to the practitioner if no one else—that he has some selfhood and personal autonomy beyond the grasp of the organization.

IV

If a function of secondary adjustments is to place a barrier between the individual and the social unit in which he is supposed to be participating, we should expect some secondary adjustments to be empty of intrinsic gain and to function solely to express unauthorized distance—a self-preserving "rejection of one's rejectors."[12] This seems to happen with the very common forms of ritual insubordination, for example, griping or bitching, where this behavior is not realistically expected to bring about change. Through direct insolence that does not meet with immediate correction, or remarks passed half out of hearing of authority, or gestures performed behind the back of authority, subordinates express some detachment from the place officially accorded them. An ex-inmate of the penitentiary at Lewisburg provides an illustration:

On the surface, life here appears to run almost placidly, but one needs to go only a very little beneath the surface to find the whirlpools and eddies of anger and frustration. The muttering of discontent and rebellion goes on constantly: the *sotto voce* sneer whenever we pass an official or a guard, the glare carefully calculated to express contempt without arousing overt retaliation. . . .[13]

Brendan Behan provides a British prison illustration:

The warder shouted at him.
"Right, sir," he shouted. "Be right along, sir," adding in a lower tone, "You shit-'ouse."[14]

Some of these ways of openly but safely taking a stand outside the authorized one are beautiful, especially when carried out collectively. Again, prisons provide ready examples:

How to express contempt for authority? The manner of "obeying" orders is one way. . . . Negroes are especially apt at parody, sometimes breaking into a goose-step. They seat themselves at table 10 at a time, snatching off caps simultaneously and precisely.[15]

When the sky pilot got up in the pulpit to give us our weekly pep talk each Sunday he would always make some feeble joke which we always laughed at as loud and as long as possible, although he must have known that we were sending him up. He still used to make some mildly funny remark and every time he did the whole church would be filled with rawcous [*sic*] laughter, even though only half the audience had heard what had been said.[16]

Some acts of ritual insubordination rely on irony, found in the wider society in the form of gallows gallantry and in institutions in the construction of heavily meaningful mascots. A standard irony in total institutions is giving nicknames to especially threatening or unpleasant aspects of the environment. In concentration camps, turnips were sometimes called "German pineapples,"[17] fatigue drill, "Geography."[18] In mental wards in Mount Sinai Hospital, brain-damage cases held for surgery would call the hospital "Mount Cyanide,"[19] and staff doctors were:

typically misnamed, being referred to by such terms as "lawyer," "white-collar worker," "chief of crew," "one of the presidents," "bartender," "supervisor of insurance" and "credit manager." One of us (E.A.W.) was called by such variations as "Weinberg," "Weingarten," "Weiner" and "Wiseman," . . .[20]

In prison, the punishment block may be called the "teagarden."[21] In Central Hospital, one of the wards containing incontinent patients was sometimes felt to be the punishment ward for attendants, who called it "the rose garden." An ex-mental patient provides another illustration:

Back in the dayroom Virginia decided that her change of clothing represented Dressing Therapy, D.T. Today was my turn for D.T. This would have been rather amusing if you had had a good stiff drink. Of paraldehyde. The Juniper Cocktail, as we call it, we gay ladies of Juniper Hill. A martini please, we more sophisticated ones say. And where, nurse, is the olive?[22]

It should be understood, of course, that the threatening world responded to with ironies need not be one sponsored by an alien human authority, but may be one that is self-imposed, or imposed by nature, as when dangerously ill persons joke about their situations.[23]

Beyond irony, however, there is an even more subtle and telling kind of ritual insubordination. There is a special stance that can be taken to alien authority; it combines stiffness, dignity, and coolness in a particular mixture that conveys insufficient insolence to call forth immediate punishment and yet expresses that one is entirely one's own man. Since this communication is made through the way in which the body and face are held, it can be constantly conveyed wherever the inmate finds himself. Illustrations can be found in prison society:

"Rightness" implies bravery, fearlessness, loyalty to peers, avoidance of exploitation, adamant refusal to concede the superiority of the official value system, and repudiation of the notion that the inmate is of a lower order. It consists principally in the reassertion of one's basic integrity, dignity, and worth in an essentially degrading situation, and the exhibition of these personal qualities regardless of any show of force by the official system.[24]

Similarly, in Central Hospital, in the "tough" punishment wards of maximum security, where inmates had very little more to lose, fine examples could be found of patients not going out of their way to make trouble but by their very posture conveying unconcern and mild contempt for all levels of the staff, combined with utter self-possession.

V

It would be easy to account for the development of secondary adjustments by assuming that the individual possessed an array of needs, native or cultivated, and that when lodged in a milieu that denied these needs the individual simply responded by developing makeshift means of satisfaction. I think this explanation fails to do justice to the importance of these undercover adaptations for the structure of the self.

The practice of reserving something of oneself from the clutch of an institution is very visible in mental hospitals and prisons but can be found in more benign and less totalistic institutions, too. I want to argue that this recalcitrance is not an incidental mechanism of defense but rather an essential constituent of the self.

Sociologists have always had a vested interest in pointing to the ways in which the individual is formed by groups, identifies with groups, and wilts away unless he obtains emotional support from groups. But when we closely observe what goes on in a social role, a spate of sociable interaction, a social establishment—or in any other unit of social organization—embracement of the unit is not all that we see. We always find the individual employing methods to keep some distance, some elbow room, between himself and that with which others assume he should be identified. No doubt a state-type mental hospital provides an overly lush soil for the growth of these secondary adjustments, but in fact, like weeds, they spring up in any kind of social organization. If we find, then, that in all situations actually studied the participant has erected defenses against his social bondedness, why should we base our conception of the self upon how the individual would act were conditions "just right"?

The simplest sociological view of the individual and his self is that he is to himself what his place in an organization defines him to be. When pressed, a sociologist modifies this model by granting certain complications: the self may be not yet formed or may exhibit conflicting dedications. Perhaps we should further complicate the construct by elevating qualifications to a central place, initially defining the individual, for sociological purposes, as a stance-taking entity, a something that takes up a position somewhere between identification with an organization and opposition to it, and is ready at the slightest pressure to regain its balance by shifting its involvement in either direction. It is thus *against something* that the self can emerge. This has been appreciated by students of totalitarianism:

In short, Ketman means self-realization *against* something. He who practices Ketman suffers because of the obstacles he meets; but if these obstacles were suddenly to be removed, he would find himself in a void which might perhaps prove much more painful. Internal revolt is sometimes essential to spiritual health, and

The Underlife of a Public Institution

can create a particular form of happiness. What can be said openly is often much less interesting than the emotional magic of defending one's private sanctuary.[25]

I have argued the same case in regard to total institutions. May this not be the situation, however, in free society, too?

Without something to belong to, we have no stable self, and yet total commitment and attachment to any social unit implies a kind of selflessness. Our sense of being a person can come from being drawn into a wider social unit; our sense of selfhood can arise through the little ways in which we resist the pull. Our status is backed by the solid buildings of the world, while our sense of personal identity often resides in the cracks.

NOTES

1. When stagecoach travelers in Europe in the fifteenth century might be required to share an inn bed with a stranger, courtesy books laid down codes of proper bed conduct. See Norbert Elias, *Uber den Prozess der Zivilisation* (2 vols.; Basel: Verlag Haus Zum Falken, 1934), Vol. II, pp. 219–21, *"Uber das Verhalten im Schlafraum."* On the sociology of sleep I am indebted to unpublished writings of Vilhelm Aubert and Kaspar Naegle.

2. Holley Cantine and Dachine Rainer, eds. *Prison Etiquette* (Bearsville, N. Y.: Retort Press, 1950), p. 78. Compare the things that small boys stash in their pockets; some of these items also seem to provide a wedge between the boy and the domestic establishment.

3. T. E. Gaddis, *Birdman of Alcatraz* (New York: New American Library, 1958).

4. Behind informal social typing and informal group formation in prisons there is often to be seen a removal activity. Caldwell provides some interesting examples of prisoners on such kicks: those involved in securing and using drugs; those focused on leatherwork for sale; and "Spartans," those involved in the glorification of their bodies; the prison locker room apparently serving as a muscle beach; the homosexuals; the gamblers, etc. The point about these activities is that each is world-building for the person caught up in it, thereby displacing the prison [Morris G. Caldwell, "Group Dynamics in the Prison Community," *Journal of Criminal Law, Criminology and Police Science* 46 (1956): 656].

5. Melville devotes a whole chapter of his *White Jacket* to illicit gambling aboard his frigate. Herman Melville, *White Jacket* (New York: Grove, n. d.), chap. 73.

6. The getaway role of reading in prison is well described in Brendan Behan, *Borstal Boy* (London: Hutchinson, 1958); see also Anthony Heckstall-Smith, *Eighteen Months* (London: Allan Wingate, 1954),*"The prison library offered a fairly good selection of books. But as time went by I found myself reading merely to kill time—reading everything and anything I could lay my hands on. During those first weeks, reading acted as a soporific and on the long early summer evenings I often fell asleep over my book."*

Kogon provides a concentration-camp example: *"In the winter of 1942–43 a succession of bread thefts in Barracks 42 at Buchenwald made it necessary to establish a nightwatch. For months on end I volunteered for this duty, taking the shift from three to six o'clock in the morning. It meant sitting alone in the day room, while the snores*

326

of the comrades came from the other end. For once I was free of the ineluctable companionship that usually shackled and stifled every individual activity. What an experience it was to sit quietly by a shaded lamp, delving into the pages of Plato's Dialogues, *Galworthy's* Swan Song, *or the works of Heine, Klabund, Mehring! Heine? Klabund? Mehring? Yes, they could be read illegally in camp. They were among books retrieved from the nation-wide wastepaper collections."* (Eugen Kogon. *The Theory and Practice of Hell,* pp. 127–128. New York: Berkley, n. d.)

7. Of approximately 7,000 patients in Central Hospital, I calculated at the time of the study that about 100 received some kind of individual psychotherapy in any one year.

8. This theme is developed by Albert Cohen in *Delinquent Boys* (Glencoe, Ill.: The Free Press, 1955.

9. A detailed description of the conniving and sustained undercover effort required to score for coffee in prison is provided in Norman S. Hayner and Ellis Ash, "The Prisoner Community As a Social Group," *American Sociological Review* 4 (1939): 365–366.

10. Traditionally, the value of pursuit itself is considered relative to the wider society, as when drug addicts are defined as playing an intensely meaningful daily game against society in obtaining the daily fix, and hustlers, grifters, and delinquents are seen as working hard at the intriguing, honorable task of making money without being seen working for it.

11. This theme is suggested by McCleery: *"The present study suggests that the display of goods and privileges among inmates serves to symbolize status that must be gained by other means. The symbols declare an ability to manipulate or resist power; and the inmate body betrays a compulsion to supply these symbols to men undergoing punishment, although their only function is to resist power bravely."* Richard McCleery, "Communication Patterns As Bases of Systems of Authority and Power," in Social Science Research Council Pamphlet No. 15, *Theoretical Studies in Social Organization of the Prison* (1960), p. 60n.

12. Lloyd W. McCorkle and Richard Korn, "Resocialization within Walls," *The Annals,* CCXCIII (1954), p. 88.

13. Alfred Hassler, *Diary of a Self-Made Convict* (Chicago: Regnery, 1954), pp. 70–71. For a military example of bitching, see T. E. Lawrence, *The Mint* (London: Jonathan Cape, 1955), p. 132.

14. Behan, *op. cit.,* p. 45. Primary school children in American society very early learn how to cross their fingers, mutter contradictions, and grimace covertly—through all of these means expressing a margin of autonomy even while submitting to the teacher's verbal punishment.

15. Cantine and Rainer, *op. cit.,* p. 106.

16. J. F. N. 1797, "Corrective Training," *Encounter* 10 (May, 1958): 15–16.

17. Kogon, *op. cit.,* p. 108.

18. *Ibid.,* p. 103.

19. Edwin Weinstein and Robert Kahn, *Denial of Illness* (Springfield, Ill.: Charles Thomas, 1955), p. 21.

20. *Ibid.,* p. 61. See especially ch. vi, "The Language of Denial."

21. George Dendrickson and Frederick Thomas, *The Truth about Dartmoor* (London: Gollancz, 1954), p. 25.

22. Mary Jane Ward, *The Snake Pit* (New York: New American Library, 1955), p. 65.

23. A useful report on ironies and other devices for dealing with life threat is provided by Renée Fox in *Experiment Perilous* (Glencoe, Ill.: The Free Press, 1959), p. 170 ff.

24. Richard Cloward, "Social Control in the Prison," S.S.R.C. Pamphlet No. 15, *op. cit.,* p. 40. Some minority groups have, relative to the society at large, a variant of this nonprovoking but hands-off-me stance. Compare, for example, the "cool stud" complex among urban American Negroes.

25. Czeslaw Milosz, *The Captive Mind* (New York: Vintage Books, 1955), p. 76.

18

Brenda Danet

"GIVING THE UNDERDOG A BREAK":
LATENT PARTICULARISM
AMONG CUSTOMS OFFICIALS

This chapter presents a paradigm for the evaluation of the degree of universalism of an organization's treatment of its clients, and then applies this paradigm to the response of officials of one organization, the Israel Customs authorities, to requests of a group of its clients. Special attention is given to the question of whether latent social characteristics of clients influence officials' response to their requests. The theoretical framework elaborated here is a direct outgrowth of ideas first expressed in programmatic form in an article by Katz and Eisenstadt (1960)* in which they suggested that contact between Israeli officials and immigrants from non-Western traditional societies may be characterized by "debureaucratization." The authors speculated that these contacts may be less universalistic, impersonal, and specific in orientation than is stipulated by the Weberian ideal model of bureaucratic role relations. The focus of that article was to isolate some of the conditions affecting the degree of bureaucratization of an organization, specifically of the bureaucrat–client relationship. Here, we shall be concerned not so much with *explaining* the degree of bureaucratization present in an organization's relations with its clients as with *evaluating* or measuring it.

NOTE: This chapter is an abridged version, specially prepared for this volume, of a paper entitled, "Giving the Underdog a Break: Favoritism or Flexibility?" ms., Jerusalem, 1972, submitted for publication 1972; full details of the study can be found in the author's unpublished Ph.D. dissertation, "Petitions and Persuasive Appeals: A Content-analysis of Letters to the Israel Customs Authorities," University of Chicago (Danet, 1970). Support for the research came from National Science Foundation, grant number GS-1385. The good will of the Israel Customs authorities in allowing project members access to its files is gratefully acknowledged.

Theoretical Framework

DEBUREAUCRATIZATION

Students of formal organizations increasingly see them not as isolated self-contained entities, but in constant interaction with their environments. Eisenstadt (1969) has identified three major outcomes of this interaction. First, there is the state of balance where organizations manage to maintain their autonomy and distinctiveness, and their goal implementation is influenced only by those who are legitimately entitled to do so. This is the "ideal" degree of bureaucratization. Viewed social-psychologically, in this autonomous form of bureaucracy, there is a delicate balance between pressures to fulfill role requirements, on the one hand, and recognition of organization members and clients as people of multiple identities, on the other. Rules remain a means to an end, and there is room for flexibility in their interpretation, as when a very sick person is not made to wait in line to see the doctor in a clinic.

"Overbureaucratization" is the second type of outcome of an organization's interaction with its environment. According to Katz and Eisenstadt,* "over-bureaucratization may be characterized in terms of the formalistic segregation of a bureaucratic relationship from all other role relations (even *relevant ones*)" . . . [1960, p. 119] (italics supplied). This suggests that in one way or another, the organization comes to dominate the environment, or fails to respond to legitimate needs and demands of the environment. One expression of this state of affairs is the phenomenon of *displacement of goals,* where rules become ends in themselves, and are interpreted too rigidly (Merton, 1952).

The third general direction which an organization may take is that of "debureaucratization." "Here there is subversion of the goals and activities of the bureaucracy in the interests of different groups with which it is in close interaction." (Eisenstadt, 1969, p. 307). Whereas in the case of overbureaucratization, the organization impinges excessively on the environment, here, environmental forces illegitimately impinge on the organization, destroying its autonomy.

UNIVERSALISM–PARTICULARISM

Blau has proposed an operational definition of universalism–particularism as a characteristic of the structure of role relations in a collectivity. He starts by rephrasing Parsons' original definition:

The specific criterion of differentiation (between particularistic and universalistic orientations), therefore, is whether the standards reflected in people's orientation to one another are or are not independent of the *relationship between the status at-*

tributes of the actors and those of the objects of their orientations.... [1962, p. 161] (italics in original).

This definition is over-strict, in our opinion, since it implies that particularism could be present only if, say, a black official gave special treatment to a black client because they were of the same race. It is enough to find that persons of certain characteristics disproportionately receive more favorable treatment, *regardless* of whether the official handling the case has the same characteristics, to conclude that particularism is in evidence, though we may not be able to explain the *reason* for the particularism.

Particularistic deviations from bureaucratic rules may take two courses, which we shall speak of as *positive* and *negative* particularism, respectively. Either officials may discriminate *against* certain clients, or *for* them. Denying clients the right to goods or services to which they have a legitimate claim, usually called, simply, "discrimination," will be called here *negative particularism*. Discrimination against blacks in the United States is the most salient contemporary example. In contrast, there is *positive particularism* where certain clients receive favors to which they have no legitimate right. The use of "pull" illustrates the latter type of deviation, as when a man gets his son into college by convincing the dean, who happens to be an old friend, to have the boy accepted. In both cases, deviations occur because officials have been influenced by officially irrelevant characteristics or behavior of their clients. Consequently, both forms of particularism are evidence of debureaucratization. This is a broader view of debureaucratization than that in the paper by Katz and Eisenstadt (1960),* where only the positive variety of particularism in its various manifestations was seen as a sign of debureaucratization.

LATENT SOCIAL IDENTITIES

Wherever we go, we take with us many identities, roles, and statuses. In any given situation, usually one of these is particularly relevant, though any or all of the others may be obvious to others involved in interaction. An old man cannot hide his age, nor a beautiful woman her beauty. More subtle are characteristics of status, which may be reflected in dress or accent, for example. *Whenever these latent social identities become salient in official-client contacts, there is potential for debureaucratization,* either because they may lead to "role impingement," the overlap of one set of role obligations with another, or because officials allow personal prejudices to influence their handling of clients (Katz and Eisenstadt, 1960, pp. 119–120). Thus, an official and client who also happen to be friends find themselves in a situation where the official has an obligation—whether implicit or explicit—to help the client as a *friend* because (implicitly) one friend must help another. Where latent social identities are not obvious, clients may make them so, by consciously exploiting them, as when a VIP makes sure an official knows who he is. The use of pull, or personal influence, by clients may be defined as the calculated manipulation of role impingement in such a way as to activate obligations in the unofficial role relations involved. Actually, officials may be affected by clients' latent social identities with or without conscious efforts on clients' part to manipulate these identities to their advantage.

Design of the Study

SETTING AND SAMPLE

The data for this study are drawn from a content-analysis of letters addressed to the head office of the Israel Customs authorities, in which the primary focus was on analysis of variations in the persuasive appeals which clients of different backgrounds presented in support of their requests (see Danet, 1971). All clients were writing in connection with the import of personal goods, and had had previous personal or written contact with regional offices of the Customs. We analyzed files of 721 different clients, drawn from the years 1962 and 1959. All first and second letters written by clients were included, bringing the total number of letters in the sample to 878.[1]

As a typical commonweal organization in which contacts with clients are mandatory and highly programmed, the Customs is highly representative of organizations where the consequences of bureaucratization (the power differential, the transformation of interpersonal relations) are most in evidence (Blau and Scott, 1962, chap. 2; Thompson, 1962).* Since clients are typically weakest vis-à-vis this type of organization, it is an especially appropriate locus for an evaluation of the equity of their treatment.

TYPES OF DATA COLLECTED

Information was collected on personal attributes of clients, including their ethnic origin, occupation, length of residence in Israel, age, sex, and the sector of the labor force in which they were employed.[2] Two aspects of the response of the Customs to clients' requests were recorded. First, we coded whether the final response to the request was fully positive, partially positive, or negative (a residual category included those cases in which for some reason the final outcome had not been determined when the case was closed). Variations in this variable served as our chief index of universalism or particularism on the part of Customs officials. We also coded the length of time it took Customs officials to complete the handling of a case. Thus, the first of these measures tapped universalism with regard to *substantive aspects* of the client's request, and the second indexed universalistic handling of *procedure*. Another variable which proved important in the analysis was the type of legal difficulty in clients' cases. Seven types of difficulty were identified, and in addition, there was a group of clients who had no difficulty, who met all legal conditions set by the Customs.[3]

Results

THE RESPONSE TO CLIENTS' REQUESTS

The overall distribution of responses. In Table 18–1 we present the dis-

TABLE 18-1

Distribution of Clients by the Response of the Customs Authorities to Their Requests, and Presence or Absence of a Legal Difficulty in Their Case (Total Percentages)

RESPONSE	LEGAL DIFFICULTY		
	NO	YES	
Positive*	33%	29%	= 100%
Negative	1%	37%	(441)

*Fully or partially positive replies.

tribution of clients in total percentages classified by both the presence or absence of a legal difficulty in their case and by the response to their requests.[4] Clients having rights and receiving a fully or partially positive answer constitute 33 percent of the total (27 percent received a fully positive answer, 6 percent a partially positive one). Another 37 percent consist of those having some difficulty and consequently being completely refused. These two groups together constitute 70 percent of the total. Thus, *70 percent of all clients were treated in more or less strict universalistic fashion by Customs officials.*

The second fact worth noting in Table 18-1 is that a negligible 1 percent of all clients (5 cases) were completely turned down, despite having fulfilled all conditions set by the Customs. These may be coding errors on our part. In any case, the numbers are clearly too small for statistical analysis, and we shall conclude that *there is no evidence for overbureaucratization in the Customs' handling of its clients.* Clients are not refused by the Customs when they have a right to the item or dispensation requested.

Third, we asked, what about the 29 percent of the total who received a fully or at least partially positive reply despite the fact that they lacked rights or had some other legal problem? It appears that the Customs is "giving these clients a break"; in other words, officials have exercised discretion in these cases. We shall now check whether discretion has been applied equally among all groups of clients.

"Giving the Underdog a Break"

The influence of latent social identities: the "underdog" effect. In Table 18-2 clients having a legal difficulty are classified by four personal attributes

TABLE 18-2

The Response of the Customs Authorities to Requests of Clients Having a Legal Difficulty by Four Client Attributes and by Seriousness of Legal Difficulty (Percent Fully or Partially Positive Replies)

CLIENT ATTRIBUTES	ALL CLIENTS	SERIOUSNESS OF LEGAL DIFFICULTY*		
		SERIOUS	MODERATE	NOT SERIOUS
Ethnic origin[a]				
European	42%	35%	36%	55%
	(209)	(82)	(72)	(80)
Middle Eastern	54	41	58	82
	(46)	(17)	(78)	(21)
Occupation[b]				
High	36	25	37	53
	(125)	(57)	(51)	(53)
Low	51	45	50	48
	(74)	(29)	(42)	(25)
Employment status[c]				
Employed	37	27	39	53
	(143)	(73)	(62)	(55)
Unemployed	56	71	54	41
	(43)	(14)	(26)	(17)
Sex[d]				
Men	38	31	42	47
	(213)	(88)	(120)	(68)
Women	60	44	53	74
	(80)	(27)	(32)	(43)

*See text footnote 5; the total N's in the three seriousness-of-difficulty categories together are higher than those in the "all" category because second letters of clients were included in the finer analysis to increase the case base. Clients of all subgroups were equally likely to write second letters.

[a]European = born in Europe or the Americas, or natives of Israel whose fathers were European-born; Middle Eastern = born in the Middle East or North Africa or natives whose fathers are from those countries. Moderate, $\chi^2 = 4.6$, 1 df, $p < .05$; serious, not serious, all, n.s.

[b]High = professionals, medium- and high-level administrators; all others = low; all, $\chi^2 = 4.5$, 1 df, $p < .05$; others, n.s.

[c]All, $\chi^2 = 4.8$, 1 df, $p < .05$; serious, $\chi^2 = 10.1$, 1 df, $p < .005$; moderate, not serious, n.s.

[d]All, $\chi^2 = 10.9$, 1 df, $p < .001$; not serious, $\chi^2 = 8.1$, 1 df, $p < .005$; serious, moderate, n.s.

and by the response to their requests. We look first at the left half of the table which explores the relation between client attributes and the response, for *all* clients having a legal difficulty. The results are intriguing. Among clients of Middle Eastern origin, 54 percent received a positive reply, as compared with 42 percent among Europeans. Persons in low-status occupations receive a positive reply in 51 percent of the cases, while only 36 percent of professionals and bureaucrats with some legal problem did so. An even larger gap exists between the employed and the unemployed, and between men and women (37 percent versus 56 prcent, and 38 percent versus 60 percent, respectively).

Persons of Middle Eastern origin, both in the sample and in Israeli society generally, are concentrated in lower socioeconomic brackets than persons of European origin; moreover, persons in low-status occupations generally earn less; persons currently unemployed (at least those seeking work) need a job and a chance to establish themselves; finally, whether women are strictly at a disadvantage or not simply by being women, it seems that Customs officials are influenced by the traditional view of them as the weaker sex. *In short, it looks like the Customs authorities may be "giving the underdog a break."* There seems to be latent positive discrimination in favor of persons who need a boost to establish themselves in Israeli society. Officials seem to give special consideration to extenuating circumstances and special hardship.

Before drawing conclusions, however, we checked whether clients varied in the degree of seriousness of the legal problem in their case. Our hunch was that matching subgroups on seriousness of legal difficulty in clients' cases might cause the "underdog" effect to disappear. The data in the right half of Table 18-2 reveal that in *none* of the four tests does the "underdog" effect disappear when seriousness of legal difficulty is held constant.[5] The groups deemed "underdogs" are less likely to be refused, regardless of the seriousness of the condition missing in the case. In fact, in 10 out of 12 comparisons the underdogs do better (four of these comparisons produce statistically significant differences). Instead of washing away the underdog effect, controlling for seriousness of the difficulty indicates a specification of the effect. The less serious the legal difficulty, the more likely Customs officials are to give women and Middle Easterners a "break."

Further probing of the underdog effect. To probe the underdog effect still further, we sought answers to two questions: (1) Might it be that being unemployed was the key to officials' perception of certain clients as underdogs, and that if we controlled for employment status, the effect would disappear? (2) Are women treated indulgently simply because they are women, or is it because they have any or all of the other three underdog characteristics?

More refined analysis, in which we held constant whether or not the client was employed, revealed that it was mainly *unemployed* persons, of Middle Eastern origin and in occupations of low-earning power who got a break. A quite secondary effect involving only 16 cases was the fact that women of *high* occupational status were the ones getting preferential treatment. Thus, the *true* underdogs were Middle Eastern men in low-status occupations and out of work. Women did not get special treatment just because they were women (though it is not clear why women with professional or administrative careers did get a break).

PROCEDURAL ASPECTS OF TREATMENT OF CLIENTS

Our original expectation was that quick treatment of clients, as indexed by how soon the file was closed, was the desirable, efficient response. But the data forced us to revise this view. Clients having some legal difficulty had to wait longer for the final decision, apparently because officials gave their case extensive consideration. We dichotomized all clients into those receiving their final reply within a month. It turned out that 66 percent of those with no legal difficulty who received a positive reply had their answer within a month; among those with a difficulty who received a negative reply, 43 percent had their files closed within a month. In contrast to both of these groups were the clients who get a break; only 20 percent of them had their final reply within a month. *So getting a break takes time.* In short, we must conclude that *the procedural aspect of clients' cases appears to be fair.* Further analysis to see whether latent identities of clients affected speed of treatment indicated no latent particularism in this aspect of the response.

Summary

This chapter has applied a simple paradigm for the evaluation of an organization's handling of its clients to the context of written communication between clients and officials of the Israel Customs authorities. On the whole, we concluded, the Customs treats its clients universalistically. A high 70 percent of all cases for which there was information were relatively clear-cut—if the client had rights his request was granted, at least in part, and if he did not have rights, he was refused. Roughly a third of all clients in fact got a break, since they did not meet all legal requirements set by the Customs. If the tendency to distribute breaks had been evenly distributed throughout all subgroups in the sample, we would have concluded that the Customs was merely flexible in its response to clients. However, the evidence clearly indicated a tendency to give the underdog a break. Apparently, Customs officials—knowingly or not—deviated from the rules to help Middle Eastern men out of a job establish themselves in Israeli society.

NOTES

1. Since the head office of the Customs normally does not have contacts with the public, it is evident that all letters in the sample were from clients who had encountered a refusal or some difficulty in their dealings with officials at the regional level. Actually, 799 files were analyzed; the sample used in the analysis reported here eliminated clients who had not written themselves, but had only used some go-between, such as a lawyer, to appeal on their behalf. The core of the sample was the first 605 files opened at the head office in 1962 (20 percent of the total for that year), and another 194 were

added from 1959 (12 percent of that year's total). When it became evident that there were no differences in the data between the two years, this distinction was dropped.

2. Where information on certain of these variables was missing from clients' files, we obtained it from the files of the Registry of Residents in the Ministry of the Interior.

3. It is not clear why clients meeting all legal conditions set by the Customs appealed at all to the head office, since they should have had their requests granted at the regional level. It may be that the head office reinterpreted their case to their advantage. The coding of the various types of legal difficulties was done at first by Customs officials, and when the criteria were clear, the job was turned over to our regular coders.

4. Unfortunately, information on the response to clients' requests was missing from the files for 113 clients; and for 203 cases there is no information about the type of legal difficulty involved. Apparently, coders were unable to make a decision based on materials available in clients' files. Thus the number of cases on which Table 18-1 is based is only 441.

5. By correlating the various types of legal difficulty with the Customs' response, we developed an empirical index of how serious the difficulty was. Having no rights was a "serious" difficulty. Legal problems of "moderate" seriousness were: goods not used; goods imported from the wrong country; and goods not for personal use only. Three other difficulties were classed as "mildly" serious: item omitted from Customs declaration; item received after deadline; no driver's license.

REFERENCES

Blau, Peter M. 1962. "Operationalizing a Conceptual Scheme: The Universalism-Particularism Pattern Variable." *American Sociological Review* 27: 159–169.

Danet, Brenda. 1970. "Petitions and Persuasive Appeals: A Content-analysis of Letters to the Israel Customs Authorities." Unpublished Ph.D. thesis, University of Chicago, Department of Sociology.

———— 1971. "The Language of Persuasion in Bureaucracy: 'Modern' and 'Traditional' Appeals to the Israel Customs Authorities." *American Sociological Review*.

———— 1972. "Giving the Underdog a Break: Favoritism or Flexibility?" Submitted for publication.

Eisenstadt, S. N. 1969. "Bureaucracy, Bureaucratization and Debureaucratization." Pp. 304–311 in Amitai Etzioni (ed.), *Complex Organizations: A Sociological Reader.* 2d ed. New York: Holt, Rinehart, and Winston.

Gouldner, Alvin W. 1957–1958. "Cosmopolitans and Locals: Toward an Analysis of Latent Social Roles, I and II." *Administrative Science Quarterly* 2: 281–306, 444–480.

Katz, Elihu, and Brenda Danet. 1966. "Petitions and Persuasive Appeals: A Study of Official-Client Relations." *American Sociological Review* 31: 811–822.

Katz, Elihu, and S. N. Eisenstadt. 1960. "Some Sociological Observations on the Response of Israeli Organizations to New Immigrants." *Administrative Science Quarterly* 5 (1960): 113–133.

Merton, Robert K. 1952. "Bureaucratic Structure and Personality." In Robert K. Merton, Ailsa P. Gray, Barbara Hockey, and Hanan Selvin (eds.), *Reader in Bureaucracy.* Glencoe, Ill.: The Free Press.

Thompson, J. D. 1962. "Organizations and Output Transactions." *American Journal of Sociology* 68: 309–324.

19

James M. Henslin

TRUST AND THE CAB DRIVER

Although trust is a generalized phenomenon in society, i.e., it is found throughout society, and this analyst assumes that trust is one of the fundamental
elements of social interaction, an element without which most interaction as
we know it could not exist and without which the world would be an entirely
different place,[1] it has been subjected to very little scientific investigation or
analysis,[2] but has been part of the "taken-for-granted" aspects of "life-in-
society." In this paper we shall attempt to explicate what trust means for the
cab driver, and, more specifically, what determines whether a cab driver will
accept an individual as a passenger.

Erving Goffman in *The Presentation of Self in Everyday Life*[3] has made
observation about and developed useful concepts concerning the "front" of
performers (the expressive equipment that serves to define the situation for
the observer) that can be utilized as a conceptual framework in analyzing how
a cab driver determines whether an individual can be trusted to become a
passenger or not. Goffman says that there are three standard parts to front: a
general aspect, (a) the *setting* (background items which supply scenery and
props for the performance, e.g., furniture, décor, and physical layout), and
two personal aspects, (b) the *appearance* of the performer (the stimuli that
tell the observer the social statuses of the performer, e.g., clothing); and (c)
the *manner* of the performer (the stimuli that tell the observer the role that
the performer will play on this occasion or how he will play the role, e.g.,
being meek or haughty). Goffman adds that the audience ordinarily expects
a "fit" or coherence between these standard parts of the front.

Actors are continually offering definitions of themselves to audiences. The
audience, by "checking the fit" of the parts of the actor, determines whether
it will accept or reject the offered definition. *Where an actor has offered a
definition of himself and the audience is willing to interact with the actor on*

the basis of that definition, we are saying trust exists. Where the audience, on the other hand, does not accept the definition of the actor and is not willing to interact with the actor on the basis of his proffered definition, the situation is characterized by distrust.

Thus trust is conceptualized for our purposes as consisting of:

a. The proffering of a definition of self by an actor;
b. Such that when the audience perceives fit between the parts of the front of the actor;
c. And accepts this definition as valid;
d. The audience is willing, without coercion, to engage in interaction with the actor;
e. The interaction being based on the accepted definition of the actor, and;
f. The continuance of this interaction being dependent on the continued acceptance of this definition, or the substitution of a different definition that is also satisfactory to the audience.

Trust and Accepting Someone As a Passenger

The major definition that actors offer of themselves that cab drivers are concerned with is that of "passenger." An individual, in trying to hire a cab, is in effect saying to the cab driver, "I am (or more accurately, want to be) a passenger," i.e., I will fulfill the role-obligation of a passenger. In the driver's view, the role obligations of "passenger" include having a destination, willingness to go to a destination for an agreed-upon rate, ability and willingness to pay the fare, and not robbing or harming the cab driver. If a cab driver accepts someone as a passenger, i.e., is interacting with him on the basis of this definition, it means, according to our conceptualization of trust, that trust is present. How does the cab driver know whether he can accept someone's definition of himself as a passenger and interact with him on the basis of that definition, i.e., how does he know whether he can trust him? This is the major concern of this paper and in the rest of the paper we shall explicate as specifically as we possibly can exactly what enters into such a decision for the cab driver.

In most situations, cab drivers will accept a potential passenger as a passenger, i.e., will accept an actor's definition of himself as belonging to the category "passenger," and they almost without exception will do so when they are dispatched to an order. However, under some circumstances, especially "flag loads," the cab driver will sometimes not allow the potential passenger to become his passenger, and will refuse to allow him to ride in his cab. How does the cab driver differentiate between those he allows to become his passengers and those he does not? Difficulties that arise in answering this problem are: a given man will be refused as a passenger by one cab driver but be accepted by another, and the same man will be refused by a cab driver under one set of circumstances but be accepted by this same cab driver under another set of circumstances. In other words, the difficulty seems to be that there is nothing constant, in either the passenger or the circumstances that would offer a solution. If this is so, how can we solve the problem?

The solution lies not in looking for constants in the passenger or in the situation that are invariant in leading to trust or distrust, but rather, in taking the view of the audience, the one who is doing the trusting or distrusting, which in this case means to take the driver's perspective, in looking for the way the driver defines the features of the situation or passenger. If we follow this approach, it seems that there are four criteria that serve as the basis for accepting passengers and five for rejecting them. (To better understand what is involved in the criteria for accepting passengers, compare them with the analysis of the criteria for rejecting someone as a passenger.) The potential passenger must meet each of the four criteria successively if he is to be accepted as a passenger, i.e., only if he satisfactorily meets (a) does his meeting (b), (c), or (d) count; he must meet both (a) and (b) for (c) or (d) to count, he must meet (a), (b), and (c) for (d) to count. Cab drivers *will accept* as passengers those who in the driver's view:

a. Desire a destination or service that the driver is both willing and able to provide;
b. Appear as if they are able to provide an exchange for the driver's services that the driver defines as being equal to or more than the service was worth under the circumstances, this exchange not necessarily being monetary;
c. Appear as if they will in fact provide such an exchange; and,
d. Offer to provide an exchange that represents little or no risk to the driver (costs not too high).[4]

Thus, if the driver thinks that the potential passenger meets these criteria, the result will be trust on the part of the driver, i.e., he will view the individual as wanting to "really" be a passenger, and will be willing to interact with him on that basis. This means that, because he has accepted as valid the individual's definition of himself as belonging to the category "passenger," that he will accept him as a passenger and will trust that he will meet a passenger's obligations (i.e., will play the role of a passenger in an acceptable fashion), especially paying his fare, and not robbing or harming the driver. Failure to meet criteria (b) and (c) will lead the driver to distrust the individual and to refuse to allow him to become a passenger. (Failure to meet criterion (a) will lead the driver to refuse the individual but probably not to distrust him.)

If this analysis is valid, we should expect that drivers will not accept as passengers those who, in the driver's view:

a. Want a service or destination that the driver is unwilling or unable to deliver, e.g., a prostitute, or a destination that is too far, or in the wrong part of town for the time of day;

b. Appear to be unable to give what the driver would call a "fair exchange" for the service or trip, this being insufficient money, insufficient sexual attractability, or insufficiency in some other area that the driver would otherwise accept as "exchange," e.g., friendship or favors; or

c. Have the "exchange" but are unwilling to part with it, e.g., "Bucket loads;"[5] or

d. Meet the criteria of (a), (b), and (c), but whose exchange represents too much risk for the driver, e.g., "getting caught" concerning a sexual exchange; or

e Appear not to be wanting to "really" be passengers, i.e., they do not want to be taken to a destination for an exchange but want to get in the cab for a purpose that is unacceptable to the driver. In this latter case would be included those whom the driver thinks might be planning on robbing him or would be more likely to do so, and also those who want to use the cab or the cab driver for personal purposes that are unacceptable to the driver, e.g., the homosexual who wants the driver as his sexual partner.

On what basis does the cab driver decide that a potential passenger satisfactorily meets the positive criteria? Why does he trust that someone's definition of himself as a "real" passenger is legitimate or valid, i.e., if the cab driver is actually utilizing these criteria in determining whether an individual who says he wants to "be a passenger" is acceptable as a passenger, as we are here positing, what underlies this decision on the part of the driver? It is here, in analyzing how the cab driver "validates" a potential passenger's claim to membership in the category "passenger" that Goffman's conceptual tools prove useful.

Because the cab driver's work takes him throughout the city and forces him to interact with people of all social statuses, he is constantly exposed to many different fronts. Because of this exposure, he becomes extremely sensitive to the meaning of front and to any misfit between the parts. This sensitivity is also developed because part of his livelihood depends on it, e.g., being able to "size up" a potential customer and his ability to pay for the destination he has ordered,[6] and even his life can depend on sensitivity to fit and misfit, e.g., being able to pick up interactional cues by a potential or actual passenger in order to avoid being robbed or murdered, i.e., becoming aware of a misfit between appearance and manner.

The following ordinary example can illustrate how a lack of coherence between the three parts of the front of the potential passenger results in distrust by the cab driver.

I had let off a passenger in the middle of the block in a business district and was writing down information on this fare when a poorly dressed crippled man on crutches walked up to the cab and said:

P: You busy?
D: No.
P: Can you give me a ride?
D: Yeah, where you going?
P: Kingsland and Lotus in Wellston.
D: Kingsland and Lotus?
P: Yeah.

D: You know what it usually runs?
P: A dollar and a quarter.
D: Yeah, that's about right.

This is a fairly typical conversation except for the question by the driver, "You know what it usually runs?" This is a question that ordinarily would not be asked, but is here being asked because the driver did not trust the man who approached the cab, who was attempting to define himself as a passenger to the driver. The driver distrusts accepting this definition because the expected fit between the parts of the front is lacking. The *setting* in which the cab driver will ordinarily accept someone's definition that he is or wants to become a passenger is when the cab driver is parked at a cab stand waiting for passengers, is dispatched to an order, or is cruising about the streets looking for passengers. In this case, however, the cab driver was sitting in a cab parked in the middle of the block taking care of some personal business, and since this setting was one in which he wouldn't ordinarily expect to be approached by a passenger, he was hesitant to accept the proffered definition. In addition, the *appearance* of the performer did not fit that expected by the driver of a passenger, i.e., the driver ordinarily expects that a passenger will "look like" he can afford to pay for the trip or at least that he has the money to do so, but this passenger looked as if he couldn't afford to ride in a cab. Finally, the expected coherence between *manner* and the proffered definition of the performer as a passenger was lacking, i.e., his first question, "You busy?" was acceptable, but his second, "Can you give me a ride?" was not. It was a question, that in conjunction with the setting and appearance, made the driver think that the performer was perhaps asking for a free ride. In addition, the man did not "look like" he was wanting a cab. He was just walking down the street, and when he saw the cab, he stopped. If he had been standing on the corner attempting to "flag" a cab, the setting would have fit the definition of himself as a passenger and would have "overridden" his appearance, i.e., would have "communicated more" to the driver than his appearance such that the driver would have been willing to accept this man's definition; and his question would then also have fit the rest of his front.

Accordingly, since there was this lack of coherence between setting, appearance, and manner with the definition of himself which he wished the driver to accept, the driver did not trust that this man was a passenger, i.e., could afford to pay for a trip, and he asked, "You know what it usually runs?" in order to find out whether this man intended to and was willing to state that he could afford to pay for the trip. Only when he had received an answer that was satisfactory to the driver, the man giving an amount that both seemed reasonable and that also communicated his intention to pay for the service, did the driver accept this actor's definition of himself and "let him become a passenger" by allowing him to enter the cab and then "treating him as a passenger" by "throwing the meter" and starting to drive toward his destination. Only then was there a trust-relationship developed such that the driver could accept this man as a passenger and take him to his destination.

342

Thus, when someone defines himself as a passenger, and there is fit between the parts of his front, the cab driver accepts this as evidence that the individual satisfactorily meets the four criteria, and he trusts him enough to let him become a passenger. When, however, in the driver's view, this fit is lacking, he takes this as evidence that the person has not met the criteria, and he refuses to allow him to become a passenger.

Thus, a lack of fit between the parts of the front and the proffered definition of the performer can lead to distrust. In the above case, there was no reason to distrust the man because of the parts of this front per se. It was only when these parts of the front did not fit the acceptable definition of the performer that distrust resulted. Thus if this man had continued walking down the street, the driver would have had no reason to distrust him. But when he tried to define himself as a passenger, the lack of fit was such that distrust resulted.

Ordinarily the cab driver accepts as passengers those to whom he has been dispatched. This is because in the vast majority of dispatched orders there is a fit between the parts of the front of the potential passenger, i.e., he is where the dispatcher said he would be, and to the driver he appears to meet the four criteria listed above. This is especially the case when the driver is to pick up a passenger from a middle- or upper-class residential area during daylight hours and becomes progressively less so as the time becomes later or the neighborhood becomes more lower-class or more Negro, especially when these last three variables are combined.

From his past experiences the driver assumes that he is safer as the neighborhood becomes better. He seems to assume greater "trackability," and a corresponding greater responsibility or trustworthiness, on the part of the caller for a cab in such neighborhoods. This is especially the case when the passenger emerges from the residence to which the driver has been dispatched. The driver assumes that there is a connection between such a caller and his point of departure, i.e., responsible people whom one can trust to be "good passengers," live in homes like these, and if this caller lives there, he is that kind of person; and if he doesn't live there, he must be "known" by those who do live there since he presumably made the call from the location from which he is now emerging. It is, therefore, unlikely that this individual would be anything other than a "good passenger" because he can be "traced back" to his point of origin and his association with the residence or with the people who live in that residence, i.e., great "trackability" exists here. Those who possess the greatest amount of trackability, and in whom the drivers place the greatest trust, are "regular riders," those who routinely use cabs in their activities and who consequently become "known" to the drivers. (In many of these cases the interaction between cab drivers and regular riders moves into the personal sphere.[7])

However, this is not the case when the driver is dispatched to a potential passenger in a neighborhood where, in the driver's view, less responsible types of people live, people who are not as financially established, who do not own their own homes, people whose trackability is less. Thus, in the driver's view, the origin of his passenger is highly important in determining trust. As the neighborhood becomes poorer or "blacker," i.e., the proportion of Negroes increases, the driver views this as an indication of correspondingly less responsibility and trackability on the part of potential passengers. Accordingly, he trusts persons from these origins less, and the likelihood increases that he will reject them as passengers.

The same is true with time of day. The driver feels that daylight provides greater trackability. He is able to "get a better look at" the passenger which would serve for easier identification if it were necessary. In the daylight he is also able to observe much more about his passenger than at night which means that he can become more aware of any discrepancies or lack of fit between the parts of the front of the passenger, especially his appearance and manner. Where these parts of the front become hard to observe in darkness, they are the easier observed during daylight. Thus, in a given lower-class neighborhood, even a lower-class Negro neighborhood, the cab driver can "look over good" any potential passenger, whether the passenger has phoned for a cab or is trying to flag down the driver. This means that he is able to observe quickly and well any discrepancies between the parts of his front and, especially in the case of a flag load, determine quickly whether to stop or not. When it is night the driver is not as easily able to observe such discrepancies, and with the lateness of the hour he becomes progressively less likely to stop for passengers in such areas.

This works out in practice the following way. There are certain neighborhoods in which a driver will always enter, at any time of the night or day, for a dispatched order to a residence. These are the upper- and middle-class neighborhoods of the city. He is, however, less likely to accept a passenger who is calling from a phone booth in this area because the trackability becomes much less, because the connection between the caller and the residents of that neighborhood becomes more tenuous, i.e., it could be anyone calling from a public phone booth, including, and probably more likely, someone who doesn't "belong there."

There are other neighborhoods which drivers will both enter during the day for a dispatched order and will stop for a flag load, but to which they will go at night only for dispatched orders. It is assumed by the drivers that one can trust people in this neighborhood who call at night from their apartment for a cab, but that one cannot trust anyone flagging a cab here at night. In this type of neighborhood, novice drivers are frequently exhorted by veteran drivers to be very careful that they observe that their passenger is actually coming from the house to which they were dispatched and not from an area by the house, e.g., from between houses or by or on the porch, and if the house has a light on inside, so much the better. (If it doesn't have a light on inside it becomes difficult to tell whether the person is coming from inside the house or not. If a light is on inside, the driver can see the individual emerge from the house when he opens the door.)

Finally, there are other neighborhoods which drivers will enter for a dispatched order during the day, and perhaps reluctantly stop for flag loads during the day, but which they will not enter at night to pick up any passengers, dispatched or otherwise. This is primarily the hard-core ghetto of St. Louis. (What demand there is for cabs from this area is serviced primarily by the Negro cab firms of St. Louis. Perhaps this is partially because the inhabitants have learned that Metro and other primarily "white" companies will ordinarily not enter the area at night.)

Along with the variables of time and type of neighborhood in determining the acceptance of one's definition of himself as a passenger is also the variable of sex. A driver, under almost all circumstances, will exhibit greater trust for a female passenger than for a male passenger.[8] The following comment by a driver illustrates this trust of the female:

I was driving down Union and Delmar about two o'clock this morning, and this woman hollered "Taxi." I wouldn't have stopped at that time in the morning, but I saw it was a woman, so I stopped for her. At least I thought it was a woman. And she gets into the cab, and she turns out to be a guy all dressed up like a woman.

Aside from the humor present in this case of deviance, the driver furnishes us with a good illustration of the differential trust cab drivers have of the female. Union and Delmar is on the fringe of the ghetto, and drivers would ordinarily stop for flag loads during the day, but would not at this time of night. This driver, however, typically stops for a woman in this area at a time when, according to his own statement, he would not think of stopping for a male who was trying to flag him down.

A variable that is similar to sex that also goes into the determinants of trust is that of age. If a passenger is quite aged, the driver will have greater trust for him. I was unaware of the influence of this variable until the following took place:

About midnight I was dispatched to an apartment building where I picked up two men who appeared to be in their seventies or eighties. As we drove along I started to count the money that was in my pocket. Ordinarily every time I accumulated five dollars over enough to make change for a ten I would put the excess away to make certain that it would be safe in case of robbery. I thought to myself, "I should put this away," but then I thought, "No, these guys aren't going to rob me." It was at this point that I realized that I felt safe from robbery because of their ages.

One does not ordinarily think of a robber as being an old man. These men were not too "spry." They walked with the aid of canes and didn't look as if they were physically able to rob me.[9]

The same applies at the other end of the age continuum: children would be more trusted by drivers than adults. They too, at least the very young children, are physically incapable of carrying out a robbery or of harming the driver, and, as they became older, until they reach a certain age or size, they could do so only with difficulty.

A variable that operates in a similar fashion is the degree of sobriety of the passenger. This variable does not operate by itself, however. It operates much as a "potentiator."[10] The passenger's degree of sobriety takes on meaning for the driver only in conjunction with other variables. Thus sobriety allows the other variables to retain their meaning, but different levels of intoxication intensify the meaning of the other variables. The level of intoxication that is described as "He is high" makes those who in the driver's view meet the criteria of a passenger even more trusted. They are more likely to increase their tips and/or to be amenable to the driver's suggestions. At the same time, this level of intoxication makes those who do not meet the criteria of a passenger even less trusted. The driver views them, when they have been drinking, as being more likely than ever before to "try something funny." When intoxication is greater than "high," and one could be called "drunk," the driver has less trust of both those who meet the criteria of a good passenger and those who fail to meet the criteria. This is because of a basic unpredictability of a drunk, or as the drivers say, "Ya don't know what a drunk is gonna do." However, when intoxication is beyond a certain point and the passenger has little control over his actions (is close to being "dead drunk" or "passed out"), trust again increases. These persons become defined by the driver as those who are unable to carry out evil intentions even if they wanted to. The person inebriated to this degree, of course, easily becomes prey for the cab driver.

The secondary location, the destination to which the passenger is going, is another variable determining trust for the cab driver. In the driver's view, the passenger's destination is frequently considered to be part of the passenger himself.[11] Thus, if the driver picks up a passenger in an area that is acceptable and the passenger is going to an area that he distrusts, his distrust of the area can be transferred to the passenger whom he otherwise trusted. That is, if this same passenger were going to a location that the driver trusted, the driver would not give a second thought about this passenger, but if everything else is the same except that the passenger wants to go to an area that the driver doesn't trust, the driver will now begin to wonder about the trustworthiness of his passenger, and will begin to question the correctness of his original decision to trust this individual as a passenger. He will wonder why this passenger is going into that area, an area which the driver himself doesn't like to enter.[12] Usually the reason will become apparent, sometimes the driver eliciting the information, either directly or indirectly, and sometimes the passenger, aware of the driver's concerns, volunteering the information. Usual reasons for this discrepancy involve such things as one's place of residence versus one's place of work, e.g., a Negro domestic returning by cab to the ghetto, or continuing relationships with friends and relatives who have been unable to move out of the ghetto, or "slumming," persons who are out for "kicks" that they can't receive in their usual "haunts."

Other ways that the passenger's given destination can communicate distrust to the driver include the driver's perception of the destination as a nonlocation, i.e., one in which there is no "match" between the location given and a corresponding location in physical reality, e.g., a street address is given, and the driver is aware that the street doesn't run as far as the number indicates. In this case, too, he will seek an explanation for the discrepancy, and many times a plausible explanation exists, e.g., the person has read the number incorrectly. If a plausible explanation is not readily available, or if the individual is one for whom low trust exists, this "fiction" will lead to distrust.

If no specific destination is given, this, too, can lead to distrust. A passenger telling a driver to "just drive around" is suspect unless there is a satisfactory explanation for this unusual type of destination, e.g., a tourist who wants to see various parts of the city, a woman who wants to be driven around the park because it is a beautiful day. Where the explanation is not available, the driver is likely to suspect that the passenger might be setting him up for a robbery.

The secondary location can communicate distrust or questions on the part of the cab driver that must in some way be answered, as above, or it can also communicate trust. A passenger who gives as his destination a "good" part of town, or an area that the driver already trusts, is less likely to be under the driver's suspicion than in the above case. In some instances, the secondary location can even mitigate distrust which has developed for other reasons. For example,

It was about one A.M. I had taken a practical nurse home after her work shift and ended up in part of the ghetto. Since I was next to a stand, I decided to park there. As I was pulling into the space, I saw a man standing at the bus stop which was next to the stand, with his arm held out horizontally and wagging his finger a bit. He was a large Negro male wearing a dark blue overcoat. He opened the back door of the cab, and my first thought was, "Well, here goes! I'm going to be robbed. I'd better turn on the tape recorder and get this on tape!" After he got in the cab, he said, "I want to go to Richmond Heights. You know where Richmond Heights is?"

Although there was originally a high level of distrust of this passenger, when he gave his destination I was much assured. My perception at that time of the Negro community of Richmond Heights was that of a small community of Negroes in the midst of middle-class whites, a Negro community that was "solid," composed of Negro professional and working people. His destination was "paired" with him, and I figured that if he was going to where this class of Negro lives, I did not have to worry about being robbed.

There are many variables that affect trust that are not as easily analyzable as the above variables. Many of these are subtle interactional cues that communicate much to the driver but which are difficult to explicate. Such a variable is the "sitting behavior" of the passenger, i.e., how the passenger sits. It is possible for the passenger to sit in such a way that he communicates "evil intention" to the driver, i.e., this part of his manner doesn't fit the rest of his front or his definition of himself as a trustworthy passenger. In the above case, for example,

After I was reassured about this passenger because of his destination, I noticed in the mirror that he was sitting in a slumped-over position in the extreme right-hand side of the back seat. It seemed that he could be sitting this way in order to hide his face from me. I decided to turn around and get a good look at him. I turned around and made some innocuous comment about directions, and as I did so I noticed that he was sleeping. When he heard my question his eyes popped open, and he began to respond. It was then obvious that he was just starting to go to sleep. I was again reassured.

Another type of sitting behavior that lessens a driver's trust of his passenger concerns single passengers. A single passenger will almost invariably sit on the right-hand side of the back seat (the side diagonal from the driver), or, at times, in the front seat opposite the driver. The driver views either of these positions as being appropriate for his passenger. Occasionally, however, a passenger will sit directly behind the driver in the back seat. This ordinarily makes the driver somewhat uncomfortable and somewhat wary of the passenger. He begins to wonder why the passenger is sitting there. Interaction between the driver and passenger is more difficult in this position, and it is more difficult for the cab driver to "keep tabs" on what his passenger is doing. One reason for this sitting behavior that strikes the cab driver is that the passenger might be sitting in such a position in order to cut his visibliity (unable to be easily seen through the rear view mirror or when the driver turns around while he is driving) and thus his trackability through identification. The passenger's sitting behavior is important for the driver because it makes certain activities possible. Thus, in this case, the driver feels uncomfortable because this is one way he could be set up for a robbery. Consequently, he attempts to determine if this is the reason or not, and in so doing he searches for other logical reasons that might explain his passenger's sitting behavior. A reason that is acceptable is that the passenger is trying to view something on the street (e.g., particular buildings, scenery) that can be best viewed from that side of the cab. Another reason that helps explain the behavior, but is less acceptable, is that the passenger climbed into the cab from that side instead of the usual side, frequently the case with flag loads or when the driver has pulled up on the wrong side of the street for a dispatched order. This reason is less acceptable, however, because most passengers when they enter the cab from the "wrong" side slide across the seat to the usual position. The driver must still account for the passenger's failure to move to this position. One such satisfactory account is that the passenger is going on an extremely short trip. Another is that the passenger wishes to minimize the communication opportunities for personal reasons, e.g., he just doesn't feel like talking to anyone.

Very similar to "sitting behavior" would be all the subtle interactional cues which members of society learn and come to associate with "intention" of an actor, cues that give direction for appropriate response, whether these cues communicate happiness, anger, trust, unfamiliarity, distrust, or whatever. Cab drivers, as individuals who have been socialized into both "general" society (i.e., they have learned the applicable general cultural traits such as gestures), and into a particular subculture (i.e., they have learned all the nuances of a particular occupational group's speech, gestures, etc.), possess, along with other members of society, standardized ways of interpreting the interaction in which they are involved or which they witness. This would range from the "look" of somebody, e.g., "sneaky, slitty eyes," to body posture and beyond. Cab drivers, then in stereotypical ways, interpret and react to others on the basis of symbols into which they have been socialized. These include those that apply to trust. It is obvious that there are any number of such cues, gestures, or symbols that lead to trust or distrust. Most of these are beyond the scope of this analysis except to state the obvious, that when those appear to which the driver has the "feeling of distrust attached," he will distrust the bearer of the communication, the passenger in this case.

An example of something to which the meaning of distrust has become attached is the sound of one's voice. This was the manifest variable leading to distrust in the following case:

DISPATCHER: Twenty third and Choteau ((   )) . . .
DRIVER: ((   ))
DISPATCHER: It's fine if you can't. Don't take any chances . . .
DRIVER: ((   ))
DISPATCHER: I don't like the order myself. *I don't like the sound of the man's voice* . . .

This order was given at 1:10 A.M., and the dispatcher himself was answering incoming calls. According to his statement, there was something about the caller's voice that made the dispatcher reluctant to dispatch a cab. But what was it about the caller's voice that led to this reaction? It is this type of variable, although it is both interesting and important in determining trust, to which our data unfortunately do not lend themselves for analysis.

As the dispatcher has a vital role in the communication process of dispatching drivers to passengers, so the dispatcher can play a crucial role in determining whether a driver will trust a potential passenger to become an actual passenger or not. For example, there are times when the dispatcher alerts the driver to his own distrust of the passenger, as in the above case. The above recorded conversation concluded with:

DISPATCHER: No. It is not a Missouri Boiler order! It is not a Missouri Boiler order! It's a terminal railroad man on Twenty third and Choteau, on twenty third street north of Choteau . . .
DRIVER: ((   ))
DISPATCHER: Let me know if you get the man or if you do not get him . . .

The driver, who wants and needs the order at this slack period of his shift, tries to tie the order in with the "known and trusted." That is, workers getting off the swing shift at Missouri Boiler sometimes take cabs, and they can be trusted. Perhaps this is such an order. But the dispatcher, showing his impatience with the driver's lack of knowledge that the address he gave is not that of Missouri Boiler, tells him that it is not that kind of order and that the man should be carefully approached if the driver is going to take the order.

Trust and the Cab Driver

The dispatcher then does an unusual thing, he makes the dispatched order optional at the discretion of the driver. Ordinarily a dispatched order becomes a "sacred thing" to the driver. It is the opposite of optional. It is a responsibility for which the driver assumes completion and for which he can be fired if he fails to complete. Yet here the dispatcher openly announces that this order is optional. The caller, because of some unrevealed aspect of his voice, is not trusted. In the view of the cab driver and of the dispatcher, the cab driver does not need to accept the responsibility for completing an order when the passenger cannot be trusted.[13]

The dispatcher when he is able, offers assurance to drivers when they do not have enough cues to know whether they can trust a passenger or not. The following illustrates how trust can develop such that the dispatcher is able to assure the driver that he can trust the potential passenger:

DISPATCHER: You have to go in the rear to the court to get in there, Driver. We had that last night, so it's alright. . . .

The dispatcher is assuring the driver that the order is acceptable, that the people will be waiting, i.e., that it won't be a no-go, and that the people waiting are acceptable as passengers, i.e., although the driver must drive where he is reluctant to go, in the back where it is perhaps dark, that it is all right to do so, that this is not a set-up for a robbery. How can the dispatcher give such assurance? As he states, they had an order out of there the night before, and it turned out to be an acceptable passenger. In this case, the setting, "in the rear of the court at night," did not fit the driver's estimation of acceptability for trusting someone to become a passenger, "in the rear of the court at night," but because the dispatcher has had a previous rewarding experience with this lack of fit he knows that it is all right and is able to so assure the driver.

The passenger whom I had who best incorporates most of the above variables of distrust within a single case and who illustrates a couple of variables which have not been explicated was the following:

About 2:00 A.M. I was dispatched to just within the ghetto, to a hotel which also serves as a house of prostitution. My passenger turned out to be an elderly male Negro, quite drunk, who chose to sit in the front seat. He ordered me to take him to East St. Louis and said, "We're going to a rough neighborhood. Lock your doors. Roll up your windows."

The passenger then began talking to himself. As he did so I thought he was talking to me, and I said, "What did you say?" He looked up and said, "None of your business!" He then continued talking to himself. As we passed the Atlas Hotel in 4200 block of Delmar, he made the comment that he should have stopped there and seen someone, but that since we had already passed it I should go on. I said, "No, that's all right. I'll take you there," and I drove around the block to the hotel. He got out and was about to leave when I said, "I'll wait for you, but you'll have to pay what's on the meter." He became rather angry, gave some money, and then urinated against the side of the cab. I drove on without him.

This man was distrusted because he was a stranger, a male, a Negro, at night, had been drinking, was coming from the edge of the ghetto, going to a ghetto area, which area was "unknown" to the driver, and acted irrationally by speaking aloud to himself.

The driver has less trust for someone who acts irrationally just as most members of society would have less trust for someone who exhibited this type of behavior, i.e., because the individual is irrational, predictability of his behavior decreases. And to trust someone means that one can predict his behavior on the basis of acceptance of his identity. This is what cannot be done with someone who is irrational, i.e., who does not act as we have learned that "ordinary" persons will act.

The driver has less trust for an area that he does not "know," i.e., an area in which he lacks previous experience with its "layout" and thus in which he cannot easily maneuver his cab and plan and carry out routes, because "control" in such situations passes from the driver to the passenger who possesses such knowledge. To enter an interaction with someone with greater control over the situation requires trust that the other individual will not use this control to his advantage and your disadvantage, in this case such things as robbery or not paying the fare.

The variables leading to greater or lesser trust on the part of the cab driver, and his corresponding willingness to allow someone to become his passenger are summarized in Table 19-1.

Summary and Conclusion

The purpose of this chapter has been to examine a very common, ordinary, everyday variable, a fundamental element of social interaction, that of trust. The specific framework that has been utilized in this examination and analysis has been that of the world of the cab driver, the specific setting being that of cab driver-passenger interaction. A conceptualization and definition of trust was formulated. This conceptualization was then examined by asking and answering the basic question, "What leads to trust or distrust for the cab driver such that he will accept or reject an individual as a passenger?" Various variables going into the make-up of trust for the cab driver were then specified as they had been observed when the author drove a cab. The major variables include the type of order, the time, the characteristics of the location type, the characteristics of the passenger, the behavior of the passenger, and the behavior of the dispatcher. These variables were seen to be correlated with positive or negative experiences which lead to the formation of stereotypes held by the cab driver which, in turn, when examined for "fit" with a proffered definition, lead to trust or distrust.

TABLE 19-1

The Variables Which, in the Cab Driver's View, Lead To Greater or Lesser Trust of One Who Wants To Be (or Has Become) a Passenger

CHARACTERISTICS OF LOCATION

TRUST	TYPE OF ORDER	TIME	MATCH WITH PHYSICAL REALITY	SOCIAL CLASS	RACIAL MAKE-UP	DRIVER'S KNOWLEDGE OF	ILLUMINATION AND HABITATION
HI	Dispatched order (caller)	Day	Matches (a location)	(a) Upper class (b) Middle class	White	Known to driver	Light, inhabited area
LO	Flag load	Night	Doesn't match (a non-location)	Lower class (poverty area)	Negro (ghetto area)	Strange to driver	Dark, deserted area

CHARACTERISTICS OF PASSENGER / BEHAVIOR OF PASSENGER

TRUST	SOCIAL CLASS	RACE	SEX	AGE	SOBRIETY	EMERGENT BEHAVIOR	SITTING BEHAVIOR WHERE	SITTING BEHAVIOR HOW	RATIONALITY OF BEHAVIOR
HI	(a) Upper class (b) Middle class	White	Female	(a) Very old (b) Very young	(a) Sober (b) "High" (c) Very drunk	Seen to emerge from primary location	(a) In rear, diagonal from driver (b) In front	"Open sitting"	Acts rationally
LO	Lower class (poverty)	Negro	Male	Ages between above	(a) Sober (b) "High" (c) Drunk	Not seen to emerge from primary location	In rear, behind driver	Sitting that seems to conceal passenger	Acts irrationally

PREVIOUS EXPERIENCE WITH A GIVEN VARIABLE / DISPATCHER / SUMMARY OF THE VARIABLES OF THIS TABLE

TRUST	PREVIOUS EXPERIENCE WITH A GIVEN VARIABLE	DISPATCHER	SUMMARY OF THE VARIABLES OF THIS TABLE
HI	Positive experience: "Known that can be trusted"	(a) Dispatches order without comment (b) Offers assurance	Matches any stereotype the driver has of a trusted category
LO	(a) Negative experience: "Known that cannot be trusted" (b) No experience: "Not known whether can be trusted"	Dispatches order with a warning	Matches any stereotype the driver has of a distrusted category

NOTES

1. This is essentially the point made by Isaacs, Alexander, and Haggard (1963), whose definition, with Garfinkel's, comes closest to my own, when they state ". . . trust is one of the important determinants of the subjective world" (p. 468) and ". . . trust forms such an important part of the basis of the current social structure that without trust and trustworthiness we could not have our form of society," (p. 462), and that trust "determines the overall basis for both degree and quality of perceptions of, and orientations to, the world" (p. 461).

2. The major exceptions are in the field of psychology; and this only recently, primarily in the last decade and a half. The few attempts at studying this phenomenon (either direct studies of or passing references to) include those by Brehm and Lipscher (1959), Deutsch (1954, 1958, 1960, 1962), Evans (1964), Farr (1967), Garfinkel (1963), Harford (1965), Hughes and Hughes (1952), Isaacs, Alexander, and Haggard (1963), Kamm (1960), Kelley and Ring (1961), Lawton (1964), Loomis (1958, 1959), Mullinger (1956), Murdock (1966), O'Donovan (1965), Read (1962), Rekosh and Feigenbaum (1966), Sandler (1966), Secord and Backman (1964), Solomon (1957, 1960), and Wrightsman (1966).

In these studies there is no agreement as to what trust actually is, or of what it consists. Consequently, trust has been conceptualized and defined in the literature in a number of differing ways. These include viewing trust as the willingness to wait for a preferred reward under various circumstances (Lawton, 1964); as cooperation (Wrightsman, 1966); as the expectation of the occurrence of an event where this expectation leads to behavior which the individual perceives to have positive motivational consequences if the expectation is confirmed and negative motivational consequences if it is not (Deutsch, 1954, 1960, 1962; Solomon, 1957; Loomis, 1958); as an affective attitude primarily directed outward, involving a sense of comfort, confidence, and reliance that certain acts and behavior will or will not occur (Isaacs, Alexander, and Haggard, 1963), as free and confidential communication (Hughes and Hughes, 1952), as a feeling—not further defined (Secord and Backman, 1964); and as taking for granted the constitutive expectancies or the basic rules of the game (Garfinkel, 1963).

One can readily see the lack of agreement that currently exists among social scientists on defining the concept of trust. Accordingly, a definition of trust develops in this chapter, a definition that will of necessity not include all previous uses of the term, but a definition that, we hope, is useful in analyzing certain behaviors of the cab driver.

3. Goffman (1959), pp. 22–30.

4. The above analysis is essentially in exchange theory terms. For a simplified, schematic presentation of exchange theory, see Secord and Backman (1964), pp. 253 ff. For a more complete analysis see Blau (1964).

5. A "bucket load" is the cab drivers' term for a passenger who refuses to pay his fare, generally by leaving the cab "to get some money" and never returning or getting out of the cab while it is stopped at a light and "melting into" the crowd.

6. The cab driver, like other members of society, isn't always correct in his "sizing up" of potential passengers. He, too, is subject to being taken in by con men, by those who convince their audience that they have the "fit" of a trusted category (cf. Goffman, 1959, footnote p. 18). This can be very costly for the driver, as witness the following:

"A Chicago taxicab driver showed up at police headquarters yesterday with a meter reading $368.05 and a passenger with an empty wallet.

Trust and the Cab Driver

"The driver, Andrew Jones, said he picked up his fare at a Chicago hotel about 6 A.M. Sunday and arrived with him in Washington at 8 A. M. yesterday after spending 26 hours and $14 for gasoline en route.

"He said the passenger, a Washington man whom police declined to identify, told him he had friends in Washington who would cash his check. On arrival, he said, the passenger admitted that this was not so.

"Officers at the Hack Inspectors Bureau were trying to determine whether a crime had been committed, and if so, who had jurisdiction." (*St. Louis Post-Dispatch*, March 22, 1966)

7. The above is true for Metro Cab which does not allow "personals," i.e., a passenger who is allowed to phone the company and ask for "his" driver and the company will dispatch that particular driver to "his" passenger, regardless of spatial rules. Where this is allowed, it is obvious that this is one step closer to "maximum trust." Personals would be more common in smaller towns; but they also exist in St. Louis with some of the smaller cab companies.

A specific type of regular rider is the "charge customer," the passenger who has a charge account with Metro, and, instead of paying cash, he fills out and signs a charge slip. Like many other charge accounts in our society, he is billed monthly by the company.

8. This was evidenced by the incredulity and shock Metro drivers expressed when during the Christmas season of 1964 it was learned that a female passenger had robbed a cab driver.

9. I assume that the health of an individual would be another such variable, that is, if an individual were sick or weak the driver would have fewer reservations about accepting him as a passenger. One's perception of health could of course be erroneous. The individual could be faking his illness or even be forced into robbery, due to needs caused by his illness. He could, of course, also be faking his sex (see quote above), his residence, his social class, and his agedness. But we are here speaking of the driver's perceptions as they relate to trust and the acceptance of a passenger, not the accuracy of his perceptions.

10. A potentiate or potentiator is a term used by chemists to refer to a substance that makes the action of the other chemicals more powerful or effective or active. It is different from a catalyst because it is consumed in the reaction. I am indebted to Elliot G. Mishler for this analogy.

11. Since cab drivers have low trust of Negroes, i.e., are reluctant to enter interaction with them on a cab driver-passenger relationship, Negroes, even in good neighborhoods, have a difficult time getting a cab. Godfrey Cambridge writes about this problem in "My Taxi Problem and Ours," *Monocle*, VI No. 1 (Summer, 1964), 48–52, where he corroborates the point above by saying that a reason for this difficulty in New York is that the cab drivers think that the passenger might be wanting to go to Harlem. I am indebted to Marcello Truzzi for bringing this article to my attention.

12. In addition to the ghetto and other low-class "tough neighborhoods," other areas of the city that will elicit distrust, unless there is an adequate "account" given, are areas of the city that are relatively deserted, especially at night, such as a small back street or dead-end street with few or no lights, or a warehouse or riverfront section of town.

13. It is again, of course, irrelevant whether the passenger can, in fact, be trusted. It is the driver's perception of trust that matters.

REFERENCES

Blau, M., *Exchange and Power in Social Life*. New York: John Wiley & Sons, Inc., 1964.

Brehm, Jack W., and David Lipscher, "Communicator-Communicatee Discrepancy and Perceived Communicator Trustworthiness," *Journal of Personality*, XXVII, No. 3 (1959), 352–61.

Deutsch, Morton, "Trust and Cooperation—Some Theoretical Notes." New York: Research Center for Human Relations, New York University, 1954.

———, "Trust and Suspicion," *Journal of Conflict Resolution*, II (1958), 265–79.

———, "Trust, Trustworthiness, and the F Scale," *Journal of Abnormal and Social Psychology*, LXI (1960), 138–40.

———, "Cooperation and Trust: Some Theoretical Notes," in *Nebraska Symposium on Motivation*, ed. M. R. Jones. Lincoln, Neb.: University of Nebraska Press, 1962.

Evans, Gary, "Effect of Unilateral Promise and Values of Rewards upon Cooperation and Trust," *Journal of Abnormal and Social Psychology*, LXIX, No. 5 (1964), 587–90.

Farr, James N., "The Effects of a Disliked Third Person upon the Development of Mutual Trust." Paper read at the American Psychological Association, New York, September 1957.

Garfinkel, Harold, "A Conception of and Experiments with 'Trust' as a Condition of Stable Concerted Actions," in *Motivation and Social Interaction: Cognitive Determinants*, ed. O. J. Harvey. New York: The Ronald Press Company, 1963, pp. 187–238.

Goffman, Erving. *The Presentation of Self in Everyday Life*. Garden City, N.Y.: Doubleday Anchor Books, 1959.

Gouldner, Alvin H., and Helen P. Gouldner, *Modern Sociology: An Introduction to the Study of Human Interaction*. New York: Harcourt, Brace & World, Inc., 1963.

Harford, Thomas C., Jr., *Game Strategies and Interpersonal Trust in Schizophrenics and Normals*. Doctoral dissertation, Boston University Graduate School, 1965.

Hughes, E. C., and Helen M. Hughes, *Where People Meet*. New York: The Free Press, 1952.

Isaacs, Kenneth S., James M. Alexander, and Ernest A. Haggard, "Faith, Trust, and Gullibility," *The International Journal of Psycho-Analysis*, XLIV, No. 4 (1963), 461–69.

Kamm, B. A., "Confidentiality in Psycho-analysis," *Samiksa*, XIV, Nos. 1–4 (1960), 24–27.

Kelley, Harold H., and Kenneth Ring, "Some Effects of 'Suspicious' versus 'Trusting' Training Schedules," *Journal of Abnormal and Social Psychology*, LXIII (1961), 294–301.

Lawton, Marcia Jean, *Trust As Manifested by Delay of Gratification in a Choice Situation*. Doctoral dissertation, Northwestern University, 1963.

Loomis, James L., *Communication and the Development of Trust*. Doctoral dissertation, New York University, 1958.

———, "Communication, the Development of Trust and Cooperative Behavior," *Human Relations*, XII (1959), 305–15.

Mellinger, G. D., "Interpersonal Trust As a Factor in Communication," *Journal of Abnormal and Social Psychology*, LIII (1959), 304–9.

Murdock, Peter H., *The Development of Contractual Norms in the Interdependent Dyad with Power Differentiation*. Doctoral dissertation, University of North Carolina, 1965.

O'Donovan, Dennis, "Detachment and Trust in Psychotherapy," *Psychotherapy: Theory, Research and Practice, II,* No. 4 (1965), 174–76.

Read, William H., "Upward Communications in Industrial Hierarchies," *Human Relations,* XV (1962), 3–15.

Rekosh, Jerold H., and Kenneth D. Feigenbaum, "The Necessity of Mutual Trust for Cooperative Behavior in a Two-Person Game," *Journal of Social Psychology,* LXIX, No. 1 (1966), 149–54.

Sandler, David, *Investigation of a Scale of Therapeutic Effectiveness: Trust and Suspicion in an Experimentally Induced Situation.* Doctoral dissertation, Duke University, 1965.

Secord, Paul F., and Carl W. Backman, *Social Psychology.* New York: McGraw-Hill Book Company, 1964.

Solomon, Leonard, *The Influence of Some Types of Power Relationships on the Development of Trust.* Doctoral dissertation, New York University, 1957.

————, "The Influence of Some Types of Power Relationships and Game Strategies on the Development of Interpersonal Trust," *Journal of Abnormal and Social Psychology,* LXI (1960), 223–39.

Wrightsman, Lawrence S., "Personality and Attitudinal Correlates of Trusting and Trustworthy Behaviors in a Two-Person Game," *Journal of Personality and Social Psychology,* IV, No. 3 (1966), 328–32.

20

Milton S. Davis

VARIATIONS IN PATIENTS' COMPLIANCE WITH DOCTORS' ADVICE: AN EMPIRICAL ANALYSIS OF PATTERNS OF COMMUNICATION

Introduction

This chapter stems from a larger study of the major social, psychological, and physical factors that account for variations in patients' compliance with doctors' orders. The investigation considered (a) the extent of patient non-compliance, and (b) the range and nature of factors that may lead to or help explain these variations. The factors reported in this paper represent a continuation of the analysis of dimensions that characterize doctor-patient interaction.[1]

In principle, the range of factors that may account for variations in patients' compliance is immense. The following set of assumptions, however, guided the larger investigation from which this report stems.

a. Individuals who go to a doctor have in common the fact that something is troubling them, but differ more or less in their *personal characteristics.*
b. In some measure, these personal characteristics are taken into account by the doctor so that variations occur in the nature of *the regimen* prescribed for each patient.
c. After being told their regimens, patients may discuss and assess the doctors' advice with paramedical and other *influential* persons, i.e., relatives, friends, and associates, whose opinions on the matter they value.
d. Such influences interact with the personal characteristics a patient brings to

Milton S. Davis, "Variations in Patients' Compliance with Doctors' Advice: An Empirical Analysis of Patterns of Communication," *American Journal of Public Health* 58 (1968): 274–288. Reprinted by permission.

the situation, the nature of the regimen, and the nature of *the doctor-patient relationship,* to produce *patterns of compliance* with the doctor's orders.

PATTERNS OF COMPLIANCE

To label patients compliant or noncompliant without elaboration is misleading. The medical regimen is ordinarily a composite of recommendations, and a patient may comply with all, some, or none of the advice. Different degrees of compliance also characterize each regimen, and assuming that the patient complies at all, it is clear that he may do so consistently or intermittently through time. A review of the literature demonstrates a range from 15 to 93 percent of patients reportedly noncompliant.[2] This wide range is not surprising when the variety of populations, the various methods of data collection, and the different medical problems investigated are considered. Nevertheless, a pattern emerges when these studies are examined as a whole. Regardless of the differences, at least a third of the patients in most studies failed to comply with doctors' orders.

Patient characteristics. A review of the literature on noncompliance evidences conflicting conclusions regarding what demographic attributes characterize a noncompliant patient. Although many factors have been investigated, they are not dealt with consistently in each study and the results are inconclusive. Therefore, it is only possible to cull some impressions about what patient characteristics influence noncompliant behavior. It seems that females are somewhat more likely to default than males[3]; that older people,[4] patients in lower socioeconomic status groups,[5] and patients with little education[6] are least likely to follow doctors' orders.

One might expect that physical characteristics of patients would affect variations in patient compliance. Most studies, however, focus on a population with a particular diagnosis, and comparative findings are few. Patients with long-term illnesses are reportedly more compliant if they are given careful instruction,[7] and the urgency of an acute illness has been related to compliance.[8]

Studies concerned with psychological characteristics of patients have shown that noncompliant patients can be identified by examining coping mechanisms,[9] dependency,[10] and defensiveness and externalization.[11] One author suggests that fear arousal is necessary for acceptance of medical advice.[12]

Regimen. A suggested medical regimen usually combines prescriptions (behavior to be initiated) and proscriptions (behavior to be prohibited).[13] Most patients, however, choose to comply with two out of three regimens and select those which are the least difficult.[14] Restrictions which necessitate relinquishing personal habits are the most difficult to follow—unlike medications which are the easiest. Compliance with one specific regimen appears to affect adherence with others.[15] However, no relationship was found between follow-through with regimens which require patient self-care and compliance with advice involving the patient in clinic procedures.[16] The former, regimens which require patient judgment, are more closely associated with noncompliance. There is also agreement that the more complex regimens affect increased noncompliance.[17] These findings evidence a need for more explanation and presentation of advice in the least complex manner.

Personal influence. It is possible that influence from family members, friends, and associates may conflict with the medical advice and counteract the doctor's potential authority. But there is also the possibility that these extra-medical influences will reinforce the doctors' recommendations. Family discord is closely associated with noncompliance,[18] while availability of local help and family cohesiveness during crises are associated with increased levels of compliance.[19] The more stable home situation is perhaps associated with positive reinforcement of medical advice.[20] Such positive reinforcement is particularly functional when one considers that the patient is not able to relate to his doctor with the same frequency and intensity as he does with family, friends, and co-workers.

Doctor-patient relationship. Few empirical investigations have dealt with the way in which interaction between patient and doctor influences patient compliance. Those who have studied this factor empirically have been concerned with perceptions of doctors and patients and have not considered objective measurement of the doctor-patient interaction or how this might influence the patient's decision regarding compliance.[21] This may account for incongruent findings. For example, in one report, barriers in doctor-patient communication could not account for patient noncompliance.[22] Another study shows that communication between doctor and patient is less important than the psychological readiness of the patient.[23] However, when doctors fail to clearly convey the significance of a regimen to the patient, there is a reciprocal failure on the part of the patient to comply.[24] Reciprocity seems to affect compliance, whether between a very docile approval-seeking patient and a nurturant doctor, or a psuedo-independent patient and an aloof doctor.[25] While there is not complete agreement on exactly how the doctor-patient relationship affects compliance, most investigations do recognize the importance of communication and explanation.[26]

Hypothesis and Design of the Study

While a full range of factors affecting compliance is recognized and was investigated in the larger study, this chapter is particularly concerned with the ways in which dimensions of doctor-patient interaction relate to patient compliance. It is hypothesized that patterns of communication which deviate from the normative doctor-patient relationship will be associated with patients' failure to comply with the doctors' advice.

359

STUDY GROUP

The study group consists of 154 *new* patients seen by 76 junior physicians (fourth-year medical students) who regularly care for patients in the clinics, and 78 senior (attending) physicians assigned to the general medical clinic of a large general voluntary teaching hospital. A *new* patient had either never been to the general medical clinic before, or had not attended the clinic for at least one year. Patients were excluded from the sample who: (a) had a chief complaint which indicated that they would probably be sent to another clinic after one visit; (b) came regularly to one or more other hospital clinics (although they were considered *new* to the general medical clinic); (c) sought follow-up care of a condition already diagnosed and well known to the patient; or (d) had a language or hearing problem.[27]

Survey data were collected on a random sample of clinic patients prior to this investigation to describe and characterize patient experiences in the general medical clinic. The composition of the present study population compares favorably with the estimated clinic population based on that survey.[28]

DATA COLLECTION AND ANALYSIS

Prior to the initiation of the present study, exploratory data were collected from doctors and patients over successive patient visits to the general medical clinic to evaluate the relative merits of various technics for studying doctor-patient interaction.[29] On the basis of this exploratory work, it was decided that data could most feasibly be collected by a combination of (a) tape recordings, (b) survey methods—including interviews and questionnaires—and (c) a content analysis of patients' medical records.

Tape recording of interaction. A method developed by Robert F. Bales, Interaction Process Analysis, was adapted for this research.[30] With this method, all doctors' and patients' verbal communication is coded into 12 categories of action (see Table 20-1). Scores representing the amount of activity devoted to each of the 12 categories were computed separately for each doctor and patient and transferred onto code sheets from which IBM cards were punched. Data analysis involved correlating an independent measure of patient compliance with four types of data derived from the interaction process analysis. First, the relative volume of participation by doctor and patient was determined; second, communication profiles for doctor and patient were compared; third, by manipulating category scores, indexes of difficulties encountered in the interaction were measured; and fourth, a factor analysis was performed. Although the latter analysis was not in Bales' original formulation, it was employed here to discover what additional dimensions in the doctor-patient relationship might account for variations in patients' compliance. This chapter is primarily concerned with the factor analysis data.

Interaction Process Analysis is an expensive method requiring extensive time for tape recording, transcribing, coding, and analyzing data.[31] Con-

Milton S. Davis

TABLE 20-1

Bales' Categories for Interaction Process Analysis

1. Shows solidarity, raises other's status, gives help, reward.
2. Shows tension release, jokes, laughs, shows satisfaction.
3. Agrees, shows passive acceptance, understands, concurs, complies.
4. Gives suggestion, direction, implying autonomy for others.
5. Gives opinion, evaluation, analysis, expresses feeling, wish.
6. Gives orientation, information, repeats, clarifies, confirms.
7. Asks for orientation, information, repetition, confirmation.
8. Asks for opinion, evaluation, analysis, expression of feeling.
9. Asks for suggestion, direction, possible ways of action.
10. Disagrees, shows passive rejection, formality, withholds help.
11. Shows tension, asks for help, withdraws out of the field.
12. Shows antagonism, deflates other's status, defends or asserts self.

sequently, only two crucial periods of interaction were recorded: first, the doctor's formulation (presentation of medical regimen and diagnosis to the patient) during the primary visit; and second, the entire interaction between doctor and patient at the time of the patient's revisit. The latter was recorded to examine changes in the doctor-patient relationship.

A total of 223 doctor-patient interactions were subsequently coded. Of the 154 doctor-patient pairs in the study group, 80 had both visits taped, 39 had only the first visit, 24 only had the second, and 11 had no tapes at all. Reliability in coding averaged 85 percent, rather good considering the subjective nature of the material.[32]

Survey methods. Personal interviews and a self-administered questionnaire were used to study the perceptions of doctors and patients with reference to their own specific role obligations and the role expectations of the other.

During the exploratory phase of the study, a series of questionnaires and interview schedules was developed and pretested. Data were subsequently collected from the patient study group by means of four interviews: one before the primary visit, one after that visit, and one after the second and third clinic visits. However, because of variations in patients' illnesses, the number of appointments, and the formulation of medical regimens on any specific

361

visit, it was necessary to allow the interviewers a certain amount of leeway in the administration of the various interview schedules. In addition, a self-administered questionnaire was completed by each physician treating a study patient.

Content analysis of patients' medical records. Some months after the survey data were collected, a chart review was designed to collect demographic data, a listing of all regimens recorded by the doctor, and a record of the proportion of broken appointments during a six-month period.

INDEX OF COMPLIANCE

A variety of indexes have been employed in other studies to measure compliance, some based on subjective reports, others on objective physical measurements.[33] In this study, the composite index of compliance includes patients' perceptions of their compliant behavior, doctors' perceptions of the patients' compliant behavior, and an independent review of patients' medical records. The inclusion of these three types of data to measure noncompliant behavior overcomes many of the difficulties inherent in accepting the patients' word, the doctors' word, or the medical records as the sole source of information.

The compliance score is a weighted average of patient follow-through with two types of recommendations ordered by the doctor. First, recommendations may involve patient initiative at home or at work. This category includes prescription and nonprescription medications, recommended diets, changes in rest habits and worrying, limitation of smoking and alcoholic consumption, and changes in work activities. Second, recommendations may also require patient participation in the hospital organization. Here we examined diagnostic procedures, specific treatments, referrals to specialty clinics, and revisits to the clinic. Medical records were used to ascertain a list of specific regimens. In addition, patients were asked if any *other* regimens were recommended by the doctor. Some patients reported advice which the doctor did not list in the medical record.[34]

After it was discovered which orders were recalled, the patient was asked how closely he followed these recommendations. The responses were coded for each regimen as follows: (0) none of the time, (1) very seldom, (2) less than half the time, (3) compliant most of the time, and (4) all of the time. The physicians were also asked how closely the patient followed the advice and these responses were coded similarly. When the responses of the physician and the patient were not in agreement, an average was taken of the two. A patient was categorized as *not at all compliant* with regard to those regimens reported by the physician but not recalled by the patient. We assumed that patients who did not recall a recommendation when asked were not following the advice. The proportions of broken appointments for revisits and referrals and diagnostic tests were also coded according to congruent categories and included in the composite index. For each type of recommendation, a weight was assigned indicating the relative importance of the regimen.[35]

Results

EXTENT OF NONCOMPLIANCE AND DEMOGRAPHIC DIFFERENCES

In this study group, 37 percent of the patients were classified as non-compliant and 63 percent were classified as compliant. This rate of compliance, in accordance with the findings of the literature review, indicates that while the majority of patients follow their doctors' advice, over one-third of the patients simply do not do what they are told.

The data from the present study show, contradictory to many reports, that there is no significant relationship between compliance and any of the demographic characteristics investigated. This finding is, nevertheless, noteworthy. No variations in patient compliance can be attributed to demographic characteristics peculiar to the patient, i.e., age, sex, marital status, religion, education, or occupation. This supports the contention that dimensions in the doctor-patient relationship are more fruitful avenues for explaining variations in patient compliance.[36]

INTERACTION BETWEEN DOCTOR AND PATIENT

Presumably, all doctors and patients have certain ideas about the kind of relationship they *should* have, and the kind of roles they are expected to play.[37] The way in which doctors and patients initially behaved and whether or not they continued to conform to expected ways of behavior was examined in an earlier paper.[38] Failure to adhere to medical advice *after* the doctor visit was related to deviant communication *in* the doctor-patient relationship. There was a reversal in roles over successive doctor visits. While the doctor was directive and emotionally neutral in the primary visit and the patient passively conformed with his role, data from the revisit suggest that this conformity was only momentary. In the second visit, many doctors passively accepted the patient whose participation was increasingly active. Noncompliant behavior was further explained by increased difficulty of communication, and attempts by doctors and patients to control each other.[39]

FACTOR-ANALYZED DIMENSIONS OF DOCTOR-PATIENT INTERACTION

The 12 categories of interaction (Table 20-1), in and of themselves, have a theoretical significance which describes the structure and process of group interaction.[40] The doctor-patient profiles and the indexes suggested by Bales represent only a few ways of combining the 12 categories. Furthermore, they did not account for much noncompliance. In order to discover some other dimensions, a factor analysis on the interaction categories was completed. The method of factor analysis was selected for its advantage in permitting the grouping of interaction categories in a way which is independent of any a priori thought. It was expected that discovery of such factors would further

TABLE 20-2
Primary Loadings and Weights for Categories Defining Factors in Doctor-Patient Interaction (N = 152)

FACTOR I
MALINTEGRATIVE BEHAVIOR

LOADING	WEIGHT	
.72	.58	Patient: Shows antagonism, deflates other's status, defends or asserts self.
.66	.50	Doctor: Disagrees, shows passive rejection, formality, withholds help.
.52	.36	Patient: Disagrees, shows passive rejection, formality, withholds help.
.36	.11	Patient: Shows tension, asks for help, withdraws out of field.

FACTOR II
ACTIVE PATIENT — PERMISSIVE DOCTOR

LOADING	WEIGHT	
.80	.37	Doctor: Agrees, shows passive acceptance, understands, concurs, complies.
−.72	.39	Patient: Agrees, shows passive acceptance, understands, concurs, complies.
.63	.36	Patient: Gives orientation, information, repetition, confirmation.
.46	.23	Patient: Gives opinion, evaluation, analysis, expresses feeling, wish.

FACTOR III
SOLIDARY RELATIONSHIP

LOADING	WEIGHT	
.95	.79	Patient: Shows solidarity, raises other's status, gives help, reward.
.53	.28	Patient: Shows tension release, jokes, laughs, shows satisfaction.
.36	.11	Doctor: Shows solidarity, raises other's status, gives help, reward.

FACTOR IV
NONDIRECTIVE ANTAGONISM

LOADING	WEIGHT	
.84	.65	Doctor: Gives opinion, evaluation, analysis, expresses feeling, wish.
.52	.28	Doctor: Shows antagonism, deflates other's status, defends or asserts self.
−.49	.40	Doctor: Gives orientation, information, repetition, confirms, clarifies.

FACTOR V
INFORMATIVE NONEVALUATIVENESS

LOADING	WEIGHT	
.99	.82	Doctor: Gives suggestion, direction, implying autonomy for others.
−.48	.24	Doctor: Gives orientation, information, repeats, clarifies, confirms.

FACTOR VI
NONRECIPROCAL INFORMATIVENESS

LOADING	WEIGHT	
.85	.68	Doctor: Asks for orientation, information, repetition, confirmation.
−.63	.49	Doctor: Gives orientation, information, repeats, clarifies, confirms.
.36	.12	Patient: Gives orientation, information, repeats, clarifies, confirms.

TABLE 20-2 (Continued)

FACTOR VII
EVALUATIVE CONGRUENCE

LOADING	WEIGHT	
.49	.59	Patient: Agrees, shows passive acceptance, understands, concurs, complies.
−.45	.46	Patient: Asks for opinion, evaluation, analysis, expression of feeling.
.41	.42	Doctor: Agrees, shows passive acceptance, understands, concurs, complies.
−.35	.34	Doctor: Asks for opinion, evaluation, analysis, expression of feeling.

FACTOR VIII
ENTREATIVE INQUIRY

LOADING	WEIGHT	
.69	.77	Patient: Asks for orientation, information, repetition, confirmation.
.51	.52	Patient: Asks for suggestion, direction, possible ways of action.

FACTOR IX
TENSION BUILD-UP

LOADING	WEIGHT	
.68	.73	Doctor: Shows solidarity, raises other's status, gives help, reward.
.54	.52	Patient: Shows tension, asks for help, withdraws out of the field.
.41	.42	Doctor: Shows tension, asks for help, withdraws out of the field.

FACTOR X
TENSION RELEASE

LOADING	WEIGHT	
.54	.58	Doctor: Shows tension release, jokes, laughs, shows satisfaction.
.51	.43	Patient: Shows tension release, jokes, laughs, shows satisfaction.

our knowledge of dimensions of doctor-patient interaction which ultimately could be related to variations in patient compliance.

The rates for the 12 interaction categories for doctor and patient were correlated to form a 24 x 24 product moment correlation matrix. Principle factors were extracted with unity as the diagonal value. Ten factors, judged salient on the basis of the magnitude of factor loadings, were rotated to oblique simple structure by the Promax procedure.[41] Each of the ten factors is defined by a particular group of categories. A list of the factors with the loadings and weights for each category appears in Table 20–2.

Seven of the 24 categories were heavily loaded on more than one factor and consequently were differentially weighted for each dimension. To compute scores, the weight of the factor loading was multiplied times the rate of doctor-patient activity which fell into the categories.

The ten factors represent empirically determined dimensions of doctor-patient communication. The label for each factor is an arbitrary name intended to summarize the interaction categories defining that dimension.

Factor I, *malintegrative behavior,* characterizes the type of doctor-patient communication which exhibits negative social-emotional interaction. Both participants appear to be formal, show passive rejection, and withhold help from the other. The patient shows antagonism toward the doctor and simultaneously withdraws from the situation. What we find here is a dimension measuring deviant interaction.

Factor II, *active patient—permissive doctor,* represents a pattern of communication between an authoritative patient and a doctor who passively accepts the authoritative position taken by the patient. The patient is likely to present his own evaluation and analysis of the situation and shows little acceptance of what the doctor says. It is assumed that a doctor-patient relationship which exhibits a high score on this factor is deviant from the normative doctor-patient interaction.

Factor III, *solidary relationship,* is indicative of communication characterized by friendly behavior on the part of both doctor and patient. Positive social-emotional interaction reckons high in this factor. The patient is able to show satisfaction with the interaction and release much of the tension which arises from the situation.

The communication in which Factor IV, *nondirective antagonism,* is high, suggests an antagonistic doctor who neglects to give the patient information, explanation, or orientation. He confines his activity to expressing opinions and feelings about the situation.

Factor V, *informative nonevaluativeness,* typifies the doctor who gives a great deal of direction to the patient but does not present any diagnosis or evaluation.

Items defining Factor VI, *nonreciprocal-informativeness,* reflect the way in which doctors collect information in order to make a diagnosis. The doctor asks for information from the patient and the patient cooperatively orients the doctor. In this case, however, the doctor also withholds information from the patient. There is no feedback.

Factor VII, *evaluative congruence,* measures the successful solution of the problems introduced by lack of agreement on values and expectations. The doctor and patient agree on what they consider important and beneficial for their relationship.

An encounter scoring high on *entreative inquiry,* Factor VIII, illustrates how a patient who desires information communicates in order to determine what the problem is and how he can resolve it. This type of patient does not wish the doctor to withhold any information. He asks for orientation, information, and analysis.

Factor IX presents one way doctors manage interaction saturated with tension. High scores on the factor *tension build-up* indicate that both doctor and patient show a great deal of tension regardless of the doctor's attempts to achieve reintegration by communicating in a friendly manner.

Factor X, *tension release,* is a corollary of Factor IX. Here the doctor and patient exhibit tension release through joking, laughing, and showing some satisfaction with the relationship.

COMPLIANCE AND FACTORS OF DOCTOR-PATIENT COMMUNICATION

It was hypothesized that those patterns of communication deviant from prescribed institutional doctor-patient relationships will result in patients' failure to comply with doctors' advice. Scores for the ten factors for each doctor-patient pair were computed for the first visit and the revisit, and subsequently correlated with patients' compliance.

First, there is very little association between what occurs in the primary visit and later compliance. In the first visit, not one of the factors was significantly associated with later patient compliance. In the revisit, however, five of the ten factors were associated with patients' compliance. Table 20–3 shows

TABLE 20-3

Product Moment Correlations and Levels of Significance for Doctor-Patient Interaction Factors and Compliance Behavior

		PRIMARY VISIT (N = 119)		REVISIT (N = 104)	
INTERACTION FACTORS		r	p	r	p
I.	Malintegrative behavior	− .141	> .05	− .260	< .01
II.	Active patient − permissive doctor	− .132	> .05	− .304	< .01
III.	Solidary relationship	.072	> .05	.173	> .05
IV.	Nondirective antagonism	− .040	> .05	− .236	< .01
V.	Informative nonevaluativeness	− .070	> .05	.040	> .05
VI.	Nonreciprocal informativeness	− .029	> .05	− .315	< .01
VII.	Evaluative congruence	.102	> .05	.123	> .05
VIII.	Entreative inquiry	− .031	> .05	− .053	> .05
IX.	Tension build-up	− .081	> .05	− .060	> .05
X.	Tension release	.108	> .05	.223	< .05

a significant correlation between compliance and *malintegrative behavior* (Factor I). The greater the malintegrative behavior in the interaction, the less likely the patient will follow the doctor's orders after he leaves the doctor's office.

There is also a negative correlation between compliance and Factor II, *active patient—permissive doctor*. When a patient acts in an authoritative manner with a permissive doctor, the doctor's position is threatened and the patient is unlikely to comply. Similarly Factor IV, measuring the extent to which a doctor is nondirective in an antagonistic way, is also negatively correlated with compliance. When a doctor confines his activity to analysis of the situation and the expression of his opinions, he is likely to promote noncompliance. The opposite type of behavior, however, does not insure compliance. Factor V, indicative of a minimum of analysis and evaluation and a maximum of direction on the doctor's part, is not significantly related to compliance. These data suggest that compliance is a function of a delicate balance of direction and evaluation presented in a manner which is acceptable to the patient.

Compliance is also a function of reciprocal interaction.[42] Noncompliance was significantly associated with Factor VI, *nonreciprocal-informativeness*. Apparently it makes little difference how much information the patient requests (Factor VIII), but when the doctor takes time to collect information without giving any feedback, the patient will probably react in a reciprocal deviant or noncompliant way.

It is interesting to note that only three of the ten dimensions iterated in the factor analysis measure positive rapport in the interaction (*solidary relationship, evaluative congruence,* and *tension release*), and only one of these, *tension release,* is significantly related to patient compliance. When tension is built up, it effects malintegration, but if released through joking or laughing, the possibility of patient adherence to the medical regimen is increased.

Factor III, measuring the amount of friendly rapport in the relationship, is not significantly correlated with patient compliance. As the relationship between the doctor and patient becomes friendly, strains are created which interfere with their role functions. It may be easier then for a patient to ignore the advice of a friendly physician than one who is formal and authoritative. If the friendly doctor's authority is undermined, the patient may be as likely to accept the advice of a friend as that of the doctor.

This is also evident when Factor VII, *evaluative congruence,* is examined. Doctors and patients who are on the same wave lengths, who agree on what they consider desirable, right, and proper, may communicate more effectively, but this activity is unrelated to the patient's later compliance.

In sum, the hypothesis relating patient noncompliance and deviant patterns of communication is supported by these data. Caution, however, is recommended when interpreting the findings. The nature of each factor is such that a negative correlation between compliance and any factor does not imply that the absence or reverse of that factor is positively correlated with compliance. For example, while *malintegrative behavior* is negatively correlated with compliance, the absence of such behavior does not necessarily affect compliance. As indicated above, compliance is not affected by the extent to which the interaction is characterized as a *solidary relationship*. One should also note that while these data evidence some statistically significant correlations, the associations are relatively small. Furthermore, the factors iterated in this particular investigation have not been standardized. Consequently, they are descriptive characteristics of this particular population of doctor-patient relationships. The significance of this research would be increased greatly if, in further studies, these factors are employed as independent variables to investigate compliance in medical as well as other settings.

Summary and Discussion

Communication between doctor and patient ideally necessitates a certain degree of reciprocity. Each person has certain rights and obligations. When the doctor performs a service, the patient is obligated to reciprocate: first, by cooperating with the doctor in their interaction; and second, by complying with the medical recommendations once he leaves the doctor's office. We have seen, however, that there are deviations from these norms. The data reported in this study, collected by means of tape recordings of doctor-patient interaction and supplemented with a series of patient interviews, a self-administered questionnaire completed by physicians, and a content analysis of patients' medical records, were analyzed to determine the extent of deviant patient behavior *within* and *outside* the doctor-patient relationship.

Thirty-seven percent of the patient group disregarded what their doctors advised. A factor analysis suggested some patterns of communication which help explain noncompliance. While interaction in the primary doctor visit was not associated with later compliance, the data suggest that revisits between an authoritative patient and a physician who passively accepts such patient participation may promote patient noncompliance. Effective communication is impeded when doctors and patients evidence tension in their relationship. Unless this tension is released, noncompliance may result, regardless of the doctor's efforts to achieve solidarity. And when doctors seek information from patients without giving them any feedback, the patient is unlikely to follow the doctor's orders once they are formulated.

Implicit in this discussion of noncompliance is the problem of controlling patient behavior. In the doctor-patient relationship, whether in private practice, hospital clinic, or on a ward, the doctor must rely on his ability to establish good rapport in order to inculcate in his patient a positive orientation and commitment to the relationship so that ultimately the patient will follow his advice. In order to do this, it becomes necessary for the doctor continually to explore and diagnose the social and psychological facets of his interaction with his patients as well as the manifest medical problem.

NOTES

1. In another paper, preliminary findings relating compliance to dimensions of doctor-patient interaction were reported. Davis, M. S. Deviant Interaction in an Institutionalized Relationship: Variation in Patients' Compliance with Doctors' Orders. Paper presented before the Medical Sociology Session, Sixth World Congress of Sociology, Evian, France (Sept.), 1966.

2. A systematic review of compliance literature may be found in Davis, M. S. Variations in Patients' Compliance with Doctors' Orders: Analysis of Congruence Between Survey Responses and Results of Empirical Investigations. J. Med. Educ. 41,11: 1037–1048, pt. 1 (Nov.), 1966.

3. Dixon, W. M.; Stradling, P.; and Wooton, I. Outpatient PAS Therapy. Lancet 273:871–873, 1957. Luntz, G. R., and Austin, R. New Stick Test for PAS in Urine. Brit. J. Med. 1:1679–1683, 1960. Morrow, R., and Rabin, D. L. Reliability in Self-medication with Isoniazid. Clin. Research XIV, 2:362 (Apr.), 1966. Wynn-Williams, N., and Arris, M. On Omitting PAS. Tubercle 39:138–142, 1958.

4. Cobb, B.; Clark, R. L.; McGuire, C.; and Howe, C. D. Patient-Responsible Delay of Treatment in Cancer. Cancer 7:920–925, 1954. Davis, M. S., and Eichhorn, R. L. Compliance with Medical Regimens: A Panel Study. J. Health & Human Behavior 4:240–249, 1963. Schwartz, D.; Wong, M.; Zeitz, L.; and Goss, M. E. W. Medication Errors Made by Elderly, Chronically Ill Patients. A.J.P.H. 52,12:2018–2029, 1962.

5. Cobb, B., et al., op. cit. Donabedian, A. and Rosenfeld, L. S. A Follow-up Study of Chronically Ill Patients Discharged From Hospital. Pub. Health Rep. 79:228, 1964. Hardy, M. C. Psychologic Aspects of Pediatrics: Parent Resistance to Need for Remedial and Preventive Services. J. Pediat. 48:104–114, 1956. Johannsen, W. J.; Hellmuth, G. A.; and Sorauf, T. On Accepting Medical Recommendations. Arch. Environ. Health 12:63–69, 1966. MacDonald, M. E.; Hagverg, K. L.; and Grossman, B. J. Social Factors in Relation to Participation in Follow-up Care of Rheumatic Fever. J. Pediat. 62:503–513, 1963. Mather, W. Social and Economic Factors Related to Correction of School Discovered Medical and Dental Defects. Pennsylvania M. J. 62:983–988, 1954. Pragoff, H. Adjustment of Tuberculosis Patients One Year After Hospital Discharge. Pub. Health Rep. 77:671–679, 1962. Watts, D. D. Factors Related to the Acceptance of Modern Medicine. A.J.P.H. 56,8:1205–1212, 1966.

6. Bates, F. E., and Ariel, I. M. Delay in Treatment of Cancer. Illinois M. J. 49: 361–365 (Dec.), 1948. Davis, M. S., and Eichhorn, R. L., op. cit. Johnson, W. L. Conformity to Medical Recommendations in Coronary Heart Disease. Paper presented at the annual meeting of the American Sociological Association, Chicago (Sept.), 1965. Pragoff, H., op. cit.

7. Abramson, J. H.; Mayet, F. G.; and Majola, C. C. What Is Wrong with Me? A Study of the Views of African and Indian Patients in a Durban Hospital. South African M. J. 35:690–694 (Aug. 19), 1961.

8. Ambuel, J. P.; Cebulla, J.; Watt, N.; and Crowne, D. Doctor-Mother Communications. Midwest Society Pediat. Res. 65:113–114, 1964.

9. Cobb, B., et al., op. cit.

10. Ellis, R. The Relationship between Psychological Factors and Remission of Duodenal Ulcer. Unpublished doctoral dissertation, University of Chicago, 1964.

11. Hellmuth, G. A.; Johannsen, W. J.; and Sorauf, T. Psychological Factors in Cardiac Patients. Arch. Environ. Health 12:771–780 (June), 1966.

12. Leventhal, H. Fear Communications in the Acceptance of Preventive Health Practices. Bull. New York Acad. Med. 41,11:1144–1168 (Nov.), 1965.

13. For a discussion of the content of normative prescriptions and postscriptions, see Mizruchi, E., and Perrucci, R. Norm Qualities and Differential Effects of Deviant Behavior: An Exploratory Analysis. Am. Sociol. Rev. 27:391–399, 1962. See also, Hollander, M. The Psychology of Medical Practice. Philadelphia: W. B. Saunders, 1958.

14. Davis, M. S., and Eichhorn, R. L., op. cit.

15. Davis, M. S. Predicting Non-compliant Behavior. J. Health & Social Behavior 8:265–271, 1967. Johannsen, W. J., et al., op. cit.

16. Berkowitz, N. H.; Malone, M. F.; Klein, M. W.; and Eaton, A. Patient Follow-through in the Out-Patient Department. Nursing Res. 12:16–22, 1963; and Patient Care as a Criterion Problem. J. Health & Human Behavior 3:171–176, 1962.

17. Davis, M. S. J. M. Educ., op. cit. Ley, P., and Spelman, M. S. Communications in an Out-Patient Setting. Brit. J. Social and Clinical Psychol. 4:114–116, 1965. Riley, C. S. Patients' Understanding of Doctors' Instructions. M. Care 4,1:34–37 (Jan.-Mar.), 1966.

18. Elling, R.; Whittemore, R.; and Green, M. Patient Participation in a Pediatric Program. J. Health & Human Behavior 1:183–191, 1960. Ku, R., and Jordan, G. A Study of Self-Administration of Isoniazid in Children. Health Research Training Program, New York City Department of Health, 1964, pp. 1–11. Wallace, H. M., et al. Study of Follow-up of Children Recommended for Rheumatic Fever Prophylaxis. A.J.P.H. 46,12:1563–1570, 1956.

19. Eichhorn, R. L.; Riedel, D. C.; and Morris, W. H. M. Compliance to Perceived Therapeutic Advice. Proceedings of the Purdue Farm Cardiac Seminar. W. H. M. Morris (ed.). Lafayette, Ind.: Agricultural Experiment Station (Sept.), 1958, pp. 65–68. Pragoff, H., op. cit.

20. Abramson, J. H., et al., op. cit. Davis, M. S., and Eichhorn, R. L., op. cit. Watts, D. D., op. cit.

21. The single exception here is the doctoral dissertation by Ellis, R., op. cit.

22. Berkowitz, N. H., et al., op. cit. Johnson, W. L., op. cit.

23. Johannsen, W. J., et al., op. cit.

24. Davis, M. S., and von der Lippe, R. P. Discharge from Hospital against Medical Advice: A Study of Reciprocity in the Doctor-Patient Relationship. Social Science & Med. 1:336–342, 1968. Hoffman, R. The Doctor's Role: A Study of Consensus, Congruence and Change. Doctoral dissertation, University of Nebraska, 1958. Sapolsky, A. Relationship between Doctor-Patient Compatability, Mutual Perception and Outcome of Treatment. J. Abnorm. Psychol. 70,1:70–76, 1965. Sobel, R., and Igalls, A. Resistance to Treatment, Explorations of the Patient's Sick Role. Am. J. Psychotherapy 18:562–573, 1964.

25. Ellis, R., op. cit.

26. Abramson, J. H., et al., op. cit. Ambuel, J. P., et al., op. cit. Cobb, B., et al., op. cit. Davis, M. S., and Eichhorn, R. L., op. cit. Elling, R., et al., op. cit. Leventhal, H., op. cit. Ley, P. and Spelman, M. S., op. cit. Mohler, D. N.; Wallin, D. G.; and Dreyfus, E. G. Studies in the Home Treatment of Streptococcal Disease. New England J. Med. 252:1116–1118, 1955. Riley, C. S., op. cit. Robbins, G. F.; Conte, A. J.; Leach, J. E.; and MacDonald, M. Delay in Diagnosis and Treatment of Cancer. J.A.M.A. 143:346–348, 1950. Ullmann, A., and Davis, M. S. Assessing the Medical Patient's Motivation and Ability to Work. Social Casework XLVI, pp. 195–202, 1965. Watts, D., op. cit.

27. Interviewers were instructed to drop patients judged to be noninterviewable. Because of insufficient numbers of suitable new patients coming to the clinic at certain times, an interviewer occasionally attempted to administer the first interview schedule to someone he hoped would be suitable but who, in fact, was not. Ten such patients were eliminated because of language barriers, hearing difficulties, and inappropriate medical problems. Another five patients were dropped from the study at the request of the physician, two because of the sensitive nature of their problems, and one because her doctor felt that the study was too distracting for her. (He insisted that she had been so fascinated by the tape recorder that she had ignored him completely.) A number of doctors and patients expressed reservations about the tape recorders but only one patient and one doctor refused to be taped. Three others were dropped from the study because they refused to be interviewed. Finally, ten patients were eliminated from the study group because the interviewer assigned to the case either failed to or was unable to follow them properly. Altogether, 32 patients were dropped from the study population.

28. Turgeon, L., and Long, D. A Study of New Patients in the General Medical

Variations in Patients' Compliance with Doctors' Advice

Clinic. Research Memorandum, Comprehensive Care and Teaching Program, New York Hospital-Cornell University Medical Center (Feb.), 1965 (mimeo). The sample included patients seen in October 1962; the present report is based on a sample of patients seen between November 1964 and June 1965. Data comparing demographic characteristics of the study population with the estimated composition of the clinic population based on the 1962 survey are available upon request.

29. The exploratory phase of the research was supported by United States Public Health Service Grant (MH08458-01), and was entitled "Dimensions of Compliant Doctor-Patient Relationships."

30. Bales, R. F. Interaction Process Analysis. Cambridge, Mass.: Addison-Wesley Press, 1951. While interaction process analysis has been employed experimentally and to study the interaction between doctor and patient in a psychotherapeutic situation, it has not been used in an investigation of interaction in a medical situation.

For the reader who wishes to examine other methods of recording interaction see: Adler, L. Mc. A Scale to Measure Psychotherapy Interactions. University of Southern California School of Medicine. Los Angeles, 1964 (mimeo). Carter, L. F. Recording and Evaluating the Performance of Individuals as Members of Small Groups. Personnel Psychology 7:477–484, 1954. Carter, L.; Haythorn, W.; Meirowitz, B.; and Lanzetta, J. A Note on a New Technique of Interaction. J. Abnorm. & Social Psychol. 46:258–260, 1951. Chapple, E. D. The Interaction Chronograph: Its Evolution and Present Application. Personnel 25:295–307, 1949. Dittman, A. T. The Interpersonal Process in Psychotherapy: Development of a Research Method. J. Abnorm. & Social Psychol. 47:236–244, 1952. Dollard, J. A Method of Measuring Tension in Written Documents. Ibid. XLII, pp. 3–32, 1947. Freedman, M. B.; Leary, T. F.; Ossonio, A. G.; and Coffey, H. S. The Interpersonal Dimension of Personality. J. Personality 20:143–161, 1951. Guetzkow, H. Unitizing and Categorizing Problems in Coding Qualitative Data. J. Clin. Psychol. 6:47–58, 1950. Heyns, R. W., and Lippitt, R. Systematic Observational Techniques. The Handbook of Social Psychology. Lindzey, G. (ed.). Reading, Mass.: Addison-Wesley Publishing, 1954, pp. 370–404. Lennard, H. L., and Bernstein, A. The Anatomy of Psychotherapy. Chapter II, Methodology, New York: Columbia University Press, 1960. Matarazzo, J. D.; Saslow, G.; and Matarazzo, R. G. The Interaction Chronograph as an Instrument for Objective Measurement of Interaction Patterns During Interviews. J. Psychol. 41:347–367, 1956. Melbin, M. Field Methods and Techniques: The Action-Interaction Chart. Human Organization 12:34–35, 1953. Murray, H. A. Content Analysis Method for Studying Psychotherapy. Psychol. Monogr. LXX:13, 1956. Psathas, G. Problems and Prospects in the Use of a Computer System of Content Analysis. Sociol. Quart. (forthcoming). Ruesch, J.; Block, J.; and Bennett, L. The Assessment of Communication: I. A Method for the Analysis of Social Interaction. J. Psychiat. 35:59–80, 1953. Stenzar, B. The Development and Evaluation of a Measure of Social Interaction. Am. Psychol. 3:266, 1948. Stone, P. J.; Dunphy, D. C.; Smith, M. S.; and Ogilvie, D. M. The General Inquirer: A Computer Approach to Content Analysis. Cambridge, Mass.: Massachusetts Institute of Technology Press, 1966.

31. Four coders worked in pairs, each pair coding together for a week. Every week partners were changed to produce the greatest uniformity in coding and to minimize the chance of developing rigid coding idiosyncracies. The coders listened to each recording unitizing the dialogue on transcripts and indicating statements of affect. This was done individually and then pairs were compared. Any disagreements were resolved through discussion, or if necessary by relistening to the tape. Coding was then done individually and the two code sheets compared. Again differences were resolved through discussion and relistening to the interaction. Any disagreements which could not be resolved were referred to the other two coders during the period set aside for that purpose each day. When the coding was completed there was some concern that increased familiarity with the code might cause some significant differences in coding

between tapes done at the beginning and at the end of the coding period. A random sample of visits from the early tapes was recoded and 4 percent of the answers were changed. However, when a random sample from all the other tapes was taken and recoded, 3 percent of the codes were changed from one category to another. It was concluded, therefore, that a certain insignificant percentage of codes would be changed regardless of how many times the interactions were recoded.

32. Bales, R. F., op. cit., Chapter 4. By coding after the observation of doctor-patient interaction, many of the difficulties of reliability of categorizing were eliminated. The problem of reliability of attribution and unitizing was nonexistent because the transcription was utilized and interaction was unitized and attributed to doctor or patient prior to the coding process.

33. For a comparison of indexes of compliance, see Davis, M. S., and Eichhorn, R. L., op. cit.; and Davis, M. S. J. Health & Social Behavior, op. cit.

34. Several patients were administered specific regimen and compliance sections of the interview when regimens were not recorded by the doctor either in the patient's medical record or the doctor's questionnaire. Occasionally, the physician made a suggestion, e.g., "Don't worry about yourself," "Maybe you should lose some weight," and so on, which was not meant as a specific recommendation.

35. For example, consider a patient who (a) was advised to make six clinic visits during the period he received medical care, (b) received a prescription for a single medication, (c) was told to cut down on his smoking, and (d) was advised to eliminate alcoholic beverages.

According to the chart review, the patient kept only three of his appointments (50 percent broken appointment rate). The patient reported that he had cut down on his smoking as recommended and took the medication most of the time. He did not recall the doctor telling him anything about alcoholic beverages. The doctor reported, in the questionnaire, that the patient did not take his medications at all, but had cut down on his smoking. According to the doctor, the patient had not curbed his drinking habits at all.

With regard to the clinic visits, the patient was given a score of "3," compliant most of the time (each patient was allowed a proportion of broken appointments before he was considered deviant). For the medication regimen, he was given a score of "1.5," the average of the disagreement "3+0." The doctor agreed that the patient had indeed complied with the smoking regimen and the patient was given a score of "4," compliant all of the time. With regard to the alcohol regimen, the patient was scored as "0," not at all compliant. Accordingly, the compliant profile for the patient is as follows:

REGIMEN	COMPLIANCE SCORE		X	WEIGHT	=	WEIGHTED SCORE
a. Clinic visits	"3"	Most of the time		(1)		3
b. Medication	"1.5"	Less than half the time		(2)		3
c. Smoking	"4"	All of the time		(2)		8
d. Alcohol	"0"	Not at all		(1)		0
				6		14

The composite index of compliance is the sum of the weighted scores divided by the sum of the weights. In this case, the index is equal to 14/6 or 2.3, compliant less than half the time.

36. More detailed data relating extent of compliance and demographic variables

can be found in an earlier paper: Davis, M. S. Sixth World Congress of Sociology, Evian, France, op. cit.

37. Coser, R. L. Life on the Ward. East Lansing, Michigan State University Press, 1962. Kasl, S. V., and Cobb, S. Health Behavior, Illness Behavior and Sick Role Behavior. Arch. Environ. Health 12:246–266 (Feb.), 1966. Mauksch, H. O., and Tagliacozzo, D. M. The Patient's View of the Patient Role. Department of Patient Care Research, Presbyterian-St. Luke's Hospital. Publication 2, Chicago, Ill. (Mar.), 1962. Mechanic, D., and Volkart, E. H. Illness Behavior and Medical Diagnoses. J. Health & Human Behavior 1:86–94, 1960. Parsons, T. The Social System. Glencoe, Ill.: The Free Press, 1951, Chapter X.

38. Davis, M. S. Sixth World Congress of Sociology, Evian, France, op. cit.

39. Ibid.

40. Bales, R. F. Theoretical Framework. Chapter 2, op. cit.

41. Hendrickson, A. E., and White, D. O. Promax: A Quick Method for Rotation to Oblique Simple Structure. Brit. J. Statist. Psychol. 17:65 (May), 1964. The relations among the factors of the oblique solution range from .22 to −.29. Most of the items have a high factor loading on one factor and a low loading on the remaining factors. Only items with a factor loading of .30 or greater were used to define a factor.

42. Gouldner, A. W. The Norm of Reciprocity: A Preliminary Statement. Am. Sociol. Rev. 25:161–178 (Apr.), 1960. A paradigm of types of doctor-patient reciprocity can be found in Davis, M. S., and von der Lippe, R. P., op. cit.

21

Robert Rosenthal and Lenore Jacobson

PYGMALION IN THE CLASSROOM

The basic question to be answered in this chapter is whether in a period of one year or less children of whom greater intellectual growth is expected will show greater intellectual growth than undesignated control-group children. There are also four important subsidiary questions. If there were some advantages to a child whose teacher had favorable expectations for his intellectual development, would these expectancy advantages be greater for:

1. Children in the lower grades or higher grades?
2. Children in the fast track, or medium track, or slow track?
3. Children of one sex rather than the other?
4. Children of minority group or nonminority group status?

The Major Variables

AGE

The folk knowledge of our culture, current theories of human development, especially psychoanalytic theory, and the work of the developmental and experimental psychologists and of the ethologists are in agreement on the importance of age as a factor in determining the degree to which an organism can be shaped, molded, or influenced (Scott, 1962). In general, the younger the organism, the greater is thought to be the degree of susceptibility to social influence. In his classic monograph, Coffin (1941) concluded that influenceability increased from infancy to ages seven to nine but decreased after that. More recently in a summary of the evidence bearing on

From *Pygmalion in the Classroom: Teacher Expectation and Pupils' Intellectual Development* by Robert Rosenthal and Lenore Jacobson. Copyright © 1968 by Holt, Rinehart and Winston, Inc. Reprinted by permission of Holt, Rinehart and Winston, Inc. (Original title of chapter, "The Magic Children of Galatea," chap. 7, pp. 72–85.)

overt social influence on children, Stevenson (1965) reported the greater influenceability of five-year-olds than twelve-year-olds, a finding consistent with Coffin's summary. Both Coffin and Stevenson were writing about more overt social influence than the subtle, unintended influence of teachers' prophecies. Still, it would be interesting to know whether influence processes of a more subtle, unintended form would also show younger children to be the more susceptible.

ABILITY

We are also interested in learning whether the children of three ability tracks differ in the degree to which they profit from the teachers' favorable expectations. In the case of ability, however, the literature is not so helpful in telling us what we might find. Stevenson (1965) suggested that susceptibility to social influence may not be too contingent on the child's intellectual status, and we know that the three tracks differ considerably in average IQ. One of the most recent discussions of intellectual gains is by Thorndike (1966) who reports that there are only modest correlations between initial intellectual status and changes in intellectual status. In the present research, in any case, we are not so much interested in gains per se but rather in the excess of gain that might be shown by the "special" children over the "ordinary" un-designated childen. In short, we are interested in differences among the tracks in the degree of expectancy advantage that may be found, but we hardly know what to expect. The matter is further complicated by the fact that the other two variables in which we are interested, sex and minority group status, are not independent of track placement. Boys tend to over-populate the slow track relative to girls who tend to overpopulate the fast track. Mexican children, Oak School's minority group, tend to overpopulate the slow track and underpopulate the fast track.

SEX

Whether boys or girls are the more susceptible to social influence processes depends on whether the influencer is male or female (Stevenson, 1965). Since the overwhelming majority of Oak School's teachers are females, the findings from research with lady influencers interest us most. Those findings, summarized by Stevenson (1965), suggest that boys should be the more suspectible to social influence. As in the case of the children's age, however, the social influence processes employed were neither unintended nor very subtle. Effects of teachers' expectations are likely to be both.

MINORITY GROUP STATUS

The reasons for our interest in the variable of minority-group status need little justification. So much of the literature on the disadvantaged child focuses on the minority-group child that "disadvantaged" almost means "minority group." One of the best known publications dealing with the disadvantaged is called *Youth in the Ghetto*. We shall be especially interested, then, if expectancy advantages occur at all, in whether they benefit minority-group children more or less than nonminority-group children.

At Oak School the minority-group child is Mexican. The definition of a minority-group child in this research, however, was more stringent than simply whether the name was Mexican. To qualify as a "minority-group child," either the child himself or his parents had to come from Mexico, Spanish had to be spoken at home, and the child had to be present for the administration of certain procedures. These procedures, in connection with another study (Jacobson, 1966), included administration of an IQ test in Spanish, a test of reading ability, and the taking of photographs of the child himself. Within this sample of Mexican minority-group children there were variations in how "Mexican" each child looked. A group of ten teachers with no connection to Oak School or its children rated each photograph on "how Mexican the child looked." The definition of how clearly Mexican a child "really" looked was the average rating of all ten teachers. These ratings were highly reliable. The average rating of the same children by the teachers of Oak School was correlated .97 with the ratings of the judges who were not associated with Oak School.

Intellectual Growth

EXPECTANCY ADVANTAGE BY GRADES

The bottom row of Table 21-1 gives the overall results for Oak School. In the year of the experiment, the undesignated control-group children gained over eight IQ points while the experimental-group children, the special children, gained over twelve. The difference in gains could be ascribed to chance about 2 in 100 times ($F = 6.35$).[1]

TABLE 21-1

Mean Gain in Total IQ after One Year by Experimental- and Control-Group Children in Each of Six Grades

| | CONTROL | | EXPERIMENTAL | | EXPECTANCY ADVANTAGE | |
| | | | | | | ONE-TAIL |
GRADE	N	GAIN	N	GAIN	IQ POINTS	$p < .05$[a]
1	48	+12.0	7	+27.4	+15.4	.002
2	47	+7.0	12	+16.5	+9.5	.02
3	40	+5.0	14	+5.0	−0.0	
4	49	+2.2	12	+5.6	+3.4	
5	26	+17.5(−)	9	+17.4(+)	−0.0	
6	45	+10.7	11	+10.0	−0.7	
Total	255	+8.42	65	+12.22	+3.80	.02

[a]Mean square within treatments within classrooms = 164.24.

Pygmalion in the Classroom

The rest of Table 21–1 and Figure 21–1 show the gains by children of the two groups separately for each grade. We find increasing expectancy advantage as we go from the sixth to the first grade; the correlation between grade level and magnitude of expectancy advantage ($r = -.86$) was sig-

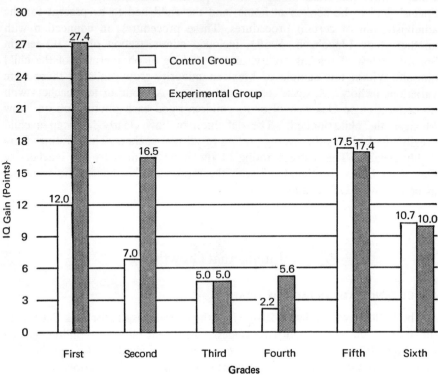

FIGURE 21-1. Gains in Total IQ in Six Grades.

nificant at the .03 level. The interaction effect, or likelihood that at different grades there were significantly greater expectancy advantages, was significant at the .07 level ($F = 2.13$). (Interactions, however, are not sensitive to the ordering of differences unless one makes them so with further statistical efforts; that is, the p of .07 is conservative.)

In the first and second grades the effects of teachers' prophecies were dramatic. Table 21–1 shows that, and so does Table 21–2 and Figure 21–2. There we find the percentage of experimental- and control-group children of the first two grades who achieved various amounts of gain. In these grades about every fifth control-group child gained twenty IQ points or more, but of the special children, nearly every second child gained that much.

So far we have told only of the effects of favorable expectancies on total IQ, but Flanagan's TOGA yields separate IQs for the verbal and reasoning spheres of intellectual functioning. These are sufficiently different from each other so it will not be redundant to give the results of each. In the case of

FIGURE 21-2. Percentages of First and Second Graders Gaining Ten, Twenty, or Thirty Total IQ Points.

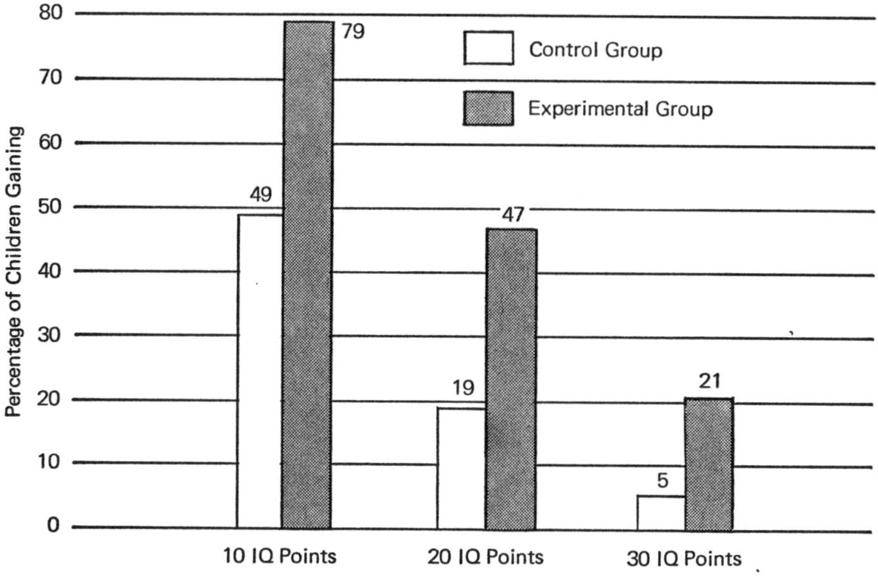

verbal IQ the control-group children of the entire school gained just less than eight points, and the special children gained just less than ten, a difference that could easily have arisen by chance. The interaction term was not very significant ($p < .15$) so that we can not conclude greater expectancy advantage at some grade levels than at others. But we do have a special interest now in the first and second graders, and it will do no harm to see what happened there in particular. In those combined grades, the control-group children gained 4.5 verbal IQ points, and the special children gained exactly 10 points more, or 14.5. If we may have the t test (even though the interaction effect was not significant) we would find $t = 2.24$, $p < .02$, one-tail. For grades three through six the control gained 1.6 points more than the experimental group, a difference not nearly significant. Table 21–3 summarizes these results.[2]

TABLE 21-2

Percentages of First and Second Graders Gaining at Least Ten, Twenty, or Thirty Total IQ Points

IQ GAIN AT LEAST	CONTROL $N = 95$	EXPERIMENTAL $N = 19$	ONE-TAIL p OF DIFFERENCE
10 points[a]	49%	79%	.02
20 points[b]	19	47	.01
30 points	5	21	.04

[a]Includes children gaining twenty and thirty points or more.

[b]Includes children gaining thirty points or more.

TABLE 21-3

Mean Gain in Verbal IQ after One Year by Experimental- and Control-Group Children in Grades One-Two and Three-Six

GRADES	CONTROL		EXPERIMENTAL		EXPECTANCY ADVANTAGE	
	N	GAIN	*N*	GAIN	IQ POINTS	ONE-TAIL $p < .05$[a]
1-2	95	+4.5	19	+14.5	+10.0	.02
3-6	174	+9.6	49	+8.0	−1.6	
TOTAL	269	+7.79	68	+9.85	+2.06	

[a]Mean square within = 316.40.

The advantage of favorable expectations showed itself more clearly in reasoning IQ as shown in Table 21–4. For the school as a whole, the ad-

TABLE 21-4

Mean Gain in Reasoning IQ after One Year by Experimental- and Control-Group Children in Grades One-Two and Three-Six

GRADES	CONTROL		EXPERIMENTAL		EXPECTANCY ADVANTAGE	
	N	GAIN	*N*	GAIN	IQ POINTS	ONE-TAIL $p < .05$[a]
1-2	95	+27.0 (−)	19	+39.6 (+)	+12.7	.03
3-6	160	+9.1 (−)	46	+15.9 (+)	+6.9	.06
TOTAL	255	+15.73	65	+22.86	+7.13	.005

[a]Mean square within = 666.58.

vantage of favorable expectations was a seven point net gain in reasoning IQ ($F = 6.98$), and there were no significant differences in the six grades in degree of expectancy advantage.[3] Once again, the younger children benefited most. While we are not especially interested in the magnitude of IQ gain of the control group, it does seem remarkable that the younger children of even the control group should gain so heavily in reasoning IQ. Table 21–1 shows that control-group children gained substantially in total IQ and not only at the younger ages where we might expect practice effects to be most dramatic. There is no way to be sure about the matter, but it may be that experiments are good for children even when the children are in the untreated control group.

EXPECTANCY ADVANTAGE BY TRACKS AND SEX

None of the statistical tests showed any differences among the three tracks in the extent to which they benefited from teachers' favorable prophecies. That was the case for total IQ, verbal IQ, and reasoning IQ. When the entire school benefited as in total IQ and reasoning IQ, all three tracks benefited;

and when the school as a whole did not benefit much, as in verbal IQ, none of the tracks showed much benefit. For all three IQ measures, the tendency was for the middle track, the more average children, to benefit most from being expected to grow intellectually, but the difference could easily have occurred by chance.

In total IQ, girls showed a slightly greater advantage than boys of having been expected to show an intellectual spurt; but to see what really happened we must look at boys' and girls' expectancy advantages for the two subtypes of IQ. Table 21–5 shows the gains in all three types of IQ by boys and girls

TABLE 21-5

Mean Gain in Three IQ Scores after One Year by Experimental and Control Boys and Girls

| | CONTROL | | EXPERIMENTAL | | EXPECTANCY ADVANTAGE | |
	N	GAIN	N	GAIN	ONE-TAIL IQ POINTS	p < .06
Total IQ						
Boys	127	+9.6	32	+12.5	+2.9	
Girls	128	+7.3	33	+12.0	+4.7	.04
Verbal IQ						
Boys	136	+8.4(−)	34	+13.9(+)	+5.6	.06
Girls	133	+7.2	34	+5.8	−1.4	
Reasoning IQ						
Boys	127	+19.2	32	+15.3	−3.9	
Girls	128	+12.3	33	+30.2	+17.9	.0002

of the experimental and control groups. In verbal IQ it was the boys who showed the expectancy advantage (interaction $F = 2.13$, $p = .16$); in reasoning IQ it was the girls who showed the advantage, and it was dramatic in size (interaction $F = 9.27$, $p = .003$). Just why that should be is not at all clear. On the pretest, boys had shown a higher verbal IQ than girls (4.4 points), and girls had shown a higher reasoning IQ than boys (8.5 points). Apparently each group profited more from teachers' prophecies in the area of intellectual functioning in which they were already a little advantaged.[4]

It was mentioned earlier that expectancy advantage was not dependent on placement in any one of the three tracks. That conclusion is modified when we examine expectancy advantages in the three tracks separately for boys and girls. Only for reasoning IQ is there a statistically significant effect (triple interaction $F = 3.47$, $p < .04$). Table 21–6 shows the excess of gain in reasoning IQ by the experimental over the control boys and girls in each of the three tracks. We already knew that girls showed the greater expectancy advantage in reasoning IQ, and from Table 21–6 we see that this was significantly truer in the medium track, the track with the more average children.

We knew also that girls are over-represented in the fast track. These are the brighter girls from whom a lot is already expected. The slow track girls

Pygmalion in the Classroom

TABLE 21-6

Excess of Gain in Reasoning
IQ by Experimental over
Control Boys and Girls in
Three Tracks after One Year

TRACK	BOYS	GIRLS
Fast	−2.6	+9.1
Medium	−12.0	+42.0[a]
Slow	−0.3	+12.5
Total	−3.9	+17.9

[a]$p = .00003$, one-tail.

tend to be relatively very slow at Oak School, and we know that girls only rarely are placed there, and that they represent a real challenge to Oak School's teachers. Of the middle-track girls there is little to say—teachers tend to find them uninteresting; preexisting expectations about their intellectual ability are neither favorable as in the fast track nor very unfavorable and challenging as in the slow track. Perhaps when teachers are given favorable expectations about these children a greater increment of interest results than when expectations are given of girls in the outer tracks. That is a possible explanation of the greater effect in the average track of teachers' favorable expectations for girls' intellectual growth. Why the growth should be in reasoning IQ in particular is not at all clear, but we do know that for the girls in this experiment when there are advantages of teacher prophecies they tend to occur in the reasoning sphere of intellectual functioning.

A pupil's sex turned out to be a factor complicating the amount of expectancy advantage found in the three tracks. Sex also complicated the magnitude of expectancy advantage found in the younger children of the first two grades compared to the older children of the upper four grades. Table 21–7 shows the number of IQ points by which the gains of the experimental-group children exceeded the gains of the control-group children. These expectancy advantage scores are shown separately for each of the three IQ measures for boys and girls in the lower and upper grades. For total IQ, although the "special" boys of the lower grades did profit from being expected to grow intellectually, the girls of the lower grades gained nearly three times as many IQ points as a function of favorable expectations (triple interaction $F = 2.96$, $p = .09$). For verbal IQ there was no difference between boys and girls at either grade level in the amount of profit from favorable expectations (triple interaction $F < 1$), although, as we learned earlier, boys and girls of the lower grades were helped more than children of upper grades three through six. For reasoning IQ, boys and girls at different grade levels did show very different magnitudes of expectancy advantage. Boys in higher grades performed better in contrast to girls in lower grades who performed better when they were expected to do better (triple interaction $F = 8.14$, $p < .005$). Most of that effect was due to the extraordinary performance of

382

TABLE 21-7

*Excess of Gain in Three IQ
Scores by Experimental over
Control Boys and Girls in Two
Grade Levels after One Year*

	BOYS	GIRLS
Total IQ		
Grades 1-2	+6.1	+17.1[b]
Grades 3-6	+2.3	−0.1
Verbal IQ		
Grades 1-2	+10.8[a]	+9.5
Grades 3-6	+2.8	−5.8
Reasoning IQ		
Grades 1-2	−10.7	+40.2[c]
Grades 3-6	+3.6	+10.0[a]

[a] $p < .05$, one-tail (or .10 two-tail).
[b] $p < .0002$, one-tail.
[c] $p < .00002$, one tail.

the first- and second-grade girls of the experimental group who gained over forty IQ points more than did the control-group girls of the first and second grade.

To summarize our somewhat complex findings involving pupil's sex as a factor, we may say most simply that girls bloomed more in the reasoning sphere of intellectual functioning, and boys bloomed more in the verbal sphere of intellectual functioning when some kind of unspecified blooming was expected of them. Furthermore, these gains were more likely to occur to a dramatic degree in the lower grades. That susceptibility to the unintended influence of the prophesying teacher should be greater in the lower grades comes as no special surprise. All lines of evidence tend to suggest that it is younger children who are the more susceptible to various forms of influence processes. The influence of a teacher holding favorable expectations may not be so very different. Why the boys gained more in verbal IQ when expected to gain intellectually, and why the girls gained more in reasoning IQ is not so easily explained. Earlier we did mention the possibility that children profit more from vague teacher expectations in those spheres of intellectual functioning in which they tend to be slightly advantaged to begin with. In Oak School, the pretest verbal IQs were higher for boys than for girls by over four points; the pretest reasoning IQs were higher for girls than for boys by over eight points.

EXPECTANCY ADVANTAGE BY MINORITY-GROUP STATUS

In total IQ, verbal IQ, and especially reasoning IQ, children of the minority group were more advantaged by favorable expectations than were the other children though the differences were not statistically significant.

For each of the Mexican children, the magnitude of expectancy advantage

Pygmalion in the Classroom

was computed by subtracting from his or her IQ gain the IQ gain made by
the children of the control group in his or her classroom.[5] The resulting
magnitudes of expectancy advantage were then correlated with the "Mexican-
ness" of the children's faces. Table 21-8 shows the correlations obtained

TABLE 21-8

*Correlations between Mexican Facial Characteristics and
Advantages of Favorable Expectations after One Year*

	BOYS		GIRLS		TOTAL	
	N	r	N	r	N	r
Total IQ	7	+.70[a]	9	−.14	16	+.27
Verbal IQ	7	+.54	10	−.11	17	+.21
Reasoning IQ	7	+.75[b]	9	−.01	16	+.14

[a]$p = .08$, two-tail.
[b]$p = .05$, two-tail.

among Mexican boys and girls when expectancy advantage was defined by
total, verbal, and reasoning IQs. For total IQ and reasoning IQ, those Mexican
boys who looked more Mexican benefited more from teachers' favorable
expectations than did the Mexican boys who looked less Mexican. There is
no clear explanation for these findings, but we can speculate that the teachers'
preexperimental expectancies of the more Mexican-looking boys' intellectual
performance was probably lowest of all. These children may have had the
most to gain by the introduction of a more favorable expectation into the
minds of their teachers.

Some Discussion

The results of the experiment we have described in some detail provide
further evidence that one person's expectations of another's behavior may
come to serve as a self-fulfilling prophecy. When teachers expected that certain children would show greater intellectual development, those children
did show greater intellectual development. For the basic year of the experiment, the self-fulfilling prophecy was in evidence primarily at the lower grade
levels; it is difficult to be certain why that was the case. A number of interpretations suggest themselves, and these are not mutually exclusive.

First, younger children are generally regarded as more malleable, less fixed,
more capable of change, more subject to the effects of critical periods (Scott,
1962). It may be, then, that the experimental conditions of our experiment
were more effective with younger children simply because younger children
are easier to change than older ones. (It should be recalled that when we

speak here of change we mean it as change relative to control-group change. Table 21-1 showed that even fifth graders can change dramatically in IQ, but there the change of the experimental-group children was not greater than the change of the control-group children.)

A second interpretation is that younger children within a given school have less well-established reputations within the school. It then becomes more credible to a teacher to be told that a younger child will show intellectual growth. A teacher may "know" an older child much better by reputation and be less inclined to believe him capable of intellectual growth simply on someone else's say-so.

A third interpretation is a combination, in a sense, of the first two. It suggests that younger children show greater gains associated with teachers' expectancies not because they necessarily *are* more malleable but rather because they are believed by teachers to be more malleable.

A fourth interpretation suggests that younger children are more sensitive to and more affected by the particular processes whereby teachers communicate their expectations to children. Under this interpretation, it is possible that teachers react to children of all grade levels in the same way if they believe them to be capable of intellectual gain. But perhaps it is only the younger children whose performance is affected by the special things the teacher says to them, the special ways in which she says them, the way she looks, postures, and touches the children from whom she expects greater intellectual growth.

A fifth interpretation suggests that the effects of teachers' expectations were more effective in the lower grade levels not because of any difference associated with the children's age but rather with some correlated sampling "errors." Thus it is possible that the children of the lower grades are the children of families that differ systematically from the families of the children of the higher grade levels.

A sixth interpretation also suggests that the greater IQ gain in younger children attributable to teacher expectation is a result of sampling "error," not in the sampling of children this time but in the sampling of teachers. It may be that in a variety of demographic, intellectual, and personality variables, the teachers of the younger children differed from the teachers of the older children such that they may have (1) believed the communications about their "special" children more or (2) been more effective communicators to their children of their expectations for the children's performance.

There is some evidence to suggest that teachers of the lower grades do in fact differ from the teachers of the upper grades of Oak School. Two administrators who were well acquainted with all the teachers rated them on overall effectiveness as teachers. The two administrators agreed well in their ratings ($r = +.88$) and, although there were many exceptions, teachers of the lower grades were judged to be more effective teachers by both administrators (average r between effectiveness and teaching grade $= -.57$, $p < .02$).

The finding that only the younger children profited after one year from their teachers' favorable expectations helps us to understand better the results of two other experimenters, Clifford Pitt (1956) and Charles Flowers (1966). Pitt, it will be recalled, divided his sample of fifth-grade boys into three groups. For one group he reported the boys' IQ scores to the teachers after having arbitrarily added ten points. For another group he reported the boys' IQ scores after having deducted ten points. For the third group he reported the boys' actual IQ scores. Pitt found that there were no effects on school achievement at the end of the year of teachers having been given false information about their pupils' IQ.

The results of our own study suggest that after one year, fifth graders may not show the effects of teacher expectations though first and second graders do. Pitt's study differed in too many ways from our own to make direct comparisons possible, however. Pitt did not, for example, retest the children on IQ per se but only on school achievement. More important perhaps, is the fact that Pitt's teachers knew their pupils for nearly two months before being given pupils' IQ scores. That was long enough for teachers to have developed realistic expectations of pupils' performance more powerful than the expectations that could have been induced by adding or deducting IQ points.

The equivocal results of Flowers' experiment are also not directly comparable to our own data. Flowers' pupils were also older children (seventh graders) and each child had many different teachers rather than just one. Perhaps the effect of teachers' expectations were diluted by being distributed over many teachers. In the case of Flowers' study, we must bear in mind, too, that the classes arbitrarily labeled as brighter had been assigned different teachers than had been assigned to the control-group classes. Therefore, any differences between the experimental- and control-group classes could have been due to differences in the quality of teachers assigned to each.

NOTES

1. The reader interested in the more technical aspects of the design and analysis of experiments will recognize our presentation as following the plan of a multifactorial analysis of variance with interest focused on the main effect of treatments, the two-way interactions of treatments by grades, treatments by tracks, treatments by sex, and treatments by minority-group status by sex. All other possible three-way and higher-order interactions yielded one or more empty cells or a number of cells with Ns so small as to weaken any confidence in the results even though the analyses were possible in principle.

All two-way and three-way analyses had unequal and nonproportional Ns per cell, and Walker and Lev's (1953) approximate solution was employed. Since all double interactions were computed directly and also were estimated in one or more of the three-factor analyses of variance, it should be pointed out that whenever the discussion is of a simple interaction, the F test was based on the two-way analysis rather than on the three-way analysis because the greater N per cell of the two-way analysis provided a more stable estimate. When a given double interaction, however, also entered into a significant triple interaction, that fact is indicated in the text, and the interpretation of the two-way interaction is modified accordingly. The main effect of treatments was of course obtained in each of the analyses of variance, and p values associated with the Fs ranged from .05 to .002.

When we consider classrooms as the sampling unit ($N = 17$), we find that in eleven of the seventeen classes in which the comparison was possible (one class was inadvertently not posttested for reasoning IQ) children of the experimental group gained more in total IQ than did children of the control group. The one-tail ps associated with the sign test, the Wilcoxon matched-pairs, signed-ranks test, and the t test for correlated means were .17, .06, and .03, respectively. . . .

2. Considering classrooms as the sampling unit ($N = 18$), we find children of the experimental group gained more in verbal IQ than did children of the control group in twelve of the eighteen classes. The one-tail ps associated with the sign test, Wilcoxon test, and t test were .12, .23, and .25, respectively. . . .

3. Considering classrooms as the sampling unit ($N = 17$), we find the advantage of favorable expectations to occur in fifteen of the seventeen classrooms. The one-tail ps associated with the sign, Wilcoxon, and t tests were .001, .003, and .003, respectively. . . .

4. This footnote will serve to illustrate the complexity of nature and the need for noncomplacency in the behavioral researcher. Preliminary results of a study conducted with Judy Evans give just the opposite results and with an equally significant probability level. The same basic experiment conducted at Oak School was repeated in two elementary schools located in a small Midwestern town. Unlike Oak School, which drew its pupils from a lower-class community, these schools drew their pupils from a substantial middle-class community. Oak School's student body included a large proportion of minority-group members; the two Midwestern schools did not. The mean pretest total IQ at Oak School was 98, compared to the pretest total IQ of 105 found in these Midwestern schools. Eight months after the teachers had been given the names of their "special" children, retests were administered. The results of the studies at the two schools were sufficiently similar that the results could reasonably be combined. No expectancy advantage was found for either boys or girls as measured by total IQ or verbal IQ. For reasoning IQ, however, the results were opposite to those found at Oak School. Now it was the boys who showed the benefits of favorable teacher expectations. Those who had been expected to bloom gained over sixteen IQ points compared to the less than nine gained by control-group boys. Among the girls it was the control-group children who gained about fifteen IQ points while those of the experimental group gained just over five IQ points. (The interaction F was 9.10, $p < .003$.) In these schools, just as in Oak School, boys had shown higher pretest verbal IQs than girls while girls had shown higher pretest reasoning IQs than boys. Therefore, in these middle-class schools it was not true that each sex benefited most from favorable teacher expectations in those areas in which they were already somewhat advantaged. At the time of this writing there appears to be no ready explanation for this dramatic and very highly statistically significant reversal ($p = .00004$) in the two studies. But now we know for sure that Oak School's results, like the results of all behavioral experiments, are not universal.

5. All of the control-group children in each classroom were employed as the basis of comparison rather than just the Mexican children. This was done to provide a more stable estimate of control-group gains, there being too few Mexican children in some classrooms. Among the children of the control group there was a high rank correlation between the IQ gains of the Mexican and non-Mexican children; $+.74$ for the fifteen classrooms in which the comparison could be made ($p < .003$). The corresponding correlation between IQ gains of all children and just the Mexican children was $+.90$ ($p < .001$).

REFERENCES

Coffin, T. E. "Some conditions of suggestion and suggestibility." *Psychological Monographs* 53, no. 4, 1941 (whole no. 241).

Flowers, C. E. Effects of an arbitrary accelerated group placement on the tested academic achievement of educationally disadvantaged students. Unpublished doctoral dissertation, Teachers College, Columbia University, 1966.

Jacobson, Lenore. Explorations of variations in educational achievement among Mexican children, grades one to six. Unpublished doctoral dissertation, University of California, Berkeley, 1966.

Pitt, C. C. V. An experimental study of the effects of teachers' knowledge or incorrect knowledge of pupil IQ's on teachers' attitudes and practices and pupils' attitudes and achievement. Unpublished doctoral dissertation, Columbia University, 1956.

Scott, J. P. "Critical periods in behavioral development." *Science* 138 (1962): 949–958.

Stevenson, H. W. "Social reinforcement of children's behavior." In L. P. Lipsitt and C. G. Spiker (eds.), *Advances in Child Development and Behavior*, Vol. 2. New York: Academic, 1965.

Thorndike, R. L. "Intellectual status and intellectual growth." *Journal of Educational Psychology* 57 (1966): 121–127.

Walker, Helen M., and J. Lev. *Statistical Inference*. New York: Holt, Rinehart and Winston, 1953.

PART IV

Making Organizations
Work for People:
Strategies for
Innovation and Change

W E HOPE it is plain by now that we are not simply neutral observers, coldly recording the passing scene, but that we have some feeling for the problems raised in these readings. Our own work on officials and clients has been carried out in Jerusalem, and we have some ideas about what can be done here. In fact, we think the classical problems of official–client relations —red-tape, long lines, and the like—are more prevalent in Israel than the United States today. Other problems of organization–public relations are nearly universal, particularly those having to do with public control of bureaucracy. But some are almost uniquely characteristic of the United States in the late 1960s and 1970s. In this introduction and the readings in this Part, we focus attention on the kinds of proposals which are being made these days. There is no pretense here at representativeness; obviously, there are hundreds of proposals that could not be included. Nor is this Part based primarily on research, as the other Parts were.

Many of the authors represented in the previous chapters surely feel as we do. Indeed, while their works were primarily research-oriented, many have quite specific implications for action. Consider Sjoberg (1966)* for example. His chapter, in Part I, points out how ignorant poor people are of their rights. One of the chapters in this Part, which describes the new role of the ghetto lawyer, is really a response to Sjoberg and his colleagues. This is a proposal for a high-status go-between who will not shrink from representing lower-class clients. It is also a message addressed to social workers about their professional obligations. Perhaps this is all too utopian—it is not even clear who will pay the ghetto lawyer, or how social workers can resist the normal temptations to raise their own professional status by dealing with higher-status clients—but Sjoberg's article, obviously, has a number of implicit suggestions for action.

Or consider Milgram's (1963)* chapter, also in Part I. If Milgram is correct, the dynamics of child and adult socialization have taken a very undesirable turn. Whether or not the same kinds of reactions are to be found in other less bureaucratic cultures, Milgram clearly has a message for the next edition of Dr. Spock: train children to beware of the uncritical acceptance of the dictates of (even legitimate) authority.

In the discussion that follows we shall return repeatedly to the selections considered previously in the context of our discussion of current proposals for innovation and change.

Inefficiency, Inhumanity, Inaccessibility

We suggested in the Introduction that the three major complaints voiced against bureaucracy are that it is inefficient, inhuman, and inaccessible. As we have seen, the problem of inefficiency may well be the ironic result of oversocialization of officials, and perhaps of clients too, to the bureaucratic regimen. This is the unanticipated consequence of bureaucratization which Merton (1952) pointed out in his famous essay. Perhaps he is wrong; or perhaps things have changed. So, at any rate, suggests Kohn (1971),* though he has nothing to say about efficiency, of course. Whatever the case, it seems to us helpful to begin to think of two, not just one, criteria of efficiency. There is the efficiency of procedure-oriented organizations, which can presumably be improved with advanced mechanization; and there is the efficiency of the service-oriented organizations which must struggle with the question of what proportion of the whole person to treat and still get the job done well. This is one of the questions of Blau's (1960) employment agency. As far as we can see, very little attention has been given to the problem of efficiency in dealing with clients. There exist very many studies—empirical and theoretical—on the subject of bureaucratic efficiency, but almost all of them have to do with increasing productivity in the factory, or reorganizing the structure of authority in a government office, or keeping closer tabs on expenditures in a television station. This is what the management consultants do. But where are the studies of efficiency in dealing with clients— and what, indeed, are the criteria for measuring efficiency? There surely must be work on this subject—perhaps in the private files of organizations—but we have nothing in hand.

It is even more curious that the problem of the alleged inhumanity of the social relations of bureaucratic organizations should also be so conspicuously unstudied. The flourishing human relations approach to the study and treatment of organizations caught hold many years ago, but again, as far as we know, this work does not deal directly with problems of the relationships between organizations and their clients. Whyte's (1946) proposals for restaurants are exceptions that come to mind. Another exception is Catrice-Lorey's (1966)* proposals for humanizing the service offered by French social security offices to their members.

The problem of inaccessibility is a direct result of the growth of tremendous concentrations of power, whether in government agencies or in private corporations. It reflects both the feeling of powerlessness in the individual client, and the problem of how democratic societies can retain active control over their ever-expanding organizations.

It is to the problem of control that most suggestions for organizational reform are addressed, and this emphasis is clearly reflected in the readings that follow. This fact does not make efficiency and humanity less important subjects for our attention and concern, however. In fact, strategies to improve controls over bureaucracy will *also* bring improvements in these two other problem areas. In other words, the three problems are *related*. Thus, if clients feel more efficacious vis-à-vis big organizations the deleterious effects of the impersonality of bureaucracy may be reduced. Schemes for decentralization and/or "citizen participation" will by definition reduce the scale of big organizations, making face-to-face encounters in a more personal atmosphere possible. And controls like the institution of the ombudsman, described below, should not only obtain redress of grievances for the "little man," but ultimately improve the overall efficiency of service to the public.

It seems that far more proposals have been put forward for increasing the environmental constraints on bureaucracy than for changing either the organizational structure or the situational setting. Since this book is organized in terms of these three headings, it may be useful to group the various proposals in the same way.

Situational Proposals

Those who have been attracted by problems of the situation of contact are researchers like Sommer (1966) or Hall (1960). Sommer's specialty as a psychologist is in the spatial ecology of human relationships. His diagnosis that the furniture arrangements in a geriatric ward discouraged conversation led to the introduction of square tables and chairs, and as a result, the aging patients talked to each other more than they had before. More generally, rearrangement of the physical environment is one type of strategy for change.

Changing the character of interaction between official and client is also Lombard's (1955) idea. He is concerned over the misperceptions of saleswomen about their customers and their wants, and proposes ways in which the department store might go about changing these. He believes that this is best done by starting at the top: changing the criteria by which executives evaluate sales women, and then changing saleswomen's evaluations of customers. In the best tradition of human relations counseling, Lombard proposes the use of training groups to achieve these purposes.

Changing the Organization

Lombard's proposal is perhaps even better classified as changing the organization. His emphasis, like that of other human relations practitioners, is on training designed to make individuals working in organizations more sensitive to each other's needs and perceptions. The idea of using training groups as a technique to improve the interpersonal skills of workers has attracted a good deal of attention in the last ten years or so, particularly in the form known as "T-groups" (T for training; e.g., Schein and Bennis, 1965). Prominent among the goals of its proponents is the notion of "power equalization" (cf. Leavitt, in March 1965), or minimizing the effects of hierarchical differences in the organizational structure. As we have noted elsewhere, this approach assumes, quite explicitly, that there is a conflict between organizational and personal needs, and its emphasis is on maximizing self-actualization of the individual as the main organization problem, rather than increasing organizational efficiency. But while this kind of training might lead to real improvements in relationships with clients on the whole, the method, as far as we know, has not been applied to this end. Also, this kind of "organizational sociotherapy" does not appear to be practical as a general remedy.

More specifically structural suggestions for change derive from the work of others. For example, the idea that organizations should have more readily available channels for complaint is implicit in the work of Bar-Yosef and Schild (1966).* The idea that people waiting on line deserve to be correctly channeled by a kind of floor manager has recently come into vogue. One sees hostesses patroling the queues of people waiting to buy a ticket and board an airplane or those waiting on line in front of the teller's window in the bank. The free income tax advice available in person and over the telephone provide a similar directive service.

Thomas's (1959) paper on the influence of organizational and community size on role definitions of social workers implies that smaller service organizations may be better able to maintain personalized service to their clients. A more radical presentation arguing for some of the same things is Goodman's *People or Personnel* (1968), which calls for decentralization of organizations—especially people-serving ones, in order to restore the personal touch and a sense of psychological community.

Catrice-Lorey's (1966)* reading on the French social security system suggests, for example, that the office hours of the various offices are frequently set for the convenience of the workers rather than the public. Her reference to "hostesses and green plants" implies attention to the physical and personal atmosphere of the offices. Most important of her suggestions, however, is that of recruiting officials of a higher cultural and educational level, and then giving them intensive training to develop a service orientation.

But in more long-term perspective, Catrice-Lorey's work raises the larger issue of the nature of work with clients in bureaucratic organizations. If we are correct in assuming, as we have freely done thus far, that procedure-oriented organizations will become increasingly computerized, then let the process be hastened whereby one purchases stamps and toothpaste from machines and orders groceries electronically. And, at the same time, why not try to move in the direction of professionalization of the service-oriented organizations? There are many new professions of this sort—osteopaths, public relations counselors, even social workers. Or, if full professionalization seems exaggerated, there are a variety of semiprofessional statuses such as physiotherapists or tourist guides (cf. Etzioni, 1969). The object of this approach would be to make today's procedure-oriented officials into semi-professionals possessing a body of expert knowledge, a service ideal, and a more cosmopolitan commitment to the profession beyond the boundaries of the organization itself. At the same time, the hierarchical structure of their organizations would also be transformed, modeled after the kinds of bureaucracies which incorporate professional workers. This emphasis is rather more lenient than that of Goode (1961), who in his sermon to the librarians informs them that they do not yet qualify for admission to professional status because they have no real knowledge of clients' needs (as distinct from their wants) and no real body of scientific knowledge on which to base their profession.

Changing the Environment

Most of the proposals for change concentrate *outside* the organization and the situation of contact. There is a large variety of suggestions here, some tried and some untried.

COUNTERORGANIZATION AND CITIZEN PARTICIPATION:
THE PROPOSALS AND THE DEBATE

The most radical of the suggestions we shall cite calls for the overthrow of specific bureaucratic organizations, by quite nonviolent means. This is Cloward and Piven's (1966) call for all legitimate beneficiaries of government social welfare agencies to apply for their rights and thus paralyze the organization by its inability to keep up with demand. The object is to do away with this particular kind of welfare bureaucracy, although the guaranteed annual income which would replace it would also be administered by a bureaucracy —though not a bureaucracy that requires regular face-to-face contact. The ultimate goal of the "welfare rights movement," as it calls itself, is to end poverty, and as such, has widespread appeal, partly because it dovetails with the growing movement for *consumer* rights.

Whatever the achievements of this movement so far, welfare recipients have participated in demonstrations and organized demands for improved rights across the nation (Cloward and Piven, 1967) and have dared to defy welfare authorities. Even if the long-term disruption of the welfare system is not in sight, hundreds of poor people have become aware of their rights and have, at least in the short run, participated in some aspect of the activities inspired by the welfare rights movement.

Activist-sociologist Frank Riessman criticizes Cloward and Piven for overemphasizing income and underemphasizing the importance of satisfying work. His proposal calls for "New Careers for the Poor" (1969, chap. 3) and is based on the idea of restructuring work in the growing human-services occupations so that the poor are coopted as paraprofessionals while acquiring an education. This would be functional for both the organization and the rehabilitated person: professional organizations are short of help and many of their functions can be performed by less highly trained persons. But most important, opportunities for education and training while on the job will help the poor person pull himself up the social ladder. Moreover, participation of the poor within the organization will lead to better service to clients because professionals will have more time to do the things they do best. And, no less important, the paraprofessionals will serve as mediators between the organization and its clients because of their greater ease in communicating with clients of like sociocultural characteristics and values. In principle this strategy proposes not merely to acknowledge that the poor have difficulties in coping with the complexities of modern society (as we did in Part I)—but to *end poverty*. Thus, by restructuring the organization, Riessman ultimately hopes to restructure *society*. Both he and Cloward and Piven seek to end poverty, though the means by which they propose to do this are different.

Riessman's program derives ultimately from the themes of "counter-organization" and "citizen participation" as part of the war against poverty and the poverty-serving bureaucracies. Neither of these themes is altogether new, though they have been given some fresh slants in the turbulent 1960s. In an influential analysis of the problems of mass society, Kornhauser (1959) recommended voluntary organizations as a means to bridge the gap between the elites and the masses. Counterorganization in unions, PTAs, neighborhood block clubs, and so on was to give the atomized individual in mass society a sense of participation and efficacy. Seeman's (1966) research on the relationship between membership in such organizations and feelings of powerlessness has borne out Kornhauser's hypothesis. A person's feelings of self-reliance and power are associated with whether he belongs to an organization that has some control over his occupational destiny. The more active he is in that organization, the more efficacious he feels. Less optimistic is the other part of Seeman's research, which finds that people who feel powerless are less able even to *learn* role-relevant information than those who feel more powerful.

A well-known activist who had been working for years with techniques of counterorganization was the late Saul Alinsky. As early as the 1940s, Alinsky published a book called *Reveille for Radicals* (1946) in which he described the need for people's organizations in poor communities. Silberman's article (1964) on Alinsky's activities in Chicago describes his success in organizing the poor people of the Chicago slum of Woodlawn into an association known as The Woodlawn Organization (TWO), in order to combat exploitation by local stores charging high prices and excessive interest on credit purchases. Other targets of TWO's activities were slum landlords and poor schools.

Silberman adds a sociotherapeutic dimension to Alinsky's tactics, suggesting that he turned the apathetic and dependent poor into dignified efficacious citizens.

Despite Alinsky's fame, not all have been so enthusiastic about his disruptive tactics, which range from rent strikes to sit-ins to walk-outs (cf. Riessman, 1969, chap. 1; Rose, and Sherrard and Murray, in Spiegel, 1968). More serious is the claim (Riessman, 1969, chap. 1) that Alinsky was not a genuine radical—that only the rhetoric, and not the goals, are radical—that he had no major program for social change on a national level. Riessman claims that Alinsky overestimated the numbers of people he had organized, and that even the effectiveness—short term or long term—of his tactics is in doubt. What is important for our general discussion of strategies to strengthen clients is that Alinsky has become a symbol of counterorganization, a champion of the underdog. But, as we shall see, the romantic halo surrounding the mystique of "the power of the poor" and of "citizen participation" has sadly worn thin in the last five years.

The Community Action Programs established under the Economic Opportunity Act of 1964 which opened the War on Poverty, called for "maximum feasible participation of the residents of the areas and the members of the groups" involved in local programs. The wide range of programs set up included Head Start, Neighborhood Legal Services, and job training programs. By January 1966, the fifty biggest cities had CAPs. Urban renewal activities also called for wide-ranging citizen participation.

Much has since been written about the failure of these programs to help the poor in any serious way. One reason was that, unfortunately, citizen participation and counterorganization are global terms whose meaning were left vague in much of the legislation (Krause, 1968; Moynihan, 1970). Krause's analysis of citizen participation as an ideology clarifies some of the other reasons for the failures. Most prominent are perhaps two factors: while the *target* groups of urban renewal programs were the poor, the groups whose *interests* were actually served by these programs were typically the better-off, including the businessmen in the district being rehabilitated. In the case of the CAPs, the poor were both the target group and the group whose interests were being served, but, according to Krause and Moynihan, pressure on Washington from local groups (typically middle class) opposing the new activities led to a "cooling down" of plans for change. Thus the reasons for the failure of citizen participation in the two cases were different, but the outcomes the same. Second, Van Til and Van Til (1970) add that citizen participation strategies failed to distinguish between (1) participation in an *advisory* capacity only, versus (2) actual sharing in the *implementation* of plans, or (3) *policymaking* itself. One result was that citizen participation became a slogan to which people paid lip-service only.

There appears to be consensus both among academics and social activists today (e.g., Wilson, 1966; Moynihan, 1970; Crain and Rosenthal in Spiegel, 1968; Van Til and Van Til, 1970) that, in Wilson's words, "effective local planning requires *less,* not more citizen participation" [p. 29]. The controversy goes on, and we cannot hope to resolve it here, except to note that there are some who, even after due consideration of the inefficiencies and complications, still advocate the pursuit of effective citizen participation (e.g., Cahn and Cahn, in Spiegel, 1968). No doubt, the seventies will see further efforts to "save" citizen participation. Moynihan concludes:

Social science research has for decades established the high correlation between social class and the level of social participation: high-high; low-low. It may be that participation is more an effect than a cause, and that until there have been fundamental economic changes in the life of poor populations, these other qualities can only be achieved at the great costs in civility which Alinsky, nothing if not unflinching in his consistency and honesty, has repeatedly avowed [1970, p. 163].

While the problems of the poor and the welfare rights movement have dominated the scene in the 1960s, the consumers' rights movement is an effort in an entirely different area which has also gained momentum. The problems of the consumer vis-à-vis producers and distributors were recognized earlier (e.g., Etzioni, 1958; Caplovitz, 1963) but strategies for control are a much newer development. As Schrag (1970)* comments in the opening line of his article, "The consumer's central civil right is the right to get his money's worth." Schrag, who heads an investigative staff for the New York City Department of Consumer Affairs, lists a series of new strategies for strengthening the position of consumers vis-à-vis sellers. First is the need to make going to court easy and financially feasible. Legislation includes such services for the genuinely poor in some places, but for the better-off it is often hard to find an address from which to get help. Second, a trend is underway to pass legislation which will make unconstitutional some of the tricks by which dealers have exploited consumers in the past. At the state level this has already been done in New York. Another promising device is what is called "class action"—a lawsuit in which one consumer sues for a refund not only for himself but for all other victims of a particular merchant.

Schrag and his colleagues work for consumers' rights at two levels: at the level of the individual consumer and his particular problem, and at the level of reform of the legal system guaranteeing consumers' rights on behalf of *all* consumers. These activities in the private sector are in some ways analogous to the function of the ombudsman in government bureaucracy; in the short run he seeks redress of grievances for particular individuals, but in the long run he too works for improvement in the general level of administration.

Like Schrag, Ralph Nader is trained as a lawyer. His activities have been institutionalized as the Center for the Study of Responsive Law in Washington, which has become a symbol of the right to demand high quality goods and services. With teams of volunteers, he investigates a very wide range of problems of concern to the general public, from radiation health hazards, to coal mine safety, to cyclamates, to air and water pollution. The objects of his scrutinizing investigations are both government agencies (The Interstate Commerce Commission, The Department of Agriculture's Pesticides Regulation Division) and private industry (General Motors).

MEDIATING MECHANISMS AND REGULATORY AGENCIES

It is ironic that the three-letter agencies established during Roosevelt's New Deal for the very purpose of *regulating* large and small organizations in the public interest have recently come under criticism. In the 1960s this was one of the targets of Goodman's *People or Personnel.* Analyzing the growth of centralized big government in America, he charged that "the regulatory agencies, sponsored by the older liberalism, have become accomodations with the giant monopolies, rather than means of pluralizing" [Goodman, 1968, p. 29]. Nader and his team have taken over the responsibility of documenting this charge, with the publication of three volumes in 1970, each of which attacks a different government agency (Turner, 1970; Esposito and Silverman, 1970; Fellmeth, 1970*). Thus Fellmeth argues that the Interstate Commerce Commission excludes the public from the decision-making process; suppresses important studies of commission functions and transportation problems; rubber-stamps railroad mergers; is allowing passenger railroad service to die; looks the other way while home-moving services cheat the customer; and so on. At the same time, the Federal Communications Commission (FCC) is being chastised by maverick Commissioner Nicholas Johnson (1970) in trying to mobilize viewers to take an active part in challenging the almost automatic renewal of the licenses of radio and television stations.

Still, some of the profoundest hopes for improvement of bureaucratic services are being placed on "mediating mechanisms" of various kinds. These are not counterorganizations, but links between the citizen and the bureaucracy, to provide the information, the social support, and the justice which are often so sorely needed. The magic word here is ombudsman, the "client's man" vis-à-vis government bureaucracy in Scandinavia, who reviews various mechanisms for the control of public administration in the interest of the public. Gellhorn (1966)* compares the institution of ombudsman with the "procurator" (in Russia); the administrative inspection bureau (Japan); the Question Hour in Parliament (in Britain). It is important to distinguish between before-the-fact and after-the-fact handling of the problem. After-the-fact mechanisms for the redress of grievances are suited to the investigation of the complaints of *individuals,* while before-the-fact legislation can set standards for equitable and responsive treatment for the public at large. Thus, in another chapter from Gellhorn's book, he discusses the casework function of congressmen in Washington, who maintain large staffs to handle individual complaints and requests.

Important developments in providing legal services to the disadvantaged have occurred in the last ten years. In Part I we reviewed some of the difficulties of the average citizen, particularly people of low income and education, in making their way around the maze of bureaucratic regulations and procedures. Potential welfare recipients typically don't know their rights; even middle-class citizens don't necessarily know how they can legitimately reduce their income tax without professional advice; and as we note below exploited consumers are often unaware that they can sue the persons or organization who duped them. Matthews and Weiss (1967)* spell out what can be done to help the poor get good legal services, and explain why the lawyer, as opposed to other types of mediators, is especially appealing to the underdog: traditionally, the lawyer does not prejudge the merits of the case from the viewpoint of the organization; rather, he does his best for the client alone. And unlike social workers who often perceive their clients in terms of middle-class values, the lawyer treats his client as a moral equal. Very much the same line of argument is found in the writings of Cahn and Cahn on the problems of the poor (e.g., Cahn and Cahn, 1964).

Another type of mediating mechanism which has attracted attention recently is what is know as Citizens' Advice Bureaus or Neighborhood Information Centers (Kahn, *et al.*).* The English Bureaus are mainly staffed by volunteers, and are designed to be maximally accessible to the public. As the overview of their activities shows, they perform an unusually wide range of services, from personal support during a crisis to supply of information about availability of services and citizens' rights, even to informal advocacy for clients seeking to establish eligibility for certain rights. Kahn and his colleagues discuss the applicability of the British experience to the American scene, and develop a set of recommendations for the establishment of similar neighborhood centers for American cities.

These mechanisms have come to supplement, but probably not to supercede, such old and new devices as radio and television confrontations between clients who feel victimized and their bureaucratic adversary, letters to the editor, and even—in traditional settings—professional petition-writers who offer their typewritten services in the entrance halls of the formidable government bureaucracies. Nor should one forget the courts as a mediating mechanism, though Gellhorn describes some of the difficulties in redressing client grievances through the courts.

PROTECTING PRIVACY

A final area of public concern over the inroads made by bureaucracy is the theme of the *invasion of privacy,* which, as suggested in the Introduction, is a special case of the general problem of the control of bureaucracy. Here too the 1960s have seen a continuing and heated debate about the nature and extent of the problem and the remedies available for it (e.g., Westin, 1967; Rosenberg, 1969; Packard, 1964; Michael, in Taviss, 1970; Miller, 1971). Westin argues that a host of new techniques of physical, psychological, and data surveillance have been invented as by-products of the technological advances of the 1960s. It is now cheap and simple to penetrate into the private life of individuals in ways unforeseen; and, as he well documents, more and more organizations, both private and public, are doing it. In the concluding chapter of his book, he proposes a set of analytic criteria for the reevaluation and redefinition of American cultural norms about personal privacy, and reviews a set of strategies for the guarantee of that privacy, such as the development of intra-organizational restraints on misuse of these new techniques and the invention of scientific countermeasures against them (just as in warfare, every new weapon generates a new counterweapon). At the same time he recommends government action through legislation to control unreasonable invasions of privacy.

Introduction to the Readings in This Part

Gellhorn's comprehensive review of the forms of redress available to the citizen-client in different times and places opens this section. The role of the ombudsman is carefully analyzed and compared with alternate forms of formal intervention in the client's behalf. The next three selections treat various efforts to mobilize communities and their resources for the purpose of strengthening the client's hand in his dealings with big organizations. Matthews and Weiss outline the challenge to first-rate lawyers of the legal frontier in the urban slum. The workings of the neighborhood Citizen's Advice Bureau of England are described by Kahn and his colleagues. Consumer advocate Schrag reports on how organized consumers can make their weight felt.

Finally Fellmeth describes the failure of the Interstate Trade Commission to regulate the activities of home movers, and makes specific recommendations for improved service to the public. Perhaps it is a coincidence that most of these men are lawyers. Perhaps it is not.

REFERENCES

Alinsky, Saul. *Reveille for Radicals.* Chicago: University of Chicago Press, 1946.
Bar-Yosef, Rivka, and E. O. Schild. "Pressures and Defenses in Bureaucratic Roles." *American Journal of Sociology* 71, no. 6 (May 1966): 665–673.
Blau, Peter M. *Bureaucracy in Modern Society.* New York: Random House, 1956.
Cahn, Edgar S., and Jean C. Cahn. "The War on Poverty: A Civilian Perspective." *Yale Law Journal* 73, no. 8 (1964): 1317–1352.
———. "Citizen Participation." In *Citizen Participation in Urban Development, Volume 1—Concepts and Issues,* edited by Hans B. C. Spiegel, pp. 211–224. Washington, D.C.: Center for Community Affairs, NTL Institute for Applied Behavioral Science, 1968.
Caplovitz, David. *The Poor Pay More.* New York: Free Press, 1963.
Cloward, Richard A., and Frances Fox Piven. "A Strategy to End Poverty." *The Nation* 202 (May 2, 1966): 510–517.

Part IV

———. "Birth of a Movement." *The Nation* 204 (May 8, 1967): 582–588.

Crain, Robert L., and Donald B. Rosenthal. "Community Status as a Dimension of Local Decision Making." *American Sociological Review* 32 (1967): 970–984.

Esposito, John C., and Larry J. Silverman. *Vanishing Air: The Ralph Nader Study Group Report on Air Pollution*. New York: Grossman, 1970.

Etzioni, Amitai. "Administration and the Consumer." *Administrative Science Quarterly* 3, no. 2 (1958): 251–264.

———, ed. *The Semi-Professions and Their Organization*. New York: Free Press, 1969.

Fellmeth, Robert. *The Interstate Commerce Omission: The Ralph Nader Study Group Report on the ICC and Transportation*. New York: Grossman, 1970.

Gellhorn, Walter. *Ombudsmen and Others*. Cambridge: Harvard University Press, 1966.

Goode, William. "The Librarian: From Occupation to Profession?" *The Library Quarterly* 31, no. 4 (1961): 306–318.

Goodman, Paul. *People or Personnel*. New York: Vintage, 1968.

Hall, Edward T. "The Silent Language in Overseas Business." *Harvard Business Review* 38, no. 3 (1960): 87–96.

Johnson, Nicholas. *How to Talk Back to Your Television Set*. Boston: Little, Brown, 1970.

Kohn, Melvin. "Bureaucratic Man: A Portrait and Interpretation." *American Sociological Review* 36 (1971): 461–474.

Kornhauser, William. *The Politics of the Mass Society*. Glencoe: Free Press, 1959.

Krause, Elliot A. "Functions of a Bureaucratic Ideology: Citizen Participation." *Social Problems* 16, no. 2 (Fall 1968): 129–143.

Leavitt, Harold J. "Applied Organizational Change in Industry: Structural, Technological, and Humanistic Approaches." In *Handbook of Organizations*, edited by James G. March, pp. 1144–1170. Chicago: Rand McNally, 1965.

Lombard, George G. *Behavior in a Selling Group*. Cambridge: Graduate School of Business Administration, Harvard University Press, 1955.

Matthews, Arthur R., and Jonathan A. Weiss. "What Can Be Done: A Neighborhood Lawyer's Credo." *Boston University Law Review* 67, no. 2 (1967): 231–243.

Michael, Donald N. "The Privacy Question." In *The Computer Impact*, edited by Irene Taviss, pp. 169–181. Englewood Cliffs: Prentice-Hall, 1970.

Miller, Arthur. *The Assault on Privacy*. Ann Arbor: University of Michigan Press, 1971.

Moynihan, Daniel P. *Maximum Feasible Misunderstanding*. New York: Free Press, 1970.

Packard, Vance. *The Naked Society*. London: Longmans, 1964.

Riessman, Frank. *Strategies Against Poverty*. New York: Random House, 1969.

Rose, Stephen C. "Saul Alinsky and His Critics." In *Citizen Participation in Urban Development, Volume I—Concepts and Issues*, edited by Hans B. C. Spiegel, pp. 162–183. Washington, D.C.: Center for Community Affairs, NTL Institute for Applied Behavioral Science, 1968.

Rosenberg, Jerry M. *The Death of Privacy*. New York: Random House, 1969.

Schein, Edgar H., and Warren G. Bennis, eds. *Personal and Organizational Change Through Group Methods*. New York: Wiley, 1965.

Schrag, Philip G. "Consumer Rights." *Columbia Forum* 13, no. 2 (Summer 1970): 4–10.

Seeman, Melvin. "Antidote to Alienations—Learning to Belong." *Trans-Action* 3, no. 4 (1966): 34–39.

Sherrard, Thomas D., and Richard C. Murray. "The Church and Neighborhood Community Organization." In *Citizen Participation in Urban Development, Volume I—Concepts and Issues*, edited by Hans B. C. Spiegel, pp. 184–205. Washington, D.C.: Center for Community Affairs, NTL Institute for Applied Behavioral Science, 1968.

Silberman, Charles E. "Up from Apathy—The Woodlawn Experiment." *Commentary* 37, no. 5 (May 1964): 51–58.

Sjoberg, Gideon, Richard A. Brymer, and Buford Farris. "Bureaucracy and the Lower Class." *Sociology and Social Research* 50, no. 3 (April 1966): 325–337.

Sommer, Robert. *Personal Space: The Behavioral Basis of Design.* Englewood Cliffs: Prentice-Hall, 1969.

Thomas, Edwin J. "Role Conceptions, Organizational Size, and Community Context." *American Sociological Review* 24 (1959): 30–37.

Turner, James S. *The Chemical Feast: The Ralph Nader Study Group Report on Food Protection and the Food and Drug Administration.* New York: Grossman, 1970.

Van Til, Jon, and Sally Bould Van Til. "Citizen Participation in Social Policy: The End of the Cycle?" *Social Problems* 17, no. 3 (Winter 1970): 313–323.

Westin, Alan F. *Privacy and Freedom.* New York: Atheneum, 1967.

Wilson, James Q. "The War on Cities." *The Public Interest* 3 (1966): 27–44.

22

Walter Gellhorn

CONFINING PUBLIC ADMINISTRATION
WITHOUT CRIPPLING IT

Nobody likes being governed. Even so, everybody save philosophical anarchists and nostalgic inhabitants of some pre-twentieth-century dream world accepts the necessity of continuously active government. Organized power makes the wheels of life go round, makes modernity feasible. Restraint and coercion can destroy citizens' freedoms, but can also enlarge them—as they do when government acts affirmatively to protect physical well being, to maintain social services that diminish life's pains and pressures, to ensure against the devastations of unemployment, illness, and old age, to provide educational facilities and cultural amenities. "Fundamental human rights" and "civil liberties" can remain mere verbal abstractions in environments not suitably influenced by political force. The expectant freedom of the twentieth century has been marked by enlargement of governmental responsibility, not by constriction of governmental authority.[1]

But no society worthy of respect can gaily march toward its defined goals (whatever they may be) without caring whom it tramples underfoot en route. That is why country after country has sought protections against oppressive, mistaken, or careless exercises of public authority. That is why in the United States, as elsewhere, thought is directed to safeguarding individuals without barring social movement.[2]

Destroying all bureaucracies would of course create more perils than were eliminated. Bureaucrats—public servants, public officials—design as well as execute policies to meet problems that government attacks in behalf of the governed. They constitute a "levelling, rationalizing force" that makes

Walter Gellhorn, "Confining Public Administration without Crippling It," chap. 1 in *When Americans Complain: Governmental Grievance Procedures* (Cambridge, Mass.: Harvard University Press, 1966), pp. 3–57. Reprinted by permission of the Harvard University Press from Walter Gellhorn, *When Americans Complain: Governmental Grievance Procedures*. Copyright 1966 by Walter Gellhorn.

for consistency in dealings with the public.[3] Yet even their admiring friends worry about bureaucrats—or, to use a kindlier word, administrators—because of their supposed susceptibility to "certain persistent maladies." These W. A. Robson has identified as excessive sense of self-importance, indifference to the feelings or convenience of others, obsessive adherence to established practice regardless of resulting hardship, persistent addiction to formality, and astigmatic inability to perceive the totality of government because of preoccupation with one of its parts.[4] When these maladies exist, they may not be instantly recognized and treated, because administrative work often occurs beyond the gaze of professional observers. Moreover, many of the individuals with whom administrators deal offensively "are likely to be anonymous and the injustices invisible."[5]

The maladies just described are in fact probably no more widespread among civil servants than among human beings generally. But since public officials are human beings (despite occasionally heard suggestions to the contrary), some administrators no doubt suffer some of these maladies some of the time. Success in detecting and treating the ailments is a measurement of good government. Whether or not they are endemic or only sporadic, insensitivity and arrogance and inflexibility and incompetence—and the invisible injustices they produce—are unendurable in all but the most despairing societies. People who live in organized communities can accept—indeed, must accept—the idea of harness; but they need never accept harness so ill-fitting that it constantly rubs its wearers raw.

Administrative Critics

Self-perpetuating bureaucracies that impose their uncontrolled will upon the citizenry are more often encountered in fiction than in real life. Legislatures, courts, and special tribunals have long been, and now continue to be, external examiners of administrators. They mark the boundaries of what officials may permissibly do, and they have the power to make officials pay attention.

No nation is likely to throw away the tools with which it has built protections against official overaggressiveness. Many countries, none the less, reflect the feeling that additional tools could be used to advantage. Tremendously enlarged governmental activity has been occurring during decades when mounting educational levels have encouraged citizens to think for themselves instead of supinely accepting whate'er befalls. Since more and more befalls and since citizens are more and more capable of saying they wish it had not, investigating and appropriately responding to demands and complaints have become major undertakings almost everywhere.

In this connection a significant worldwide movement toward reliance on systematized, professionalized critics of administration can be discerned. Administrative critics, unlike courts, cannot overturn decisions. Unlike legislatures, they cannot issue new directions. They are commentators and counselors, not commanders; their eye rests upon public administration, but they are not themselves superadministrators to whom all others defer.

Later pages will reflect in greater detail the operations of three prominent types of administrative critics—the ombudsman, the procurator, and the impersonal administrative inspection bureau. These three types are mere samples of current development. Perhaps one might better refer to current emphasis than to current development, since the ombudsman's beginnings in Sweden go back to 1809 and the procurator's beginnings in Russia go back to Peter the Great. Indeed, history suggests counterparts in far distant antiquity. But history alone does not account for the present-day popularity of these models or of comparable organs of criticism elsewhere.

Among these comparable organs may be mentioned the State Comptroller of Israel, who, not content with reviewing expenditures of public moneys, also investigates complaints that public officials have used wrong means to reach fiscally permissible ends.[6] His recommendations carry great weight because administrators respect the qualifications of his staff members, the public trusts their objectivity, and the legislature weighs his reports with care.[7] Auditors General in several South American countries have manifested a somewhat similar eagerness to deal with the suitability of administrative action as distinct from its narrow legality.[8] The famous Austrian Court of Accounts, or Rechnungshof, has no doubt spurred this kind of development, for it has significantly inquired (ostensibly in behalf of the parliament) into officials' efficiency as well as into their financial regularity; the Rechnungshof is a prime example of how administrative oversight can be achieved under the guise of reviewing budgets and accounts.[9] Public Service Boards in the states of Australia—theoretically concerned merely with personnel administration and management methods—act directly on complaints against civil servants that, if well grounded, could possibly lead to disciplinary proceedings.[10] Improvisations with like effect have occurred in numerous countries, sometimes without even a semblance of formal structure or authorization. Polish newspapers, for example, have become investigators as well as reporters of complaints, and serve actively as the people's tribunes. And American legislators absorb themselves so actively in constituents' conflicts with law administrators that they have little time left for thinking about the laws they enact. Developments like these serve as reminders that the means of elaborating existing safeguards are myriad and that no patented device has been approved for universal use.

The point to be made, very simply, is that protective mechanisms against official mistake, malice, or stupidity are much in demand.[11] Whatever materials can be grasped for the purpose are being used to construct "a fence along the administrative road, not a gate across it."[12]

OMBUDSMEN

Among governmental additives now widely discussed, the Scandinavian ombudsman system ranks high in popularity—possibly because it seems so easy to understand. The ombudsmen in Sweden, Finland, Denmark, Norway, and New Zealand—men of recognizedly great professional distinction—function as general complaint bureaus to which everyone can turn, at little or no cost, to complain about an administrator's naughty acts or failures to act. Then the complainant can relax, having placed his trust in the National Father Figure.

The responsibilities and powers of ombudsmen vary from country to country. Some have the capacity to initiate prosecutions; others can, at most, exclaim in horror. Some are expected to roam the land, dropping into public offices with little or no warning in order, presumably, to take idlers by surprise or to prevent sweeping dirt under the rug; others remain steadily at their own desks. Some can look into the affairs of Cabinet Ministers; others stop at the departmental level.

Their common attributes are more significant than their dissimilarities:

1. All are instruments of the legislature but function independently of it, with no links to the executive branch and with only the most general answerability to the legislature itself.
2. All have practically unlimited access to official papers bearing upon matters under investigation, so that they can themselves review what prompted administrative judgment.
3. All can express an ex officio expert's opinion about almost anything that governors do and that the governed do not like.
4. All take great pains to explain their conclusions, so that both administrators and complaining citizens well understand the results reached.

They are, in fine, prominent administrative critics. When they find fault, administrators are likely to listen to what they say. When they find no fault, complainants are likely to be persuaded by their reasoning. And when they see a chance to make everybody tolerably happy by sensibly adjusting desires, they adeptly seize "the possibility of some hitherto undiscussed arrangement that will let both parties have what they want without undue cost to either."[13]

PROCURATORS

Procurators are multitudinous ombudsmen in the Soviet Union and to a much lesser extent in other countries whose legal systems the U.S.S.R. has influenced. They are law enforcement officers—prosecuting attorneys, in short. But their duties go beyond securing citizens' observance of penal laws. They are supposed to be the guardians of legality, and in that capacity must see that officials as well as citizens fulfill their obligations. Hence they can be appealed to by anyone who thinks an administrator is doing more or less than the law says is proper. Whether the grievance be about the sanitation of the railway station, the failure to observe factory safety regulations, the promulgation of *ultra vires* rules, or the exaction of a "voluntary contribution" toward the cost of a new public enterprise, citizens can ask the local procurator's office (of which two thousand are to be found in the U.S.S.R.) to spring to action as the official defender of socialist legality. To a striking extent citizens do ask and procurators do respond.

Like ombudsmen, procurators have access to files and can give advice, both substantive and procedural, about the issues they perceive. Moreover, they have a heavy club behind their backs, since they can (at least in theory) prosecute those whose behavior flouts procuratorial notions about permissible administration. The procurators are so numerous, however, that they lack personal distinction; their range of vision, being geographically confined, does not encompass the entire sweep of public administration; and their insulation against external pressures is far from being as complete as the ombudsmen's. Hence the parallelism between procurators and ombudsmen is not at all precise. They nevertheless do function as administrative critics, and they can claim considerable accomplishments in that role.

ADMINISTRATIVE INSPECTION BUREAU

Japan, whose traditionally acquiescent citizenry had until recently shown little enthusiasm for challenging administrative irregularities, has created a highly decentralized bureau to be the critic of other bureaus. Beginning merely as an efficiency expert or Organization-and-Methods consultant, the Administrative Inspection Bureau has become in late years a wide-open grievance office, soliciting all manner of individual complaints about the conduct of public affairs. With fifty offices scattered throughout the country and with the unpaid aid of more than 3,500 "local administrative counselors," the Bureau inquires into the merits of grievances or, almost without reference to the merits, attempts to eliminate irritations by negotiating acceptable settlements. Some 5,000 cases are being disposed of monthly. The results seemingly soothe most of the complainants without unsettling the administrators. Hence the system must be accounted a definite success.

The Bureau's administrative criticism tends, however, to be rather shallow. Too many persons deal too uncoordinately with too diverse grievances in too inconsistent ways to be able to achieve large-scale improvement of public administration. A goodly number of mistakes are being corrected at low levels (which is where they occur), but in a piecemeal way that does not assure their future avoidance. The Japanese system, in sum, has not yet discovered how to derive general lessons from isolated episodes, nor how to place emphasis on prophylaxis instead of cure. In this respect the dispersed Administrative Inspection Bureau, speaking as it does through many local throats, is not so coherent a teacher as an ombudsman whose authoritative voice can be heard throughout the land. Yet the Japanese bureau of administrative criticism has already significantly reduced governmental frictions. Officials have become increasingly conscious that, even in the nation's remotest corners, authorized critics are able and willing to pounce upon their judgments and their conduct. This may lead to intellectual and behavioral refinements that would otherwise develop much more slowly.

Later pages will continue the discussion of what administrative critics can sometimes accomplish. At this point we may simply underscore that the nature of their office gives them influence, but withholds from them the power to direct or restrain. That power lodges chiefly in more conventional governmental organs, the legislature and the judiciary, which are powerful, indeed. Why is anything needed beyond the basics of constitutional authority?

The Legislative Will

DEFINING THE LIMITS OF AUTHORITY

Legislatures control administrators. That is axiomatic, since administrators never generate their own authority, but derive it from explicit or implicit statutory grants and only rarely from constitutional provisions. Hence legislatures can prevent official excess by defining tightly what administrators may allowably do. Narrow power is not easy to abuse in any far-reaching way.

The trouble with that course is its inflexibility. The administrator whose permissible range of judgment is restricted cannot make very many bad choices, but he cannot make good ones, either. His life may become easier when doing his job requires him merely to have a well-conditioned reflex that will produce a decision when the appropriate bell rings. But automaticity may not be the highest form of public service.

Moreover, rigid statutory instructions impose tremendous workloads on hard-pressed legislatures. They have constantly to reexamine petty details that might better have been turned over to subordinates. In Massachusetts, for example, the General Court recurrently enacts minute laws affecting particular highways, corporations, and insurance programs because nobody else has been empowered to deal with them.[14]

So long as the human mind cannot foretell every combination and permutation of circumstance and so long as advance agreement cannot be reached about what to do when the unforeseen occurs, legislative rules cannot possibly be devised to govern everything. That does not mean abandoning rulemaking altogether. No doubt legislatures can sometimes draw clearer guidelines than they now provide.[15] If, however, they were to pile rule on top of rule in an effort to anticipate every occurrence, spontaneous responses to life's realities would become impossible in the end unless everyone were quietly to forget that rules had been made. A few years ago the transportation companies of New York were intractably at odds with their employees. Finally, instead of striking, the employees began undeviatingly to obey the extensive working rules their employers had laid down. The havoc created by the rules' observance caused the companies' quick capitulation. The moral of the lesson is that means chosen for curbing wrongminded acts must stop short of curbing sensible judgment as well.

PROCEDURAL PRESCRIPTIONS

More than any other country the United States has attempted to achieve administrative justice by prescribing the steps administrators are to take along the way. Administrative power has been given extensively, but administrators have been commanded to observe procedural regularities before formulating conclusions.[16]

The importance of fair administrative procedures cannot easily be exaggerated. By facilitating the flow of pertinent information and the expression of relevant opinion, they lessen the risk of imperfect judgment. Much highminded effort has gone into refining the administrative process, and much of the effort has had rewarding effects.

To some extent, however, the reform movement has defeated its own purposes by telling administrators to act as though they were judges even when they are not. "The more closely that administrative procedures can be made to conform to judicial procedures," declared a Hoover Commission task force, "the greater the probability that justice will be attained in the administrative process."[17] This presupposes that justice has in fact been attained by judicial procedures in the courts themselves, a proposition few informed circles would accept unqualifiedly. It presupposes, too, that essentially similar methods can be used for many dissimilar types of cases.[18] "Judicial procedures" can add costs and delays without adding very much justice.[19] They can weight the scales against the very persons whose protection has been sought and who most need the supposed advantages of the administrative process: cheapness, speed, informality, and finality of expert judgments.[20] These have been traded away for methods that stress the creation of trial records appellate judges can understand. Contestants are often thoroughly exhausted by the administrative remedies they must exhaust before seeking judicial review, and so they wearily drop cases that might be adjudged meritorious.

Moreover, fixation on the importance of administrative procedures sometimes distracts attention from fundamental substantive choices. When, for example, an inadequate supply of commodities or services necessitates a scheme of allocation among competing applicants, steps to overcome the scarcity are infinitely more important than elaboration of the allocation procedures; "in the long run it is better to make more telephones available than to construct an ingenious appeals system for those who are refused telephones."[21] British procedures for compulsorily purchasing land needed for public purposes aroused bitter dissatisfaction which virtually disappeared when a new law raised the scale of compensation.[22] American crop support and other agricultural subsidy laws seem to be administered with very slight procedural tension, probably because the statutory policies are generous and good working relations have been cultivated among those affected.[23] In short, improving the procedures for settling disputes is no substitute for laws aimed at reducing the likelihood that disputes will arise.

None of this suggests, however, that methods are insignificant or that they have now reached perfection. The experience of administrative critics in countries outside the United States strongly suggests the contrary. Almost without exception they have, for example, detected need for greater administrative ingenuity in bringing current information about policies and procedures to the notice of affected parts of the public, especially those "who cannot be expected to have a detailed knowledge of their rights and duties or to employ experts to advise them."[24] This fully accords with conclusions reached in America concerning the need for disclosure of administrative attitudes and internal organization.[25] Better public information services depend, however, on ampler budgetary allowances for preparing, printing, distributing, and periodically revising bulletins that the laity can understand. Resistance to large "information services" continues because many legislators fear they may develop into self-serving propaganda agencies.

Beyond the need for broad educational programs, foreign experience has underlined the importance of explanations addressed directly to those whom administrative determinations affect. Many complaints, the administrative critics have discovered, reflect misconceptions about what has been decided or misunderstanding of the administrative reasoning. When the matter has been clarified, disgruntlement has changed to acceptance (if not always to contentment). In formally contested proceedings American law stresses the need for administrative "findings of fact and conclusions of law," which often prove to be opaque formulations that little justify the time devoted to preparing them. Some risk exists that in the United States, as in Sweden, passion of having faultless papers in the file may undercut passion for getting on with the job. In most countries administrators have resisted their critics' moderate advice to explicate their decisions in a simple manner that may enhance their acceptability and, more subtly, simultaneously "provide an incentive to the authority to found its decision on reasons which will stand up to criticism."[26] They have seemingly feared that attaching a statement of the reasons that support each decision would prove too heavy a task for already burdened personnel or would make for routinized expressions conveying little meaning. Possibly a new procedural requirement could be laid down by law that an administrative authority must explain a decision whenever an adversely affected person requests, and must then stand upon those reasons if the decision be challenged subsequently. Without causing a needlessly large workload this would eliminate the misunderstandings that now seemingly generate contests and would also force administrators to rest conclusions on grounds that "will stand up to criticism." Administrative procedures need not be laborious in order to be efficacious.

LEGISLATIVE ENFORCEMENT

Legislative commands, whether concerning policies or procedures, are not invariably heeded by the officials addressed. Judicial review, to be considered in later pages, is the usual means of determining whether officials have remained within the limits set by law. Legislatures themselves engage in very considerable policing of administration, and have done so forcefully. They have some powerful weapons. Investigations, appropriations pressures, "watchdog committees," and the like have kept lawmakers closely in touch with law administrators.[27] At times, indeed, they have become so close as to be virtually indistinguishable, causing the executive branch acute fear lest it lose its identity altogether.[28] Legislative organization is ill-suited, however, to deal with specific instances as distinct from broader tendencies, with alleged injustice to an individual as distinct from programs at large.[29] Legislators do of course engage in "constituents' casework." By and large, this is a personal, not an institutional enterprise, though sometimes influential committee members may use their posts to squeeze administrative judgments.

THE QUESTION HOUR

Occasionally one hears a wistful allusion to the Question Hour in the House of Commons, coupled with the wish that American legislators had a similar means of forcing upon the mightiest executives accountability for their subordinates' invasions of citizens' rights.[30] Since many Britons cling to their forefathers' faith in the efficacy of the Question Hour, Americans may be forgiven for viewing it with a respect heightened by the enchantment distance lends.

The fact seems to be, nevertheless, that the Question Hour's accomplishments are dim and few. Four times weekly, for less than an hour, private Members can interrogate Ministers about the acts of administrative units for which they are responsible. Questions have occasionally made Ministers squirm in an effort to justify subordinates' acts and, very occasionally, their squirming has had dramatic consequences. Moreover, the sheer possibility that shortcomings may be publicly challenged seemingly reminds British administrators to exercise power circumspectly. Still, the timetable of the House permits only twenty-odd questions during the Question Hour, most of them about things other than administrative errors and omissions.[31] Altogether, only two or three hundred matters in the nature of constituents' grievances about public administration can be ventilated during an entire session of Parliament.[32] Some put the figure much lower.[33] Although backbenchers may hugely enjoy the cross-examination of ministers, its value is largely symbolic.[34] It produces few changes in favor of complainants and is little more than a flickering reminder of ministerial accountability.[35]

This no doubt accounts for the quickened pace of recent British discussion about administrative procedure and judicial review, closely resembling that to be heard in American scholarly, professional, and political circles.[36] It accounts, too, for the search for other mechanisms of administrative control, continuously available and not manipulatable by those whose work has been criticized.

Of course a number of controls already exist. Britain's admirable Tribunals of Inquiry Act of 1921, for example, provides for high-powered investigations of maladroit administration. But the machinery it contemplates is too ponderous for casual use.[37] "Sledgehammers," S. A. de Smith has remarked, "ought not to be used as nutcrackers."[38] Members of Parliament cannot readily crack open the grievances reported to them; they usually "act merely as a post-box," a British barrister has caustically said, "passing on a complaint or problem to the appropriate department for comment or action."[39] This reflects their inability to get at the relevant documents. Self-justifying findings by those whose conduct has been criticized do not always carry conviction despite the traditional confidence in Britain's civil service, but those who remain unconvinced have no effective means of going behind the findings when they relate to complaints too minor to rouse national concern or shake a Cabinet's stability.[40] The Council on Tribunals, a fifteen-member body established in 1958 to advise about the conduct of formal proceedings, can investigate complaints about administrative imperfections within its sphere, but has no authority to deal with the mass of public administration that is not "quasi-judicial."[41]

Because these various protections against civil servants' "insolence of office" left too many uncovered areas, the British Government proposed in late 1965 to create a Parliamentary Commissioner for Administration. When requested by members of the Commons, he would investigate complaints of maladroit or oppressive official conduct—with power to examine departmental files himself instead of having to be dependent upon self-investigation by those complained against.[42] Questions in the House do not suffice.

Judicial Control

Looking to the judiciary to forestall bad law administration—or, what is perhaps more important, to secure affirmatively good law administration—has its drawbacks, too. Judges are wonderfully capable watchmen, but they are inert except when summoned; their "correction of abuses," as Lon Fuller well reminds, is "dependent upon the willingness and financial ability of the affected party to take his case to litigation."[43] The relatively small volume of judicial review cases in federal courts suggests that willingness and financial ability do not coincide often.[44]

Willingness may be shaped by factors other than money and time. Economic pressure to accept a debatable administrative determination may be awesome. A former general counsel of the Federal Communications Commission, who has characterized the Commission's policy decisions as bordering on gun-at-the-head jurisprudence, asserts for example that telecommunications licensees simply modify their operations to accord with administrative views because they cannot run the risks of challenging them.[45] Licensees of all descriptions—and nowadays almost every occupation operates within a licensing system[46]—are especially prone to yield "voluntarily" to official pressures an objective mind might well conclude should never have been imposed.[47]

In this respect licensees resemble persons whose violations of regulatory laws may be penalized by judicially imposed fines, but who may escape "the psychic pain of being prosecuted" if they accept the administrative enforcement agency's offer to compromise or mitigate the penalty. Alleged violators tend to bargain away their theoretical opportunity to have full judical review of the issue of violation, preferring not to bear the financial burdens and uncertainties of litigation. A "kind of administrative blackmail," a careful scholar has said, extorts away the will to use the courts.[48]

JUSTICIABILITY

Those who do have the will and the money to use the courts are not invariably free to do so. Judicial review may sometimes be specifically precluded by law, thus immunizing policies that might shrivel if a searchlight were turned upon them.[49] Much more frequently, "technicalities" that go to the heart of judicial processes—problems of timing and standing and jurisdiction—may block access to courts.[50] Yet matters that do not fit into the pattern of cases and controversies for whose resolution courts were designed may be gravely significant for society as a whole as well as for its individual members.

Kenneth Davis has recently revealed the Immigration and Naturalization Service's reliance on dubiously valid "operations instructions" when exercising discretionary power in 700,000 cases annually.[51] The secret law system, he declares, is "unjust, illegal, and inexcusable." Probably no court will ever appraise the accuracy of that description; nobody, as matters stand, may be in a position to frame a question so specific that judges must respond. An administrative critic, if one existed, would be less confined by notions of "standing" and "timing" that beset applicants for judicial review, and could therefore proceed readily to examine the propriety of the Service's administrative behavior.

LEGALLY RECOGNIZED RIGHTS

Active doubt persists about the very existence of legally cognizable rights in connection with public welfare activities involving literally millions of people.[52]

Questionable and sometimes actively offensive practices affecting welfare recipients have grown without effective challenge in the courts. Early morning searches of the homes of female "home relief clients" provide a glaring example.[53] Investigators' demands for entry into impoverished homes have been coupled with threats to terminate relief payments if entry be barred. The substantive theories behind the searches may be sustainable: A male who shares the delights of a lady's bed may perhaps have to share the burdens of paying for it as well; or the presence of too many unsanctified daddies in mommy's arms may suggest that children are being raised in an unwholesome environment. Even if these propositions be sound, atrocious means of giving them effect are unjustifiable—though very possibly they are beyond the reach of judicial review.

Difficulties of obtaining a judicial ear into which grievances can be poured are not confined to lowly social elements. Whether, for example, a student in a publicly supported institution of higher learning can demand "due process" when affected by an academic decision that may shape his whole future is by no means clear, because perhaps students have no "right" to education despite its being a virtual necessity and not a mere indulgence.[54] Persons wishing to do business with the government or hold public jobs or operate under licenses or obtain a subsidy or share in using public resources have an equally uncertain position. Possibly none of them has a "legally protected interest" entitling him to challenge official acts.[55]

A general policy declaration plainly aimed at a going business has been held to raise no justiciable issue.[56] A decision to "redevelop" an urban area cannot be challenged by the property owners and tenants who will be evicted.[57] A business concern cannot complain that a competitor has been illegally subsidized.[58] A labor union, acting in behalf of its threatened members, cannot ascertain whether an official interpretation of a statute is sound until the interpretation has been concretely applied.[59] The uncertainties in this area are so numerous that the leading American academic authorities on the subject sharply disagree about what past decisions mean and about what future decisions should say.[60]

JUDGES AS TEACHERS

Despite all these limiting factors, American judges, probably more than any others in the world, function not simply as adjudicators, but also as educators—educators of citizens concerning their rights, educators of officials concerning the boundaries of their power. Sooner or later, issues that elsewhere provide the meat of continuing political debate become compressed into personalized questions to which judges attempt to give definitive answers.[61]

Sometimes the questions judges are asked about public administration can be answered confidently. Sometimes, however, the proprieties of what public employees have done must be measured by elastic tapes, not precision gauges. When seeking the meaning of broad constitutional language that has been invoked in narrow cases, courts must gather it "not from reading the Constitution but from reading life itself."[62] How is that done? By identifying principles of justice "so rooted in the traditions and consciences of our people as to be ranked as fundamental."[63] Or by disapproving governmental procedure unless it "comports with the deepest notions of what is fair and right and just."[64] Even after the judges have somehow determined to their satisfaction the principles that are tradition-rooted and deepest among the competing conceptions of rightness, their task does not end. Having articulated the American conscience, they must take pains to see that their teachings have been heard.

Consider as an example the Supreme Court's efforts to instruct a numerous group of public employees, the police. Physical or psychological pressures can extort confessions; everybody knows that to be true. Everybody knows, too, that "voluntary" confessions have often been made to police whose questioning was more forceful than polite. After long temporizing, the Supreme Court finally held that even a seemingly unextorted confession could not be used at all if obtained when the suspect was in prolonged detention or had no access to legal advice.[65] Plainly enough, this was educational effort masquerading as rule of law. The court was telling police that terrorization is not a currently approved method of crime investigation; the bulldozer can never yield results usable in a courtroom. Somewhat similarly, when police continued to sin despite earnest judicial sermons against unwarranted searches, the courts finally decided that illegally obtained evidence could not be used at all at a trial, no matter how pertinent or persuasive. By forbidding the introduction of objectively reliable evidence the judges hoped to discourage "the lawless activities of law enforcement officials."[66] Because nobody else seemed intent upon halting police malpractice, the courts thought they must undertake to do that job themselves. Courts have set lawbreakers free in order to drive home a lesson to policemen who had grown careless of citizens' rights. The soundness of the pedagogical device is still debated, the repercussions of its use still detectable.[67]

None of the preceding discussion is meant to suggest that judicial review should be abandoned as useless or that the present measurements of its availability are immutably fixed. Although American courts cannot constitutionally be transformed into general law offices, required to give advice concerning legal perplexities that have not ripened into actual conflicts, legislatures no doubt can and very probably should authorize more extensive opportunities for review than now exist.

When all the advantages of judicial review have been taken into proper account, however, realists will still recognize that the possessors of legal rights cannot or will not always defend them if litigation is required. Judicial supervision will perforce continue to be random.

That is why other countries have established grievance bureaus other than courts to which an aggrieved person may choose to take his case even when judicial review is possible.[68] If he does so, he loses complete control over his own case, so to speak—his analysis of the problem, his arguments concerning rights or wrongs, his advocacy of a particular position are not heard as they might be were he a party to litigation. On the other hand, he is freed from the costs in strain, time, or money that might have deterred his presenting a case for judicial consideration. The ordinary citizen is assisted, in Justice Arthur Goldberg's words, "in seeing that the law is not administered with an evil eye or an uneven hand."[69]

The grievance bureaus—or administrative critics as they have been called elsewhere in this chapter—have been significantly freer than courts to grapple with the problems just discussed. Take the matter of "standing," for example. Administrative critics have had little difficulty in recognizing the actualities of controversy and in coming to grips with them. The question they have asked is, simply, whether official conduct has had impact—and, if it has, they have evaluated matters that remain effectively unchallengeable in American courts.

Or take distressing practices like "midnight raids" of welfare clients' homes, which rest on the victims' unwilling "consent." Welfare departments have in essence bought off a few lawsuits by outraged persons whose benefits had been terminated. Responding to challenge by actually increasing the amount of relief payments previously made, administrators have satisfied the challengers, leaving no controversy for judicial consideration. An administrative critic's attentive interest, one may safely guess, would not have flagged. His eye, which looks forward more than backward, would have remained firmly fixed upon the administrative practice itself and would not have wavered either because the original complainant was a supplicant or, later, was paid to be contented.

Or take the matter of covert or explicit official pressures that cause licensees and others to swallow instead of to fight what is obnoxious to them.[70] Flexibility, which assuredly includes capacity to compromise, is on the whole a governmental virtue, not a vice. Its occasional misuse should not lead to its being discarded. But judicial review is not proving to be an altogether practical means of limiting vice without eliminating virtue. The grievance bureaus in other lands have well served as examiners of questionable exercises of discretionary authority. A person who fears open battle with an administrative power may explain his problem to the administrative critic, the official watchman against abuse, who then suitably shields the complainant's identity while investigating the problem the complaint symptomatizes.

Or take the educational difficulties of American judges, faced by a stark choice between tolerating lawless law enforcement and freeing criminals. Ombudsmen in five countries have energetically educated police officers. Because they never leave the classroom, they may have been more effective teachers than American judges, whose attention has necessarily been discontinuous. People who think they have been ill-used have simply written the ombudsman, who has then assumed the burden of pursuing inquiries. The ombudsman's primary purpose has been to smooth the rough edge of public administration rather than to catch wrongdoers. External to law enforcement agencies, yet influential with them, each country's ombudsman has been successful in encouraging self-policing that has lessened abuses American judges have had to battle nearly alone.

The Continental System

Britain's and America's are of course not the only well trod paths toward administrative justice. Legality has long been prized by the more sophisticated European nations, where its chief exponents and upholders have been a highly professionalized, highly self-righteous bureaucratic elite.

Professor Fritz Morstein Marx has brilliantly described how the higher civil service in France, Germany, and Austria generated administrative law concepts that forced officials to defend their acts; observing the law (and being able to prove it had been observed) became for continental officials "a matter of honor" and "the hallmark of the tried-and-true career man in public service."[71] Administrative law was more than an element of preparation for a career; it was a branch of knowledge virtually held in trust by the administrators.

Hierarchic controls, enabling affected citizens to appeal readily from one to another level of administration, stimulated subordinate officials to be careful. The involvement of mounting thousands of public officers in the supposed "government of laws" made consistency increasingly difficult, however, and sometimes utilitarian considerations or the temptation to be self-justifying overrode all else. "Someone was needed to look in from the outside—one having the right to ask all kinds of questions, to examine all kinds of files, to weigh all kinds of explanations. . . ."[72] Administrative courts, providing an external and yet not foreign check upon operating officials, developed as a relatively easy next step. Staffed by men who understood administration because they themselves had been a part of it, they sought to harmonize individual protection with the official efficiency needed for completion of large tasks.

The French Conseil d'Etat may well be the finest flowering of the continental system of administrative justice.[73] Embracively supervising administrative decisions and simultaneously advising the cabinet, the parliament, and the civil service concerning all phases of public administration—that is, both redressing past grievances and proposing steps that may avoid their recurrence—the Conseil d'Etat has been a model many have sought to copy, though, alas, with small success.[74] Serving as the General Staff of the public service as well as the custodian of justice, the Conseil looks at the matters before it "not only with the judicial eye of those trained to suspect government but with the administrative eye of those charged with maintaining it."[75] Its rigorous objectivity, professional competence, and political independence have been acclaimed.[76] Its inventiveness in "subjecting the totality of public life in France to a system of ethical concept" not discoverable in any written law has been applauded.[77]

Yet this great tribunal and counselor has not overcome all difficulties. Swollen caseloads were alone enough to defeat its purposes, for contests often remained undecided for as long as five years. In 1953 subordinate administrative tribunals were created at the prefectural level to reduce the congestion. Although the French review procedures now in force are not so fully adversarial as those of America, they necessitate fairly active participation by the complainant. An unsuccessful suitor may have to pay costs. The use of lawyers is often advisable and sometimes mandatory. Resort to the French administrative courts, as to the ordinary American courts, is therefore not a simple matter for the common man.[78]

Considerations like these have led a warmly respected member of Sweden's Supreme Administrative Court to doubt that even well developed administrative courts can effectively deal with the "many thousands of decisions of a more or less legal character" that daily emerge from modern society's official organs. Despite the attempted simplicity of tribunals like the Conseil d'Etat, "it is always a ticklish business for a private person to appeal a decision which he believes to be incorrect. This is especially true of people who cannot afford the services of a lawyer, who have no administrative experience, or who have no connections with persons knowledgeable about administrative matters. . . . Furthermore, in most countries administrative law courts normally cover only judicial wrongs and mistakes; but often it is the decisions involving both law and expedience that cause most trouble for the private individual; in such cases there is a need of an independent authority to which the citizen may turn without strict formality."[79]

More about Administrative Critics

None of what has been said is an argument for supplanting existing means of dealing with conflicts between wielders of governmental power and those affected by it. Every country that now relies on legislative controls or on procedural rules or on judicial review or on administrative courts wants to keep what it has—though, to be sure, discussion can be heard everywhere about refining present practices and requirements, and a few isolated voices can be heard calling for really radical change. Starting on an entirely new tack has little appeal. The Conseil d'Etat is not going to be imported into the United States, and British newspapers are not going to assign their drama critics instead of their political analysts to review the Question Hour in Commons. The familiar institutions do, after all, work. They fit national habits—or, perhaps, national habits have grown to fit them. Expunging the past, always a painful exertion, is not worth undertaking unless the past's future projection means perpetuating discernibly grave defects.

Keeping what one has does not, however, foreclose adding to it. Without displacing any of the established instrumentalities, administrative critics could possibly fill chinks in the protection of individuals against adminstrative irregularities. The following pages deflect various beams of light that foreign experiences shed on that possibility.

GREAT OAKS FROM TINY ACORNS GROW

Of all the varieties of administrative critics in the world, ombudsmen on the Scandinavian model have had the best press. They are sometimes spoken of as though they were miracle men instead of directors of public grievance bureaus, trying as best they can (and on the whole successfully) to reduce inflammations.

By and large ombudsmen have dealt with small illnesses, not with major diseases. They have been society's family doctors, binding up relatively minor wounds, prescribing for discomforts not likely to become disasters, and pointing paths to healthful living. The most difficult cases and those requiring a long course of treatment have usually been referred to specialists. Lesser aches and lacerations can become serious if not timely treated, and constant irritation may even produce a malignant growth. So it is with the abuses of official power.

The able English judge who writes under the name of Henry Cecil has pertinently summarized the matter in this parable:

An omnibus conductor has considerable authority in his omnibus. He can't tell people to take their hands out of their pockets or to stop sucking sweets but he can order people about to a substantial extent. Few conductors abuse this power but some do. Such abuses cannot do much harm, although they can start an unfortunate train of events moving. If a conductor is rude to a business man, it may rankle until he reaches his office. He may find there that a clerk has made a mistake. Normally he would have overlooked it, but, unconsciously, in order to be avenged for the conductor's rudeness, he creates a fuss about it all and makes some unwarranted remarks to the clerk. Eventually the clerk is provoked into answering back and is given a week's notice. This may lead to all sorts of domestic complications.

"Lost your job, have you? What am I going to use for housekeeping, tell me that?"

"It wasn't my fault, really, Mary." No, it wasn't. It was the conductor's.

So, even the abuse of authority on that very small scale can have serious effects. And, conversely, good manners and helpful conduct, even on a small scale, can start a chain reaction of a happier kind.[80]

Ombudsmen everywhere have tried to encourage those happier chain reactions by becoming instructors in administrative deportment.[81] They have also resolved bitter arguments that, even if technically justiciable, would almost certainly never be taken to court—the Swedish fisherman's disagreement with a game warden's interpretation of the law, the Norwegian craftsman's demand that a licensing authority return his expired license certificate as a keepsake, the Danish citizen's quarrel with policemen who retained his fingerprint record after exonerating him of the crime for which he had been arrested, the Finnish townsman's dissatisfaction with local officials who insistently advised him how to be a good neighbor when all he wanted was to be left alone, the New Zealand horticulturist's dismay when the Agriculture Department minimized the virtues of hybrid plum trees without adequately testing them.

One may say that these are petty affairs, but they are not petty to those whom they immediately touch. And, anyway, most of life, individual and collective, consists of petty affairs. Immediate episodes have broader implications, too. When an ombudsman takes the sting out of situations like those just mentioned, he is setting a future example as well as salving a past hurt. The presence of an "Auditor-General of human relations accounts" (as the New Zealand ombudsman once described himself) constantly reminds officials that their acts touch beings, not cases—people, not papers.

PROTECTING PUBLIC SERVANTS

Almost all discussions of this kind acquire a slightly accusatory tone. The bureaucrat, the writer seems to hint, is a beast to be kept at bay. The weapons at hand seem too few, too ineffective. More must be done, apparently, to protect the good citizens against officials passionately devoted to victimizing them.

The present discussion may have had a bit of that tone, too. By way of amends, the explicit statement may now be made that American public servants are typically loyal to their assigned functions, reasonably respectful without being obsequious, and at least as rational as those to whom their duties may relate. Roughly one out of six gainfully employed Americans draws his income from the public treasury at one or another level of government. All of them know how it feels to be governed, for all of them are subject to the activities of other public employees except in the tiny area of their own governing. To suppose that so large a segment of the population is peculiarly beset by mental and temperamental deficiencies would be absurd. A phase-by-phase comparison of administration, private and public, might be far more favorable to the public side than is commonly conceded.[82]

Still, after all the kindly thoughts have been expressed, some power wielders are going to be inept. Then the process of over-generalization, which assuredly must be one of the most widespread of all self-indulgences, begins again. Demonstrable instances of bureaucratic incompetence, insensitivity, or injustice have far too often been viewed as typical instead of aberrational. When respect accorded the public service sinks, the chances of its becoming a proudly professional adjunct of democracy sink correspondingly.

An extremely valuable by-product of public grievance machinery abroad has been reinforced confidence in civil servants. Administrative critics have found only a minor fraction of complaints to be sustainable. External investigation of surrounding circumstances and objective analysis of official conclusions have not only exonerated administrators against whom complaints had been lodged, but have also persuaded the public at large (and usually the complainants themselves) that justice has indeed been done. Administrative mistakes, when discovered, have been rectified without exaggerating their significance, just as judges' errors are daily detected and corrected by appellate courts without shaking confidence in the entire judicial system; they are usually accidental crushings, not intentional wrongs. Genuine grievances do indeed exist, but they are far outnumbered by complaints by the chronically querulous, the psychopathically hostile, and the simply mistaken. Only when sober sifting has been undertaken can proper attention be paid to the truly aggrieved and, at the same time, proper support be given to those who truly serve.[83] Without exception, every country that leans heavily on ombudsmen or other administrative critics has strengthened its civil service in the process of solacing those whom civil servants have offended.

THE FORCE OF SWEET REASON

Criticism is of little moment if nobody pays attention to it. How much coercive force does an official critic of public administration need in order to give his words weight?[84]

The ombudsmen in Sweden and Finland are prosecutors as well as persuaders. They can hale unheeding administrators into court, charged with the crime of being unmannerly, lazy, or inefficient (or something more serious, of course). But prosecutions of officials are now rare; reason has supplanted compulsion. The Danish ombudsman, too, carries a club, for he can order prosecution or other disciplinary action against an errant administrator; in point of fact, however, he has never used his club, choosing instead to gain genuine acceptance of his recommendations without having to rely on punitive proceedings. The Norwegian and New Zealand ombudsmen have no weapons at all other than the support of public opinion and as yet untested parliamentary sympathy; and still, though no punishment awaits recalcitrants, administrators have heeded their advice readily.

Similarly, the Japanese grievance buerau—the Administrative Inspection Bureau—appeals to reason, not to force, when it thinks that officials should retrace their steps. Even in Eastern European countries which have traditionally leaned heavily on authoritarian pressures and the possibility of penalties to keep administrators in step, administrative critics rely on calm counsel much more than on dire threats. The Soviet procuracy (which does indeed have power to prosecute) has expressed increasingly polite opinions about sound administration and has remained urbane even when the opinions have not been accepted instantly; Polish procedures presuppose the effectiveness of appeals to administrative reason rather than to administrative fear; the Yugoslav Bureau of Petitions and Proposals negotiates without ever snapping out a command.

The pattern of persuasion—and it has been successful persuasion, one may add—in all these countries suggests something about the grievance machinery itself. Were administrative critics to see themselves as extirpators of malefactors in office, no doubt they would need a full set of sanctions to do their job. When, however, inquiry into past errors is aimed not at determining individual fault but at producing a more satisfactory future, punitive powers lose their relevance. Somewhat to everyone's surprise, the official grievance bureaus have not often been asked to castigate individuals. The complaints reaching them have tended to be impersonal, directed chiefly at administrative organizations collectively, only rarely at identified administrators. They have challenged procedures and policies and procrastination much more often than personally objectionable conduct. A review of official files has usually sufficed to disclose the relevant facts; the taking of testimony and other aspects of formal trials have almost never seemed to be useful. Even when an administrative critic has found fault with the outcome of a particular case, the fault has infrequently had to be attributed to an individual official. Rather, from the specific instance the critic has sought to draw useful generalizations about better ways of handling similar matters when next encountered; giving a spanking for past shortcoming has seemed less important than giving guidance. The spanking, when necessary, has been done by others. Disciplinary proceedings have been initiated by superiors who had been embarrassed by comments upon their subordinates' failings; department heads, having humbly apologized for staff members' carelessness, have taken pains to avoid similar discomfitures in the future; in rare instances resignations at the highest level have followed an administrative critic's censorious remarks.

A gentle war against bureaucratic sin can be won, of course, only when the warrior's own integrity and objectivity are beyond doubt—and when, moreover, the bureaucracy as a whole has pride in itself.[85] If officials think of themselves, and are thought of by others, as partisan tools instead of as public servants, external criticism of their methods, manners, and morals becomes a sheer irrelevancy.[86] It follows that an administrative critic's acceptance is likely to be greatest in the very societies that need him least. External criticism triumphs most easily when it concentrates on but a few lapses from customarily high standards of fairness and efficiency.

Yet this proposition can be overstated. More important than a brightly polished civil service is a society agreed upon its objectives and, in general, upon the measurements of proper political behavior. A public grievance bureau, no matter how honored its personnel, can gain acceptance of its critical views only if they reflect and apply accepted social norms. External critics cannot remake public administration in their own image. They can do much to make it match society's image of it. That is what has been happening in late years in the countries of Eastern Europe, and it has been happening despite lessened reliance on harshly applied sanctions.[87]

THE CULT OF PERSONALITY

Because the Scandinavian ombudsman has lately become so popular a figure at home and abroad, opinion has formed that public grievance machinery functions well only when personally manipulated by a singularly exalted man.[88] If this be accurate, external criticism of administration could have slight success where large populations would generate too many grievances for one man to review—a proposition, as others have observed, producing the sorry conclusion that nothing should be done because the demand is so great."[89]

True enough, the ombudsmen have become significant figures in their respective homelands. Officials listen when an ombudsman speaks because they know his expressions are nonpolitical, usually well informed, and likely to command journalistic, legislative, and popular support if needed. His singularity does facilitate his being recognized as a distinguished authority; he is not merely one well-intentioned man among a host of others. But this does not really establish that grievance evaluation need be a monopolistic pursuit.

Even in the Scandinavian countries, monopoly is not the rule. Sweden has two ombudsmen, not one; a third lurks in the shadows under the title of "deputy" and a fourth under the title of Chancellor of Justice, while public prosecutors also share in work that, in popular mythology, belongs to a single ombudsman.[90] Finland's ombudsman is paralleled by a Chancellor of Justice. An ombudsman for military affairs works side by side with the Norwegian ombudsman who is concerned with civil administration. Only in Denmark has the ombudsman been a true monopolist; almost singlehandedly dealing with the entire range of governmental activity. The New Zealand Ombudsman has no direct competitors, but has a narrower jurisdiction than his Danish counterpart.

In much more populous Japan and Russia, not even a pretense of personalism remains. The Administrative Inspection Bureau in the former and the Procuracy in the latter have been able to effect at least some "bureaucratic reform" throughout government despite being large organizations themselves. They have received and acted upon complaints in much the same way as ombudsmen, and have induced sounder decisions in particular cases as well as strengthened procedures for future use. Their size has not discernibly diminished their stature. In other contexts public administrators have accorded high respect to collegial, depersonalized bodies (the French Conseil d'Etat and the British Treasury are examples), and no reason dictates that they should withhold it in this field. From the public's point of view, personalism seems not so important as sheer identifiability. A grievance bureau will clearly be a failure if the public cannot find it when needed.

Doing a large job in a large country is obviously more difficult and necessitates more complex organization than doing a smaller job in a smaller country. That is not the same as saying that a big job cannot be done at all.

THE IMPORTANCE OF PROPHYLAXIS

In public administration as in personal health, prevention is far more important than cure. The large-scale operations of the bureaucratized Japanese and Soviet administrative critics have failed to emphasize this, and their failure may indeed be inherent in their size. When many persons in decentralized offices deal discontinuously and separately with the incoming flow of citizens' complaints, the full dimensions of the problems they reflect may not be perceived. Instead, each complainant's file may be closed when his particular difficulty has been overcome, without anyone's becoming aware that related complaints may suggest the need of wider inquiries and perhaps more sweeping results.

So, for example, scattered dissatisfactions with the freight-trucking services of Japanese common carriers have been treated as isolated episodes, not as warning signals that the adequacy of existing public transportation controls may need re-examination. The administrative critic who disposed of each complaint knew nothing of the others, and as a consequence their possible interrelationships remained unnoticed. Had similar grievances passed through the hands of an ombudsman's few aides, awareness of their places in a pattern would have been far more likely. Sweeping improvements can be generated by what might at first seem to be a minor mishap. Thus, a Danish ministry's methods of handling mail were completely overhauled after one or two irate correspondents had complained to the ombudsman about the ministry's unresponsiveness. The ombudsman's inquiries into the causes of that irritation had a rippling effect throughout the ministry. Before the ripples had subsided, controls were in operation from the minister's office all the way down to the mail room to forestall future complaints.

Smallness of size does not, however, absolutely guarantee sensitivity to the implications of cases in progress. The Finnish ombudsman's office, for example, has at times indulged a seemingly ungovernable passion for detail, without becoming even mildly aroused by broader issues. Whether administrative critics be few or many, they must constantly remind themselves that prophylaxis should be a major objective of their work.

THE DANGER OF INSIPIDITY

Watching out for administrative misbehavior has such obvious merits that its less obvious demerits may be overlooked. One of these is its tendency to create too bland an administration. The process of eliminating needless irritations may remove useful abrasiveness, too.

Edmund Burke wisely counseled against superfluous governmental restraints; "it ought to be the constant aim of every wise public council," he urged, "to find out by cautious experiments, and with cool rational endeavors, with how little, not how much, of this restraint the community can subsist; for liberty is a good to be improved, and not an evil to be lessened." That is good doctrine now, just as it was when it was said nearly two hundred years ago. Once the need for public action has been determined, however, the end in view calls for forthright administration, since few laws accomplish their purposes unaided. The gravest danger in today's world is not positive government that reflects the conclusions of wise public councils. It is flabby, erratic, ineffective execution of policies adopted in response to active needs.

The administrative critics have strengthened, not weakened, public administration by attacking concededly obnoxious behavior—needlessly slow dispatch of business, rudeness in manner, unwillingness to explain decisions, unprincipled inconsistency in handling objectively similar cases. Exposing imperfect administration has both solaced the wounded and stimulated self-corrective measures that have lessened the risk of "blunders which leave lasting stains on a system of justice."[91] Informed criticism by highly qualified, highly respected outsiders has certainly paid its way.

One of the hidden costs should, however, be pulled into the open: Awareness that someone is constantly peering over their shoulders causes some public servants to become too timid instead of too bold. Not long ago a senior Swedish administrator caustically appraised the consequences of continuous oversight: "'Officials who want to be sure not to get into trouble don't try to find the quickest and simplest ways to do their jobs, but the safest. I have rarely heard of anyone's being held up before the public as a horrible example because he was not being vigorous enough. Nowadays the civil service needs vigor, but it isn't really encouraged to have it." His views were echoed by a police official who, speaking about his fellow officers, asserted: "None of those fellows worries about being punished for doing too little, but he knows he can get into plenty of trouble for doing too much." A third official, praising the soundness of an admonition by the ombudsman, added: "That criticism caused me a lot of trouble, though. My own committee became so cautious I had difficulty getting anything at all done, even the good things that needed doing very badly."[92]

Inhibiting the determined performance of duty is not a necessary result of attacking undesirable official action. The possibility of that unintended aftermath of critical inquiries is great enough, nevertheless, to warrant thoughtful countermeasures.[93] Insensitive administration must not be supplanted by insipid administration.

THE DANGER OF OVERRELIANCE

External criticism gives rise to a second risk—the risk of complacency. Too many persons seem willing to suppose, on much too little evidence, that God's in his heaven, all's right with the world of public administration so long as somebody like an ombudsman is keeping an eye on operations. That is an extremely dangerous fallacy. Administrative critics do not produce good government. They cannot themselves create sound social policies. They have no capacity to organize a competent civil service. They are at their best when calling attention to infrequent departures from norms already set by law or custom, at their weakest when seeking to choose among competing goals or to become general directors of governmental activity.

Administrative critics have sometimes themselves inflated the public's expectations. The Soviet Union's Procuracy, for example, has done good work in assuring that administration accords with legality, but often claims to be exercising a broader "general supervision" over every state functionary—on the theory that all incompetence is illegal. "General supervision" has not accomplished very much. It has perhaps heightened awareness of the giant difference between criticizing ineptitude and creating aptitude.

Ombudsmen, too, have been tempted to seem omnipotent. They then stub their own toes in the process of trampling on others'. In 1964, for example, the Swedish ombudsman proceeded against a provincial governor for inactivity in conducting civil defense training programs. This, he felt, was a dereliction of duty, as indeed perhaps it was. Forcing the governor to turn to civil defense may, however, have made him turn away from something else of even greater significance, a matter concerning which an external critic could scarcely expect to be fully informed. The same thing happened at about the same time across the world in New Zealand, whose ombudsman instructed high officials to get on with the job of creating a civil defense organization although they believed they should attend to other urgent work. The Danish ombudsman has confidently considered whether the Foreign Office had adopted an adequate personnel security program, whether tax revenues were being spent properly, and whether the organization of departmental offices could be improved upon. These illustrative episodes suggest that an outside observer's limited capability has been prudently recognized only intermittently, to say the least. Instead of modestly acting like critics, ombudsmen have sometimes behaved a bit like The Father of the Country. This encourages the citizenry to rely unduly upon their benign superintendency to see that all is well.

Without further belaboring, the conclusion can be stated that administrative critics are on sounder ground when dealing with omissions of specific duties owed to identifiable persons or groups than when building new governmental policies or castigating generalized failures of law administration.[94] Issues that concern the public at large without focusing upon individuals may perhaps best be left to political controls instead of to the judgment of a jack of all trades.[95]

That would not impose total abstinence upon administrative critics. Their observations might, indeed, be important generators of concern about problems whose existence might otherwise pass unnoticed. The ombudsman in Finland, for example, directly informs parliament whenever he detects governmental failure to execute a legislative resolve. Since the failure may not reflect administrative incompetence, but inadequate financing, unclear statutes, or conflicts between one legislative command and another, the Finnish ombudsman does not presume to denounce every gap between law in the books and law in action. Instead, he serves primarily as a watchman against specific faults (with which he does concern himself) and secondarily as a mere reporter when he discovers broader problems calling for large policy choices others should make.

NOTES

1. The verbalisms of older constitutions have usually ignored this, but not so those of emerging nations, which emphasize social obligations rather than concepts like "liberty, equality, and fraternity." See L. Hamon, "Les Tendances Constitutionelles des Etats Ayant Accédé à l'Indépendance," *23 Etudes de Droit Contemporain* n.s. 409 (1962); D. G. Lavroff and G. Peiser, *Les Constitutions Africaines* vol. I (1961). And compare J. N. Hazard, "Negritude, Socialism and the Law," 65 *Columbia Law Review* 778 (1965). See also D. V. Cowen, "African Legal Studies—A Survey of the Field and the Role of the United States," in H. Baade, ed., *New Law for New Nations* 9, at 26, 31 (1963); D. H. Bayley, *Public Liberties in the New States* chap. VI (1964).

2. Compare "The Recognition of Human Rights in Eastern Europe." *Bulletin of the International Commission of Jurists* no. 24, at 4–7 (1965).

3. W. A. Robson, *The Governors and the Governed* 17 (1964).

4. *Ibid.* at 18. An American writer has compiled an even more devastating set of charges against public administration: "inefficiency, undue delay and expense, prejudgment of controversies, absence of clear rules, ex parte influences, capture by regulated industries, lack of expertise, excessive power of staffs, inadequate personnel, corruption, and lack of coordination—and these by no means exhaust the list." M. G. Shimm, Foreword, 26 *Law and Contemporary Problems* 179 (1961). But compare B. Chapman, "The Ombudsman," 38 *Public Administration* 303, 307 (1960), reflecting the opinion that civil servants have been subjected to unduly "savage and vicious attacks" while "almost daily instances of far worse cases of partiality and prejudice in magistrates' courts" invoke no more than "a shrug from those most furious in their denunciation of the Civil Service."

5. C. Frankel, "Bureaucracy and Democracy in the New Europe," 93 *Daedalus* 471, 481 (1964).

6. The State Comptroller acted upon 1,900 complaints submitted by the public in 1963, 1,500 in 1962, 1,300 in 1961. About a fifth concerned unsatisfactory handling of applications, discourtesy, and so on. *See 14th Ann. Rep. of State Comptroller of Israel* 15–16 (1964). The State Comptroller himself asserts that he "carries out the functions of an institution which exists in several countries and is known in the Scandinavian countries as the Ombudsman." *State Control in Israel* 9 (1965). A similar remark appears in *15th Ann. Rep.* 15–16 (1965), which also notes that 2,000 grievances were handled in 1964.

Israeli interest in the concept of the ombudsman and recognition of its relationship to the work of the State Comptroller are reflected in L. Boim, *The Ombudsman* (Jerusalem, 1965).

7. E. Samuel, "Control of the Executive in Israel," 73 *South African Law Journal* 171, 178 (1956).

8. *Argentina:* Auditor General of the Nation and Tribunal of Accounts, Decree Law 33.354, Dec. 31, 1956, chaps. VIII, IX; *Chile:* Office of Comptroller General, Law No. 10.336, May 29, 1952, Arts, 1, 10, 13; *Colombia:* see G. Garzonineto Combarigo, *Algunos Aspectos del Control Fiscal Nacional en Colombia* 78–88 (Bogota, 1961).

9. The example may be increasingly followed by the recently established "Supreme Chamber of Control" in Poland; see the chapter on Poland in Walter Gellhorn, *Ombudsmen and Others: Citizens' Protectors in Nine Countries* (Cambridge, Mass.: Harvard University Press, 1966), hereafter cited as Gellhorn, *Ombudsmen*. And compare Finan-

cial Management in the Federal Government, Sen. Doc. No. 11, 87th Cong., 1st Sess. (1961), analyzing existing and proposed legislation in the area of federal financial management.

10. The National Public Service Board is directed to exercise critical oversight of the activities and methods of each government department. Negligent, inefficient, or otherwise incompetent officials may be fined, reduced in rank or pay, transferred, or dismissed. Sec. 17, Public Service Act 1922–1950, IV *Commonwealth Acts 1901–1950*, p. 3349.

11. Perhaps one should note, in passing, that the demand for protective mechanisms can lead toward "traditional" as well as toward "novel" devices. Thus, for example, what Americans regard as thoroughly conventional, old fashioned judicial review has been advocated in Poland and the Soviet Union and has already been widely adopted in Yugoslavia. See also J. Martonyi, "Le Contrôle Jurisdictionnel des Actes de l'Administration," 10 *Revue de Droit Contemporain* 73 (no. 2, 1963).

12. D. C. Rowat, "An Ombudsman Scheme for Canada," 28 *Canadian Journal of Economics and Political Science* 543, 556 (1962).

13. The quoted phrase comes from L. L. Fuller, "Irrigation and Tyranny," 17 *Stanford Law Review* 1021, 1031 (1965), discussing the qualities needed by good negotiators of complex agreements.

14. Massachusetts Legislative Research Council, Reduction of Workload of the General Court 48–51, Sen. Doc. No. 990 (1965). Fraternal societies in Massachusetts must receive statutory approval of changes in their benefit plans. Insurance department officials have said that legislative changes often occur without adequate knowledge of the actuarial soundness of the funds concerned.

The same sort of problem arises, of course, when state constitutions tie too tight knots in the ropes that bind administrative judgment. See The Problem of Simplification of the Constitution, N.Y. Legislative Doc. No. 57 (1958) at pp. 7ff. During a recent period of twenty-five years, for instance, the people of Louisiana had to adopt 219 amendments of constitutional specifications in an only partly successful race to keep their government abreast of changed circumstances.

15. Administrative agencies, too, can themselves do more in the way of laying down regulations that will guide both citizens and officials, instead of leaving everything to discretionary judgments after the event. See R. F. Fuchs, "Agency Development of Policy through Rule-Making," 59 *Northwestern Law Review* 781 (1965); D. L. Shapiro, "The Choice of Rulemaking or Adjudication in the Development of Administrative Policy," 78 *Harvard Law Review* 921 (1965). Compare H. Friendly, *The Federal Administrative Agencies* vii (1962): The most signal fault of administrative agencies is "the failure to develop standards sufficiently definite to permit decisions to be fairly predictable and the reasons for them to be understood." But compare M. Cohen and J. Rabin, "Broker-Dealer Selling Practice Standards: The Importance of Administrative Adjudication in Their Development," 29 *Law and Contemporary Problems* 691, 714 (1964), strongly supporting "the flexibility afforded by the case method."

16. The United States has not been alone in stressing procedural improvement. Even countries with markedly different traditions and legal systems have moved strongly in the same direction. See, e.g., discussion of the Yugoslav and Polish codes of administrative procedure in Gellhorn, *Ombudsmen*.

17. Commission on Organization of the Executive Branch of the Government, Report of Task Force on Legal Services and Procedures 138 (1955).

18. Elsewhere I have sought to develop at greater length why "judicial procedures" do not fit all needs. See "Administrative Procedure Reform: Hardy Perennial," 48 *American Bar Association Journal* 243 (1962). The "principle of impartial adjudication" works well when the factors that bear upon a decision and the weight to be given

them can be understood in advance, and when the immediately affected parties possess the information on which decision must rest.

19. See, e.g., W. K. Jones, Licensing of Truck Operations by the Interstate Commerce Commission (March 1962), a mimeographed report prepared for the Administrative Conference of the United States; G. E. and R. D. Hale, "Competition or Control: Motor Carriers," 108 *University of Pennsylvania Law Review* 775 (1960); E. Hutchinson and G. M. Chandler, "Evidence in Motor Carrier Application Cases," 11 *Vanderbilt Law Review* 1053 (1958). Delay is reflected in mounting backlogs of unresolved controversies, which in federal agencies grew at the rate of 29 percent (3,500) during a recent biennium. Administrative laziness was not to blame, for the agencies were highly productive even though unable to surmount the inflow of new cases. See Sen. Judiciary Subcommittee on Admin. Prac. and Proc., Sen. Rep. No. 119, 89th Cong., 1st Sess. at p. 6 (1965).

20. This has happened, for example, in connection with tenants' petitions in rent control matters and adjudicating workmen's compensation claims. Forty years ago Reginald Heber Smith's trailblazing study of poor persons' inability to utilize existing disputes resolution mechanisms, spoke admiringly of administrative organs that would lessen the disadvantages of poverty; see *Justice and the Poor* 98 (1924). Some of the hopes then expressed have remained only partly realized. As to somewhat cumbersome methods for passing on occupational injury cases, see G. Spielmeyer, ed., *Ascertaining Entitlement to Compensation for Industrial Injury* 198–209, 218–226 (Intl. Inst. Admin. Sciences, 1965).

21. A. W. Bradley, "The Redress of Grievances," [1962] *Cambridge Law Journal* 82, 89; and see D. C. Holland, "A British Ombudsman," 1 *Solicitors' Quarterly* 147, 154 (1962).

22. Compare the Franks Committee Report—Report of the Committee on Administrative Tribunals and Enquiries 61 (Cmnd. 218, 1957)—discussing the Town and Country Act 1947 and maintaining that the inadequate compensation it contemplated creates "dissatisfaction" which is "bound to remain" despite the fairness of condemnation procedures. After the Act was amended in 1959, the dissatisfaction diminished.

23. For an excellent comparative study of well-accepted administration in a difficult field, see A. Heilbronner, *Prevention of Cattle Diseases* 28–39 (Intl. Inst. of Admin. Sciences, 1965), discussing the application of compensation plans for the benefit of farmers whose livestock must be destroyed to prevent the spread of disease.

24. *New Zealand Ombudsman's Report 1964*, at 11. And see W. A. Robson's discussion of "We and They: The Problem of Communication," in *The Governors and the Governed* 35–50 (1964).

25. Sec. 3 of the Federal Administrative Procedure Act requires each agency to publish a description of its organization, procedures, and substantive rules. Other sections of the law require publication of formal notices. Both the scope of the present publication requirements and the adequacy of their observance have been criticized frequently. See, e.g., F. C. Newman, "Government and Ignorance," 63 *Harvard Law Review* 929 (1950); "Comments on Proposed Amendments to Section 3 of the Administrative Procedure Act," 40 *Notre Dame Lawyer* 417 (1965); and see also Sen. Rep. No. 1219, 88th Cong., 2d Sess. (1964), challenging the adequacy of the present Sec. 3.

The other side of the coin is suggested by a U.S. Bureau of the Budget pamphlet, *War on Waste*, published on Dec. 31, 1964, pointing out at p. 43 that President Johnson had personally appealed to the heads of all administrative organs to eliminate all unnecessary publications. The result: "During the first half of this year, more than 500 pamphlets and other publications have been dropped by various agencies of the Government, which, together with other production economies, has resulted in an estimated saving of almost $3 million."

As to the actual availability of information to persons who need to know where to go for what, see Hearings before the Joint Committee on the Organization of the Congress, 89th Cong., 1st Sess., Part 10, pp. 1855–1856 (1965).

26. G. Powles, "The Procedural Approach to Administrative Justice," 1965 *New Zealand Law Journal* 79, 81. One may note that no such requirement rests on courts. The United States Supreme Court in 1963–64 disposed of 2,401 matters on its docket, but wrote opinions in only 123 cases. In early 1966 the Appellate Division of the Superior Court of New Jersey was ordered by that state's supreme court to write fewer opinions and to "devote the time thus saved to the hearing and decision of additional cases." *N.Y. Times,* Jan. 7, 1966, p. 31, col. 8.

27. For general discussion of federal legislative controls of administration and references to relevant materials, see W. Gellhorn and C. Byse, *Administrative Law* 166–195 (4th ed. 1960); compare Financial Management in the Federal Government, note 9 (above), at 199–208, referring to congressional inability to supervise adequately and accurately the appropriation and use of funds.

28. See, in this connection, President Johnson's veto of the Military Authorization Act of 1965, H.R. 8439, 89th Cong., 1st Sess. (1965), which would have drawn Congress into decisions to abandon obsolete military installations. The veto message is printed as H. Doc. No. 272, 89th Cong., 1st Sess. (1965). And see also R. E. Neustadt, *Presidential Power* 92–93 (1959).

29. But compare F. C. Newman and H. J. Keaton, "Congress and the Faithful Execution of Laws," 41 *California Law Review* 565 (1953); and see W. Gellhorn and L. Lauer, "Congressional Settlement of Tort Claims against the United States," 55 *Columbia Law Review* 1 (1955). For illustrative use of a simple substitute for legislative action on claims, see discussion of the Swedish ombudsman's recommendations that compensation be granted in Gellhorn, *Ombudsmen.*

30. See, e.g., Testimony of Professor J. K. Pollock of the University of Michigan, June 7, 1965, in Hearings before the Joint Committee on the Organization of the Congress, 89th Cong., 1st Sess., Part 5, p. 702 (1965). And see R. Heller, *Strengthening the Congress* 27 (145).

31. Despite the great growth of administrative activities, the time available for questions—only 45 to 55 minutes—has remained unchanged since 1906. D. N. Chester and N. Bowring, *Questions in Parliament* 271 (1962).

32. See *The Citizen and the Administration: The Redress of Grievances* 36 (1961). This report is usually called the Whyatt Report; Sir John Whyatt was director of research for the sponsoring organization, "Justice," the British section of the International Commission of Jurists.

33. Dr. Donald Johnson, a respected Conservative member from Carlisle, has been quoted as saying that throughout the 1956–57 session only 144 grievance cases were brought forward during Question Time, and of these fully three-quarters had to do with colonial and commonwealth administration, so little attention was being paid to administration in the home sphere. T. E. Utley, *Occasion for Ombudsman* 39 (1961).

34. The questions addressed to Ministers have usually been preceded by considerable correspondence and interviews, but the House as a whole knows little of the matter. "The majority of the members present, who will never have heard of the issue before," Mr. Utley declares (at p. 40), "will witness an exchange on the merits of which they are quite incapable of forming a judgment. There will be sheer contradictions of fact between the Question and the reply; the Minister having made due inquiries, is satisfied that Mrs. Smith was not struck by an officer of the Potato Marketing Board; the Member will assert that he has evidence to the contrary; the Minister will aver that he has examined the evidence which does not convince him; the Member will ask whether the Minister in the circumstances will agree to an independent inquiry; the Minister will say that he sees no cause for such an inquiry."

35. See S. E. Finer, "The Individual Responsibility of Ministers," 34 *Public Admin-*

istration 377, 394 (1956), asserting that individual responsibility has little substance because party discipline has affected the House's capacity to act. And see also G. Marshall, "Ministerial Responsibility," *Political Quarterly* 256 (1963).

36. See, e.g., H. W. R. Wade, *Towards Administrative Justice* (1963); S. A. de Smith, *Judicial Review of Administrative Action* (1959). Professor de Smith, the leading English writer on judicial review, has described the courts' attitude as "unambitious conservatism"; he says that, despite considerable agitation for change, the law about judicial remedies remains "highly technical and full of pitfalls" and litigation is likely to be "expensive and protracted." S. A. de Smith, "Anglo-Saxon Ombudsman?" 33 *Political Quarterly* 9, 11, 12 (1962).

37. Tribunals of Inquiry or similar Departmental Inquiries were launched to investigate charges of maladministration only nine times during a span of forty years. Whyatt Report, note 32 (above), at 43. For discussion of a similar, more frequently used investigatory device in an American state, see E. H. Breuer, *Moreland Act Investigations in New York* (1965); J. E. Missall, *The Moreland Act* (1946).

38. "Anglo-Saxon Ombudsman?" 33 *Political Quarterly* 9, 11 (1962).

39. A. A. deC. Hunter, "Ombudsman for Britain?" 4 *Journal of the International Commission of Jurists* 150, 156 (1962).

40. The Whyatt Report, note 32 (above), remarked at 39–40: "Although framed as an interrogatory for the purpose of Parliamentary procedure, a Parliamentary Question which raises a complaint of maladministration is not so much a request for information as an accusation against a Government Department that it has failed to discharge its duties properly . . . But no matter how thorough the work of the Department may be in preparing the answer, the process contains two inherent weaknesses: first, the investigation is carried out by the Department whose conduct is impugned, and secondly, it is based upon documents which are not available to the complainant or indeed to anyone other than the Department. The investigation, therefore, is not impartial in the sense that it is conducted by an independent authority having access to all relevant documents and it is inevitable in these circumstances that the complainant should feel that the Department has been judge in its own cause and for that reason, if for no other, should feel dissatisfied with the process."

41. Tribunals and Inquiries Act, 1958, 6 & 7 Eliz. 2, c. 66. See H. W. R. Wade, *Towards Administrative Justice* 81–95 (1963), and "Council on Tribunals," 1960 *Public Law* 351; N. D. Vandyk, "A Collective Ombudsman?" 104 *Solicitors' Journal* 357 (1960), and "Watchdog at Work," 105 *Solicitors' Journal* 601 (1961). As to the separate Scottish Committee of the Council on Tribunals, see N. Gow, "An Ombudsman for Scotland?" *Scots Law Times*, June 25, 1960, at 119.

42. The Parliamentary Commissioner for Administration, October 1965, Cmnd. 2767, para. 6, 9.

43. L. L. Fuller, *The Morality of Law* 81 (1964).

44. For some relevant statistics showing that "judicial review is not an hourly or daily occurrence in the lives of administrative agencies," see "Administrative Procedure Reform," note 18 (above), at 245–246. And see also K. C. Davis, Administrative Law Treatise, 1965 Supp. at 11.

Compare C. Abrams, "The City Planner and the Public Interest," 8 *Columbia University Forum* no. 3, 25 at 27–28 (1965): "Where the executive and legislative branches of government cannot lead, it is futile to expect the judiciary to offer much help . . . The proliferation of administrative agencies, such as local zoning commissions, school boards, urban renewal, housing and city planning departments has been accompanied by an increase in the effective power of these agencies, and our courts are simply unequipped to review their findings or discover abuses. Only where there is a glaring perversion of power will the courts now intervene, and most perversions are becoming increasingly undiscoverable."

45. W. E. Baker, "Policy by Rule or Ad Hoc Approach—Which Should It be?" 22 *Law and Contemporary Problems* 658, 665 (1957).

46. See C. A. Reich, "The New Property," 73 *Yale Law Journal* 733, 734 (1964); W. Gellhorn, *Individual Freedom and Governmental Restraints* chap. III (1956).

47. Compare R. M. Benjamin, *Administrative Adjudication in the State of New York* 267 (1942): "The State Liquor Authority often cancels a license and immediately issues a new license for the remainder of the annual license period. The actual effect...is to subject the licensee to a monetary penalty in the amount of the cost of his new license...; and the procedure is optional with the licensee in the sense that he is under no obligation to take out a new license. Another method, used by the Department of Agriculture and Markets, combines the Commissioner's power to revoke or suspend a milk dealer's license with the Commissioner's power to compromise rights of action for monetary penalties . . . ; as an alternative to revocation or suspension, the Department often offers a licensee the option of voluntarily paying a monetary penalty. The State Athletic Commission sometimes actually revokes a boxer's license in addition to imposing a monetary penalty, the understanding being that the license will be restored upon payment of the 'fine.' "

48. D. H. Nelson, "Administrative Blackmail: The Remission of Penalties," 4 *Western Political Quarterly* 610, 620 (1951). And see the same author's *Administrative Agencies of the U.S.A.* 186 (1964).

49. Selective Service and Veterans Affairs are among the broadly important administrative activities that courts are instructed to ignore. In 1965 Selective Service officials threatened to hasten the military involvement in Vietnam. See *N. Y. Times*, Dec. 23, 1965, p. 1, col. 7. The Selective Service system was designed to meet military manpower needs, not to discourage political agitation; but the courts had no power to inquire into the purity of the administrative purposes. As for the unreviewable determinations of the Veterans Administration, see F. Davis, "Veterans' Benefits, Judicial Review, and the Constitutional Problems of 'Positive' Government," 39 *Indiana Law Journal* 183 (1964).

50. For extensive exploration of these problems see L. L. Jaffe, *Judicial Control of Administrative Action* chaps. 4, 10, 12, 13 (1965).

51. K. C. Davis, Administrative Law Treatise, 1965 Supp., § 4.16, pp. 102–112.

52. H. W. Jones, "The Rule of Law and the Welfare State," 58 *Columbia Law Review* 143 (1958), was among the first to insist upon the need of extending legal protections in the welfare state where, he concluded (at 156), "the private citizen is forever encountering public officials of many kinds: regulators, dispensers of social services, managers of state-operated enterprises. It is the task of the rule of law to see to it that these multiplied and diverse encounters are as fair, as just, and as free from arbitrariness as are the familiar encounters of the right-asserting private citizen with the judicial officers of the traditional law." But compare Flemming v. Nestor, 363 U.S. 603 (1960), holding that old age benefits under the Social Security Act are not an "accrued property right" and may therefore be snatched away unless the snatching is "utterly lacking in rational justification."

53. See C. A. Reich, "Midnight Welfare Searches and the Social Security Act," 72 *Yale Law Journal* 1347 (1963).

54. See W. Seavey, "Dismissal of Students: 'Due Process,' " 70 *Harvard Law Review* 1406, 1407 (1957). And compare C. Byse and L. Joughin, *Tenure in American Higher Education* 171–197 (1959); "Private Government on the Campus—Judicial Review of Expulsions," 72 *Yale Law Journal* 1362 (1963). But see Dixon v. Alabama State Board of Education, 294 F.2d 150 (5th Cir., 1961), cert. den. 368 U.S. 930 (1961), holding that a college student could not be summarily expelled. State statutory requirements sometimes assure deliberation before a pupil can be excluded from school, see Bishop v. Rowley, 165 Mass. 460, 43 N.E. 191 (1896); Morrison v. Lawrence, 186 Mass. 456, 72 N.E. 91 (1904).

55. For effective discussion of all these relationships between the individual and his government, see C. A. Reich, "The New Property," 73 *Yale Law Journal* 733 (1964). For a demonstration that conceptions about "property" are susceptible to major change, see N. Hecht, "From Seisin to Sit-in: Evolving Property Concepts," 44 *Boston University Law Review* 435 (1964). Compare "Administrative Procedure Reform," note 18 (above), at 248: "... in large areas of government, procedural safeguards are at present virtually absent because of the old-fashioned notion that fair and careful procedures are not necessary when mere 'privileges' are at issue. This a very grave gap indeed. If, for example, the benefactory, contractual, service and employing activities of the government be added together, one must conclude that 'privileges' have become in many respects more important than 'rights.' Virtually no attention is being directed to the administrative procedures involved in these tremendously significant phases of governmental activity." And see also, as to similar problems abroad, D. C. Holland, "A British Ombudsman," 1 *Solicitors' Quarterly* 147, 151–153 (1962).

56. Hearst Radio, Inc. v. Federal Communications Commission, 167 F.2d 225 (D.C. Cir., 1948).

57. Gart v. Cole, 166 F.Supp.2d 129 (S.D.N.Y., 1958), aff'd 263 F.2d 244 (2d Cir., (1959), cert. den. 359 U.S. 978 (1959).

58. See M. Eisenberg, "Judicial Standing in Subsidy Cases: Availability of Review Should Be Expanded," 41 *American Bar Association Journal* 718 (1955).

59. International Longshoremen's and Warehousemen's Union v. Boyd, 347 U.S. 222 (1953).

60. Compare L. L. Jaffe, *Judicial Control of Administrative Action* chap. 13 (1965), and K. C. Davis, Administrative Law Treatise, 1965 Supp. chap. 22.

61. Compare F. Frankfurter, "Chief Justices I Have Known," 39 *Virginia Law Review* 883, 895 (1953).

62. F. Frankfurter and J. M. Landis, *The Business of the Supreme Court* 310 (1928).

63. Snyder v. Massachusetts, 291 U.S. 97, 105 (1934).

64. Solesbee v. Balkcom, 339 U.S. 9, 16 (1950).

65. See McNabb v. United States, 318 U.S. 332 (1943); Mallory v. United States, 354 U.S. 449 (1957); Escobedo v. Illinois, 378 U.S. 478 (1964); and, for background, see Gellhorn *American Rights* 24–28 (1960).

66. People v. Cahan, 44 Cal. 2d 434, 282 P.2d 905 (1955); and see also Mapp v. Ohio, 367 U.S. 643 (1961), in which the Supreme Court upheld "the right to privacy free from unreasonable state intrusion" and "closed the courtroom door ... to evidence secured by official lawlessness." W. R. La Fave, "Improving Police Performance Through the Exclusionary Rule," 30 *Missouri Law Review* 391, 566 (1965).

67. Compare Y. Kamisar, "On the Tactics of Police—Prosecution Oriented Critics of the Courts," 49 *Cornell Law Quarterly* 436 (1964), and F. E. Inbau, "More About Public safety v. Individual Civil Liberties," 53 *Journal of Criminal Law, Criminology, and Police Science* 329 (1962). See also "A Forum on the Interrogation of the Accused," 49 *Cornell Law Quarterly* 382 (1964); M. G. Paulsen, "Safeguards in the Law of Search and Seizure," 52 *Northwestern Law Review* 65 (1957); P. M. Bator and J. V. Vorenberg, "Arrest, Detention, Interrogation, and the Right to Counsel," 66 *Columbia Law Review* 62 (1966). As to the difficult problem of retroactively applying Supreme Court teachings to previously closed cases, see Linkletter v. Walker, 381 U.S. 618 (1965), denying habeas corpus relief to a prisoner whose conviction, based on illegally obtained evidence, had become final before Mapp v. Ohio, note 66 (above), had decided that such a conviction is constitutionally impermissible. And see P. J. Mishkin, "The High Court, the Great Writ, and the Due Process of Time and Law," 79 *Harvard Law Review* 56 (1965). See also Tehan v. United States ex rel. Shott, 382 U.S. 406 (1966).

68. The New Zealand Ombudsman, unlike his counterparts in Scandinavia, is not to

investigate an administrative act that can be reviewed "on the merits of the case" by any court. The 1965 proposal of the Labour Government for a British "parliamentary commissioner for administration" contemplates that "he will have discretion to act if he thinks that the remedy open in the courts is not one which the complainant could reasonably be expected to use, but this will not affect anyone's right of access to the courts." Cmnd. 2767, para. 8 (1965).

69. A. J. Goldberg, "Equality and Governmental Action," 39 *New York University Law Review* 205, 215 (1964).

70. The extent of grudging acquiescence because of the fear of official reprisals has not been measured in America, but the time is ripe for a thorough study. Comment on related attitudes in Japan appears in Gellhorn, *Ombudsmen.*

71. "Administrative Regulation in Comparative Perspective," 26 *Law and Contemporary Problems* 307, 318 (1961).

72. *Ibid.* at 323.

73. For well-informed, enthusiastic accounts, see C. E. Freedman. *The Conseil d'Etat in Modern France* (1961); C. J. Hamson, *Executive Discretion and Judicial Control* (1954); R. Grégoire, "The Conseil d'Etat," 8 *Canadian Public Administration* 505 (1965). And see also M. Letourneur, "Le Contrôle de l'Administration par le Juge Administratif," 1964 *Public Law* 9.

74. W. A. Robson, *The Governors and the Governed* 32 (1964): "I have no doubt that the French *Conseil d'Etat* is a much more effective and impressive organ of judicial control of the Executive than any which exists in the common law countries. But this great institution has not been successfully implanted in any other country. The Councils of State which have been established in Italy, Belgium, Greece, Egypt, and elsewhere are mere shadows of the original institution from which they take their name; and none of them has attained a position at all comparable to that enjoyed by the French *Conseil d'Etat.*"

75. T. E. Utley, *Occasion for Ombudsman* 36 (1961).

76. See, e.g., G. Langrod, "The French Council of State: Its Role in the Formulation and Implementation of Administrative Law," 49 *American Political Science Review* 673 (1955).

77. R. A. Newman, "The Role of Equity in the Harmonization of Legal Systems," 13 *American University Law Review* 8, 10 (1963). But compare K. C. Davis, "Ombudsmen in America," 109 *University of Pennsylvania Law Review* 1057, 1061–1062 (1961), criticizing the Conseil d'Etat for insensitivity to the need for procedural safeguards of fairness. Compare, however, C. H. Fulda, "A Proposed 'Administrative Court' for Ohio," 22 *Ohio State Law Journal* 734, 738 (1961), citing Conseil d'Etat cases to show that the "fundamentals of what we call procedural due process are jealously guarded."

78. See R. W. Brewster, "The Tribunaux Administratifs of France," 11 *Journal of Public Law* 236 (1962); L. N. Brown, "The Reform of the French Administrative Courts," 22 *Modern Law Review* 357 (1959). For further discussion of procedural aspects of the French administrative law system, see N. Questiaux, "How Administrative Courts Meet the Need," in D. C. Rowat, ed., *The Ombudsman* 217 (1965). Mme. Questiaux, herself a member of the Conseil d'Etat, concludes that the system (despite its procedural difficulties) works on the whole satisfactorily to the citizenry. "More often than not," she says, "attacks and criticisms against the system come from the administration."

79. K. Holmgren, "The Need for an Ombudsman, Too," in D. C. Rowat, ed., *The Ombudsman* 225, 227 (1965). And see also I. M. Pedersen, "The Ombudsman and Administrative Courts," in the same volume at 231. Judge Pedersen contends that administrative courts do not deal effectively with minor errors of procedure and conduct in which "the importance of the issue is out of proportion to the annoyance felt by the

citizen." She points also (at 233) to the "any borderline cases where the courts may be competent, but where even a very angry citizen may feel that it is too much to bring his case before a court."

80. H. Cecil, *Alibi for a Judge* 14–15 (Michael Joseph Ltd., 1960).

81. W. A. Robson asserts that "There is nothing more infuriating than arrogance or conceit on the part of an official, while a friendly and helpful attitude can leave a favourable impression of a lasting nature. This is true even though the behaviour of the official may not in either case affect the decision or the action of the public authority concerned." *The Governors and the Governed* 20.

82. Public service organizations usually apply higher entry standards than most private employers enforce. Much work performed by official hands came there because, in the first place, it had been wretchedly performed by private bureaucracies that had previously had it in charge, or because private bureaucracies' shortcomings led to demands for public supervision.

83. Compare L. J. Blom-Cooper, "An Ombudsman in Britain?" 1960 *Public Law* 145, 151; S. A. de Smith, "Anglo-Saxon Ombudsman?" 33 *Political Quarterly* 9, 19 (1962). And see Robson, *The Governors and the Governed* 20–21, remarking that "If we want public servants to behave well towards us we must behave well towards them" and calling on social psychologists, sociologists, and political scientists to give attention to the "difficult operation" of enhancing the public esteem in which politicians and civil servants are held.

84. For a skeptical answer to that question, see S. Krislov, "A Restrained View," in D. C. Rowat, ed., *The Ombudsman* 246, 253–254 (1965): ". . . the historical experience of the United States with committees and boards established without powers, operating only with moral authority, does not lend support to an expectation of compliance with their findings."

85. Compare the largely unsuccessful effort to cope with discreditable public administration described by L. A. Viloria, "The Presidential Complaints and Action Committee in the Philippines," in D. C. Rowat, ed., *The Ombudsman* 153–161: (1965).

86. Compare R. L. Harris, "The Role of the Civil Servant in West Africa," 25 *Public Administration Review* 308 (1965), showing the debilitating consequences of official acts that are conventionally shaped by technically and administratively improper considerations.

87. Even in the best administered societies judicially applied penal laws remain necessary, of course, to deal with isolated instances of true criminality, such as embezzlement or extortion. An external critic's gentle adjurations are out of place when positive lawlessness comes to light.

88. See, e.g., K. W. B. Middleton, "The Ombudsman," 5 *Juridical Review* n.s. 298, 303 (1960): "The effectiveness of the office of Ombudsman depends essentially on his personal prestige and could hardly survive if he were nothing more than the head of a government department"; L. J. Blom-Cooper, "An Ombudsman in Britain?" [1960] *Public Law* 145, 149: "If he ever became a department the value of the institution would disappear. A bureaucracy upon a bureaucracy spells inanition."

89. See Blom-Cooper, note 88 (above), at 148; Rowat, "An Ombudsman Scheme for Canada," 28 *Canadian Journal of Economics and Political Science* 543, 549.

90. A commission in late 1965 recommended a new division of responsibility between the two existing ombudsmen, without eliminating other officials who do ombudsmanlike work. Statens Offentliga Utredningar, *Riksdagens Justitieombudsmän* (Stockholm, 1965).

91. The quoted phrase is from Justice Robert H. Jackson's dissenting opinion in Shaughnessy v. United States ex rel. Mezei, 345 U.S. 206, 225 (1953).

92. Compare K. C. Davis, "Administrative Powers," 63 *Harvard Law Review* 193, 225 (1949): "Administrative apathy is all the more insidious because of its silence. A

defeat of legislative will through inaction usually harms only an inarticulate general public and is likely to pass unnoticed. Abuses of an affirmative character are less dangerous because they usually damage interests which are vocal or vociferous. Fear of bureaucracy has overemphasized excessive zeal and has underemphasized administrative apathy."

93. The New Zealand ombudsman seems to have had this thought much in his mind, for he has sought out occasions to say favorable as well as unfavorable things about administrative bodies, apparently believing that good work can be encouraged by a pat on the back as well as by a kick on the backside. See further discussion of this matter in Gellhorn, *Ombudsmen*.

94. The above distinction is reflected in many American court decisions, typified by Walsh v. LaGuardia, 269 N.Y. 437, 199 N.E. 2d 652 (1936). That case involved a citizen's suit to compel New York's mayor and police commissioner to enforce the law against operation of unlicensed buses. The court refused the desired order, saying that responsibility for sound municipal government was lodged elsewhere than in the courts, which were not so organized as to enable them "conveniently to assume a general supervisory power." An earlier Illinois case, People ex rel. Bartlett v. Dunne, 219 Ill. 346, 76 N.E. 570 (1906), had reached a similar conclusion when suit was brought against Chicago's mayor to make him enforce laws which unquestionably forbade selling liquor on Sundays. The court declined to issue a command that would commit it "to control and regulate a general course of official conduct and enforce the performance of official duties generally." A court cannot suitably tell an official to adopt a general course of action (as distinct from completing a particular duty), because doing so would necessitate the court's determining "in very numerous instances whether he had persistently, and to the extent of his power and the force in his hands," performed the duties imposed on him by law. Compare Powell v. Katzenbach, F.2d (D.C. Cir., 1965), holding that a court will not command the Attorney General to prosecute alleged lawbreakers.

95. For example, "A complaint about the shortage of maternity beds in a hospital area could hardly be dealt with responsibly except by the authority with power to provide a new maternity hospital; and the decision of this body would in turn be subject to the Government's current plans for capital development in the National Health Service at large." A. W. Bradley, "The Redress of Grievances," [1962] *Cambridge Law Journal* 82, 92.

23

Arthur R. Matthews, Jr., and Jonathan A. Weiss

WHAT CAN BE DONE: A NEIGHBORHOOD
LAWYER'S CREDO

"Are you talking about the New Jerusalem?" says the citizen.
"I'm talking about injustice," says Bloom.
"Right," says John Wyse.
"Stand up to it then with force like men."

—James Joyce, *Ulysses*

A new romanticism about poverty supposedly spreads both in the United States and abroad. We hear it is based on idealism and expressed with exuberance—almost as if the existence of poverty was not known to other men of other countries at other times. "The poor" have been rediscovered. Poverty, we can assume, is at least the extreme of inequality of money—some citizens forced to do without while others have all the money they need even for luxuries. Some agree, moreover, with what Franklin Delano Roosevelt said at his second inauguration: "The test of our progress is not whether we add more to the abundance of those who have much; it is whether we provide enough for those who have too little."[1]

Inequality has been a traditional concern of lawyers, since lawyers are dedicated to justice or, in part, the even distribution of the law's benefits and sanctions depending on acts and, perhaps, intrinsic worth. Moreover, a lawyer is dedicated to his client and sworn to uphold his interests, so that when he deals with the poor, the lawyer must be concerned with the inequality he confronts for his client.

Commensurate with the new rhetoric of poverty has been the development of Neighborhood Legal Services Projects, as one expression of the lawyer's

Arthur R. Matthews, Jr., and Jonathan A. Weiss, "What Can Be Done: A Neighborhood Lawyer's Credo," *Boston University Law Review* 47 (1967): 231–243. This chapter originally appeared in 47 *Boston University Law Review* 231 (1967). Reprinted by permission.

concern for justice to the poor and equality of treatment in the courts. Such projects can be a tremendous force for the good, worthy of the highest ideals of the profession, and their successful fulfillment is a realization in concrete terms of some of the express goals of the poverty program.

The thesis of this chapter is that a neighborhood lawyer, by practicing in complete and dedicated manifestation of the traditional ideals of legal represen-, sentation, can create a climate of justice, a culture of equality, and an achievement of greater equality, dignity and hope for the poor. We shall develop this thesis by first outlining the traditional doctrine of representation; then by delineating some recognized constituents of the continued deprivation the poor endure; then by detailing how really adequate legal representation can help ameliorate this deprivation; and conclude by suggesting a credo for the neighborhood lawyer to follow in applying traditional notions of representation and present knowledge about the poor in his day to day work with and for the poor client.

Fundamental to the notion of legal representation is the doctrine of attorney-client relationship. The distinguishing characteristic of the relation between lawyer and client is that the lawyer is client-oriented. The lawyer is the agent of the client and the client the principal.[2] If a client chooses a course of action and seeks counsel, it is not for the lawyer to pass judgment on the client's personal worth or the social value of the client's project unless such advice is solicited or expected. The lawyer is there to serve the client's desires. A lawyer chooses not his cases, causes, or clients with complete freedom; for once the attorney-client privilege attaches, he must respect the client's desires which in many instances may not even be compatible with what the lawyer thinks are his client's best interests. The lawyer counsels and advises, but the client ultimately decides. A lawyer provides for his client all the legal skills a client needs to effectuate his purpose. In effect he does for the client all he would do in his own behalf, given his special knowledge and skills, had he the same aims and expressed goals as the client. Except for computations of time, cost, and effort in determining the advisability of litigation or other activity when advising his client, the lawyer's duty is to be his client's advocate. It is therefore not his duty to pass judgment, even on the final legal merits of the case. His advocacy of his client's cause makes the system work —as an officer of the court, he produces all he can in his client's favor, meeting the material presented by the opposing advocate, and awaits the judgment of the judicial system.

The lawyer has functions to perform in addition to presenting the position of the client since he has knowledge and experience the client does not possess. To fulfill his client's desires he must use these skills. Often this obligation involves counseling beyond the strictly legal. For example, in corporate practice, as in labor management situations, the lawyer is often one of the parties negotiating a contract. In dealing with real estate closings, dangers are described; and in advising businessmen, tax lawyers have learned to skirt up to the edge of the law in the use of technicalities on behalf of their clients.

Once involved in litigation, the lawyer, in effect, generates most of the case. It is not mere rhetoric that allows a lawyer to say, in ancient and honorable language, "Comes now the plaintiff, by and through his attorney, and says. . . ." and to sign for his client as an agent under civil procedure. To assert all possible legal theories that may advance the client's cause, to cover all litigational possibilities, the lawyer must create the armaments, the pleadings, the driving force of a case. Not to do so is to fail the client's interests by not equipping the system to accommodate the expression of his desires as fully as possible.

The poor are, to an extent, a mystery to others not so classified. Yet, almost all poverty literature commentators agree that the poor are characterized in general by passive rather than active reactions to every day situations,[3] by dependence. Moreover, for the poor, "the system" is an enemy—the law, for example, has often been the instrument of rather than a bulwark against the oppressors.[4] In addition, Mr. Justice Frankfurter has reminded us of the relevance in our own time of the words of Anatole France: "The law, in its majestic equality, forbids the rich as well as the poor to sleep under bridges, to beg in the streets, and to steal bread."[5] When they cease being passive and dependent, the poor tend to go outside the "system" and outside the "law," to violence, destruction, and abnormal public activity. Even demonstrations, laudable and properly protected by the Constitution, are unusual, and often run athwart local laws—which are, of course, probably wrong.[6] The orderly and sophisticated processes of democratic government, regarded as normal and rational by the middle class, are perceived by the poor either as mysteries in which often they are accidentally victimized, or as oppression clear and simple. The societal relations of the poor in many parts of this country are reminiscent of a feudal kingdom in which they survive by paying fealty to various lords: the rent man, the grocery man, the policeman, the furniture store man—against whom they have no rights they really know or can exercise, but merely standard expectations of what to give and what they may expect to receive in return. One observing the everyday lives of such citizens in many parts of this country must observe that these citizens have not yet graduated from "status" to "contract."[7]

In short, as most acknowledge, but few specify, poverty means not only real financial inequality but a resultant or at least a concomitant psychological inequality which needs to be surmounted. Moreover, there are other real inequalities, political and social, which may be no less important either causally, descriptively, or essentially. Without specifying these, let us merely focus on the two inequalities of money and psychological weakness that experts believe have traditionally characterized the American poor. We contend that these two types of inequalities, the one real and the other psychological, are very closely related and mutually reinforce each other so that if poverty programs are to fulfill their goals, and neighborhood legal services to have any impact, they must strive towards the simultaneous elimination of both. Their mutual dialectical importance, often overlooked, also must receive explicit recognition and remedying.

Often, psychological inequality is an excuse used by some for saying that the poor cannot be helped much, when actually it is a real inequality that is at stake. For instance, the Moynihan report[8] goes to great length to characterize the psychological inequality supposed to be associated with the Negro poor, but this report reveals a surprising lack of awareness of the factors of real inequality which contribute to this psychological inequality. Because the Moynihan report on the Negro family did not enumerate the many actual injustices and real inequalities, which have and still are contributing factors to the situation of the American Negro family, it was received by many as the forerunner of a new racism, couched in the language of the social sciences, buttressed by impersonal, ostensibly irrefutable, statistical data, bearing the official stamp of approval of the sophisticated, liberal intelligentsia. Because it presented only one side of the story, and because of its implicit moral connotations, it inevitably evoked a quick and angry response from the Negro community.

On the other hand, many commentators overlook the psychological aspects of poverty. These individuals would lead us to believe that poverty and injustice can be overcome if only a few new statutes on consumer credit and landlord-tenant laws are passed or a few major decisions are won in the appellate courts. This group blissfully overlooks the plethora of legal rights and defenses now available to the poor but which are not exercised.[9] True it is that not many are exercised, because the poor have had no lawyers, and what they need are many more lawyers. The old common law doctrine of the law accommodating itself to reality by the whole legal process's involvement in economic or social spheres would seem to call for more lawyers, not more law, at least immediately—and it is the contention of the authors that such a position, at least now, makes sense. But beyond this, even where there is some awareness of the existence of legal remedies among the poor, even when there are lawyers available, and even where lawyers actually represent the poor, the poor sometimes do not receive the full benefit for psychological reasons. These psychological handicaps also need to be removed, and although a major step in that direction would be the removal of real barriers to equality, some change of climate and attitude seems to be essential as well.

In recognition of the need for a change in climate and attitude, the new romantic poverty cliché of "participation by the poor" has sprung up. Such a cliché has the dangerous aspect of being yet another version of "go out and inherit a department store." The idea that voting blocks or even at best "local pressure groups" have a major effect on political decisions strikes the authors as naive given the existence of money, corruption, and back-rooms in politics. To suggest that whatever political decisions such groups might effect will have major historical impact is unrealistic. And any implication that the poor are downtrodden as the result of some inherited guilt of nonparticipation by their political fathers ought to be rejected as both naive and dangerous. Finally, it should be pointed out that the poor as well as the rich have the moral right, and should be able to ignore politics and concern themselves instead with the arts, with leisure, with pleasure and with personal fulfillment as they choose.

The controversy over the extent to which the poor should participate in their forthcoming "salvation" has obscured more fundamental issues. In retrospect, the notion of "consensus," embodied in section 202(a) of the Economic Opportunity Act of 1964,[10] appears somewhat misguided. The war on poverty, in effect, proposes to underwrite a revolution of the poor. To be sure, the poverty program contemplates a revolution carried out more or less within the framework of the democratic process, but it is a revolution, nonetheless. And while "consensus" may ultimately be a result, certainly one does not begin with consensus. Moreover, the cynical could assert that little groups and even larger demonstrations are often but token voices with very little real political effect. Demonstrations, for example, frequently seem less the result of organized planning to achieve a specific objective, than a bit of emotional hoopla which is an end in itself, and tolerated by the authorities only because the demonstration is itself its own goal, and hence, harmless.

Nevertheless, the unthinking fixation on participation by the poor, misleading and perhaps dangerous as it may be, points up one important issue. The poor, caught in lives of daily horror, living in the status of fiefdom, often do not recognize their own dignity as men. They do not seek the rights others do because they are led to believe they cannot receive them and therefore implicitly are not worthy of them. Frustration, bitterness, and anger are the least products of this—a lower estimation of the self can hardly help but be associated with it. Hence, it is the lack of genuine individual accomplishment in a whole series of related life enterprises, because of a variety of factors, some real, some imagined, and some psychological, that accounts for the origins of Harrington's observation: "There is, in a sense, a personality of poverty. . . the other Americans feel differently than the rest of the nation. They tend to be hopeless and passive, yet prone to bursts of violence; they are lonely and isolated, often rigid and hostile."[11]

It is often such an American, poor, often inarticulate, hostile, suspicious and distrustful, with whom the lawyer will be dealing in the neighborhood law office. As a group, the profession can work towards the elimination of the real inequality; as private practitioners, by the role they play, and by their activity, they can help these individuals secure their rights, and by eliminating a particular existent inequity, help these clients realize their own particular worth and dignity. The lawyer can, in a peculiar way, perform both these functions because, interestingly enough, the traditional lawyer-client relationship which has so well served the middle and upper classes, the merchants, the railroads, the corporations, and the consumer credit industry has the characteristics we have sketched.

The poor person who comes to the lawyer for help will usually receive two benefits which concretize the two above-mentioned notions of aiding the poor.

On the one hand, the lawyer can, often just by his presence alone, change the balance of advantage. The fact that a lawyer has time to devote to his client's case—time that must be matched by the time of the opposing lawyer —may well influence a decision, as may the mere fear of lawyers. Tactics may have tremendous effects. Just as delaying an antitrust suit may save millions, so letters of inquiry, interrogatories, and the like may buy useful time and harass the opponent into effective settlement. Since very often real equities and legal rights do exist for the poor, the lawyer can actually be successful in representing a poor client. By removing a barrier to happiness or desire in American society with traditional legal methods, the lawyer also accomplishes the end of blunting the feelings of psychological inequality and alienation from the "system" which have built up over a lifetime. The human experience of the poor person working with a lawyer who is "his" lawyer alone, begins to create new attitudes. Here is a representative of the law, who on the one hand is part of the "system" and yet is operating to make the poor person's lot better—using the "system" and what he can do within the law and the legal system for the poor person's benefit. Next, of course, any success brings psychological results—the poor person now knows that the law and the "system" can be used to benefit him. But, perhaps most important is what results by virtue of the attorney-client relationship.

The attorney-client relationship is established from the outset as one of confidentiality. The attorney, though representing the law and working within a traditional legal framework, is in the poor person's "corner." When "push comes to shove" the lawyer is committed to the poor person and can be counted on. Needless to say, this commitment is perhaps most effective psychologically for juveniles. It is maintained, for example, that in Negro families, children grow alienated from their family and come to hate their parents at an early age.[12] In the juvenile court in the District of Columbia, there are many cases of parent against child, for under the law of the District of Columbia a parent may turn his child in for being "beyond control."[13] The result is an alignment of parent and prosecutor against the child. If the child has a lawyer, and if counsel can bring other forces to bear to aid the child, the youth has a sense of worth and dignity; at the moment when all authoritarian figures seem arrayed against the child, there is one person in authority who provides him with recognition—his counsel. In such situations, the lawyer by acting as the advocate of the client provides the poor person, the juvenile, the deserted, in short the outcasts and rejects of society, the sorely needed psychological support simply by assuming the role his profession obligates him to assume. As Mr. Justice Fortas has recently reminded the juvenile court of the District of Columbia: "The right to representation by counsel is not a formality. It is not a grudging gesture to a ritualistic requirement. It is of the essence of justice."[14]

Often the poor man comes to the lawyer supposing that real barriers cannot be overcome, and he is surprised to find a professional person willing to act as his advocate. Often a neighborhood lawyer has to find out what the person

443

really wants, what really is worrying him, because the poor person has so little faith in the lawyer and the law's remedies or knows so little of the law and his rights. Sometimes a client does not even take the confidentiality requirement seriously until the lawyer persuades him of his good faith. The lawyer cannot go to the poor; the poor must come to the lawyer. But once the objective is learned, and the client perceives that the lawyer is acting on his behalf and is committed to leave no stone unturned in pursuit of the client's desires and interests, changes occur. A process of discovery occurs for the poor client, as he watches the drama of advocacy unfold. The poor man learns and commences to understand the workings of advocacy as he sees the process performed alive before his eyes. In a sense, the advocacy of the attorney is learned by the client, or perhaps, by a form of osmosis is somehow communicated to the poor client and, hopefully, through him to his associates and his family. He begins to gradually awake from a slumber of passivity and ineffectualness, to perceive that the powerful can be resisted, that lawyers and the legal system can redress more grievances than he had imagined and can operate *against* those in power as well as *for* those in power.

Moreover, a neighborhood lawyer is not just a lawyer for emergencies, as is even the best of the legal aid lawyers. He has an office in the neighborhood and often lives in the neighborhood or nearby. It is possible to say "hello" to him on the street, wave to him from a car, and drop in when worried for advice. In short, a continuing relationship exists and a real lawyer-client relationship can be developed. The neighborhood lawyer becomes more than simply an *ad hoc* advocate or emergency advisor, here one moment and gone the next; rather, a continuity develops to the point of relationship.

Also, just as a good corporation lawyer or tax lawyer gives advice which is not always strictly legal, so the neighborhood lawyer can enlist those aids and advices that help the client's desires—as long as they are not preachments, but aids enlisted for specified interests and desires. Again, this is most valuable in the case of children. For example, neighborhood legal service attorneys can aid school children in problems with school administration. Here, where a lawyer is more a matter of leverage than of legal advocacy, his advice can be of help in realizing that the system is, at base, rational, and that there are ways to promote individual interests within a rational system. Here again, the lawyer is often filling the gap left by a departed parent for a child who has no one else to turn to. A similar phenomenon is the entrance of the neighborhood lawyer into administrative law, government law, and welfare regulations. For the lawyer's continuous presence provides reassurance, provides grounds for a belief that the system can work rationally, and establishes a guide to achievement of the person's own interests.

Finally, lawyers are human. It is impossible to practice law for the poor in a slum without becoming emotionally involved in some cases, causes, and with some people—the establishment of some emotional contact may, in fact, turn out to be one of the most valuable fruits of such a program.

The lawyer, thus operative, differs from the others who come in contact with the poor. The midtown Manhattan study found that popular definitions (those of the middle class viewing the poor) tend to be accepted by the poor themselves as correct. Take the following view: "The American man who is not earning a good living is not considered to be a 'man' and his morality as well as his virility and mental health, is open to question."[15] Such a view is often accepted by the poor, a group often out of work; ironic as it is, it is nevertheless probably a psychological reality. No attorney, however, can accept such a view. First, his job is to find out the specific grievance of the client and try to alleviate it by the application of appropriate legal remedies as effectively as possible. Unless he assumes that the client has the right to the relief sought, he can hardly represent him. The lawyer's solution, instead of "working with" the individual as some caseworkers do, with the possible implication that the cause of misery and lower social status is self-caused, is to try to work through and within the system in a combative manner for the client. Rather than turning the attention of the client towards his own life and problems, or indicating that the system has no help, the lawyer acts as the client's agent in the system. Law is, after all, at least in part, the doctrine that problems can be isolated and that criteria can be applied to them to resolve differences. A problem, a dispute, can be resolved by a decision based on arguments relevant to that issue.

In this sense, law operates as a safety valve.[16] Advocacy by professionals within a framework of legal rules is a healthy operation. The grievances of the poor are thereby channeled into the legal system where they can, for the most part, be resolved peaceably rather than fester to become antisocial drives capable of igniting the fires of revolution in the streets. The wishes of the poor and the outcast, unless channeled towards healthy fulfillment or psychological resolution, may be lost in reality. A battle of rich and poor in court is preferable to a riot of the poor against those with money in the streets of Watts, just as the trial by jury is preferable to the trial by combat.

Again, the contrast with traditional social workers is important to understand. An advocate treats his clients at least as moral equals. Social workers try to orient them to society's precepts and values. The lawyer will take even antisocial desires and try to give them concrete fulfillment inside the legal system and "society" itself. The lawyer respects the individual and his desires—puts the place for answers in activities and the legal system, rather than posing the answers and an acclimation to a culture from which the individual may be "alienated" (and perhaps rightly so). In this sense, the lawyer is client-orinted, and may provide better psychological help than the social worker. The lawyer is, in short, not the judge. The lawyer who can steer a client through the experience of legal process with the result that the client feels he has been "fairly" treated is psychologically important to every litigant. For the time being, the poor perhaps need more than others an outside agent to provide answers for their felt concrete needs—at least in addition to whatever supportive techniques social workers may provide. It should be noted, of course, that a good lawyer will enlist good social workers to help his client if the client desires such service, in much the same way as a competent tax lawyer might enlist an accountant or a business expert.

It is important to stress that the lawyer as a participant in social change does so from his office and from the courts, and not from pulpits or soap boxes. It is not by organizing block clubs or picketing that the lawyer has effect (though he may aid in these) but in a more traditional legal framework. The respect and hence the influence lawyers may have in a community will be based on their relationship with individual clients who come to their offices seeking counsel, advice, and positive action. If these individuals do not receive the advocacy which they seek, the other groups of which they are a part will also turn away from the lawyers.

We should make two caveats clear at this juncture. First, it is true that the poor need advocates in places other than courts and agencies. They need them before legislatures and before the court of public opinion. Secondly, the few attorneys who will be available to the poor are not enough. Yet, we need state that the few attorneys are a beginning, an example, at least a breach in the wall. A good lawyer operating in the neighborhood and serving his clients can demonstrate a real living concern for the people in the neighborhood— a concern that even the most beautifully and elegantly phrased statute in a law book cannot express. By actually being present in the neighborhood, by subordinating the client's interests to nothing, the lawyer can overcome the real barriers to equality and by example and by involvement help the poor to stand up to injustice "with force like men."

To do this, the following credo provides an outline.

1. Once the attorney-client relationship has attached, the traditional client loyalty must be paramount. The only interest, ideals, and desires the lawyer should follow are those of his client and he should leave no stone unturned in their pursuit. It is wrong for him to tell his client what he the lawyer, or he the middle-class citizen, thinks of the client's desires, past conduct, or projected desires or to stop short of the all out representation he would provide for a million dollar fee. For only in this way will the existent desires of the poor be communicated to the lawyer so that they can receive expression in the appropriate tribunals. And in a confidential relationship with one individual they are more likely to be accurately articulated than in some loose public meeting manipulated by those after power. Only in this way will the client recognize not only his own worth and right to his own desires, but the possibility that they can be fulfilled within a personally meaningful legal system.

2. Cases cannot be selected according to a scheme established by a poverty program or by any other group. Traditionally, the lawyer is not bound to accept all comers, but these comers could find other lawyers willing to take their fee. The poor cannot shop for lawyers or find others. As Judge Skelly Wright has recently suggested, Canon 31 should be "expunged": "If we want the public to believe that lawyers must accept clients, lawyers should begin to do just that. Until the public is convinced of the compulsory nature of a lawyer's service, every lawyer representing an unpopular client runs the risk of being tarred with unpopularity."[17] Advocates must work with the materials presented to them by clients. To reject clients whose cases do not seem to make the legal points sought to win some social revolution, that they lack the social impact desired by a theoretician, however well

intentioned, who holds a position on an advisory board, is to play a very immoral type of god. Even assuming that a lawyer can know what is good for the poor in general as opposed to the client sitting across his desk, to reject people is to alienate them not only individually but also as a group. Moreover, it is in the desperation of seeking to find a solution for a particular client's problem that lawyers find important legal theories.[18] Lawyers who represent clients do not judge what sort of law they want made. Finally, lawyers operate in a tradition of common law, with a theory that the law will expand for justice over a field of facticity presented by litigation of specific cases and controversies. To do otherwise is to make the courts legislatures where bills can be introduced only with a process of selection dictated to lawyers by outsiders—a perversion of the purpose of both the courts and the legislatures. Once the lawyer-client relationship has been established, how can any lawyer, especially a neighborhood lawyer dealing with a person whose total past experience has been one of rejection from the officials of the court and the rest of the establishment, say to this client across his desk: "Your cause is just, but it lacks the social utility without which we cannot represent you"?

3. Neighborhood lawyers should strive to become part of the neighborhoods they serve. It is their function to establish a continuity of lawyer-client relationship and to give advice as do house counsel to corporations. Their job is to be the advocate for people in the neighborhood who want to know how to achieve their desires in that community.

4. Lawyers in a poor neighborhood should recognize that the "horror" is so great that forthright advocacy alone will often produce beneficial results—it will air issues and begin to make law. When discontented with their clients or their aspirations, neighborhood lawyers should recognize that if slums produced ideal citizens, we should seek not to abolish them, but to promote them. Rather than being repelled by the inadequacies of their clients, neighborhood lawyers should seek to represent them vigorously, to change the system to accommodate their human worth, their dignity and their desires—the system that in part has made them what they are and makes them suffer the way they do.

5. A lawyer in a neighborhood should ultimately remember that he is human and that his clients are human too. While there are demonstrable differences between the poor and other citizens, preoccupation with the differences should not obscure that great area of common humanity which both the poor and the not-so-poor share. Terms such as passivity, dependency, and even the notion of poverty itself, are in the ultimate analysis, abstractions. They are of little help when the client lays his troubles on the lawyer's desk. His is not the role of a Prometheus bringing the fire of middle-class truths to their dull hovels. He, too, can learn, can discover the range of meaning in human experience. In operating for and with the poor, the lawyer should begin to understand and then to communicate to his own community and to mankind at large, those truths the poor can communicate, individually and collectively, and also the truth and force of what it is to lead that style of life.

These reflections we leave with the reader as the passionate position of some, with the sincere hope that they will stimulate thought and reflection on the part of others. We leave it with the reader as one credo, one analysis, in the hope that some day real answers may be found, and true justice achieved for those individuals who make up the poor.

NOTES

1. Second Inaugural Address, January 20, 1937.
2. See Sparer, Thorkelson & Weiss, The Lay Advocate, 43 U. Det. L.J. 493, 514–15 (1966).
3. Duhl, The Urban Condition (1963); Reisman, Cohen & Pearl, Mental Health of the Poor (1964).
4. Alinsky, Reveille for Radicals (1946); Smith, Justice and the Poor: A Study of the Present Denial of Justice to the Poor (1919); Silberman, Crisis in Black and White (1964); cf. Law Day Address by Robert F. Kennedy, University of Chicago School of Law, May 1, 1964.
5. Griffin v. Illinois, 351 U.S. 12, 23 (1956) (concurring opinion).
6. See, e.g., Brown v. Louisiana, 383 U.S. 131 (1966); Shuttlesworth v. City of Birmingham, 382 U.S. 87 (1965).
7. Maine, Ancient Law (1861). But see Williams v. Walker-Thomas Furniture Co., 350 F.2d 445 (D.C. Cir. 1965); Comments to Uniform Commercial Code § 2–302. Judge Danaher, dissenting in Williams, argued: "Many relief clients may well need credit, and certain business establishments will take long chances on the sale of items, expecting their pricing policies will afford a degree of protection commensurate with risk." 350 F.2d at 450. Quaere the assumption that the poor are bad credit risks; in the instant case $1,400 of $1,800 had been paid by a consumer receiving welfare payments of $218 a month. If the argument is only an economic one, i.e., the taking of "long chances," why should not the risk remain with the "business establishment"?
8. Office of Policy, Planning, and Research, Dept. of Labor, Negro Family, Case for National Action, March 1965.
9. See, e.g., cases cited in Weiss, Book Review, 37 Geo. Wash. L. Rev. 627, 632 n. 16 (1967). Often the poor do not know how to articulate their grievances, often believe they do not have a remedy when in fact they have one and do not state their problem. Either they expect miracles or nothing at all, and often they do not trust anyone initially—hence the importance to lawyers of the privilege of confidentiality. Lawyer-client relations, generally, pose a similar problem generically; the difference is one of degree. Similarly, the poor citizen is as likely to fear crime and violence as the middle-class citizen, and the fact that the poor citizen lives in an area where crime is more frequent does not reduce his fears, but heightens them and reinforces the inequality of selective enforcement of criminal law. See Brown, Manchild in the Promised Land (1966).
10. 78 Stat. 516, 42 U.S.C. § 2782 (a) (1964).
11. Harrington, The Other America 120 (1963).
12. Silberman, op. cit. supra note 4. But cf. Gregory, Nigger 42 (1963): "[T]he social worker . . . said, 'We have reason to suspect you are working, and you can be sure I'm going to check on you . . .' Momma, a welfare cheater, a criminal, who couldn't stand to see her kids go hungry, or grow up in slums and end up mugging people in dark corners. I guess the system didn't want her to get off relief, the way it kept sending social workers around to be sure Momma wasn't trying to make things better." For an articulation of how the lawyer's role differs from that of at least some social workers, see Cahn & Cahn, The War on Poverty—A Civilian Perspective, 73 Yale L.J. 1317, 1334–36 (1964).
13. D.C. Code Ann. § 11-1551(a)(1)(B)(Supp. V 1966); see, e.g., In re Sippy, 97 A.2d 455 (D.C. Munic. Ct. App. 1953). Whatever the meaning of "habitually beyond control," many lawyers familiar with these matters in the District of Columbia

share the opinion that the majority of juvenile cases involve this question. Upon notification by the parent, the juvenile authorities take the child into custody i.e., to jail. See e.g., Elmore v. Stone, 355 F.2d 840 (D.C. Cir. 1966) (Separate Opinion of Bazelon, C.J.); Clayton v. Stone, 358 F. 2d 548 (D.C. Cir. 1966) (Separate Opinion of Bazelon, C.J.). It may be weeks before the matter comes up for preliminary hearing. Unless the complaint is withdrawn, (or if the parent never signed a petition), commitment to a reformatory generally follows.

14. Kent v. United States, 383 U.S. 541, 561 (1966). The extent to which the juvenile court, ostensibly serving the child, has, wittingly or unwittingly, in practice attached criminal stigma and criminal treatment has been a subject of widespread comment. Allen, The Borderland of Criminal Justice (1964); Hartung, Crime, Law and Society (1965); Matza, Delinquency and Drift (1965); Note, Juvenile Delinquents: The Police, State Courts and Individualized Justice, 79 Harv. L. Rev. 775 (1966); Note, District of Columbia Juvenile Delinquency Proceedings: Apprehension to Disposition, 49 Geo. L.J. 322 (1960).

15. Langer & Richard, Life Stress and Mental Health 457 (1963). See also Briar, Welfare From Below: Recipients' Views of the Public Welfare System, 54 Calif. L. Rev. 370 (1966). Recently, economists have offered proposals that, in separating "jobs" from "income," may pull the rug out from the view quoted in the text; see the suggestion for a "Negative Income Tax" in Friedman, Capitalism and Freedom 190–92 (1962), and a proposal for a guaranteed income in Theobold, Free Men and Free Market 192–93 (1963); see generally, Galbraith, The Affluent Society (1958).

16. See generally, Arnold, The Symbols of Government (1935).

17. Wright, The Renaissance of the Criminal Law: The Responsibility of the Trial Lawyer, 4 Duquesne U.L. Rev. 213, 223 (1966).

18. In the experience of one of the authors it was only after an apparently mundane juvenile problem produced just such a frustration that, in a context of continued client contact, the case reached appellate proportions, and beginning (hopefully) of decent treatment for juveniles in the District of Columbia. See Elmore v. Stone, 355 F.2d 840 (D.C. Cir. 1966); Clayton v. Stone, 358 F.2d 548 (D.C. Cir. 1966).

24

Alfred J. Kahn, Lawrence Grossman, Jean Bandler, Felicia Clark,
Florence Galkin, and Kent Greenwalt

THE BRITISH CITIZENS' ADVICE
BUREAUS: AN OVERVIEW

The local British Citizens' Advice Bureau is a neighborhood center whose stated purpose accurately describes its operation:

To make available to the individual accurate information and skilled advice on the many problems that arise in everyday life; to explain legislation; to help the citizen to benefit from and use wisely the services provided to him by the state.

The widely displayed and recognized symbol of the CAB is an owl—he is wise but does not talk.

The Bureaus were created at the outbreak of World War II to help Britons through the confusion and hardship war would bring. Whether in the immediate aftermath of a bombing or to handle continuing problems of rationing, separation and housing, persons of all social classes found the service invaluable. Today a network of 466 CAB's throughout Great Britain answer more than one million inquiries a year. The offices are nonsectarian and accessible; their personnel generally friendly. They are staffed by trained volunteers and paid personnel in a 70:30 ratio, which varies with the locality, working with the help of a central, professional staff at the National CAB office. They are looked to for aid by a wide cross-section of the public.

CAB workers are prepared to answer requests for any type of information, listen to problems, make home visits, fill out forms or write letters for an inquirer, or make informal referrals to public or voluntary agencies and to specialists such as lawyers. They are supplied with a comprehensive directory of social legislation, rules, regulations, and instructions on how to use these

Alfred J. Kahn, Lawrence Grossman, Jean Bandler, Felicia Clark, Florence Galkin, and Kent Greenwalt, "The British Citizens' Advice Bureaus: An Overview," in *Neighborhood Information Centers: A Study and Some Proposals* (New York: Columbia University School of Social Work, 1966), pp. 16–36. Reprinted by permission of Alfred J. Kahn.

laws. They have guides to resources, public and voluntary, available to those in need of help. This information is provided and continually updated by the National CAB office.

No appointment is needed at a CAB; callers are welcome to walk in off the street. All discussions are confidential. The inquiries are categorized and tallied each month, and CAB records become a source of impartial evidence for those studying the needs and problems of the British citizen and the adequacy of services designed to help him.

Although partially financed through government grants, CAB's are sponsored and run by local committees of citizens and representatives of public and voluntary agencies in their areas. They work closely with the agencies, and have succeeded in becoming an integral part of Britain's social service system.

The National CAB Council emphasizes "the unique contribution CAB can make to prevention because, being nonspecialist and informal, the inquirer is more likely to 'drop in for a chat' at an early stage of his problem when he may not even recognize his need for social work help; and knows too that his use of the CAB will not label him as a person with a problem."

Wartime CAB's were on the spot in trailers and makeshift offices as soon as bombings ended, to help victims locate next of kin and to make emergency arrangements. The growth of CAB during the bombings and its use by all persons is unique and the base for an image which cannot be reproduced. As put by one of our consultants, the CAB is "now traditional enough on the voluntary scene to become part of the 'good and the true.' " As such, it continues to have local and national governmental support.

Yet it is also a fact that CAB began as a function and then became an organization. Those concerned with meeting social needs in the United States must therefore separate in their analysis these two aspects.

What is the nature of the CAB as an organization—or rather as a loose federation of many local organizations? What does it do? What is the connection between what it does and its method of operation?

Our first section is largely descriptive.

The Bureaus in Action

An American visitor to a number of CAB's throughout Britain recently wrote the following, which conforms to our own observations:

Each local CAB decides the hours it will be open each day; most of them also are open at least one evening a week. The offices are unpretentious, easy to reach, informal. The walls have posters, neatly tacked up, colorful reminders of the citizen's need to file taxes by a given date or consider adult education courses at the local college. Leaflets are available on the counter—many of them free, although most have a small price. . . . The volunteers in the office are friendly. Visitors are welcomed. On one occasion when we visited a CAB bureau at closing time, we found the volunteer quite weary; even so, she was willing to spend time talking with us and with a man who came in off the street after us. . . . There was a marked friendliness and helpfulness about all the offices we visited, except in ————.

CAB's set their own hours to meet local needs. Several visited in middle-sized cities were open only from 10 A.M. to noon and from 2 to 4 P.M. Longer hours and some evening service are more common in big cities. There is a tendency to avoid 24-hour coverage or telephone answering service since it is not an emergency service. Another organization, the Samaritans, handles suicide threats and similar emergencies.

Location apparently is an important factor; Bureaus have reported a marked decrease in inquiries when their offices are moved to out-of-the-way spots. One Bureau visited was a small storefront office at a busy city intersection. The rooms were dark, disorderly, yet informal and friendly and one felt far more at home than in some glittering business-like atmospheres. Three workers answered inquiries; one was almost continuously on the telephone. This office reports that many of its initial inquiries are by phone, but the calls are almost always followed by a personal visit. A record is kept of each request and these are tabulated at the end of each month under ten subject headings, along with the total number of calls, and sent to the central or regional CAB office. The workers make an effort to give the inquirer some privacy and all records are confidential.

Generally, the workers observed seem to have all the time in the world, and much patience. They meet with some inquirers again and again, occasionally visit homes, explore resources, and try to give the help needed.

Although the Bureaus encourage inquirers to help themselves, the workers also will take action on their behalf: write letters, fill out forms, do accounts, make appointments, telephone other agencies to explain the problem. An example is one CAB worker, who for weeks was in daily communication with a homeless, crippled man. The worker made dozens of telephone calls and wrote at least half a dozen letters before successfully finding the inquirer a place to live.

Frequently, the true problem does not emerge immediately. An inquiry about finding an apartment for a teen-age girl led the worker to realize after subsequent visits that the girl was pregnant and had run away from home. The problem of an elderly widow who was unable to subsist on a pension led to a discussion of her previous life, from which the CAB worker discovered that the woman was entitled to other support of which neither she nor the government insurance office had been aware.

CAB workers on occasion will mediate a dispute—between a store manager and a dissatisfied customer, or a landlord and his tenants.

To the question of how far a worker should go with an inquirer, or when does CAB work become casework, the answer depends on the availability of casework services and on the professional-volunteer balance of the particular Bureau's staff. CAB workers are urged to use public and voluntary case-work services to the greatest possible extent. When there is no local family casework organization, the CAB worker must become the intermediary be-tween the inquirer and whatever resources are available.

For the most part, CAB's lack a follow-up process. The only way the worker can evaluate the quality of service the inquirer gets is if he returns to the worker with his problem unsolved—or if the inquirer, his family or friends make subsequent use of the CAB.

A person might come to the CAB merely for an opportunity to pour out his troubles in confidence to an uninvolved and sympathetic listener. He might come to get leads as to possible alternative actions, based on the specialized information in CANS (see below) and the general knowledge of the worker. He might arrive knowing that he needs referral to a specialist, such as a lawyer or another agency. Or he might need the help of the CAB to identify his basic problems and to accept referral and help.

CAB's receive telephone inquiries and may offer information and advice over the telephone, but the preference is for an office visit, and an inquirer will often be invited to drop in. On occasion, a report from a third party that a person in need cannot get to the office will lead to a home visit, as will other special circumstances. There are, however, no firm statistical data about home and office contacts; usually a person enters the office to ask for information or help.

Some offices receive a significant volume of mail inquiries which are an-swered by mail. Others do little of this. Systematic data are not available.

An American observer is struck by the CAB range, which contrasts with the usual scope of a social agency in the United States. CAB's are concerned with landlord-tenant problems and with housing, with consumer problems and social security rights, with educational and training services and medical services. They are truly intermediaries between the individual and the statutes and bureaucracies of a social welfare-oriented state. They give information and advice, listen, help in concrete ways or refer inquirers to specialized serv-ices. They are part of the social welfare network but far broader than social work as understood by most Americans.

The exact balance between giving information and tying it to the indi-vidual is hard to measure. One unverified estimate is that 60 percent of the inquiries are handled by giving the information and 40 percent go beyond this. The CAB central staff sees expertise in information as the foundation of its work and the entry to other services.

The scope of the concerns and the relative balances among areas is sug-gested by the following national compilation (with no breakdown among in-formation, advice and referral), see the table on p. 454.

While the categories intrinsically are not completely revealing for United States purposes, these illustrations, selected from a group made available by the National office and not edited for present purposes, provide further clari-fication:

TYPE	1962	1963	1964	1965
1. Communications and Travel: Travel, emigration, currency regulations, customs regulations, sending gifts abroad, etc.	35,620	31,470	29,250	24,684
2. Education and Training: Grants, scholarships, apprenticeships, schools, further education, community activities, etc.	29,840	30,600	30,800	24,684
3. Employment: Conditions of work, regulations, holiday pay, employer/employee agreements, Ministry of Labour rehabilitation centers, accidents at work, employer's liability, etc.	66,660	68,760	71,920	61,415
4. Civic, Local and National Information: Organizations, local authority and other offices, places of interest and times when they are open to public, reference data and requests for special information, etc.	257,250	271,140	275,840	230,413
5. Family and Personal: Noncontributory pensions, old people's welfare, care of children, affiliation, family budgeting, change of name, making a will, probate, letters of administration, naturalization, problems of overseas people, financial and material needs, national assistance, matrimonial, income tax, etc.	316,970	333,000	344,620	282,348
6. Insurance: Schemes in other countries, national insurance, private insurance, etc.	35,720	35,390	34,130	27,396
7. Health and Medical: General practitioner services, dentists and opticians, hospital services, convalescence, prevention and aftercare services of the local authority, public health departments and voluntary organizations, etc.	42,060	36,060	38,970	36,224
8. Property and Land: Housing, town and country planning, conveyancing charges, mortgages, loans and sureties, landlord and tenant problems, etc.	273,940	282,690	267,310	227,203
9. Service and Ex-Service Questions and War Pensions: Recruitment, careers in the service, discharge, war pensions, etc.	15,330	13,860	10,340	7,741
10. Trade and Manufacture: Businesses, regulations, licenses, consumer advice and information, hire purchase and credit sales, unsatisfactory goods, estimates and contracts, etc.	76,090	84,430	94,980	80,708
Total	1,149,480	1,184,400	1,198,190	1,003,219

Kahn, Grossman, Bandler, Clark, Galkin, and Greenwalt

CATEGORY 1—COMMUNICATIONS AND TRAVEL

A bureau in Wales received a letter from a French girl living in France who was going to marry an American and then come to a Welsh University to study for a year. She wanted to know if her husband would be able to get a job while he was in Wales with her. Having checked the situation with the various ministries concerned, the bureau replied explaining that to do so the husband must have a work permit which he could only obtain after he had gotten a job in England; and also suggested various authorities and businesses in the area who would be prepared to offer him suitable jobs.

CATEGORY 2—EDUCATION AND TRAINING

A bureau received an inquiry about the possibility of obtaining a subsistence allowance for the wife and two children of a man who had been accepted at their local Agricultural College for a year to study general agriculture. He had received the maximum educational grant from the Local Education Authority but could get nothing extra for his dependents. As the children were only 2 and 4 it would be extremely difficult for the wife to work. C.A.B. headquarters suggested a number of charities who might be approached, particularly those connected with agriculture and also advised the bureau worker to see if the inquirer had any connections with the Army as regimental funds can often be helpful. It was also suggested that the College itself might well be approached.

CATEGORY 3—EMPLOYMENT

She is a young deserted wife and has been in trouble with the police. Her parents will not have her at home and, wherever she takes a job, her prison sentence goes against her. She needs accommodation and employment. On the advice of the Discharged Prisoners Aid Association, C.A.B. telephoned to the Salvation Army who arranged to see her and do what they can for her.

CATEGORY 4—CIVIC, LOCAL AND NATIONAL INFORMATION

At what time can the changing of the guard at Buckingham Palace be seen? What is the address of the Criminal Inquiries Compensation Board? How can a telegram from the Queen be arranged for a centenarian? When does the coarse fishing season open? In which district of London would it be best to try and hitch a lift to Scotland?

CATEGORY 5—FAMILY AND PERSONAL

He brought his small child to C.A.B. His wife has been under treatment at a mental hospital and is said to be quite unfit to care for a child. He and the child have been staying with the paternal grandparents. Last week when he went home, he found that his wife was in occupation, having discharged herself from the hospital. She is demanding to have the child with her. He feels inclined to let her have the child in order "to bring matters to a head." He is not prepared to make a home with his wife again. As the child is under treatment at a children's hospital, C.A.B. made an appointment for the father to see the hospital almoner this afternoon and strongly advised the father to accept whatever medical advice was given. The procedure for claiming custody of a child through the Court was explained to him.

He came to C.A.B. to ask where he could find accommodations for himself, his young wife and son. The choice at present lies between his mother's home or her mother's home. They had been living with his mother till friction arose and his wife went back to her home saying she will not return till he finds accommodation. Their name is down with the L.C.C. for housing but with little prospect of

455

success. His mother-in-law lets lodgings and could take them in as she has a larger house but he is not sure if he wants to go. His own mother has given up her work to look after the little grandson.

He had a long talk with C.A.B. on the pros and cons of the situation and in the end seemed to realize that the longer he and his wife are apart, the worse it will be; also the child is fretting for his own mother. He will see the wife this evening and try to come to some arrangement with her parents until they can get their own accommodation. He cannot leave the district as his work is involved.

A neighbor came to the bureau on behalf of Mrs. H., who was too embarrassed to do so herself. A home visit revealed that she was the mother of six children, with a mentally sick husband, and that she had incurred a debt of £14 with the grocer while he was an in-patient in a mental hospital. Mrs. H. did not dare tell her husband about her debt when he came out of hospital for fear of upsetting his mind again. It was not possible to ask his regimental association for money because his signature would be required. An approach to the local British Legion produced a grant from funds to pay off the debt, clothing was obtained through SSAFA, and later the C.A.B. helped to find part-time employment for Mrs. H.

CATEGORY 6—INSURANCE

Her mother and father are separated. Her father is drawing a retirement pension. Is her mother entitled to a retirement pension in right of his insurance? C.A.B. telephoned to the Ministry of National Insurance who advised that the old lady should be eligible for 30/ a week and should apply to her local office about it.

CATEGORY 7—HEALTH AND MEDICAL

Mrs. A. telephoned the bureau very upset about a bachelor brother aged 28. She had not seen him for five years and he had suddenly called on her and stated he was being persecuted—his landlady was trying to poison him and the furniture was electrified. He stayed overnight but left the following morning having acted strangely. His speech was sometimes incoherent. He telephoned the sister the next evening to say he was sleeping rough and did not know what he had been doing all day. He wanted to come back to her. The woman was advised to have him back and get in touch with a general practitioner. The next day she telephoned the C.A.B. again, saying that no local g.p. would see him as he was not on their list. We eventually found a willing doctor and the patient was seen. Urgent psychiatric treatment was immediately arranged.

CATEGORY 8—PROPERTY AND LAND

A bureau received a number of complaints about an estate agent who after the customer had signed an agreement making him the sole agent for their house, sold the house for considerably more than was agreed and pocketed the difference. On reading the agreement, described as "a harsh and unconscionable document" by a legal adviser, they found that they had in fact agreed that the estate agent should have "all monies over and above that figure as his profit."

The bureau contacted both professional organizations concerned with estate agents but although one had received a complaint about this man before they were unable to help as he was not a member of their associations.

Note: At that particular time the Home Office was promoting a bill requiring the registration of estate agents and this agent's agreement was gratefully received by the Home Office from C.A.B. headquarters as clearly demonstrating the need for this.

He is eighty years old and has lived for the last twenty years in a ground floor furnished room. His landlord died and a relative took over the house and has told the old man that he must leave as the accommodation will be needed by the owner who is getting married. The old man suffers with heart trouble and must have a ground floor room. Where can he go? C.A.B. explained that the landlord will have to give him four weeks written notice before getting possession and, in the meantime, C.A.B. will make inquiries for him about Homes. This was done and after some search, the L.C.C. interviewed him and placed him on their list for a Home.

CATEGORY 9—SERVICE AND EX-SERVICE QUESTIONS

AND WAR PENSIONS

A serviceman serving in Germany wrote to C.A.B. headquarters asking us to send him our booklet on "Buying a House" and any other advice we could give him about building a bungalow for his retirement in four years' time.

We wrote back to him enclosing the booklet and giving some general advice about building a house and asked him to write to us again if we could give him some more help.

He wrote giving us details of his land and telling us of his desire to have a small holding which would help keep him and his wife on their pension. We wrote in confidence to the C.A.B. in the area concerned asking them about the local position and if they would help Sergeant H. in getting planning permission etc., for his house. We then referred Sergeant H. to the bureau who, knowing the local people and firms, would be in a much better position to help him.

CATEGORY 10—TRADE AND MANUFACTURE

She supports a small daughter and herself with aid from the National Assistance Board. She was persuaded by visiting Salesmen to sign an agreement for the purchase of educational books to the value of £25 although she told them she could not afford to pay. She thought the offer came through the school authorities. When the books arrived, she posted them back at a postal cost of 10/. The firm have told her that it was a credit sale and the books are not returnable. She came to C.A.B. to ask what she could do.

With her permission, C.A.B. wrote to the firm explaining the home financial position and suggesting that it was unlikely to be the policy of the firm to hold a customer to an agreement into which she had entered unwillingly. The firm agreed to cancel the transaction.

Sources of Advice and Information

Relevant to the understanding of what these offices do is their distinction between information and advice. In the words of the CAB manual *Advising the Citizen:* "The difference between them would seem to lie in the fact that advice involves interpretation. An informant confines himself to presenting the facts in as orderly a manner as possible; an advisor helps the inquirer to interpret them and relate them to his own particular situation. He does not, however, direct the inquirer to any particular decision. Advisor and inquirer may together seek a solution of the difficulty, but the choice as to which of the two possible alternatives should be adopted, or whether a solution is accepted or rejected, remains the inquirer's; and this must be understood by both sides."

Both information and advice are provided by CAB's. Backup for the information comes from the following sources, available for use by the staff:

1. *Citizens Advice Notes (CANS)*. A comprehensive digest, in looseleaf form, clearly indexed, of social legislation, governmental and voluntary services and their regulations, the rights of citizens, all types of resources, and résumés of reports of committees studying pertinent subjects. It is kept up to date by periodic supplements, and is obviously the definitive work in the field of aid and service to individuals. More than 3,500 subscribers outside the CAB's, including many government officials on all levels, use it in their work. CANS is a publication of the parent body, the National Council of Social Services, but is basic to the CAB operation.

2. A monthly *Information Circular,* with digests of new legislation and useful general information, such as new educational or voluntary services, dates of elections, etc. The circular's information appears in permanent form in the subsequent CANS supplement.

3. Periodic *Supplementary Circulars,* each dealing in detail with a subject of importance, e.g., legal aid and advice. A circular describes a new law, the requirements for individuals wishing to benefit from it, and detailed instructions for making use of it, with descriptions of necessary forms, their numbers, etc.

4. The *Information Department* of the National CAB Council. This office of professionals is available to local CAB's to locate obscure information, help solve a tough problem, or to serve as a channel of referral to a government agency or office.

5. A quarterly *Bulletin of Information* for non-CAB workers—such as clergymen and schoolteachers—in rural areas who come in contact with the general public, containing a summary of recent information put out by the National CAB Council, or reports made by CAB's on specific subjects (such as consumer problems or property laws), so that these individuals can be aware of what CAB's are doing and can send people to them.

A last, significant source of information and help to CAB workers is a thorough knowledge of neighborhood resources. This is obtained during the training period, when the prospective CAB worker meets local government and agency officials, hears them speak on their work, visits their offices and is encouraged to form a close relationship of mutual assistance and understanding. This frequently is the only resource when a problem goes beyond a request for clear-cut information or advice, when the job becomes one of putting people in touch with people. Each local unit has a roster of experts who may be telephoned for guidance when a request is complex and not readily dealt with in the office.

In this connection, many Bureaus keep registers of local specialized groups and services. The CAB's are sometimes the only place where this information is available by geographic area. Such groups or agencies frequently provide the key to the solution of many intangible human problems, such as the dependency of the aged, the loneliness of unattached individuals and the inability of a foreigner, a released mental patient or prisoner to adjust to neighborhood life.

For the general public, the local Bureaus provide a variety of excellent booklets, displayed on tables, to be picked up and taken home. Available at the CAB's visited by the study staff were two booklets on adult education courses with course descriptions, times and locations; *Your Guide to Dental Treatment, under the National Health Service; House Improvement Grants; The Young Foreign Worker . . . Useful Information; The Redundancy Payments Scheme* (this was in the CAB within a week after the Act which it explains had come into force); *Legal Aid and Advice; The 1965 Rent Act; National Health Service Maternity Care;* and *Buying a House* and *Renting a Home—a Guide for Landlord and Tenant.* These latter two were put out by the National CAB Council in response to questions put to the local Bureaus. Also on the tables were consumer advice booklets, a complete guide to London public transportation, and a questionnaire from a local borough councilor on whether the borough had adequate laundry facilities.

Some Bureaus also make their information available to the general public by writing letters to the press and by sponsoring lectures.

Operations

CAB's are locally incorporated by committees of representatives of statutory and voluntary agencies on the local level and unaffiliated community leaders. The national office operates a registration scheme. Local groups with appropriately constituted committees, which train their staffs and meet other conditions, can obtain certification.

The local CAB continues to be independent, however, and assures its own funding. The service is locally run. It is therefore not surprising that local CAB's tend to present a public image emphasizing one or another type of problem and service. In addition, we may assume regional differences in needs. Thus the 16 CAB's in inner London or the 70 in Greater London cannot be expected to yield statistical pictures identical with the others which make up the national total of 466. Some CAB's find themselves very busy with questions about low-cost housing or consumer problems, while others are occupied with requests for help to the mentally ill. A few seem to be entering, slowly, into problems related to racial tensions. In the so-called new towns many inquiries concern problems in family and personal life. Volunteers are fewer, because of a smaller pool of available retired people or mothers whose children have completed school.

The wartime beginnings and the wide range of interest and competence endow the CAB's with characteristics especially attractive to Americans: they are nonsectarian, nonpolitical, nondiscriminatory and stigma-free. The user is not a patient or a recipient. He is a person who is assumed to be competent and his requests are taken at face value until experience shows otherwise. He has a right to confidentiality and privacy. The Bureaus are accessible to members of all social classes, although the more prosperous and better educated, who are less often without needed information and advice or have access to other resources, such as private attorneys, tend to use the services less. Most users apparently are lower middle class and working class, but no specific data are available. We could not determine whether the most disorganized among the poor and multiproblem families, who reach no service in the United States unless one reaches out to them, fare any better with a CAB, which leaves most initiative to inquirers.

As will be seen in the next section, there are variations among CAB's in reaching out to those needing help, the extent to which they take a request literally or probe more deeply and even in whether users are regarded as peers or as less competent unfortunates. Certain issues reside in these variations and must be considered by Americans who would seek to adapt the service for themselves. To illustrate briefly by way of introduction: In central London and one other city, the CAB's are conducted by the family service agency and are professionally staffed. They serve as intake for family counseling. This obviously affects perceptions, image, case load, and outcome and creates a different situation than in CAB's in which the staff is all volunteer and nonprofessional.

It is of special interest, in view of the expanding Neighborhood Legal Services in poverty areas in the United States, that CAB's at one time included legal aid staffs. Later, a report of their experiences contributed to the passage in 1949 of Britain's Legal Aid and Advice Act. Currently, CAB's refer to the legal aid system but also draw on their panels of consultant lawyers for specialized purposes. They are reported as performing a valuable case-finding and referral function for legal services as well as sifting out cases better resolved outside of the legal system.

Staffing

The CAB's boast of their amateur status, but staffing is mixed. While the national totals show volunteers to professionals in a 70 to 30 ratio, the London units are almost completely professionally staffed and units in sparsely settled localities might be completely volunteer. (The 36 CAB's operated by local authorities and the professionally run ones in London also recruit volunteers, but their role is not well developed in these Bureaus.)

In many there is one professional person or local secretary, plus a staff of part-time volunteers. A small office might have six volunteers, a large one as many as 36. One middle-sized city visited, for example, has a social worker as full-time secretary, trainer, director and coordinator, plus 16 volunteers who provide coverage for a five-day week of 10 A.M. to 12 noon, 4 P.M. to 6 P.M. Volunteers also were available to cover evening hours twice weekly.

To find volunteer workers the local sponsoring committee advertises in various media. All candidates must complete application forms and appear before a selection committee. There does not seem to be any shortage of candidates, and those who become workers generally find it an absorbing and satisfying experience, according to one professional CAB director. The prospective worker must take a local preliminary training course of 12–16 lectures, supplemented by observation, visits, reading and private study. Recommended guide lists specify topics, and suggest possible lectures. The volunteer must be willing to accept almost continual further training in new areas of knowledge, take refresher courses, participate in study groups and specialized courses such as "Law Relating to Consumers," "Housing and Real Estate Taxation," and so on.

There is a strong emphasis on field observation, personal contact with service agencies and an understanding of who does what, instead of merely a knowledge of what is, or should be, offered. All the initial and continuing training is planned in consultation with the National CAB Council and its advisory officers. In some areas, universities provide teachers and help plan courses.

While specific data are not available, in general the volunteers are heavily drawn from retired civil servants and middle-class housewives. Their dedication is most impressive and their expertise sometimes outstanding. Also significant is the reported regularity of attendance by volunteers.

There is debate as to whether the positive picture presented here is not too frequently marred by fragmentary coverage (each volunteer giving too little time each week to become an integral part of the operation), lack of sufficient expertise (are sixteen lectures plus agency visits and refresher courses enough for such complex matters?) and insufficient variation in volunteers' backgrounds (should inquirers not find people like their neighbors in a CAB?).

The CAB's perceive their combination of part-time volunteers and full-time professionals as one of their great assets. The volunteers bring to the service a wide range of skills and experience not available among professional social workers. The professionals bring specialized knowledge and experience plus adherence to professional ethics and standards. As seen by the CAB's, the volunters also provide the informality, accessibility, and willingness to seek imaginative solutions outside normal channels, which is sometimes difficult for professionals.

However, there is some tendency both to extol the virtues of amateurism and volunteers (whose training, at best, creates expertise in legislation and resources and not diagnosis), while talking simultaneously of the CAB's capacity to go beyond the immediate problem to the more basic need.

Organization

The National CAB Council, a voluntary coordinating body, is an autonomous constituent unit of Britain's National Council of Social Service. County and regional CAB organizations are represented on the National CAB Council, which is the central policy body. The Council's secretary is, in effect, the national executive director. The CAB's rely heavily on the National Council's CANS (*Citizens Advice Notes*), and receive secretariat and headquarters costs subsidies. Two government departments join the Council in meeting a budget of about $180,000. A national staff of 20 organizes CAB's, conducts training courses, assists and certifies new CAB's, takes on difficult inquiries, prepares memoranda and evidence in response to ministerial or commission requests and provides leadership for experimentation and innovation. Ten of the staff members were added recently to strengthen the field operation and develop new units on the basis of a national subsidy.

Each CAB is independent, with a voluntary relationship to a national framework involving standards and patterns of operation. But each CAB is somewhat dependent on the National organization for its name, training, information manuals and bulletins, expert consultation on complex matters and channels to national government. A local CAB may be started either by a group of interested citizens or by National CAB advisers in consultation with local governmental bodies. A series of local public meetings is then held to discuss the need for a CAB and a sponsoring committee of leading citizens is formed. Generally included are lawyers, doctors, children's officers (local child welfare workers), clergy, teachers, representatives of social agencies and civic groups, officials from local government. "Without such representative support," says the booklet, *Advising the Citizen*, "the bureau could not be established. . . . One reason why CAB's have succeeded in gaining acceptance by people of all races, creeds and classes is that they have been established for these citizens by these citizens."

CAB's are financed in large part by grants-in-aid from the local government unit, as is permitted by the 1948 Local Government Act. Besides providing cash, the local authority might offer office space, utilities or telephone service. Some Bureau offices are located in the Borough Halls or libraries. They seek to remain impartial among agencies, recognized and respected by official agencies, without representing any particular partisan point of view. Thirty-six of the 466 CAB's are run by local authorities rather than by nongovernmental local committees.

The Bureau workers say that the average citizen recognizes the advantage of a Bureau's nonstatutory status. They believe that he can tell his problems more freely to an unofficial listener and can accept unpalatable information more easily from a worker who is not a governmental official. The CAB staff believes that this independent status enables CAB's to take whatever action is best for the inquirer without feeling the pressure of political considerations. Whether this can ever be completely true, particularly of an organization that receives its financial support from local government, remains a question for observers.

A Window

CAB's do more than dispense information and help to individuals. Through their day-to-day contact with a wide section of the population, they acquire a unique range of knowledge of community and individual problems and the adequacy of services. The CAB's, in fact, have been described as a "window on the man in the street." Some view them as a major force for counteracting impersonal bureaucratization. The data collected from the CAB's by the National Council are valuable for appraising the quality and adequacy of services, for considering the need for new legislation or for developing changes of procedure or administration. These data are extensively used.

The CAB sees its records as a sensitive instrument which measures the condition of the general public without the bias of a particular profession or interest group. No local CAB need become a party to local issues or pressure groups in order that its recommendations be heard since the data are channeled and assembled in the national office. Occasionally, a local CAB will compile similar material relating either to issues within local purview or to national matters, but this is not usual. There are observers in Britain who urge more advocacy on policy matters by local CAB's.

The value of CAB data is well known to governmental officials and to study groups or committees inside and outside government. "Hardly a week goes by," according to the National CAB Council Report, "without the headquarters officers having to decide whether or not to contribute evidence to some inquiry or study." CAB material has contributed to the passage of legislation on rent and housing, on legal aid and the protection of the consumer. In general, the National CAB assembles evidence in response to central government inquiries rather than routinely monitoring its experience and reporting.

In addition to giving evidence, CAB's are available as field stations to try out new governmental forms or procedures or to advise on their development. They are thus sources of feedback and channels in a two-way communication between bureaucratic government and the man in the street.

They also serve a semi-ombudsman function, as they follow up to help an individual perhaps unfairly treated. Problems of this kind are often solved by telling a person of his rights, calling a local official, consulting with the local unit's advisory panel members or referring the matter to the National CAB to have it taken up in the appropriate ministry. Sometimes the individual inquirer might not be helped, but new legislation or administrative procedure might be launched. Most often the help consists of talking out a person's special situation with the responsible department or ministry. The CAB sees itself as interpreting a person's situation or need but not as representing him before a tribunal in the sense of some new United States urban community development, antipoverty and neighborhood legal services.

Most recently, CAB has received additional national funding in appreciation of the fact that its general expansion is a way of strengthening consumer services. This has not involved any departures in mode of service or in reporting, since the CAB regards itself as unspecialized.

It should be noted that most of the CAB evidence and reporting is of the case-illustration and impressionistic variety. An amateur, citizen-observer status is sought and preserved. As put by one CAB official, questions may be asked to help a person, not to assemble data. CAB staff point to signs of effectiveness and wish to preserve this approach. Others, who would prefer exact counting, careful research and more professional evaluation, tend to deprecate the usefulness of the CAB as a "window."

Functions and Qualities—A First Listing

Why consider a CAB or something like it for the American scene? Our exploration to this point suggests that certain of the CAB *functions* and *qualities* may have general significance. These are listed here as they guided our more intensive exploration of CAB operations and as they provided focus in the study of what is available in New York and elsewhere in the United States. As will be noted, we subsequently elaborate the listing.

FUNCTIONS

Information. Used as a broad term (as in Neighborhood Information Center) information includes such functions as advice, steering, referral and making available literature and pamphlets. Used in a more restrictive sense, to contrast with advice and referral, for example, information involves the answering of questions about services, facilities, programs, laws, eligibility, etc. But this service is not individualized for the inquirer. Included are the simple inquiries (where is the library?) and the more complex (at what age will my son cease to draw social security benefits?).

Advice. Here an individualized interpretation is called for on how a given program, rule, facility or situation may be applied to an inquirer or his representative. Judgment might be involved about the capacities of the inquirer or his representative, the priorities to be accorded to needs, the way that services and facilities should be approached. Collateral clearances and consultation might be involved. The service might be terminated by the advice or could lead to referral or steering.

Steering. This is a specific form of advice, involving the suggestion that the person in need of service or information go to a particular agency or facility. However, unlike the referral, the interviewer does not establish the contact or facilitate the transfer.

Personal help and emotional support. The inquirer might not be prepared to accept advice, referral or steering or might not need it. The entire service might consist of occasional friendly "chats" or the giving of reassurance, which keeps a dependent or slightly disturbed person functioning in the community. Or the inquirer might need help, once or periodically, in writing a letter, filling out an application or report form (housing, insurance claim) or making a phone call. Sometimes the personal help involves arranging for emergency shelter (for a homeless family or a runaway adolescent), or assisting overwhelmed people to cope with a serious personal catastrophe of another kind. At times, the inquirer needs to be accompanied to a clinic, service agency or appeals tribunal and helped to interpret his situation. Occasionally, there is personal counseling or casework.

Referral. This is a specific form of advice involving the suggestion that the person in need of service or information go to a specific agency or facility. The interviewer establishes the contact and might make a specific appointment, send a report or explanation and even escort the person in need of service.

Feedback. Either out of experience with rendering service to individuals or by conducting specific surveys or inquiries, an information and referral service might report to appropriate authorities, agencies or the public at large about needs, questionable policies, opinions, defects in administration of services, etc. Such feedback might originate in specific outside requests (from governmental agencies or planning bodies, for example) or might be a continuing aspect of the agency's responsibility.

Advocacy. An information and referral service might consider it important to help an inquirer to establish his eligibility for a program, service or grant (advocacy focused on service to the case). Where deemed necessary, a CAB might seek reconsideration of decisions, or review of existing policies, because they cause hardship to a client or group of clients, produce inadequate help or do not address priority needs (advocacy oriented to changes in policy, law and administrative procedure).

Case-finding. This function is a by-product of an information service as defined in the broad sense. It involves recognition of a need, a problem or illness which is not the reason for the initial entry into the service, *but which is deemed worthy of community attention.* It leads to an attempt to render advice, referral or steering with reference to the new problem, no matter what the original request.

Community facilitation service during crises. Certain services might originate in an emergency or crisis. Thus, during a transportation stoppage, a Bureau could arrange community transportation pools. A CAB is a normal center for emergency services in a flood or power blackout, recalling the community facilitation service during World War II out of which the British CAB's developed.

QUALITIES

Formal functions alone do not constitute the essence of the CAB. What attracts the observer are actual or potential qualities, here described in the idealized form. They provide some of our yardsticks both in Britain and the United States.

An "open door" atmosphere. Everybody is made to feel welcome. This is the one place where *any* inquiry is "within function" and an attempt always will be made to get the answer. The physical setting is attractive and does not in itself demean the user. The office is open most of the day and is easily reached. Telephoning is not discouraged and the staff visits the home if a request is made or an urgent need described.

Expertise. Information and advice are backed by staff training, comprehensive basic manuals, periodic bulletins and inservice courses to up-date information about laws and facilities. When a local center does not have an immediate answer it may draw upon expert local consultants and a central service. The inquirers have reason to have confidence in an interviewer's answers.

Range. Unlike information services set up for special illnesses (heart, TB), special categories (aged, unemployed), special groups (Jewish, Lutheran, Catholic, etc.), special services (social work, education), the Bureau has wide range. An inquirer might be concerned with taxes, installment buying, tenant problems, social security, marital problems, and so on. Range is essential to maintaining an "open door."

Service to all social classes. While there will be different use on the basis of economic status, education and other factors, the center itself is available to all community members. Its services, location, mode of operation and the way it presents itself to the public are designed to avoid the stigma often associated with public assistance offices or clinical services.

Confidentiality. Advice and information are given on a confidential basis. The request and problem are shared with others only when the inquirer's permission is given. Only when the community, the inquirer or another person is seriously endangered by this confidentiality is this rule suspended on a carefully predetermined and announced basis.

Nonpartisanship and nonsectarianism. These qualities are essential to the open door.

Unbiased case channeling. This is the evaluation of a person's needs, and the recommendation of service, from a perspective free of the predilections of specialized agencies, professions, or social theories. The assumption is that a situation has been created in which all relevant professional orientations or concepts of agency function have equal chance of being of use, so that the information given reflects the best general community judgment about how the client will best be served. With no vested interest in any program, the Bureau does not have to use or defend any specific one.

Accountability. Of the several forms of accountability, *case* accountability is most relevant. One sets up reporting-back or follow-up procedures to determine whether the contact has been made, a service begun, a problem solved.

Our further exploration of the CAB's helped deepen our understanding of these functions and qualities. Issues emerged relevant to their balance, relationships, priorities, and conditions.

25

Philip G. Schrag

CONSUMER RIGHTS

The consumer's central civil right is the right to get his money's worth. In theory, the competitive market system and the law of contracts are designed to ensure that he does—that having chosen from a variety of products, the consumer's expectations will be fulfilled. Nevertheless, few, if any, Americans have never been "taken" by a magazine salesman, a television or automobile repairman, or simply a fast-talking store clerk.

Sometimes, the consumer's expectations go unfulfilled for reasons having nothing to do with misleading advertising or high-pressure sales tactics. For example, American manufacturers are now finding the cost of quality control to be so great that they are frequently willing to accept a high rate of defective products; it is cheaper to replace merchandise for those who complain, than it is to ensure that few defective products are distributed, even when the defects pose a hazard to human safety. In 1969, 10 percent of the automobile parts tested by the National Safety Bureau failed to comply with federal safety standards. Price-fixing conspiracies may also deny buyers their money's worth, but more often, limited competition, particularly in low-income areas, produces the same effect whether or not anyone is "at fault."

But consumers' expectations are also defeated by retailers who lead them to expect too much, and by laws that are inappropriate to a mass consumer economy, particularly one in which credit plays so large a role.

The frequency of exaggerated or otherwise incorrect statements about merchandise can only be appreciated, I think, by carrying around a pad of paper for a day and noting every instance—in storewindow advertising, in newspapers, on television, in conversations with merchants, and on coffeeshop menus—where the seller isn't quite telling the truth. We have become so used to exaggeration and half-truth that we are insensitive to it, at least on a con-

Philip G. Schrag, "Consumer Rights," *Columbia Forum* 13, no. 2 (Summer 1970); pp. 4-10. Copyright © 1970 by Random House, Inc. Reprinted from *The Rights of Americans: What They Are—What They Should Be,* edited by Norman Dorsen, by permission of Pantheon Books, a division of Random House, Inc.

scious level. The absurd statements (that a cleanser is "stronger than dirt") and pictorial deceptions (the loading of marbles into a bowl of soup to make the vegetables rise to the surface and appear dense) employed on television by major producers seem harmless individually but are numbing in the aggregate. Examples of such "puffing" have played a large role in dulling us into thinking that we have no right to expect accuracy from sellers, and in our having less than total sympathy for those who accept salesmen at their word.

But whether they buy a $1,200 stereo console or a can of soup, consumers who make purchases based upon erroneous or exaggerated claims are not without rights. Indeed, the law has worked out quite a sensible set of rules defining precisely the relief to which such buyers are entitled. These rules comprise the law of misrepresentation and the law of warranties. It may seem startling to the millions of housewives who have argued for hours with merchants who refused to take back unacceptable products, but the basic rule is this: whenever a salesman makes more than a plainly trivial mistake in describing merchandise, the customer is entitled to his money back, even if the salesman's error was unintentional. Virtually any material misrepresentation entitles the consumer to a refund.

Many different types of falsity are common. For example, sellers may incorrectly describe the quantity or quality of merchandise. They may misrepresent a product's average lifetime, the uses to which it can be put, or the identity, location, and qualifications of the manufacturer. Salesmen, particularly those who work from door to door, have also been known to misrepresent their own authority, connections, or qualifications.

Not infrequently, false statements are made concerning the existence of bargains or discounts (as in perpetual "going-out-of-business" sales), the reasons for such discounts, or their amounts. An example of this is the "bait and switch" technique. A store advertises a bargain, such as a $14 sewing machine. The machine is shown to the customer, but the salesman describes only its inadequacies. Perhaps it even breaks down during the demonstration. Then the customer, having been lured into the store, is shown a more expensive model.

It doesn't make any difference whether the falsity originated with the seller or was simply passed on by him from the manufacturer. Nor does it matter that the customer could easily have investigated and learned the truth. The buyer is entitled to his refund, though he must be prepared to return the merchandise.

A refund merely returns the buyer to his original condition before the sale: he has received financial restitution, but he still lacks the product or service he wanted to purchase. If the seller has breached what the Uniform Commercial Code calls a "warranty," however, the buyer is entitled to damages; he may keep the merchandise and obtain from the merchant an amount of money representing the difference in value between what he got and what he was promised.

"Warranties" in this connection mean far more than the pieces of cardboard with scalloped borders that are often found packaged with new appliances. They include any promises made by the seller. Any statement of fact or promise about a product is a warranty, as is any description of the goods. Even if a salesman says nothing, but merely shows the consumer a floor sample, he warrants that what the consumer buys will be just like the sample.

The consumer's protection under warranty law goes even further. The law implies that in any sale of goods by a merchant, he warrants that they are "merchantable," which means, essentially, that they work. In other words, a salesman who palms off on a customer a stereo set that does not work, or a chest of drawers that falls apart within a week, has breached his warranty —even if he never made any promises about the goods.

Notwithstanding all of these rights, consumers are in terrible trouble. The structure of rights, so elegant on paper, is more theoretical than real. The middle-class buyer of a non-functioning stereo may be lucky and get a refund; if so, it is probably because the store to which he went wanted his continued business. He would feel sheepish, however, demanding a refund from his grocer because a package of frozen food promised more quantity and better quality than was actually inside. The low-income consumer is in much greater trouble, because retailers in his neighborhood are much less likely to be interested in good will; therefore he will have difficulty obtaining redress in a friendly way when he has been victimized, even on a large purchase.

If friendly settlement is impossible (and the 42,000 complaints annually to the New York City Department of Consumer Affairs alone suggest that this is often the case), consumers must look to the courts. That is where the theoretical structure of consumers' rights breaks down, for consumers are invariably unable to obtain the oldest and most fundamental civil liberty— a day in court. The barriers that the legal system has erected to consumer litigation go a long way toward explaining the relative unconcern of merchants and manufacturers about truthful selling and the quality of their products.

The prime barrier is the cost of litigation. An individual lawsuit is enormously expensive, no matter what the suit involves. Experienced lawyers charge from $40 to $100 an hour. Assuming that it takes two hours to interview a client, an hour to write a complaint, two hours to research the law, and two hours to try the case, the simplest litigation would cost each side at least $300 in legal fees alone. But no case is that simple, if it is done well. Each side's lawyer will spend many additional hours tracking down and interviewing friendly witnesses (for example, other consumers who bought the same type of merchandise from the same salesman), examining under oath the parties and witnesses on the other side in pretrial discovery proceedings, making and resisting motions for further discovery, etc. The merchant may try to avoid the process server, or claim that the suit was begun in the wrong court, or engage in any of a thousand dilatory tactics. And, of course, when it is all over, he may appeal. On top of legal fees are costs for investigation, expert witnesses (such as a furniture expert to testify that a chest bought by a consumer would probably fall apart within a week), process servers, court costs, and stenographic fees. The result is that litigation over a $50 case may cost each side more than $1,000.

Theoretically, each side must pay its own legal fees, regardless of who wins the case. However, in most states, consumer contracts may lawfully provide that if the merchant sues the consumer and wins, the consumer pays the merchant's legal fees. Since merchants' lawyers write the contracts, they do not provide for the payment of counsel fees to a consumer who sues successfully. So in reality, the consumer pays his own lawyer if he wins, and both lawyers if he loses.

As if this were not enough to keep consumers out of court, the law has special devices for defeating challenges by those who buy on credit—a group that includes most low-income purchasers of furniture and appliances. The credit buyer is, after all, in a special position. He has the merchandise at a time when he has delivered only a small part of the price (the down payment) to the merchant. In low-income neighborhoods, it is common that "the payments outlast the goods"; that is, the misrepresentation, or fraud, or breach of warranty, may become obvious to the buyer—if the merchandise falls apart, for instance—before the merchant has all his money. The credit purchaser has it in his power, at least temporarily, to effect rough justice. He can throw the costs of misrepresentation upon his creditor by cutting off his payments.

The creditor in such circumstances, however, is armed and dangerous. He may invoke a clause in all his contracts providing that the goods remain his until they are fully paid for, and he may repossess them at any time without first going to court. Creditors will jump-start a partially paid-for car in front of buyer's house during the night, and drive it off. Repossession of household goods is rarer, since creditors are forbidden to commit breaches of the peace in repossessing, but there have been such cases—like that of the frightened woman who was warned not to call her husband at work while a crew disconnected the washing machine in her basement and carried it off on a truck.

Having repossessed the merchandise, a merchant may sell it and sue the buyer for the difference between what the buyer owes him and the amount realized by the repossession sale. This will usually be almost as much as the buyer's debt, because repossessed goods generally bring a very low price. Of course, the creditor adds to the bill the expenses incurred in the repossession and sale.

Since a given creditor or merchant will have hundreds of collection cases each year, he will benefit from the economies of large-scale operation that are not available to consumers. For example, he may be able to hire an attorney on a salary rather than a fee basis. Or he can obtain a "bulk discount" from a collection lawyer. The lawyer, in turn, benefits from the volume in another way. Only a small percentage of consumers who are cheated seek professional help—9 percent, according to David Caplovitz' pioneering study, *The Poor Pay More* (The Free Press, 2nd ed., 1967). Of this number, only a portion see lawyers who try to help them, and of those lawyers, only a few put up any sort of a fight. The collection lawyer, then, can afford to make some settlement with those few consumers who might make trouble, because he can easily sue the vast majority of consumers without opposition. Ninety-nine percent of the consumers sued in Manhattan never appear to defend themselves, and therefore lose by default. As a result, their creditor extracts the amount of the judgment from their bank accounts or by garnisheeing their wages.

While these circumstances facilitate use of the courts as a prime means of collecting debts from buyers, other procedures and legal rules further deny buyers the chance to be heard. There are three principal devices: "confession of judgment," "wage assignment," and "holding in due course."

"Confession of judgment" is fortunately limited to a few states. By this device, consumers who buy on credit surrender their rights not only to claim fraud and breach of warranty as reasons why they have discontinued payments, but also the right to notice of a lawsuit against them. This is accomplished by a clause in the installment contract that designates the seller's own attorney as the buyer's lawyer in the event that he stops paying. Thus, the merchant's lawyer can appear in court for the buyer, and admit that the buyer is withholding his payments for no good reason; the court then automatically enters a judgment against the buyer. The buyer never even knows about the lawsuit until it is over, and he realizes that his salary is being garnisheed.

A "wage assignment" is a document signed by the debtor at the time he obtains credit. If he stops payments for any reason, his creditor may show the wage assignment to the debtor's employer, who is then legally required to pay the creditor part of the employee's wages every week. The employee is denied a hearing, and even prior notification of the proceeding. If the employee had some reason to stop paying—for instance, if he had been cheated —the burden is on him to obtain a court order to allow him to tell it to a judge.

A similar device, called the "pre-hearing wage garnishment," was held unconstitutional by the Supreme Court in a 1969 test case brought by the N.A.A.C.P. Legal Defense Fund. The court held that it deprived wage earners of their property without prior notice and hearing. According to that ruling, many creditors' practices could be considered unconstitutional, especially confessions of judgment and wage assignments.

The "holder-in-due-course" doctrine, used by creditors in about 45 states, has two forms. In one variety consumers buying on credit sign their names twice: once on a contract and once on a promissory note, which contains the phrase "pay to the order of [creditor]." This has no special meaning to consumers, but a very special meaning to judges. When sold for cash to a third party, such as a bank or a finance company, the note becomes an almost unassailable instrument for the collection of money—regardless of the seller's deception or the condition of the product sold by the original store. For example, imagine that a consumer buys a television set on credit, and that the store immediately sells the note to a finance company, which becomes the "holder in due course." Even if the television is never delivered, the buyer has no justification for stopping his payments. The finance company has no legal responsibility for any misrepresentations or other violations of law committed by the store. Legally and practically, it is easier for a consumer to defend a suit brought against him by a store (for nonpayment) on the grounds of misrepresentation or breach of warranty, than it is to pay a holder-in-due-course finance company in full, and then spend years trying to sue the store for misrepresentation. Yet that is what is required when the use and resale of a note strips the buyer of his right to defend himself.

In some states (even ones that prohibit the use of notes in consumer sales), consumer contracts may contain a clause whereby the buyer agrees to waive his right to defend himself against a finance company or bank that bought the contract from the seller. In New York, this waiver is effective only if the finance company (1) tells the consumer it has bought his contract, (2) warns him of the waiver, and (3) hears nothing from him for 10 days. But the statutorily prescribed warning consists of a single sentence of 125 words:

Notice:
1. If the within statement of your transaction with the seller is not correct in every respect; or
2. if the vehicle or goods described in or in an enclosure with this notice have not been delivered to you by the seller or are not now in your possession; or
3. if the seller has not fully performed all his agreements with you; you must notify the assignee in writing at the address indicated in or in an enclosure with this notice within 10 days from the date of the mailing of this notice; otherwise, you will have no right to assert against the assignee any right of action or defense arising out of the sale which you might otherwise have against the seller.

I have never met a consumer who understood and acted upon the warning. Of course, even if a consumer did understand it, he would have no protection against latent defects that might not appear until months later.

Protecting the retail buyer, then, is largely a job of improving the consumer's opportunity to confront his abuser. Several approaches to this problem will be attempted in the 1970s.

The first way is to improve consumer representation in court. Until the late 1960s the lack of contested consumer litigation could be explained in large part by the lack of consumer lawyers. Even consumers who recognized their problems and sought help couldn't find it. The private bar by and large was not interested or could not afford to get involved, and legal aid societies were already too overburdened to take on such complicated and time-consuming litigation, which usually involves small amounts of money. The first crack in the system was the emergence of new legal institutions that began to represent consumers. Work on the front lines came from the neighborhood offices of the Office of Economic Opportunity Legal Services Program, staffed by aggressive, issue-oriented young lawyers. Support came from institutions like the National Office for the Rights of the Indigent, the National Consumer Law Center at Boston College, and the National Institute for Education in Law and Poverty at Northwestern Law School. Since the O.E.O. offices were not dependent upon fees, they could afford to spend more money on some cases than the amount of money at issue in the litigation, and consumer issues began reaching appellate courts.

These offices cannot do the job alone. They do not exist in many areas of the U.S., particularly in the South. O.E.O. offices in Northern cities are often deluged with housing and welfare litigation, involving more pressing emergencies than consumer disputes. And even where there are O.E.O. offices with adequate resources, they may not assist people who do not qualify as "poor." Consumers who earn $4,000 ($2,500 in some states) or more still have nowhere to go.

So, the private bar must be mobilized to represent the bulk of deceived consumers. But members of the private bar are unlikely to enter this field unless they receive remuneration. An obvious source of money for such encouragement might come from the deceiving merchants and manufacturers themselves; if deception has been built into packaging or advertising, the cost of correcting the deception should fall upon the packager or advertiser. The attorney who wins a consumer suit should be entitled to a counsel fee commensurate with the time he has had to spend on the case; this fee should be included in the court's award. Although the principle of taxing the losing party with counsel fees is an abrogation of the usual American rule, there are some precedents for it in statutes encouraging litigation in the public interest, particularly in civil rights laws. Congress extended the principle to consumer protection in the Truth-In-Lending Act, although it remains to be seen whether the courts will award sufficiently high fees to attract the private bar to the cause.

Another way to reduce the overall cost of consumer recourse might be to remove such disputes from the regular courts. Small claims courts were intended to serve this purpose, but many communities have not established them; in others, they have been turned into collection agencies for creditors. In cities where they do work, such courts attempt to enable the consumer to press his claim without a lawyer, informally, without special knowledge of judicial procedure.

But the legislators and judges who design these institutions seem unable to imagine a truly informal judicial body; even good small claims courts tend to impose procedural requirements that boggle the mind of most laymen, and are incomprehensible to those who have little education. For example, the would-be small claims plaintiff in New York City must comb city records to determine whether the store that cheated him is Gypsum Furniture or Gypsum Furniture, Inc. An error here could doom his suit.

In addition, low-income consumers are as reluctant to go to night court "downtown" as middle-class citizens are to amble through the ghetto after dark. It is to be hoped that truly informal, decentralized "people's courts" will spring up in the next few years.

There has also been some discussion among consumer groups of arbitration as an alternative to litigation. Until arbitration projects are tried and evaluated, it is impossible to know whether this process is really cheaper and fairer than litigation; the answer may depend on the effectiveness of individual arbitrators. A serious stumbling block, however, is the distrust consumers and merchants alike have for arbitration. Consumers fear that arbitrators will "split the difference" rather than enforce their rights, while merchants are wary that a more accessible grievance institution will multiply claims made against them. Probably the agreement of merchants in a neighborhood to submit to arbitration will only result from massive pressure by local groups.

It seems likely that confessions of judgment, wage assignments prior to hearing, and the holder-in-due-course practice will be abolished by reform legislation or constitutional challenge during the 1970s. (The New York law, for example, has just been modified so that finance companies suing on contracts signed after February 1971 cannot claim to hold in due course. However, the law still forbids consumer suits against finance companies or refunds of payments already made to credit companies.) But it is probable that even if the holder-in-due-course device is eliminated, a new practice will accomplish the same circumvention of consumers' rights. Merchants will refuse to permit contracts, insisting instead that consumers borrow money to pay them cash, or charge purchases to credit cards issued by banks. The salesman will tell a customer to use such a card, or to go down the street to the small loan company (or bank, if banks yield to consumer pressure to make loans to low-income borrowers) and obtain a check to pay for the product. If the merchandise subsequently breaks down, and the store has conveniently gone out of business, the loan company or bank will have an even better claim to be unconcerned than the finance company (which, under holder-in-due-course procedure, buys the actual contract) does now. All the bank did was lend money to the customer. It didn't even ask what the money was for.

Clearly, if abolition of the holder-in-due-course doctrine is to be meaningful, at least some types of direct lending institutions will have to be liable on consumer claims of deception and defective merchandise. A bank (or loan company) might be liable for a merchant's violations of consumers' rights unless the bank could prove that it had, within three months before the sale in question, investigated the seller and determined that the store was financially sound (and therefore capable of honoring its continuing warranty obligations) and that the store engaged only in fair and lawful practices. This standard would shift the burden of proof from the consumer to the bank.

The consumer would not have to prove a conspiracy between the bank and the store; rather, to obtain the special privileges of a holder in due course, the bank would have to show efforts on its part to police the practices of those for whom it is a lifeline.

Another promising device is the class action, a type of lawsuit in which one consumer sues to obtain not only a small refund for himself, but also similar relief for every other victim of a merchant's abusive practice. Sometimes, the victims are dispersed, and since there is no way of identifying them, class actions are not possible. But when purchases are made on credit, or when a store has kept delivery receipts, hundreds of cheated customers can be aided if class actions are allowed.

Class actions permit consumers to utilize the same kind of economies of scale that collection attorneys have been enjoying for years; they permit a large number of similar transactions to be treated as one, for the practical purpose of litigation. A lawyer need be paid only once to try the case, but hundreds or even thousands of buyers participate in the judgment. Class action suits are also attractive to members of the private bar, because judges usually allow the lawyer a generous fee out of the total proceeds, to reward him for helping so many people.

Unfortunately, while every state has a law on its books permitting class actions, many have procedural rules or court decisions that as a practical matter forbid them. Thus far, experience with class actions has not come from consumer cases, but rather from antitrust, fraudulent securities, and civil rights cases. The reason is that these lawsuits are based upon federal laws or the Constitution and are therefore usually initiated in the federal courts, which liberally permit class suits. Misrepresentation and breach of warranty, however, are claims derived from the laws of the states, and must therefore be made in state courts, which treat class suits more suspiciously.

Currently, a primary goal of the consumer movement is to liberalize procedures for class action suits. California and Illinois courts have recently rendered decisions permitting consumers to sue as a class, in cases involving taxicab overcharges and overcharges to six million revolving account customers. A setback occurred in May, when the New York Court of Appeals, construing a statute identical to that of California, rendered class actions in New York virtually impossible. But dozens of test cases, begun by legal services offices, are proceeding in many other states. And half a dozen bills pending in Congress would permit the federal courts, with their liberal rules for hearing class action suits, to hear consumer class actions where the alleged violation affected interstate commerce. Senator Joseph Tydings and Representative Robert Eckhardt have sponsored bills to permit class actions in federal courts whenever substantial numbers of consumers have been victimized by violations of state law.

The Nixon administration opposes these bills, and would permit class actions only after a federal agency successfully sued the violator. This restriction would subject the injured consumers to the caprices of bureaucratic politics, the shortage of staff in overburdened and underfunded enforcement agencies, and the delays of two successive lawsuits, each of which would be likely to take at least two years. The administration argues that the class action device will be abused, and that fee-hungry lawyers will bring frivolous cases against legitimate industry. But nonmeritorious cases have been rare in the five states that liberally permit consumer class actions, and the device has not been abused by antitrust and securities fraud lawyers who use it routinely as an effective supplement to government regulatory activities. Class actions are big cases requiring significant investments of time by attorneys who will be compensated only if they win; this fact alone will lead lawyers to accept those cases where consumers have been hurt and to reject border-line cases.

The shortest route to justice for consumers might be avoidance of the judicial process altogether. Organized consumer groups might do more to obtain relief for their members by direct action than by hiring lawyers. Strangely, only Philadelphia has such an organized movement. There, the Consumer's Education and Protection Association (C.E.P.A.) investigates a complainant's grievance, and if it believes it to be valid, will picket the offend-ing merchant or bank in force. Such tactics usually succeed in obtaining a refund. In return for C.E.P.A.'s help, the complainant is obliged to join the organization and agree to picket for others when called upon. C.E.P.A. is constantly expanding its membership and power, and by invoking the First Amendment has successfully fought off several attacks upon it in the courts.

So far, C.E.P.A. has limited itself to obtaining individual relief for indi-vidual complainants. But such an organization, if sufficiently powerful to lead a successful boycott, might obtain concessions from merchants that transcend individual cases; concerted action might, for example, force a merchant to rewrite his contracts or his advertising, reform his collection techniques, stock higher quality merchandise, or consent to arbitration of customer griev-ances. Consumer unions might even adopt the labor movement model, seek-ing mass support to bargain collectively with merchants or manufacturers.

Similarly, committed consumer lawyers, or those retained by consumer organizations, might, by employing sufficiently threatening legal tactics such as class actions and suits for punitive damages, be able to obtain significant concessions from merchants by withdrawing or settling proposed litigation. The merchant could settle the suit by entering into a contract with the plain-tiff, for the benefit of all of the other members of the community and enforce-able by any of them.

Improved consumer protection may also come from government agencies, which have not been very effective in the past. A key experiment in con-sumer advocacy is now getting underway in New York City's Department of Consumer Affairs, the nation's first municipal consumer agency. Under the New York City Consumer Protection Law of 1969, all deception in the sale of consumer goods and services is unlawful, including deception by exag-geration, ambiguity, innuendo, and failure to state material facts. The law permits the City to sue for mass restitution on behalf of all the citizens deceived by a particular seller's practice, and to settle on behalf of individual consumers so that they don't have to go to court on their own to obtain restitution. It remains to be seen whether such intervention by agencies will result in significant improvement in consumer protection, or whether municipal administrations will be unable to cope with the volume of consumer victimization that occurs.

If consumers, their organizations, their lawyers, and interested government agencies become accustomed to using such tactics, and if those measures prove to be effective, they might also be employed to attack consumer problems at ever-higher levels. For example, consumer class actions for price-fixing under the antitrust laws, or class suits based on massive violations of manufacturers' warranties, might induce the producers themselves to insure high-quality, reasonably priced merchandise and to banish deceitful advertising techniques. The abuse of consumers is based on an inequality of bargaining power and an inequality in the ability to press claims; redressing these imbalances must be the major priority for the consumer movement in the seventies.

26

Robert Fellmeth

HOME MOVING

March 10, 1969

Dear Senator Magnuson:
   ... There is a ludicrously wide credibility gap between the charming advertising by the moving industry, and actual performance and ethics.... Moving is a difficult enough task without being cheated in the bargain! Whatever Congress can do to force movers to be good Americans will be appreciated by hundreds of thousands of citizens yearly!

Yours sincerely,
Mrs. T . . . E . . . R . . .

Riverside, California
February 21, 1969

Dear Senator Magnuson,
   ...I would like to know who the ICC is protecting. It is a government agency supported by the people, not by any private industry.
   The cost of a legal suit for a private citizen between states is prohibitive and that is why moving companies ignore letters and complaints.
   I have contacted the ICC and they say they cannot help me.

Very truly yours,
R . . . F . . . E . . .

Orlando, Florida
July 11, 1969

Dear Mr. Nader,
   ...I wrote the ICC and they did nothing about it to this day except to advise me that they are investigating. . . . I believe that ICC is a price-fix monopoly that tells the van lines how much to charge to protect them—no free enterprise and the heck with the consumer.... I am sure that you would be the one to wake this situation up, including the ICC.

Sincerely,
S . . . G . . .

Interstate Commerce Commission
Bureau of Operations
219 South Dearborn St.
Chicago, Illinois
February 17, 1969

Dear Mr. P . . .
. . . This Commission has no jurisdiction over claims for delay, however, and if you are unable to reach a satisfactory agreement with the carrier your recourse is to an appropriate civil court. . . .

Very truly yours,
R . . . M . . .
District Supervisor

Interstate Commerce Commission
Washington, D.C. 20423
February 14, 1969

Dear Senator Magnuson,
. . . The Interstate Commerce Commission does not have jurisdiction to settle loss or damage claims. If the parties fail to reach an amicable settlement, proper recourse is had by filing suit in a court having appropriate jurisdiction. . . .

Sincerely,
Virginia Mae Brown, Chairman

Columbus, Ohio
February 6, 1969

Dear Senator Magnuson,
A year having now passed since my experience with interstate movers . . . I have concluded that:
Government is decidedly pro-industry and contra-citizenry. . . .
The ICC in my case was useless, but they write lovely letters.

Sincerely yours,
D . . . W . . . C . . .

Household moving is a unique service among those under ICC regulation, and the home moving consumer may need even more protection by a public regulatory agency than other consumers in the area of transportation. The individual home owner transferring his earthly belongings to a new city is not a businessman shipping his goods to market, and as a result is at a distinct disadvantage vis-à-vis the trucker. His is a one-time move, and he lacks the promise of future business as an incentive for good service and honest billing. He is unfamiliar with trucking and therefore naive about tariffs and industry practices. There are other disadvantages, which he shares with all "small" shippers who need the services of truckers under ICC jurisdiction. His shipment is relatively costly per pound and requires careful handling, but the ICC has been less than eager to supervise the handling and storing of household goods. Perhaps the most important disadvantage of the small shipper is that he lacks legal *bargaining* power, the power to enforce his rights either in the courts or through the ICC. The big trucking company knows this individual cannot afford a private lawsuit. It also knows that he cannot bend the regulatory process to his purpose the way the large shipper or carrier can. He cannot afford, as they can, a staff to sit at the ICC to scrutinize every tariff filed, and protest when it is applicable to himself. He does not read the Federal Register or know when there are Commission proceedings that might concern him. He could not hire a lawyer and enter the proceedings even if he were to have notice. He is a sideline participant, trusting in and needing the protection that must be actively initiated and administered by the ICC.

Individual Americans paying for their own moves comprise roughly one-third of the movers' annual business. Another third is made of "national account" traffic, employee moves paid for by companies with large contracts with the movers. The final third consists of military moves, made under contracts between the D.O.D. and private moving companies. Though these latter two-thirds give rise to their share of complaints, they are not of concern here because in each case the shipper—the large company or D.O.D.[1]—holds out the prospect of large contracts as an inducement to good service. The Department of Defense, moreover, pays for all damage incurred by military personnel during moves. The individual in such situations moves under the protection of the large company or D.O.D. contract and thus is not as urgently in need of ICC protection as the unaffiliated consumer.

The nation's 183 intercity movers collected $600 million in 1968, one-third of which came from individual household moves. One in five Americans —40 million—moves annually. The practices of the movers have stirred thousands of complaints on the local, state, and federal level. The ICC reports receiving over 5,000 complaints per year—a very high figure considering how unfamiliar the public is with the ICC. Congressional mail, especially that of Warren Magnuson, Chairman of the Senate Commerce Committee, is increasingly full of complaints as Congress shows growing interest in consumer affairs. And while the ICC itself has not devoted much long-range policy planning attention to the problem, moving consumes more and more of the agency's staff time. A field agent near the headquarters of several of the large national movers reports spending 30 percent of his time on home moving, although the problem was officially considered to be only 5 percent of his responsibilities.

The estimate is often the consumer's first step into the troubled waters of household moving. Although the price of a move will be determined by the actual weight and distance regardless of the estimate, the moving companies usually quote the customer a figure he can "expect" to pay. While the customer is told that the estimate will not be binding, the industry practice is to induce business by quoting low estimates. Many customers, receiving a low estimate, think that even though the actual weight will ultimately be determinative, they "somehow" might get a bargain.

The customer does not really feel the crunch of the low estimate until delivery. Almost without exception, the movers require full payment in cash or certified check on delivery. No personal checks are accepted. Thus, if the estimate was low, and the customer did not provide enough for the actual charge, he must either get together the needed cash in a strange city in two hours or else watch his possessions go off to the storage warehouse. . . .

In part, the estimates problem stems from the structure of the industry. Movers normally operate through local agents, who are not regular company employees. These agents are paid according to the moves they book. Once the move is booked, these agents normally bear no responsibility for its satisfactory completion. Thus, the agent's incentive is to book as many moves as he can, and low estimates are one way to raise the number.

Several solutions have been proposed for the problem of underestimates. One is to make estimates binding. The industry contends that people would then show the mover only a portion of what they intended to ship. It would seem that an inventory taken at the time of the estimate could solve that problem. Tht industry also contends, in phrases reminiscent of the Granger movement of the 1880s, that binding estimates would encourage what is known as "rebating"—movers deliberately quoting low estimates to capture business. It is not clear how such price competition would harm consumers, whether it is called "rebating" or anything else. So long as maximum rate levels were enforced, consumers would have everything to gain from a possible discount. A second solution to the problem of low estimates was proposed the last time the ICC reconsidered its regulations for home movers in 1961. The rule would have required the movers to accept payment of the estimate on delivery, and defer payment of any excess charges for at least ten days.

The Commission rejected this proposal out of sympathy with the industry's contentions. The movers argued that they would not be able to collect many of the deferred payments, and that the amount would, in effect, be lost. Again they used the magic word "rebate." The Commission showed considerably more sympathy with this hardship when coming from the movers than when its analog is voiced by consumers. How the public can collect overcharges or damage claims from the large moving companies, once cash has been paid on delivery, is not even considered a problem by the ICC—which had no consumer representative at its rule-making hearing.[2]

In short, the Commission had before it evidence of a practice which was subjecting large numbers of American consumers to great hardship. By the Commission's own figures, out of 829,038 moves made in 1960, there were 66,920 overestimates of 10 percent or less; 107,402 underestimates of more than 10 percent; and 71,753 underestimates of 20 percent or more. Yet the Commission decided that deferral of the excess was too harsh on the industry. The movers proposed, and the Commission accepted, an "alternative," whereby the movers would file with the Commission each month a list of all underestimates of 10 percent or more. How this industry-proposed "rule" will effectively deter overestimating is not clear. But unchallenged by public counsel or by an alert Commission, the movers succeeded in having it written into the proposed Code of Federal Regulations provision.

When questioned by the authors about this decision, the Commissioners' answers were predictable. One Commissioner, asked about the possibility of making estimates binding, remarked only that "rebates" might result. Another said that people would cheat and hide encyclopedias under clothes and fill the refrigerator with junk.

Lest there be any possibility that the mover might be legally bound to his estimate, or that the consumer have any bargaining power with regard to price, the Commission has enacted into its regulations (176.10a): "The shipper [customer] shall not be permitted or required to sign the 'Estimated Cost of Service Form.'" (If he did sign it, both parties might be bound by its terms.)

Hide and Seek

Many consumers have discovered, too late, that once the loaded van drives off, their possessions have begun an uncharted and untraceable journey. Very possibly the van is headed not out on the road, but back to the local warehouse where the belongings will be stored until another van picks them up. The extra handling and the conditions under which possessions are stored in such unauthorized warehousing are a major cause of loss and damage. The precarious timetables involved in such deposit and pickup arrangements frequently cause substantial delays in delivery. Had a customer been told of such arrangements beforehand he might well have opted for a mover who would carry his load directly. Yet the ICC makes no requirement of disclosure and prescribes no standards for warehousing or handling of shipments en route. Even if a mover does carry the load directly, without warehousing, a family's possessions may have to be transferred from one truck to another in an "interlining" arrangement. Such interlining is often necessary because in the ICC's mode of regulation some carriers are limited in the area in which they can operate. Because of the Commission-imposed fragmentation, the load must be transferred between two or more van lines to get to its destination. Sometimes a load is transferred between vans of the same line when one is going closer to the destination point than the other. Such interlining, along with imposing added costs on the industry and thus on the consumer, is, like warehousing, a major source of loss and damage. It also creates uncertainty as to the location of one's possessions en route. Some families have waited hours, days, even weeks for their possessions to be delivered, and have called the national mover only to discover that the company itself does not know where the shipment is.

Although interlining is a practice which the home owner would like to know about before he engages a company to haul his family possessions, the ICC does not require notice of interlining until immediately before the truck drives away, and then only if the exact arrangements are *known* to the mover.

This regulation, as originally proposed in the 1961 rule-making proceeding, would have required disclosure under *all* circumstances; but the Commission bowed to the industry demand that the phrase "when these are known" be added. Thus a mover need only claim that he did not know in advance what interlining arrangements he would make, and he escapes prosecution under the section. The ICC regulations actually make it advantageous to him *not* to chart carefully a customer's move in advance.

This Commission capitulation is symptomatic of the ICC's attitude toward the home moving industry. To have required disclosure of interlining arrangements under *all* circumstances would have required the industry to tighten its organization. It would have made the movers prearrange the details of the shipment of a customer's goods, rather than subject the customer to all the vagaries of *ad hoc,* last minute arrangements. Such regulatory pressure would have subjected the movers to the discomfort of change. The ICC was unwilling to apply it.

The Waiting Game

Before a family can even confront the damage and delays caused by warehousing, interlining, and careless handling, however, it must first get its possessions onto a van. Very frequently, vans arrive hours or days after the time or date promised. Such delays can be extremely burdensome to the customer. Often a family must vacate a home or apartment by a certain time; it may also have an obligation to arrive at the destination on a particular day. Such obligations aside, it is a trial simply to manage a family when one's appliances, utensils, and household items have been packed away. An obvious alternative would be to call another van line, but it is difficult if not impossible to arrange for a move on such short notice. Although the customer has made no legal commitment to a particular line until the bill of lading is signed from the time he "books" with a particular company, he has effectively cast his die. . . .

As the movers assert, late pickups are often not their fault, at least not directly. A delay on one pickup or delivery, whether a customer's or the mover's fault, can set back a mover's entire schedule. But mostly pickup delays are a result of overbooking. Business-hustling local agents, paid according to the business they book, take on, free of liability, more customers than their company realistically serve in the time promised. Another cause of delay to the average customer is the industry practice of rolling out the carpet for "King George." When a van is needed to carry a load paid for by a national account, it will be diverted from "John Smith" even if Mr. Smith placed his order for service far in advance. Affording such special treatment to national accounts would seem a violation of the sections of the Interstate Commerce Act prohibiting preferential treatment, but the Commission has neither passed a regulation against it nor even shown an awareness of the problem.

In 1960 the ICC found in a sample study that movers delivered later than the date promised 30 percent of the time. Delays of days and weeks are common, and senators have received complaints of delays upwards of one month. Mr. and Mrs. W. D. were assured by a local agent that their possessions would be in Columbus, Ohio, when they themselves arrived. The shipment was a month late and the family had to pay $625 in motel, restaurant, and laundry expenses. Mrs. E. F. S. of Brooklyn, New York, wrote of friends, "The people in question not only suffered the annoyances mentioned, but the expense of one week's motel lodging both in New York and Arizona."

The ICC regulations do not require delivery on the date promised, leaving eager agent-bookers free to make extravagant promises. The regulations require only that the bill of lading note a "preferred delivery date or the period of time within which delivery of the shipment may be expected" (S1056.8). The section is carefully worded to avoid subjecting the movers to legal liability for the promise. The "General Information for Shippers of Household Goods," which movers are required to give to customers, reads, "Unless expedited service is to be rendered . . . the carrier is not obligated to deliver your goods on any particular day, but only to deliver within a reasonable time." More important, the "time within which" clause is often buried in a small space on the bill of lading so that the customer may not even be aware that he has no right to expect delivery on the exact date promised. Furthermore, by slipping a lengthy "time within which" into the small space in the crowded and unintelligible bill of lading, the mover affords himself an easy "out."

The ICC regulations help to immunize the movers from liability for late delivery. As provided by § 1056.8(c) as long as the mover notifies the customer once of any delay in delivery, he has fulfilled his duty under the regulations. Yet mere notification mitigates only a part of the customer's grief; the worst hardships—the living expenses, the waiting, the calls to the national headquarters of the movers—must still be borne.

The Commission is remarkably inattentive to the customer's need for an *effective remedy*. Even if the mover does not comply with the Commission's innocuous notice requirements, he is liable to the Commission only. There is no provision in the ICC regulations, such as remission of a part of the transportation cost, which will benefit the customer and actually alleviate his plight. The customer himself does not even have a right of action under the act. The only present value of the regulations to the customer is their deterrent effect, yet ICC enforcement of the regulations is so infrequent, and the fines for their violation so slight, that a mover might well choose to violate them rather than incur the expense of delivering on time. Lax enforcement denies the customer whatever protection there might be in the deterrent value of the regulations.

The customer's only recourse in such a case is to sue the mover in court. The attorney's fees usually preclude this remedy, and even without the attorney's fees the common law standard is in the mover's favor. Movers are required only to deliver with "reasonable dispatch," usually interpreted as the fastest possible service under the circumstances. A consumer might find it hard indeed to prove that a mover had not done his best under the circumstances, and the expense of assembling sufficient evidence would put the endeavor beyond most people's means.

Early deliveries present similar problems. Often the uncertainties of a mover's schedule result in a load arriving at its destination long before the customer. In such cases, the load is automatically taken to the storage warehouse, where it is subjected to loss and damage, and the customer must incur the cost both of storage and delivery. "Reasonable dispatch" can mean early as well as late, weighted as it is to the mover's, not the customer's convenience. One might think it reasonable that the movers provide free storage when they deliver a load early. As one victim of an early delivery put it, "Whose fault was it that our belongings went into storage?" But here again the movers intone phrases like "rebate" and "unfair advantage" and the ICC nods in agreement.

Mr. and Mrs. R. D. H. of Lansing, Michigan, were handed a $162 storage bill upon arrival from Los Angeles because their possessions had arrived ten days earlier than the Los Angeles agent had promised. The ICC regulations provide no help for people like Mr. and Mrs. H. because, by the grim irony of ICC regulations, a return of the storage fee might be deemed by the Commission an illegal "rebate."

The Summer Rush

The movers usually blame these service deficiencies—late pickups, late deliveries, warehousing, and interlining en route—on the "summer rush." It is true that Americans prefer to move during the summer and, as a result, over 50 percent of the movers' business falls between May and September. Customers expect good service in the summer months largely because they are promised it by local agents. Perhaps more would move off-season if they were given an honest appraisal of the difficulties of providing satisfactory service in the summer. The movers claim that they lack the equipment to handle this business, but fail to add that they do nothing to alleviate or discourage the summer rush. On the contrary, they encourage it, and they have acted in concert to defeat those among them who would act differently.

In September 1968 an application by Republic Van and Storage to reduce certain of its off-season rates by 10 percent was rejected by a three-Commissioner division of the ICC. According to the *Wall Street Journal*, "The request was opposed by most major moving companies, at least some of which, it is understood, would have difficulty offering a similar slack season discount. . . . Republic sought approval of the discount to relieve demands on business in the peak June-September period." Republic appealed the decision and its plan was approved over a year later by the full Commission. The case is but another illustration of an industry attempt, this time unsuccessful, to use the ICC to suppress competitive pressure that might result in better service to the public.

In fact, the inability of the moving industry to handle the summer rush is due mainly to its own structural flaws. Without competition from other kinds of transportation, and protected by the rate bureaus and ICC regulations, the movers have not been subject to pressure to modernize. Routing, for example, is done on an *ad hoc* basis; as shown above, the movers are not sure what will happen to a person's belongings even after they are picked up. Communications between drivers, agents, and central dispatchers and officers are deficient.

Some of the structural weaknesses contributing to summer service deficiencies are actually fostered by "regulation." The parceling out of separate "operating territories" to individual carriers, and the reluctance with which the ICC extends them, creates a need for continual interlining. The lack of coordination between different van lines servicing the same territory means that much excess capacity goes unused, even in the summer months. Often a delayed pickup is not caused by the unavailability of a moving van; the cause is that a van of the particular van line with which the customer booked is not available. Another van line might have a van sitting in the customer's own city, two-thirds full, waiting for another order to carry a full load to the very place the customer is going, but without coordination between the van lines, both customer and the two-thirds loaded van continue to sit. The ICC might reasonably *require* such coordinated service, especially in light of the industry's admissions that it cannot handle the summer surge of business. The requirement could be considered a fair exchange for the antitrust exemption granted to the industry's tariff-making bureaus—thereby making the antitrust exemption work in the customer's behalf as well as in the carrier's.

In spite of the seasonal nature of the moving business, there might be more fancy than substance to the summer rush alibi for service failures. In 1967 the American Mover's Conference did a study of the complaints it received according to month of delivery. It would appear that there is a constant ratio between complaints received and deliveries made. For example, assuming that the movers make roughly half the deliveries in February as they make in July, they receive complaints on an almost identical proportion of the moves for each month.

Complaints Received, by Month of Delivery: 1967

January	67	July	109
February	51	August	90
March	45	September	83
April	40	October	38
May	49	November	20
June	86	December	08

The Tariff Mess

To the typical family man, the tariffs charged by a household mover might have been brewed in a witches' kettle. They are highly complicated, and most people never even see them. Tariffs are documented in tomes on file at the mover's headquarters and in a room on the seventh floor of the ICC headquarters in Washington. Thus, when the typical American is handed a bill in the front yard of his new home, he has no idea what the basic rate structure is, or whether it was fairly applied. The billing process takes place at the national company headquarters, usually hundreds, if not thousands, of miles away.

Unfortunately, billing "errors" are not infrequent. One source close to the industry (a former veteran traffic manager for one of the largest home movers) estimates that of the twelve million Americans who moved in 1969, at least one-half were overcharged and did not know it. During an interview he documented an example: a customer was charged a "stair charge" (an extra assessment for carrying furniture upstairs) of $121, at a rate which applies to business, not household moves. "This guy doesn't know a bill of lading[3] from a bale of hay or a tariff from a telephone book," was the expert's comment.

Often billing "errors" are merely the inadvertent misapplication of complicated tariffs. Typing, decimal, and addition errors are also common. Errors frequently occur when a clerk multiplies the weight by the mileage instead of by the rate per mile. Along with these clerical errors, there is the "bumping" of weights by the movers themselves. "Bumping" is the trade term for intentionally increasing the scale weight of a shipment. The practice is prohibited by federal regulations, but it occurs nevertheless. For example, different tractors will be used when getting the "tare," or weight before loading, than the weight after loading. Or two loads will be put on the same van, a weight taken, and both customers charged for the combined weight. Two practices expressly forbidden by the federal regulations also occur: getting tare weight with an empty gas tank and filling the tank before getting the loaded weight (which adds up to 600 pounds), and taking the loaded weight with men and equipment in the truck—while these were not on the truck when the tare was taken. Although customers have a right to watch the weighing, few can because of the pressures of moving day. Even if they do, however, they have no way of knowing what was on the van when the tare was taken, before their own possessions were loaded. Such weighing practices are difficult if not impossible to prove after the fact. The industry source says that about 20 percent of at least one company's weights are bumped.

An ICC field agent, by his own admission not a vigorous enforcer of home moving regulations, says of weight bumping, "There is more of it than I would like to see."

Errors occur in the packing process as well. Some shippers are billed for containers which were not used. Also when the movers do the packing, they sometimes use excess filler material so as to use and charge for more cartons.

Most home owners accept the mover's charges, assured by the ICC certificate number on the side of the truck that the movers are "regulated" and that somebody must therefore be watching them. In fact, nobody is watching over the billing process—moving bills are not audited. As to the scrutability of the tariffs themselves, the ICC has revealed no sensitivity to the individual home owner's needs for a more simplified rate schedule than those which only the shipping departments of large businesses can interpret. The Commission, which has the power to initiate complaints, lacks the manpower to do so and has not attempted to acquire that manpower. A section chief at the Commission reveals that with 2,000,000 shipments of all kinds per day, it is impossible for his staff to police this area. Instead, he must rely on complaints. Shippers, he adds, usually do not know when the tariffs have been misapplied, and they do not know enough about the ICC to complain even if they were aware of a misapplication. This section chief goes on to note that the *business* shipper does not complain because he can always pass his increased costs on to his customers. But the homemoving customer has nobody to whom to pass on his expense.

Even if the tariffs were applied as written, however, they are not likely to be "just and reasonable" as required by Section 316(a) of the Interstate Commerce Act. The movers' rates have never been subjected to the rigorous scrutiny which competition automatically forces upon rates of different carriers. First, contrary to common misconception, the ICC does not set or prescribe movers' rates. It merely requires that rates be published and filed. It has the *power* to challenge the rates, but it never does. Second, again contrary to the common notion and to the movers' communications to their customers, they do not have to charge the same rates. The Commission merely compels them to adhere to the tariffs they file.

The movers are permitted, under special provisions of the Interstate Commerce Act which exempts them from antitrust regulations, to engage in price fixing by belonging to "rate bureaus." Since all, or virtually all, movers belong to the rate bureaus, they will generally not challenge the rates the bureaus file. Further, in home moving there is no competition from other modes of transportation. Thus home movers enjoy virtual freedom from the downward pressure on rates that might be exerted either by competing truckers or by other modes. Their customers, consisting of the unorganized public, lack the awareness and power to protest the rates filed by the moving industry at the ICC.

One of the special executions from even minimal ICC scrutiny which the moving industry enjoys has to do with rate increases. Most carriers are required to submit, annually, sufficient economic data to justify the rates they charge. Whatever the shortcomings of the Commission's rate judging formulae, at least the other carriers must meet them. Evidently, however, the movers have convinced the Commission that their rate increases are so infrequent that it would not be worth the expense to file sufficient cost data annually to justify their rates.

A source close to the industry claims that the movers increase their tariffs infrequently only because they jack them up 300 percent more than necessary each time. Thus they can operate profitably for a long time without changing rates, and they do not undergo annual Commission review. The Commission does not even demand justifying cost figures when the movers *do* up their rates. One high official in the ICC's Bureau of Accounts admits that when the movers filed their last rate increase, they did not bring in enough data to show the boost was needed, but the Commission let them have the increase anyway, demanding only a promise that they would bring in sufficient data at the *next* increase. According to this official, the Cost Section does not make independent investigations of the movers' costs, but relies instead on their own annual reports, which he described as "cursory."

It is questionable whether moving rates are based in any way on costs. In fact, it is difficult to ascertain *how* the movers arrive at their rates. In part, the movers' rates are straight mileage rates, applicable in any part of the country. Thus, a move between equidistant points in the Rocky Mountains would cost the same as a move over flat southern terrain, even though the labor and trucking costs might be vastly different in each case. It would appear either that the rates for the low-cost moves are subsidizing the high-cost moves or else that reasonable profits are being made on the high-cost moves and exorbitant profits on the low-cost moves. This appears to be the case in a move between Boston, Massachusetts, and Champaign, Illinois, or between Meridian, Mississippi, and Oakly, Kansas. As an expert in moving tariffs has observed, the labor costs would be much lower in the southern move than in the northern, yet the tariffs applied are identical.

It would appear from other indices that ICC regulation is maintaining moving rates at artificially high levels. In some instances, the rates for interstate moves are *more* than those for intrastate moves of equal distance, not under ICC jurisdiction. For example, a tariff expert has pointed out that a home owner moving four thousand pounds of possessions from St. Louis, Missouri, to Kansas City, Missouri—252 miles—pays $5.05 per hundredweight. His neighbor, moving from St. Louis, Missouri, to Kansas City, Kansas—255 miles—pays $6.07 per hundredweight, plus higher packing charges.

So-called "directional" differences are another aspect of the movers' tariffs which invite explanation. The movers' tariffs provide that between certain points it costs more to move in one direction than in another. For example, a family moving four thousand pounds from Chicago to Milwaukee pays $5.00 per hundredweight, or $200 (not including packing and insurance). His Milwaukee counterpart moving to Chicago pays $4.01 per hundredweight, or $160.40.[4]

The ICC has not questioned whether a backhaul problem exists between two such points at Milwaukee and Chicago, or whether other cost or demand factors justify the differential. And it is not clear that moving vans go back and forth along the same route like railroads or transcontinental truckers. It would seem that instead they crisscross along irregular routes, going where there are loads to carry. In short, the directional differentials found in the home moving industry invite the attention of anyone concerned about carriers' rates, as the ICC purportedly is.

If moving rates merely invite suspicion, the tariffs for packing charges are clearly irrational. Most carriers adhere to two tariffs. One applies between any two points in the United States except points entirely within eleven western states, Canada, and Baja, California; the second applies between points in these latter places, and from these places to the Provinces and El Paso, Texas.

Each of these tariffs has two identical schedules of packing charges. A lengthy analysis of these tariffs reveals evident economic discrimination by the movers resulting from different charges for the same service. The packing bill of a man moving from Klamath Falls, Oregon, to Omaha will be 8.5 percent lower than that of his next-door neighbor moving by the same agent and van line to Denver, Colorado.

The present tariff structure, based on mileage, encourages the unwarranted manipulation of moving charges. The rates change at intervals of miles, for example every twenty miles. Between Chicago and Washington, one rate applies for from 661 to 680 miles, then a different rate applies between 681 and 700 miles. It is very easy, according to this same expert, for a mover to add or subtract two or three miles on a move which is near the "breakpoint." Such an "error" of only one or two miles can change the rate from ten to twenty cents per hundredweight; an error of ten miles can change it from fifty to seventy-five cents per hundredweight. This is another of the billing "errors" which is nearly impossible for the average customer to discover, and which the ICC refuses to investigate.

C.O.D. Only

In most dealings with "unregulated" business, the customer has an ace in the hole against service inadequacies: if he has suffered loss because of poor service, or damage to his possessions, he can simply withhold payment until the damage is adjusted. With the blessings (and sanctions) of the ICC, however, the movers require cash on delivery. Thus the customer does not even have the option of stopping a check once he has paid the movers. No matter how good the individual consumer's credit rating, most moving companies will extend credit only to their national accounts.

The special circumstances of household moving make it impossible to withhold payment in the absence of prior credit agreement. The driver has the owner's goods on his truck. Many drivers will not even open the doors until they have the cash in hand. . . .

The consumer is up against a wall. If he balks on payment, his possessions go off to the warehouse where they accumulate storage charges until he changes his mind and decides to pay.

The refusing of credit to individual home owners is simply one more industry practice sanctioned by the Commission regardless of its effect upon the consumer. The ICC-prescribed "Important Notice to Shippers of Household Goods," which the movers must give to customers, reads as though the Commission itself endorsed the practice: "The carrier *will require* payment in cash, money order, or certified check before unloading your goods, unless credit arrangements were made beforehand. Be prepared in case the actual charges demanded at this time are greater than what was estimated." (49CFR § 1056–12[a]) While this statement does not say that credit is not allowed, the ICC-prescribed notice gives the C.O.D.-only policy the color of law. Complaint letters to Congressmen indicate that movers often tell their customers that they are not *allowed* to grant credit.

That the movers do grant credit to their national accounts is clearly recognized by the Commission. In sanctioning the systematic denial of credit to individual consumers, the Commission appears to be endorsing discriminatory treatment and preferential service in behalf of the national accounts, in violation of the Interstate Commerce Act.

Even the favored national accounts, however, are considered less important—judging by Commission responses—than the moving companies themselves. In a ruling decided in May 1969[5] some of the national accounts requested that the Commission extend from seven to fifteen days the length of time for which credit could be extended to them. They needed this time, they told the Commission, to coordinate the payment of moving bills with their other bills and to check the bills against the tariffs. The Commission denied the request for an extended credit period. In the same proceeding, however, it granted the movers' request for more time in which to send out bills. The Commission was sympathetic to the movers' bookkeeping problems—that it took them time to amass the billing data from their scattered local agents—but not to the analogous bookkeeping problems of the shippers.

The Commission's policy of sanctioning the denial of credit to individuals represents a policy choice, placing upon the customer the burden of trying to recoup an overcharge or a damage claim from the company, after payment has been made in full. In light of the industry's rusty machinery for responding to such attempts, the burden is considerable. The burden could have been put upon the industry to collect a disputed charge, as it is in most un-"regulated" areas of business. In view of the industry's economic and legal bargaining power advantages over the consumer, one might question if the burdens have been allotted fairly.

Of all the consumer problems under ICC jurisdiction, none has caused more grief and loss to the public than the loss and damage to possessions entrusted to household movers. The ICC found in 1960 that over one-half the complaints it received regarding household moving concerned loss and damage. It further found that claims were filed with movers on *one-quarter of the shipments tendered,* and that one-fifth of these claims were never even acknowledged by the movers. (The Commission did not study the adequacy of settlements on claims which were acknowledged.)

The situation has not improved since 1960. Between July 1, 1967, and September 15, 1968, the Commission received, according to then Chairman Paul Tierney, 962 complaints within and 4,581 complaints not within ICC jurisdiction. Since the Commission regards all loss and damage complaints as "nonjurisdictional," and since no other problem is put to the Commission in such quantity, the overwhelming majority of these "nonjurisdictional" complaints appear to concern loss and damage.

A brief look at industry practices reveals why claims handling engenders so much dissatisfaction. The customer is at a disadvantage from the start, because drivers are assessed the first $50 of every claim. When they inventory a shipment on the bill of lading they describe every piece as "marked," "scratched," "gauged," "chipped." Complaint letters reveal that brand-new furniture has been so described.

One letter related that a brand-new playpen was inventoried "torn, soiled, scratched," and a brand-new coffee table "scratched, top and sides." Another said, "My own bill of lading indicated bad scratches on four pieces of furniture which came through the move completely unscratched."

The driver's notations are scrawled in code on a cramped inventory list, and during the rush of moving day a harried customer rarely feels he can check the list item by item. Housewives are understandably reluctant to second-guess and antagonize the drivers loading the belongings.

Thus the customer begins his move with a contract describing his belongings as damaged. The shipment is then subjected to incalculable handling deficiencies en route—warehousing, interlining, crowding, etc. Heavy chests and boxes are put on top of sofas. Foam cushions from couches are used as padding to protect automobiles.

In order to complete a delivery, a driver will often pick up helpers from a street corner. Such help is cheaper than regular help, and an owner-operator working on a commission can pocket the difference. Local agents bear no responsibility for loss or damage, and are not eager to help. Drivers, though supposedly liable for the first $50, know that their companies are virtually immune from claims. "Well, file a claim," or "Call the company," has been the reply to more than one customer who has complained to the driver of the condition or handling of his wares.

Collection for loss and damage is extremely difficult for the customer because, as a former ICC attorney has pointed out, the roots of the problem lie in the structure of the industry itself. The movers are self-insured, and they handle loss and damage claims themselves. But they have never "tooled-up" to handle this part of their business adequately, and there has never been pressure from consumers or from the ICC to compel them to do so. Thus, as complaints document by the hundreds, the movers continue to disregard estimates, demand purchase receipts for items bought years ago, apply outlandish depreciation rates, and contradict their local agents when the latter authorize repairs. None of these practices violate ICC regulations, and most customer claims are too small to justify the expense of suing a moving company.

Had the Commission invested half the energy in devising remedies within its authority that it has spent denying its authority and defending that denial, consumers might find the scales tipped slightly more in their favor. But the Commission has vigorously and continuously denied authority over loss and damage claims. Complaint letters referred to the Commission by Congress are answered with the Chairman's cheery regrets that the Commission "does not have jurisdiction to settle loss and damage claims." In a recent letter to the Senate Commerce Committee, expressing her opinion on a proposed bill, the Chairman used variations of the phrase "the Commission has no power to adjudicate loss and damage claims" three times within one and one-quarter pages.

The Commission rarely seems to consider what it could do or what the complainant really wants it to do. Most of the complaint letters do not ask it to *settle* a claim, but merely to force the mover to settle it. Some letters detail a whole list of grievances of which a damage claim is just one. Yet they all get the same response. It is as though a man staggered into a doctor's office covered with blood, told the doctor he had a gash in his head, a slit down his back, and a broken tooth, and the doctor replied, "Sorry, I don't fix broken teeth."

When questioned about the extent of the Commission's authority over claims-handling practices, Chairman Brown told us that she would have to "investigate" the matter. Her hearing examiner, Richard D. Heironimus, echoed in another interview that the Commission should investigate its authority over claims. Had Chairman Brown merely consulted the Commissions own files, she might have found the answer to the question. In response to the identical query, a recent Chairman sent a letter to a Congressional Committee spelling out with extensive legal precedent the extent of the Commission's authority over claims practices. His letter recognized that the Commission has "consistently held" that it did not have the authority to "determine the merits . . . of *particular* loss and damage claims" (emphasis added) but that the Commission *"does possess the authority to regulate* the carriers' *practices and tariff rules* on the subject." (Emphasis added.) The letter pointed out that the Commission had exerted this authority regarding shipments of grain and eggs. Furthermore, had Chairman Brown read the 1964 household goods rule-making decision, she would have found the Commission announcing publicly that "the examiner was correct in finding that the Commission has the duty to require reasonable practices by the motor carriers in the handling of loss and damage claims."

Home movers, unlike carriers of grain and eggs, are subject to *no* ICC regulations prescribing "reasonable" claims-handling procedures which are clearly unreasonable. The act does not require that every standard of reasonableness be spelled out in a regulation before the Commission can prosecute. The Commission's authority to determine *fitness* is another enforcement tool which has lain idle. When one-quarter of the annual household moves provoke loss and damage claims, a carrier's procedures for settling these claims might be deemed an important part of his "fitness." But that criterion is never applied to challenge operating authorities.

The Commission has been equally timid in rule making, and so far has applied only the most superficial of remedies to the problem. In the 1964 rule-making decision, it issued a regulation requiring the mover to acknowledge receipt of a damage claim within thirty days, and to make a definite offer of denial within 120 days. Although this regulation does prevent the movers from ignoring damage claims, as they had done 20 percent of the time, it is only the most meager of beginnings. It merely requires that a customer be told "no" instead of having to infer it from silence. The customer is still without help in achieving a just and reasonable settlement. And as with so many of the Commission's regulations, there is no redress for the consumer even if the mover violates the regulation. A mover prosecuted for not responding to a damage claim at most pays a fine to the government. The customer, the one actually hurt by the practice, gets nothing.

A first step in dealing adequately with the claims problem would be to regulate the practices which give rise to loss and damage claims. The Commission should prohibit such damage-causing practices as warehousing and interlining without the customer's permission, and the hiring of cheap, untrained, temporary labor from street corners. It should set standards for warehousing, and for equipment and padding used on the vans. It should impose more liability on drivers and local agents.

A second step would be to guarantee the customer a fair hearing on his claim. Merely requiring some response to his claim hardly insures the consumer of an adequate settlement. An often mentioned solution would require ICC arbitration of consumer claims. One ICC bureau head objected that binding arbitration would deny the customer of his right to a trial, but individual home owners do not really have this right when they cannot afford to exercise it. Commissioner Kenneth Tuggle objected that the Commission should not become a small claims court.[6] It is true that the Commission should not plunge any deeper than necessary into a time- and manpower-consuming case-by-case approach, but the Commission itself would not have to be the arbitrator. It would merely have to prescribe standards for arbitration. A possible prototype for such arbitration already exists. In the "unregulated" New York-New Jersey metropolitan area, loss and damage claims have been entrusted to the arbitration of the Office of Impartial Chairman. According to that Office's director, it receives complaints from customers, investigates the mover's records, holds a hearing, and renders a decision binding and confirmable in the New York State Supreme Court. Most complaints are settled in two weeks, and the service is free to the public. If the Chairman's description is accurate, this office could be a model for a reasonable claims procedure which the ICC might require of the movers under its jurisdiction.

The prescription of reasonable claims procedures, whatever form it takes, will require imaginative and exploratory use of the ICC's authority. It is even possible that the ICC would need new legislative authority to act effectively in this area—but the Commission has yet to make a gesture toward trying. One wonders whether the much postulated lack of authority is an obstacle or an alibi. Sources on Capitol Hill reveal that the Commission has never asked Congress for added authority in this area. According to the Commission staff, it does not really want it. Congress should look carefully at the ICC's performance with regard to claims procedures, and either give it the authority it may require, or else transfer regulation of the home movers to an agency more responsive to the public need.

What Is to Be Done

In order to change the nature of ICC regulation so that the home moving public—rather than commercial industry interests—benefits from the agency's protection, the following recommendations are worth serious consideration:

1. Remove the movers' antitrust immunity regarding rates, so that consumers will be able to benefit from price competition, and so that rates will not be artificially maintained to provide profits for the less efficient operators.
2. Reduce or abolish restrictions on routes and lower requirements for entry in the home moving industry, so that

    a. Existing demand will be more adequately served;
    b. Innovation will be facilitated and encouraged;
    c. Better service will be achieved by reducing the need for interlining;
    d. Competition will be encouraged.

3. Conduct an annual cost analysis of movers' rates for maximum rate ceilings.
4. Provide public counsel to represent the public in all home moving matters before the Commission.
5. Require the simplification of tariffs, and their publication in a form which customers can understand.
6. Simplify and clarify the bill of lading—the basic contract between mover and customer.
7. Prescribe standards of accountability of local agents to customers, so that there will be less dispersal of responsibility. Encourage the internal simplification of the industry so that authority is more centralized.
8. Reduce wherever possible the need for litigation with regard to customer claims by
    a. Requiring the establishment of a no-fault, administratively run insurance system to replace the present system of litigating claims. Make recovery rest only upon a prima facie showing of loss or damage (including loss due to *delay*). At the very least, prescribe reasonable claims-handling procedures for the movers, possibly arbitration. Congress should provide the ICC with whatever legislative authority it may need to act effectively in this area.
    b. Revising the regulations so that penalties for violation directly benefit the customer. (For example, provide a return of a percentage of the charges if delivery is late.)
9. As a less desirable alternative to 8b, enact legislation to allow for recovery of reasonable attorney's fees in successful actions for loss or damage (including loss or damage due to delay). Such legislation would discourage litigation in the long run by encouraging movers both to provide more careful handling, and to offer more reasonable settlements.
10. Require the extension of credit to customers meeting prescribed requirements.
11. Require the extension of credit on all amounts exceeding the estimate by 10 percent.
12. Require the mover to meet the promised pickup and delivery dates, allowing for a reasonable leeway provided customer is informed in advance of this leeway. As in 8b, require mover to forfeit part of charge to customer for failure to meet promised date.
13. Require the prior consent of the customer to any warehousing or interlining of his shipment en route.
14. Prescribe standards for
    a. Packing, handling, and warehousing;
    b. Equipment and padding used on vans;
    c. Drivers and helpers (eliminate picking up help at street corners);
    d. Handling of complaints and relations with public (eliminate such practices as evasion of long-distance inquiries from customers).
15. Provide stricter enforcement of ICC weighing regulations.
16. Require the movers to provide industry-wide "clearing-houses" at population centers, so that if one company cannot meet a promised pickup date, the customer might locate a van of another company which can accommodate him.

NOTES

1. "Multi-representation," a practice whereby a local mover will become an "agent" of several different moving companies and thereby take advantage of the D.O.D.'s practice of rotating contracts among competing carriers, is beyond the scope of this report.

2. The bargaining and legal power of a large company to collect an unpaid claim (a normal part of any business) vis-à-vis the power of the average consumer to collect an overcharge seemed lost on the Commission, as did the incredibly high frequency of industry underestimates and overcharges.

3. The contract between home owner and mover.

4. Such directional differentials are not unknown where carriers experience a backhaul problem; that is, where most or all of the available traffic is going in one direction, and only by substantially lowering the rates for the backhaul can a carrier utilize capacity which would otherwise be completely unutilized. The railroads and transcontinental truckers often experience this problem.

5. *Ex Parte MC-1* (sub. no. 1).

6. The Commission seems not to mind massive adjudication of such matters as whether carrier x will be allowed to carry cocoa beans as well as coffee beans between points y and z, however.

Bibliography

The following bibliography is divided into seven sections. Many articles and books could have been classified in more than one section. To save space, we have placed each item in the category to which it makes the greatest contribution. The first contains references dealing with the general theme of bureaucracy as a problem for sociology and for society. The second section contains books and articles on the influence of environmental factors on official–client relations. Next is a section on organizational goals and their influences, and on various aspects of organizational structure and their consequences for relations with the public. Situational factors, as developed in Part III, is the theme of the materials listed in the fourth section. A fifth involves the general topic of remedies and strategies for innovation and change with respect to official–client relations. A group of papers on methodology has been collected in the sixth section. Since the field of bureaucracy and the public is so new, there are few general methodological papers treating this subject specifically. Much of the work on developing techniques for studying interaction generally are applicable, of course, and therefore some of this work is included. Several papers are listed on general methods for studying organizations because they contain ideas which are potentially applicable to the study of relations between officials and clients. The reader should also note that many papers included elsewhere for their substantive content also contain methodological ideas. A last section contains a number of source books with additional articles and references. Etzioni's two readers as well as Vollmer and Mills' and Blau and Scott's texts are all comparative, containing materials on different kinds of organizations; the others are devoted to particular professional areas.

General: Bureaucracy As a Problem for Sociology and for Society

Albrow, Martin. *Bureaucracy.* London: Pall Mall Press, 1970.

Bendix, Reinhard. "Bureaucracy and the Problem of Power." *Reader in Bureaucracy,* edited by Robert Merton, Alisa Gray, Barbara Hockey, and Hanan C. Selvin, pp. 114–134. Glencoe, Ill.: Free Press, 1952.

Bennis, Warren G., and Philip E. Slater. *The Temporary Society.* New York: Harper Colophon Books, 1968.

Bensman, Joseph, and Bernard Rosenberg. "The Meaning of Work in Bureaucratic Society." In *Identity and Anxiety: Survival of the Person in Mass Society,* edited by Maurice Stein, Arthur J. Vidich, and David Manning White, pp. 181–197. Glencoe, Ill.: Free Press, 1960.

Blau, Peter M. *Bureaucracy in Modern Society.* New York: Random House, 1956.

Caplovitz, David. *The Poor Pay More.* New York: Free Press, 1963.

Crozier, Michel. *The Bureaucratic Phenomenon.* Chicago: University of Chicago Press, 1964.

Bibliography

Downs, Anthony. *Inside Bureaucracy.* Boston: Little, Brown, 1967.

Etzioni, Amitai. "Administration and the Consumer." *Administrative Science Quarterly* 3, no. 2 (1958): 251–264.

Glazer, Nathan. "Negroes and Jews: The New Challenge to Pluralism." *Commentary* 38, no. 6 (1964): 29–34.

Goodman, Paul. *People or Personnel.* New York: Vintage, 1968.

Gouldner, Alvin. "Red Tape As a Social Problem." In *Reader in Bureaucracy,* edited by Robert Merton, *et al.,* pp. 410–419. Glencoe, Ill.: Free Press, 1952.

——. "Metaphysical Pathos and the Theory of Bureaucracy." *American Political Science Review* 49, no. 2 (1955): 496–507.

Hofstadter, Richard. "Antitrust in America." *Commentary* 38, no. 2 (1964): 47–53.

Howton, William. *Functionaries.* Chicago: Quadrangle Books, 1969.

Katz, Elihu, and Brenda Danet. "Communication between Bureaucracy and the Public: A Review of the Literature." In *Handbook of Communication,* edited by Wilbur Schramm, Nathan Maccoby, Ithiel de Sola Pool, Leonard Fein, and Fred Frey. Chicago: Rand McNally, in press.

Kohn, Melvin L. "Bureaucratic Man: A Portrait and an Interpretation." *American Sociological Review* 36 (1971): 461–474.

Kornhauser, William. *The Politics of Mass Society.* Glencoe, Ill.: Free Press, 1959.

Martindale, Don. "The Invasion of Privacy." In *Institutions, Organizations and Mass Society,* pp. 523–527. Boston: Houghton Mifflin, 1966.

Merton, Robert K. "Bureaucratic Structure and Personality." In *Reader in Bureaucracy,* edited by Robert K. Merton, *et al.,* pp. 361–371. Glencoe, Ill.: Free Press, 1952.

Michael, Donald N. "The Privacy Question." In *The Computer Impact,* edited by Irene Taviss, pp. 169–181. Englewood Cliffs, N.J.: Prentice-Hall, 1970.

Milgram, Stanley. "Behavioral Study of Obedience." *Journal of Abnormal and Social Psychology* 67 (1963): 371–378.

——. "Some Conditions of Obedience and Disobedience to Authority." *Human Relations* 18 (1965): 57–76.

Miller, Arthur. *The Assault on Privacy.* Ann Arbor: University of Michigan Press, 1971.

Mills, C. Wright. "The Condition of Modern Work." In *White Collar,* pp. 224–238. New York: Oxford, 1951.

Nisbet, Robert A. *The Sociological Tradition.* New York: Basic Books, 1966.

Packard, Vance. *The Naked Society.* London: Longmans, 1964.

Peabody, Robert L., and Francis E. Rourke. "Public Bureaucracies." In *Handbook of Organizations,* edited by James G. March, pp. 802–837. New York: Rand McNally, 1965.

Presthus, Robert. *The Organizational Society.* New York: Vintage, 1965.

Reich, C. A. "Individual Rights and Social Welfare: The Emerging Legal Issues." *Yale Law Journal* 74 (1965): 1245.

Robson, W. A. *The Governers and the Governed.* London: Allen and Unwin, 1964.

Rosenberg, Jerry M. *The Death of Privacy.* New York: Random House, 1969.

Rourke, Francis E., ed. *Bureaucratic Power in National Politics.* Boston: Little, Brown, 1965. Especially chap. 5, "Controlling Bureaucratic Behavior."

Rovere, Richard H. "The Invasion of Privacy: Technology and the Claims of Community." In *The Dilemma of Organizational Society,* edited by H. M. Ruitenbeck. New York: Dutton and Co., Inc. 1963.

Smith, Michael P. "Self-Fulfillment in a Bureaucratic Society: A Commentary on the Thought of Gabriel Marcel." *Public Administration Review* 29, no. 1 (January–February, 1969): 25–32.

Strauss, E. *The Ruling Servants.* New York: Praeger, 1961.

Thompson, Victor A. "Bureaucracy in a Democratic Society." In *Public Administration and Democracy,* edited by Roscoe Martin, pp. 205–228. Syracuse, N. Y.: Syracuse University Press, 1965.

Weber, Max. "Bureaucracy." In *From Max Weber,* edited by H. H. Gerth and C. Wright Mills, pp. 196–244. New York: Galaxy, 1958.

——. *The Theory of Social and Economic Organization.* New York: Free Press, 1965.

——. "Bureaucratization." In *Max Weber and German Politics,* edited by J. P. Mayer, Appendix I, pp. 95–99. London: Faber and Faber, 1943.

Whyte, William F., Jr. *Organization Man.* New York: Simon and Schuster, 1956.

Environmental Factors: Culture and Community

BUREAUCRATIC SOCIALIZATION

Becker, Howard, *et al. Boys in White.* Chicago: University of Chicago Press, 1961.

Crowne, Douglas. "Family Orientation, Level of Aspiration, and Interpersonal Bargaining." *Journal of Personality and Social Psychology* 3, no. 6 (1966): 641–645.

Denhardt, R. B. "Bureaucratic Socialization and Organizational Accommodation." *Administrative Science Quarterly* 13, no. 3 (December 1968): 441–450.

Eisenstadt, S. N. *From Generation to Generation: Age Groups and Social Structures.* New York: Free Press, 1956.

Erikson, Erik H. *Childhood and Society.* New York: Norton, 1950.

Feldman, Jacob. *The Dissemination of Health Information.* Chicago: Aldine, 1966.

Janowitz, Morris, Deil Wright, and William Delany. *Public Administration and the Public.* Ann Arbor, Mich.: University of Michigan Institute of Public Administration, 1958.

Katz, Elihu, and S. N. Eisenstadt. "Some Sociological Observations on the Response of Israeli Organizations to New Immigrants." *Administrative Science Quarterly* 5 (1960): 113–133.

Kohn, Melvin. *Class and Conformity: A Study in Values.* Homewood, Ill.: Dorsey Press, 1966.

Koos, Earl. "Metropolis—What City People Think of Their Medical Services." In *Patients, Physicians, and Illness,* edited by E. Gartly Jaco, pp. 113–119. Glencoe, Ill.: Free Press, 1958.

Levy, Sidney J. "The Public Image of Government Agencies." *Public Administration Review* 23, no. 1 (March 1963): 25–29.

McClelland, David. *The Achieving Society.* New York: Van Nostrand Reinhold, 1961.

Merton, Robert K., George C. Reader, and Patricia L. Kendall, eds. *The Student Physician: Introductory Studies in the Socialization of Medical Education.* Cambridge, Mass.: Harvard University Press, 1957.

Miller, Daniel R., and Guy E. Swanson. *The Changing American Parent.* New York: Wiley, 1958.

Naegle, Kasper D. "Clergymen, Teachers and Psychiatrists," *Canadian Journal of Economics and Political Science* 22 (1956): 46–52.

Pratt, Lois, *et al.* "Physicians' Views on the Level of Medical Information among Patients." In *Patients, Physicians, and Illness,* edited by E. Gartly Jaco, pp. 222–229. Glencoe, Ill.: Free Press, 1958.

Sears, Robert B., Eleanor E. Maccoby, and Harry Levin. *Patterns of Child Rearing.* Evanston, Ill.: Row and Peterson, 1957.

Seeman, Melvin. "Alienation, Membership, and Political Knowledge; A Comparative Study." *Public Opinion Quarterly* 30, no. 3 (Fall, 1966): 353–367.

Bibliography

Whiting, J. W. M., and Irwin L. Child. *Child Training and Personality*. New Haven: Yale University Press, 1953.

Wilcox, Herbert. "The Cultural Trait of Hierarchy in Middle Class Children." *Public Administration Review* 28, no. 3 (1968): 222–235.

CROSS-CULTURAL COMPARISONS

Abegglen, James C. *The Japanese Factory*. Glencoe, Ill.: Free Press, 1958.

Abraham, C. M. "Police in a Welfare State." *Indian Sociology* 2, no. 2 (February 1960): 64–72.

Ahmad, Muneer. *The Civil Servant in Pakistan*. London: Oxford, 1964.

Almond, Gabriel, and Sidney Verba. *The Civic Culture*. Boston: Little, Brown, 1965.

Banfield, Edward C. *The Moral Basis of a Backward Society*. Glencoe, Ill.: Free Press, 1958.

Barzini, Luigi. *The Italians*. New York: Bantam, 1965.

Bayley, David H. "The Effects of Corruption in a Developing Nation." In *A Sociological Reader on Complex Organizations*, edited by Amitai Etzioni, 2d ed. New York: Holt, Rinehart and Winston, 1969.

Berger, Morroe. *Bureaucracy and Society in Modern Egypt*. Princeton: Princeton University Press, 1957.

————. "Bureaucracy East and West." *Administrative Science Quarterly* 1 (March 1957): 518–529.

Berkhead, Guthrie S., ed. *Administrative Problems in Pakistan*. New York: Syracuse University Press, 1966.

Blom, Raimo. "Public Opinion about the Functioning of Social Institutions," *Acta Sociologica* 13, no. 2 (1970): 110–126.

Bradburn, Norman M. "Interpersonal Relations within Formal Organizations in Turkey." *Journal of Social Issues* 19 (January 1963): 61–67.

Caiden, Gerald E. *Israel's Administrative Culture*. Berkeley: University of California, Institute of Governmental Studies, 1970.

Carmi, Yair. "Favoritism in the Israel Civil Service." *Public Administration in Israel and Abroad, 1967* 8 (1968): 58–69.

Caudill, William. "Around the Clock Patient Care in Japanese Psychiatric Hospitals—The Role of the Tsukisoi." *American Sociological Review* 26 (1961): 643–655.

Danet, Brenda, and Harriet Hartman. "Coping with Bureaucracy: The Israeli Case." *Social Forces* in press.

————. "On 'Proteksia': Orientations toward the Use of Personal Influence in Israeli Bureaucracy." *Journal of Comparative Administration* 3 (1972): 405–434.

Dror, Yehezkel. "Nine Main Characteristics of Governmental Administration in Israel." *Public Administration in Israel and Abroad, 1964* 5 (1965): 6–17.

Eldersveld, S. J., U. Jagannadham, and A. P. Barnabas. *The Administrator and the Citizen in a Developing Democracy*. Glenview, Ill.: Scott, Foresman, 1968.

Fallers, Lloyd A. *Bantu Bureaucracy*. Chicago: University of Chicago Press, 1965.

Field, Mark G. *Doctor and Patient in Soviet Russia*. Cambridge, Mass.: Harvard University Press, 1957.

Friedl, Ernestine. "Hospital Care in Provincial Greece." *Human Organization* 16, no. 4 (1958): pp. 24–27.

Hall, Edward. *The Silent Language*. New York: Fawcett Premier, 1966.

Hamilton, B. L. St. J. *Problems of Administration in an Emergent Nation: Jamaica*. New York: Praeger, 1964.

Heady, Ferrel. *Public Administration: A Comparative Perspective*. Englewood Cliffs, N.J.: Prentice-Hall, 1969.

Kearney, Robert N., and Richard L. Harris. "Bureaucracy and Environment in Ceylon."

In *Readings in Comparative Public Administration,* edited by Nimrod Raphaeli, pp. 306–324. Boston: Allyn and Bacon, 1967.

Kiani, Acquila. "People's Image of Bureaucracy." In *Bureaucracy and Development in Pakistan,* edited by Inayatullah, pp. 377–398. Academy Town, Peshawar: Pakistan Academy for Rural Development, 1962.

Kriesberg, Martin, ed. *Public Administration in Developing Countries.* Washington, D.C.: Brookings Institution, 1965.

La Polombara, J., ed. *Bureaucracy and Political Development.* Princeton: Princeton University Press, 1963.

Marriott, McKim. "Western Medicine in a Village of Northern India." In *Health, Culture and Community,* edited by Benjamin D. Paul, pp. 239–268. New York: Russell Sage, 1955.

Milne, R. S. "Mechanistic and Organic Models of Public Administration in Developing Countries." *Administrative Science Quarterly* 15, no. 1 (March 1970): 57–67.

Mitchell, Austin. "The People and the System: Some Basic Attitudes." *New Zealand Journal of Public Administration* (September 1968): 19–35.

Presthus, Robert V. "The Social Bases of Bureaucratic Organization." *Social Forces* 38 (1959): 103–109.

————. "Weberian vs. Welfare Bureaucracy in Traditional Society." *Administrative Science Quarterly* 6 (December 1961): 1–24.

Raphaeli, Nimrod, ed. *Readings in Comparative Public Administration.* Boston: Allyn and Bacon, 1967.

Richardson, Stephen A. "Organizational Contrasts on British and American Ships." *Administrative Science Quarterly* 1 (1956): 189–207.

Riggs, Fred. *Administration in Developing Countries.* Boston: Houghton Mifflin Co., 1964.

Strauss, E. *The Ruling Servants: Bureaucracy in Russia, France and Britain.* New York: Praeger, 1961.

SUBCULTURAL AND CLASS DIFFERENCES

Bloom, Samuel W. *The Doctor and His Patient.* Glencoe, Ill.: Free Press, 1965.

Blum, R. H. *The Management of the Doctor-Patient Relationship.* New York: McGraw-Hill Co., 1960.

Briar, Scott. "Welfare from Below: Recipients' Views of the Public Welfare System." In *The Law of the Poor,* edited by Jacobos Tenbroek, pp. 46–61. San Francisco: Chandler Publishing Co., 1966.

Brill, Norman O., and Hugh A. Storrow. "Social Class and Psychiatric Treatment." In *Mental Health of the Poor,* edited by Frank Riessman, *et al.,* pp. 68–75. New York: Free Press, 1965.

Clark, Burton. "The Organization-Clientele Relationship." In *Adult Education in Transition,* pp. 85–86. Berkeley and Los Angeles: University of California Press, 1958.

Croog, Sydney H. "Interpersonal Relations in Medical Settings." In *Handbook of Medical Sociology,* edited by Howard E. Freeman, *et al.,* pp. 241–271. Englewood Cliffs, N.J.: Prentice-Hall, 1963.

Falk, Gerhard J., "The Public's Prejudice against the Police." *American Bar Association Journal* 50 (August 1964): 754–757.

Farberman, Harvey A., and Eugene A. Weinstein. "Personalization in Lower Class Consumer Interaction." *Social Problems* 17, no. 4 (Spring 1970): 449–457.

Graham, Saxon. "Socio-Economic Status, Illness, and the Use of Medical Services." In *Patients, Physicians, and Illness,* edited by E. Gartly Jaco, pp. 129–134. Glencoe: Free Press, 1958.

Hausknecht, Murray. "The Blue-Collar Joiner." In *Blue-Collar World,* edited by Arthur

Bibliography

B. Shostak and William Gomberg, pp. 207–215. Englewood Cliffs, N.J.: Prentice-Hall, 1964.

Hoggart, Richard. "'Them' and 'Us.'" In *The Uses of Literacy*, pp. 62–68. Boston: Beacon, 1961.

Hunt, Raymond G., *et al.* "Social Status and Psychiatric Service in a Child Guidance Clinic." *American Sociological Review* 23 (February 1958): 81–83.

Levens, Helene. "Organizational Affiliation and Powerlessness: A Case Study of the Welfare's Poor." *Social Problems* 16, no. 1 (1968): 18–32.

Levin, Jack, and Gerald Taube. "Bureaucracy and the Socially Handicapped: A Study of Lower-status Tenants in Public Housing." *Sociology and Social Research* 54, no. 2 (1970): 209–219.

Lieberson, Stanley. "Ethnic Groups and the Practice of Medicine." *American Sociological Review* 23 (1958): 542–549.

Marsh, Paul, *et al.* "Anomia and the Utilization of Three Public Bureaucracies." *Rural Sociology* 32, no. 4 (December 1967): 435–445.

Martin, John M. "Socio-Cultural Differences: Barriers in Case Work with Delinquents." *Social Work* 2 (1957): 22–25.

Miller, S. M., Pamela Roby, and Alwine A. de van Steenwijk. "Creaming the Poor." *Trans-Action* (June 1970): 39–45.

Muller, Charlotte. "Income and the Receipt of Medical Care." *American Journal of Public Health* 60, no. 4 (1965).

Overall, Betty, and H. Aronson. "Expectations of Psychotherapy in Patients of Lower Socio-economic Class." In *Mental Health of the Poor*, edited by Frank Riessman, Jerome Cohen, and Arthur Pearl, pp. 76–87. New York: Free Press, 1965.

Plaja, Antonio Ordonez, *et al.* "Communication between Physicians and Patients in Outpatient Clinics: Social and Cultural Factors." *Milbank Memorial Fund Quarterly* 46, no. 2, part I (April 1968): 161–213.

Rein, Martin. "The Strange Case of Public Dependency." *Trans-Action* 2, no. 3 (March-April 1965): 16–23.

Rosenblatt, Daniel, and Edward A. Suchman. "The Underutilization of Medical-Care Services by Blue-Collarites." In *Blue-Collar World*, edited by A. B. Shostak and W. Gomberg, pp. 341–349. Englewood Cliffs, N.J.: Prentice-Hall, 1964.

Rosenfeld, Jona M. "Strangeness between Helper and Client: A Possible Explanation of Non-Use of Available Professional Help." *Social Service Review* 38 (March 1964): 17–25.

Saunders, Lyle. *Cultural Difference and Medical Care: The Case of the Spanish-Speaking People of the Southwest.* New York: Russell Sage Foundation, 1954.

Simmons, Leonard C. "'Crow Jim': Implications for Social Work." *Social Work* 8, no. 3 (July 1963): 24–30.

Sjoberg, Gideon, Richard A. Brymer, and Buford Farris. "Bureaucracy and the Lower Class." *Sociology and Social Research* 50, no. 3 (April 1966): 325–337.

Werthman, Carl, and Irving Piliavin. "Gang Members and the Police." In *The Police: Six Sociological Essays*, edited by David J. Bordua. London: Wiley, 1967.

Zeitz, L. "Survey of Negro Attitudes toward Law." *Rutgers Law Review* 19 (1965): 288–303.

Zola, Irving Kenneth. "Culture and Symptoms: An Analysis of Patients' Presenting Complaints." *American Sociological Review* 31. no. 6 (October 1966): 615–630.

———. "Illness Behavior of the Working Class: Implications and Recommendations." In *Blue-Collar World*, edited by A. B. Shostak and W. Gomberg, pp. 350–361. Englewood Cliffs, N.J.: Prentice-Hall, 1964.

ORGANIZATIONS AND THE COMMUNITY

Banton, Michael. *The Policeman in the Community.* London: Tavistock, 1964.

Eisenstadt, S. N. "Bureaucracy, Bureaucratization, and Debureaucratization," *Administrative Science Quarterly* 4 (1959): 302–320.

Freidson, Eliot. "Client Control and Medical Practice." *American Journal of Sociology* 65 (1960): 374–382.

Liberman, Robert. "Personal Influence in the Use of Mental Health Resources." *Human Organization,* 24, no. 3 (Fall 1965): 231–235.

Litwak, Eugene, and Henry J. Meyer. "A Balance Theory of Coordination between Bureaucratic Organizations and Community Primary Groups." *Administrative Science Quarterly* 11, no. 1 (June 1966): 31–58.

Lyle, Jack, and Herbert S. Dordeck. "Communication Crisis Points in Urban Development." Paper presented to International Conference on Future Research. Kyoto, Japan (April 1970).

Mayer, John E., and Aaron Rosenblatt. "The Client's Social Context: Its Effect on Continuance in Treatment." *Social Casework* (November 1964): 511–518.

Reiss, Albert J., Jr., and David J. Bordua, "Environment and Organization: A Perspective on the Police," in *The Police: Six Sociological Essays,* edited by David J. Bordua, pp. 28–45. London: Wiley, 1967.

Stinchcombe, Arthur. "Social Structure and Organization." In *Handbook of Organizations,* edited by James G. March, pp. 142–193. Chicago: Rand McNally, 1965.

Thomas, Edwin J. "Role Conceptions, Organizational Size, and Community Context." *American Sociological Review* 24 (1959): 30–37.

Intra-Organizational Goals and Structure

GOALS

Berk, Bernard B. "Organizational Goals and Inmate Organization." *American Journal of Sociology* 71, no. 5 (March 1966): 522–534.

Coser, Rose L. "Alienation and Social Structure: Case Analysis of a Hospital." In *The Hospital in Modern Society,* edited by Eliot Freidson, pp. 231–265. Glencoe, Ill.: Free Press, 1963.

Cressy, D. R. "Prison Organization." In *Handbook of Organizations,* edited by J. G. March, pp. 1023–1070. Chicago: Rand McNally, 1965.

Daniels, M. J. "Affect and Its Control in the Medical Intern." *American Journal of Sociology* 66 (1960): 259–267.

Grusky, Oscar. "Organizational Goals and the Behavior of Informal Leaders." *American Journal of Sociology* 65 (1959): 59–67.

———. "Role Conflict in Organizations: A Study of Prison Camp Officials." *Administrative Science Quarterly* 3 (1958–1959): 452–472.

Katz, Elihu, and Brenda Danet. "Petitions and Persuasive Appeals: A Study of Official-Client Relations." *American Sociological Review* 31, no. 6 (December 1966): 811–22.

Lefton, M., and W. R. Rosengren. "Organizations and Clients: Lateral and Longitudinal Dimensions." *American Sociological Review* 31 (1966): 802–810.

Little, R. W. "The 'Sick' Soldier and the Medical Ward Officer." *Human Organization* 15 (1956): 22–24.

Martinez, Thomas M. "Why Employment Agency Counsellors Lower Their Clients' Self-Esteem." *Trans-Action* 5, no. 4 (March 1968): 20–25.

Parsons, Talcott. "The Mental Hospital As a Type of Organization." In *The Patient and the Mental Hospital,* edited by Milton Greenblatt, *et al.* Glencoe, Ill.: Free Press, 1957.

Perrow, Charles. "Hospitals: Technology, Structure and Goals." In *Handbook of Organizations,* edited by James G. March, pp. 910–971. Chicago: Rand McNally, 1965.

Bibliography

Stein, W. W., and Oetting, E. R. "Humanism and Custodialism in a Peruvian Mental Hospital." *Human Organization* 24 (1964): 278–282.

Street, D. "The Inmate Group in Custodial and Treatment Settings." *American Sociological Review* 30, no. 1 (February 1965): 40–54.

Thompson, James D. "Organizations and Output Transactions." *American Journal of Sociology* 68, no. 3 (November 1962): 309–324.

———, and W. J. McEwen. "Organizational Goals and Environment: Goal Setting As an Interaction Process." *American Sociological Review* 23 (1958): 23–31.

Wilensky, Harold L. "The Professionalization of Everyone?" *American Journal of Sociology*, 70 (1964–1965): 137–158.

HIERARCHY AND CONTROL STRUCTURE: GENERAL

Aiken, Michael, and Jerald Hage. "Organizational Alienation: A Comparative Analysis." *American Sociological Review* 31, no. 4 (August 1966): 497–507.

Bell, Gerald. "Formality vs. Flexibility in Complex Organizations." In *Organizations and Human Behavior,* edited by Gerald D. Bell. Englewood Cliffs, N.J.: Prentice-Hall, 1967.

Bidwell, Charles, and Rebecca Vreeland. "Authority and Control in Client-Serving Organizations." *Sociological Quarterly* 4, no. 3 (1964): 231–242.

Blau, Peter M. *The Dynamics of Bureaucracy.* Chicago: University of Chicago Press, 1964.

Catrice-Lorey, Antoinette. "Social Security and Its Relations with Beneficiaries: The Problem of Bureaucracy in Social Administration." *Bulletin of the International Social Security Association* 19 (1966): 286–297.

Etzioni, Amitai. "Organization Control Structure." In *Handbook of Organizations,* edited by James G. March, pp. 650–677. New York: Rand McNally, 1965.

Francis, R. G., and R. C. Stone. *Service and Procedure in Bureaucracy.* Minneapolis: University of Minnesota Press, 1956.

Jacobs, Jerry. "Symbolic Bureaucracy: A Case Study of a Social Welfare Agency." *Social Forces* 47 (1969): 413–432.

Janowitz, Morris, and William Delaney. "The Bureaucrat and the Public: A Study of Informational Perspectives." *Administrative Science Quarterly* 2 (1957): 141–162.

Kahne, Merton J. "Bureaucratic Structure and Impersonal Experience in Mental Hospitals." *Psychiatry* 22 (November 1959): 363–375.

Mitchell, John. "Cons, Square-Johns, and Rehabilitation." In *Role Theory: Concepts and Problems,* edited by B. J. Biddle and E. J. Thomas, pp. 207–212. New York: Wiley, 1966.

Pearlin, L., and M. Rosenberg. "Nurse-Patient Social Distance and the Structural Context of a Mental Hospital." *American Sociological Review* 27 (1962): 56–65.

Rosengren, W. R. "Organizational Age, Structure and Orientations toward Clients." *Social Forces* 47, no. 1 (September 1968): 1–11.

Rubington, E. "Organizational Strains and Key Roles." *Administrative Science Quarterly* 9, no. 4 (March 1965): 350–369.

Seeman, Melvin, and John W. Evans. "Stratification and Hospital Care: I. The Performance of the Medical Interne." *American Sociological Review* 26 (1961): 67–80.

———. "Stratification and Hospital Care: II. The Objective Criteria of Performance." *American Sociological Review* 26 (1961): 193–204.

Whyte, William F., ed. "When Worker and Customer Meet." In *Industry and Society,* edited by William F. Whyte. New York: McGraw-Hill, 1946.

———. *Human Relations in the Restaurant Industry.* New York: McGraw-Hill, 1948.

Wilcox, Herbert G. "Hierarchy, Human Nature and the Participative Panacea." *Public Administration Review* 29, no. 1 (January-February 1969): 53–63.

BUREAUCRATIZATION OF PROFESSIONAL SERVICES

Ben David, Joseph. "The Professional Role of the Physician in Bureaucratized Medicine." *Human Relations* 11 (1958): 255–274.

Corwin, R. G. "The Professional Employee: A Study of Conflict in Nursing Roles." *American Journal of Sociology* 66 (1961): 604–615.

Croog, Sidney H. "Interpersonal Relations in Medical Settings." In *Handbook of Medical Sociology*, edited by Howard E. Freeman, *et al.*, pp. 241–271. Englewood Cliffs, N.J.: Prentice-Hall, 1963.

Ferguson, R. S. "The Doctor-Patient Relationship and 'Functional' Illness." In *Patients, Physicians and Illness*, edited by E. Gartly Jaco, pp. 433–439. Glencoe, Ill.: Free Press, 1958.

Freidson, Eliot. *Patients' Views of Medical Practice.* New York: Russell Sage Foundation, 1961.

———. "The Organization of Medical Practice." In *Handbook of Medical Sociology*, edited by Howard Freeman, *et al.* Englewood Cliffs, N.J.: Prentice-Hall, 1963.

Goode, William. "The Librarian: From Occupation to Profession?" *The Library Quarterly* 31, no. 4 (1961): 306–318.

Haug, Marie, and Marvin B. Sussman. "Professional Autonomy and the Revolt of the Client." *Social Problems* 17 (1969): 153–161.

Litwak, Eugene. "Models of Bureaucracy Which Permit Conflict." *American Journal of Sociology* 67 (1961): 177–184.

Rosengren, William R., and Mark Lefton, eds., *Organizations and Clients: Essays in the Sociology of Service.* Columbus: Merrill, 1970.

Scott, Richard W. "A Case Study of Professional Workers in a Bureaucratic Setting." Ph.D. dissertation, Department of Sociology, University of Chicago, 1961.

Simon, Abraham J. "Social Structure of Clinics and Patient Improvement." *Administrative Science Quarterly* 4 (1959): 197–206.

PAYMENT

Field, Mark G. "The Doctor-Patient Relationship in the Perspective of 'Fee-for-Service' and 'Third Parties' Medicine." *Journal of Health and Human Behavior* 2, no. 4 (Winter 1961): 252–262.

Roemer, Milton I. "On Paying the Doctor and the Implications of Different Methods." *Journal of Health and Human Behavior* 3 (1962).

PEER-GROUP RELATIONS

Blau, Peter M. "Orientations toward Clients in a Public Welfare Agency." *Administrative Science Quarterly* 5 (1960): 341–361.

Coleman, James S., Elihu Katz, and Herbert Menzel. *Medical Innovation.* New York: Bobbs-Merrill, 1966.

Menzel, Herbert. "Integration, Innovation and Marginality." *American Sociological Review* 25 (1960): 704–713.

ORGANIZATIONAL SIZE

Shuval, Judith T. "Ethnic Stereotyping in Israeli Medical Bureaucracies." *Sociology and Social Research* 46, no. 4 (1962).

Thomas, E. J., and C. F. Fink. "Effects of Group Size." *Psychological Bulletin* 60 (1963): 371–384.

Bibliography

TOTAL INSTITUTIONS

Aubert, Vilhelm, and Oddvar Arner. "On the Social Structure of the Ship." *Acta Sociologica* 3 (1958): 200–219.

———. "A Total Institution: The Ship." In *The Hidden Society,* pp. 259–287. Totowa, N.J.: Bedminster, 1965.

Bettelheim, Bruno. "Individual and Mass Behavior in Extreme Situations." In *Readings in Social Psychology,* edited by Eleanor Maccoby, Theodore Newcomb, and Eugene Hartley, pp. 300–310. New York: Holt, Rinehart and Winston, 1958.

Caudill, William. *The Psychiatric Hospital As a Small Society.* Cambridge, Mass.: Harvard University Press, 1958.

Cressey, Donald R., ed. *The Prison: Studies in Institutional Organization and Change.* New York: Holt, Rinehart and Winston, 1961.

Dornbusch, Sanford M. "The Military Academy As an Assimilating Institution." *Social Forces* 33 (1955): 316–321.

Goffman, Erving. *Asylums,* pp. 1–24. Garden City, N.Y.: Doubleday Anchor, 1961.

Jones, Maxwell. *Beyond the Therapeutic Community.* New Haven: Yale University Press, 1968.

Levinson, D. J., and E. B. Gallagher. *Patienthood in the Mental Hospital.* Boston: Houghton Mifflin, 1964.

Roth, J. "Information and the Control of Treatment in Tuberculosis Hospitals." In *The Hospital in Modern Society,* edited by E. Freidson, pp. 293–318. Glencoe: Free Press, 1963.

Schwartz, Morris S., and Charlotte Green Schwartz, et al. *Social Approaches to Mental Patient Care.* New York and London: Columbia University Press, 1964.

Stanton, A. H., and M. S. Schwartz. *The Mental Hospital.* New York: Basic Books, 1954.

Strauss, A., et al. "The Hospital and Its Negotiated Order." In *The Hospital in Modern Society,* edited by E. Freidson, pp. 147–169. Glencoe: Free Press, 1963.

Zurcher, Louis A., Jr. "Sailor Aboard Ship: A Study of Role Behavior in a Total Institution." *Social Forces* 43, no. 3 (March 1965): 389–400.

Situational Factors: The Physical and Social Setting

INTERPERSONAL STYLES AND STRATEGIES

Bar-Yosef, Rivka, and E. O. Schild. "Pressures and Defenses in Bureaucratic Roles." *American Journal of Sociology* 71, no. 6 (May 1966): 665–673.

Berne, Eric. *Games People Play: The Psychology of Human Relationships.* New York: Grove Press, 1964.

Danet, Brenda. "The Language of Persuasion in Bureaucracy: 'Modern' and 'Traditional' Appeals to the Israel Customs Authorities." *American Sociological Review* 36 (October 1971): 847–859.

———, and Michael Gurevitch. "Presentation of Self in Appeals to Bureaucracy: An Empirical Study of Role-Specificity." *American Journal of Sociology* 77, no. 6 (May 1972): 1165–1190.

Fox, Renee. *Experiment Perilous.* Glencoe, Ill.: Free Press, 1959.

Goffman, Erving. *The Presentation of Self in Everyday Life.* Garden City, N.Y.: Anchor Books, 1959.

Henslin, James M. "Trust and the Cab Driver." In *Sociology and Everyday Life,* edited by Marcello Truzzi, pp. 138–158. Englewood Cliffs, N.J.: Prentice Hall, 1968.

Johnson, Walter L., and Helen M. Simon. "Some Aspects of the Interaction of Public

Health Nurses and Patients in Home Visits." *American Journal of Public Health* (January 1961).

Miller, Dorothy, and Michael Schwartz. "County Lunacy Commission Hearings: Some Observations of Commitments to a State Mental Hospital." *Social Problems* 14, no. 1 (1966): 26–35.

Rosenberg, Morris, and Leonard I. Pearlin. "Power Orientations in the Mental Hospital." *Human Relations* 15, no. 4 (November 1962): 335–350.

Stone, Gregory P. "City Shoppers and Urban Identification: Observations on the Social Psychology of City Life." *American Journal of Sociology* 60 (1954): 36–45.

Strodtbeck, Fred L., and Marvin Sussman. "Of Time, the City and the 'One Year Guarantee': The Relations between Watch Owners and Repairers." *American Journal of Sociology* 61 (1956): 602–609.

Weinstein, E. A., and Paul Deutschberger. "Some Dimensions of Altercasting." *Sociometry* 26, no. 4 (December 1963): 454–466.

LATENT SOCIAL IDENTITIES

Bradley, Trudy. "An Exploration of Caseworkers' Perceptions of Adoptive Applicants." *Child Welfare* 45 (October 1966): 433–443.

Brown, Luna Bowdoin. "Race As a Factor in Establishing a Casework Relationship." *Social Casework* 31, no. 3 (March 1950): 91–97.

Curry, Andrew E. "The Negro Worker and the White Client: A Commentary on the Treatment Relationship." *Social Casework* 45, no. 3 (March 1964): 131–136.

Danet, Brenda. "Giving the 'Underdog' a Break: Favoritism or Flexibility?" Jerusalem, 1972, submitted for publication.

Evans, F. B. "Selling As Dyadic Interaction." *American Behavioral Scientist* 7 (May 1963): 76–96.

Filbush, Esther. "The White Worker and the Negro Client." *Social Casework* 46, no. 5 (May 1965): 271–277.

Gochros, Jean S. "Recognition and the Use of Anger in Negro Clients." *Social Work* 11, no. 1 (January 1966): 28–34.

Gold, Ray. "Janitors versus Tenants: A Status-Income Dilemma." *American Journal of Sociology* 57 (1951): 486–493.

Gouldner, Alvin. "Cosmopolitans and Locals: Toward an Analysis of Latent Social Roles." *Administrative Science Quarterly* 2 (1957–1958): 281–306, 444–480.

Haney, C. Allen, Kent S. Miller, and Robert Michielutte. "The Interaction of Petitioner and Deviant Social Characteristics in the Adjudication of Incompetency." *Sociometry* 32 (1969): 182–196.

Joseph, Alice. "Physician and Patient: Some Aspects of Inter-Personal Relations between Physicians and Patients, with Special Regard to the Relationship between White Physicians and Indian Patients." *Applied Anthropology* 1, no. 4 (1942): 1–6.

Mamamoto, J., et al. "Racial Factors in Patient Selection." *American Journal of Psychiatry* 124 (1967): 630–636.

Nagel, Stuart S. "The Tipped Scales of American Justice." *Trans-Action* 3, no. 4 (1966): 3–9.

Stark, Francis B. "Barriers to Client-Worker Communication and Intake." *Social Casework* 40, no. 4 (April 1959): 177–183.

INFLUENCES OF TIME AND SPACE

Berkman, Paul L. "Life Aboard an Armed-Guard Ship." *American Journal of Sociology* 51 (1945–1946): 380–387.

Brown, E. L. "Newer Dimensions of Patient Care: The Use of the Physical and Social Environment of the General Hospital for Therapeutic Purposes." *Sociological Quar-*

509

terly 4 (1963): 83–84.

Cressey, P. *Taxi Dance Hall*. Chicago: University of Chicago Press, 1932.

Davis, Fred. "The Cabdriver and His Fare: Facets of a Fleeting Relationship." *American Journal of Sociology* 65 (1959): 158–165.

Eldersveld, S. J. "Bureaucratic Contact: Dimensions and Relevance for Public Attitudes." *Indian Journal of Public Administration* 12 (1965): 216–235.

Hall, Edward T. "The Silent Language in Overseas Business." *Harvard Business Review* 38, no. 3 (1960): 87–96.

———. *The Hidden Dimension*. Garden City, N.Y.: Doubleday, 1966.

Riggs, Fred W. "The 'Sala' Model: An Ecological Approach to the Study of Comparative Administration." In *Readings in Comparative Public Administration*, edited by Nimrod Raphaeli. Boston: Allyn and Bacon, 1967.

Sommer, Robert. *Personal Space: The Behavioral Basis of Design*. Englewood Cliffs, N.J.: Prentice-Hall, 1969.

Stinchcombe, Arthur L. "Institutions of Privacy in the Determination of Police Administrative Practices." *American Journal of Sociology* 69, no. 2 (September 1963): 150–160.

EXPECTATIONS, INTERACTION, AND OUTCOMES

Biddle, Bruce J., *et al*. "Shared Inaccuracies in the Role of the Teacher." In *Role Theory: Concepts and Research*, edited by Bruce J. Biddle and Edwin J. Thomas, pp. 302–310. New York: Wiley, 1966.

Davis, Milton S. "Variations in Patients' Compliance with Doctors' Advice: An Empirical Analysis of Patterns of Communication." *American Journal of Public Health* 58 (1968): 274–288.

Eaton, Joseph W. "The Client-Practitioner Relationship As a Variable in the Evaluation of Treatment Outcome." *Psychiatry* 22 (1959): 189–195.

Guttman, Louis, and Uriel Foa. "Social Contact and an Interpersonal Attitude." *Public Opinion Quarterly* 15, no. 1 (1951): 43–53.

Heine, Ralph W., and Harry Trosman. "Initial Expectations of the Doctor-Patient Interaction As a Factor in Continuance in Psychotherapy." *Psychiatry* 23 (August 1960): 275–278.

Kadushin, Charles. "Social Distance between Client and Professional." *American Journal of Sociology* 67, no. 5 (March 1962): 517–531.

Kutner, Bernard. "Surgeons and Their Patients: A Study in Social Perceptions." In *Patients, Physicians, and Illness*, edited by E. Gartly Jaco, pp. 384–397. Glencoe, Ill.: Free Press, 1958.

Lennard, Henry L., and Arnold Bernstein. "Expectations and Behavior in Therapy." In *Anatomy of Psychotherapy*, chap. 4. New York: Columbia University Press, 1960.

Lombard, George F. *Behavior in a Selling Group*. Cambridge, Mass.: Graduate School of Business Administration, Harvard University Press, 1955.

Rosenthal, Robert, and Lenore Jacobson. *Pygmalion in the Classroom*. New York: Holt, Rinehart and Winston, 1968.

Making Organizations Work for People: Strategies for Innovation and Change

RESTRUCTURING THE ORGANIZATION

Argyris, Chris. *Integrating the Individual and the Organization*. New York: Wiley, 1964.

Bennis, Warren G., Kenneth D. Benne, and Robert Chin. *The Planning of Change:*

Readings in the Applied Behavioral Sciences. 2d ed. New York: Holt, Rinehart and Winston, 1969.

———. *Changing Organizations: Essays on the Development of and Evolution of Human Organization.* New York: McGraw-Hill, 1966.

Leavitt, Harold J. "Applied Organizational Change in Industry: Structural, Technological and Humanistic Approaches." In *Handbook of Organizations,* edited by James G. March. Chicago: Rand McNally, 1965.

Miller, S. M. "Some Thoughts on Reform." In *Blue-Collar World,* edited by A. B. Shostak, and W. Gomberg, pp. 298–306. Englewood Cliffs, N.J.: Prentice-Hall, 1964.

———, and Pamela A. Roby. *The Future of Inequality.* New York: Basic Books, 1970.

Schein, Edgar H., and Warren G. Bennis, eds. *Personal and Organizational Change through Group Methods.* New York: Wiley, 1965.

Strauss, E. "Remedies against Bureaucratic Defects." In *The Ruling Servants,* chap. IV. New York: Praeger, 1961.

COUNTERORGANIZATION AND CITIZEN PARTICIPATION:
THE PROPOSALS AND THE DEBATE

Alinsky, Saul. *Reveille for Radicals.* Chicago: University of Chicago Press, 1946.

Cahn, Edgar S., and Jean Camper Cahn. "Citizen Participation." In *Citizen Participation in Urban Development, Volume I—Concepts and Issues,* edited by Hans B. C. Spiegel, pp. 211–224. Washington, D.C.: Center for Community Affairs, NTL Institute for Applied Behavioral Science, 1968.

Cloward, Richard A., and Frances Fox Piven. "A Strategy to End Poverty." *The Nation* 202 (May 2, 1966): 510–517.

———. "Birth of a Movement," *The Nation* 204 (May 8, 1967): 582–588.

Cousens, F. R. "Indigenous Leadership in Two Lower-Class Neighborhood Organizations." In *Blue-Collar World,* edited by A. B. Shostak and W. Gomberg, pp. 225–234. Englewood Cliffs, N.J.: Prentice-Hall, 1964.

Crain, Robert L., and Donald B. Rosenthal. "Community Status As a Dimension of Local Decision Making." *American Sociological Review* 32 (1967): 970–984.

Kramer, Ralph M. *Participation of the Poor: Comparative Community Case Studies.* Englewood Cliffs, N.J.: Prentice-Hall, 1969.

Krause, Elliot A. "Functions of a Bureaucratic Ideology: Citizen Participation." *Social Problems* 16, no. 2 (Fall 1968): 129–143.

Moynihan, Daniel P. *Maximum Feasible Misunderstanding.* New York: Free Press, 1970.

Riessman, Frank. *Strategies Against Poverty.* New York: Random House, 1969.

Rose, Stephen C. "Saul Alinsky and His Critics." In *Citizen Participation in Urban Development, Volume I—Concepts and Issues,* edited by Hans B. C. Spiegel, pp. 162–183. Washington, D.C.: Center for Community Affairs, NTL Institute for Applied Behavioral Science, 1968.

Seeman, Melvin. "Antidote to Alienation—Learning to Belong." *Trans-Action* 3, no. 4 (1966): 34–39.

Sherrard, Thomas D., and Richard C. Murray. "The Church and Neighborhood Community Organization." In *Citizen Participation in Urban Development, Volume I—Concepts and Issues,* edited by Hans B. C. Spiegel, pp. 184–205. Washington, D.C.: Center for Community Affairs, NTL Institute for Applied Behavioral Science, 1968.

Sigel, Robert S. "Citizens Committees—Advice vs. Consent." *Trans-Action* 5, no. 4 (March 1968): 47–52.

Silberman, Charles E. "Up from Apathy—the Woodlawn Experiment." *Commentary,* 37, no. 5 (May 1964): 51–58.

Tannenbaum, Arnold S. "Unions." In *Handbook of Organizations,* edited by James G. March, pp. 710–763. New York: Rand McNally, 1965.

Bibliography

Van Til, Jon, and Sally Bould Van Til. "Citizen Participation in Social Policy: The End of the Cycle?" *Social Problems* 17, no. 3 (Winter 1970): 313–323.

Wilson, James Q. "The War on Cities." *The Public Interest* 3 (1966): 27–44.

Zurcher, Louis A. "The Leader and the Lost: Case Study of Indigenous Leadership in a Poverty Program Community Action Committee." *Genetic Psychology Monographs* (1967): 23–93.

CONSUMERS' RIGHTS

Esposito, John C., and Larry J. Silverman. *Vanishing Air: The Ralph Nader Study Group Report on Air Pollution.* New York: Grossman, 1970.

Fellmeth, Robert. *The Interstate Commerce Omission: The Ralph Nader Study Group Report on the I.C.C. and Transportation.* New York: Grossman, 1970.

Mueller, Marti. "Nader: From Auto Safety to a Permanent Crusade." *Science* 166 (1969): 929–983.

Roth, Julius. "Who's Complaining: The Inhibitions of the Dissatisfied Consumer." *Trans-Action* 2, no. 5 (July-August 1965): 12–16.

Schrag, Philip G. "Consumer Rights." *Columbia Forum* 13, no. 2 (Summer 1970): 4–10.

Turner, James S. *The Chemical Feast: The Ralph Nader Study Group Report on Food Protection and the Food and Drug Administration.* New York: Grossman, 1970.

MEDIATING MECHANISMS

Anderson, Stanley V., ed. *An Ombudsman for American Government?* New York: American Assembly, Columbia University Press, 1968.

Cahn, Edgar S., and Jean C. Cahn. "The War on Poverty: A Civilian Perspective." *Yale Law Journal* 73, no. 8 (1964): 1317–1352.

Carlin, Jerome E., Jan Howard, and Sheldon L. Messinger. "Civil Justice and the Poor." *Law and Society Review* 1, no. 1 (1966).

Carrow, Milton. "Mechanisms for the Redress of Grievances against the Government." *Administrative Law Review* 22, no. 1 (October 1969): 1–37.

Cloward, Richard A., and Richard M. Elman. "Advocacy in the Ghetto." *Trans-Action* 4 (December 1966): 27–35.

Gellhorn, Walter. *Ombudsmen and Others.* Cambridge, Mass.: Harvard University Press, 1966.

———. *When Americans Complain: Governmental Grievance Procedures.* Cambridge, Mass.: Harvard University Press, 1966.

Inkeles, Alex, and Kent Geiger. "Critical Letters to the Editor of the Soviet Press: Areas and Modes of Complaint." *American Sociological Review* 17, no. 6 (1952): 694–703.

Kahn, Alfred J., Lawrence Grossman, Jean Bandler, Felicia Clark, Florence Galkin, and Kent Greenwalt. *Neighborhood Information Centers: A Study and Some Proposals.* New York: Columbia University School of Social Work, 1966.

Matthews, Arthur R., and Jonathan A. Weiss. "What Can Be Done: A Neighborhood Lawyer's Credo." *Boston University Law Review* 67, no. 2 (1967): 231–243.

Rowat, Donald C., ed. *The Ombudsman: Citizen and Defender.* London: Allyn and Unwin, 1965.

Simmons, Ozzie. "The Clinical Team in a Chilean Health Center." In *Health, Culture, and Community,* edited by Benjamin D. Paul, pp. 325–348. New York: Russell Sage, 1955.

Sussman, Leila. *Dear FDR: A Study of Political Letter Writing.* Totowa, N.J.: Bedminster, 1963.

Research Methods

Bales, R. F. *Interaction Process Analysis*. Cambridge, Mass.: Addison-Wesley Press, 1951.

Barton, Allen H., and Bo Anderson. "Change in an Organizational System: Formalization of a Qualitative Study." In *A Sociological Reader on Complex Organizations*, edited by Amitai Etzioni, pp. 540–558. New York: Holt, Rinehart and Winston, 1969.

Dittman, A. T. "The Interpersonal Process in Psychotherapy: Development of a Research Method." *Journal of Abnormal and Social Psychology* 47 (1952): 236–244.

Foa, Uriel G. "The Foreman-Worker Interaction: A Research Design." *Sociometry* 18 (1955): 226–244.

Hall, R. H. "The Concept of Bureaucracy: An Empirical Assessment." *American Journal of Sociology* 69 (1963–1964): 32–40.

Katz, Elihu, Michael Gurevitch, Tsiyona Peled, and Brenda Danet. "Doctor-Patient Exchanges: A Diagnostic Approach to Organizations and Professions." *Human Relations* 22, no. 4 (August 1969): 309–324.

————, Brenda Danet, and Tsiyona Peled. "Petitions and Prayers: A Method for the Content-Analysis of Persuasive Appeals." *Social Forces* 47 (1969): 447–463.

Landsberger, H. A. "Interaction Process Analysis of the Mediation of Labor Management Disputes." *Journal of Abnormal and Social Psychology* 51 (1955): 552–559.

Lennard, Henry L., and A. Bernstein. "Methodology." In *The Anatomy of Psychotherapy*, chap. 2. New York: Columbia University Press, 1960.

Longabaugh, Richard. "A Category System for Coding Interpersonal Behavior As Social Exchange." *Sociometry* 26 (1963): 319–344.

Matarazzo, J. D., G. Saslow, and R. G. Matarazzo. "The Interaction Chronograph As an Instrument for Objective Measurement of Interaction Patterns During Interviews." *Journal of Psychology* 41 (1956): 347–367.

Melbin, M. "Field Methods and Techniques: The Action-Interaction Chart." *Human Organization* 12 (1953): 34–35.

Murray, H. "A Content Analysis Method for Studying Psychotherapy." *Psychological Monographs* 70, no. 13 (1956).

Ruesch, J., J. Block, and L. Bennett. "The Assessment of Communication: A Method for the Analysis of Social Interaction." *Journal of Psychiatry* 35 (1953): 59–80.

Scott, W. Richard. "Field Methods in the Study of Organizations." In *Handbook of Organizations*, edited by James G. March, pp. 261–304. Chicago: Rand McNally, 1965.

Stenzar, B. "The Development and Evaluation of a Measure of Social Interaction." *American Psychologist* 3 (1948): 266.

Stone, P. J., D. C. Dunphy, M. S. Smith, and D. M. Ogilvie. *The General Inquirer: A Computer Approach to Content Analysis*. Cambridge, Mass.: MIT Press, 1966.

Wager, L. Wesley, and George A. Miller. "Hypothetical Situations and Particularistic Requests: A Test in Three Hospitals." *Human Organizations* 28, no. 2 (1969): 119–127.

Weick, Karl E. "Laboratory Experimentation with Organizations." In *Handbook of Organizations*, edited by James G. March, pp. 194–260. Chicago: Rand McNally, 1965.

Additional Sources

The following books contain many references and/or articles not included in this bibliography:

Blau, Peter M., and W. Richard Scott. *Formal Organizations: A Comparative Approach.* San Francisco: Chandler, 1962.

Etzioni, Amitai, ed. *A Sociological Reader on Complex Organizations.* 2nd ed. New York: Holt, Rinehart and Winston, 1969.

————. *The Semi-Professions and Their Organization.* New York: Free Press, 1969.

Freidson, Eliot. *The Hospital in Modern Society.* New York: Free Press, 1963.

March, James G., ed. *Handbook of Organizations.* Chicago: Rand McNally, 1965.

Scott, W. Richard, and Edmund H. Volkart. *Medical Care: Readings in the Sociology of Medical Institutions.* New York: Wiley, 1966.

Thomas, Edwin J., ed. *Behavioral Science for Social Workers.* New York: Free Press, 1967.

Vollmer, Howard M., and Donald L. Mills. *Professionalization.* Englewood Cliffs, N.J.: Prentice-Hall, 1966.

Zald, Mayer N. *Social Welfare Institutions: A Sociological Reader.* New York: Wiley, 1965.

Name Index

Name Index

Delany, William, 86n, 166
Deutsch, Morton, 353n
Deutschberger, Paul, 284
Diamond, Sigmund, 76
Dickson, W. J., 212
Dorsen, Norman, 468

Eaton, Joseph, 160, 202, 205
Eckhardt, Robert, 476
Edell, Laura, 162
Eisenstadt, S. N., 14, 18, 34, 37–38, 40, 73–88, 188n, 191, 284, 289, 290, 293
Eldersveld, S. J., 34, 35
Elias, Norbert, 326n
Eliav, Arie, 73
Erikson, Eric, 37
Esposito, John C., 399
Etzioni, Amitai, 10, 160–161, 299n, 395, 398
Evans, F. B., 279
Evans, Gary, 353n
Evans, John W., 165
Evans, Judy, 387n

Fallers, Lloyd, 87n
Fanshel, David, 200
Farr, James N., 353n
Farris, Buford, 34, 35, 40, 61–72, 391
Feigenbaum, Kenneth D., 353n
Feldman, Jacob J., 137
Fellmeth, Robert, 399, 401, 479–498
Field, Mark G., 162, 169
Flanagan, J. C., 378
Flowers, C. E., 386
Fortas, Abe, (Justice), 443
Fox, Renee, 282, 327n
France, Anatole, 440
Francis, Roy G., 197, 243n
Frank, J. D., 123
Frankfurter, Felix, (Justice), 440
Freeman, Howard E., 169
Freidson, Eliot, 36, 161, 204, 205
French, John R. P., Jr., 178
Frenkel-Brunswik, Else, 123
Freud, S., 11, 111
Friedrich, C. J., 123
Friendly, H., 429n
Fuchs, F. R., 429n
Fullex, Lon, 413

Gallagher, Eugene B., 166
Gans, Herbert, 67
Garfinkel, Harold, 353n
Gellhorn, Walter, 10, 399, 400, 401, 404–437
Gerth, H. H., 32, 137, 138, 151
Gibb, H. A. R., 60n
Glaser, Daniel, 106n
Glazer, Nathan, 16, 21, 68

Goffman, Erving, 5, 18, 170, 211n, 275, 276, 277, 285, 308, 317–328, 338, 354n
Goldberg, Arthur, 417
Goldhamer, H., 300
Goldstein, Joseph, 106n
Golkin, Florence, 450–467
Gomberg, A. B., 25
Goode, William, 395
Goodman, Paul, 23, 394, 399
Gouldner, Alvin W., 18, 75–76, 77, 87n, 243n
Greenwalt, Kent, 450–467
Grimes, Michael D., 152n
Gross, Neal, 299n
Grossman, Lawrence, 450–467
Grusky, Oscar, 210n, 213, 214, 215, 219–220, 221, 224, 225–226n
Guest, Edgar A., 116–117
Gurevitch, Michael, 277

Haggard, Ernest A., 353n
Hall, Edward T., 34, 138, 393
Hammond, Peter B., 211n
Hamon, L., 428n
Haney, C. Allen, et al., 279
Hanson, Robert, 225–226n
Harford, Thomas C., Jr., 353n
Harrington, Michael, 442
Harris, R. L., 436n
Hartley, E. L., 225n
Hartman, H., 35
Hartung, Fred E., 449n
Hawkes, Robert W., 208
Hayner, Norman J., 327n
Hecht, N., 434n
Heckstall-Smith, Anthony, 326n
Heider, Fritz, 178
Heironimus, Richard D., 494–495
Henslin, James M., 281, 285, 338–356
Hitch, Charles J., 62
Hofstadter, Richard, 7
Holland, D. C., 434n
Hollingshead, August B., 154n
Horowitz, Uri, 73
Hughes, Everett C., 5, 243n, 353n
Hughes, Helen M., 353n
Hull, C. Hadlai, 154n

Isaacs, Kenneth S., 353n

Jaco, E. Gartly, 284
Jacobson, Lenore, 284, 286, 375–387
Janowitz, Morris, 86n, 166, 212, 213, 214
Johnson, Donald, 431n
Johnson, Lyndon B., 36, 68, 430n, 431n
Johnson, Nicholas, 399
Jones, Frank E., 86n, 87n
Jones, H. W., 433n
Jones, Maxwell, 170

516

Subject Index

quirer, 452, 466; public image of, 459; qualities of, 451, 461, 466; records of, 463; scope of, 453–457, 466; staff of, 460–461. *See also* official-client relationship

Citizens' Advice Notes (CANs), 453, 458; and Citizens' Advice Bureaus, 462

civil rights, 404, 434*n*, 468–478. *See also* disadvantaged classes; rights; universalism

civil servants. *See* bureaucrats

class action, 398, 476, 478

class differences. *See* subcultures

classical model of bureaucracy. *See* ideal model of bureaucracy

client: attitudes of, 247, 250; demands and pressures, to deviate from bureaucratic norms, 289, of response to, 405; interests of, vs. interests of officials, 178; organization of, 17; participation of in social security organization in France, 246, 247–248, 252; power of, 180, 181, 190*n*, 247–248, 250; role of, 174, perception of, 175, 288, socialization to, 174, 288; selection of by bureaucracy, 63–64

client-centered bureaucracy. *See* service organizations

coercion. *See* power, types of: coercive

commitment: activation of (influence-attempt), 178, 179; and bargaining position, 295; of bureaucrat, 295

commonweal organizations, 159; appeals to, 181, 277. *See also* Israeli Customs Authorities; service organizations

communications: channels of, 283, and culture, 283, and official-client interaction, 19, in Poland, 406; of intention, 174–190, 329–337; patterns of in doctor-patient relationship, 357–374; and police, 105; problems of (intercultural), 34, 487; profiles of, 360; with public in social security administration, 246. *See also* persuasive appeals

community: size of and interpersonal relations in organizations, 35

Community Action Programs (CAPs), 397

community organization. *See* neighborhood organization

comparative administration research: framework for, 52

comparative sociology, 245

complaints: channels for, 394; about moving industry, 481; responding to, 405. *See also* persuasive appeals

compliance: with doctors' orders, 357–374, effect of communication difficulties in doctor-patient visit, 278, effect of feedback from doctor, 278, effect of struggle to control relationship, 278, and reciprocal interaction, 368, 369; index of, 362, 373*n;* patterns of, 358–359. *See also* conformity

conflict of demands, 133, 134, 160

conformity: in bureaucrats, 39; of child, 111; enforcement of, 206, 221–222; index of, 139; to official bureaucratic procedures, 231; promises of in appeals, 180; as response to client and organizational cross-pressures, 297. *See also* compliance; obedience; rigidity

congressmen: casework function of, 399

consumer: expectations of, 468; lower class vs. middle class, 470–471, 477; organization of, 395, 398, 401, 477–478; power of, 480; protection of, 480; representation, in courts, 472–473, on Interstate Commerce Commission, 482; rights of, 398, 468–478. *See also* law, and buyers vs. sellers; lawyers, and buyers vs. sellers

Consumer's Education and Protection Association (CEPA), 477

contact with bureaucracy: facilitation of, 24; in Germany, Italy, Mexico, 49; in Great Britain, U.S., 48; initial, 204; and persuasive appeals, 177, 180; and socialization to client role, 184; voluntary vs. mandatory, 160

contingencies in official-client transactions, 195, 197

control: of administrators by legislatures, 409, 412; of British Ministers by Question Hour, 412; centralization of, in custodial vs. treatment-oriented prisons, 223, in social security administration, 252; formal vs. informal, 214; internalized, 108, 110-111, 112; judicial, 413–418; of lower-class client by bureaucrats, 65; of movers' industry, 496–497; in prison, 221–222, 227*n;* specificity of, over member, 193; state vs. internal, 252, 256; strategies for programmed vs. heuristic roles, 198, 202. *See also* authority; power; supervision

coping with bureaucracy, 17; and lower classes, 34–35; police, prosecutors and jurists, 96. *See also* remedies; socialization, to bureaucracy

corporate structure: efficiency of, 62

corruption: of formal authority system, 223; in Italy and Mexico, 49

Council on Tribunals, 413

counterorganization: influence of custodial-therapeutic orientation on, 161; as rebellion against bureaucracy, 277; as remedy, 24–25, 68, 395–399. *See also*